Sports Marketing

Sam Fullerton

Eastern Michigan University

McGraw-Hill
Irwin

Boston   Burr Ridge, IL   Dubuque, IA   Madison, WI   New York   San Francisco   St. Louis
Bangkok   Bogotá   Caracas   Kuala Lumpur   Lisbon   London   Madrid   Mexico City
Milan   Montreal   New Delhi   San Juan   Seoul   Singapore   Sydney   Taipei   Toronto

SPORTS MARKETING

Published by McGraw-Hill/Irwin, a business unit of The McGraw-Hill Companies, Inc., 1221 Avenue of the Americas, New York, NY, 10020. Copyright © 2007 by The McGraw-Hill Companies, Inc. All rights reserved. No part of this publication may be reproduced or distributed in any form or by any means, or stored in a database or retrieval system, without the prior written consent of The McGraw-Hill Companies, Inc., including, but not limited to, in any network or other electronic storage or transmission, or broadcast for distance learning.

Some ancillaries, including electronic and print components, may not be available to customers outside the United States.

This book is printed on acid-free paper.

1 2 3 4 5 6 7 8 9 0 QPD/QPD 0 9 8 7 6

ISBN-13: 978-0-07-110658-0
ISBN-10: 0-07-110658-8

www.mhhe.com

I am honored to dedicate this book to the memory of Dr. H. Robert (Bob) Dodge.

Over our 32-year relationship, I was fortunate to be associated with Bob in several capacities. Among them was that he was my first marketing professor at Memphis State University. It was his insight and enthusiasm that led me to become a marketing major and then to pursue an MS degree in marketing. My first position in the academic world as an instructor at Pittsburg State (KS) University came about solely because of his trust and encouragement. My second position at Northern Illinois University allowed me to accompany Bob as he assumed the position as the head of the Marketing Department at NIU. I could even sense a fatherlike pride when I informed him of my decision to enroll in the doctoral program at Michigan State University. Over the years, we collaborated on many projects, including three textbooks, more than 20 national and international publications, a research grant from the state of Michigan, and several consulting projects. At the time of his death, we were laying the foundation for this text. During his memorial service, I recounted the roles that Bob played in my life. He was my teacher, my mentor, my colleague, and my boss. Above all else, he was my friend and I miss him greatly.

While this dedication is primarily designed to express my gratitude to Bob for his unwavering support, it is also designed to encourage the users of this book—students and teachers alike—to never overlook the importance of developing long-lasting, mutually beneficial relationships. Without that type of relationship in my life, this book would never have become a reality. So if you find the book useful in your career, understand that much of the credit belongs to my dear friend, Bob Dodge.

Brief Contents

Contents

PART THREE
THE MARKETING OF SPORTS 279

15
Segmentation of the Sports Market 280

16
Product Decisions in Sports Marketing 295

17
Distribution Decisions in Sports Marketing 318

18
Pricing Decisions in Sports Marketing 340

22
Controversial Issues in Sports Marketing   434

About the Author

Sam Fullerton *Eastern Michigan University*

Sam Fullerton was awarded BBA and MS degrees in marketing from Memphis State University. He earned his doctorate in marketing from Michigan State University. Dr. Fullerton is currently a professor of marketing at Eastern Michigan University where his teaching emphasis is sports marketing. He has also taught sports marketing and sponsorship courses at the University of Michigan and Waikato University in New Zealand.

By his own admission, he played a lot of sports as a kid but never excelled at any. He did once bowl on TV (and lost) as a 12-year-old. However, he was—and remains today—an avid sports fan. Over the years he has achieved some measure of sports success. He has several rounds of even-par golf, including his most recent at the University of Illinois course. He is also an accomplished bowler; his official average in league competition has exceeded 200 for the past 15 years, with his highest average of 216 recorded during the 2001–02 season. His accomplishments include three perfect games that have been certified by the American Bowling Congress.

Among his favorite diversions are travel, photography, and classic cars. He has visited more than 30 countries, which provided the opportunity to learn about and enjoy sports such as rugby, cricket, and netball. And the travel has presented numerous opportunities to use his camera. While textbooks do not necessarily represent the best forum for displaying these creative abilities, he took the vast majority of the photographs in this book. Finally, he loves fast cars. He maintains a 1982 Corvette that he bought new, but his treasured vehicle is a 1967 Plymouth GTX. The muscle car takes him back to the late 1960s when he once won his class in an NHRA drag racing meet in his native Memphis, Tennessee.

Dr. Fullerton is the president of the Sports Research Institute of Plymouth, Michigan. In this capacity, he has consulted for numerous organizations, including sporting goods retailers, publications, golf course operators, and the state of Michigan. His research on fans and sponsorship has been published in journals and presented at conferences across the globe. He feels fortunate to work in a profession that provides so much gratification. The ability to teach college students the intricacies of marketing, coupled with the opportunity to focus on sports, has meant that there has never been a morning when he dreaded to go to work.

Preface

The discipline of sports marketing has grown in stature despite there being no consistent agreement as to exactly what the discipline encompasses. As sports have moved into the category of big business, new approaches to teaching the subject have surfaced. Textbooks focused on marketing principles with a few sports examples sprinkled in began to fill the void for students and professors. But few have taken an in-depth look at the applications of strategies germane to the discipline. This textbook has been conceived and designed in an effort to move sports marketing into a new arena. It recognizes the recreational nature of the industry but emphasizes that the focus has begun to shift to the bottom line. While many traditionalists may lament that transition, others view it as an opportunity. As a result, the need to develop effective marketing strategies has never been more important. Upon completing a course using this book, students should have a better understanding of how to apply strategies and tactics within the sports marketing environment.

The discipline of sports marketing encompasses two broad perspectives. The one that will probably most readily come to the student's mind is that of the *marketing of sports products*. This type of marketing might involve questions such as

- How do we get more people to attend a sports event?
- How do we increase the size of the various media audiences?
- How do we attract more participants?
- How do we sell more sports-related products?

To most people, questions such as these represent the totality of sports marketing. However, this misconception fails to recognize the immensely important component of *using a sports platform as the foundation for the marketing of nonsports products*. Tiger Woods's endorsement of Tag Heuer watches, Coca-Cola's sponsorship of the World Cup of Soccer, the use of venue naming rights such as those seen at FedEx Field, and the sale of merchandise bearing a sports organization's trademarks and logos such as Antigua shirts that incorporated the Olympic rings design are all examples of marketing through sports. This textbook is an effort to address both perspectives.

Content

As evidenced by the preceding discussion, this textbook reflects an effort to provide the most comprehensive overview of the sports marketing environment available within the textbook market. While intertwined, the two broad perspectives of sports marketing are quite different. Indeed, many universities have separate courses on the marketing of sports and marketing through sports. Whether the book is used in a single semester or over two separate courses, it will provide students with insight that cannot be gained from a casual examination of the literature or the Internet.

Every effort was made to provide a sports-related example to illustrate how marketing concepts can be applied in that environment. Sports, athletes, teams, and stadia from around the globe are referenced. Marketing is becoming more global every day, and sports marketing is no different in this regard. There is also an abundance of information available on the Internet if you just know where to find it. Appendix A provides a listing of the URLs for many sports and sports marketing organizations around the world. Students are encouraged to use this reference to augment their learning experience.

After an introduction to the field of sports marketing in Chapter 1, the next 13 chapters focus on how marketers use sports as a platform for developing their strategies and tactics. Chapter 2 provides a broad overview of the techniques used to market through sports. Chapters 3 through 11 provide the basis for developing and assessing a comprehensive traditional sponsorship proposal. While the emphasis is on sports properties, the material will lead the students through the steps required to develop a proposal for many other types of properties available to prospective sponsors. At the end of Chapter 11, students should be able to complete a comprehensive written proposal and develop a sales presentation designed specifically for the prospect. Not only does the material provide insight for the sellers, but it also provides a basis for understanding on the part of the buyer. As such, this material represents a vital area that can be the basis for a class, group, or individual project. Chapters 12 through 14 provide detailed coverage of three special forms of sponsorship. The pros and cons of celebrity endorsements, venue naming rights, and licensing are discussed. Upon the completion of Chapter 14, students will have a solid understanding of how marketers such as Coca-Cola and Ford use a sports platform as the foundation for many of their marketing efforts.

Chapters 15 through 19 provide detailed coverage of the marketing of sports products. This includes strategic initiatives involving target market and marketing mix decisions. For students who are new to the marketing discipline, the marketing mix represents the set of four controllable variables that comprise the marketers' strategic domain. These variables are the decisions regarding the products being sold, the techniques involved in the distribution of the products, the pricing strategies employed, and the various promotional tools that are available to the marketer. One chapter is devoted to the process of identifying target markets and each of the four variables of the marketing mix. Coverage encompasses spectator sports, participation sports, and a broad array of sports-related products such as sporting goods and athletic shoes. Basic marketing principles are introduced in each of these chapters, and specific sports examples are provided as a means of illustrating how these concepts are applied in the sports environment.

The final three chapters examine issues germane to both marketing perspectives—the marketing of nonsports products through sports and the marketing of sports products. The issues discussed in the final chapters can have a profound impact on a marketer's accomplishments. Recognizing the importance of customer retention, Chapter 20 provides a detailed perspective of relationship marketing practices within the sports marketing industry. The role of technology, especially the Internet, is discussed in Chapter 21. While the emphasis is on the Internet, the role of other innovations such as virtual imaging and mobile technology are discussed. And finally, acknowledging that sports marketing is often subjected to intense scrutiny and criticism by many people, the text concludes with a chapter addressing many of the controversial issues that raise the ire of our critics. These controversies are grouped according to the five essential elements of marketing strategy: target markets, products, distribution strategies, pricing concerns, and criticisms regarding promotional practices.

The text takes a strong international focus. Examples that cover a broad array of sports, teams, and athletes are used to make the book relevant to students across the globe. This can be a positive learning experience, as students find out a little more about sports not commonly played in their home countries. But in this age of globalization, we will witness a geographic expansion of many of these sports. And for those students who will be working within the domains represented by the marketing of mainstream products through sports, it is imperative that they recognize these global opportunities.

Ancillary Package

A comprehensive ancillary package accompanies this text. For instructors, we offer an Instructor's Resource CD-ROM that includes the Instructor's Manual and PowerPoint slides developed by the author. We also included a test bank in MS-Word and our easy to use computerized test generator, EZ-Test. The test questions were written by Betty Pritchett.

Additional resources are found on our textbook website at www.mhhe.com/fullerton1e. Instructors can access the Instructor's Manual and the PowerPoint slides at the site for quick download. Other appropriate resources will be provided on a time-sensitive basis. For students, support materials include links to the Web sites referenced in the text, chapter summaries, learning objectives, and multiple-choice quizzes for self-assessing study. This array of materials will facilitate both the task of teaching sports marketing and the learning process on the part of the students.

—Sam Fullerton

Acknowledgments

No project of this scope is ever completed without the assistance of many important people. There are several who I would like to thank. First is the sponsoring editor for this project, Barrett Koger. Barrett showed both patience and faith that we would reach closure within a reasonable time frame. Her rapid response to any question was greatly appreciated. I must also thank Robin Reed of Carlisle Publishing Services, the developmental editor for the book. Her role in putting the final project together and interacting with the reviewers resulted in a text that is better than I imagined. Barrett and Robin definitely added value to this finished product. I would also like to express gratitude to my longtime McGraw-Hill/Irwin representative, Brian Murray. Brian was a student of mine some 25 years ago at Michigan State University. He was my first point of contact when this book was still in the conceptual stage. I can only hope that this book is as successful as Brian has been.

There were five reviewers who were quick to offer praise when it was warranted but also willing to provide constructive criticism when they thought the book could be improved. There is no doubt that the changes emanating from their comments have made this book more insightful and more user-friendly. My sincere thanks are extended to the following people.

Jeffrey M. Buck
Anderson University

Gary Donnelly
Casper College

Katherine Bohley Hubbard
University of Indianapolis

Susan Logan Nelson
University of North Dakota

Susan K. Osborne
Friends University

Without naming names, I would also like to thank the many sports marketing students I have had the privilege to teach at Eastern Michigan University, the University of Michigan, and Waikato University in New Zealand over the past 10 years. As I see former students who now work for organizations such as NFL Films, NASCAR, the St. Louis Blues, and the Chinese Sports Information Institute, I am reminded of why this job is so rewarding. I also appreciate the willingness of representatives of the Detroit-area sports teams to provide insight to my students while concurrently enlightening me. Finally, I must thank my late colleague Bob Dodge. It was Bob who first envisioned the housing of a sports marketing class within our Department of Marketing some 15 years ago. The dedication earlier in the book illustrates the debt that I owe Bob for his incredible contributions to the sports marketing discipline and my own academic career.

The Foundation of Sports Marketing

Part One provides a broad overview of the sports marketing environment. It provides an introduction to the concepts of marketing through sports and of the marketing of sports. It looks at the economic impact of the industry and identifies an array of career opportunities for students interested in sports marketing.

CHAPTER ONE

Introduction to Sports Marketing

Learning Objectives

- Be able to differentiate among sports marketing domains.
- Learn how the sports marketing discipline has evolved.
- Understand the economic impact of the industry.
- Identify career opportunities.

There is little doubt that the field of sports marketing has emerged as a key area in business over the past 30 years. Despite this acknowledged growth, there is still considerable confusion as to what types of activities comprise the domain of sports marketing. Most outside observers recognize the role of marketing in the task of creating demand for spectator sports, participation sports, and sports equipment. However, these same observers often fail to acknowledge the role that sports can play in the marketing of mainstream products and services such as fast food and cellular telephone service. Those working in the field of sports marketing must recognize the breadth of the industry and understand both domains.

The key objective of this book is to provide aspiring sports marketers with insight into both domains. The book is divided into two major sections. First, it will address the task of marketing nonsports products using sports as a primary platform. We refer to this as *marketing through sports*. Then the focus shifts to the strategic initiatives used in the *marketing of sports* products and services.

Marketing Through Sports

Astute marketers have long recognized the role that sports can play in the marketing of their products. Marketers of Wheaties cereal first incorporated athletes and sports themes in the product's packaging as early as 1933. Figure 1.1 shows a recent Wheaties box featuring golf legends Tiger Woods and Jack Nicklaus. Prior to that, the manufacturer of Jockey underwear capitalized on the endorsement of the most famous athlete in Major League Baseball in an effort to influence the consumers' purchase behavior. The endorsement contract with Babe Ruth was implemented in 1921. Other early efforts to market through sports include Gillette's decision to become involved with televised boxing matches in the 1940s with its sponsorship of "Friday Night at the Fights." In an unusual strategy, football's Joe Namath was shown in a TV commercial wearing L'eggs pantyhose in the 1960s. Miller Brewing began its strategy of using retired athletes to sell its Lite Beer in the 1970s, and the Los Angeles Olympics was recognized for the opportunities that the event provided for a large number of sponsors to reach their own target markets in 1984.

FIGURE 1.1
Replica of Wheaties Box Featuring Golf Legends

Marketing through sports flourished in the 1990s and continues to represent a key strategic domain for marketers today. Within this domain, there are two types of strategies: traditional and sponsorship. *Traditional strategies* represent efforts to incorporate sports into the firm's marketing efforts. For example, one recent McDonald's advertisement featured children being rewarded with a trip to McDonald's after winning their game. *Sponsorship strategies* feature a greater level of integration of sports into the marketing strategy. There are four strategies that represent specific applications of sponsorship principles. They are traditional sponsorship, venue naming rights, licensing, and endorsements.

Traditional sponsorship involves the creation of an official relationship between a marketer and some noteworthy sports property. For example, Coca-Cola is an official sponsor of the upcoming Olympic Games. *Venue naming rights* are based upon the marketer's ability to have its name attached to a physical facility. A recent example is Petco Park. In this case, the Major League Baseball stadium in San Diego is designated by the name of a major retailer of pet products in the United States. The third strategy, *licensing,* is a contractual agreement that allows a marketer to use valuable trademarks and brand names of a sports property. Inexpensive T-shirts increase in value by a substantial amount as soon as a sports team's logos are printed on them. Finally, marketers can use *endorsement strategies.* Popular athletes such as Tiger Woods and David Beckham are often used to gain attention and influence selective demand for a variety of products. Chapters 3 through 14 take a comprehensive look at each of these four sponsorship strategies.

In addition to sponsorship strategies, products are marketed through sports using a variety of traditional approaches. Advertising can incorporate a sports theme; packaging can feature sports activities; products can be sold at sports venues. These traditional strategies involve the exploitation of opportunities provided by the sports environment by carefully considering target market decisions and by establishing product, promotion, pricing, and distribution strategies that can be used to influence demand within the firm's selected target markets.

The various strategies for marketing through sports that were introduced in this chapter are listed in Box 1.1. The key component of these strategies is that each involves the use of a sports platform in the marketing of nonsports products. These strategies will be the focus of Chapters 2 through 14.

Marketing of Sports

The more commonly acknowledged aspect of sports marketing involves the proactive efforts that are designed to influence consumer preferences for a variety of sports products and services. But even this domain is often not fully understood. There is a question of exactly what falls into the category of sports products and services. From the most basic perspective, this category is comprised of three subcategories. They are

- Access to spectator sports events.
- The provision of venues for participation sports.
- Sporting goods and apparel.

STRATEGIES FOR MARKETING THROUGH SPORTS   1.1

- Traditional strategies
- Sponsorship strategies
  - Traditional sponsorship
  - Venue naming rights
  - Licensing
  - Endorsements

Access to Spectator Sports Events

For the first time in the team's history, the Boston Red Sox sold out of tickets for each of their 81 home games during the 2004 season. Conversely, the Montreal Expos played some of their scheduled home games in San Juan, Puerto Rico, and then moved their franchise to Washington, DC, to begin the 2005 season. The Expos' problem was that they simply could not sell enough tickets to remain economically viable. Many sports marketing efforts focus on initiatives that can be effective when attempting to sell tickets within the team or event's target markets. Teams have long used promotions such as ladies day and the businessman's special to attract spectators. More recently, teams have emphasized giveaway promotions such as bobblehead dolls and inflatable "thunder sticks." Teams have created family pricing in an effort to make their games affordable. To be more family-friendly, some teams have established family seating areas where the consumption of alcoholic beverages is prohibited. Clearly, there is a wide array of strategies and tactics that can be used to sell tickets. The key for the sports marketer is an understanding of the target markets and the implementation of strategies that are consistent with those target markets.

> To be more family-friendly, some teams have established family seating areas where the consumption of alcoholic beverages is prohibited.

Ticket sales are critically important to the financial success of any team or event. And with the increased number of media options available today, yet another focus is the delivery of sports broadcasts to the media-based audience. Sports marketers are involved with a wide range of events. One recent attempt to categorize these events referred to the *sports event pyramid.*[1] This pyramid consists of five distinct levels with each successively higher level incorporating a broader geographic scope. Figure 1.2 depicts the hierarchy represented by the sports event pyramid.

FIGURE 1.2
The Sports Event Pyramid

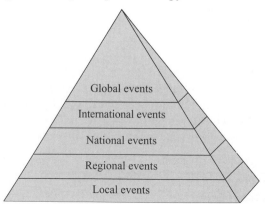

Global events
International events
National events
Regional events
Local events

At the lowest level, *local events* are dominated by the ability to attract spectators from a relatively small geographic area. For such events, the narrow focus will typically consist of the local community. Minor league hockey, high school sports, and local amateur competitions such as a city golf tournament find it difficult to generate much interest from even the most avid sports fan outside of the local area. Because of their small budgets, marketing efforts tend to be quite modest.

If marketing strategy can be used to broaden the level of interest in a local event, it might climb to the second level of the pyramid. *Regional events* comprise the second level. While these events do not generate significant interest at a national or international level, they can be extremely popular within a broader geographic area of a single country. The Boston Marathon has a significant following throughout the northeastern region of the United States. Regional events may attract spectators and TV viewers from areas beyond the local area where the event is staged. There is often a meaningful role for sports marketing as the event organizers attempt to attract spectators and seeks to move the event to the next level of the pyramid.

The third level is characterized by *national events*. These events are important to a large portion of the population of one or two countries. The Stanley Cup hockey playoffs appeal primarily to Canadians and Americans. A cricket or netball test match between Australia and New Zealand is closely watched by citizens of those two countries. In the United States, the NCAA Final Four produces such fan fervor that it is the culmination of a period commonly referred to as *March Madness*. The championship games for professional sports leagues in many countries attract both a large live audience and a large TV audience from across the country. Sports marketing plays a significant role in this type of sports environment.

Events that generate interest in a number of countries fall into the *international events* category. The competition itself may be limited to a single geographic area, but its appeal transcends national borders. The Wimbledon Tennis Tournament is played in England, but it attracts fans and viewers in many countries, especially Belgium, Australia, and the United States. The same may be said for the Tour de France cycling race. In fact, the Tour de France itself now includes race segments outside of France. Multicountry competitions such as the Davis Cup tennis tournament, the Commonwealth Games, the Ryder Cup golf tournament, the America's Cup Yachting Regatta, and Super 14 rugby matches include participants and fans from several countries.

Events that were once best classified as national events may move to this international category with the help of effective marketing. The NFL's Super Bowl was best described as a national event at its inception in 1967. But today it is broadcast across the world. The 2004 game was broadcast in 229 countries and territories by a total of 47 international broadcast organizations. It is estimated that the broadcast was viewed by one billion people.[2] Clearly, the Super Bowl has used aggressive marketing to move itself higher in the event pyramid. In fact, it could easily be argued that the Super Bowl has actually achieved a status that places it in the top category, that of global events.

The top level of the pyramid is comprised of *global events*. There are relatively few events that have been able to attain this lofty designation. Events in this category are not only broadcast to a global audience, but fans throughout the world are captivated by the competition. National pride and patriotism can be impacted by the results. The two preeminent events in this category are the Olympic Games and the World Cup of Soccer. These events will draw billions of TV viewers from all over the world. These events are expensive to stage, so marketing has become a crucial element for their financial success.

> As an event moves up the pyramid, it is likely to be perceived as a more viable opportunity for a company to market its products through the sports event.

Another key point is that as an event moves up the pyramid, it is likely to be perceived as a more viable opportunity for a company to market its non-sports products through the sports event. Larger live and media-based audiences mean that marketers can reach more consumers. This allows organizers to sell broadcast rights for sizable sums of money because the broadcasters can command higher rates for the advertising time during the broadcast of the event. For example, the cost for 30 seconds of advertising time during the most recent Super Bowl broadcast exceeded $2.4 million. These types of events also appeal to companies seeking to align themselves with the event via an official sponsorship. The fees charged to sponsors of premier global events such as the World Cup of Soccer can easily exceed $40 million.

> Fees charged to sponsors of premier global events such as the World Cup of Soccer can easily exceed $40 million.

The Provision of a Venue for Participation Sports

Consumers today enjoy more leisure time than did any previous generation.[3] This increase has been important to sports marketers as they compete to earn a larger share of the consumers' discretionary time. Sports must now compete with the arts and other providers of entertainment, including other sports marketers. While the organizers of a local golf tournament may compete with the local basketball team for spectators, they must also compete with television, theaters, and museums for the consumers' time and money. Also important, consumers today are more inclined to participate in sports activities, and this participation is a direct competitor to the marketer of spectator sports.

Favored sports activities vary from one country to another. As with every marketing endeavor, marketers in every country must be attuned to the preferences within their markets. Another key consideration is that many of these participation sports can be undertaken by consumers who neither own nor maintain the facilities in which the participation takes place. For instance, surfboarding participants generally use public beaches as the site for engaging in their sport. Runners often use local roads as their venue of choice. Hunters generally use public lands as their hunting destination.

Some members of these groups use privately owned venues that are maintained to meet their recreational needs. Participation sports such as golf and downhill skiing generally require the resources of an outside service provider. Runners and others who participate in fitness sports often rely on the resources of fitness club operators. Instead of running on a public street, many find the cushioned tracks at the climate controlled, traffic-free facilities of Gold's Gym to be a superior alternative. Even hunters and those who enjoy fishing may find that privately controlled hunting reserves and lakes provide a less crowded environment as well as a greater likelihood of success. Inline skaters and skateboarders are seeking safer options that not only meet their needs but also meet with less public resistance from citizens who fear the potential danger that these activities present when participants choose to use public streets, walkways, and parking areas.

Other activities generally require facilities that are operated by an outside provider. In some cases, these facilities are maintained by local government agencies. Examples include swimming pools, tennis courts, and skating rinks. But in most cases, privately owned facilities offer a superior option to publicly owned and operated facilities. While some tennis players might opt to play at a public park, others prefer to play at a private racquet club.

For some participation sports, the most viable option for the typical consumer is the use of privately owned and operated facilities. The expense of building and maintaining a golf course makes individual ownership unfeasible for all but the wealthiest consumers. As a consequence, golfers generally play on courses owned by someone else. A golf course may be owned and operated by a local government or a private corporation. Privately owned courses may be open to the public or they may require a membership in order for the golfer to gain access to the course. Other participation sports that generally require special facilities include racket sports such as squash and racquetball, skiing and snowboarding, and ten-pin bowling. The 35 most popular participation sports and activities in the United States are shown in Table 1.1. The list illustrates the variety of activities and the array of opportunities that are available to sports marketers.

Sports marketers must stay abreast of changes in the supply and demand for facilities dedicated to each of the participation sports that are popular within their markets. The popularity of golf has been on an upswing, thus we have seen new courses opening each year. Conversely, bowling has seen a steady decline in its number of participants in the United States. These declining numbers have led to the closure of existing bowling facilities, and only limited resources are now being devoted to the construction of new bowling establishments. Ironically, both of these trends seem to have changed direction within the last two years. The golf market fell slightly in 2003 while the bowling market benefited from significant growth.

TABLE 1.1
Most Popular Sports in the United States in 2003

Source: Anonymous, "SGMA Sports Participation Trends," August 2004, www.SGMA.com (accessed August 28, 2004) Reprinted with permission of SGMA.

Activity	Number of Participants	Growth from 2002
Swimming (recreational)	96,400,000	4.1%
Walking (recreational)	88,800,000	4.5
Bowling	55,000,000	3.5
Bicycling (recreational)	53,700,000	0.3
Fishing	53,000,000	3.0
Free weights	51,600,000	6.9
Camping	51,000,000	2.4
Treadmill exercise	45,600,000	4.9
Stretching	42,100,000	9.7
Billiards/pool	40,700,000	3.0
Hiking	40,400,000	6.7
Fitness bicycling	37,900,000	(0.1)
Fitness walking	36,100,000	0.8
Basketball	35,400,000	(3.1)
Stationary cycling	31,000,000	6.4
Resistance machines	30,000,000	7.7
Cardio kickboxing	28,000,000	4.3
Golf	27,300,000	(1.8)
Volleyball	20,300,000	(5.6)
Target shooting	19,800,000	12.7
Darts	19,500,000	(1.1)
In-line skating	19,200,000	(10.8)
Football	18,000,000	(4.0)
Soccer	17,700,000	0.2
Abdominal machine/device	17,300,000	0.0
Tennis	17,300,000	5.9
Ice skating	17,000,000	17.3
Aerobics	16,500,000	2.5
Softball	16,000,000	(3.4)
Horseback riding	16,000,000	9.3

Marketers involved in participation sports seek to develop strategies to retain current participants and to attract new ones. Still other sports marketers understand that participation often requires special equipment. This recognition leads us to the third category in the marketing of sports, namely the creation of demand for sporting goods and apparel.

Sporting Goods and Apparel

This third category for the marketing of sports is comprised of two types of products: those used in participation sports and those that represent keepsakes, replicas, and souvenirs from spectator sports events. Consumers might purchase a basketball in order to play games at their local playground or they might purchase a replica ball that includes the team and league logos as well as replica signatures of the players on that team.

Many sports such as golf, skiing, and tennis generally require participants to personally own their equipment. Some, such as bowling, provide basic equipment for free or for a nominal rental fee. Regardless, the marketers seek to influence demand for their equipment. New players and participants take up a sport and purchase new equipment. Current players often seek to upgrade their own equipment in order to take advantage of technological advances. The player's objective is often simply that of improving one's proficiency at his or her chosen sport. A new golf club that hits the ball farther, a new tennis racket with a larger sweet spot, and a bowling ball with stronger hooking characteristics can provide the incentive for participants to abandon their existing equipment in an effort to improve their play.

New players, novices, and experts have different expectations regarding new products. A young bowler who plays primarily for social reasons may want a bowling ball that glows under the ultraviolet lights used during "Cosmic Bowling." An expert may own several bowling balls that react differently when thrown. These experts are far more likely to spend a large sum of money on a ball that possesses the newest technological advance. And while the social bowler may purchase equipment at a general merchandise store, the expert is far more likely to be a patron of a pro shop that specializes in bowling equipment. Effective marketing is directed by an understanding of who is participating in a given sport, why they are participating, and what benefits they are seeking from their participation. This knowledge allows sports marketers to capitalize on many of the opportunities that exist within the marketplace.

Many fans of spectator sports will purchase one or more souvenirs that can be used as a remembrance of attendance at a particular event or as a visual means of demonstrating support for a team, event, or player. Some of these products may serve a purpose beyond simply being a souvenir. A ball may bear a team's logo, but it can still be used for recreational purposes by the fan. A team shirt may reflect the fan's support for that team, but it can also be worn as part of the fan's daily attire.

New merchandising strategies extend beyond the event venue. Retailers have begun to appear at regional shopping malls, and many retail sites have emerged on the Internet. Sports marketers need to understand the appeal that these types of products have and develop a marketing strategy that capitalizes on that demand. The product component of marketing strategy will be expanded and explored in detail in Chapter 16.

The Need for a Sports Marketing Curriculum

"Within the span of a single generation, sports marketing has evolved from a two-bit enterprise into a big business bonanza."[4] The sheer scope of sports marketing highlights the need to develop educational programs that teach the fundamental aspects of the discipline. It is a global phenomenon with enormous economic consequences. A generation ago, there was little formal training on the tasks involved in the marketing of sports. And beyond using advertising during the broadcasts of sports events, there was virtually no coverage of the use of sports as a platform for the marketing of non-sports products.

Business curricula have been slow to incorporate sports marketing as part of a degree program. This is changing, however, as we are witnessing a significant growth in the number of courses and programs that feature sports marketing. Some programs such as the sports marketing program in the Business School at ESSEC in France have even begun to secure corporate sponsors. With sound marketing principles being incorporated within the sports marketing curriculum, future practitioners will be better prepared to implement strategies that capitalize on the opportunities presented by the sports environment.

Evolution of Sports Marketing as an Educational Discipline

Just as the practice of sports marketing has evolved over the years, so has the curriculum that is used to train aspiring sports marketing practitioners. Early efforts simply involved the consideration of the marketing of sports; virtually no attention was paid to the strategic initiatives used to market everyday products through sports. Marketing curricula sometimes incorporated a limited number of sports examples within the principles of marketing class or treated it as one area that could be used to illustrate the concept of services marketing.

The most comprehensive coverage was initially provided in sports management courses that were taught in programs featuring leisure studies, health, physical education, recreation, sports administration, and kinesiology. The programs initially featured a single sports marketing course that focused primarily on the marketing of sports. They may have incorporated travel and tourism as we began to give additional consideration to the role that sports played in the consumers' planning of their vacations. Consumers traveled to watch their favorite teams play games away from home; they took golf vacations. The economic impact began to be noticed. Still, sports marketing primarily emphasized the methods for putting more fans in stadium seats and to increase participation levels in sports such as golf and tennis.

Television was limited to a small number of stations in each media market, and viewers received a limited amount of sports programming each week. But TV and radio broadcasts began to be recognized for their potential to reach a firm's target markets. As a result, the idea of marketing through sports became more important. It could be argued that the explosion in media options created by cable TV was a turning point in the evolution of sports marketing. The discipline began to incorporate a more pronounced business orientation in both theory and practice.

Despite this newfound business orientation in the practice of sports marketing, this focus was slow to be incorporated within the curriculum of most business and management schools. Its integration was typically limited to a single elective course that was part of the undergraduate marketing program. More attention began to be paid to activities such as sponsorship and advertising during sports broadcasts. Marketing through sports was emerging as a key aspect of the sports marketing environment.

Finally, comprehensive sports marketing and sports management programs began to emerge. The early development again was concentrated in the programs that featured leisure studies or health, physical education, and recreation. Graduate programs that granted advanced degrees in sport management were developed. For these graduate degrees, complementary courses needed to be developed. These new courses often included facilities management, sports law, finance, ethics, and the media. Business-oriented programs that have developed sports marketing concentrations have begun to include courses such as sports economics, sponsorship, the marketing of sports, and marketing through sports. Because of the interdisciplinary nature of the sports environment, university programs often involve courses from two or more curriculum areas. A common alliance is that of physical education and marketing.

> Today's curriculum represents an amalgamation of strategies that emphasize both the marketing of sports and the marketing of nonsports products through sports.

The primary point of the preceding discussion is that the early focus was on the marketing of sports, but that today's curriculum represents an amalgamation of strategies that emphasize both the marketing of sports and the marketing of nonsports products through sports. In addition to this evolution, we have witnessed a growth in the number of universities offering degrees with a major that features the business component of the sports environment. More graduate programs have also emerged. These developments represent global phenomena with programs being introduced in universities in many countries across the world.

Economic Impact

Sports and the related industries that serve the sports industry can have a tremendous impact on local, national, and global economies. Because of the recognition of this benefit, there have been a number of recent efforts that emphasized the calculation of estimates for the financial impact of some sport or a specific sports event. Similar estimates have also been developed in an effort to assess the impact of art exhibits, local festivals, and a variety of other nonsports events.

Municipal governments use the economic contributions to offset financial incentives that are granted and costs that are incurred as a result of playing host to a team or an event. These estimates are also used to help government agencies determine how resources should be allocated when promoting these sports products to the public.

Economic estimates range from those involved with a single, one-day event such as a boxing match to an event that stretches over an extended period of time such as the Olympic Games. There have been estimates of the broader impact of golf on the economy of a state. Finally, from a macro perspective, there have been efforts to gauge the aggregate impact of the sports industry on the national economy. These types of studies are summarized in Table 1.2.

TABLE 1.2
Types and Examples of Economic Impact Studies

Category	Example
One-day event	Boston Marathon
Multiday event	America's Cup Yachting Regatta
Participation/recreation activity	Golf in the state of Arizona
Professional team or arena	New York Yankees
Aggregate	American Gross Domestic Sports Product (GDSP)

APPLICATION OF THE MULTIPLIER   1.2

Initial estimate of direct economic impact	$5,000,000
(times) the appropriate multiplier	1.7
Adjusted estimate	$8,500,000

Components of Economic Impact Estimates

These estimates generally incorporate one or two key components. First is the level of direct spending by consumers involved in the engagement of the various sports activities. For an event, this component will include revenues from the sale of tickets and related merchandise at the event venue. It will also incorporate other related expenditures that result from the event, including public transportation, local accommodations, restaurant meals, gasoline, and other entertainment expenditures. Some estimates include compensation paid to participants and other local employees when that money is expected to remain in the local economy for which the measurement is being developed. For a participation sport or recreation activity, many of these same economic considerations are incorporated. For instance, downhill skiers not only purchase lift tickets, but they may take a plane to the resort city, stay in local accommodations, and patronize local restaurants and bars.

A second component is an adjustment that reflects the fact that the initial expenditures support subsequent economic activity. For instance, the money paid by a golfer for greens fees does not simply lie dormant. Employees, service providers, and taxes are paid before the profits can be counted. Individuals who are paid by the golf course operators may spend their money in the local community as well. In a manner of speaking, each dollar is actually spent more than once. The adjustment tool used to revise the estimate is called the multiplier. The *multiplier* represents the number of times that each dollar will be spent before it "leaks out" of the economy under scrutiny.[5] Clearly the value of the multiplier depends upon how quickly the money exits the economy. Money that tends to stay longer will produce a higher value, whereas money that is quickly removed will result in a lower value.

To apply the multiplier, the initial estimate for the direct expenditures is increased by the percentage that is reflected in the multiplier. If the initial estimate of economic activity was $5,000,000 and the multiplier was 1.7, then the revised estimate is $8,500,000. Box 1.2 illustrates this type of adjustment.

The typical multiplier reportedly ranges between 1.3 and 3.0. Multipliers make sense for local estimates because the events and activities tend to bring new money into the economy, money that might not otherwise be available to local workers and merchants. Conversely, it may be argued that multipliers should not be used for national events because the resultant revenues may simply represent a reallocation of the consumers' expenditures. If a person chooses to play golf instead of attending a play, it isn't new money to the national economy. However, for events that attract international fans and participants, multipliers may be relevant. For instance, when Brazilian soccer fans spent money at a World Cup event in Germany, there was a new infusion of economic activity in Germany that otherwise would not have existed.

One-Day Events

From a relatively narrow perspective, efforts to estimate the economic impact of events that last a short period of time are often undertaken. In many cases, these events are not staged in the same location each time. For example, the Super Bowl is played in a different city each year. Not only is economic activity generated on the day of the event, but the economy will also benefit from the short-term run-up in activity. Participants, fans, and the media use local hotels and restaurants. They rent cars and purchase souvenirs. They create the need for temporary jobs. Revenues from both income taxes and sales-based taxes will increase. After virtually every major event, there are media reports that indicate the estimated economic impact of the event. Event organizers and area politicians tout these estimates as justification for incurring the expenses associated with staging the event.

> A recent Super Bowl in Atlanta was estimated to have brought 94,000 visitors and produced a $215 million economic bonanza.

Some estimates specify the number of visitors to an area as well as the economic infusion resulting from an event. A recent Super Bowl in Atlanta was estimated to have brought 94,000 visitors and produced a $215 million economic bonanza.[6] In Australia, the Queensland state government looked to the Indy 300 race as a tool to help rescue a struggling economy. Pre-race estimates speculated about producing 700 new jobs, 175,000 visitor nights in local accommodations, and a $40 million (U.S.) contribution to the state's economy.[7]

Multiday Events

Many major events extend for a period of several days or longer. A typical PGA golf tournament takes place over one entire week, with qualifying, practice rounds, pro-am competitions, and the actual tournament competition. The Summer Olympic Games extend over 17 days. The World Cup of Soccer extends over several weeks, and the America's Cup Regatta takes several months from start to finish. Beyond the world of sports, a rock concert may last only one night, but an art exhibit may take place over several weeks or months.

Prior to the 2004 Olympic Games in Athens, economists were forecasting a net impact that would result in a 1 percent increase in the Greek gross domestic product (GDP). While much of this increase was directly related to attendance at the various events, it was also believed that Greece would host an additional one million tourists because of its status and the favorable publicity received as an Olympic destination.[8] For the 2000 Olympic Games in Sydney, the estimated one-month infusion to the Australian economy was $1.4 billion. The first balance-of-trade surplus for Australia in several years was attributed to the Games. That same year, the America's Cup Yachting Regatta was staged in New Zealand. An estimated $187 million was pumped into the New Zealand economy based on spending from international visitors, governmental bodies, competing yachting syndicates, and the media.[9]

The growth trend associated with this type of event has been difficult for organizers and governments to ignore. For example, consider the estimate that indicated that the 2004 Ryder Cup competition directly created a $150 million injection into the southeastern Michigan region where the event was staged.[10] This figure was almost double the estimate for the 2002 Ryder Cup that was held in Warwickshire, England. While noting an economic impact of $78 million, the director of economic development for the Warwickshire area indicated that the event was "a tremendous boost to the local economy. It's not just spending on hotels and entertainment, but many of the spectators will bring partners who will go shopping or visit the sights."[11]

> It's not just spending on hotels and entertainment, but many of the spectators will bring partners who will go shopping or visit the sights.

Similar estimates are often developed for nonsports events. For example, it was estimated that an exhibit of Vincent Van Gogh's paintings at the Detroit Institute of Arts pumped some $93 million into the metropolitan Detroit economy.[12]

Participation Sport or Recreational Activity

Recently there have been several notable efforts to estimate the economic activity that can be attributed to a particular sport or recreational activity. In many regards, this process is similar to that of estimating the impact of events such as a one-day race. Fans attending not only spend money on tickets; they also purchase lodging at temporary accommodations, restaurant food, gasoline, and a variety of other goods and services. And though it is a one-day event, the duration of activity associated with it is often extended over a period of time. Using similar measurement techniques, the state of Michigan develops estimates of the economic impact of its two-week deer-hunting season, and South Carolina and Michigan scrutinize the impact of golf on those states' economies over the course of the calendar year. One recent estimate for Michigan indicated that golf created a yearly infusion of $950 million to the state's economy.[13]

> One recent estimate for Michigan indicated that golf created a yearly infusion of $950 million to the state's economy.

Professional Team or Arena

Local governmental officials often use estimates of economic impact as a justification for expending tax money and other resources to support a bid to acquire a new sports franchise or to retain an existing one. One prevailing belief is that construction jobs will be created by virtue of the need to build a new stadium or arena. A variety of other jobs will also be created; these range from lower-paid seasonal jobs at the venues to highly paid executives and athletes. Each of these individuals will earn income and pay taxes. They will also spend money on local housing and at local retailers. In addition to this economic infusion, spectators will spend money at the sports venue. The visiting team may also have a large following of its supporters. These visiting fans also spend money on local goods and services.

While it is apparent that a sports team can drive economic activity, the exact economic impact is difficult, if not impossible, to measure. Estimates may involve a monetary amount, or they may be based upon forecasts of measures of increases in local employment. The projections may focus on a single year, or they may represent forecasts that encompass a number of years over an extended period of time.

The Virginia Baseball Stadium Authority was recently formed in an effort to convince Major League Baseball to move the existing Montreal team to the Northern Virginia–Washington, DC area. The group also had to convince local residents and government officials that the team would make a meaningful contribution to the local economy. They cited estimates for the construction of a new baseball park and annual inflows that would result from operations.

The construction of the stadium was projected to last two years. The project would create 3,384 jobs that would generate almost $9 million in tax revenues. Following its completion, the stadium was projected to create 3,938 full-time jobs that would result in some $20.8 million per year in tax revenues for the state and local governments. Overall, for the first 30 years, the estimated impact for the affected government entities was some $266.4 million.[14] It is important to note that these estimates simply look at tax collections and they do not consider the significant impact that the team might have on local businesses.

Another comprehensive study was undertaken by the city of Arlington, Texas, in its effort to determine the contributions of the local Major League Baseball team. The assessment took four categories into account. The economic impact was deemed to have been derived from franchise operations, visiting team personnel spending, patron spending, and out-of-stadium miscellaneous activities. It also considered two types of economic output: direct and induced. The net result was that the stadium activities were projected to contribute approximately $155 million to the city's economy. The categories and the corresponding estimates are summarized in Table 1.3.

TABLE 1.3
Economic Impact Study–Arlington, TX

Source: W. Schaffer, "The Sports Industry: Definitions and Reappraisals," unpublished paper, Southern Regional Science Association, April 1997.

Categories	Total Economic Impact
Franchise operations	
Tickets	$81,521,000
Parking revenue	10,166,000
Concessions/souvenirs	33,419,000
Category total	$125,106,000
Visiting team personnel spending	
Hotel	$208,000
Restaurant	132,000
Category total	$340,000
Patron spending	
Hotel/lodging	$5,224,000
Restaurants/bars	8,055,000
Grocery stores	4,181,000
Car rental/gasoline stations	3,118,000
Convenience stores	2,339,000
Other retail	1,559,000
Category total	$24,476,000
Out-of-stadium miscellaneous activities	
Category total	$5,130,000
Total economic impact	$155,052,000

Aggregate Economic Impact

There have been broad-based estimates that were designed to provide a measure of the overall economic impact of the sports industry on a large economy such as a state or an entire country. The biggest dilemma faced by those seeking to implement this type of measurement process is that of reaching agreement on exactly what constitutes the sports industry domain. In other words, what should be measured? While measurement may be relatively simple when the focus is a single event such as the Super Bowl, it becomes more complex when the focus shifts to estimates for events such as the Olympics that take place over an extended period of time. When the objective becomes one of determining the aggregate economic impact of sports, the task becomes significantly more difficult. Perhaps the most problematic issue is the failure to accurately define the sports industry.[15] To fully assess the economic impact, there is a need to consider three primary sectors. According to one source, these three sectors are

- Sports entertainment.
- Sports products.
- Sports support organizations.[16]

When activities in these sectors are measured, the aggregate economic impact can be calculated. Much the way a nation's total economic output constitutes its gross domestic product, a comparable measure can be tailored to the sports industry. This measure has been specified as the *gross domestic sports product (GDSP)*.[17] A good starting point is an understanding of exactly what components make up each of these three sectors. They are summarized in Table 1.4. The lists shown are designed to provide an understanding of each sector. While each list is a representation of its domain, they are far from complete. This difficulty in identifying the components of sports marketing makes the measurement of GDSP even more difficult.

There have been limited efforts to compute the GDSP over the years. One somewhat dated estimate for the United States is from 1995. The figure of $151.9 billion made sports

TABLE 1.4
The Components of the GDSP

Sports Entertainment	Sports Products	Sports Support Organizations
Spectator sports tickets	Sporting goods	Consulting firms
Pro and amateur	Sports-related goods	Advertising agencies
Participation sports fees	Apparel	Sports law services
Spectator sports concessions	Footwear	Agents
Spectator sports souvenirs	Videos	League offices
Pari-mutuel betting receipts	Magazines	Sports organizations
Sports museum/display receipts	Licensed products	NCAA
Related tourism	Sports investment	USOC
	Construction	
	Stadia	
	Golf courses	
	Ski resorts	
	Swimming pools	
	Net sports exports	

the eleventh largest industry in the United States and comprised slightly more than 2 percent of the overall GDP.[18] Thus, if we take the GDP from government statistics that are published each year, we can develop a rough estimate of the GDSP by multiplying the GDP figure by 2 percent. For example, the estimate for the American GDP in 2003 was $11.0 trillion.[19] Thus 2 percent of that value, or $220 billion, would represent the portion that is estimated to be devoted to the sports industry in 2003.

A major concern is that expenditures on sports products and services are likely to be growing faster than the overall economy. Thus, it is likely that the 2 percent figure is low, thereby resulting in a conservative estimate for the American GDSP. Care should also be taken not to assume that the 2 percent figure is applicable in the task of estimating the GDSP for countries other than the United States. Still, by any measure, it is evident that sports are a major force in a nation's economy. It is this force that has led to the growth of jobs for those seeking employment in the sports marketing industry.

Career Opportunities in the Field of Sports Marketing

As evidenced by the increased emphasis on economic considerations, it is obvious that, for many, the sports industry has evolved into a form of business where the focus is on the bottom line. This focus has resulted in an increased need for individuals who are trained in marketing. In many cases, this training takes the form of a traditional marketing curriculum. But the growth of the industry has created an increased demand for employees with education and experience specific to the field of sports marketing. This growth is a global phenomenon with the most significant increases occurring in Australia, China, Europe, and North America.

> The growth of the industry has created an increased demand for employees with education and experience specific to the field of sports marketing.

The career opportunities include jobs within both key domains of sports marketing. Specifically, there is a need for employees with skills required for the effective marketing of a myriad of sports products as well as for individuals who are adept at using the sports environment to facilitate the marketing of nonsports products.

How can we sell more tickets to a golf tournament? What techniques can be used to get more golfers to play a particular course? Can a marketing strategy be designed so as to create a preference for a particular brand of golf ball? And how can golf be used as part of a strategic initiative designed to support the marketing of a luxury automobile? Clearly, there are many opportunities to work within the field of sports marketing. The following discussion is meant to highlight some of these career opportunities.

Internships

First and foremost, students who are interested in working in the sports marketing industry should seek to be placed in an internship program prior to graduation. This is especially true for anyone seeking to be involved in the marketing of sports. Most professional teams seek interns in a variety of career paths. While these encompass many dimensions of marketing such as sponsorship sales, ticket sales, and corporate promotions, they also include other business functions such as accounting, hospitality, and human resources.

> Students who are interested in working in the sports marketing industry should seek to be placed in an internship program prior to graduation.

The upside of these internships is the networking that allows students to develop relationships with practitioners in the sports industry. They also allow one to gain experience in the field, and this experience is often a key asset upon graduation. Interns may even discover that while it is the sports industry, it is still a job that is quite demanding of their time. The downside is that most internships are unpaid. It is the simple law of supply and demand. There are few positions and many students seeking them, thus the cost of hiring an intern is quite low. Students need to look at the short-term sacrifice as a means of gaining long-term satisfaction with a career in the exciting world of sports marketing.

Many professional teams, organizations, and facilities post internships on their websites. Some even allow potential applicants to receive e-mail notifications when new openings are posted. Students should invest the time to explore the websites of targeted employers and seek all available information. Consider some of the following internship and career opportunities.

Sales

As with many industries, the field of sports marketing has a need for professional salespeople. In the marketing of sports, account representatives are employed to sustain relationships with season ticket holders. These representatives are points of contact with consumers and organizations that have purchased season tickets. Another area is that of group sales; these professionals work with both consumers and organizations that are interested in purchasing a large number of tickets for a limited number of events.

In the task of marketing through sports, a key sales area is that of selling sponsorship opportunities. Representatives of events, teams, and facilities interact with businesses that might benefit from such an association. Sponsors seldom seek ways to spend their money; rather, sports organizations approach them with sponsorship proposals. Salespeople may also be used to solicit potential advertisers who seek to reach their target markets during radio and TV broadcasts, in printed event programs, and with an array of venue alternatives such as stadium signage. The field of sales presents an array of entry-level and senior-level opportunities for those individuals who are interested in a career in the sports marketing industry.

Advertising

While many sports organizations depend upon advertising agencies, some will maintain an in-house staff for certain advertising tasks. This may involve copywriting, graphics design, and the purchase of media space and time. Those working in this area may be creating advertising or managing a promotional campaign for their own sports organization. Alternatively, they may be providing similar services for clients who are seeking to use sports as a platform for marketing their own products. Advertising is an essential element for the marketers of sports as well as those involved in marketing through sports.

Marketing Research

Every industry today has the opportunity to operate more effectively when they have enhanced their knowledge of the marketplace. Sports marketing has begun to aggressively seek information about fans, participants, and the competition. Professional teams are engaging in customer satisfaction surveys. Economic impact studies often involve surveys designed to solicit feedback on consumer behavior. The recognized value of and the need for this type of information have created demand for employees (and consultants) with research skills.

Hospitality

Many businesses use sports as a tool for entertaining clients, employees, and business associates. This may involve facilities such as a luxury suite at a major venue or a private tent at a local event. Salespeople are used to market a broad array of hospitality alternatives. A key aspect of hospitality is the management of food and beverage services.

Facilities Management

Sports and special event venues represent significant investments for governmental, university, and sports entities. Many venues seek a variety of entertainment alternatives. While a stadium may host 81 Major League Baseball games in a season, management often seeks an array of events to create an additional revenue stream and to better utilize the available resources. Stadia and arenas may feature concerts, circuses, alternative sports events, and other exhibitions. The facilities manager must schedule events while avoiding conflicts. Food and beverages must be ordered. A manageable workforce must be maintained. This job involves skills in marketing, sales, human resources, planning, and hospitality.

Public Relations

Most teams, leagues, events, and associations seek positive public relations regarding their operations and role within the community. Public relations professionals write press releases and interact with the local media. Generally speaking, the objective is to gain favorable publicity that enhances the image of the sports entity in the eyes of the public. Written and oral communications skills are extremely important for those seeking employment in this facet of the sports marketing industry.

Agents

Many individuals pose the question of how they can become an agent. This most often involves the representation of an athlete, but it can also involve the licensing of registered trademarks. Since this job is based on contract law as well as intellectual property rights, the aspiring agent should have a good grasp of the legal environment as well as fundamental business principles. Some player agents work as independent contractors while others are employed by major representation firms such as the International Management Group (IMG).

Retailing

The sale of sports equipment and apparel is often achieved via the use of channels of distribution that feature sports specialty stores. While one might readily envision the salesperson's role in this environment, many other career opportunities exist. Store management and purchasing are two key areas for employment. Even in large, diverse retail operations, there may be a need for purchasing agents who specialize in sports-related products. Also important are those who manage storage and distribution centers in an effort to coordinate a market's supply and demand.

Sponsorship Purchasing

While the job of selling sponsorships was discussed earlier, there is a need for sponsorship experts on the buyer's side as well. Organizations such as Visa International and McDonald's are inundated with sponsorship proposals. There is a need to evaluate the proposals and invest only in those that represent the proper fit for the prospective sponsor. Thus, the task is one of eliminating sponsorship proposals that are not likely to generate an acceptable return on the sponsor's investment. While this is important for all organizations, jobs of this type are likely to exist only within large corporations that invest in a number of different types of promotional efforts.

Sponsorship Evaluation

Many consulting firms have emerged in recent years. Among those important to the sports industry are those that seek to evaluate the impact of a sponsorship over the course of an event or season. A. C. Nielsen is best known for its TV ratings; however, it has recently introduced a new service that is designed to provide sponsors with an estimate of the economic value of their sponsorships. Other companies employ people to develop similar measures and to sell their services to sponsors.

Participation Center Management

A key dimension in the sports industry is the participation market. Consumers play golf, ski, bowl, and engage in fitness activities. More often than not, these types of activities take place away from the participant's home. Golf course operators and fitness centers must market their services in an increasingly competitive environment. The operators of a ski resort want you to choose skiing over a golf vacation. Furthermore, they want you to select their resort over that of a neighboring competitor. Customer acquisition and customer retention are based upon the marketing efforts used by the staff of the center.

Career Trends

There continues to be substantial growth in the demand for employees who are trained to work in the business side of the sports industry. Major growth continues in Australia, China, Europe, and North America. The skills sought by employers tend to emphasize sales and marketing. Other critical areas are the media and the Internet. Recognizing this trend, colleges and universities have begun to incorporate more sports marketing and sponsorship courses as part of their curriculum. Students seeking employment in the sports marketing industry should take advantage of these newer course offerings. They should also consider seeking an internship prior to graduation. The experience gained and the networking opportunities can be critical points of differentiation among students seeking to get their foot in the door of the sports marketing arena. Sports will continue to gain stature as a marketing platform. This will help sustain the growth in the demand for sports marketing practitioners.

> Sports will continue to gain stature as a marketing platform; this will help sustain the growth in the demand for sports marketing practitioners.

Closing Capsule

There are two primary domains in the sports marketing environment: the marketing of sports and marketing through sports. Companies have long used sports as a platform for selling their products. Athletes are featured on packaging and endorsements for products ranging from breakfast cereals to laser eye surgery. Venue naming rights have emerged as a popular and effective means of getting a marketer's name in front of the public. The sale of officially licensed merchandise continues to grow at a rapid pace. But perhaps the most dramatic use of sports as a marketing tool involves the use of traditional sponsorship. From large, expensive events such as the Olympics to small local events such as a charity golf tournament, sponsorship continues to represent a popular way of cutting through advertising clutter and reaching potential customers.

> Sponsorship continues to represent a popular way of cutting through advertising clutter and reaching potential customers.

The marketing of sports includes the tasks of getting more people to attend an event or watch it on TV, influencing demand for sporting goods and apparel, and providing facilities for participants in sports such as golf, skiing, and aerobics. Spectator sports events range from small local competitions to those with enormous global implications. Regardless of the geographic scope of the event, marketing can play an instrumental role in its financial success. Participation sports vary significantly from one country to another; in fact, there are regional differences within many ethnic and geographically diverse countries such as the United States. Marketers must recognize these differences and not treat the market as a homogeneous collection of individuals who can be reached with a single universal strategy.

The marketing of sporting goods and apparel has changed significantly in recent years. Efforts have been made to widen interest in sports such as basketball, rugby, and cricket. The Internet has made it easier to reach a global market. Retailers such as Wal-Mart, Carrefours, and Kmart have more of an international presence than ever before. Retailing has changed as large superstores have come to dominate the retail environment, and distribution channels have gotten shorter. Marketers have had to adapt to these dramatic changes in order to effectively reach those consumers who are predisposed to purchase a vast array of sporting goods.

Colleges and universities have recognized the economic power of the sports industry as well as the need to develop skills among their students seeking a career in the business of sports. As a result, new programs have been developed. These range from the introduction of a single sports marketing course to doctoral programs in sports administration. These curricula continue to evolve, and today they have a stronger business focus than ever before. Clearly, the task of marketing through sports has gained importance in today's marketing curriculum.

The acknowledgment of the power of the sports industry is based, in part, on the recent emphasis on measuring the economic impact of sporting events and activities. From one-day events such as a boxing match to overall estimates of a country's gross domestic sports product, there has been an increased effort to quantify the impact that sports have on local, national, and global economies.

> Aspiring sports marketers should not confuse it with playing a game. It is a job, one that demands time, energy, commitment, and knowledge.

There are numerous opportunities for careers in sports marketing. While an interest in sports helps make the job more enjoyable, it alone will not be sufficient for the aspiring sports marketer. Students are encouraged to seek internships with professional teams and sports organizations. In this capacity, they will develop skills and build a network of references for full-time jobs upon graduation. Marketing and communications skills are crucial for those seeking permanent employment in the sports industry. But aspiring sports marketers should not confuse it with playing a game. It is a job, one that demands time, energy, commitment, and knowledge.

Review Questions

1. Briefly explain the two domains of sports marketing.
2. Why do you think that the marketing of products through sports has gained so much attention over the past 20 years?
3. What are the four types of sponsorship that were discussed in this chapter? Identify an example of each within your home country.
4. Explain the sports event pyramid.
5. Why are sports marketing curricula at universities increasing their emphasis on business principles today?
6. Why has there been an increased emphasis on economic impact studies?
7. Briefly explain the GDSP.
8. Explain why multipliers are often used to adjust estimates of economic impact.
9. Why are internships considered so important for students who anticipate seeking employment in the sports marketing industry?

Endnotes

1. D. Shani and D. Sandler, "Climbing the Sports Event Pyramid," *Marketing News,* August 26, 1996, p. 6.
2. D. Barrand, "Super Bowl to Reach 1 Billion," January 29, 2004, www.sportbusiness.com/news/index?news_item_id=153630 (accessed October 13, 2005).
3. S. Hofacre and T. Burman, "Demographic Changes in the U.S. into the Twenty-First Century: Their Impact on Sport Marketing," *Sport Marketing Quarterly* 1, no. 1 (1992), pp. 31–36.
4. R. Monts, "To Market, to Market," *Detroiter,* January–February 1998, pp. 33–36.
5. A. Meek, "An Estimate of the Size and Supported Activity of the Sports Industry in the United States," *Sport Marketing Quarterly* 6, no. 4 (1997), pp. 15–21.
6. "Big News down South," October 18, 2000, www.nfl.com/news/001018supermoney.html (accessed November 1, 2000).
7. G. Ansley, "Queensland Looking to Indy 300," *New Zealand Herald,* August 16, 2003.
8. D. Barrand, "Athens to Get Economic Boost," August 28, 2003, www.sportbusiness.com/index?news_item_id=152321 (accessed October 13, 2003).
9. "Sport Boosts Economics," *SportBusiness International,* December 2000.
10. R. King, "Event Is Ticket to Schmooze," *Detroit News,* June 13, 2004, pp. 1B, 8B.
11. S. Gerlis, "Ryder Cup's $78 Million Cash Boost," September 25, 2002, www.sportbusiness.com/news/ index?news_item_id=148555 (accessed October 13, 2005).
12. J. Colby, "Van Gogh Exhibit Is $93 Million Work of Art," September 22, 2000, www.detroitnews.com /2000/metro/0009/23/a01-123697.htm (accessed October 13, 2005).
13. R. Dodge and S. Fullerton, "Michigan Golf: Attitudes, Play & Economic Impact," October 21, 1997, www.webgolfer.com/sportsresearch/golf_report/golf_content.html (accessed October 13, 2005).

14. "New Baseball Team Would Create 3,384 Jobs," January 20, 2003, www.espn.go.com/mlb/news/2003/0120/1496072.html (accessed October 13, 2005).

15. "Economics Research Associates Project 15652," *Economic and Fiscal Impacts for the Proposed NFL Stadium in Arlington, TX,* August 30, 2004, p. 34.

16. Meek, "An Estimate of the Size and Supported Activity of the Sports Industry in the United States."

17. Ibid.

18. Ibid.

19. "News Release: Gross Domestic Product and Corporate Profits," *BEA News,* September 29, 2005, www.bea.gov/bea/newsrel/gdpnewsrel.htm (accessed October 13, 2005).

Marketing Through Sports

Part Two begins with an assessment of the four domains in sports marketing. Once these are identified, the focus is on the use of sports as a tool for the marketing of nonsports products. In some cases, marketing through sports involves the traditional elements common to effective marketing strategies. With traditional strategies, the marketer's task is one of aligning its product, distribution, pricing, and promotion strategies with its selected target markets while incorporating a sports overlay. The other broad approach to marketing through sports involves the implementation of some form of sponsorship. These include traditional sponsorship, endorsements, venue naming rights, and licensing.

CHAPTER TWO

Marketing Through Sports

Learning Objectives

- Learn strategies for marketing through sports.
- Identify elements of mainstream strategies.
- Reinforce understanding of marketing mix.
- Learn about new promotional tools.

The sports marketing environment encompasses two distinctly different domains. While there is quick acknowledgment of efforts designed to increase demand for spectator sports, participation sports, and a variety of other sports-related products, the task of selling non-sports products through the application of a sports platform is largely overlooked. This is unfortunate because it is this domain in which many marketers will work as they seek to implement sports marketing strategies. This text will address both domains; however, the objective of this chapter is to acquaint the reader with the various ways in which marketers can use a sports overlay in their task of implementing effective marketing strategies for nonsports products. Once the marketer has decided to use sports as the foundation for its marketing strategy, the next question concerns the level of integration. Based upon the nature of the marketer's relationship with sports, these strategies can be classified into two broad categories: traditional strategies and sponsorship-based strategies.

Traditional strategies involve the basic components of a marketing strategy: a target market and a corresponding marketing mix. As such, these strategic initiatives involve no official relationship with a sports entity such as a league, team, or player. Conversely, *sponsorship* involves an array of activities whereby the marketer attempts to capitalize on an official relationship with an event, a team, a player, or some other sports organization such as the NCAA, the IOC, or FIFA. This chapter will focus on traditional strategies; the various types of sponsorship-based strategies will be discussed in depth in Chapters 3 through 14.

The Sports Marketing Environment

When the discussion focuses on the role that sports play in the task of marketing products, it is useful to consider two key dimensions. When differentiating among products, an appropriate classification is the simple designation of sports products and nonsports products. In the consumer market, *sports products* can include a variety of goods, including tickets to an event, participation in a sport, sports equipment, and sports apparel. This represents only a partial listing as there are certainly many other products in the consumer market as well as the business-to-business market that would also fall into the sports product category. *Nonsports products* include those that are not directly related to a sport;

FIGURE 2.1
The Sports Marketing
Environment Matrix

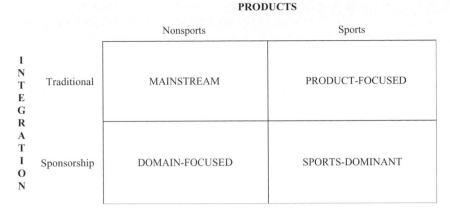

examples would include automobiles, medical services, fast food, consumer electronics, and beverages such as milk, beer, and colas.

> Traditional strategies represent a lower level of integration in that marketers simply implement strategies with a sports overlay.

The second dimension was briefly addressed in the introduction of this chapter; it considers the extent to which sports are integrated within the firm's marketing strategy. This designation considers two broad categories of strategies: traditional and sponsorship. *Traditional strategies* represent a lower level of integration in that marketers simply implement strategies with a sports overlay. For this type of strategy, the marketer is not relying upon an official relationship with the particular sports property that is referenced in the firm's marketing efforts. For example, when a company chooses to advertise during the TV broadcast of a sports event, a basic decision to incorporate sports at a fundamental level has been made. In addition to advertising, many other strategic components can be incorporated in an effort to create a sports overlay. A much higher level of integration is present when the strategy involves sponsorship. With *sponsorship strategies,* companies invest significant resources in an effort to be recognized as having an official relationship with the sports property; these companies then attempt to achieve their marketing objectives by developing strategies that capitalize on those sponsorships.

We have now identified the two key dimensions in the sports marketing environment: products and integration. Using these two dimensions, a basic framework for describing the sports marketing environment can be developed. Figure 2.1 illustrates this framework. The two dimensions allow for the identification of four strategic domains within the sports marketing environment.

An Overview of the Sports Marketing Environment

Mainstream strategies are characterized by the use of traditional marketing strategies that incorporate some element of sports in the effort to sell nonsports products. The marketer might opt to use a sports theme and advertise its products in sports-related media that effectively reach its customers. A key aspect of mainstream strategies is that the marketer's efforts are not based upon a relationship with the sports property that is used to create the sports overlay within the firm's marketing efforts. A bank that advertises in a sports magazine or during a TV broadcast of a sports event has integrated sports at a rudimentary level. As such, this domain represents the lowest level of involvement of sports within the sports marketing environment.

Many marketers officially align themselves with sports properties via some form of sponsorship. The nature of this relationship reflects a higher level of integration of sports within the sports marketing environment. A common strategy involves a sponsor that uses sports to effectively market nonsports products. This combination emphasizes strategies that are classified as *domain-focused*. In an effort to sell more fast food, McDonald's advertising and packaging feature its official partnership with the Olympic Games. Volvo uses its sponsorship of a high-profile sailing event to strengthen the public's perception of the carmaker as one that is exudes prestige while concurrently emphasizing safety and technology. While the strategic initiatives that augment the sponsorship are important, the foundation for the resultant strategy is that the sponsor is highly integrated within in the sports environment. It will seek to implement strategic initiatives that allow it to capitalize upon its position within the sports domain.

Efforts to market sports products using traditional strategic initiatives when the marketer has no official relationship with another the sports property are classified as *product-focused strategies*. These initiatives may or may not involve a sports theme beyond the product offering. If a marketer of athletic shoes drops prices and provides incentives for the retailers, it is apparent that these specific strategic decisions are independent from the sports environment. However, since the product is sports-related, the strategy still falls within the sports marketing environment. Within this product-focused domain, it is also possible for the marketer to employ strategies that incorporate sports themes even when there is no official sponsorship contract with the sports entity that is featured in the marketer's strategy. A sporting goods retailer might choose to give away free caps at a baseball game. If this strategy is the result of the retailer providing compensation for the right to distribute the caps and not on the basis of an official sponsorship, then it can be classified as a product-focused strategy. Clearly, there are varying levels of involvement of sports for strategies within this domain.

The final domain, *sports-dominant strategies,* is characterized by official sponsors that are selling sports products. Because of the role of sports in both the product and integration dimensions, this domain reflects the greatest reliance on sports-oriented initiatives. Strategies in this domain can be very effective when appealing to customers who are excited by the sports that are used in the implementation of the specific strategic components; for example, adidas sells sporting goods and it uses advertising that complements its sponsorship of the World Cup of Soccer. This consistency produces the synergy that is characteristic of the sports-dominant domain.

Traditional Strategies for Nonsports Products

The primary objective for this chapter is to provide insight into the mainstream marketing domain. As such, we will emphasize how marketers of nonsports products utilize a sports platform to achieve their objectives. While examples from the other three domains will be introduced as a means of comparing one domain to another, strategies outside of the mainstream category are examined more fully later in this text. Domain-focused strategies will be examined in Chapters 3 through 14, and product-focused strategies and sports-dominant strategies will be discussed in Chapters 15 through 22.

To reiterate the key point that was made earlier in this chapter, *traditional strategies* represent a company's efforts to utilize sports in its marketing efforts when that company has no official relationship with the sports property. Sports simply provide a favorable environment in which the marketer can implement strategic initiatives designed to capitalize on the opportunities available to marketers within that environment.

> Effective strategy is based upon the recognition that different groups of customers must be approached with initiatives designed specifically for them.

As was noted earlier, the basic elements of any marketing strategy are a target market and a corresponding marketing mix. The implication is that effective strategy is based upon the recognition that different groups of customers must be approached with initiatives designed specifically for them. It is also essential to remember that most marketers employ multiple strategies at any one time. As we move away from mass marketing, there is an understanding that an undifferentiated strategy is not very effective when attempting to appeal to a heterogeneous market. To effectively implement traditional strategies, the two basic elements must be understood. Therefore, this chapter begins with a brief overview of the concepts of target markets and the marketing mix.

Target Markets

The designation of one or more target markets is based upon the identification of market segments that are deemed attractive by the marketer. To accomplish this task, there must first be an acknowledgment that the aggregate market is quite heterogeneous. Strategy, therefore, begins in earnest with the process of *market segmentation* when the mass market is subdivided into a number of smaller more homogeneous groups of consumers.

Markets may be segmented on several different bases. Historically, the most common basis has been demographics. When *demographics* are used, segments may be defined on the basis of gender, age, race, income, education, and marital status as well as a number of other variables of this type. Marketers may opt to use one or more of these variables in the segmentation process, but it is important to understand that the number of segments increases dramatically as the number of variables employed increases. Using gender, two segments will be defined: male and female consumers. The use of broad categories of marital status would also result in the delineation of two segments: single and married consumers. If the two variables are used concurrently, then the result is the identification of the four market segments:

- Single females
- Single males
- Married females
- Married males

Although demographics have long been the basic criteria used for many segmentation strategies, other variables may also be used. *Geographic* variables consider the consumers' location. Segmentation may be based upon one's country of residence; for instance, residents of Canada, the United States, and Mexico may be deemed to be three distinct segments. Within any one country, many regional differences often exist. Differences among consumers in the southern United States and the northern part of the country may dictate a need to designate them as unique segments. Many countries, especially large ones, possess an array of regional differences, including language, slang terms, recreational activities, and dietary preferences. Another geographic designation is the nature of the community. Is it

COMMON BASES FOR MARKET SEGMENTATION 2.1

- Demographic
  - Basic classification data such as gender, income, race, and age
- Geographic
  - Country
  - Region of country
  - Urban, suburban, rural
- Psychographics (lifestyle)
  - Attitudes
  - Activities
  - Interests
  - Opinions
- Product-related variables
  - Usage rates
  - Brand loyalty
  - Benefits sought

urban, suburban, or rural? In many instances, consumption patterns are quite different even though the segments are located in close proximity to each other.

Psychographics represent the third basis for segmentation. Typically, this basis would involve the delineation of groups based upon their attitudes, activities, interests, and opinions. One segment could be liberal while another is conservative. One might have an affinity for the arts while another demonstrates a fondness for hunting. These examples illustrate why the term *lifestyle* is often used as a synonym for psychographics. These variables capture key considerations in the day-to-day life of the consumer.

The final category is relatively broad. *Product-related variables* encompass a variety of issues. Is the consumer a heavy user or a light user; is brand loyalty exhibited or does the consumer readily switch from one brand to another; what benefits are being sought from the product?

Marketers must determine the most relevant bases to use in the task of segmentation. Then consideration must be given to how the individuals are to be grouped using those bases. For example, if age is to be used, how many groups should be created and how should the age groups be defined? A key consideration in selecting the bases is to use only those where there is reason to believe that purchase behavior is related to each criterion. In other words, if men and women are deemed to be identical in regard to the marketer's strategic initiatives, then gender should not be used to segment the market. The bases for market segmentation are summarized in Box 2.1.

With the basic premise of segmentation now understood, it is imperative to recognize the distinction between market segments and target markets. Segmentation has facilitated the process of breaking down a heterogeneous population into a number of smaller, more homogeneous groups. These smaller groups are referred to as *market segments*. With this process completed, the marketer must turn to the task of assessing each of the defined market segments and selecting one or more of them to pursue with efforts aimed at selling products to members of the selected segments. The segments that are selected are classified as *target markets*.

TABLE 2.1
Market Segments and Target Markets

Group	Market Segment	Target Market
Single females	Yes	No
Single males	Yes	No
Married females	Yes	Yes
Married males	Yes	No

If a marketer chooses to segment on the basis of gender and marital status as was shown in the earlier example, then there are four market segments. Now the question becomes one of deciding which of the four segments to pursue. For the sake of illustration, consider a product that primarily appeals to women. Further research indicates that the product is attractive to married consumers. As a result, the company designates married women as its sole target market. Table 2.1 summarizes this situation.

While reviewing Table 2.1, it is important to remember that selection may encompass more than one target market. It was noted earlier that most marketers today engage in multisegment strategies. In fact, it is possible that each segment can be designated as a target market. In this example, such a designation would require the marketer to develop four marketing mixes, one for each target market.

The Marketing Mix

The second essential element of a marketing strategy is the marketing mix. The *marketing mix* can be defined as the set of four controllable variables that are manipulated in an effort to achieve a firm's stated marketing objectives. These variables are often referred to as the *four P's*; they are price, product, place, and promotion.

Price refers to the amount to be charged to the buyer. In this regard, price represents what the buyer will relinquish in exchange for the product. *Product* refers to the tangible and intangible attributes that the customer is purchasing. The product also includes the services associated with the purchase, the brand name, guarantees, packaging, and the benefits associated with the purchase and use of the product. *Place* is another term for distribution. How will the product transported in the channel of distribution; what types of stores will it sold through; and how many dealers does the prospective purchaser have to choose from when making the purchase? Finally, there is the *promotion* variable. Marketers have an array of promotional tools from which they can select. While the most readily acknowledged are advertising and personal selling, there are two others that the marketer needs to consider. Sales promotion includes activities such as the distribution of free samples, discount coupons, and items such as calendars, golf balls, and ballpoint pens that bear the marketers' brand names and logos. The fourth promotional tool is public relations aimed at generating favorable publicity for the marketer. This set of four tools is commonly called the *promotional mix*. Box 2.2 provides a brief review of the components of the marketing mix.

With a firm understanding of the concept of the marketing mix, the job at hand now becomes one of designing an appropriate marketing mix for each of the selected target markets. Since each target market is different from all others in some meaningful way, the firm's objectives are more attainable when each marketing mix addresses these differences. Pepsi-Cola has created products such as Diet Pepsi, Pepsi Edge, Pepsi Max, Crystal Pepsi, Pepsi One, and Mountain Dew with specific target markets in mind. The other variables within the marketing mix are tailored to support the product strategy that is directed toward each target market.

The preceding discussion was meant to be a review for readers who have previously taken some courses in marketing. For those studying marketing for the first time, it was

THE MARKETING MIX

- Price
- Product
  - Tangible goods
  - Intangible service
  - Packaging
  - Brand name
  - Guarantees
  - Benefits
- Place (distribution)
  - Physical distribution
  - Types of stores used
  - Intensity of distribution
- Promotion
  - Advertising
  - Personal selling
  - Sales promotion
  - Public relations/publicity

designed to provide the insight needed to understand the process of developing a comprehensive marketing strategy. For both groups, dare we say segments of students, these strategic initiatives will also be important when the discussion addresses the marketing of sports. For now, however, the emphasis will be on the use of traditional strategic components when a sports overlay is being used in the marketing of nonsports products.

Mainstream Strategies

For the purpose of this text we have identified two classes of products: nonsports and sports. Similarly, we have acknowledged two types of strategies for marketing products through sports: traditional and sponsorship. In considering the marketing of nonsports products with traditional strategies, we emphasize the selection of target markets and the development of a corresponding marketing mix for each designated target market. However, the environment in which we are operating is sports. So a typical question might be: How can we use soccer to appeal to one of our target markets with a marketing mix designed to sell more minivans, or what type of beverage appeals to avid runners? This section of the text attempts to address questions such as these.

Target Markets

In many cases, the target market of the organization seeking to develop the consumers' interest in its products will coincide with the target market of a sports property. It is sports' ability to provide access to the organization's target markets that makes the marketing of products through sports viable. Marketers that have a good understanding of their own customers will align themselves with sports entities that allow them to develop strategies designed to capitalize on the similarities of the two organizations' target markets. Once identified, the emphasis becomes one of developing a marketing mix that corresponds to the target market. In this respect, marketing through sports is no different than any other marketing effort.

> It is sports' ability to provide access to the organization's target markets that makes the marketing of products through sports viable.

Beer companies seeking to reach adult males may align with football; they may use football themes in advertising or they might reach an agreement with a bar owner to feature its brands at discounted prices during the broadcast of an important game. Mountain Dew uses advertising featuring X-treme sports as a means of reaching its 13–25-year-old, male target market. Cadillac uses golf to appeal to an older, more affluent market. In a theme that will be dominant in this book, the marketer needs to find the appropriate match with a sports entity that can provide access to its own target markets. Once this decision has been made, the focus shifts to the four variables of the marketing mix.

Price

Because of the costs associated with sponsorship, many marketers shy away from domain-focused strategies. But even when the marketer is considering a mainstream strategy, some options have costs that can be a barrier. For example, traditional advertising during high-profile events can be characterized by prohibitive costs; for example, it was earlier noted that a 30-second ad during the 2006 Super Bowl cost more than $2.4 million. A common concern is that alignment with sports and athletes can be very expensive, and this cost is invariably passed on to consumers in the form of higher prices. It is this concern that leads many marketers to adopt a mainstream strategy that incorporates sports at the most basic level. Instead of higher prices, marketers intent on the implementation of a mainstream strategy generally seek ways in which they can provide discounted prices while projecting an informal relationship with sports.

A producer of hot dogs might offer its product to operators of sports venues at a discounted price. While that discount is not likely to be passed on to spectators in attendance, it may be the determining factor that persuades the venue operator to sell one particular brand rather than that of a competitor. Once the manufacturer has been selected, it can capitalize on the opportunity in which it is likely to have a monopoly with no direct competition. Another benefit is that fans who purchase and enjoy the hot dog at the sports venue may shift their own purchase behavior in favor of that brand. Resultant purchases at the supermarket do not have to rely on discounted pricing.

A second example of a mainstream strategy is the combination of a discounted price with a sports-oriented promotion. A brewery might engage in a cooperative effort with a bar to allow its beer to be featured in promotions and sold at a reduced price during the broadcast of popular sports events. Other bars often offer discounted food during broadcasts of games played by local teams. Examples such as these will be explored further in the upcoming discussion of the implementation of product and promotion decisions in the application of mainstream strategies.

Yet another perspective is that effective marketing is typically designed to increase sales. Undoubtedly, this is the goal of many marketers that attempt to create an association with sports. If the anticipated increase in demand does materialize, then there is a corresponding need to increase production. The typical result is the achievement of economies of scale. As production goes up, the cost of producing each item should go down. The lower cost has the potential to translate into lower prices. If a price decrease is not forthcoming, then the firm's profits will increase. These resources may be put back into research and development for new products or into other strategic initiatives such as increased levels of advertising. Alternatively, any increased profits may be distributed to stockholders in the form of stock dividend payments.

It is evident that there is no clear outcome or strategy when considering the creation of a sports overlay in the development of a mainstream strategy. Marketers that associate themselves with sports often manipulate their prices and offer special deals. Retail prices may vary depending upon the product's availability and the type of stores in which the product is sold. Clearly all elements of the marketing mix must be coordinated if they are to be effective.

Product

When discussing product-related issues, it is important to remember that the sports marketing environment is comprised of two products categories: sports and nonsports. When the objective is to sell sports products via the application of a traditional marketing strategy, the marketer is operating within the product-focused domain. For instance, the objective of advertising during the broadcast of the X Games may be to create a preference for Burton snowboards. Less directly related, but recognizing that its product is still associated with sports, the likely goal of Gatorade's advertising during a Major League Baseball game is to increase the demand for its sports drink. Because these efforts involve sports products, they fall within the product-focused domain rather than the mainstream domain. The important point of differentiation among the strategies is that within the mainstream domain, sports are not part of the marketer's core product, but they are still key considerations in the development of one or more of the elements of the marketer's strategy.

When considering nonsports products, we shift away from products that are used in or otherwise associated with sports. For example, Budweiser Beer spends considerable money for advertising during sports broadcasts, in sports publications, and on sports sponsorships. But the question here involves the way in which a marketer such as Budweiser incorporates sports as a part of its marketing strategy. In this regard, it is often difficult to differentiate between mainstream strategies and those that fall into the category of domain-focused strategies. Is the strategic initiative simply an effort to invoke a sports theme, or is it being implemented in an effort to support an official sponsorship with a sports property?

> The absence or presence of a sponsorship relationship with the sports property is the key distinction between mainstream and domain-focused strategies.

Much of the effort for both nonsports and sports products involves a variety of sponsorship options. Strategies that feature sponsorship incorporate a higher level of integration of sports into the firm's strategy; therefore they fall within the domain-focused and sports-dominant categories. These important strategic initiatives are discussed in future chapters; however, the emphasis in this chapter continues to be the assessment of mainstream strategies where marketers attempt to incorporate sports into their traditional strategies in the task of marketing nonsports products. In essence, the marketer is often attempting to convert its nonsports product into a de facto sports product in the minds of members of its target market.

The hospitality industry has witnessed a substantial growth in the number of sports bars. These establishments offer televised sports programming as one means of attracting customers. Many will incorporate food and beverage specials during the broadcast of certain events. Also, in many cases, the sports bar will subscribe to programming packages that will allow patrons to watch events that they either cannot receive at home or that they would have to pay a substantial fee to access. In this case, the TV programming has become part of the bar's product portfolio. They are selling food, drinks, and sports entertainment. Chicago's Hard Rock Café has specials that start an hour prior to the kickoff of the Monday Night

FIGURE 2.2
Selling a Product
Through Sports

Football games. Included are discounts on chicken wings and Sam Adams beers. Figure 2.2 illustrates a tabletop promotion that is designed to alert customers to the availability of sports programming that sports programming is available to them.

The travel industry also uses sports as a means of increasing business. Travel agencies partner with hotels, airlines, charter bus companies, and restaurants to offer package tours. In many cases, these tours are designed as road trips that allow fans to travel to watch their favorite team play a game away from home. In some cases, rather than a travel package deal, a hotel will partner with a local team. For example Adam's Mark Hotel in St. Louis offers a package that includes tickets to a St. Louis Cardinals baseball game, overnight accommodations, parking, and an authentic personalized baseball bat. While many of the purchasers of this package are fans of the Cardinals' opponents, it also attracts Cardinal fans from the area who are seeking the convenience of accommodations in close proximity to the stadium, who don't want the hassle of pregame and postgame traffic, or who like the idea of having a Major League bat with their name engraved on it. Similarly, the Essex Hotel in Chicago offers a package for Chicago Bears games. The package includes two game tickets, overnight hotel accommodations, complimentary parking, and two complimentary drinks at the hotel bar. Regardless of the motivation, the hotels benefit from their incorporation of sports as a component of their product strategy.

Tag Heuer sells expensive upscale watches. In an intriguing augmentation of its assortment of products, it bundled one of its models of watches with the eligibility to compete in a golf tournament that it was staging. The tournament dubbed the "Link Challenge" allowed the 100 buyers of the special edition Tag Heuer Link Challenge 2004 watch at a price of $2,100 to gain entry into the invitation-only tournament.[1] Although the actual watch and its brand name were important parts of the product strategy, some people likely bought the watch in order to participate in a competition that purposely excluded most consumers. This strategy was as much about ego and sports as it was about knowing the correct time. A similar strategy has been implemented by Visa whereby holders of the Visa Signature credit card are provided access to "members-only" events such as the one held at the world-renowned Pebble Beach Golf Course. Visa expects that this benefit for its cardholders will provide the marketer with a competitive advantage, especially within the target market that is comprised of golfers.

According to most contemporary definitions, packaging is also part of the product decision. Many packages today incorporate sports themes even when there is no official relationship with the sport being featured on the packaging. For example, Kodak has used its official Olympics connection on the packaging of film. It has also used more generic sports themes on packaging in combination with similarly themed promotional displays that feature Kodak products at supermarkets and discount retailers. Similarly, Crunch and Munch has used generic images of basketball on the packaging of its popular snack food.

It is evident from this discussion that it is often difficult to distinguish among the four strategic domains in the sports marketing environment. While it is easy to recognize the difference between nonsports and sports products, the marketer's level of integration is more difficult for outsiders to determine.

Place (Distribution)

When considering the marketing of nonsports products through sports, decisions relevant to the place variable typically involve the ability to sell one's products at a specific retail outlet, the types of outlets at which the marketer's products will be available, and the intensity of the retail coverage within a geographic market. For each of these, sports has the potential to make a positive contribution that will enhance the marketer's bottom line.

Companies often seek the opportunity to sell their products at sports venues. This opportunity often involves an official sponsorship, but there are numerous examples where the marketer has simply negotiated with team management or venue operators for the rights to sell its products during events staged there. Marketers of different brands of beverages and snack foods readily recognize the benefits associated with being sold at a sports stadium. In many cases, the number of available brands is limited to those of a single supplier, thus the competition is locked out of an important captive market. Many new stadia are being built as older ones are being replaced. Additionally, multipurpose stadia have fallen into disfavor. Instead of a single stadium that hosts multiple sports, special purpose venues are being built. The resultant growth in the number of new stadia has created new distribution opportunities for marketers.

> Growth in the number of new stadia has created new distribution opportunities for marketers.

Another recent example involved the 2004 Ryder Cup golf matches. Events of this type are noted for the sale of officially licensed merchandise; they are also noted for the number of attendees from outside of the geographic area where the event is staged. As an international competition, many of the Ryder Cup spectators were visiting from foreign countries. The purchase of souvenirs and other merchandise was inconvenient for the buyers who would have ordinarily had to consider carrying a shopping bag around the golf course all day and then packing it in their luggage for their trip home. FedEx made it more convenient for the consumer while simultaneously benefiting from increased sales. The company set up a booth outside of the main merchandise shop to allow buyers to ship their purchases to their friends, relatives, or even to themselves. With international shipments averaging $60 and domestic customers spending about $20 per shipment, FedEx was able to generate thousands of dollars in revenue that otherwise would not have been attainable.[2]

It is not just the actual venues that are important to the marketers. The geographic market may play an important role too. An effort by Budweiser to sell NASCAR-inspired "eight-packs" was initially limited to three markets: Charlotte, Darlington, and Atlanta. These three cities all feature major NASCAR competitions. Spokespersons for Budweiser indicated that they planned to have the special packaging available in all major NASCAR race markets within a year of its introduction. So while the packaging might not be seen in San Francisco, it will be available in Daytona Beach.

The type of outlets at which a marketer's products will be sold is also a key consideration. Marketers that utilize a sports theme may seek to have their products available at sporting goods stores. In the introductory stage of the product life cycle, the manufacturer of Quench gum used a sports orientation as a means of getting its product on the retail shelves and at checkout locations in a number of sporting goods stores. Quench was able to gain access to a market segment that the traditional producers of gum found to be elusive. Similarly, convenience foods that are positioned to sell to hunters can find a place on the shelves of sporting goods retailers. Not only does it address the needs of a segment, but it is also characterized by a high profit margin. Both of these facts provide strong incentives for the retailer.

> Quench was able to gain access to a market segment that the traditional producers of gum found to be elusive.

Retailers understand that a sports theme can represent a powerful sales proposition. This can induce more store owners to embrace the idea of stocking and selling the marketers' products. As a result, the intensity of the distribution of these products can increase. Simply stated, the marketer's products are available at a larger number of retail outlets. This can be extremely important, especially for low-priced, consumer convenience goods.

Promotion

The final element of the marketing mix is promotion. It is perhaps the easiest variable to use in the effort to develop a sports overlay for the implementation of a mainstream strategy. Each component of the promotional mix is viable for the marketer that is attempting to incorporate sports within its marketing strategy. In addition to the four commonly acknowledged components of the promotional mix, there are also four emerging strategies. These eight mainstream approaches for promoting products are listed below and briefly discussed on the following pages. These promotional tools include

- Advertising
- Personal selling
- Sales promotion
- Public relations/publicity
- Product placement
- Virtual advertising
- Hospitality
- Internet

Advertising

Companies choose to advertise on televised sports programs that appeal to their own target markets. Other advertising strategies include paying for signage at an event venue and advertising in the event's program that is either sold or distributed free of charge at the venue. In some cases, this advertising is done to complement an official sponsorship; such was the case with McDonald's advertising during the broadcast of the Olympic Games. But in most cases, no formal relationship exists. For instance, Monster.com chose to advertise during the Super Bowl because the broadcast would reach its own target market. Monster.com had no official relationship with the NFL or the Super Bowl.

Live sports in general are viewed as safer investments than general entertainment programming. This viewpoint has fueled the redirection of many marketers' promotional resources toward sports programming. For example, for NFL programming during the 2004 season, Anheuser-Busch reported a "greater presence"; Domino's Pizza shifted $10 million in resources to the Monday Night Football broadcasts; General Motors tripled its advertising expenditures on NFL broadcasts; and Visa more than tripled its number of new ads shown during NFL broadcasts.[3]

Without a doubt, the most noteworthy sports vehicle for a single commercial in the United States is the Super Bowl. Many companies have used the Super Bowl's high TV ratings as a means of reaching millions of consumers. Perhaps the most noteworthy example is the 60-second commercial in 1984 that introduced the Apple Macintosh computer. More recently, Coca-Cola used it as a way of introducing Surge, its entry to compete with Pepsi's Mountain Dew. Likewise, Frito-Lay saw it as an appropriate mechanism for the introduction of its new Wavy brand of potato chips. Movie studios have also begun to use the expensive, high-reach advertising as a way of creating awareness for new films that they are prepared to release. While this tactic may be considered expensive with a cost exceeding $2.4 million for 30 seconds, it can still be cost effective by virtue of its reach. With a TV rating between 40 and 45 percent in the United States, the game can easily reach a domestic audience approaching 90 million viewers. The ability to reach this number of viewers explains why the Super Bowl is considered to be an effective tool for creating awareness of a new product. Table 2.2 provides a historical perspective of the cost, reach, and cost effectiveness of the Super Bowl since its inception in 1967.

Given the costs shown in Table 2.2, it is evident that advertising on high-profile events is not an option for many marketers. In addition to the cost, there is a question of whether the advertiser is spending money to reach viewers who are not part of its own target market. The X Games can be used to reach the 12–25-year-old male segment; the WNBA is relatively cost effective in reaching a younger, female audience. Lower costs and better targeting are two reasons marketers are using this type of alternative sports programming. Regardless of the scope of the event, there is one undeniable requirement.[4] Who is watching and what are their purchasing habits?

> In order to effectively use advertising during any sports programming, the marketer must have a good understanding of the audience.

TV has also evolved to the point where the idea of *broadcasting* is being replaced by the concept of *narrowcasting*. With the growth of cable and satellite delivery services, consumers have more access to networks with a specific focus. While this phenomenon is not limited to sports, the proliferation of sports networks has underscored the viability of this type of programming as a way of reaching consumers. Across the globe, we have seen the birth of networks that feature a single sports genre 24/7. Golf, tennis, rugby, collegiate sports, and motor sports are just a few examples. Advertising on these networks is comparatively inexpensive and more focused on a defined market segment.

While the discussion to this point has focused on TV programming, there are many other media that feature sports. Some are quite broad and cover an array of sports; others are very narrow and provide more in-depth coverage of a single sport. Magazines such as *ESPN: the Magazine* and *Sports Illustrated* are examples of vehicles that provide breadth in their coverage and reach sports fans in general. Conversely, *Baseball Digest* and *Rugby World* are two examples of publications that feature depth over breadth; they cover one sport, and advertisers can use them to reach a much more narrowly defined target market.

Another emerging sports medium is talk radio. Across the world, we have witnessed a growth in the number of radio stations devoted to sports programming, sports commentary, and audience call-ins. Listeners tend to be highly involved sports fans. Not only can the advertiser assure a good demographic fit with its own target market, but it is reaching fans who are more likely to be motivated by the marketer's involvement in sports.

Advertisers also have many opportunities to deliver their messages at the event venue. Many spectators purchase printed programs that provide information about the event. Inevitably, this program will include advertising for many local and national companies. Such advertising may be a good way for a local restaurant to reach a target market when the

TABLE 2.2
History of Super Bowl Advertising

Source: Adapted from www.adage.com/page.cms? pageId=685 (accessed September 20, 2004).

Year	Price	Rating	Viewers	CPM*
1967	$ 42,000	23.0	N/A	N/A
1968	54,000	17.8	N/A	N/A
1969	67,500	36.8	N/A	N/A
1970	78,200	39.4	44,270,000	$1.77
1971	72,000	39.9	45,270,000	1.57
1972	86,000	44.2	56,640,000	1.52
1973	103,500	42.7	53,320,000	1.61
1974	107,000	41.6	51,700,000	2.07
1975	110,000	42.4	56,050,000	1.96
1976	125,000	42.3	57,710,000	2.17
1977	162,000	44.4	62,060,000	2.61
1978	185,000	47.2	78,940,000	2.34
1979	222,000	47.1	74,740,000	2.97
1980	275,000	46.3	76,240,000	3.60
1981	324,300	44.4	68,290,000	4.75
1982	345,000	49.1	85,230,000	4.05
1983	400,000	48.6	81,770,000	4.89
1984	450,000	46.4	77,620,000	5.80
1985	500,000	46.4	85,530,000	5.85
1986	550,000	48.3	92,570,000	5.94
1987	575,000	45.8	87,190,000	7.17
1988	600,000	41.9	80,140,000	7.49
1989	675,000	43.5	81,590,000	8.29
1990	700,000	39.0	73,852,000	9.48
1991	800,000	41.9	79,510,000	10.06
1992	800,000	40.3	79,590,000	10.05
1993	850,000	45.1	90,990,000	9.34
1994	900,000	45.5	90,000,000	10.00
1995	1,000,000	41.3	83,420,000	11.99
1996	1,100,000	46.0	94,080,000	11.69
1997	1,200,000	43.3	87,870,000	13.66
1998	1,300,000	44.5	90,000,000	14.44
1999	1,600,000	40.2	83,720,000	19.11
2000	2,100,000	43.3	88,465,000	23.74
2001	2,050,000	40.4	84,335,000	24.30
2002	1,900,000	40.4	86,801,000	21.89
2003	2,100,000	40.7	88,600,000	23.70
2004	2,250,000	41.4	89,800,000	25.06

* CPM = cost per thousand (cost of reaching each 1,000 viewers).

consumers are in close proximity to the restaurant. Advertisements may also be displayed on the scoreboard or other signage throughout the venue. Commercial messages may be read over the public address system. Many venues have rotating signs that change periodically throughout the event. It is these *Dorna boards* that are perhaps the most popular type of venue-based advertising. They can alternate the display of as many as 28 different messages. Spectators in the arena are exposed to its messages as are the TV viewers at home. It has been estimated that a Dorna board ad during an NBA game creates an average exposure for TV viewers of two minutes and 50 seconds.[5]

> It has been estimated that a Dorna board ad during an NBA game creates an average exposure for TV viewers of two minutes and 50 seconds.

Finally, advertisers of nonsports products often use sports themes as a way of gaining recognition in the marketplace. Foster's Beer implemented a campaign that was a parody of Olympic events. Canon used a sports theme to demonstrate how its cameras could allow the consumer to take sharp pictures, even when the subject was a fast-moving sports competition. More recently, Snickers implemented a campaign with a general sports theme for the introduction of its new Snickers Marathon Energy Bar. Even the brand name, Marathon, projects an image of sports.

Personal Selling

The use of sports in the task of selling products is relevant in both the consumer and business-to-business (B2B) markets. Personal selling is often the predominant promotional tool in the B2B arena. Thus, it is safe to assume that the sports environment provides more meaningful opportunities for salespeople working in the B2B sector. That notwithstanding, sports can also present opportunities for salespeople seeking to generate a preference for their products and for establishing and nurturing relationships with prospects and clients in the consumer market.

A common application involves the distribution of complimentary tickets for events that customers and prospects enjoy. Many marketers maintain season tickets for teams that reside in their community. These same marketers often purchase tickets for annual and special events that are staged in close proximity to their offices and those of their customers. These tickets may be given to prospects as part of the salesperson's effort to overcome their resistance. They may also be given to long-standing customers in an effort to reinforce the relationship between the marketer and the individual customer.

For many of these same events, the marketer may have access to a luxury suite. New stadia are being constructed with an emphasis on corporate hospitality opportunities. Special events provide hospitality facilities for marketers that want to be able to entertain various constituencies at events such as the Ryder Cup golf matches, the America's Cup Yachting Regatta, and the NFL's Super Bowl game. In many cases, members of the firm's sales force will have significant influence in the determination of which customers will be invited to use the facilities. Such efforts to reward one's best customers are designed to strengthen the customer's attachment to the marketer. Practices such as this are included in a set of activities within the task of customer relationship management (CRM). There are two constraints to this aspect of CRM. First, the customers must be genuinely interested in the event to which they are being invited. Admission to a company's luxury suite at a hockey game will have little impact if the customer is not interested in hockey. This is especially problematic because of the second constraint; these events often take place during the nonworking hours of the customers' day. Will the customers devote six hours of their discretionary time to attend an event that doesn't excite them? The answer is, probably not.

Many people believe that a golf course is a perfect venue to conduct business; so many firms actually maintain memberships in private clubs. These memberships allow company employees to play golf and to use other facilities such as tennis courts, restaurants, and bars. Salespeople often take advantage of this access by inviting their associates, clients, customers, and prospects to join them. Such a strategy can be an effective approach to CRM. One caveat is that some clubs have been under increased scrutiny because of exclusionary membership policies that have made it difficult for women and minorities to reap this type of benefit. With that scrutiny, more businesses have been pressured to withdraw their memberships from clubs that many people deem to be discriminatory.

> Businesses have been pressured to withdraw their memberships from clubs that many people deem to be discriminatory.

In the consumer market, each of the aforementioned examples is available to the salesperson. Financial services companies such as Morgan Stanley allow agents and brokers to provide such sports-related incentives to their clients. The ability to interact with clients on a casual basis or the goodwill that is generated by providing the client with tickets to a local team's game can impact the relationship between the marketer and the customer in a favorable manner.

It is noteworthy that several large firms have begun to prohibit the provision of such perks to their employees. Ford's policy is that they are simply not allowed. Even meals that are customarily paid for by the salesperson are prohibited. The rationale is that Ford is seeking to ensure that purchases are made on a rational basis, not on the basis of which marketer can provide the best personal benefits.

Sales Promotion

The sales promotion category encompasses a broad spectrum of tools that are designed to accomplish a variety of goals. Strategies that involve sales promotion are extremely important to marketers of consumer goods. Examples include specialty advertising, discount coupons, free samples, consumer expos, customer loyalty reward programs, contests, point-of-sale displays, and premiums.

Specialty advertising typically involves the placement of a marketer's logo, trademark, or brand name on products that are given to and retained by consumers for some period of time. For example, calendars may be kept by the recipient for a year or more.

FIGURE 2.3
Example of Specialty Advertising

Figure 2.3 illustrates a calendar that was mailed to prospects by a local real estate agent. The calendar featured the schedule of the local NFL team and two major universities in the area.

Another common product that is distributed in both consumer and B2B markets is a package of golf balls that display a marketer's logo. These balls are kept and used until they are discarded or lost. The golfer, his or her playing partners, and any subsequent user of the ball will be exposed to the logo. Figure 2.4 is an advertisement by Titleist that is appealing to its B2B customers to use this type of sales promotion technique.

Discount coupons are often distributed at sports venues. They may be incorporated into the back of the tickets or simply distributed to all patrons as they enter the arena. The coupons may be distributed in a myriad of ways. One intriguing promotion at a recent Pensacola Ice Pilots game in the East Coast Hockey League involved the random dropping of coupons from a small radio-controlled blimp. Another application was the distribution of a "fan book" at one of the home games of the NFL's Indianapolis Colts. This book included approximately 200 discount coupons for products from retailers including restaurants, cellular telephone accessories, jewelers, and automobile service providers. The cover of the fan book is shown in Figure 2.5.

Away from the sports venues, marketers can still seek to reach the sports-oriented market segments. One popular brand of candy bar that is sold by Nestlé in America is Baby Ruth; its sports marketing strategy involved the provision of a coupon for a free game of bowling with the purchase of a multipack of the product. Figure 2.6 illustrates the packaging that was

FIGURE 2.4
Titleist Ad for Logo
Golf Balls

used for this promotion. While the effort may have generated more interest in the sport of bowling, it was designed to sell Baby Ruth candy bars.

Free samples of products may be distributed at sports venues. Though this strategy often involves an official sponsorship, this type of promotional opportunity can be negotiated with teams and venue officials. Absopure passes out free samples of its bottled water at

FIGURE 2.5
Indianapolis Colts
Fan Book

college football games played at Michigan Stadium. Some golf courses provide free samples of suntan lotion to their patrons.

Consumer expos are a type of trade show where an industry displays its products and promotes its services to those in attendance. A popular form of the consumer expo is the golf show. Consumers pay to visit, and they receive information on courses and equipment. It is also common for companies that reach the same target markets to promote their nonsports products. Car companies and home builders may find this type of promotion to be very cost effective.

Customer loyalty programs are designed to encourage repeat patronage. Perhaps the most widely recognized nonsports example is the frequent-flier program that is offered by virtually every airline in the market. Consumers tend to be more loyal to a particular carrier because they understand that their loyalty will be rewarded with free flights in the future. While some sports teams have started to implement their own loyalty programs, the combination of a nonsports product or service and a sports entity has been rare. Possible applications would be free tickets or free sports equipment to consumers who purchase a designated amount of the mainstream marketer's products over time. For example, Campbell's Soup will provide an array of products, including sports equipment, to schools that collect a specified number of labels from Campbell's products. Parents and other consumers who recognize this benefit may shift their purchase behavior and become more loyal to the Campbell brand.

The use of *contests* typically involves offering an opportunity to attend a particular sports event as a prize. Marketers of consumer goods recognize the importance that many of their customers place on sports, and they see this promotional tool as a way to enhance those consumers' purchase intentions. The media also employ this approach. Local radio and TV stations often provide opportunities for their listeners and viewers to win tickets to games played by their local teams. For example, during the 2005 NBA finals, a local Detroit radio station offered listeners the chance to win an all-expenses-paid trip to see their team play in the final series in San Antonio. In the nonmedia environment, Coors Beer provided the winner of one of its contests with tickets to the NCAA College Basketball Final Four, and a marketer of recreational vehicles in Indianapolis staged a contest that featured several sports-related prizes with the grand prize being 10 free tickets to a home game of the NFL's Indianapolis Colts. This marketer's advertisement was printed in the aforementioned Indianapolis Colts Fan Book.

Point-of-sale (POS) display is another commonly used sales promotion tool that is particularly relevant for companies that emphasize the consumer market. Signage and posters at retail stores are designed to attract the consumer's attention. Consumer affinity for sports has led many marketers to use sports themes in their retail displays. While this approach is more effective when there is an official sponsorship in place, that type of relationship is not mandatory. For example, a pain reliever could use a POS sign featuring a model as a tennis player. A nutritional beverage for kids might incorporate a soccer theme into a poster that will be displayed at retail stores that sell the beverage. The ability to use POS display and have the consumer associate a particular brand with sports has the potential of creating a competitive advantage for the marketer.

The final category of sales promotion to be discussed here is that of premiums. *Premiums* represent free products that are provided to purchasers of a specific product; often these premiums are sports related. For example, one might purchase a box of cereal and receive free trading cards. In an intriguing promotion, one retailer of BMW automobiles offered purchasers of each new car free parking for the Ryder Cup golf matches that were staged at a nearby golf course. While the latter example may have stretched the limits of consumer response, it does illustrate that marketers do believe that appropriate sports-oriented premiums will help in the task of motivating consumers to purchase their brands of products.

Public Relations/Publicity

The fourth and final element of the traditional promotional mix is public relations (PR) and the resulting publicity. Marketers often affiliate themselves with a sports organization for philanthropic reasons. In some cases, these alliances are based upon official sponsorship relationships. But in other situations, the affiliation is viewed as a way for the marketer to align itself with the sports organization in a beneficial manner. One of those benefits is the ability to gain positive PR within the market.

One example of such a relationship is Bayer Pharmaceutical Company's use of a football theme in an initiative called "Tackling Men's Health." The company sought to create awareness for methods of preventing, detecting, and treating a variety of illnesses including prostate cancer, cardiovascular disease, and diabetes.

Other programs are tied to team performance. Companies agree to donate a designated sum of money each time that a particular result is achieved. Donations for home runs in baseball, quarterback sacks in football, and three-point shots in basketball represent potential donation criteria. Throughout the season, the team and local media will report the amount that has been donated to the charitable cause. Spectators at the event as well as those watching on TV will tend to view this in a positive manner, thus the relationship with the public has been enhanced. Both the sports organization and the company may incorporate this initiative within their Web sites thereby alerting more people to the donations while soliciting outside donations as well. Press releases can also result in positive stories in the local media. Properly executed, such PR efforts can create a more positive perception regarding the company. Though it is often difficult to incorporate public relations into the effort to market products through sports, opportunities do exist. So the marketer should consider how public relations will work in concert with its advertising, personal selling, and sales promotion strategies to create an effective promotional mix.

Emerging Promotional Strategies

Beyond the traditional promotional mix, several emerging techniques have come to the forefront in the effort to market products through sports. It is appropriate to consider product placement, virtual advertising, hospitality and the Internet as viable tools when developing a comprehensive promotion plan to support a mainstream sports marketing effort. These tools represent the next focus for the continuation of this discussion of promotion and its role in the marketing mix.

Product Placement

Marketers most readily associate product placement with the motion picture industry. Since Reese's Pieces appeared as an integral part of the movie *E.T.: the Extraterrestrial,* marketers have sought opportunities to have their products placed in such a visible entertainment property. The practice has continued to flourish and is now an important part of TV programming.

Marketers can pay a fee to have their products seen and perhaps even mentioned by name in TV programming and movies that feature a sports theme. Note that we are not necessarily speaking of the broadcast of actual sports events; rather, the theme of the program or movie is sports. Pepsi-Cola and Budweiser were both acknowledged in the motion picture *Dodgeball*. Similarly, the TV program *Hustle* that was broadcast on ESPN and documented the life of Pete Rose was replete with product placements.

New placement opportunities have recently surfaced in the video game market. One of the industry leaders is EA (Electronic Arts) Sports. The company produces games that feature current players in representations of actual venues. The games also include signage around the field of play. In an interesting twist, companies with venue naming rights for the actual stadium or arena are required to pay a fee to EA Sports to have their name incorporated within the game. Other companies that seek this type of signage and product placement are also required to pay for that exposure.

Placement during actual games is generally achieved via some type of reciprocal agreement where the products are provided to the athlete, team, or event organizers free of charge. David's Sunflower Seeds are routinely seen during broadcasts of Major League Baseball games. Gatorade has a strong sidelines presence during National Football League games.

Marketers may begin to more seriously consider actual sporting events as opportunities for product placement. The allure of having one's products appear during sports programming is growing and the benefits are too substantial to ignore.

> The allure of having one's products appear during sports programming is growing and the benefits are too substantial to ignore.

Virtual Advertising

Virtual advertising may well fit into the advertising category in the future, but its newness, uniqueness, and technology-basis merit special attention today. Virtual advertising is signage that is not seen by fans at the venue; it is only visible to viewers watching on TV. In fact, the signs do not really exist. They are computer generated, thus they are advertising's concept of virtual reality. While virtual advertising has applications for prerecorded TV broadcasts, it has gained its notoriety in the realm of live sports broadcasting.

Computer-generated images can be strategically placed so that they are visible to TV viewers. Nonadvertising applications have included informational graphics regarding race drivers, the first-down line that can be seen during most broadcasts of college and professional football games, and the projected path of the cricket ball in an effort to judge whether it would have struck the wicket or not. (Cricket fans will recognize this as an effort to assess the leg-before-wicket (LBW) call.) But it is virtual advertising that commands our attention as it has been touted as the "next big thing to hit sports advertising."[6] Because of its similarity to signs at the venue, it is often referred to as *virtual signage*. Virtual placement is also possible in recorded broadcast materials. The technology is capable of inserting a sign or a representation of a package that did not exist when the show was originally recorded. This type of computerized product placement was recently used on the syndicated broadcasts of the popular *Law & Order* show on the TNT network.[7]

During a recent Indianapolis 500 race, virtual signage could be seen for Oldsmobile and SAP. During the Brickyard 400, viewers saw virtual advertisements for Pennzoil and Miller Beer. During many broadcasts of Major League Baseball games, computer-generated signage is positioned behind home plate so that it is directly in the line of sight for viewers when the center-field camera is focused on the pitcher. The benefits are significant. Because of the enhanced revenue stream for teams and venue operators, some new stadia are being designed to maximize the opportunities for applying virtual imaging technology. The new Petco Park in San Diego is one example of a new facility that was constructed with virtual advertising opportunities in mind.

> Petco Park in San Diego is one example of a new facility that was constructed with virtual advertising opportunities in mind.

While Americans are familiar with sports that have numerous breaks in the action, many sports played internationally do not have these convenient interruptions in play. A typical soccer game is played in two 45-minute halves. Likewise, rugby is played in two 40-minute halves. While there is a break between the halves, each half is completed with no stops in the action. On the other hand, baseball has natural breaks between innings or when a team changes pitchers; football has breaks after a team scores or when there is a change in the team with possession of the ball. Basketball has designated points in the game where media time-outs or other mandatory time-outs are scheduled. It is these breaks where TV broadcasters would typically insert their advertising.

In games without such breaks, the advertisers have historically been precluded from any chance of reaching the viewers during the course of the game. One option has been for the broadcaster to consider breaking away from the action to show advertisements. This is obviously risky as a team could score or some other significant occurrence might happen while the network is in its commercial break. Another option is to not show any advertising during the course of the action, but this impacts revenue in a meaningful way. Virtual advertising can help overcome this limitation. This may explain why virtual imaging technology was embraced in Europe before it began to make inroads into the U.S. broadcasting industry.[8] Signage can be placed on the field of play, in the bench area, in the fan sections, or in other areas where it is visible to the TV viewers. The technology is capable of creating realistic images so that viewers perceive them to be actual signs, not virtual images.

Another advantage is that the signs can be changed during the course of the broadcast. For baseball games, several different advertisers will typically purchase the space behind home plate. Figure 2.7 illustrates one of the different signs that were displayed during the recent broadcast of a Major League Baseball game.

Broadcasters and venue operators also have the opportunity to regionalize their advertisements. Anyone familiar with magazines understands that the ad on one page of a magazine sold in New York City may be completely different from the ad on the same page of the same magazine that is sold in Atlanta. Such is the basis for regionalization. The virtual imaging technology facilitates this same type of customization. The sign seen at midfield of the soccer pitch on the signal beamed to Amsterdam may be different from the one that appears during the broadcast in London. As can be seen from these examples, regionalization may involve multiple cities in a single country or broadcasts that are received in two or more countries. The virtual signage in Montreal may be in French; the same space is in English in Memphis while it appears in Spanish in Mexico City. And of course, the ads may be for completely different products.

FIGURE 2.7
Example of Virtual Signage During an MLB Game

Two of the major problems with traditional TV advertising are zipping and zapping. Commercials come on and the viewer *zips* from one channel to another. When televised programming has been recorded by a viewer, commercial breaks are often *zapped* by fast forwarding through them when the video is being replayed. Since virtual signage appears during the course of the action, it is not vulnerable to zipping and zapping.

> Since virtual signage appears during the course of the action, it is not vulnerable to zipping and zapping.

The last potential advantage is one that is subject to question on the basis of ethics. Virtual imaging can be used to obscure or replace an actual sign. While an advertiser might relish the idea of replacing a competitor's actual sign with a virtual sign of its own, the question of whether such a strategy would be an acceptable practice needs to be considered. If a company has paid for the right to have its name appear on the stadium scoreboard, is it ethical for the broadcaster to electronically manipulate the image so that it appears to be blank, with a competitor's name, or with the name of another marketer from an industry that is not in direct competition with the company that has paid for the actual signage at the venue?

Internet

There are numerous ways in which marketers can use sports-oriented Web sites to generate interest and demand for their products. Many Web sites that are maintained by sports properties routinely sell advertising space. By purchasing this space, the marketer reaches a segment that should be similar to one of its own target markets. The advertising can create an association of the marketer's brand with the sports entity. As a result of this presumed relationship, consumers may be more receptive to this type of advertising. The Web site will likely measure the number of hits that it achieves, so the advertiser's reach can be verified. When the Web site offers a link to the advertiser's site, the advertiser can also measure its *click-through rate,* which is the number and percentage of consumers who viewed the original Web site and then clicked on the advertiser's icon in an effort to acquire more information. Another advantage is that it is not viewed as a nuisance in the way that *pop-up* ads are. Some high profile examples of this type of promotion include

Xbox on fifa.com, Dell Computers on SI.com (Sports Illustrated), Hampton Inn (Hilton Hotels) on pga.com, and Orbitz Travel on espn.com.

Pop-up ads can also be used, but they tend to be less effective. New software for many Internet browsers has been designed to block these ads. Still, their use represents an inexpensive way to reach consumers. A recent surfing expedition through a variety of sports Web sites produced the following set of examples. Tickle Matchmaking and On-line Dating popped up on football.com; a site offering other promotions at freegames-source.com was displayed while viewing nhl.com; an ad for Publishers' Clearing House popped up while the mlb.com Web site was on the screen; and an American Express ad appeared during the viewing of the pga.com Web site. In some cases, the appearance of these ads is actually approved by the sports property as it is compensated for each click-through from its site. In other cases, the ads are not sanctioned by the Web site and appear either at random or on the basis of the primary emphasis of the Web site being visited by the user.

A third Internet-based approach is to tie in with one of the search engines such as Yahoo or Lycos. Marketers can pay the operators of many search engines for a prioritized link with key search terms. When an individual enters specific search terms, not only does the engine seek matches from the database, but it also identifies the Web sites for those organizations that have paid to be associated with one or more of those key search terms. These are often listed first and identified as *sponsored sites*. Practitioners have begun to refer to this strategy as *search marketing*. For example, a recent search using the single term, rugby, on the MSN search engine resulted in the identification of eBay and Discount Rugby Hotels as sponsored sites. In an interesting example, the use of "golf" as the sole search term resulted in the identification of a Volkswagen retailer and placed it first on the list of "golf" Web sites identified in this search.

> Marketers can pay the operators of many search engines for a link with key search terms.

Mainstream marketers can also choose to incorporate some element of sports into their own Web sites. Wheaties Cereal has long been recognized for its involvement in sports. Endorsements by notable athletes and packaging that incorporates sports and key sports figures are both part of Wheaties' long-standing marketing strategy. More recently, its Web site has also featured a sports overlay. A recent viewing of the www.breakfast-of-champions.com Web site featured a partnership with the American College of Sports Medicine. The Web site also includes a link to their "champions list" where visitors can click on and view an image of an actual Wheaties box that featured one of the many athletes who have appeared on their packaging over the past 70 years. The McDonald's USA Web site displays an image of four kids who just won their first game. While there is no indication as to what sport was involved, visitors to the Web site are told that the kids' reward for winning was a McDonald's Happy Meal.

The Internet has become an important tool for marketers worldwide. The preceding discussion outlined ways in which marketers can use the sports environment in developing their own strategies for selling nonsports products. The use of the Internet to market sports products will be discussed later in this book in Chapter 20.

Hospitality

Sports provide companies with many opportunities to entertain clients, customers, and employees. As was discussed earlier, hospitality can also play a key role in the personal selling strategy of the firm. Yet not all hospitality directly involves personal selling. Many sponsorships include resources to facilitate these hospitality efforts; however,

FIGURE 2.8
2004 Ryder Cup
Hospitality Area

such opportunities exist beyond the realm of sponsorship. Companies can simply purchase hospitality rights at many major events. Hospitality is also a key consideration regarding a corporation's decision to purchase or rent a luxury suite at a major sports venue. New stadia and arenas today are being designed to optimize the use of the available space, and the result has been the allocation of more space devoted to luxury suites.

Among the amenities of most hospitality and corporate suite facilities are food and beverage catering, private restroom facilities, and video monitors. Many of the events that are staged on an irregular basis and those played at venues not generally designed for spectator sports will construct temporary structures for hospitality purposes. These structures may be as simple as a large tent or as complex as a furnished banquet hall.

The PGA's staging of the Ryder Cup is the perfect example of the use of hospitality. According to the "Official PGA Corporate Hospitality Guide," there are many reasons to use this type of promotion. The list includes enhanced image among customers, targeted networking, inspiring customer loyalty, ability to spend "quality" time with clients and prospects, the provision of incentives for your own sales force, the competition may be there, and it has a proven record of success.[9] These are compelling reasons to invest in corporate hospitality. The options that were available at the 2004 Ryder Cup were reported to range from a table for 10 guests at the Champions Club for a price of $60,000 to a "corporate chalet" that would accommodate between 100 and 150 guests at prices ranging up to $350,000. In all, officials sold out of the nearly 300 hospitality areas to a list of customers that included KPMG, Ford Motor Company, and General Motors.[10] Figure 2.8 is a photo of one of the hospitality areas at the 2004 Ryder Cup matches.

Closing Capsule

The field of sports marketing encompasses two distinct components. While most of the attention focuses on how to market spectator sports and other sports products, there is a tendency to overlook the important process of marketing nonsports products through sports. The emphasis here concerns questions like How can sports help us sell more M&M's? or How can sports improve the recognition of Nextel among consumers?

By considering the type of products sold and the nature of the relationship between the marketer and the sports property that is used in the firm's marketing efforts, four strategic domains can be identified. This chapter introduces examples from all four domains, but the emphasis is on mainstream strategies that are represented by efforts to sell nonsports products by marketers that have no official sponsorship involvement with the sports property.

Many times, the answers to the aforementioned questions involve official relationships with a sports property. These strategies include traditional sponsorships, endorsements, licensing, and venue naming rights. However, marketers can use traditional strategies when aligning themselves with sports properties. These traditional strategies do not involve an official relationship between the marketer and the sports property. Rather, they simply involve the creation of a sports overlay and coordinating it with the development of a marketing strategy by properly selecting target markets and by developing an effective marketing mix for each designated target market.

When considering mainstream strategies, perhaps the most commonly applied element of the marketing mix is promotion. Despite this, it is still important for marketers to understand how the price, product, and place variables can be used to market products through the sports environment. And within the promotion variable itself, several emerging strategies have received increased attention over the past few years. These include product placement, virtual advertising, hospitality, and Internet applications.

Of all the promotional techniques discussed in this chapter, the one that has been scrutinized the most is virtual advertising. This technique involves the insertion of computer-generated images into TV broadcasts. In this way, virtual signage can appear in places where no actual signage exists. While it was first embraced in Europe where many of the popular sports do not include natural breaks where TV advertisements can be aired, it is widely used on sports broadcasts in the American market today.

The second major phenomenon is the Internet. By virtue of the number of people that it reaches and its 24/7 availability, the Internet is fast becoming a basic component of most firms' promotional strategy. Marketers can advertise on sports-oriented Web sites, with pop-ups, through search engines, or by incorporating a sports theme on their own Web sites. They can also use a variety of sports themes on their own Web sites even though they are not involved in the marketing of sports products.

Marketers of all types of products continually seek ways to attain a sustainable competitive advantage over other firms within their industries. Using the sports environment to develop effective mainstream strategies represents one approach that is used by many marketers of nonsports products. As this chapter has demonstrated, companies with no official relationship with a particular sports property can still adjust their marketing mixes in an effort to effectively reach their target markets through sports. However, in those cases where an official relationship is deemed beneficial or perhaps even essential, marketers must consider the various sponsorship opportunities available to them. These domain-focused strategies will be the emphasis of Chapters 3 through 14

Review Questions

1. What is meant by the term *traditional strategy* as it relates to the integration of sports in the firm's marketing efforts?

2. What variables are commonly used in the task of market segmentation?

3. How is a target market different from a market segment?

4. Using a sports overlay, develop a mainstream strategy that could be used to reach a key target market for personal computers. Be certain to give a specific description of the target market.

5. Explain the four domains of the sports marketing environment. Give an example for each domain; use examples that are not given in this chapter.

6. What are the four variables in the marketing mix? What are the four traditional tools in the promotional mix?

7. Super Bowl advertising is very expensive. How can an expenditure exceeding $2,400,000 for 30 seconds be justified?

8. What are Dorna boards?

9. What is specialty advertising? Why is it so widely used in the task of marketing through sports?

10. What is product placement?

11. Explain the concept and the advantages of virtual advertising.

12. How can the Internet be used for strategies aimed at marketing nonsports products through sports?

Endnotes

1. C. Britcher, "TAG's New Tournament," April 14, 2004, www.sportbusiness.com/news/index?news_item_id=154264 (accessed October 13, 2005).

2. "FedEx Rings up Business at Ryder Cup," *Crain's Detroit Business*, September 20–26, 2004, p. 30.

3. T. Howard, "Advertisers Get in the Game," *USA Today,* September 30, 2004, p. B4.

4. T. Taylor, "Audience Info the Key to Sports Marketers," *Marketing News,* January 18, 1999, p. 10.

5. J. Heckman, "For Marketers, Camera Angles Score Best," *Marketing News,* August 30, 1999, pp. 1, 9.

6. S. McMurray, "Virtual Ad Makers Hope for Real Dollars," *Sports Sense,* June 1, 1998, p. 5.

7. D. Goetzl, "TBS Tries Virtual Advertising," *Advertising Age,* May 21, 2001, p. 8.

8. H. Méndez. "Virtual Signage: The Pitfalls of 'Now You See It, Now You Don't,'" *Sport Marketing Quarterly* 8, no. 4 (1999), pp. 15–21.

9. "Official PGA Corporate Hospitality Guide," 2004, www.pga.com/rydercup/events_hospitality.html (accessed May 5, 2004).

10. R. King, "Event Is Ticket to Schmooze," *Detroit News,* June 13, 2004, pp. 1B, 8B.

CHAPTER THREE

Introduction to Sponsorship

Learning Objectives

- Be able to differentiate between advertising and sponsorship.
- Learn the advantages of each tool.
- Identify five categories for sponsorship opportunities.
- Distinguish between self-evident and strategic linkages.
- Learn the trends in spending on sponsorships.
- Understand how ambush marketing and leveraging play roles.
- Identify special cases of sponsorship.
- Create awareness of controversies regarding sponsorship.

Although the traditional elements of the promotional mix have long been used to market products through sports and special events, it is evident that sponsorship has emerged as a key strategic initiative for many marketers today. The practice has become so common-place that many marketers have begun to stress the need for sponsorship to be incorporated with all of the firm's promotional efforts. As a result, marketers today have begun to expand the scope of their traditional promotional mix. Not only is sponsorship being included, but marketers are also seeking to develop cohesive strategies where all of the elements complement each other. The result is that marketers now speak of their *integrated marketing communications (IMC)* plan.

The concept of an IMC plan will be discussed throughout the remaining chapters of this text. Not only is it an essential element of the strategy for marketing products through sports, but it is also crucial in the task of marketing the vast array of sports products. The five components of an integrated marketing communications plan are identified in the following list.

- Advertising
- Personal selling
- Sales promotion
- Public relations/publicity
- Sponsorship

While we must always consider the potential role that each of the elements can play in the development of a firm's marketing strategy, the focus will now shift to sponsorship. This chapter will provide a broad overview of the concept; the next few chapters will provide a detailed description of the key considerations. Several special cases of sponsorship will be introduced in this chapter; they are also focal points in later chapters.

Overview of Sponsorship

On May 30, 2004, the Coca-Cola 600 was underway at Lowe's Motor Speedway. Because it was part of NASCAR Nextel Cup, all of the drivers were aware of the importance of a high finish. Though he drove a strong race, Michael Waltrip in the NAPA Auto Parts Chevrolet could manage only a second-place finish. So who was the winner?

Some would argue that there were many winners. While Jimmie Johnson's car won the race, that was not the only competition of interest to many observers. Coca-Cola, Nextel Cellular Service, Lowe's Home Improvement Stores, Chevrolet Automobiles, and NAPA Auto Parts retailers were all sponsors that gained considerable value from this race. Fans at Lowe's Motor Speedway and TV viewers at home were all exposed to a concerted effort to gain an advantage in the marketplace by a vast array of sponsors. These companies, and many others, spend millions of dollars each year on sponsorships from which they expect to gain significant exposure in key target markets. Additionally, sponsorship is instrumental in the effort to achieve a number of business objectives beyond exposure. To these marketers, the winner of the race is important, but not as important as the winner of the sponsorship competition. In order to fully understand this mind-set, we must first develop an understanding of the concept of sponsorship.

Sponsorship versus Advertising

There is a great deal of confusion regarding the concept of sponsorship. For many years, people have tended to consider sponsorship to be synonymous with advertising. Perhaps this misconception can be attributed to the terminology that has been routinely used by broadcasters of sports and special events. When going into an advertising break, TV announcers often proclaim, "We will be back after these words from our sponsors." With this proclamation, the announcers may have helped to perpetuate the misconception that advertising and sponsorship are synonyms.[1] Therefore, the initial objective of this chapter is to differentiate these two promotional tools.

Advertising

Advertising has been defined as "any paid, non-personal communication through various media about a business firm, not-for-profit, product, or idea by a *sponsor* identified in a message that is intended to inform or persuade members of a particular audience."[2] The use of the term *sponsor* as part of the accepted definition may cause further confusion regarding the difference between advertising and sponsorship.

> Announcers may have helped to perpetuate the misconception that advertising and sponsorship are synonyms.

Advertising emphasizes mass media techniques for the delivery of a standardized message. These media include television, radio, magazines, newspapers, and outdoor advertising. Recent emphasis has also been given to direct mail and Internet advertising. In some situations, advertising has advantages over sponsorship; in other cases, the reverse is true. The following discussion highlights the advantages for advertising.

Persuasive Message

The ability to deliver a persuasive message provides advertising with a significant advantage over sponsorship when the marketer is attempting to communicate product attributes, benefits, and competitive advantages based upon a superior set of attributes and benefits. An automobile manufacturer can communicate the fuel efficiency of a sporty new model. A pharmaceutical company can promote that its vitamins help protect consumers from specific illnesses. An Internet service provider might advertise that its DSL connection is faster than traditional dial-up service.

Standardization

Because advertising uses printed and spoken words to deliver its messages, marketers are able to compose ads that deliver the standardized message that they are seeking to convey to the target market. This helps assure that the message that is communicated is what the marketer actually sought to convey. Furthermore, each person who is exposed to the advertisement is presented with the same message.

Guarantee of Number of Consumers Reached

Since advertisers purchase time on the electronic media and space in the print media, they can be guaranteed a specific level of exposure. While they may know that they have 30 seconds on a TV program or half a page in a popular magazine, these numbers are not the critical element in determining the advertisement's potential impact. More important is the *reach;* how many consumers will be exposed to the ad? Print media know their circulation numbers; electronic media have prior estimates of each program's rating. Given this information, advertisers have a reasonable estimate of the audience that they will reach.

> Advertisers have a reasonable estimate of the audience that they will reach.

In many cases, TV networks will provide guarantees that the audience will meet or exceed a predetermined level. Consider NBC's broadcast of the 2004 Olympics in the United States. NBC promised and delivered a TV rating of 14.5 percent. Conversely, the 2000 Olympics in Sydney failed to achieve the targeted rating. When that happened, NBC was forced to provide make-goods. For the media and its advertisers, *make-goods* are resources that are provided for free to advertisers to compensate for the inadequate reach. These resources typically take the form of free advertising. For the Sydney Olympics, NBC provided additional advertising during the Olympic broadcast at no charge to the advertisers. When the TBS network failed to deliver the guaranteed rating of 3 percent for its inaugural Goodwill Games, advertisers were given enough free time on other sports programming on TBS to make up for the original shortfall.

> Make-goods are resources that are provided for free to advertisers to compensate for the inadequate reach.

Evaluation

Although the evaluation of the effectiveness of any promotional tool is difficult, it is generally accepted that such measurements are easier to implement for advertising than they are for sponsorship. Measures such as cost per thousand (CPM) are deemed appropriate for advertising but not for sponsorship. Similarly, there are several techniques that are widely used for measuring the impact that advertising has on sales. Some of these techniques, in addition to emerging measurement methodologies, are beginning to be applied to sponsorship. These methods and applications are discussed later in this text.

Turnkey

Whereas advertising may be viewed as a stand-alone promotional tool, that is not the case with sponsorship. The turnkey concept relates to this stand-alone capability. Duraliner, a manufacturer of inserts for the cargo beds of pickup trucks, once spent its entire advertising budget on a single commercial during the Super Bowl. The results were outstanding as the company experienced a substantial increase in its sales. While advertising can often stand alone, sponsorship cannot. Sponsors must spend considerable money on other promotional efforts that are designed to support its sponsorship; otherwise it will likely fail to accomplish its goals.

Sponsorship

While sponsorship takes many forms, the International Events Group (IEG) has defined sponsorship as a relationship between a marketer and a property in which the marketer pays a cash or in-kind fee in return for access to the exploitable commercial potential associated with the property.[3] For example, Coca-Cola recently paid $65 million for the rights to associate itself with the International Olympic Committee (IOC) for a four-year cycle. Nextel will pay $70 million per year for 10 years for the right to be officially aligned with NASCAR via the Nextel Cup series of races. (Because of the 2005 merger of Nextel and Sprint, the competition will be recognized as the Sprint Cup beginning with the 2007 season.) While these two examples reflect expensive deals with high-profile events, many sponsorships involve much smaller financial commitments and far less prestigious properties. Examples in this category include Budweiser's sponsorship of the Illinois State Fair, Sunoco's involvement with the Independence Day fireworks in Philadelphia (see Figure 3.1), and Oakley Sunglasses' sponsorship of the sports teams at Long Beach Polytechnic High School.

FIGURE 3.1
Sunoco's Welcome America Program

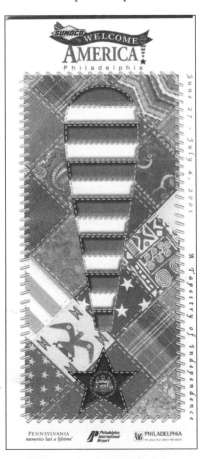

Typical benefits of sponsorship include the likelihood of significant exposure to signage that identifies the sponsor and its brands. These images will be seen by spectators at specific events and by those who watch the events on TV. But unlike advertising that delivers its message with strong words and images, sponsorship's constraints make it virtually impossible to deliver a persuasive message. Likewise, there are seldom guarantees regarding a sponsor's level of exposure. Their signs might receive considerable exposure or none at all. For example, if a race car that is sponsored by Marlboro Cigarettes is contending for the lead, spectators and TV cameras will focus on the car thereby providing significant exposure for the Marlboro logo on the side of the car. However, if the car crashes on the first lap, any hope for exposure has vanished.

Although we have already acknowledged that advertising is superior to sponsorship in several regards, sponsorship is not without its own advantages. These include credibility, image, prestige, internal morale, distribution rights, and access to a live audience.[4] These advantages are the subject of the next section of this chapter.

Credibility

Gatorade has a sponsorship contract with the National Football League (NFL). When consumers see the Gatorade cooler on the sidelines during the game, they are likely to think that the product does indeed have merit. The belief is that it must work, otherwise the NFL would not use it; this presumption establishes the credibility that Gatorade is seeking from its sponsorship.

Image

Volvo recently acquired the title sponsorship rights to a round-the-world yacht race. The automaker believes that its association with a sport and an event that appeal to an upscale target market enhances its image. Furthermore, there is a belief that yachting connotes an image of safety and new technology. Both of these are consistent with the image that Volvo seeks to nurture with its other promotional activities.

Prestige

Marketers choose to associate with elite properties in an effort to enhance their own prestige. While most sponsors do seek to achieve an acceptable return on their sponsorship investment, others seek relationships that consumers will look upon in a favorable way. American Telephone and Telegraph (AT&T) admittedly takes a qualitative perspective when assessing the impact that its association with the Olympics has on its image in the eyes and minds of American consumers.[5]

Internal Morale

Employees are often given opportunities to be involved with a sponsored property. They may be able to attend the event or participate in the entertainment of their company's customers at the event. They witness their company's involvement when the sponsorship features local events. All of these serve to enhance morale within the sponsor's firm.

Sales Opportunities

This benefit provides the sponsor with the opportunity to sell its products at the event venue. For example, Coors beer is sold at Coors Field. Another sales opportunity can involve the property itself. If new TV monitors are needed for the luxury suites at an arena, preference may be given to a vendor such as Philips Electronics that has sponsorships with many sports properties.

Access to a Live Audience

Advertising reaches viewers indirectly. On the other hand, sponsorship delivers a live audience at the venue. Not only might this enhance consumer receptivity to the sponsor's message, but it also provides access to fans for the distribution of free samples, for use as respondents to marketing research surveys, and for the ability to get immediate feedback from consumers. The immediacy of this live audience cannot be duplicated with traditional advertising.

Table 3.1 provides a summary of the comparison of advertising and sponsorship. It documents that each promotional tool has its own strengths and weaknesses. Marketers must assess each tool when developing their own integrated marketing communications plans.

TABLE 3.1
Comparison of Advertising and Sponsorship

Source: *IEG's Complete Guide to Sponsorship: Everything You Wanted to Know about Sponsorship* (Chicago: IEG, Inc., 1999), pp. 40–41.

Advertising Is Superior	Sponsorship Is Superior
Persuasive message	Credibility
Delivers standardized message	Image
Can guarantee reach	Prestige
Evaluation	Internal morale
Turnkey	Sales opportunities
	Access to a live audience

Sponsorship Categories

There are five recognized categories of sponsorship available to marketers:

- Sports.
- Entertainments, tours, and attractions.
- Cause-related marketing.
- Festivals, fairs, and annual events.
- Arts.

Sports represent the most common sponsorship category; in North America, some 69 percent of all sponsorship dollars are devoted to this category. Historically, the most expensive contracts have been in sports; this reality has been a key factor in sports' domination of the sponsorship market. Examples of this type of relationship include that of McDonald's sponsorship of FIFA and the World Cup of Soccer, the adidas sponsorship of intercollegiate athletics at the University of Tennessee, Vodafone's sponsorship of the Manchester United Soccer team, Amway's decision to sponsor a snooker tournament in China, and South African Airlines' partnership with the International Cricket Council's (ICC) World Cup of Cricket.

The category that represents the second-largest aggregate sponsorship investment is that of *entertainment, tours, and attractions*. This category has grown to 10 percent of the market on the strength of several high-budget music deals. Typical of this category are Ameriquest Mortgage Company's sponsorship of the 2005 Rolling Stones concert tour, Stacker's recognition as the official energy drink of the 2004 Ozzfest, Nokia's status as the presenting sponsor of Hard Rock Live, Virgin Megastores' recognition as the exclusive retail sponsor for Summerfest 2003 (a large music festival in Milwaukee), and Coca-Cola's designation as the official soft drink of Six Flags Amusement Parks. To illustrate the potential importance of this source of revenue for properties in this category, it has recently been reported that the reemergence of the Lollapalooza Tour is dependent upon new funding from corporate sponsors.[6]

> The reemergence of the Lollapalooza Tour is dependent upon new funding from corporate sponsors.

Category three is represented by *cause-related marketing (CRM) endeavors*. Approximately 9 percent of the sponsorship dollars in North America are invested in relationships that feature what might best be characterized as charitable organizations. This may be done on a large-scale basis for major health care providers, educational institutions, animal welfare funds, and public broadcasting. However, many marketers view local causes as an opportunity to become involved in their communities for modest investments. Because of their local nature, these relationships are often referred to as *grassroots* sponsorship. Examples of high-profile sponsorships of CRM efforts include Delta Airlines' association with the Elton John AIDS Foundation, Nestlé and its affiliation with the Ronald McDonald House charities, Whirlpool's sponsorship of Habitat for Humanity, and Starwood Hotel's relationship with the American Society for the Prevention of Cruelty to Animals (ASPCA). On a grassroots basis, the list would include John Hancock Financial Services' involvement with the Jimmy Fund, a cancer research organization in Boston. A second example is Kroger, a large grocery retailer chain, and its sponsorship of the Celebrity Classic Benefiting the Children's Hospital in Cincinnati, Ohio.

Festivals, fairs, and annual events comprise the fourth category, one that attracts approximately 7 percent of the sponsorship dollars in North America. Generally, these events are recurring in that they are staged each year. As with CRM, some of these are quite large and attract a large TV audience in addition to a significant live audience. Holiday parades may have large national prominence; events such as Mardi Gras in New Orleans and Carnival in Rio de Janeiro are examples of annual events that attract both national and international attention. In the aftermath of the destruction in New Orleans that was caused by Hurricane Katrina, organizers of Mardi Gras were forced to seek new sources of funding in the form of corporate sponsors. The first marketer to sign on as an official sponsor of Mardi Gras was Glad trash bags. The relationship resulted in a payment of some $200,000 to the organizers of this famous annual event. Other events in this category include expositions such as large auto shows, award shows on TV such as the Academy Awards, and a variety of trade shows. An example of a sponsor that has sought to capitalize on this type of relationship is Olympus Cameras through its relationship with the New York Fashion Week; the combination of photography and fashion is a logical fit. Many of the smaller events in this category also present grassroots opportunities. State fairs and festivals that are staged in small, local communities are seeking a cash infusion because many state and local governments have become reluctant to fund these types of activities. Examples of these grassroots opportunities include Budweiser's association with the Tennessee Renaissance Festival and the sponsorship of the Swallows (of Capistrano) Day Parade by a local automobile dealer, Capistrano Ford.

The smallest category at 5 percent is the *arts*. This involves sponsorships that focus on the visual or performing arts such as a symphony orchestra concert series or a museum exhibit.[7] There are numerous current or recent sponsorships, including American Airlines and the Boston Pops, Audi and the San Diego Symphony, Ford Motor Company and the Three Tenors Concert tour, M&T Bank and the Rodin art exhibit at the Albright-Knox Art Gallery in Buffalo, New York, and the Hotels.com sponsorship of the Museum of Modern Art in Paris, France.

Overview

It is estimated that the sports category is the recipient of the vast majority of sponsorship dollars that are spent today. Though there has been some fluctuation in the share attained by each of the five categories over the years, the variation has been relatively modest. Clearly, there are numerous opportunities for sponsors. Some are expensive while others are much more reasonably priced. The figures presented in the previous paragraphs represent expenditures in North America, but each category is available on a global basis. While the examples cited generally focused on North American sponsorships, several international relationships were also identified. The next few chapters discuss the issues that are germane to sponsorship, and they will continue to highlight the international dimension of sponsorship in today's marketing environment.

Key Concepts

A sponsorship involves two participating parties: the sponsor and the sponsee. To be effective, these participants must have a sound understanding of three key concepts: linkages, leveraging, and ambush marketing. Each of these considerations will now be introduced.

The fundamental premise to understand is that there are two parties involved in any sponsorship endeavor. These two parties are the sponsor and the sponsee. The *sponsor* is the party that provides compensation in order to be officially associated with a specific property. The *sponsee* is the property that provides value by virtue of that association. For example, in one of the most widely recognized sponsorship relationships today, Coca-Cola is the sponsor whereas the Olympic Games represent the sponsee. For this sponsorship—or any other sponsorship—to be effective, both the sponsor and the sponsee must understand the linkages that are available and the potential roles of leveraging and ambush marketing.

Marketers seek sponsorships that provide access to their target markets. This access is generally characterized as a *linkage*. Many of these linkages are readily apparent. For instance, when Nike sponsors an Olympic sports team, it is evident that many of the products sold by Nike are routinely used in that type of competition. Athletes wear Nike apparel; the game may be played using sports equipment that bears the Nike brand. This type of linkage is deemed to be *self-evident*.[8] Sponsors benefit because consumers readily understand their relationship with the property. In this example, the relationship between Nike and the team is apparent. Nike attempts to capitalize on this awareness by selling more of its products to its target markets. Beyond sports, an example of a self-evident linkage would be an electronics company such as Sony sponsoring a concert by a popular singer or musical group.

With *strategic* linkages, the sponsor's products are not prominently used during the staging of the event.[9] For example, Volvo is the primary sponsor of the prestigious Volvo Ocean Race, and Ford is involved with professional golf. The rationale in these cases is that the target markets for the sponsor and the sponsored event are similar. Volvo has reason to believe that the fans of yacht racing are the same consumers who purchase its automobiles. Thus, the sponsorship provides a strategic linkage in the form of access to Volvo's target market. One organization that has been able to capitalize on its ability to provide strategic linkages is the Susan G. Komen Breast Cancer Foundation and its "Race for the Cure." Because of the enhanced image and the ability to connect with women in the marketplace, companies such as American Express, Ford Motor, Lee Jeans, the U.S. Postal Service, New Balance, Kellogg, and Avon have all become involved with this important cause.

The concept of *leveraging* is based on the premise that all sponsorships must be supported with strategic efforts that are designed to enhance the effectiveness of the sponsorship. It is shortsighted to simply pay the sponsorship rights fees and assume that the market will recognize the relationship. Companies often develop an integrated marketing communications plan that incorporates an array of promotional efforts designed to draw attention to the sponsorship. In addition to promotion, special packaging or commemorative products may be introduced. Regardless of how the strategy is implemented, leveraging is an essential element of each sponsor's strategy.

> It is shortsighted to simply pay the sponsorship rights fees and assume that the market will recognize the relationship.

Finally, sponsors must be alert to the possibility of ambush marketing. Nonsponsors use *ambush marketing* efforts to create the impression that they are associated with an event when, in reality, no official association exists. An example that will be discussed at length later in this text is Wendy's effort to ambush McDonald's official sponsorship of the Olympics. By using sports themes and former Olympic athletes in its TV advertising that aired when the Olympics were being staged, Wendy's misled many consumers into believing that it, not McDonald's, was the official fast-food sponsor of the Olympic Games.[10] The ethics of this type of strategy were questioned by many, but clearly it provided immediate benefits for Wendy's while having a detrimental impact on McDonald's. Sponsors must anticipate the types of ambush marketing efforts that their competitors will implement. Clearly, an effective leveraging strategy can help minimize the detrimental impact that an ambush marketing campaign can have on the consumers' ability to recognize official sponsors.

Spending on Sponsorship

Worldwide expenditures on sponsorship in 2004 were $27.9 billion. The estimated figure for 2005 was $30.4 billion. This 9 percent growth rate was primarily driven by increased expenditures in Australia, China, and North America. Still, spending grew in real terms in every region of the world. Table 3.2 provides an overview of spending levels and trends over the period from 2004 through 2005.

When assessing expenditures, it is also noteworthy to examine the list of companies that spent the most money on their global sponsorship activities. The most recent data are from 2003. A quick look at the top 20 spenders shows that sponsorship is a global phenomenon. It can also be seen that in order to make the top 20, a company had to spend more than $51 million on sponsorship fees. These figures are reported in Table 3.3.

Spending in North America

North American expenditures on sponsorship were expected to rise to $12.09 billion in 2005, a figure that represents an 8.8 percent increase from 2004 levels. The growth was expected to be driven by modest increases in the budgets of companies that were previously active in sponsorship and by companies entering the sponsorship environment for the first time. Also of interest is the anticipation that much of the increase would be fueled by an abundance of small deals rather than expensive, high-profile contracts. The projected growth in North American expenditures fell slightly below the anticipated overall global growth rate of 9 percent.[11]

TABLE 3.2
Worldwide Spending on Sponsorship

Source: *IEG Sponsorship Report*, 23, no. 24 (December 27, 2004), pp. 1, 5. Reprinted with permission.

Region	2004 Level	2005 Level	Growth Rate (2004–05)*
Europe	$7.8 B	$8.4 B	8.1%
Pacific Rim	5.2 B	5.8 B	12.3
Central and South America	2.3 B	2.5 B	7.4
North America	11.1 B	12.1 B	8.8
Rest of world	1.5 B	1.6 B	4.0
Overall	$27.9 B	$30.4 B	9.0

*Rounding of yearly data produces small level of rounding error; statistics in growth rate column are accurate.

TABLE 3.3
Sponsorship's Largest Global Spenders

Source: "Sports Big Spenders," *SportBusiness International,* July 2004, pp. 14–15. Data from The World Sponsorship Monitor, published in the U.K. by Sports Marketing Surveys.

Rank	Company/Brand	Reported 2003 Expenditures (US$)
1	Nextel	$761,890,000
2	Nike	521,821,000
3	GE	200,000,000
4	adidas	199,048,500
5	Reebok	169,574,000
6	MasterCard	131,862,000
7	T-Mobile	130,949,500
8	Bank One	125,000,000
9	Barclays	112,250,000
10	Toyota	108,999,500
11	Sony PlayStation	102,473,498
12	MBNA	96,000,000
13	Ford	77,549,500
14	Amstel	72,000,000
15	Qatar	63,000,000
16	Vodafone	62,424,500
17	Diadora	62,350,000
18	Citizens Bank of Pennsylvania	57,000,000
19	Budweiser	51,823,500
20	Pepsi	51,097,000

As we consider the role that sponsorship plays in a firm's integrated marketing communications plan, it is interesting to look at the growth rates for the three mass media components: advertising, sales promotion, and sponsorship. Table 3.4 provides a brief historical perspective. A quick review of the data reveals that the rate of growth for sponsorship spending has substantially exceeded the growth rates of both advertising and sales promotion. Although more money is still spent on advertising and sales promotion, it is evident that sponsorship is closing the gap.

> Much of the increase will be fueled by an abundance of small deals rather than expensive, high-profile sponsorship contracts.

TABLE 3.4
Advertising, Sales Promotion, and Sponsorship Growth

Source: *IEG Sponsorship Report* 23, no. 24 (December 27, 2004), p. 5. Reprinted with permission.

Year	Advertising	Sales Promotion	Sponsorship
2005 (est.)	6.4%	5.1%	8.8%
2004	7.4	4.7	8.4
2003	5.2	4.2	6.2
2002	2.8	5.6	4.0
2001	−4.1	−5.6	7.0
2000	9.9	6.3	14.0
1999	6.8	7.4	12.0
1998	7.1	4.2	15.0
1997	6.6	3.3	9.0
1996	7.6	4.6	15.0
1995	7.7	4.6	11.0

Special Cases of Sponsorship

On the preceding pages, the discussion focused on issues germane to traditional sponsorship. Beyond this, there are three special cases of sponsorship that merit the marketer's attention. These strategic initiatives are endorsements, venue naming rights, and licensing.

Whether these initiatives truly fit the definition of sponsorship may be subject to question. Yet they do possess the key consideration; the marketer is attempting to capitalize upon its official association with a property, event, or individual. When effectively implemented, these types of sponsorship initiatives can complement the marketer's promotional strategy and facilitate the achievement of the firm's goals and objectives. Each of these three strategies is introduced in the following discussion, and a comprehensive examination of each is provided in later chapters.

Endorsements

Endorsements are generally thought of within the context of traditional advertising, but they are often characterized as *personality sponsorships*. They involve the use of a celebrity who is consistent with the market segment that is being targeted with the advertisement. These celebrities include current athletes like Tiger Woods, retired athletes such as Michael Jordan, entertainers such as Cybill Shepherd, politicians such as former U.S. Vice President Bob Dole, and a variety of other noteworthy individuals such as Sarah Ferguson, the Duchess of York.

These celebrities are compensated for allowing their likenesses to be used in advertising. They also often provide testimonials regarding the merits of the products that they are paid to endorse. In many cases, the endorser will actively participate in some of the marketer's activities. They may attend press conferences announcing a new product introduction or participate in corporate activities. For example, when Arnold Palmer endorsed products for Lanier Worldwide, he attended a trip that was awarded to the firm's top salespeople, with the highest performers earning the opportunity to play a round of golf with a golfing icon that many people still idolize. Figure 3.2 illustrates an advertisement that features a celebrity endorsement.

Venue Naming Rights

This strategy involves a payment by a company or individual in exchange for the right to have a facility bear the name of its naming rights sponsor. In sports, this strategy involves the stadia and arenas where the competition takes place. Many refer to venue naming rights in sports as *stadium sponsorship*. It must be acknowledged, however, that many of the naming rights opportunities that exist today are not in the sports domain. While most readers will quickly acknowledge the rationale for Reebok attaching its name to a soccer stadium, the logic is not so evident when scrutinizing the relationship between a financial services company such as Edward Jones and a football stadium. Yet the St. Louis Rams of the NFL play their home games at the Edward Jones Dome. Beyond sports, recent contracts have created identities such as the Kodak Theatre in Los Angeles and the Mattel Children's Hospital at UCLA.

The similarity to sponsorship is evident. The most common application involves a marketer's payment to become intimately associated with a sports facility. When done correctly, the parties will find the relationship to be mutually beneficial. Figure 3.3 illustrates some of the major signage at the Lexus Centre in Melbourne, Australia.

Licensing

The final special case of sponsorship is licensing. With this strategy, marketers pay for the right to produce and sell merchandise that bears the trademarks of another organization. This array of merchandise typically includes clothing, sports equipment, banners, coffee mugs, and a variety of other miscellaneous items.

FIGURE 3.2
Ad Featuring
Celebrity
Endorsement

It is important to note that not all sponsors of a property, a team, or an event necessarily have the right to sell or give away any merchandise that bears the sponsored organization's trademarks. That right is conveyed in contracts that allow the marketer to be classified as a licensee. It is these licensees that offer *officially licensed merchandise* to the market.

Overview of Special Forms of Sponsorship

Clearly, the practices of celebrity endorsements, venue naming rights, and licensing do not fit the exact structure of traditional sponsorship. Yet they are consistent with the basic premise.

FIGURE 3.3
Venue Naming
Rights—Lexus Centre

In each case, the two parties enter into a mutually beneficial relationship that is predicated upon the exchange of resources. Each of these modes of sponsorship can effectively use sports in the task of marketing products in both consumer and business-to-business markets.

This chapter has provided an introduction to traditional sponsorship and three nontraditional sponsorship approaches. The next 11 chapters provide a comprehensive discussion of the application of each of these strategies. At the end of this section of the text, there should be a clear understanding of how and why companies seek to market their products through the sports environment.

Controversial Issues

As with promotion in general, there are often concerns that the high cost of sponsoring a premier event adds to the costs that are passed along to consumers in the form of *higher prices* for the sponsor's products. There is a concern that the high cost also provides an *advantage for large, multinational corporations (MNCs)*. These MNCs have the financial capacity to invest millions of dollars on sponsorships and their leveraging programs, whereas smaller companies are simply unable to devote the requisite resources. So the concern is that the financial advantage translates into a marketing advantage for these large, global corporations.

Another criticism that is often voiced concerns the *absence of an obvious fit* between the sponsor and the event or property that is being sponsored. When Nike sponsored the Kenyan cross-country ski team for the Olympic Games, the critics were quite vocal. The African country has no snow, so why would it have a ski team? The athletes' performance paled in comparison to Olympic standards, so Nike was criticized for subjecting the Kenyans to certain failure. The sponsor's argument was that it allowed two athletes who otherwise would not have had the opportunity to compete and enjoy the Olympic experience to benefit by virtue of its support. Therefore, they should be commended for embracing the ideals of the Olympic Games. It must also be remembered that strategic linkages between the sponsor and the market are not always readily apparent. At first glance, one might question the logic of Tide laundry detergent sponsoring a NASCAR racing team. But virtually every race fan purchases detergent for their household, so the fit between Tide and NASCAR is both present and effective.

Strong criticism has been directed toward *sponsors whose products are deemed to be unwholesome.* Perhaps the best example is tobacco products. Public concern in many countries has led some governments to impose new restrictions that prohibit this type of sponsorship. Australia and the United States have both placed significant restrictions on the marketers of cigarettes. Questions may also be raised about sponsorships involving alcoholic beverages; is it appropriate for a beer company to sponsor a car racing team? Should anyone, especially children, be subjected to signs bearing the names of sponsors who sell drugs aimed at correcting male impotence? Many will say no, but both Major League Baseball and NASCAR have prominent displays of signage promoting Viagra. Products such as these will inevitably lead to questions regarding their appropriateness, thus both the sponsor and the sponsored property should anticipate the criticism prior to initiating the relationship.

Closing Capsule

Sponsorship is being incorporated into many firms' integrated marketing communications plans as they use the sports environment to create both interest and demand for their products. Billions of dollars are spent each year as sponsors attempt to gain an advantage over their competitors by becoming involved with events and properties that are of interest to their target markets. And while the vast majority of these investments involve sports, there are many other opportunities beyond sports that are available to marketers today.

Many people confuse the concepts of advertising and sponsorship. Advertising is a mass media–oriented approach for the dissemination of a standardized message to those who choose to be exposed to a specific advertising medium. Sponsorship reaches consumers who choose to watch or attend an event by virtue of the association between the sponsor and the event. Each of these promotional tools possesses some advantages over the other.

There are five categories of properties and events that are available to the prospective sponsor. By attracting 69 percent of the sponsorship dollars, sports is by far the largest category in North America. The remaining four categories each command between 5 and 10 percent of the expenditures. In descending order, they are entertainment, tours, and attractions; cause-related marketing; festivals, fairs, and annual events; and the arts. Clearly, today's marketers have a broad array of properties and events from which sponsorship opportunities can be selected.

> Sponsorship is a global phenomenon with a significant presence in every region of the world.

Global spending on sponsorship in 2005 was expected to reach $30.4 billion. Sponsorship is a global phenomenon with a significant presence in every region of the world. Several large multinational corporations devote more than $100 million each year to sponsorship. These expenditures continue to fuel a steady growth in the financial commitments made by sponsors.

Sponsorships are selected, in part, on the basis of their linkages to target markets. Self-evident linkages exist when the sponsor's products are a visible component of the staging of the event; for example, adidas provides uniforms and rugby balls for the New Zealand Rugby Football Union. Strategic linkages exist when the sponsor and the sponsored property have similar target markets. The Olympic Games provide Coca-Cola with the opportunity to reach many consumers who purchase soft drinks.

To be effective, sponsorships should be leveraged. This refers to the array of strategic initiatives that are designed to support the sponsorship and reinforce the relationship in the consumers' minds. A sound leveraging program will help to minimize the negative impact of ambush marketing; these represent efforts by nonsponsors to create the misperception in the marketplace that they are affiliated with the property. Ambushing has become more commonplace and can significantly diminish the value of the relationship.

> A sound leveraging program will help to minimize the negative impact of ambush marketing.

While most firms focus on traditional sponsorship, there are several special cases of sponsorship that can be used as part of a firm's marketing strategy. One case is endorsements; for instance, Tiger Woods' endorsement of TAG Heuer watches is referred to as a *personality sponsorship*.[12] Another recent example is Nike's new contract with Serena Williams. The second special case is venue naming rights. While this strategy is most often associated with sports arenas, a variety of other types of facilities are recognized by the names of sponsors that have paid for this right. Finally, there is licensing. This strategy involves the conveyance of the right to use an organization's trademarks on merchandise offered by another marketer. For example, adidas sells a variety of items that incorporate the logos of the University of Tennessee.

While sponsorship is viewed as a sound marketing strategy, it is not immune from criticism. With companies spending millions of dollars to sponsor premier properties, there is a concern that these costs are passed along to consumers in the form of higher prices. On a similar note, because small firms cannot afford to become involved with premier properties, many believe that large multinational corporations have an advantage. Some sponsorships seem to defy logic as critics question the appropriateness of relationships such as the one between the Kenyan cross country ski team and Nike. Finally, sponsorship often involves products that may be deemed unwholesome or inappropriate for some reason. In this regard, the tobacco industry's relationship with motor sports has been questioned for many years.

> When properly conceived and executed, sponsorship can be an effective tool.

Sponsorship involves far more than simply paying a fee to be associated with a property. Marketers have many options and must select the opportunity that represents the best fit. Inadequate assessment is the cause of failure for many sponsorships. It is a very complex process, but when properly conceived and executed, sponsorship can be an effective tool. The following chapters are designed to provide insight into the process that helps assure that sponsors are making wise investments.

Review Questions

1. Differentiate between advertising and sponsorship.
2. What advantages does sponsorship have over advertising?
3. What are the five categories of properties available for sponsorship opportunities?
4. Select an event and identify one sponsor that has a self-evident linkage and one with a strategic linkage for the event.
5. Briefly describe the concept of leveraging.
6. Briefly describe ambush marketing.
7. Briefly discuss endorsements. Find an example of an endorsement that you think is ineffective. What are your reasons for thinking as you do?
8. What are the most common concerns about sponsorship?
9. What are make-goods?
10. What are grassroots events?

Endnotes

1. S. Fullerton and D. Taylor, "A Comparison of New Zealand and American University Students' Views of Various Aspects of Sponsorship," *The Challenge: Sport Management beyond 2000,* January 2000, pp. 20–21.
2. L. Boone and D. Kurtz, *Contemporary Marketing 2005* (Mason, OH: Southwestern Publishing, 2005), p. G1.
3. *IEG's Complete Guide to Sponsorship: Everything You Wanted to Know about Sponsorship* (Chicago: IEG, Inc., 1999), p. 42.
4. Ibid., p. 40.
5. G. Levin, "Sponsors Put Pressure on for Accountability," *Advertising Age* (1994), pp. S1, S4.
6. P. Farrell, "Corporate Sponsors May Be Key to Lollapalooza's Return," January 15, 2003, www.mtv.com/news/articles/1459531/20030114/story.html (accessed October 13, 2005).
7. *IEG's Complete Guide to Sponsorship,* p. 40.
8. B. Cornwell, "Sponsorship-Linked Marketing Development," *Sport Marketing Quarterly* 4, no. 6 (1995), pp. 13–24.
9. Ibid.
10. H. Schlossberg, *Sports Marketing* (Cambridge, MA: Blackwell Publishers, Inc., 1996), pp. 40–47.
11. "Sponsorship Spending in North America," 2004, www.sponsorship.com/learn/ northamericas-pending.asp (accessed October 13, 2005).
12. "Sports Big Spenders," *SportBusiness International,* July 2004, pp. 14–15.

CHAPTER FOUR

Sponsorship Objectives and Components

Learning Objectives

- Identify five key sponsorship objectives.
- Learn how important each objective is.
- Understand the concept of matching.
- Learn the potential components of a sponsorship plan.
- View a comprehensive example of a sponsorship.

As sponsorship objectives continue to evolve to a focus on return on investment, both the sponsor and the property (sponsee) must anticipate the types of goals that will be sought by the marketer. Once these have been sufficiently identified and prioritized, the sponsorship program should be designed accordingly. Negotiations will focus on the components of the sponsorship that are available to the prospective sponsor. The property must attempt to match its sponsorship plan to the needs of the prospect. Event organizers and property owners must be aware of the reality that there are numerous sponsorship opportunities available to the marketer and that the final selection will be predicated upon which opportunity best satisfies the marketer's needs.[1] Both parties understand that it is not just the cost associated with a sponsorship that drives the final decision.

Sponsorship Objectives

While there are a number of specific objectives that may be sought by the sponsor, they can be categorized so as to identify five broad objectives:

- Drive sales.
- Improve image.
- Create greater awareness.
- Provide hospitality opportunities.
- Enhance employee morale.

A meaningful question becomes one of what specific goals fall within each of these five broad categories.

> Sponsorship objectives continue to evolve to a focus on return on investment.

Drive Sales

Since most sponsorships focus on the bottom line, the most important objective for most marketers is to increase sales via better market penetration and growth in market share. A marketer can seek to establish a *sustainable competitive advantage (SCA)* over competition by virtue of its relationship with a sponsored property. In many cases, consumers are more prone to purchase and tend to be more loyal to products and brands that sponsor events or other properties that the consumer admires. For example, research has shown that fans of particular NASCAR events and drivers recognize sponsors and express a preference for their products over those of their competition. As a result, NASCAR sponsors have become far more diversified with the array including beer (Miller Genuine Draft), chemical companies (DuPont), retailers (Home Depot), pharmaceutical products (Viagra), and laundry products (Tide). In some cases, a sponsor's participation in an event contractually precludes any competitor's involvement, thus the advantage attained by the sponsor is difficult for competition to neutralize. For example, Fuji Film's sponsorship of the World Cup of Soccer guarantees that competitor Kodak will not be allowed any official association with the event.

Merchandising and channel issues are also related to the objective of driving sales. The event itself might be an important channel of distribution with the sponsor's products being sold at the various venues. Furthermore, the sponsorship can result in greater cooperation by traditional retailers. If retailers believe that the sponsorship will be effective, then they will be more prone to increase shelf space and display point-of-sale promotional materials. This participation by retailers should result in increased market share for the sponsor. From yet another promotional perspective, a sponsorship can give a marketer a chance to showcase its products. Firestone Tires has used race teams for the Indianapolis 500 for this purpose. This presence can help *shape consumer attitudes* in a way so as to achieve an advantage or overcome a disadvantage.

Another specific objective is that of *overcoming advertising restrictions*. Across the world, there are classes of products that are prohibited from advertising using traditional media. The most noteworthy is the category of tobacco products. When the prohibition of cigarette advertising took effect in the United States in 1975, the tobacco industry sought alternative promotional tools. Thus was born the strong, important relationship between motor sports and the tobacco companies. NASCAR's most important series of races was designated the Winston Cup. As a result, the Winston brand name and logo have appeared in a variety of media, including some that tobacco companies are prohibited from using for advertising. However, the critics' concerns have been addressed, and countries such as Australia and the United States have begun to impose new restrictions on tobacco sponsorships that have either precluded future sponsorship opportunities or caused tobacco companies to reassess the role of sponsorship in their existing integrated marketing communications plan. Effective with the 2004 season, the Winston sponsorship was replaced by a new sponsor, Nextel.

With the proliferation of advertising, companies are seeking ways to *cut through advertising clutter*. TV commercials have become shorter and more numerous, not to mention more expensive. Advertising pages in newspapers and magazines have increased. Consumers are exposed to an explosion of "pop-up" ads on the Internet. As a result, it is increasingly difficult for advertising to deliver an effective message that the consumer will acknowledge and remember. Sponsorship has been touted as one way to circumnavigate that clutter.

Companies are seeking ways to cut through advertising clutter.

For most events, the number of sponsors is limited; for example, the 2006 World Cup of Soccer was limited to 15 official sponsors, thus guaranteeing each sponsor a comparatively clutter-free environment. It is worth noting that many event sponsors have begun to articulate concerns that the sponsorship environment is becoming too cluttered as well. For example, the 15 official sponsors for the 2006 World Cup of Soccer represent a 50 percent increase over the 10 official sponsors for the 1994 tournament. Recently, event organizers such as those involved with the 2000 Sydney Olympics have begun to reassess this situation and impose new smaller limits on the number of sponsors allowed. The argument that less (fewer sponsors) is more (better results) is the emphasis for these event organizers. In an acknowledgment of this premise, FIFA recently announced a decision to reduce the number of official sponsors from 15 to 6 effective with the 2010 competition.

Finally, sponsorships can be used to *reach small segments and niches* in the marketplace. Oakley reaches a small segment with its involvement in Professional Beach Volleyball. Powerbar has used its designation as the official energy bar of the Boston Marathon to reach a small segment defined on the basis of lifestyle. These small segments can be very important to any marketer, even the large multinational corporations, as evidenced by adidas' sponsorship of the Boston Marathon.

Improve Image

Though not mutually exclusive from the objective of driving sales, a key strategic initiative for a sponsorship program is that of improving the image of a company, product, or a brand. One goal is that of *attaining positive public relations*. Marketers often seek opportunities to sponsor cause-related marketing (CRM) events. McDonald's has a long-standing relationship with the Muscular Dystrophy Association; FedEx has a newer relationship with St. Jude's Children's Hospital through their association with the PGA's Memphis Open. Another way to attain good PR is by sponsoring events for which there are strong emotional ties within the market. Steinlager Beer's sponsorship of Team New Zealand's entry in the America's Cup Yachting Regatta, Nike's sponsorship of the Brazilian national soccer team, British Airway's involvement with the national rugby team of South Africa, and Kodak's involvement with U.S. Olympics are examples of sponsorships that have resulted in a number of positive stories. This is enhanced when consumers are convinced that the sponsors' involvement makes the team more competitive and increases the likelihood that it will win. The sense of pride and patriotism is one on which the sponsor can capitalize by creating a positive image for itself.

Another way to generate good PR is by seeking sponsorship opportunities that *enhance the company's community involvement and portray it as a good corporate citizen*. From a sports perspective, this can be achieved via the sponsorship of local amateur sports and facilities. Sponsoring a team of local kids or having its name attached to a venue where they play can help achieve an improved local image. A large car dealer in Plymouth, Michigan, is the corporate sponsor for a local baseball/softball field (Don Massey Park). From a nonsports perspective, marketers can seek opportunities to be involved with local events. Local fairs and festivals often represent fund-raising opportunities for local organizations as well as a significant source of community pride. Sponsoring such events can allow the marketer to capitalize on this community involvement and pride. The aforementioned small city of Plymouth, Michigan, is very proud of its annual Ice Festival that brings in carvers from all over the world. Rock Financial has chosen to sponsor that event in recent years in an effort to enhance its image and community involvement. Signage used to create more public awareness of that involvement and to improve its image within the community is shown in Figure 4.1.

FIGURE 4.1
Sponsor Signage at Local Festival

A traditional marketing tactic is that of repositioning a product or brand. In this case, the marketer is attempting to modify the perception of the company and the products as seen by the consumer. American carmaker Buick has used golf, Tiger Woods in particular, to *shape consumer attitudes*. The brand has had an old-fashioned image. Their sponsorships within the sport of golf used Tiger Woods to reach a younger market and nurture the perception that Buick can appeal to a younger, more contemporary market and lifestyle.

The final approach to image enhancement is via *philanthropy*. While some might opt to position philanthropy as a major objective in its own right, others will recognize is as yet another way in which the sponsor can create a better image. This goes beyond the concept of cause-related marketing in that the objective is simply to make a donation to a worthy cause. Still, we would be remiss if we failed to acknowledge the positive feedback that such donations evoke.

Create Greater Awareness

As marketers introduce new products or enter new geographic markets, they recognize that the initial task in getting consumers to purchase their products is to create awareness. Even as they seek to increase market share via better penetration of existing markets, they seek ways to *increase their visibility* in the marketplace. This is also important when companies are changing a brand name. Andersen Consulting's name change to Accenture was facilitated by its sponsorship of a PGA golf tournament. Marketers will often seek associations with high-profile events that draw large attendance, significant TV viewership, and high levels of exposure in the news media.

Provide Hospitality Opportunities

Sponsorship can provide expanded opportunities by using a sports event as a forum for entertainment. This may include opportunities to simply *attend the event*. It may also include a variety of additional entertainment alternatives. Hospitality areas can provide a *number of amenities* to those granted access. Food and beverage service, private restroom facilities, premium parking locations, TV monitors, and preferred seating represent a few of the amenities not available to the general public. The objective of this hospitality is to reward customers, prospects, and suppliers. As such, it should also encourage a continued relationship with the sponsor. It is but one component of a relationship marketing program designed to create goodwill and a sense of loyalty. In the long run, this should also drive sales. One of the many hospitality tents available at the 2004 Ryder Cup matches is shown in Figure 4.2.

FIGURE 4.2
Ryder Cup
Hospitality Facility

Enhance Employee Morale

Just as an event can be used to entertain customers and suppliers, it can serve as an *entertainment opportunity for employees*. This may be used as a way to *reward high-performing employees*. In this case, the employees' morale should be enhanced because of the recognition received. It also affords these high performers the opportunity to interact with their peers. These hospitality areas may also be used to *entertain employees in general*. Today's emphasis on team building can be promoted by providing employees with a treat and allowing for the informal interaction among employees at different levels within the organization.

For these events that have a humanitarian nature, sponsorship can evoke a *sense of pride and involvement for the employees*. The idea that they work for a company that cares is not only effective in eliciting positive public relations in the press, but it is also effective with formal organizations such as unions and informal organizations such as the sales force.

Importance of Each Objective

The International Events Group (IEG) queried sponsorship decision makers about the relative importance of an array of objectives. Their basic conclusion was that enhancing brand loyalty was deemed to be the most important objective of a sponsorship program. Close behind this objective is that of increasing awareness or visibility. That was followed by the creation of a desirable image within the target market. The results of this study are summarized in Table 4.1.

TABLE 4.1
Importance of Sponsorship Objectives

Source: "Performance Research/IEG Study Highlights What Sponsors Want," 2001, www.sponsorship.com/learn/decisionmakerstudy.asp (accessed October 13, 2005).

Objective	% Rating Importance Level of 9 or 10*
Increase brand loyalty	68%
Create awareness/visibility	65
Change/reinforce image	59
Drive retail/dealer traffic	45
Showcase community/social responsibility	43
Stimulate sales/trial/usage	35
Sample/display/showcase products/services	35
Entertain clients/prospects	31

*On a 10-point scale, where 10 is "extremely important."

TABLE 4.2
Relative Importance of Sports Sponsorship Objectives

Source: Adapted from R. Irwin and W. Sutton, "Sport Sponsorship Objectives: An Analysis of Their Relative Importance for Major Corporate Sponsors," *European Journal for Sport Management* 1, no. 2 (1994), pp. 93–102.

Sport Sponsorship Objective	Mean*
Increase sales/market share	6.14
Increase target market awareness	6.07
Enhance general public awareness	5.88
Enhance general company image	5.47
Enhance trade relations	4.60
Enhance trade goodwill	4.55
Involve community	4.48
Alter public perception	4.15
Enhance employee relations	3.84
Block competition	3.68
Develop social responsibility	3.13
Develop corporate philanthropy	3.12

* On a scale of 1 to 7.

A second study also assessed the perceived importance of a variety of sponsorship objectives. The results summarized in Table 4.2 are consistent with the IEG study in that the focus on increased sales and market share are viewed as the most important objectives in the eyes of corporate sponsors.[2]

Matching Sponsorship Objectives with Sponsorship Components

Once there is an understanding of what the sponsor wants to achieve, the next task is to negotiate a sponsorship package that incorporates the components that will maximize the likelihood that those goals will be reached. Potential sponsors may be seeking different outcomes, thus every sponsor will not want the exact same set of components in return for their financial commitment. While many events have a standardized package whereby every sponsor is provided with the same components, event organizers should recognize that even a little flexibility in the negotiation process can pay dividends. In those situations where the event is seeking a single sponsor, flexibility is easy. Every effort should be made to provide the sponsor with a package that meets its needs. The event will benefit from the ability of the sponsor to achieve its goals. Upon the expiration of a sponsorship contract, companies must decide whether to renew or not, and the likelihood of renewal is much higher when the sponsor is satisfied with the outcome. This raises the question of what the event can provide; what are the key components of the sponsorship package?

> Every sponsor will not want the exact same set of components in return for their financial commitment.

Sponsorship Components

For a sponsorship to be a win–win relationship where both the sponsor and the sponsee benefit, considerable attention must be paid to the components of the sponsorship plan. From the sponsor's perspective, this involves the designation of the features that will help the sponsor achieve its strategic goals. While we cannot overlook the benefits received by the sponsee, the essential part of the sponsorship proposal will outline the components available to the sponsor. Many potential sponsors have a thorough understanding of the array of components that will best assist them in their marketing efforts. For example, Visa International has an entire group within its corporation whose job it is to assess sponsorship proposals.

They will eliminate those that fail to provide the means of achieving the marketing objectives associated with the potential sponsorship program. They will also be involved in negotiating the components that they will receive in exchange for the cash and value-in-kind (VIK) provided to the sponsee.

Category Exclusivity

Sponsors generally expect to be protected from direct competition for the event that they are sponsoring. For example, it would be difficult to convince Nestlé to spend significant monies sponsoring an event when its competitor, Mars, is allowed to be a sponsor as well. Many event organizers offer such protection by providing category exclusivity. This component of many major events prohibits the simultaneous participation of direct competitors in opposing sponsorship roles. It is assumed that a company will be more likely to invest resources in a sponsorship program if its competitors cannot officially participate. This may also increase the potential income for the event because the sponsor is willing to pay more for this component.

When negotiating category exclusively, the potential sponsor would prefer complete protection from any competition. The trade-off for the event is that increased levels of protection reduce the number potential sponsors by precluding many companies from participating.

Consider the earlier example for Nestlé. If Nestlé is an official sponsor and is granted category exclusivity, then no other candy and confectionary company will be allowed to participate in a sponsorship capacity. The fact that Cadbury or Mars cannot participate eliminates them from the list of potential sponsors. This raises the question of how much protection should the event organizers provide.

Major events with expensive sponsorship packages may have several levels for their programs, and each level may provide different levels of exclusivity. For example, the World Cup of Soccer distinguishes among sponsors, marketing partners, and regional supporters. Sponsors for the 2006 tournament expected to be protected from competitor's participation as one of the components in return for their $40 million (U.S.) investment. This level of protection is high. For example, McDonald's has an ongoing sponsorship relationship with FIFA and the World Cup. The category exclusivity granted to McDonald's means that none of its competitors are allowed to be involved at any level, thereby effectively precluding restaurants such as Burger King and Pizza Hut from any association with the event. The question of whether a hamburger restaurant is in the same category as a pizza restaurant may need to be addressed in the negotiation process between the potential sponsor and the sponsee. In some cases, category exclusivity is defined in narrow terms focused on the sponsor's most prominent products as they relate to the event. In other cases, wide latitude is given and the sponsor is protected in all categories in which it has a meaningful presence.

> In some cases, category exclusivity is defined in narrow terms focused on the sponsor's most prominent products.

Another question regarding category exclusivity goes beyond the sponsorship designation. For the World Cup, competitors of sponsors are allowed to have no official relationship with the event. The contract with McDonald's mandates that no restaurants, be they a large chain or a small family diner, can so much as buy advertising space in game-day programs. When the TV broadcast is controlled by the event, competitors may not be able to purchase time for TV advertisements during the broadcast of the event. Such controls not only provide additional value to the sponsor, but they also make ambush-marketing efforts (where competitors attempt to convince consumers that they are a sponsor) more difficult to implement.

An example of broad protection is shown in the following example. It illustrates the vast array of categories in which McDonald's has been protected in its ongoing sponsorship program with the World Cup of Soccer. The depth of that protection is best appreciated by reviewing the last few reserved categories on the list.

World Cup 1994, McDonald's "Reserved Categories"

- Hamburger
- Cheeseburger
- Filet of Fish
- 1/4 lb. Cheeseburger
- Big Mac
- McChicken Sandwich
- McNuggets, 6 pieces
- McNuggets, 9 pieces
- McNuggets, 20 pieces
- McDLT
- Small Fries
- Medium Fries
- Large Fries
- Egg McMuffin
- Handheld Sandwiches
- Big Breakfast
- Hotcakes and Sausage
- Hash Browns
- Sausage McMuffin w/Egg

- Garden Salad
- Chef's Salad
- Side Salad
- Chunky Chicken Salad
- Happy Meal/Hamburger
- Happy Meal/Cheeseburger
- Happy Meal 4/6 piece McNuggets
- Pizzas
- Cooked Bone-in Chicken
- Prepared Fajitas, Burritos
- Prepared Spaghetti/Hot Dogs
- Any national restaurant chain
- Any quick-service restaurant
- Any quick-service café restaurant
- Sit-down coffee shops
- Lunch centers
- Small café/cafeteria
- Any convenience food store
- Any family restaurant

Signage

Marketers understand the potential value that signs provide as a component of their sponsorship package. Signage will be seen not only by the fans who are attending an event, but also by TV viewers throughout the market. Many sporting events are replayed by cable and satellite programming providers, so the signs may be seen by some fans more than once, or the replay may reach viewers who did not see the game either in person or during the original real-time broadcast.

Signage helps the sponsor reinforce the fact that it is officially associated with the event. It is this issue that causes sponsors to designate signage as one of the most important components of a sponsorship program. Typical of this type of signage is that of Coors Field in Denver, which is shown in Figure 4.3.

There will always be questions regarding the number of signs at a venue, their location, their size, and whether the signs are actually present at the venue or computer-generated. Another key issue is the presence of signage for nonsponsors. Even signs that are not associated with competitors of actual sponsors add to the clutter and potentially diminish the effectiveness of the sponsorship.

The number of signs provided to each sponsor is also a critical issue. The event organizers worry about clutter detracting from the event, while sponsors want their signs seen throughout the venue. In response to this concern, the Canadian Football League (CFL) recently implemented new restrictions on the number of signs that could be displayed at the

FIGURE 4.3
Signage at
Coors Field

various stadia. This reduction was achieved via fewer sponsors being allowed to display fewer signs. The CFL argued that it had increased the value of signage by reducing the clutter. Despite the concern surrounding clutter, some sponsorship proposals will provide for increased signage for an increased fee. For example, the 1994 World Cup of Soccer had 10 official sponsors (at the highest level). Sponsors like MasterCard and Philips Electronics had to decide between the options of having two signs or four signs at each stadium where games were taking place. The difference in cost was $6.5 million (U.S.). A sponsorship using two signs cost $11 million; the four-sign option was $17.5 million.

Another issue is the location of signs. Olympic sponsors at the highest level (known as TOP sponsors, an acronym for The Olympic Partners) spend some $65 million (U.S.) for a sponsorship. One point of contention has been the IOC's reluctance to allow signage within the competitive venues. In arguing for increased access to place signs within the venues, sponsors, most notably Coca-Cola, have argued that sponsor Panasonic has its logo on video replay monitors and the Swatch logo appears on timing devices. Coca-Cola is reportedly making some progress and gaining some concessions regarding signage and product placement within the venue, but there remains considerable opposition to greater sponsor exposure within the venues.[3] Outside of the Olympic environment, however, numerous prominent signage opportunities exist.

There are certain areas of a competitive arena where more action takes place. TV cameras and fans' eyes spend more time focused on these areas. Center ice at a hockey game is a valuable location as are the area directly behind home plate at a Major League Baseball game and the midfield area of the soccer pitch (field). Another valuable spot is the player interview area; in this case, the signage will be seen by TV viewers upon the completion of the event, a time when the fans' emotions are often at their highest levels. Secondary signage may also be located in congregation areas at the arena. Concession areas and other gathering points can be used to reach those in attendance. For example, it has been noted that one of the most effective locations for signage at professional golf tournaments is at the concession vending areas.

The size of the signs is often dictated by event organizers. Sponsors at the same level will generally have signs of equal size. If the event has a single sponsor, then signage size becomes more of a negotiation point. There is a trade-off in deciding between actual signs and computer-generated (virtual) signs. Actual signs are seen by the spectators in the stands and by the TV viewers, whereas virtual signage is seen only by the TV viewers.

FIGURE 4.4
Virtual Advertising

Actual signage is inflexible, but virtual signage can be changed during the course of the event and from one geographic market to another. Virtual signage can also be animated for greater impact. Event organizers worry that animated signage might detract attention from the actual event. Figure 4.4 illustrates the use of virtual advertising by a sponsor during a recent TV broadcast.

The final issue concerns the presence of signage referring to nonsponsors at a venue. Many venues have naming rights deals and sponsorship deals that include signage for the sponsor. On occasion, events will be scheduled for a venue and signage conflicts will occur. The 2003 Rugby World Cup encountered such problems. The governing body overseeing the tournament (Rugby Football Union) was negotiating in an effort to play some of the tournament games in New Zealand. One condition was for each venue to be a *clean stadium,* one that is void of signage. This would allow the RFU to place signage at each venue without worrying about conflicts between the World Cup sponsors and other sponsors at the venue. Stadium operators were told that they would have to remove all references to brands, including the brand identifiers on TV monitors in the luxury boxes, signage on the scoreboards, and signage around the pitch. When the New Zealanders were unable to guarantee clean stadia, the games were pulled from New Zealand and scheduled in Australia.

Signage is a crucial element in the sponsorship program. It is also a potential source of major conflict. Sponsors want to maximize their signage while minimizing clutter. As a result, negotiations regarding signage can be quite contentious.

Rights to Use Event Trademarks and Logos

Virtually every organization and event has one or more registered trademarks that cannot legally be used without the trademark owner's permission. Sports leagues have taken precautions to protect their names as they are viewed as valuable assets. In addition to brand names, other symbols and slogans may also be protected from unauthorized use. Not only do sports leagues have such trademarks and logos, but so do many teams, events, and sports organizations. In this regard, sports marketing is no different from marketing in any other industry.

Consider the Olympic Games. Among the protected trademarks are the term *Olympics,* the Olympic rings logo, the representation of the Olympic flame, and the logos specific to a particular host city. For instance, in addition to the traditional Olympic trademarks, the 2000 Sydney Games had three characters that were used to depict the event and its Sydney venue. These characters—Syd, Milly, and Olly—were used to sell officially licensed merchandise.

Because of the efforts by trademark owners to protect their assets, the use of these trademarks and logos is greatly restricted. One important component of a sponsorship program is the right to use the trademarks and logos of the event being sponsored. The ability to do so allows the sponsor to implement effective leveraging programs and exhibit its association with the event by including the trademarks in advertising, packaging, and other promotional programs.

Coca-Cola used the Olympic Rings symbol on its packaging. Moro once declared itself the official energy bar of the renowned New Zealand All Blacks and incorporated the rugby team's logo on its packaging. McDonald's and Kodak have used Olympic themes and trademarks in an array of television advertising. MasterCard, one of the official sponsors of the World Cup of Soccer, was able to use a number of different FIFA trademarks in its global advertising. Figure 4.5 illustrates a sponsor's use of an event's trademark in its own marketing efforts.

FIFA has done a good job of controlling the use of its intellectual properties; the right to use specific trademarks is determined by the level of sponsorship commitment. More prominent sponsors, such as MasterCard, have greater opportunities to use the event trademarks. For the most recent World Cup of Soccer, four basic trademarks were available: the World Cup emblem, the FIFA name, the World Cup mascot, and the World Cup trophy. Rights to use these trademarks depended upon the sponsorship level for each of the companies that entered into a sponsorship relationship with the World Cup. The rights associated with each level were

- *Official sponsor:* emblem, FIFA, mascot, and trophy.
- *Marketing partner:* emblem, mascot, and trophy.
- *Official product/supplier:* emblem and mascot.
- *Regional supporter:* emblem.

FIGURE 4.5
Sponsor's Use of Event's Trademark

Efforts that utilize these various symbols are designed to strengthen the consumers' association of the sponsor with the event. One rationale for sponsorship is the belief that consumers are more favorably predisposed to a marketer's products when the marketer sponsors an event or a team that the consumers support and admire. Given this belief, the marketer should seek the right to use these assets and the event should recognize that the right to use the trademarks adds value to the sponsorship program. Properly done, it will also help decrease the level of ambush marketing efforts by nonsponsors and reduce the effectiveness of ambushing efforts that are attempted.

Distribution Rights

In recent years, sponsors have begun to emphasize the granting of distribution rights for their products at the event venue. Such distribution may simply reflect an opportunity to promote their products, or it may represent an important channel of distribution in the sponsor's efforts to reach a specific target market.

From the standpoint of promotion, the sponsor may seek opportunities to create awareness or effect the trial of its products by members of its target market. This target market is represented by the actual attendees of the event. The sponsor may distribute free samples of products or it may distribute other promotional materials such as discount coupons. Absopure Water is one of the sponsors of intercollegiate athletics at the University of Michigan. At each home football game that attracts some 110,000 fans in attendance, Absopure has facilities at which it distributes free cups of water. On a warm day, this sample is greatly appreciated by the fans. More important for the sponsor, it creates a positive association between the sponsor (Absopure) and the sponsee (University of Michigan).

The second type of distribution right is the establishment of the venue as a retail outlet. The sponsor has the right, often with category exclusivity that precludes any competitor's presence, to sell its products at the venue. As the exclusive distributor of a class of products, the sponsorship has the potential to generate considerable direct revenues. That these revenues are measurable and would not be possible in the absence of the sponsorship represents a strong selling point for the event organizers and a major advantage for the sponsor. One recent example includes Coca-Cola and the Olympics. Perhaps this relationship is best illustrated by the 1996 Olympic Games in Atlanta, the home of Coca-Cola. The distribution rights granted in the contract allowed Coca-Cola to sell its entire line of beverages, including Coca-Cola, Diet Coke, Sprite, Dasani Water, and PowerAde, at the Olympic venues. These venues included stationary concession areas and walking vendors. It also meant that no products produced by rivals such as Pepsi-Cola would be sold. This component was also part of Coca-Cola's sponsorship program with the International Cricket Council and the 2003 World Cup of Cricket competition. Comerica Bank has the venue naming rights for a stadium in Detroit; this special case of sponsorship gives Comerica Bank the right to place its ATMs within the stadium.

It is easy to see why distribution rights have become more important in recent negotiations for sponsorship contracts. The potential sponsor sees the revenue potential and the competitive advantage that the sponsorship can provide. The sponsee understands the value of this right for the sponsor and must factor it into the sponsorship fee.

Hospitality Areas

When the sponsor is seeking opportunities to entertain customers, prospects, suppliers, or employees, the provision of a hospitality area can be a meaningful component of the sponsorship plan. These can be on-site facilities where the actual event can be observed, or they can be off-site where there is greater flexibility. Examples on on-site hospitality include the granting of the use of a luxury box at a stadium or a tent along the fairway of a golf tournament. Off-site locations may include tents or other structures in parking lots or outside of the venue itself. The advantage of off-site locations is that the sponsor can accommodate more people and does not have to provide event tickets to everyone visiting the hospitality area.

In some cases, these areas are provided as part of the sponsorship program. In others, event organizers may make hospitality areas available for sponsors to purchase. This allows the establishment of hospitality areas that can accommodate the number of people that the sponsor anticipates entertaining.

As indicated earlier in this chapter, the hospitality areas provide amenities not available to the typical spectator. This can include food and beverage service, private restrooms, and television monitors. Typically, some of these services are subject to additional costs even when the hospitality area itself is included as part of the sponsorship program. For example, food and beverage service will generally add to the cost of hospitality. The growth in sponsor interest in hospitality is illustrated by examining the demand for these activities at the 2003 Rugby World Cup in Australia. This event experienced record levels of revenue with some $56.5 million (U.S.) in sales, a figure reflecting a 54 percent increase over the previous competition in 1999.

Hospitality has become more important for sponsors in recent years. It is also more important for some events and in certain types of venues. Event organizers need to determine the role that hospitality areas can play for potential sponsors while the prospective sponsors need to assess their objectives and decide whether or not hospitality areas of this type would be beneficial to them.

Complimentary Advertising

The use of the word *complimentary* may be inaccurate, as the cost is generally considered in the determination of the sponsorship fees charged by the event organizer. Still, such advertising provides incremental value to the sponsor.

Event organizers often control one or two media outlets. The most likely medium that they control is the printed event program. While fans will view the program primarily as a source of information about the event, it is also used by organizers to generate revenue. Some of this revenue is in the form of charges for advertising pages within the program. Typical advertising includes retailers and service providers in close proximity to the event venue. Examples include local restaurants, casinos, and other sports and entertainment events that are scheduled to take place in the area. It is not uncommon for a sponsorship plan to include a certain number of "free" advertising pages in the event program. The potential sponsor can easily see the monetary value of such advertising.

In some cases, event organizers also control the TV broadcast including both the event and the advertising that is shown during the broadcast of the event. In these cases, the organizer can provide a predetermined number of "free" TV spots for the sponsor to air advertisements. While complimentary advertising is not a component of every sponsorship plan, it is becoming more important in the negotiation process. Potential sponsors seek it as a way to justify the cost, while event organizers may add it in an effort to avoid discounting their sponsorship price.

A key consideration that contributes to the popularity of complimentary advertising is the way in which it can be used by the sponsor as part of a leveraging effort. In this way, it gives sponsors another way to reach the consumer and reinforce the idea that they are official sponsors, thereby combating the ambush marketing efforts of companies that seek to create the misconception that they, the ambushers, are officially linked to the event.

In some cases, the sponsor is required to purchase a contractually agreed-upon number of advertisements. The price of the sponsorship will be divided into two categories: the cost of the sponsorship and the cost associated with the purchase of advertising as stipulated in the agreement. This can not be positioned as complimentary advertising, but the net result is the same. The marketer is acknowledged as a sponsor and will have a number of advertising opportunities to promote its products and relationship with the event.

Free Tickets

Many sponsorship agreements call for organizers to provide a specified number of free tickets to the event. These free tickets have a monetary value that the sponsor can easily determine. They provide the sponsor with the opportunity to entertain customers, prospects, suppliers, and employees. Such entertainment opportunities can create considerable goodwill within these important groups. For employees, it can create a sense of esprit de corps by conveying a belief that management cares about them and wants to nurture the idea of teamwork. For suppliers, the sponsor wants to emphasize relationships while acknowledging their contributions. For customers, it is a way to reward the company's best customers and thank them for their business. It is also done in an effort to secure brand loyalty that makes it less likely that the customer will leave the sponsor in favor of one of its competitors. Hospitality opportunities emanating from the provision of free tickets to prospects may be one way that the sponsor can gain a differential advantage over its competition and generate new sales by converting those prospects into customers.

One strategy used by event organizers is to base the number of free tickets upon the sponsorship level or commitment of the sponsor. Sponsors at higher levels that also pay higher fees are provided with more free tickets than are lower-level sponsors that commit fewer resources to the event. In some cases, the top-level sponsors may be provided with a luxury box that will accommodate a stated number of guests. The World Cup of Soccer illustrates this strategy. During the competition in the United States, the free ticket distribution policy was as follows:

- Sponsors received 520 free tickets (10 per game).
- Marketing partners received 416 free tickets (8 per game).
- Official product/service providers received 312 free tickets (6 per game).
- Regional supporters received 100 to 194 free tickets, depending on location.

This component is more important when one of two conditions exist. The first is when tickets are expensive. In this case, the sponsor can see an immediate return on the investment. Second is when the tickets simply are not available through traditional outlets, the event is popular, ticket distribution is controlled, and demand for tickets exceeds supply. The sponsor may view the investment as a way to acquire tickets to a prestigious event when tickets would not otherwise be available. An example of this situation would be the Masters Golf Tournament. Ticket sales are limited to 25,000 per day, demand exceeds supply, and there is a waiting list for tickets. Tournament sponsors and event organizers both need to consider the role that free tickets play in helping determine the final composition of the sponsorship plan.

Right to Purchase Additional Tickets

The right to purchase tickets to the event can be a significant incentive when the event is historically sold out. The World Cup of Soccer finals, the Super Bowl, and the opening ceremony at the Olympics are examples of events where tickets are virtually impossible to acquire. The purchased tickets are in addition to any free tickets granted as part of the sponsorship package. In some cases, particularly those where the event is not expected to sell out, the sponsor may have the opportunity to purchase tickets at a discounted price. The event organizer must forecast demand in order to assess the available inventory of seats that can be offered to sponsors. If the event will have a large number of empty seats, the right to purchase additional tickets is of little value to the sponsor. If the event is expected to sell out, the event may want to minimize the number which can be purchased in an effort to better serve the sports fan. In some cases, the event organizers may opt not to provide any free tickets to sponsors, but they will make some tickets available for purchase.

Link on the Event Web Site

The Internet has become a major tool in the marketing of major sports events. The IOC has a comprehensive site that provides information about past and future Olympic competitions. During the events, the site provides updates on results and other news. Other events and organizations with important Web sites are the International Tennis Federation (Davis Cup tennis tournament), FIFA (World Cup of Soccer), America's Cup (yacht race), the National Football League (Super Bowl), the International Rugby Board (World Cup of Rugby), and the International Cricket Council (World Cup of Cricket). Each of these events has its own set of sponsors.

Additionally, teams competing in these competitions often have their own sponsors and their own Web sites. Team Prada, the United States Olympic Committee, the Pittsburgh Steelers, and the New Zealand All Blacks are some of the prominent organizations and teams in these types of competitions. They seek to take advantage of the international exposure given to the event while capitalizing upon the local and national support for the individual team. A review of their Web sites will underscore the current practice of providing information about each sponsor or even a direct link to the sponsors' home pages from the event Web site. Figure 4.6 illustrates the International Cricket Council's Web site page that identifies its primary sponsors for the 2007 World Cup of Cricket.

Designation

There may be certain prestige associated with the way the sponsor is able to characterize its association with the event. The typical sponsorship contract will include specific information regarding the designation that can be used in leveraging efforts and the way in which sponsors will be identified in communications and promotional efforts by the event.

Some events have different designations that depend entirely upon the level of commitment made by the sponsor. For example, the IOC designates its sponsors at the highest

FIGURE 4.6
ICC Cricket World Cup Web Site

level as TOP sponsors; TOP is an acronym for The Olympic Partners. The World Cup of Soccer has several levels all reflecting different payments to FIFA. A company contributing at the highest level is designated an "official sponsor," whereas the next level is identified as a "marketing partner."

Another strategy that has become more popular is the concept of a presenting sponsor. In these cases, the name of the event and the name of the primary sponsor are typically incorporated within a single phrase to promote the event. "The Rose Bowl presented by Citi" is an example of such a designation. Yet another approach whereby the sponsor receives even more exposure and a more prominent role is where the sponsor's name becomes the name of the event. The Heineken Open by another name was the New Zealand Open Tennis Tournament. Similarly, the NatWest Challenge is a cricket competition in the United Kingdom, and the BMW Russian Open is a tournament on the European PGA tour. Note that in each case the event itself received no specific acknowledgment with this designation.

More common is the strategy of incorporating the sponsor's name and the event name in a single designation. This is somewhat different from the presenting sponsor designation. Examples include the Nokia Sugar Bowl, the Accenture Match Play Championship, and the Diageo Championship at Gleneagles. A final sponsorship designation strategy is to attach the sponsor's name with a team. The Vodafone Silver Ferns have replaced the Silver Ferns when referring to the New Zealand netball team. Virtually every team in the Philippine Basketball Association is identified using its primary sponsor's name; examples include the Coca-Cola Tigers and the San Miguel Beermen. Similarly, in the Japanese Baseball League, the Daiei Hawks are named after their corporate owner and sponsor, Daiei Department Store. One soccer team in China is now known as the Beijing Hyundai Motor, thus leaving little doubt as to whom its primary sponsor is. This type of designation not only serves to reinforce the relationship between the sponsor and the sponsee, it also tends to discourage ambush marketing efforts. The jersey for the New Zealand rugby team, the Vodafone Warriors, is illustrated in Figure 4.7.

FIGURE 4.7
Vodafone Warriors Uniform

It is evident that sponsorship designation is yet another point of negotiation for many events. The designations should be created in an effort to provide added prestige to the sponsor, to acknowledge a major commitment to the sponsee, to provide greater recognition to the sponsor, and to reinforce the relationship between the sponsor and the sponsee in the consumer's mind. But clearly, some such designations may not be deemed appropriate for some events.

Inclusion in Event Promotions

Sponsors often view their inclusion in event promotions as a good faith effort by the sponsee to help reinforce the relationship. The basic operationalization of this component is achieved by simply including each of the sponsors' logos on promotions for the event. This includes TV advertisements, print advertisements, direct mail, posters, and outdoor media such as billboards. Another expectation is the presence of on-site displays that acknowledge all of the sponsors; this is often positioned as an event's encouragement for fans to support sponsors and as a means of expressing its appreciation to the sponsors. Since such promotions generally acknowledge all of the event's sponsors, this component is markedly different from the aforementioned signage component.

This component can be meaningful when the event will be spending a significant sum of money on traditional advertising. It is also more important when the event has a cause-related marketing (CRM) overlay. With a CRM basis, sponsors view their inclusion in event promotions as a way to nurture its image of being a good corporate citizen.

Access to Property Mailing List/Database

Most sponsors select the events with which they wish to be associated based upon the match between their target market and the market to whom the event appeals. Whether this involves self-evident or strategic linkages, the fans and spectators represent members of the sponsor's target market. Event organizers have basic information on its fans; they often have specific information on those who purchase tickets or belong to fan clubs. As a result, the event often has mailing lists (traditional and e-mail) that represent a potentially valuable resource to the sponsor. Event organizers prefer not to be associated with a mass mailing (junk or spam) that might alienate their fans, but they should recognize that access to the mailing list or database can be a component that provides value to the sponsor.

Right of First Refusal

The right of first refusal is a basic agreement that allows a current sponsor the opportunity to assess the new sponsorship program and either accept or reject it before the event solicits new sponsors. The terms and other components may change, so the sponsor must be given time to review the program, to assess the extent to which the expiring program has met its objectives, to discuss it with others within the firm, and to articulate the decision as to whether or not they will continue the sponsorship relationship with the event. A key issue in this scenario is that the sponsor is not dropped, especially in favor of a competitor, without consultation. Some companies may choose to continue a sponsorship that they deem a little too expensive or a little too ineffective simply to keep a competitor locked out. Coca-Cola might want to lock out Pepsi-Cola; adidas may look to do the same to Nike.

Most major events grant the right of first refusal. Of note is the fact that IBM was granted the opportunity to renew its sponsorship with the Olympics but decided to terminate the relationship. In the cases where the sponsors do opt out, they generally indicate that they want to go in another direction with their promotional efforts. This generally means that they are looking for promotions that are more cost efficient. In other cases, the sponsor has a long-standing relationship that has been effective and that they want to continue. McDonald's association with the Olympics and the World Cup of Soccer are two examples of continuity

TABLE 4.3
Importance of Various Sponsorship Plan Components

Source: "Performance Research/IEG Study Highlights What Sponsors Want," 2001, www.sponsorship.com/learn/ decisionmakerstudy.asp (accessed October 13, 2005).

Component	% Rating Importance Level of 9 or 10*
Category exclusivity	68%
On-site signage	53
ID in property (event) media buys	39
Broadcast ad opportunities	37
Rights to use trademarks and logos	32
Presence on event/property web site	32
Access to property mailing list/database	32
Tickets/hospitality	30

*10-point scale, where 10 is "extremely important."

that has benefited both the sponsor and the sponsee. Doubtless, McDonald's fully expects to maintain the right of first refusal for both of these events. It would be a major mistake for either of these two events to not comply with McDonald's expectations.

What Is Most Important?

The International Events Group recently completed a study in which sponsors were questioned as to which components of a program are most important to them. The results of the study are summarized in Table 4.3.

An Overview

Table 4.4 provides information specific to a recent World Cup of Soccer tournament. It illustrates the different levels of sponsorship available and the financial commitment required at each level. It also provides a summary of the components that comprise the sponsorship program at each of the levels.

A Comprehensive Sponsorship Example

One of the least expensive types of sponsorship for the World Cup of Soccer was the regional supporter. Regional supporters were solicited for each of the nine venues in which games took place, and the price associated with each region was based upon the number of games played there and the rounds of competition that took place there. Later rounds were deemed to be more important, thus more valuable than were the earlier rounds. The following summary provides an overview of the components and the costs associated with this level of sponsorship for the tournament staged in the United States.

Rights and Benefits–Regional Supporter Package

The following are the rights and benefits of the Regional Supporter package:

1. *Category/territory exclusivity:* Regional Supporters will be given exclusive category rights within their geographic region.
2. *Stadium recognition:* World Cup Marketing shall provide for each Regional Supporter visual recognition at multiple locations within the site perimeter area of the stadium for each game played at the Regional Supporter's venue. The visual recognition shall be at the discretion of World Cup Marketing and consistent with design criteria and stadium limitations. The opportunity for signage within the stadium playing field or seating area is not available.

TABLE 4.4 World Cup 1994 Sponsors Rights and Privileges

Designation Level	Sponsor	Marketing Partner	Product/Service	Regional Supporter	Equipment Supplier
Price	$17.5M–four boards $11.0M–two boards	$7.0M	$3.5M (worldwide) $2.5M (U.S.)	$160k–320k	$300k–500k (cash + vik)
Quantity	10 (fixed)	8 (fixed)	10 to 12	8 per venue = 72	10
Marketing rights					
Exclusivity	Categories	Category	Product or service	Product or service	Nonexclusive
Territory	Worldwide	Worldwide	Worldwide	Geographic area in U.S.	U.S./worldwide
Designation	Official Sponsor	Official Partner	Official Product/Service	Supporter of World Cup	Equipment Supplier of World Cup
Use of marks	Emblem, FIFA, mascot, trophy	Emblem, mascot, trophy	Emblem, mascot	Emblem (print only)	Emblem (print only)
In-camera view					
Field boards	Two or four	One	Option to purchase	Right to purchase on nonexclusive basis	Right to purchase on nonexclusive basis
TV	1st option U.S./Canada	1st option U.S./Canada	Right to purchase on exclusive basis		
Official program ad	One full-page ad	One full-page ad			
Tickets–prime/game (total)	10 (520)	8 (416)	6 (312)	25/gms x 9 gms (220)	10/1st 5 gms, 2 for rest (66)
Hospitality					
Individual corp. tents if avail.	Right to purchase	Right to purchase	Yes	Yes	Yes
Access to all areas	Yes	Yes	Access to host area	Access to host area	Access to host area
VIP transportation	Yes	Yes			
Invites to all functions	Yes	Yes	Yes	Yes	Yes
Displays/sampling	Yes	Yes	Yes	Yes	Yes

3. *Use of logo:* Regional Supporters shall have the right to use the official World Cup USA 1994 Regional Supporter logo. Regional Supporters shall have the option to designate a venue city by use of the tag line at the bottom of the logo (e.g., Regional Supporter Boston World Cup '94). Regional Supporter use of logo is allowed in print and all measured media within the designated category and territory only and per the guidelines of the World Cup graphics standards policy.

4. *Tickets:* The allocation for both complimentary tickets and option to purchase tickets are as follows:

Complimentary Tickets						
	First Round	Round of 16	Quarters	Semis	Third	Final
Boston	100	50	24	0	0	0
Chicago	100	50	0	0	0	0
Dallas	100	50	24	0	0	0
Detroit	100	0	0	0	0	0
Los Angeles	100	50	0	20	10	10
New York/New Jersey	100	50	24	20	0	0
Orlando	100	50	0	0	0	0
San Francisco	100	50	24	0	0	0
Washington, DC	100	50	0	0	0	0

Right to Purchase						
	First Round	Round of 16	Quarters	Semis	Third	Final
Boston	500	150	176	6	4	4
Chicago	500	150	10	6	4	4
Dallas	500	150	176	6	4	4
Detroit	500	0	10	6	4	4
Los Angeles	500	150	10	30	16	16
New York/New Jersey	500	150	176	30	4	4
Orlando	500	150	10	6	4	4
San Francisco	500	150	176	6	4	4
Washington, DC	500	150	10	6	4	4

- Regional Supporters shall only have the right to complimentary tickets for games in their venue.
- All numbers constitute the aggregate of tickets available for any tournament round. For example, Regional Supporters will receive an aggregate of 100 tickets for all four first-round games. They do not receive 100 tickets per game. Similarly, an Orlando Regional Supporter that seeks to purchase tickets to the semifinals may purchase a total of six tickets, not six tickets to each of the semifinals.
- Regional Supporters must designate the allocation of tickets among such games and exercise their option to purchase additional tickets within six months of executing the Regional Supporter agreement.
- Regional Supporters in Chicago can designate up to 10 complimentary and 20 rights to purchase tickets to the opening game. The remaining 90 complimentary and 480 right to purchase tickets shall be distributed among the remaining three first-round games.
- Regional Supporters' rights to final game tickets extend only to Category 2 and Category 3 tickets. As to games other than final, tickets available shall be a mix of Category 1, 2, and 3 tickets in accordance with policies developed by the Organizing Committee.

5. *VIP hospitality:* Regional Supporters shall have the right to purchase hospitality within their local venue for each holder of a complimentary ticket. Hospitality opportunities shall be consistent with policies of World Cup USA 1994.

6. *Programs:* Regional Supporters shall be given mention in local venue day-of-game programs and opportunities to purchase advertising in day-of-game and commemorative programs where applicable.

7. *Premiums:* Regional Supporters shall have the opportunity to independently contract with approved licensees through Time Warner Sports Merchandising for the purchase of premiums. Premiums can only be used to promote the Regional Supporters' business, for internal use, or to be sold in conjunction with the Supporters' products at cost or at subsidized prices and only within the designated territory.

8. *Participation:* Regional Supporters shall have opportunities, when applicable, to participate in other activities that are planned by WCOC or host committees. This participation may be at additional cost to Regional Supporters.

9. *Training site signage:* Regional Supporters shall have rights to signage to be located at all training sites in the Regional Supporter's venue. Type of signage and location shall be determined by World Cup USA 1994, Inc., and consistent with design criteria and training site limitations. Regional Supporters shall be responsible for the cost of constructing and maintaining signage.

10. *Price:* Pricing per Regional Supporter package with allowance of one buyer per region is as follows:

City	Price per Package	City	Price per Package
Boston	$240,000	New York/NJ	$280,000
Chicago	$200,000	Orlando	$200,000
Dallas	$240,000	San Francisco	$240,000
Detroit	$160,000	Washington, DC	$200,000
LA	$320,000		

Closing Capsule

Sponsorship is based upon the ability of an event to afford opportunities for a sponsor to achieve specific goals. Potential sponsors have many events from which they can choose, so they will select the events that provide the best match. Typical objectives for the sponsor include driving sales, improving image, creating greater awareness, hospitality, and enhancing employee morale. Marketers may often seek to achieve multiple objectives with a single sponsorship. Event organizers must anticipate the objectives of any potential sponsor and attempt to design a program that will increase the likelihood that these objectives will be achieved.

When designing a sponsorship program, the emphasis is on the program components. What benefits does the sponsee provide to the sponsor? There are many components that may be incorporated within the program, and it is important to note that these vary in importance depending upon the potential sponsor and its objectives. In general, the most important are category exclusivity, on-site signage, and sponsor identification in event advertising. Both the sponsor and the sponsee must prioritize these components and negotiate a program that is mutually beneficial. This win–win premise is the underlying principle of sponsorship. The sponsor achieves its stated business objectives while the sponsee is adequately compensated for providing these opportunities. A recent quote attributed to Justin Stead, vice president of Fossil, in addressing his company's decision to become a sponsor of the Davis Cup Tennis Tournament beginning in 2004 captures the essence of the sponsorship decision. Stead indicated that Fossil's primary sponsorship goal "is to find partnerships that make sense for our brand–Davis Cup is in line with this objective."[4]

Review Questions

1. What are the five primary sponsorship objectives?
2. Why is it true that the decision to sponsor an event is not primarily driven by the cost of the sponsorship?
3. Explain the ways in which merchandising and channel issues drive sales.
4. What is meant by the expression "less is more" in the sponsorship environment?
5. Identify the major components of sponsorship plans.
6. Explain the concept of category exclusivity
7. What are the benefits of virtual signage?
8. Go to a Web site for a major event. See if sponsors are identified. What types of links are given to the sponsors' Web sites?
9. According to sponsors, what are the most important components of a sponsorship program?
10. Identify a sponsor of one of the major athletic teams at your university or at a major university in your area. What do you think the sponsor's primary goals are relative to its sponsorship?

Endnotes

1. J. Kuzma, W. Shanklin, and J. McCalley, Jr., "Number One Principle for Sporting Events Seeking Corporate Sponsors: Meet Benefactor's Objectives," *Sport Marketing Quarterly* 2, no. 3 (1993), pp. 27–32.
2. D. Morris and R. Irwin, "The Data-Driven Approach to Sponsor Acquisition," *Sport Marketing Quarterly* 5, no. 2 (1996), pp. 7–10.
3. B. Horovitz, "Olympic Sponsors Push for More Play," *USA Today,* October 5, 2000, p. C1.
4. D. Barrand, "Q&A: ITF's Fossil Find," November 3, 2003, www.sportbusiness.com/news/fandc?region=global&news_item_id=153004 (accessed October 13, 2005).

CHAPTER FIVE

The Sponsorship Commitment: Resources and Duration

Learning Objectives

- See the trends in cost and time commitments.
- Learn the factors that add value to a sponsorship.
- Identify relevant pricing models.
- Differentiate between cash payments and value-in-kind.
- Distinguish between serial and once-off commitments.
- Learn the essential decisions regarding timing.

A consideration that is important to both the sponsee and the prospective sponsor is the determination of the terms of the commitment to be established by the sponsorship contract. The commitment will be stated in two terms. First and foremost is the financial consideration required from the sponsor. This includes both the cash required and the goods and services provided to the property owner. These goods and services, known as value-in-kind (VIK), may represent some or all of the financial requirements. Second is a set of timing issues germane to the sponsorship relationship. In regard to timing, it is essential to designate the timing of future payments and activities. In other words, how much is the sponsorship going to cost, when are payments due, when can the sponsor publicize the relationship, and for how long can the sponsor continue to use its official designation?

As stated above, this determination is important to both parties. It will most assuredly be part of the negotiation process. The sponsor does not want to overpay, so there must be an assessment of the value of all of the components and the anticipated performance in helping the sponsor meet its stated objectives. Similarly, the sponsee seeks to receive the fair market value for those rights granted to the sponsor. This chapter seeks to provide an answer to the question of how we determine the fair market value and thus the price of a sponsorship.

Trends

The historical trend has been characterized by continued increases in the costs associated with high-profile sports events. However, this rise has not been in evidence for all events and properties. For example, sponsorship costs associated with Formula 1 (F1) racing have been reduced by up to 50 percent, especially for those teams that do not rank at the top of the field. According to an article in the U.K. newspaper *The Times,* title sponsorship for a mid-ranking F1 team dropped from $11.3 million per year in 2000 to $6.4 million per year in 2003.[1] As sponsors have placed more emphasis on ROI, pressure has been placed on the sponsees' ability to provide opportunities to achieve an acceptable return. The costs have also driven some sponsors away from expensive properties to those costing less. The alternatives include less costly sports events as well as an array of nonsports events. DaimlerChrysler recently initiated a plan to examine more grassroots opportunities. Not only are the fees considerably less expensive, but events of this type allow the sponsor to reach smaller markets and emphasize its involvement in the local community.

> As sponsors have placed more emphasis on ROI, pressure has been placed on the sponsees' ability to provide opportunities to achieve an acceptable return.

A review of recent sponsorship agreements documents that some events have become more expensive while others have become more affordable. Thus, it raises the question as to whether or not there has been a discernable trend in the commitments required of sponsors. In general, these fees have been increasing, but clearly the potential sponsor has numerous alternatives. These alternatives have exerted some downward pressure on the events and properties that do not fall within the premier event and property category.

One intriguing trend has been that of companies forgoing long-term commitments, instead selecting opportunities to sponsor an event that encompasses a short period of time. While it may be a major event, the sponsor may stay with it for only one cycle then move on to another property. This means that property owners are constantly in the market for a replacement sponsor. For the property owner, this is referred to as *revolving sponsorships*. For the sponsors, this phenomenon is termed *property hopping*. Several events exemplify this phenomenon. The Nationwide Tour is a second-tier golf series tied to the Professional Golfers Association (PGA) in the United States. Since 1998, the title sponsorship has been held by four different marketers: Ben Hogan Golf, Nike, buy.com, and Nationwide Insurance. Similarly, the League Cup in English soccer is now the Carling Cup (Coors beer); previously it was known as the Worthington Cup and the Coca-Cola Cup. The Rose Bowl's initial presenting sponsor was AT&T; the contract expired in 2002. That sponsorship was followed by a one-year agreement with Sony PlayStation 2 in 2003 and by Citibank from 2004 through 2006.

> Coca-Cola's involvement with the Olympic Games dates back to 1928.

It is evident that the contractual commitment for sponsors and sponsees is relatively short, with the typical duration in the range of one to four years. However, most marketers accept the premise that sponsorships are more effective when there is ongoing, long-term continuity. To address this, sponsors have aggressively sought short-term contracts that provide them with the right of first refusal. With this right, sponsors can convert a series of short-term contracts into a long-term relationship. Consider for example that Coca-Cola's involvement with the Olympic Games dates back to 1928. This is not to say that long-term contracts are not struck when the conditions merit them. Nextel's 10-year contract with NASCAR and Coca-Cola's eight-year extension of its relationship with the World Cup of Soccer (FIFA) are but two examples. Additionally, when events are held on a regular but infrequent schedule, longer-term deals are often arranged. Many "World Cup" competitions are staged every four years (rugby, cricket, soccer, golf, etc.). When this is the case, it is typical for a sponsorship contract to last for that interval (or cycle); however, the bulk of the sponsorship activities occur in a shorter period of time coinciding with the time frame during which the event takes place or is newsworthy. An example is the recent signing of Lenovo, a Chinese computer company, to a four-year contract to participate as a first-tier sponsor

TABLE 5.1   Terms of Select Sponsorships

Property/Event	Sponsor	Term (years)	Sponsor's Total Commitment
NASCAR	Nextel	10	$750,000,000
National Football League (NFL)	Gatorade	8	478,000,000
FA Premier League	Barclay's	3	96,000,000
Williams Team (F1 racing)	Budweiser	5.5	95,000,000
Soccer World Cup (FIFA)	Coca-Cola	8	80,000,000
New Zealand All Blacks (NZRFU)	adidas	7	70,000,000
Olympics (IOC)	Lenovo	4	65,000,000
Saturn Ramenskove (Russian soccer)	Nafta Moscow (oil)	6	60,000,000
UEFA Championship League	Canon	3	30,000,000
PGA	Crestor	5	25,000,000
Football League Cup (U.K.)	Carling (Coors)	3	18,000,000
National Music Awards	Woolworth's	1	14,000,000
Rugby World Cup	Travelex	1	5,500,000
Sphinx (Black & Latino symphony)	Texaco	3	300,000

(TOP) for the Olympic Games cycle that includes the 2008 Games in Beijing. Another exception to the trend for shorter agreements is commonly seen in a special case of sponsorship, namely venue naming rights. The typical contract for this type of relationship ranges from 10 to 30 years, with 20 years representing the norm.

Table 5.1 provides a listing of several sponsorships throughout the world. It is evident that the terms measured in both time and financial commitments are quite varied. There is no single answer to the questions of "how long" and "how much" to commit. This puts more pressure on both the sponsor and the sponsee as they attempt to justify any sponsorship endeavor.

Factors that Provide Value

Pricing a sponsorship is difficult because the sponsor is buying the rights to an array of factors, many of which are intangible. While there are a number of tangible factors associated with most sponsorships (e.g., complimentary tickets, free advertising space in the program, and a hospitality area), the aggregate value of these tangible factors is invariably less than the fees charged for the sponsorship. Compounding this discrepancy, according to the International Events Group (IEG), the disparity between the value of the tangibles and the fees charged is even greater when the event or property is one of high prestige and profile such as the Olympics. Before a value can be assigned to any sponsorship, it is necessary to identify the set of factors that are designed to provide value for the sponsor. A good starting point is the delineation of tangible and intangible factors relevant for the sponsorship that is under consideration.

Tangible Factors

Tangible factors are those that are more evident in terms of their presence and therefore easier to assess in terms of economic value. For example, free tickets are quite tangible. If sponsors are given 20 free tickets to an event and the face value of those tickets is $50, then they provide an economic value of $1,000 to the sponsor. If signage at the event venue sells for $250,000 and two signs are included as plan components, then their economic value is $500,000.

> Tangible factors are those that are more evident in terms of their presence and therefore easier to assess in terms of economic value.

TANGIBLE FACTORS THAT ADD VALUE TO A SPONSORSHIP

5.1

- Value of complimentary tickets
- Value of hospitality areas
- Value of signage
- Value of nonmeasured media with sponsor ID (ticket backs, scoreboard)
- Value of "free" advertising during event broadcast
- Value of acknowledgment or link on event Web site
- Value of "complimentary" advertisements in event program
- Value of event mailing list
- Value of on-site distribution rights (sale and samples)
- Value of identification in event advertising
- Value of identification during event broadcast (radio and TV)

Some tangible factors are apparent, but it is often difficult to assign an absolute figure to the value that they provide. For instance, a link on the event's Web site is readily visible, but how much will it be worth to the sponsor? The answer may well depend upon the click-through rate and the extent to which there is congruence between the markets for the sponsor and the sponsee. Though less tangible, market congruence is easily assessed; however, forecasting click-through rates is potentially an inaccurate process.

A list of tangible factors that are designed to add value for the sponsor is provided in Box 5.1. It should be noted that not every sponsor receives all of the benefits listed.

The identification of the tangible factors associated with the sponsorship and the determination of the value of each represents a key step in the establishment of the final price of the sponsorship. But the task is unfinished at that point. The next step involves the identification of the intangible factors associated with the sponsorship and the estimation of the value of each.

Intangible Factors

Intangible factors are those that are impossible to see and touch. Consequently, the task of assigning a value to them is considerably more difficult. For example, one of the key sponsorship components identified in Chapter 4 was the right to use the protected trademarks and logos that are controlled by the sponsee. Undoubtedly there is value associated with this right, but it is virtually impossible to determine how much that right is worth in advance of signing a contract and exploiting that right. Components such as category exclusivity and the right of first refusal provide value, but how much? Cross-marketing opportunities with other sponsors may provide value, but it may well depend upon who the other sponsors are. For example, World Cup of Soccer sponsors Coca-Cola and McDonald's may anticipate the development of effective cross-marketing promotions. Conversely, Steinlager beer and Toyota, two sponsors of Team New Zealand in the America's Cup Sailing Regatta, may not be so optimistic about value being added by the opportunity to develop this type of marketing strategy.

> World Cup of Soccer sponsors Coca-Cola and McDonald's may anticipate the development of effective cross-marketing promotions.

Despite the difficulties in assigning a precise value, it is still imperative that the sponsor and the sponsee agree on which intangible factors are likely to impact the tangible benefits

INTANGIBLE FACTORS THAT IMPACT THE VALUE OF A SPONSORSHIP

5.2

- Event attendance
- Number of sponsors
- Sponsorship clutter
- Category exclusivity
- Right of first refusal
- Cross-marketing opportunities with other sponsors
- Past relationship with sponsee
- Continuity prospects for future
- Media coverage
- Right to use sponsee's trademarks and logos
- Extent to which sponsee's trademarks and logos are recognized by the market
- Congruence between sponsor and sponsee markets
- Prestige of sponsee's property or event
- Right to purchase additional tickets to event

to the sponsor. Some factors have a positive effect; others negatively impact the value. Box 5.2 provides a listing of many of these intangible factors that may add or subtract value for the sponsor.

With the lists of tangible and intangible factors identified, the task of determining what a sponsorship is worth is progressing, but it is still only partially complete. The IEG recommends that the parties involved next need to consider three additional categories. These include geographic reach, market factors and price adjusters.[2]

Geographic Reach

The range of categories in evaluating geographic reach begins with minor local markets (such as a small community) to global opportunities that reach more than 150 countries. In general, the greater the reach, the greater the value of the sponsorship opportunity. While the IEG's focus is on the number of markets and countries reached, it is important to take into consideration which markets are reached. An event that reaches major markets in Japan may be far more effective and thus more valuable than a similar event that reaches a comparable number of markets in a less developed country such as Vietnam. Table 5.2 lists the categories and the criteria established by the IEG for the geographic reach factor.

TABLE 5.2
IEG's Geographic Reach Categories

Source: Adapted from *IEG's Complete Guide to Sponsorship: Everything You Wanted to Know about Sponsorship* (Chicago: IEG, Inc., 1999), p. 19.

Category	Reach
Global	More than 150 countries
International	75–150 countries
Multiregional	15–74 countries in multiple regions
Multicountry	2–4 countries
National	Relevant in at least 15 of the country's top markets
Regional	Multiple markets within a single region
Statewide	Multiple markets within a single state
Local: Major market	A market
Local: Minor market	B or C market
Local: Minor market	D or E market

It may be simple to determine the magnitude of the geographic reach for a particular sponsorship opportunity, but it is more difficult to assign a value to it. The parties must take into account both the number of markets reached and the number of people in those markets. However, they must also consider the quality of those markets. The quality factor includes the desirability of reaching those markets as determined by the fit that exists when comparing who is actually reached with a description of the sponsor's target markets. These descriptions are often based upon demographics and lifestyles, but they may include a broad array of other variables as well. Consideration must also be given to the viability of the local media in the task of communicating with the sponsor's target markets. Once the extent of the geographic reach has been determined, the next task in the process of determining the price is the identification of key market factors that serve to either increase or decrease the potential value to the sponsor.

Market Factors

When adjusting prices of sponsorships on the basis of market factors, the focus is on supply, demand, and competition. It must also be acknowledged that sponsorship is not the only promotional tool available to the prospect. As noted in the previous section on geographic reach, a key consideration is that significant differences exist from market to market, further adding to the complexities associated with determining the fair market value for any sponsorship proposal.

> When adjusting prices of sponsorships on the basis of market factors, the focus is on supply, demand, and competition.

The initial market factor to consider is the *cost of sponsoring similar properties in other markets*. For instance, the cost of sponsoring an art exhibit in London may be influenced by the cost of sponsoring a similar exhibit in Los Angeles. The fair market value for a sponsorship for the National Football League in the United States might be compared to the value of a sponsorship of a soccer team in Europe's Premier League. It is essential to note that the events are not necessarily identical, but they should be comparable. In other words, don't compare the cost associated with the art exhibit in Los Angeles to the cost of sponsoring the Manchester United team of the Premier League.

The second market factor involves the *determination of the cost of sponsorship alternatives in the same market that the proposed sponsorship will reach*. Values and the subsequent prices are influenced by the supply options available to the prospective sponsors. The number of alternatives has increased dramatically over the past two decades. More sports events now routinely seek sponsors; this list includes major sports, minor sports, university sports, stadium naming rights, teams, and events. In addition to the growing list of opportunities within the sports domain, the number of nonsports options has continued to expand. In fact, some companies that have invested heavily in sports in the past have begun to explore so-called grassroots events. As companies like DaimlerChrysler move into more of the smaller, local events, the impact on demand is evident. The value of many events, even those with global reach, may experience a decline. The earlier example of Formula 1 racing is but one example of this phenomenon. Conversely, the upward trend in the demand for local sponsorship opportunities will likely increase their market values. This trend must be monitored for the foreseeable future in order to determine the long-term impact on demand and the subsequent increases and decreases in the fees charged for the sponsorship alternatives.

Next there is a need to explore the *demand for the property under consideration*. How many potential sponsors are there? Higher demand translates into higher prices unless the number of sponsorships available for the property has also increased. Fees charged for premier events such as the Olympics and the World Cup of Soccer have increased dramatically over the past few years. TOP sponsors for the Olympics have seen the fees increase from $55 million to $65 million for the current four-year cycle. Similarly, the World Cup of Soccer fees moved from $17.5 million in 1994 to approximately $40 million in 2006. The Olympics has sought to maintain a steady number of sponsorships (12) while the World Cup has an increased number (10 in 1994 versus 15 in 2006). Many local events are hard-pressed to find sponsors, thus risking cancellation. The annual Blue–Gray College Football All-Star game in the United States was canceled in 2002 because of the inability to attract a major sponsor; it was reinstated in 2003 when adequate sponsor participation was secured. When an absence of demand exists, the sponsee and its potential sponsors must consider that the property might be overpriced and that price concessions might be in order.

> The annual Blue–Gray College Football All-Star game in the United States was canceled in 2002 because of the inability to attract a major sponsor; it was reinstated in 2003 when adequate sponsor participation was secured.

The final market factor to incorporate in the pricing decision is the *cost of purchasing time and space in traditional media* such as television, radio, and newspapers in the market(s) reached by the event or property. The performance of a sponsorship is often measured by the exposure that the sponsor attains by virtue of its relationship with the sponsee. How long did the sponsor's name or logo appear on the TV during the broadcast; how many times was the sponsor's name mentioned; how often did its name appear in press coverage on radio, TV, or in the local print media? As noted in Chapter 4, sponsors often receive free advertising as a component of their program. How much would it have cost had the sponsor been required to purchase the complimentary advertisements? Expensive media markets add value to a sponsorship, and this increased value should be reflected in the fees charged for it. The following list summarizes the four market factors that influence the final price of any sponsorship.

- Cost of sponsoring similar properties in other markets.
- Cost of sponsorship alternatives in the same market.
- Demand for the sponsorship opportunity under consideration.
- Cost of purchasing time and space in traditional media in same market(s).

Price Adjusters

The fifth and final category of factors that influence the value of a sponsorship program is that of price adjusters. This category represents an eclectic assortment of situational factors that may tend to either increase or diminish the program's potential value. The IEG has identified a comprehensive set of these price adjusters. The more common concerns in this category are identified in Box 5.3. A brief overview of each of the identified issues follows.

Desirability of the Property to the Sponsor

In some cases, there is simply a strong strategic linkage between the property or event under consideration and the products sold by the prospective sponsor. They reach similar target markets. Examples of such a fit include luxury cars and yacht racing (Volvo), beer and Super 14 Rugby in Australia (Victoria Bitter), luxury automobiles and the Senior Professional Golf Tour (Cadillac), and youth-oriented soft drinks and the X Games (Mountain Dew). It is evident that this congruency between the target markets will make

PRICE ADJUSTERS THAT INFLUENCE
SPONSORSHIP VALUE

5.3

- Desirability of property to the sponsor (congruence)
- Value of the sponsor's proprietary commitment
- On-site sales rights
- Pass-through rights
- Level of the sponsor's promotional commitment
- Multiterm contract discount
- Introduction of a new co-sponsor

Source: Adapted from *IEG's Complete Guide to Sponsorship: Everything You Wanted to Know about Sponsorship* (Chicago: IEG, Inc.), 1999, p. 19.

the property more desirable to the prospect, as well as the prospect's direct competitors. This enhanced value will contribute to an environment whereby the prospect may be willing to devote more resources in order to secure the contract. Both the sponsor and the sponsee should anticipate any additional value that this fit creates.

Value of the Sponsor's Proprietary Commitment

Under some circumstances, the sponsor may be able to lay claim to some part of the sponsored property. For instance, a stadium sponsor may have signage on the scoreboard, around the field, or in the executive suites. To the extent that the stadium is used for special or unanticipated events, the signage provides extra value. A question has recently been raised about control over computer-generated (virtual) signage during TV broadcasts and who has the right to utilize it. When the sponsor has this type of "ownership" or proprietary interest, it provides additional value that may be reflected in higher fees required for the sponsorship.

On-Site Sales Rights

There are circumstances when it is logical to presume that a sponsor would benefit from the right to sell its products at the event venue. Coca-Cola sought and received exclusive rights to sell its beverages at the Olympic Games. The sale of Coca-Cola, Diet Coke, Sprite, Minute Maid, PowerAde, and Dasani Water created a revenue stream that would otherwise have been unattainable. Other examples include Little Caesar's pizza sold at University of Michigan football games and Comerica Bank ATMs located within Comerica Park in Detroit. The revenue from these sales provides value. Furthermore, the ability to exclude one's competitors from a desirable venue adds value for which prospective sponsors may be willing to pay a premium. Figure 5.1 shows one of the three Comerica ATMs that are located within Comerica Park.

Pass-Through Rights

Pass-through rights provide the sponsor with the ability to transfer some of the plan components and benefits to a third party. For example, the sponsor's on-site sales rights might be passed through (or along) to a retailer that would assume the responsibility for that aspect of the sponsorship. This allows the sponsor to capitalize on strategic alliances with its partners. Such pass-through rights may be cost-free for the partner, but in other cases the partner will be expected to share in the financial obligation to the sponsee. This may

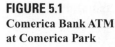

FIGURE 5.1
Comerica Bank ATM
at Comerica Park

be in the form of cash or value-in-kind. The presence of pass-through rights tends to add complexity and clutter to the sponsorship environment; therefore, this right is typically associated with higher fees for the sponsor.

Level of Sponsor's Promotional Commitment

The key issue to consider in this category is the total level of resources committed for all promotions that flow directly from the sponsor to the sponsee. For example, in those cases where the TV broadcast is controlled by the sponsee, a discount for the sponsorship fees might be granted if the sponsor agrees to purchase a specified amount of advertising time. The Nextel agreement with NASCAR is an example of this. As part of their contract, Nextel has agreed to purchase a specified amount of advertising during the broadcasts of the races in the series. Since the sponsee considers the full impact of the cash flows, a discount on the price of the sponsorship is generally open to negotiation.

Multiterm Contract Discount

The parties involved might be interested in establishing a longer-term deal than the typical contract encompasses. For example, the typical term of a contract for a TOP sponsor for the Olympics is a four-year cycle. However, it is evident that most sponsors exercise their right of first refusal and opt to renew cycle after cycle. It has been reported that the International Olympic Committee has decided to pursue contracts that incorporate more than a single cycle. An example is Coca–Cola, which has a contract through the 2020 games. At the time it was signed, the term encompassed an extension of 12 years. The sponsor was signed through the 2008 games in Beijing, thus the extension covers 3 full sponsorship cycles (4 years each) for the Olympic Games. Similarly, the IOC's contract with Swatch expires after the 2010 Winter Games, and its relationship with TOP sponsor

GE is set to expire after the 2012 Summer Games. When multiterm contracts are sought, the sponsee is often amenable to granting a discount to the sponsor. However, even in the absence of a discount for the latter part of a contract, the sponsor may realize a cost savings because it has insulated itself from increased rights fees that might occur during the course of the multiterm contract.

Introduction of a New Co-Sponsor

A new co-sponsor may open up cross-marketing opportunities. It may also add prestige to the event. The ability to develop strategic alliances and even share the costs of managing and developing a comprehensive promotional package designed to support a program with a complementary sponsor may be attractive to a prospect or even to an existing sponsor considering renewal. A recent example involved the 2004 Olympics, where sponsors Samsung and Coca-Cola worked together as co-sponsors of the 2004 Olympic Torch Relay. Added prestige brought about by a particularly noteworthy sponsor can have a halo effect and raise the perceived value of the sponsorship. So even if the sponsors do not interact in any capacity beyond the scope of their sponsorships, the mere presence of an influential sponsor can still have a positive impact on other sponsors. This enhanced value will be reflected in the price quoted by the sponsee.

Price Determination

Upon completing the task of delineating all of the factors that influence the value of the sponsorship, the sponsee must then determine the actual price. The qualitative assessment must be translated into a quantitative measure of value. To do this, the sponsee must make both the investment and the benefits measurable in the eyes of the prospective sponsor.

Make the Sponsor's Investment and Benefits Measurable

In today's environment, the conclusion of a sponsorship program is likely to be marked by an assessment of its impact. There are several methods for implementing postevent evaluation, but they are generally measured based upon some predetermined outcome such as increased level of sales during the sponsorship period. Since potential sponsors are primarily interested in measurable results, it is logical to presume that the prospect will evaluate the quoted price based upon the anticipated return on the sponsorship investment. Thus, there is a need for the sponsee to make both the investment and the anticipated benefits measurable and meaningful.

In the absence of measurable outcomes, it is difficult if not impossible for the prospect to compare alternative programs–be the alternatives one event versus another or one level of involvement versus another level for the same event. The reality is that there is no standard price. Whereas advertising looks at cost per thousand, measures such as this are not appropriate when comparing one sponsorship opportunity to another.

The starting point is to identify each component of the plan that provides benefits to the sponsor. Next is the identification of each of the market factors that influence the fair market price. Then each planned activity should be outlined. Within the context of this outline, opportunities for the sponsor to participate and attain the benefits derived from its participation must be clearly identified. It is essential that the benefits be delineated as they represent the path to the bottom line that drives most sponsorship decisions today. Finally, it is easier to support the price being asked if the sponsee can provide insight into how to measure the results attained via the implementation of the sponsorship plan.

Of paramount importance in this process is the task of getting potential sponsors to state specific objectives that they will seek to achieve with the sponsorship under consideration. In other words, the objectives of "increasing sales" or of "increasing our distribution in the retail market" are inadequate because they are far too general. Instead of increasing sales, a more specific objective might be to "increase sales by 10,000 units in the primary markets reached by the property and the sponsor's marketing plan." This objective is much easier to assign a value to. An alternative to "increasing our level of distribution" is to "increase our market coverage to 90 percent of the retailers selling products in our category."

The objectives are stated in measurable terms; however, there is another key element in this measurement process. Where did we start? In other words, the prospective sponsor must establish a *benchmark*. How would the sponsor know if it was successful in meeting its objective of increasing sales by 10,000 units if it did not know the level of sales prior to the sponsorship? As for the second objective, did the sponsor start with an 80 percent, 89 percent, or 95 level of distribution? What did the sponsorship actually accomplish? Without that benchmark, it is impossible to know.

> The prospective sponsor must establish a benchmark. How would the sponsor know if it was successful in meeting its objective of increasing sales by 10,000 units if it did not know the level of sales prior to the sponsorship?

This knowledge is also important to the sponsee. Objectives must be attainable. If the prospect establishes unrealistic expectations, it will undoubtedly be disappointed with the results. Disappointing results generally lead to higher attrition on the part of the sponsors; in other words, they will not renew their sponsorships for the next cycle. If both parties are aware of the starting point and the target, then the task of establishing and evaluating the price is easier.

Alternative Approaches to Establishing a Price

New sponsorship opportunities regularly appear in the market. New properties such as the inaugural 2006 World Baseball Classic, existing properties opting to add new sponsors (such as the World Cup of Soccer increasing its roster from 10 to 15 sponsors), and existing properties embracing sponsors for the first time (such as the Rose Bowl in 1999) all add to the supply of opportunities available to prospects. Demand is also in a constant state of change. New companies enter, existing partners leave, and current sponsors defect from one event to another, often from one category of event to another. The constant shifts in the character of supply and demand make the determination of the right price difficult.

Another factor leading to wide variations in pricing is that each of the sponsees will seek to differentiate its property from those of the competition. Whether it is the event itself or the components associated with the sponsorship plan, the lack of uniformity means that each opportunity must be judged on its own merits and cannot simply be compared to a competitor's alternative program.

It is evident that the establishment of a correct price is both essential and difficult. A price that is too low means that the property owner has failed to attain a fair market value and has forfeited potential revenue. A price too high makes the sponsorship difficult to sell. And if it is sold at a premium price, the potential problem is that the sponsor will not achieve an acceptable return on investment and will choose to terminate the relationship at the first opportunity.

So how does a property owner determine the price that is appropriate for both the buyer and the seller? In the sponsorship environment, four methods dominate this task. They are the cost-plus approach, the competitive market approach, the equivalent opportunity approach, and the relative-value approach.

The Cost-Plus Approach

Price determination based upon the cost-plus approach is similar to so-called markup pricing that is typically used in the retail marketing environment. First, the event organizers determine the actual costs that they incur in the task of providing the components specified in then sponsorship plan; then a desired profit margin is added. That margin may be an absolute, predetermined amount or it may be a predetermined percentage. For example, it could be the organizer's estimated costs plus $100,000 or its costs plus 40 percent.

Event organizers must recognize that there are many issues that need to be included in the process of determining their costs. While it is evident that there are many direct costs that are easily attributed to the plan components and benefits offered, some costs are often overlooked by inexperienced organizers. These less evident costs include administrative costs (such as secretarial support), the costs associated with providing sufficient service to the sponsor (advice on supporting promotions, meetings, producing postevent evaluation and performance reports, and other labor costs), and marketing costs (advertising, proposal development, commissions, and other sales costs). It must also be remembered that not every proposal results in a signed contract. The costs associated with all efforts, not just the successful ones must be factored in.

Once all of these costs have been allocated, the sponsee has arrived at its baseline fee.[3] The desired profit margin is then added to the baseline fee and the price is established. Event organizers are advised to give serious consideration to the profit margin. It must not drive the price of the sponsorship to a point that it is overpriced and therefore unsellable. Furthermore, it must be recognized that an adequate profit is required from each sponsorship as the profit is a significant component of the revenues that will be used to pay the costs of staging the event. When properly done, the sponsor will achieve an acceptable return on investment, the event organizers will raise enough money to cover all sponsorship costs, and the organizers will still reach their profit goals after paying all expenses. These goals vary significantly as some events such as the World Cup of Soccer seek meaningful profits whereas others such as a community parade may simply seek to cover costs and break even.

The cost-plus method is especially valid where costs must be passed on but the price quoted is not based upon the inherent value of the sponsorship per se. Local grassroots events may be less dependent upon a measurable return on investment and influenced more by the sponsor's desire to enhance its involvement and its image in a community. This pricing technique is used less frequently when establishing the price for a highly desirable, high-profile event such as the Masters golf tournament, the Olympic Games, or top teams and drivers in Formula 1 racing.

The Competitive Market Approach

In contrast to the cost-plus method of price determination, the competitive market approach is driven by conditions that exist within the marketplace. Issues such as supply, demand, competitive actions, and the ability to differentiate a property and the associated sponsorship are key considerations. Other external factors such as the social, legal, political, and economic environments also influence the final price. So rather than focus on costs, the emphasis is on providing value commensurate with that of the competing properties. The expectations of the prospective sponsors must also be taken into consideration.

Both the sponsee and the prospective sponsor are well aware that sponsorship opportunities abound in the marketplace. Some of these opportunities may be in direct competition with each other; an example would be one football team versus another. Some may represent substitute competition; for example, a football team and a rock concert may provide the same strategic linkage to the prospective sponsor's target market. Finally, the sponsee faces discretionary competition in that the prospect may select a promotional tool other than sponsorship. The proposed sponsorship for the football team may be in competition with more traditional advertising or the distribution of coupons and free samples by the prospect. Or the prospective sponsor may decide to forgo sponsorship and invest those resources in the introduction of a new product. Few prospects have unlimited resources, and they constantly evaluate their expenditures in an effort to use them as effectively as possible. As a result, they likely have a perception of the value of the sponsorship program that is being offered to them. If not, the proposal will be evaluated prior to any significant investment.

> Just like consumers, a prospect does not always base it's purchase decision upon the lowest price.

Large companies such as Visa International often have a corporate sponsorship division that bears the responsibility of screening each proposal submitted to it and developing its own estimate of the economic value of each proposal. This process allows the firm to compare the various alternatives, and it underscores the need for property owners to establish realistic prices that are consistent with the competition's offerings.

Just like consumers, a prospect does not always base its purchase decision upon the lowest price. Rather, the decision is based upon which of the alternatives provides for the best use of the resources to be expended by the firm. This philosophy is the basis of the competitive market approach.

The Equivalent Opportunity Approach

A less commonly used approach is that of determining the equivalent opportunity cost.[4] This method does not look at the cost of similar alternative sponsorships; rather, it looks at traditional media. The assumption is that if the company spends the money on a sponsorship, then it cannot spend it on other promotional tools such as TV, radio, magazine, newspaper, Internet, and outdoor advertising. Therefore, in one sense a sponsorship represents an opportunity cost.

It could be argued that this approach is not used to determine the price; rather, it is used to evaluate the price arrived at through one of the other price determination techniques. More specifically, once the sponsee has established the price, it must consider how a sponsor could spend that money if it was to purchase time and space in traditional media instead. The assessments must be made in comparable terms. In other words, if the event reaches only one local geographic market, then local media costs should be the basis. If it reaches a national audience, use media prices based on nationwide coverage. These costs are readily available on media rate cards, trade publications, and from representatives of one's advertising agency.

By comparing the price of the sponsorship to the cost of advertising in traditional media, the sponsee can scrutize the appropriateness of the price. This scrutiny may result in an adjustment, up or down, in the price. This method is similar to the competitive market approach, but it differs in that it is used to evaluate a preliminary price that has already been determined.

Relative Value Approach

Rather than looking at costs, the relative value approach emphasizes outcomes. It requires the determination of the market value of the components that are included in the plan. Part of this evaluation is based upon values that are easily determined, but another part is based upon the anticipated exposure that a sponsor will gain by virtue of its involvement. Accuracy for the first part is easy; accuracy for the second part is based on forecasts, so it is an estimate that is risky at best. That notwithstanding, this approach is the only genuine effort to relate the price of the sponsorship to the anticipated direct outcomes achieved by the sponsor.

> Rather than looking at costs, the relative value approach emphasizes outcomes.

The easily determined costs include the price of components that are available and sold to nonsponsors. For example, plans often include free advertising in the event's program. If a sponsor gets two pages free and the prevailing rate for nonsponsors is $10,000 per page, then the relative value of that component is easily calculated to be $20,000. Other components that may be available to nonsponsors on a fee basis include signage, executive suites, recognition on the video boards or in public address announcements, hospitality areas, tickets, and parking passes. Therefore, the initial task is simply to identify the components provided in the sponsorship plan and determine how much it would cost if all of these components had to be purchased.

The second part is not so easy. For a sponsorship to be effective, consumers must recognize the association between the sponsor and the sponsee. When TV viewers see a sponsor's logo on their screens, this relationship is reinforced and value is added. When the announcers mention a sponsor's name during a radio or TV broadcast, value is added. The dilemma is to assign a number that represents that value. In other words, how much is the exposure gained during the event worth?

Consider the following scenario where the fast-food restaurant chain Subway was the title sponsor of a recent NASCAR race, the Subway 400 held in Rockingham, North Carolina. A postevent evaluation revealed that during the course of the broadcast, Subway's name or logo appeared (in focus) on home TV screens for a total of 37 minutes and five seconds. Given the prevailing cost of purchasing a 30-second slot for advertising during the broadcast ($140,000), Subway received $10,833,240 worth of exposure. This value was derived by multiplying the cost of a 30-second advertisement by the number of 30-second units that the Subway name or logo appeared on TV (74.166). Additional value of $2,240,000 resulted from the announcers mentioning Subway 48 times during the broadcast, bringing the total relative value of this exposure to approximately $12.6 million. Of course, this valuation was undertaken after the event. Valuations for sales purposes take place prior to an event and are based upon forecasts for the level of exposure, a variable that is impossible to control. The methodology described is that developed by Joyce Julius and Associates, a pioneer in postevent evaluation. This methodology is discussed more fully in the chapter on postevent evaluation (Chapter 10). Table 5.3 provides estimates of value for other sponsors in the Subway 400 race.

From a price determination perspective, the sponsee will simply sum the values of the plan components and the *anticipated* exposure. The net result is a preliminary price that is a reflection of the relative value to the sponsor. Prospects may rightfully argue that 30 seconds of logo exposure during the broadcast is not as effective as a 30-second advertisement where vivid images and persuasive copy can be used. This generally results in a lower estimate of the relative value of the exposure and a reduction in the price of the sponsorship.

TABLE 5.3
Value of Exposure during the Subway 400

Source: Joyce Julius and Associates, *Sponsors Report* 18, no. 2 (2002). Reprinted with permission of Joyce Julius & Associates, Inc.

Sponsor	Exposure Time (mins.)	Mentions	Comparable Value
Subway	37:05	48	$12,623,225
Ford	17:17	25	6,005,975
UPS	8:56	2	2,594,630
AOL	8:25	1	2,403,285
Pepsi-Cola	4:23	2	1,320,480

Of course, the question of how much of a reduction is in order is subject to negotiation. This negotiation process is instrumental in the determination of the final price. Once the parties agree upon the projected value of the exposure, the likelihood of getting a signed contract is greatly enhanced.

Still to be determined are the form of the payment and a variety of timing issues. These are discussed in the following sections.

> Prospects may rightfully argue that 30 seconds of logo exposure during the broadcast is not as effective as a 30-second advertisement where vivid images and persuasive copy can be used.

Methods of Payment

There are three basic methods by which the sponsor can provide the required compensation to the sponsee. Payments are generally made in the form of cash; however, the financial commitments for some sponsorships can be met via the provision of *value-in-kind*. In many cases, the event will accept goods and services as payment because the VIK relieves the sponsee of the need to purchase these same goods and services that are required to stage the event. In other cases, the payment may be a combination of cash and VIK.

Statistics indicate that about half of all sponsorship contracts are completed solely on the basis of cash. Approximately one-quarter use only VIK, and the remaining quarter use a combination of cash and VIK. The use of VIK has gained importance in recent years, as some events are incorporating a class of sponsors that are recognized as "official suppliers" or "equipment suppliers" or some similar term. Events need outside goods and services to function. Computers, transportation, photography services, food, beverages, sports equipment, telecommunications services, video equipment, audio equipment, and apparel are examples of the types of goods and services that are needed to stage an event such as a concert, a golf tournament, or a charity fund raiser. Still, it is important to note that even "official suppliers" are sometimes required to pay a portion of the fees in cash. An effort must be made to assure that all sponsors in a single class (e.g., official supplier) are treated similarly. Since events do not necessarily require an equivalent amount of goods and services from each supplier, that imbalance may be equalized by requiring the difference to be made up in cash.

One potential point of contention regarding VIK is the calculation of the precise value of the goods and services provided by the sponsor. A pair of shoes provided to a team might have three distinct values: cost, wholesale price, and retail price. The basis used for this determination can have a pronounced affect on the amount of goods and services sought by the sponsee. As a rule of thumb, the value of VIK should be based upon what it would cost the sponsee to acquire these goods and services through the normal channels of distribution, either from the sponsor, one of the sponsor's competitors, or an intermediary such as a retailer, wholesaler, or import house.

Sponsorship Level

Many properties, especially the premier sports events, provide sponsorship opportunities at different levels. Each level is priced differently and provides sponsors with a different array of plan components. Lower-level sponsors that pay less receive fewer benefits in return.

> Different levels can be used to overcome price resistance on the part of a prospective sponsor.

TABLE 5.4
Examples of Levels of Sponsorship

World Cup of Soccer	2008 Beijing Summer Olympic Games
Sponsor	TOP VI Partners
Marketing Partner	Beijing 2008 Partner
Official Product/Supplier	Beijing 2008 Sponsor
Regional Supporter	Beijing 2008 Supplier
Equipment Supplier	

The different levels can be used to overcome price resistance on the part of a prospective sponsor. Thus, it can be helpful in the negotiation process. It can also provide opportunities for sponsors that simply cannot afford the financial commitment required from top-level sponsors to officially associate themselves with the event. Table 5.4 delineates the different levels for the World Cup of Soccer and the 2008 Beijing Summer Olympic Games.

The key consideration for the sponsee is the development of a pricing strategy that is equitable for all sponsors at all levels. A regional supporter spending $300,000 for the World Cup is just as concerned with the value of the sponsorship and its ROI as is the top-tier sponsor that is spending many millions of dollars in rights fees.

Timing

From a timing perspective, there are four key considerations. First is the duration of the agreement. Second is the time frame during which the sponsor will be allowed to utilize its sponsorship designation in other promotional activities. Third is the projected schedule for sponsee activities that will serve to identify its sponsors. And finally, there is the issue concerning the timing of the payment of the sponsorship fees.

Duration of the Agreement

The terms of the sponsorship proposal and the resultant contract will specify the length of the relationship. To a certain extent, this may be a function of the event itself. It may be a *once-off event* with no opportunity for an ongoing program. For example, sponsors of a popular rock band's farewell tour have no opportunity for continuity. Their sponsorship will essentially last for the duration of the event. And while the sponsor may engage in some supporting promotions to highlight its relationship with the band, there is no legitimate opportunity for a long-term relationship. But whether the event is scheduled for a single day (e.g., a championship boxing match), for several weeks (an art exhibit), or for several months (a concert tour), the prospective sponsor will still need to confirm the other timing issues identified in this chapter.

Many events are staged on an annual basis. Examples of these *serial events* include national championships in a number of sports such as golf, tennis, ice skating, and gymnastics. Other examples include the college football bowl games and the NFL's Super Bowl game, the UEFA Cup in European soccer, and the NPC (National Provincial Championship) in New Zealand rugby. In these cases, the decision must focus on the number of years for which the sponsorship agreement will be in force.

In other cases, the property being sponsored is not an event. For example, adidas has chosen to invest millions of dollars in a sponsorship of the New Zealand Rugby Football Union (NZRFU) and its prized New Zealand All Blacks rugby team. Among others, Nike sponsors golfers Tiger Woods and Michelle Wie as well as basketball player LeBron James. Even when the sponsorship does not involve a staged event, the duration of the contract must be determined.

Regarding the length of the contract, there are many legitimate reasons for a short-term deal. There might be an immediate short-term objective for either the sponsee or the prospective sponsor. In these situations, a one-year agreement may be deemed appropriate. Perhaps the sponsee is attempting to fill a void because of a previous sponsor dropping out. Or alternatively, the potential sponsor may be seeking a short-term promotional vehicle that can be coordinated with other elements of its marketing strategy. One example that was discussed earlier in this chapter highlights both of these situations. Upon the decision by AT&T to not renew its four-year contract as the presenting sponsor of the Rose Bowl game, event organizers needed to quickly fill the void. At the same time, Sony was preparing to introduce its new video-game console and software, the Sony PlayStation 2. In this case, both organizations saw immediate value in a one-year agreement. Upon the completion of the sponsorship for the 2003 game, they parted ways. But the one-year contract was deemed to be mutually beneficial to both parties involved.

> Once-off sponsorships are considered less effective than the ongoing serial sponsorship programs.

In most cases, however, these once-off sponsorships are considered less effective than the ongoing serial sponsorship programs. In the case of a serial program, the sponsee has an enduring stream of revenue while the sponsor has a greater opportunity to perceptually link its name and products to the sponsored event or property. Thus, there is an incentive for both entities to pursue a multiyear contract. The obvious question concerns the number of years that will be stipulated in the contract. It is a question for which there is no universally accepted answer. There exists a wide range of examples. The Barclay sponsorship with the FA Premier League covers a three-year period; the Nextel contract with NASCAR is set for 10 years; the adidas sponsorship of the New Zealand All Blacks rugby team was originally signed for seven and a half years; the stadium naming rights contract for Telstra's relationship with what was known as Stadium Australia (2000 Sydney Olympics) encompasses some eight years, and the Reebok contract with world-class basketball player Allen Iverson is characterized as a lifetime contract.

From the sponsor's perspective, a long-term contract assures continuity with minimal disruption because the sponsee may not be allowed to impose significant changes that would adversely impact the sponsor. Conversely, a long-term contract may be risky in that the sponsor may be obligated to commit resources for a sponsorship that is not effectively contributing to the achievement of the marketer's stated goals. For the sponsee, there are risks as well. Short-term contracts put the sponsee in the unenviable position of frequently negotiating new contracts either for the purpose of renewing and extending a relationship with a current sponsor or seeking a new sponsor to replace one that has opted to end the relationship. Conversely, a long-term contract locks the sponsee into a financial agreement that might be difficult if not impossible to modify until the existing contract expires. Thus, the sponsee may not be receiving the true market value for a property or event that has appreciated in value. As a result, the industry standard has evolved into a midterm time frame, generally three to four years.

In some cases, even annual events have a cyclical pattern. For example, the controversial Bowl Championship Series (BCS) that was designed to assure a national championship game for college football in the United States has a four-year cycle. As initially conceived, there were four games that comprised the series, with each venue assured the hallmark championship game every fourth year. In situations such as this, it may be appropriate to consider a contract that reflects the cycle period, four years in this case.

The cyclical pattern is perhaps more relevant for events that are not held every year. The Olympics, the Ryder Cup golf competition, the World Cup of Soccer, and the World Cup of Cricket are examples. The Ryder Cup is contested every two years, with the venue alternating between Europe and the United States every four years. Both of the afore-mentioned World Cup events are staged every four years. The Olympics represent a four-year cycle; however, this cycle includes both a summer and winter event. In general, sponsorship contracts conform to the time frame associated with the event. For example, the typical World Cup event or Olympic sponsorship will be for a term of four years. Of course, sponsors of all of the aforementioned events will have the right of first refusal when it comes time to renew their commitment to each event.

Timelines for Use of Sponsorship Designation

The Summer Olympics lasts 17 days; a typical golf tournament is contested over four days; Wimbledon tennis competition takes place over 14 days; a concert tour may last several months; a one-day international cricket match takes about seven hours to complete; and a championship boxing match may last as little as a few seconds and no longer than an hour. Given that the success of a sponsorship is enhanced by the marketer's ability to associate itself with the event, it is evident that any sponsorship must provide an opportunity for the marketer to portray itself as a sponsor for some period of time both prior to and after the event has been staged. Yet it is also important that there be no overlap of the terms such that retiring sponsors and new sponsors would be able to concurrently identify themselves as sponsors. Imagine the confusion and inefficiency of two competitors like Coca-Cola and Pepsi-Cola, one a retiring sponsor and one a new sponsor, simultaneously advertising their relationship with the same event.

An integral element of the contract is the specification of the period during which the sponsor can identify itself accordingly; the contract will also dictate when the sponsor is allowed to utilize event trademarks and logos in its promotions designed to support the sponsorship. That period will be influenced by the nature of the event, the duration of the event, the length of the contract (one year versus several), the duration of marketing activities undertaken by the event organizers, and the extent to which additional promotional efforts are anticipated to be initiated by the sponsors.

> The potential sponsor should recognize that the periods immediately preceding and following the actual event are important windows of opportunity.

The potential sponsor should recognize that the periods immediately preceding and following the actual event are important windows of opportunity. Even in those cases where there are long-term contracts or when events are staged less frequently, it is likely that the entire period will not be productive. The intent of the supporting promotional activities is to increase the likelihood that the sponsor will be associated with an event deemed important by one or more market segments. Consumer enthusiasm tends to peak just prior to the event, so that period is crucial. The postevent period is also important, especially in those geographic areas directly affected by the event. This impact may be a result of being the venue or the home of the triumphant team or athlete. The former is predictable; the latter is not.

Each sponsor should attempt to secure the rights to pre- and postevent recognition and the right to use event trademarks and logos. This period should coincide with the anticipated supporting program as established by the prospective sponsor.

Projected Schedule of Sponsee Activities That Identify Sponsors

One of the components sought by sponsors is the undertaking of activities by the event organizers or property owners that acknowledge the support of sponsors through a variety of methods of recognition. Clearly signage, if included, is relevant primarily during the course of the event. However, it is not uncommon for organizers to recognize their sponsors in their own advertising, via press releases, and on the event Web site. The question then becomes one of establishing the time frame during which the organizers will be recognizing the sponsors. When will the press releases be disseminated? What is the schedule for advertising in the various media? When will the sponsor's name first appear on the event's Web site; at what point after the event will this acknowledgment be terminated? These are key questions, and the answers will provide direction for each sponsor's promotion that is designed to support the sponsorship. As a consequence, this information should be included in the sponsorship proposal and the subsequent contract. These beginning and ending dates are often subject to negotiation, and the prospective sponsor needs to ensure that it has adequate time to strengthen the public's awareness that there is a relationship between the sponsor and the sponsee.

Timing of Payments to the Sponsee

Whether the payment is lump sum or spread out over time and whether it is all cash, all VIK, or a combination of cash and VIK, the proposal and final contract should specify exactly when all payments are due. When the contract is for multiple years, it is common for fees to be paid on an annual basis. It is also standard practice for an initial payment to be made upon the signing of the contract. When the sponsored event is staged less frequently than once a year, perhaps on a biennial basis, it is common for payments to be spread over the entire period of time. This payment is often justifiable as the sponsor may be using the event's trademarks and logos over part of, if not the entire period of time between the actual events. For example, the Olympic Games are held every two years if one considers the interval between the winter and summer games. The typical Olympic sponsorship agreement is for a period of four years. It is common for sponsors to incorporate their relationship with the event in their own promotions and packaging, even in the off years. For instance, McDonald's packaging includes the Olympic rings and its Web site includes a historical perspective of its past and future relationship with the International Olympic Committee throughout the period specified in the contract. Thus, the requirement of partial payments in off years can be justified by both McDonald's and the IOC.

Small-scale events often solicit sponsors via direct mail. This single contact is modestly effective for cause-related marketing efforts where there are few tangible benefits accruing to the sponsor. In cases such as these, the solicitation generally seeks immediate payment to the event organizer.

| **Closing Capsule** | Every sponsorship requires a commitment of resources by both the sponsor and the sponsee. The key question addressed in this chapter concerns the allocation of resources on the part of the sponsor. Stated more succinctly, What will the sponsor have to pay to start a new relationship or continue an existing relationship with a property or event? Clearly the answer to this question is important to both parties. |

Companies seem to acknowledge that sponsorships work best when given time to imprint the relationship between the sponsor and the sponsee. Coca-Cola has a relationship with the Olympics dating back to 1928. Yet one trend today is that of revolving sponsorships where properties routinely change their key partners, sometimes each year.

There are many factors that influence the market price of a sponsorship program. These include tangible factors, intangible factors, geographic reach, market factors, and price adjusters. A key consideration in the task of determining the price is the ability to make the sponsor's investment and benefits measurable. Results can be measured against sponsor benchmarks after the completion of the program and its effectiveness can easily be assessed.

The price of a sponsorship program may be determined via four approaches: cost-plus, competitive market, equivalent opportunity, and relative value. The method used depends upon the availability of relevant data and personal preference. Once the price has been determined, the form of payment must be established. Fees are paid using cash, value-in-kind, or a combination of cash and VIK. Approximately half of all sponsorships today are based solely on cash.

Many events have several sponsorship levels. Each level has a different program with different components and prices. This allows even relatively small companies to become involved with high-profile events and properties.

The final consideration is that of timing. The four key concerns regarding timing are the duration of the agreement, timelines for the sponsor's authorized use of the sponsorship designation, the projected schedule for the sponsee's activities that will identify its sponsors, and the timing of the payments.

If agreement can be reached, then a signed contract is likely to result. Then the sponsee can move on to preparing to stage the event, and the sponsor can begin to consider when and how to initiate its efforts to capitalize on its new asset, the sponsorship.

Review Questions

1. Why do you think that long-term sponsorships are more effective than spending money on a changing series of properties and events (property hopping)?

2. What is meant by the term *revolving sponsorship?*

3. Why is the value of tangible factors easier to calculate than is the value of intangible factors?

4. Briefly discuss some market factors that influence the final price charged for the sponsorship.

5. How do we make the sponsor's investment and benefits measurable?

6. Put together a pricing model for sponsoring a career fair at your university. Illustrate the use of the cost-plus approach to determine your price.

7. What is the key distinction between the cost-plus approach and the relative value approach for price determination?

8. What is meant by VIK? (Explain it; don't just give the name.) If you were organizing a three-man-team basketball tournament, which companies would represent good sponsorship prospects if you were seeking VIK as the sole form of payment?

9. Explain the use of sponsorship levels by major events such as the Olympic Games.

10. What are the key considerations regarding the concept of timing as it relates to sponsorship decision?

Endnotes

1. C. Britcher, "F1 Cut Prices for Sponsors," January 6, 2003, www.sportbusiness.com/news/? news_item_id=149767 (accessed October 13, 2005).

2. *IEG's Complete Guide to Sponsorship: Everything You Wanted to Know about Sponsorship* (Chicago: IEG, Inc., 1999), p. 19.

3. A. Grey and K. Skildum-Reid, *The Sponsorship Seeker's Toolkit* (Sydney: McGraw-Hill Companies, 1999), p. 93.

4. Ibid., pp. 95–96.

CHAPTER SIX

Ambush Marketing

Learning Objectives

- Learn what ambush marketing is.
- See why ambush marketing has become commonplace.
- Learn how to ambush.
- Learn how to protect yourself from ambushers.
- Distinguish between piracy and ambush marketing.
- Evaluate preventative measures.

One of the most important considerations in sponsorship today is that of ambush marketing. *Ambush marketing* represents efforts by nonsponsors to attach themselves to a desirable property or event. When done effectively, ambush marketing confuses consumers and diminishes the value of any actual sponsor's relationship with the property or event. As discussed earlier in the text, sponsorships are most effective when consumers recognize the relationship between the sponsor and the sponsee. Effective ambush marketing causes the consumer to mistakenly associate the ambusher with the event. Thus, some of the benefits of the sponsorship are denied the actual sponsor and attained by the ambusher. The concept of ambush marketing, techniques to implement it, examples of effective implementation, and ways to avoid it are the focal points of this chapter.

> Effective ambush marketing causes the consumer to mistakenly associate the ambusher with the event.

Ambush Marketing

The IEG has defined ambush marketing as "a promotional strategy whereby a nonsponsor attempts to capitalize on the popularity/prestige of a property by giving a false impression that it is a sponsor."[1] The definition goes on to state that ambush marketing is often used by the competitors of the property's official sponsors. Only a few years ago, the practice was viewed with such disdain that one of its critics, John Bennett of Visa, referred to American Express Company's ambush efforts as *parasite marketing*.[2]

> A parasite attaches itself to an unwilling host and takes nourishment from it.

Simply stated, ambush marketers attempt to create the impression that they are officially associated with an event when, in fact, no such association exists. Let us reconsider the reference to parasitic marketing. From a biological perspective, a parasite attaches itself to an unwilling host and takes nourishment from it. A leech or a tick may attach itself to a human being and draw nutrients from it. The leech is a parasite; the human being is an unwilling host. If left unchecked, the parasite will continue to sap the energy of its unwilling host, perhaps jeopardizing the well-being of the host. So it is with ambush marketing. The ambush marketer attaches itself to an unwilling property or event in such a way that it extracts an array of benefits to which it is not rightfully entitled. The question of how harmful ambush marketing is has been subject to some disagreement. One indisputable fact is that an official sponsor that is effectively ambushed by a competitor suffers by virtue of the diminished value of its own sponsorship rights and the inability to capitalize on all of the anticipated benefits.

How to Ambush

Whether a company is an official sponsor on the alert for possible ambushing activities by its competitors or a nonsponsor seeking to create the impression that it is officially associated with a property, it should understand the alternative strategies that might be used.

First, it is important to note what is and what is not ambush marketing. The key consideration for ambush marketing is that it represents an intentional effort to confuse the consumer as to who is and who is not an official sponsor. According to U.K. attorneys Patrick Elliot and Tony Singh, an activity should be characterized as ambushing only if the marketer is "attempting to imply, or contrive, an endorsement of a specific event; and only if that implied endorsement is damaging the revenues of the event."[3]

Advertising a product used in conjunction with an event is not by definition an ambush effort. For example, if Michelin airs TV ads during a motor sports event, it is not necessarily guilty of ambushing. The key question is whether or not Michelin attempted to deceive viewers and create the impression that it was an official sponsor. From a somewhat different perspective, consider marketing efforts such as a TV ad for a product that is not related to the event being shown. What if Porsche airs an advertisement during the broadcast of a European Professional Golfers Association when the official automotive sponsor is Volvo? The same criterion applies. Did Porsche attempt to create a false impression that it, and not Volvo, was the official sponsor? The answer lies in the message used by Porsche.

In response to allegations of ambushing Olympic sponsor Ansett Australian Airlines by airing its own series of patriotic ads, a Qantas Airlines spokesperson stated bluntly that to not advertise "would be unprofessional."[4] Stated another way, it is a natural response to attempt to neutralize the competitive advantage held by an adversary. Indeed, competition is the foundation of the Olympics.

Companies are generally quick to respond to allegations of ambushing. When accused of ambushing Ansett Australia, Qantas said it was coincidental that its advertising slogan "The Spirit of Australia" was similar to the Olympics slogan, "Share the Spirit." When Pepsi was accused of ambushing Coca-Cola's sponsorship of the National Hockey League (NHL) in Canada, it defended its actions by noting that it had used no trademarks or logos owned by either the NHL or any NHL teams. American Express defended its actions by stating that it was attempting to correct the misconception created by Olympic sponsor Visa that the American Express card could not be used in and around the geographic areas where Olympic events were being staged. When Nike was accused of ambushing adidas' sponsorship of the World Cup of Soccer, it said it had done nothing illegal. To some, there needs to be a crossing of the legal threshold before one is guilty of ambushing. In other words, since Nike did not use any of the World Cup's (FIFA) trademarks or logos in an effort to promote its products, there was no effort to associate itself with the event. And such competitive advertising should not be construed to be ambush marketing.

It is evident that there is no consensus as to exactly what constitutes ambush marketing. It is an ethical dilemma, not a legal one. It has been described as clever, devious, deceptive, parasitic, unethical, imaginative, innovative, upstaging, and cunning. For the sake of developing a consistent perspective on ambush marketing, three questions need to be answered:

- Was the activity undertaken by a nonsponsor?
- Did the nonsponsor intentionally attempt to connect itself with the event?
- Does it harm an official sponsor, the event, or both?

Why Ambush?

The driving force behind the decision to use ambushing tactics is the *high cost of rights fees*. With several major events crossing the $30 million barrier, marketers have begun to reassess the viability of sponsorship. If a company can achieve similar results without paying the rights fees, it can save considerable resources and increase the return on its marketing investment.

> Ambush marketing has been shown to work.

The second major point is that *ambush marketing has been shown to work*. There is an abundance of postevent research that documents consumer confusion as to who is and who is not an official sponsor. Consider the 1994 Olympic Games. McDonald's was the official sponsor; prior to the Olympics, 69 percent of the respondents who took part in a survey correctly identified that relationship. During the games, Wendy's engaged in an ambush campaign that featured advertising with a winter sports theme. In the postevent survey, 68 percent of the respondents incorrectly identified Wendy's as the official sponsor. For those same games, 72 percent of the postevent sample correctly pointed to Visa as an official sponsor; however, the effective ambushing campaign orchestrated by American Express resulted in some 52 percent of those surveyed identifying it as an official sponsor.[5]

Converse was a sponsor of the 1984 Olympics in Los Angeles. Nike implemented an ambush strategy by purchasing outdoor advertising space along the roads leading to the Olympic venues and displaying the Nike "swoosh." It also used former Olympic athletes Mary Decker and Carl Lewis in many of its promotions. As a result of the ambushing campaign, a consumer poll revealed that twice as many people identified Nike as an official sponsor as compared with the true sponsor, Converse. The Qantas "Spirit of Australia" campaign produced postevent results indicating that 44 percent of those surveyed believed Qantas was the official sponsor compared with only 27 percent who correctly identified Ansett Australia.[6]

These examples document that ambush marketing works. If companies can achieve better results than official sponsors without paying the enormous rights fees, then the incentive to ambush is clear. Until events or legal systems are able to implement policies that preclude efforts of this type, ambush marketing efforts will continue to grow in popularity.

Third, *consumers are not offended by companies that engage in ambush tactics*. A recent study shows that there is confusion as to who is allowed to advertise during the broadcast of any given event. For example, the majority of those polled indicated their belief that only official sponsors of the Super Bowl can advertise during the broadcast.[7] The consequences of this misconception are apparent; if one of those consumers sees an advertisement for a nonsponsor during the broadcast, then that viewer will incorrectly associate the advertiser with the event. More disconcerting, only 20 percent of the respondents agreed with the statement that they were "annoyed by companies trying to associate themselves with the Super Bowl without being official sponsors."

A study that questioned New Zealand and American university students about the appropriateness of ambush behavior further supports the premise that there is apathy on the part of consumers in regard to these tactics. Fully 50 percent of the Americans and 69 percent of the New Zealanders exhibited either a neutral stance or agreed with the summary statement that ambushers were simply making more effective use of their promotional resources.[8] The same question was posed to a national sample of consumers in the United States, and similar results were documented.[9] Until consumers are turned off by ambushers and refuse to buy from them, there will continue to be an incentive to ambush. Given current attitudes, it is apparent that the apathy will persist and that consumers will continue to simply shrug off the efforts of ambushers and view their actions as acceptable.

> Until consumers are turned off by ambushers and refuse to buy from them, there will continue to be an incentive to ambush.

Last is the fact that *attitudes within the industry may be slowly changing.* At a recent seminar in Auckland, New Zealand, an executive for adidas was asked about Nike's effort to ambush his company's sponsorship of the World Cup of Soccer. With a shrug of his shoulders, he responded, "They ambush us; we ambush them." It was but one indication that the perception of ambush marketing may be slowly evolving from parasitic to appropriate. In other words, it is becoming more prominent and it may become a more acceptable strategy for tomorrow's marketers.

Implementation of Ambush Marketing Strategies

Whether the firm is a nonsponsor or an official sponsor, it must understand the array of strategies typically employed by today's ambushers. The nonsponsors will be seeking the optimal ambush strategy to implement, whereas the official sponsor needs to be alert to the different strategies that might be used against it in an effort to dilute the value of its relationship with the event. It is also important for the event organizers to anticipate ambush tactics. This understanding allows organizers to develop strategies designed to limit ambush opportunities and to protect its sponsors.

Piracy versus Ambush Marketing

The initial consideration addresses the legality of the actions of nonsponsors. The illegal activities cross the boundary of ambushing and fall into a category characterized as *piracy*.[10] Actions deemed to be piracy generally have definitive remedies under the laws of most countries. Examples of piracy include infringements of intellectual property rights such as the unauthorized use of an event's trademarks in advertisements or the sale of counterfeit merchandise. An overt claim to be officially related to a property is another example of piracy. Transgressions such as theses are often adjudicated in a court of law. The pirates may be ordered to cease their illegal activities, and they may be forced to compensate their victims for losses incurred because of their actions.

> Actions deemed to be piracy generally have definitive remedies under the laws of most countries.

On the other hand, ambush marketing is perfectly legal in most countries. Since no laws are broken, there are no legal steps that can be taken. It is these legal strategies that are most troublesome to property owners and their sponsors. The most common of these legal ambush marketing strategies have been placed into six categories.

Ambush Marketing Strategies

The six categories of ambush marketing are

- Sponsor media coverage of the event.
- Sponsor subcategories.
- Make a sponsorship-related contribution to the players' pool.
- Purchase advertising time during the broadcast replay.
- Engage in advertising to coincide with the timing of the event.
- Use other dilution strategies.

A brief discussion of each of these categories follows. Then the next section includes a number of actual examples of how ambush strategies have been implemented in the past.

Sponsor Media Coverage of the Event

When the event is broadcast via electronic media such as radio, TV, or video streaming on the Internet, it is typically the sale of advertising that pays the costs associated with the broadcast. In most cases, the event does not control the broadcast; consequently it may have little influence over which companies are allowed to advertise during its transmission. Ambushers can purchase time to broadcast their own advertisements during the broadcast. While the advertisers do not reach the spectators and attendees at the venue, they do reach the media audience. For major events, sports or otherwise, the media audience is much larger than the live audience. The reality is that the ambusher may care very little about the attendees at the venue because the media audience represents the more important target for the marketer.[11]

Efforts of this type are legal; therefore, they are deemed by many to be legitimate competitive responses that attempt to overcome a competitive advantage held by an official sponsor of a particular event. While Fuji Film was a sponsor of the Los Angeles Olympics, a major competitor (Kodak) purchased time and ran advertisements during the TV broadcast of the event. More recently, Carlton and United Breweries' sponsorship of the Australian Football League (AFL) was legally ambushed by rival brewer Lion Nathan, which aired commercials during the broadcast of the games over the course of the season.

It is important to note that ambush marketing is not just a sports-related phenomenon. There are a number of high-profile nonsports events that have sponsors, are broadcast by electronic media, and are vulnerable to ambush marketing of this type. Live concerts and awards shows are but two examples. The point is that property owners and their sponsors can not afford to make the mistake of assuming that they are safe from ambushers simply because they are not a sports event.

> Property owners and their sponsors can not afford to make the mistake of assuming that they are safe from ambushers simply because they are not a sports event.

It is also important to determine what is being ambushed. Is it a sponsor or is it the event itself? The Kodak example is evident; its efforts were aimed at Fuji. What if the advertiser has no direct competitor associated with the event? Is it still ambushing? The earlier questions posed still need to be answered. Was the advertising done by a nonsponsor? Did the nonsponsor intentionally attempt to connect itself to the event? Does that perceived connection harm an official sponsor or the event itself, or both? If the answers to these questions are yes, then the strategy associated with the purchase of the advertising time does represent an ambush marketing effort.

Sponsor Subcategories

Adidas sponsored the most recent World Cup of Soccer. Nike sponsored several of the top teams that were competing. Nike's sponsorship of a lower category germane to the event constituted a legitimate marketing decision. In a similar scenario, Reebok sponsored the U.S. men's basketball team at the Barcelona Olympics; at a lower level, Nike sponsored several of the players on the team, including the most noteworthy, Michael Jordan.

This strategy is sometimes referred to as *ambushing up*. The term is derived from the fact that the ambusher is involved with an official sponsorship of some lower level (at a lesser cost) but uses techniques designed to create the impression that it is involved with the event at some higher level of sponsorship. Again, for the ambushing to take place, there is no need for the marketer to be targeting a direct competitor. Many events today have multiple levels of sponsorship. For example, a firm might choose to be an official supplier of the World Cup or the Olympics, but it might try to create the impression that it is a sponsor at the highest level. Some people question whether the Sydney Olympics' official service provider TNT Delivery diminished the consumers' ability to recognize UPS delivery as a TOP sponsor. This issue highlights the need to negotiate broad category exclusivity in the early stages of establishing the terms of the sponsorship contract.

Make a Sponsorship-Related Contribution to the Players' Pool

Changing rules regarding amateurism have led to a broader use of this strategy. It is commonly used for both team sports and individual sports, especially those that have international appeal. Cash or VIK may be used to fulfill this commitment. Players' salaries may be supplemented by contributions for which the contributor may be acknowledged via logos on uniforms or recognition in TV interviews. Another method of implementing this strategy is via bonus pools or prizes for winning. For example, world-class swimmer Michael Phelps is sponsored by Speedo. While this relationship best fits the previous strategy of sponsoring a subcategory of an event, there is one key point of differentiation. Speedo designated a total of $1 million to be awarded to Phelps if he were to win seven gold medals in either the 2004 or 2008 Summer Olympics. Though he did not achieve this standard at the 2004 Games, the potential for this payout generated considerable discussion and publicity. And should Phelps succeed in 2008, there is no doubt but that his prize will be discussed in the various media. Whether simply an unattained incentive or a realized prize, its availability undoubtedly caused some people to incorrectly associate Speedo with the IOC and the Olympic Games.

Purchase Advertising Time during the Rebroadcast

Events are often rebroadcast after the initial live broadcast has taken place. The original broadcast may have been on free-to-air TV, pay-per-view, or a premium cable or satellite network such as ESPN, Fox, or Sky Sports. These initial broadcasts are often very expensive for advertisers, and access may be limited by category exclusivity agreements. So it may neither be economically viable nor even possible for some companies to purchase commercial time for the original broadcast.

Many events are shown again and again after the original airing. For these subsequent broadcasts, access may not be limited, thus potentially opening up opportunities for non-sponsors that were previously excluded. Additionally, the cost of advertising time may be greatly reduced. These opportunities give companies a chance to associate themselves with an event in the minds of some key target markets. Events that are often aired well after the live competition takes place include the NFL's Super Bowl, Premier League soccer matches, Super 14 rugby matches, and Formula 1 races.

Engage in Advertising to Coincide with the Timing of the Event

Advertising designed to fit this description falls into one of two categories: themed or traditional.[12]

Themed advertising is represented by creative components that are related to the property or event being ambushed. One of the strategies used by Wendy's in its effort to ambush McDonald's Winter Olympics sponsorship was to feature former Olympic ice skating champion Kristi Yamaguchi in a series of advertisements that aired prior to, during, and after the Olympic competition. Similarly, part of the aforementioned Nike strategy when it ambushed Reebok was to feature a number of athletes, including former Olympic champion Carl Lewis.

> One of the strategies used by Wendy's in its effort to ambush McDonald's Winter Olympics sponsorship was to feature former Olympic ice skating champion Kristi Yamaguchi in a series of advertisements that aired prior to, during, and after the Olympic competition.

Themed ads do not necessarily feature famous athletes. They may instead focus on similarities with the event. If the ambush effort is directed toward a golf tournament or its sponsors, the creative aspects of the advertising could feature golf situations. Efforts directed toward the Olympics could feature competition similar to the popular events. A second component of the aforementioned Wendy's campaign was to feature the company's president in advertisements making fun of his lack of skills in his presumed efforts to ski, play hockey, or drive a bobsled. Consumers saw Wendy's advertisements with a winter sports theme broadcast during times that coincided with the Olympic Games, and many erroneously assumed a relationship between the company and the event. Similarly, Nike leased outdoor signage on the roads leading to Olympic venues in Salt Lake City. These themed billboards helped to create the impression that Nike was an official sponsor of the Winter Olympics.

The use of a *traditional advertising* strategy is represented by a company's decision to pursue its marketing objectives by countering a sponsor's advertising with its own messages. Since the marketer is simply trying to overcome the sponsor's advantage by promoting its own strengths, few would consider this strategy to be parasitic. As noted earlier, being an event sponsor does not make a company immune to efforts by competitors to create brand preference for their own products. Still, some critics view these actions to be ambush marketing efforts when the advertising is executed around the same time frame as the event, especially if the campaign represents a substantial increase in the amount of money spent in comparison to previous promotional strategies. This strategy is hampered by category exclusivity components that are common in today's sponsorship contracts. Further restricting this type of opportunity, the broadcast networks often offer sponsors the right of first refusal for purchasing advertising time. As a result, the inventory of time available for advertising may be depleted without it ever being made available to nonsponsors. However, this does not preclude the nonsponsor's ability to place advertising on alternative media such as newspapers, radio, magazines, billboards, the Internet, or other TV programming.

Other Dilution Strategies

A final category is comprised of an eclectic array of activities undertaken in an effort to dilute the advantage held by the sponsor. These strategies are often combined with techniques discussed in the five preceding categories.

A nonsponsor may *purchase tickets to an event* with which it is seeking to create the perception of an association. By distributing these tickets to customers, employees, or as prizes in contests, an association may be assumed by some people in the market. If so, the ambush effort has been effective. A key consideration with this strategy concerns the ambusher's inability to use event trademarks and logos in its promotional efforts. To do so might cross the legal boundary and turn ambushing into piracy. Furthermore, one common stipulation regarding the sale of tickets to major sports events is the prohibition of the subsequent use of those tickets as prizes in any type of contest or sweepstakes.

Another commonly used dilution strategy is the *confusion technique*. This strategy requires the ambusher to develop creative promotions that consumers naturally associate with the event or property. Steinlager Beer was an official worldwide sponsor for the 1991 World Cup of Rugby. The English rugby team is generally a strong contender; therefore it is a potentially valuable property for a sponsor. During the competition, the English team would play its "anthem," the familiar song "Swing Low, Sweet Chariot." Imagine the outrage on the part of Steinlager executives when Foster's Beer introduced its advertising theme song "Swing Low, Sweet Carry-out" sung to the same beat and tune as the English team's anthem.[13] Another creative strategy was American Express' declaration that if you went to Lillehammer, Norway, site of the 1994 Winter Olympics, you would need a passport but not a visa. Of course, its real focus was not travel documentation required to enter Norway; rather, it was directed at Visa International, one of the official sponsors of the Games.

A marketer might go so far as to *create its own event*. If it cannot sponsor a local bowling tournament or concert series, it may initiate its own. When a marketer finds itself locked out of a series of theatrical productions in a major city, it may negotiate with touring companies and local venues to develop a new series that it can sponsor. In this way, not only does the marketer control the sponsorships, but it controls the product and timing as well.

Yet another strategy is to *sponsor other events that take place in the venue* of the event being ambushed. This strategy allows the ambusher to create an indirect association with the event. Additionally, photos used in subsequent advertising further reinforce the misinterpretation that the ambusher is affiliated with an event when it is not. Remember that Ansett Australian Airlines was the official airline of the Sydney Olympics. Major competition took place at Stadium Australia outside of Sydney. Qantas Airlines sponsored the Bledisloe Cup, a rugby competition played between Australian and New Zealand national rugby teams. The event was also contested at Stadium Australia. Later advertising that featured Qantas and the stadium created further confusion as to who the official Olympic sponsor actually was. Pictures in advertising placed Qantas at Stadium Australia during the Olympic competition; that association is exactly what the ambusher was seeking to achieve. It is easy to understand why event organizers have begun to demand clean stadia devoid of any signage as a condition for staging their events in a particular city, stadium, or arena.

A tactic that was a recent source of controversy is to encourage the *wearing of clothing at an event when that clothing represents a company that is not a sponsor*. Nonsponsors often give free T-shirts to fans in the hope that they will wear them to the event. In addition to clothing, the ambush strategy may call for the distribution of flags, signs, or other items that display the logo of a nonsponsor. Ambushers have been known to orchestrate the display of their brand names and logos by, in effect, hiring *fans* to wear their shirts and wave their flags. The controversy arises when a fan is confronted and the offending items are confiscated. What the organizers perceive as an ambush marketing strategy may simply be a fan's decision. Should a fan wearing a Heineken T-shirt to an event where Budweiser is the sponsor be subject to having clothing confiscated or perhaps being denied admission to the event?

When to Ambush

The previous sections explained the concept of ambush marketing, the rationale for ambushing, and the ways in which the strategy can be implemented. The final question concerns when it represents an effective strategy.

WHEN SHOULD AMBUSH MARKETING BE CONSIDERED?

6.1

- When a firm is doing a poor job supporting its official sponsorship.
- When there is a good fit with the target market.
- When adequate resources are available.
- When there is companywide support for the strategy.
- When it does not conflict with the ambusher's existing sponsorships.
- When the ambusher is prepared for controversy.
- When it is aware of the legal restrictions.

> Ambush marketing is most effective when the official sponsor is doing a poor job of reinforcing its relationship via an effective integrated marketing communications plan.

As a point of reference, it is important to remember that ambush marketing is most effective when the official sponsor is doing a poor job of reinforcing its relationship via an effective integrated marketing communications plan. Although this is a key consideration, there are several other issues that help the prospective ambusher identify potential opportunities. These considerations are summarized in Box 6.1.

Some Examples of Ambush Marketing

While ambush marketing happens with all types of properties ranging from small, local festivals to major entertainment events, there is no doubt that the most aggressive activities take place when the stakes are the highest. Many marketers choose to ambush because the cost of sponsoring major events is so high. Or perhaps they are given no alternative except to ambush because a competitor aligned with the event has category exclusivity. As a result, ambush marketing activities take place every day. The following examples illustrate the efforts of ambush marketers across the globe.

Sydney Olympics: Official Sponsor, Nike; Ambusher, adidas

After several years of ambushing the Olympics and its sponsors, Nike finally signed on as an official sponsor. It also had another vested interest in that it sponsored one of Australia's star athletes, Cathy Freeman.

The adidas ambush strategy included hospitality and media centers that made adidas-backed athletes available to the press. Although these events were staged at sites away from the official Olympic venues, they were well covered by the various international media. Adidas also sponsored another sensational Australian athlete, swimmer Ian Thorpe. When receiving one of his gold medals, Thorpe obscured the Nike logo on his official team uniform by draping the Australian flag over his shoulders.

Sydney Olympics: Official Sponsor, Foster's Beer; Ambusher, Toohey's New Beer

Foster's supported its sponsorship by participating in athlete gatherings and corporate parties that were popular with the media. Free beer was distributed to the attendees, especially to those who were about to be photographed.

The ambush strategy by Toohey's actually ended up in court. Its advertising campaign included the tag line that it was the "beer of choice at Stadium Australia." Toohey's was using its sponsorship of the stadium as an opportunity to align itself with the Olympics. The court ruling required Toohey's TV advertising to include the disclaimer that it was not an Olympic sponsor. It is doubtful that this disclaimer did much to dispel any misconception that Toohey's was a legitimate sponsor. After all, how many people, especially sports fans in local bars, actually read the small print?

National Hockey League: Official Sponsor, Coca-Cola; Ambusher, Pepsi-Cola

Coca-Cola was the official soft drink of the NHL, the most popular sport in Canada. This relationship provided Coca-Cola with pouring rights at each of the Canadian arenas as well as the ability to utilize the logos of the NHL and its teams. For this, Coca-Cola paid the NHL some $2.6 million.

The principal element of Pepsi's ambush strategy was a contest that consisted of two components: the "Diet Pepsi $4,000,000 Pro Hockey Playoff Pool" and the "Pepsi Shoot and Score Pro Hockey Draft." Note the absence of any NHL trademarks. Literature distributed by Pepsi stated that Pepsi was not associated with the NHL, any NHL teams, or any other NHL affiliates. One of Pepsi's TV spokespersons was Don Cherry, a former NHL coach and a popular hockey commentator on the games broadcast by the Canadian Broadcasting Company. While the contest pieces named Canadian cities such as Montreal and Toronto, they did not use the team trademarks. In other words, Pepsi referred to Toronto, but not the Toronto Maple Leafs. Since Coca-Cola's contract with the NHL did not prohibit its competitors from advertising during TV broadcasts, Pepsi incorporated it as part of its ambush strategy. Advertising for the contest was aired during the playoff games, and the ads utilized a setting that featured a hockey team's dressing room. Pepsi also sponsored "Coach's Corner," a part of the game broadcast that featured Don Cherry.

Prizes were won when the game piece identified both the team that won and the number of games required to complete the best-of-seven playoff series. There was no mistaking the fact that winning was based upon NHL outcomes. And Don Cherry's relationship did nothing to dispel consumer misperceptions that Pepsi was affiliated with the NHL. In response to criticism and a court case (won by Pepsi), Pepsi acknowledged using aggressive but legitimate marketing tactics. Such is the basic premise of ambush marketing.

Major League Baseball All-Star Game: Official Sponsor, Coca-Cola; Ambusher, Pepsi-Cola

The setting for this event was ideal: Atlanta, the home of the international headquarters for Coca-Cola. The sponsor was looking to baseball in an effort to reach a market segment comprised of young kids through college-aged adults. Coca-Cola had significant signage at the game's venue, Turner Field. It also had pouring rights for the stadium.

Pepsi was a sponsor of MLB, but not the All-Star game or Turner Field. One of the ambush tactics Pepsi used was to fly the "Pepsi balloon" over the stadium during an official competition (Home Run Derby) staged the evening prior to the game itself.

New Zealand Olympic Association: Ambusher, Telecom New Zealand

Even when there is no direct competitor to be targeted with ambush marketing tactics, the strategy can still be effective when ambushing the event or property itself. Virtually every Olympic Association in every competing country has its own set of sponsors. The New Zealand Olympic Association (NZOA) is no different. Sponsorship rights conveyed by these national organizations typically provide some ability to use Olympic trademarks in

FIGURE 6.1
Official NZOA Logo
in PowerAde Ad

promotions in their home countries. In a patriotic, sporting country such as New Zealand, this level of sponsorship can be very effective.

Telecom New Zealand is the primary provider of land-based telecommunications services in New Zealand. It is also involved in a number of sponsorships throughout the country, so nobody would be surprised to see its name associated with any major event. For a unique ambush strategy directed at NZOA, the telephone company recognized that the use of *rings* created a novel opportunity: The most recognizable Olympic symbol is the set of five interlocking rings; the most basic aspect of a telephone is that it rings. Telecom New Zealand combined these two concepts to create a print ad that was used within its domestic market. The ambush ad featured the word "Ring" five times with each word printed in a different color. The colors corresponded to those of the five interlocking rings in the IOC logo. By arranging them in the appropriate order, with three "rings" set over two "rings", the ad became a parody of the actual Olympic logo. If those who saw the ad simply viewed it as a creative variation of the Olympic rings, then the ad served as an effective ambushing tool. It caused consumers to incorrectly associate Telecom New Zealand with the Olympic Games. It is this type of confusion that ambushers seek to create.

National Olympic organizations such as the NZOA can use the interlocking rings logo of the IOC. The variation for New Zealand was the incorporation of a silver fern, a symbol used with many of the country's national teams. This logo was featured in the ad for official sponsor PowerAde; see Figure 6.1. Note that the ad provides collateral support for PowerAde's sponsorship of the NZOA even though in was in the game-day program for the local (Waikato, NZ) rugby team, the Chiefs. When compared with the ambushing ad, it is evident that both have a row of three rings on top of a row of two rings. The colors associated with each ring are identical. The Telecom New Zealand ad stated that "with the Telecom mobile, you can take your own phone to the Olympics."[14] Although New Zealand courts ruled the actions legal, the company was accused by many of engaging in parasitic marketing.

Cabot 500 Anniversary Celebration: Official Sponsor, Labatt Breweries; Ambusher, Molson Breweries

Even relatively small regional events and their sponsors can be the targets of ambush marketing campaigns. Labatt's Beer was named an official sponsor of this Canadian event. The company made a sizable investment in the development of Cabot lager beer. Other promotions connecting the sponsor and the sponsee were used as well.

Molson's ambushing campaign was simple. The company ran print ads throughout the province of Newfoundland proclaiming its Black Horse Beer as the "unofficial brew of Cabot's crew." As should always be the case with ambush marketing efforts, Molson was careful not to infringe upon any protected trademarks or logos that might have resulted in legal restraints and penalties.

Protection from Ambush Marketers

Since ambush marketing is legal in most countries, the process of restraining ambushers and protecting sponsors is difficult. However, there are certain precautions and techniques that can be used to reduce the opportunities to ambush and to reduce the effectiveness of those campaigns. The origination of these precautions and techniques may be the sponsor, the sponsee, or a variety of government initiatives.

> If a sponsor understands how to ambush, then it can better assess its own vulnerability.

The first thing that the sponsor should do is *learn how to ambush*. If a sponsor understands how to ambush, then it can better assess its own vulnerability. The ability to envision how it could be ambushed should help the sponsor develop a more effective strategy to counter the efforts of ambushers. So some experts recommend that every sponsor should develop a plan to ambush itself.[15] Once the marketer understands the tactics used, it can then implement strategies designed to prevent them.

> Leveraging refers to the use of a variety of strategic initiatives that are designed to support the sponsorship.

The most important tool that can be used is primarily the responsibility of the sponsor. Every sponsorship must be effectively leveraged. *Leveraging* refers to the use of a variety of strategic initiatives that are designed to support the sponsorship and reinforce the public's awareness of the official relationship between the sponsor and the event or property to which the rights fees have been paid. This includes efforts directed toward both the consumers and the members of the channel of distribution. Sponsors should not underestimate the importance of leveraging. Given its importance, a comprehensive discussion of leveraging issues is provided in the next chapter.

Another prevention strategy is to limit a nonsponsors' ability to advertise in close proximity to the event venue. This advertising could take many forms. The easiest to control is the prohibition of advertising by anyone other than sponsors in the event venue itself. This concept has been referred to as the clean-stadium strategy. The second strategy is to limit the ability of nonsponsors from having any display of signage within a predetermined distance of the venue.

A *clean stadium* is void of any advertisements, signage, or displays of trademarks owned by any nonsponsor. Logos may need to be removed from the playing field or scoreboard. It may even include logos at concession areas or in luxury suites. There have been cases where stadium managers were directed to remove TVs or any brand identification of the TVs in suites and concession areas. In fact, it was the inability of the New Zealand Rugby Football Union (NZRFU) to assure clean stadia that reportedly led to the International Rugby Board's decision to pull the World Cup games that were scheduled for New Zealand venues and relocate them to clean stadia in Australia.

The idea of a clean stadium has been extended beyond the limits of the stadium grounds. In some cases, event organizers will mandate that no unauthorized advertising can take place within some established distance of the venue. This can include freestanding signs, signs at area stores and markets, signs painted on buildings, billboards, and even airborne displays. This strategy is difficult to implement without governmental support in the form of laws. For instance, the Atlanta Olympics received protection by the implementation of flight restrictions that limited the ability of general aviation aircraft to engage in any airborne ambushing activity. In 1997, the IOC instituted new rules that require that any city bidding for the Olympic Games must acquire the rights to all advertising space within its city limits for the month during which the Games take place. This includes all billboards, posters, advertising on mass transit vehicles, and all paintings on buildings. The estimated cost of satisfying these requirements on the part of the Athens Olympics Organizing Committee was some $10 million; however, it is generally believed that the resultant limitations on ambushing activity will make official Olympic sponsorships more valuable.[16]

Nike's prior ambushing strategy that used billboards caused organizers of the Salt Lake City Winter Olympics to consider methods to limit their ability to ambush. The result was an agreement for the organizers to secure the rights to many of the existing billboards along 70 miles of roadway through the city; these billboards were reserved for official sponsors. Besides the IOC, organizations such as the NFL and the National Collegiate Athletics Association (NCAA) have implemented similar strategies designed to restrict advertising in areas in close proximity to their events.

Efforts should be made by event organizers to *establish more control over advertising* during the TV broadcast of the event. This includes both the regularly televised advertising that we all recognize as such and the less understood tactic of virtual advertising.

Efforts to limit traditional advertising can be challenging. Broadcast networks pay large sums of money for the rights to televise popular events. They recoup these costs and seek to earn a profit by selling time to advertisers. In some cases, the broadcast is completely under the control of the event organizers. In other cases, the organizers attempt to implement restrictions that limit ambush opportunities without adversely impacting the revenue earned by the broadcaster.

Event organizers can control the advertising by one of three methods. The first is the concept of a *time-buy*. In these situations, the organizer purchases a specified block of time from the broadcaster. That block of time is under the complete control of its purchaser. The final programming will consist of the event and its attendant commercials as determined by the organizer, not the broadcaster. It is then the responsibility of the event organizer to sell advertising time in order to create a revenue stream. Ownership of the time period is crucial in regard to ambush marketing. As the owner, the organizer can control who is and who is not allowed to advertise during the broadcast. Any potential advertiser that might represent an ambushing risk will be denied access to the broadcast. The time-buy strategy is often employed for minor sports that do not generate large TV ratings; however, it is less applicable for major sports and entertainment events.

The second way in which the organizer can control the advertising is by contractually *limiting the broadcaster's ability to sell advertising time* to companies deemed unacceptable. Contracts with this restriction are generally limited to highly desirable events such as the Masters Golf Tournament, the Super Bowl, and the World Cup of Soccer. A concern is that the broadcaster may view such a policy as an intrusion that limits its ability to earn a profit. In many cases, however, the space is initially provided to sponsors on a right-of-first-refusal basis. They can purchase time, thereby leveraging their sponsorship while preventing ambushers from buying in. If sponsors fail to purchase their reserved time, then it becomes available to other marketers and may enable the ambusher to gain access to the broadcast. Sponsors must be willing to spend additional money to leverage their sponsorship rights.

Another anti-ambushing initiative is a *restriction on the use of virtual advertising* by the broadcaster. Virtual advertising is the computer-generated imagery that appears as signs on TV broadcasts. Sometimes referred to as virtual signage, these images exist only on the broadcast; they are not physically present at the venue. Because they are electronically generated, virtual signage can be superimposed anywhere there is a void. Some new stadia have even been designed and constructed so as to maximize the applications of virtual advertising. Broadcasters could place ads for ambushers on the field of play or on structures such as signs and scoreboards. As it relates to ambush marketing, the greater concern is that existing signage for a sponsor could be supplanted by virtual signage for the ambusher. While fans at the stadium would see the sponsor's sign, those watching at home would see the ambusher's sign. To prevent this type of ambush effort, event organizers have begun to include restrictions against virtual advertising in the contracts granting broadcast rights.

A strategy used with greater frequency today is one that will inevitably alienate many of the participants. Events such as the World Cup of Cricket and the World Cup of Rugby have begun to *limit the ability of teams and players to endorse brands that are not officially associated with their events.*

The International Cricket Council (ICC) has required players to sign an agreement not to endorse any products that might be perceived as rivals of any ICC sponsor. This agreement includes a period prior to and after the completion of the competition in addition to the period during which the actual competition takes place.[17] However, players will likely see this strategy as inhibiting their ability to supplement their income with endorsement opportunities.

> The International Cricket Council (ICC) has required players to sign an agreement not to endorse any products that might be perceived as rivals of any ICC sponsor.

Similarly, the Rugby World Cup organizers imposed rules that prohibit players from wearing clothing not provided by the event's official sponsor. O_2 is an official sponsor of the national teams from England, Ireland, Wales, and Scotland. The clothing provided by the team sponsor was not allowed to be worn on the playing field or at the practice facilities during the event period. It was reported that even leisure clothing provided to the English team could not be worn when the team traveled between matches from one location to another.[18] This prohibition may also be applied to sponsors other than clothing manufacturers. One sponsor of the Scottish Rugby Union is Famous Grouse (Scotch whisky). Reportedly, it considered requesting a partial refund of its sponsorship fees because it felt deprived of one of the important benefits provided under the terms of that sponsorship.

The Rugby World Cup also requires all players to convey all rights to their image to the event organizers.[19] The net effect of this strategy is that the organizer controls the ability to use photos of the players in advertisements that it, the organizer, chooses.

Many experts believe that public relations and advertising should be used to *educate consumers*. The event organizer should publicize its sponsors and express appreciation for their role in staging the event. Figure 6.2 provides an example of a print ad that was used by the South African Rugby Football Union to educate fans while acknowledging each of its principle sponsors and suppliers.

Some also believe that ambushers should be identified in an effort to embarrass them in the eyes of the public. Although few would reject the idea that positive PR that identifies and supports event sponsors can be effective, the tactic of using negative PR in an effort to shame ambushers is of dubious value. Since consumers are not really turned off by ambush marketing, identifying the ambushers is likely to have little or no impact on consumer attitudes. So educate in a positive way. Identify the sponsors and inform the consumers of the role that sponsors play in helping to stage the event and in providing entertainment opportunities for the public. If it is a cause-related marketing event, publicize the positive aspects for the beneficiary. Help the sponsors in their quest to develop recognition of the relationship between themselves and the sponsored property. Stress any benefits gained by the target markets.

> Identifying the ambushers is likely to have little or no impact on consumer attitudes.

FIGURE 6.2
Ad Used to Educate
Fans and Identify
Sponsors

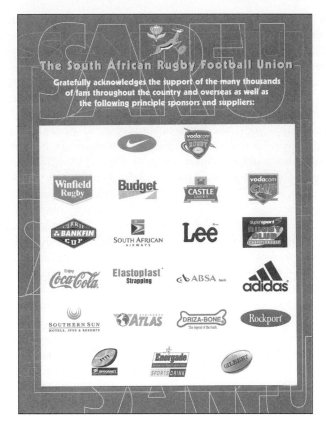

Ambush marketing efforts must continuously be identified by both the sponsor and the sponsee. Many events have begun active *surveillance programs;* these programs are not solely the responsibility of the sponsor. For example, the Detroit Red Wings use student interns to drive around the metropolitan Detroit area in an effort to identify ambush marketing efforts as well as vendors who are selling unlicensed merchandise. The term *ambush police* has been applied to these scouts. According to the Sydney Olympics brand protection manager, a team of 50 ambush police found only isolated instances of ambushing at the Olympic venues.[20]

For the Atlanta Olympics in 1996, "a dedicated task force" was "assigned to continuous surveillance."[21] At Wimbledon, officials of the Lawn Tennis Championships reportedly confiscated thousands of hats and signs bearing the names and logos of brands that were not official sponsors of the tournament.[22] A similar strategy was used by the World Cup of Cricket in South Africa. Signs, clothing, and towels distributed to spectators by ambush marketers were confiscated by the ambush police. When using this approach, care must be taken to avoid overreacting to individuals. The ICC was strongly criticized for acting too aggressively and expelling a fan who had brought a can of Coca-Cola to a game when Pepsi-Cola was the official sponsor. The ambush police must be able to differentiate between actual ambush marketing efforts and individual consumer actions. Furthermore, they must be able to legally justify any actions taken that directly impact fan choice and fan behavior.

Recently, organizers have recognized that less can be more and have thus tried to *limit the number of sponsorships to a manageable level*. As was noted earlier, FIFA has indicated an intention to reduce the number of official sponsors of the World Cup of Soccer from its level of 15 in 2006 to a more manageable level of 6 for the 2010 cycle. More sponsors can lead to more confusion, and more confusion opens the door to effective ambush marketing efforts. The strategy is designed to convince prospects that fewer sponsors will make their sponsorships more valuable. Event organizers must be able to acquire the needed sponsorship revenue with a smaller base of partners, a requirement that obviously places upward pressure on the price of the opportunities that are available. But if prospects are convinced that they will be less vulnerable to ambushers, then their perspective of the value of the sponsorship should change accordingly.

Earlier in this book, there was a discussion of pass-along rights for sponsors. It addressed the ability of a sponsor to transfer some of the benefits of its sponsorship to a third party that will likely share the costs associated with the official sponsor's rights. In some cases, event organizers have chosen to *prohibit the pass-along strategy* for fear that the entity that receives the transferred rights could use them to engage in ambush marketing. For example, consider a situation where a cola producer sponsors an event. If the cola producer can pass along its benefits to a fast-food chain that sells its brands of cola, then the fast-food restaurant might be able to use event logos in advertising and on packaging involving the cola. The net effect could be that consumers view the fast-food restaurant as a sponsor, a perception that is particularly problematic if another fast-food restaurant is an official sponsor. So while granting pass-along rights may be viewed favorably by some sponsors, the potential for abuse must be considered by property owners and event organizers.

The property or event could *incorporate the sponsor's name*. The Volvo Ocean Race leaves little room for a competitor to ambush Volvo. College football bowl games in the United States routinely incorporate a title sponsor; consider the Nokia Sugar Bowl and the FedEx Orange Bowl. In Australia, the names of the men's and women's professional basketball teams once incorporated their sponsors' names within their team moniker. Figure 6.3 shows a sign that references the teams' sponsors, Coca-Cola and Sega.

This strategy is fairly effective in those circumstances where it can be employed. One concern is that the sponsors' names are often routinely omitted in media reports or during the broadcast. For example, some Australian broadcasting concerns take a strong stance against the acknowledgment of these corporate relationships as well as stadia that are named after a corporate entity.

FIGURE 6.3
Incorporating the Corporate Sponsor's Name with the Team's Name

More recently, a number of *legal restrictions* have been implemented. Of course, the event organizers must be able to convince the various governmental bodies that protective laws are in their own best interest, otherwise it is difficult to have any beneficial legislation passed. The typical argument is that the event will benefit the local economy, and without the regulations being sought by the organizers, the event will not be staged in their city. A second concern is that laws that are enforceable in one location are not enforceable in others. For example, the laws passed to protect the Olympics in Sydney did not apply for future summer games in Athens, Beijing, or London. As a result, organizers are constantly seeking the institution of new sets of laws in new cities and countries.

Laws that provide significant protection are those that address the ability to protect trademarks and logos. While there is no universal law and enforcement of existing laws is not always vigorous, most developed countries seek to provide some measure of protection for an organization's trademarks and registered logos. Two recent efforts to strengthen existing laws and further protect events and sponsors from the unauthorized use of their trademarks and logos are associated with the Sydney 2000 and the Beijing 2008 Olympics.

The Sydney 2000 Games (Indicia and Images Protection) Act was passed in 1996 to strengthen an act passed only two years earlier. It specifically addressed logos owned by the IOC (such as the Olympic torch) and others owned by the Sydney Organizing Committee of the Olympic Games (such as Olympic mascots Syd, Olly, and Milly). This additional protection was a requirement imposed on the Australian government as a condition for being awarded the rights to stage the Games. It is noteworthy to acknowledge that laws such as these truly address issues of piracy more so than ambush marketing per se. Although legislation can protect piracy, freedom of expression makes it difficult to create rules whereby ambush marketing is illegal.

Recently, the IOC imposed similar requirements on China in relation to the 2008 Olympics and London for the 2012 Games. China has a long history of counterfeit products and trademark infringements, so the IOC and its continuing sponsors were rightfully concerned. Separate laws were passed by the city of Beijing and the Chinese national government. The laws that took effect in 2003 provide broad protection for the Olympics' intellectual property rights. They provide for an array of penalties, including confiscation, seizure of cash resources, and fines. Furthermore, criminal charges are applicable if the efforts involve fraudulent activities.[23] Legitimate rights-holders can also seek damages from violators whose efforts serve to diminish the value of their intellectual properties, namely trademarks and logos. A new set of more stringent laws in England is already in the formative stage even though the Games themselves are several years away.

In South Africa, perhaps the most stringent set of laws ever to address ambush marketing was passed prior to the World Cup of Cricket held there in 2003. The legislation made it a criminal offense to engage in ambush marketing of any event. The designation as a criminal offense meant that violators could face lengthy jail sentences if convicted. The law even allowed for the confiscation of tickets if they were distributed as part of an ambush marketing campaign.[24] The key point that differentiates these laws from those of Sydney and Beijing is that they address common ambushing strategies, not just piracy.

FIFA has created its own legal team to immediately respond to efforts to ambush its events. According to officials of the organization, the problem can be resolved with a simple phone call to the violator. However, FIFA is prepared to initiate legal action if that is deemed to be the only way to resolve the conflict.

As global organizations such as the IOC, FIFA, and the International Cricket Council gain more power, and as economic rewards for hosting their premier events continue to escalate, we can expect to see more pressure exerted on governments with the result being the passage of new laws that further restrict ambush marketing activities, even those activities that were previously legal. Box 6.2 summarizes the most common measures taken in the effort to prevent sponsors and properties from being ambushed.

Are Preventative Measures Effective?

No event is immune to ambush marketing. Events and sponsors will continue to be ambushed, especially in light of the ever-increasing rights fees required from sponsors. Event organizers and their sponsors jointly bear the burden of implementing safeguards that prevent ambush marketing attacks and protect their intellectual property rights. New legal restrictions are offering additional protection.

PREVENTATIVE MEASURES AGAINST AMBUSH MARKETERS

- Learn how to ambush
- Leverage the sponsorship
- Limit nonsponsors' ability to advertise
- Establish control over advertising during event broadcast
- Make a time-buy
- Limit broadcasters' ability to sell time
- Prohibit virtual advertising
- Limit participants' ability to endorse brands of nonsponsors
- Educate consumers
- Provide positive PR for sponsors
- Provide negative PR to shame ambushers
- Surveillance programs
- Limit number of sponsorships to a manageable number
- Prohibit pass-along strategy
- Incorporate sponsor's name
- Legal restrictions

Some will argue that ambush marketing is simply a way for an astute marketer to neutralize an advantage held by a competitor or to gain its own advantage in the marketplace. There are numerous examples cited on the previous pages that document the effective use of ambush marketing by companies both large and small.

> It is difficult for a competitor to ambush when the public is aware of who the actual sponsor is.

Perhaps the key point made earlier was that property owners and sponsors need to learn how to ambush. Only then can they recognize their own vulnerability. When this vulnerability is scrutinized, then appropriate measures designed to protect the sponsor's investment by preventing ambush marketing can be implemented. Many of the techniques are effective, but even new laws will not completely insulate the sponsor and the sponsee from the renegade marketer. Therefore, no matter what other safeguards are put in place, the sponsor must engage in a planned leveraging campaign designed to support its sponsorship. It is difficult for a competitor to ambush when the public is aware of who the actual sponsor is.

Closing Capsule

A statement from Schlossberg's early book on sports marketing provides a starting point for the closing capsule. The advice offered was, "you've got to hit consumers over the head with your message of sponsorship, or don't do it." The rationale behind that statement is threefold:

- Sponsorship is most effective when consumers recognize the relationship.
- Ambush marketing efforts will negatively impact that recognition.
- Leveraging will help to reinforce it.[25]

Piracy represents illegal activities designed to unfairly associate a marketer with a property or event. Ambush or parasitic marketing represents an array of generally legal but questionable actions likewise designed to confuse fans and consumers. There are many ways in which ambush marketing can be implemented. Perhaps the best way to avoid it is for the property owners and the sponsors to learn how to ambush. Then they are better prepared to implement safeguards that will inhibit the effectiveness of ambush efforts.

It is important to understand that ambush marketing can be very effective, especially when preventative measures are not taken by the sponsors and sponsees. Likewise, it is important to understand that consumers are not alienated by ambush marketing, so ambushers seldom need to be concerned about consumer backlash. In a concerted effort to reduce the instances of ambush marketing, several of the major events have been successful in getting new anti-ambush laws passed. If public scorn is not forthcoming, perhaps significant fines and the threat of jail time will cause marketers to rethink their plans to ambush. Still, the best weapon to use against the ambush marketer is a well-conceived leveraging plan. The issue of leveraging is the focus of the next chapter.

Review Questions

1. Differentiate between ambush marketing and piracy.
2. What are the three conditions for identifying ambush marketing?
3. Support the statement that "ambush marketing works."
4. What are the six categories of ambush marketing strategies?
5. When should a company consider using ambush marketing?
6. What methods can an event or a sponsor use to protect itself from ambushers?
7. Why are more restrictions being placed on ambush marketers?
8. IBM is one of the official sponsors of the Masters Golf Tournament. Identify one of IBM's competitors and design an ambush plan that could be used by the competitor in an ambushing effort.
9. Put together a table. In the left column, list the things that make ambush marketing unethical. In the right column, list the reasons ambush marketing is considered an acceptable practice. Based on this assessment, do you think that ambush marketing is acceptable? Identify the two key points that influenced your opinion.

Endnotes

1. *IEG's Complete Guide to Sponsorship: Everything You Wanted to Know about Sponsorship* (Chicago: IEG, Inc., 1999), p. 42.
2. G. Ruffenach, "Olympic Sponsors Will Pay Atlanta Plenty for Exclusivity and Ambush Protection," *The Wall Street Journal,* June 4, 1992), pp. B1, B4.
3. P. Elliot and T. Singh, "Ambushing the Games?" October 13, 2002, www.sportbusiness.com/news/fandc?news_item_id=148935 (accessed October 13, 2005).
4. C. Pritchard, "Sydney's Ambushers Strike Gold," *Marketing Magazine* 105, no. 4 (November 6, 2000), p. 6.
5. H. Schlossberg, *Sports Marketing* (Cambridge, MA: Blackwell Publishers, Inc., 1996), pp. 44–45.
6. J. Davidson and J. McDonald, "Avoiding Surprise Results at the Olympic Games," *Managing Intellectual Property,* no. 115 (December–January 2002), p. 22.

7. M. Lyberger and L. McCarthy, "An Assessment of Consumer Knowledge, Interest in, and Perception of Ambush Marketing," *Sport Marketing Quarterly* 10, no. 2 (2001), pp.130–37.

8. S. Fullerton and D. Taylor, "A Comparison of New Zealand and American University Students' Views of Various Aspects of Sports Sponsorship," *The Challenge: Sport Management beyond 2000,* January 2000, pp. 20–21.

9. H. Dodge, S. Fullerton, D. Moore and D. Taylor, "A Study of American Consumer Attitudes toward Sponsorship," *Sport Management: Best Research and Innovative Practice,* November 2000, p. 27.

10. S. Townley, D. Harrington, and N. Couchman, "The Legal and Practical Prevention of Ambush Marketing in Sports," *Psychology and Marketing* 5, no. 4 (1998), pp. 333–48.

11. T. Meenaghan, "Ambush Marketing: Corporate Strategy and Consumer Reaction," *Psychology and Marketing* 15, no. 4 (1998), pp. 305–22.

12. Ibid.

13. Ibid.

14. J. Curthoys and C. Kendall, "Ambush Marketing and the Sydney 2000 Games (Indicia and Images) Protection Act," *Murdoch University Electronic Journal of Law,* 8, no. 2, (2001).

15. A. Grey and K. Skildum-Reid, *The Sponsor's Toolkit* (Sydney: McGraw-Hill Pty Ltd., 2001), pp. 165–66.

16. J. Curthoys and C. Kendall, "Ambush Marketing and the Sydney 2000 Games (Indicia and Images) Protection Act," *Murdoch University Electronic Journal of Law* 8, no. 2 (2001).

17. P. Elliott and T. Singh, "All Aboard the Brandwagon," October 30, 2002, www.sportbusiness.com/news/fandc?news_item_id=148934 (accessed October 13, 2005).

18. "England Face Loss after Ban on World Cup Sponsorship," *Guardian Newspaper,* April 22, 2003, www.buzzle.com/editorials/text4-22-2003-39424.asp (accessed December 8, 2003).

19. D. Barrand, "RWC Lays Its Own Ambush," October 6, 2003, www.sportbusiness.com/new/fandc?news_item_id=152704 (accessed October 13, 2005).

20. Pritchard, "Sydney's Ambushers Strike Gold."

21. Ruffenach, "Olympic Sponsors Will Pay Atlanta Plenty."

22. M. Kleinman, "Wimbledon Acts to Halt Unofficial Ambush Activity," *Marketing,* July 5, 2001, p. 1.

23. F. Mendel and C. Yijun, "Protecting Olympic Intellectual Property," *Chinese Law and Practice,* May 1, 2003, p. 1.

24. D. Barrand, "ICC Sets Its Own Ambush," December 9, 2002, www.sportbusiness.com/new/fandc?news_item_id=146913 (accessed October 13, 2005).

25. Schlossberg, *Sports Marketing,* p. 42.

CHAPTER SEVEN

Leveraging

Learning Objectives

- Learn why leveraging is so important.
- Develop an understanding of many leveraging strategies.
- Learn how firms have engaged in leveraging programs.
- Evaluate the need to hire an outside service provider.

Throughout the earlier chapters of this book, there was a recurring theme. Sponsorship is not a stand-alone technique. Rather, it is a component of a firm's integrated marketing communications (IMC) plan. The effective implementation of any sponsorship is impacted by the execution of an array of supporting activities. Marketers must understand that the concept of integration implies that the various elements of the promotional mix must be coordinated in a cohesive plan where each element complements the others. When sponsorship is included in the mix, the collateral promotion should be designed so as to reinforce the relationship between the sponsor and the sponsee. This process is referred to as leveraging. Most sponsors allocate significant resources beyond the sponsorship rights fees to leverage their sponsorships. An effective leveraging effort is one way, perhaps the best way, to combat the efforts of ambush marketers. The key issues of how a firm supports a sponsorship and how much it spends in doing so are addressed on the following pages.

Leveraging: The Concept and Rationale

Sponsorship has been described as a license to spend more money. The basis for this statement is that any sponsorship must be incorporated as part of the firm's integrated marketing communications plan. Thus, sponsorship is not a *stand-alone* activity.

> An effective leveraging effort is one way, perhaps the best way, to combat the efforts of ambush marketers.

To be effective, consumers must recognize the official link connecting the sponsor to the sponsee. This is especially true when there is evidence that the consumers' purchase behavior will favor the sponsors of athletes, teams, sports, or events with which they associate themselves or express admiration. Nike's involvement with Australian Olympic swimming champion Ian Thorpe, the adidas association with the New York Yankees and the New Zealand All Blacks, Nextel's sponsorship of the NASCAR auto racing series, and Coca-Cola's grassroots sponsorship of the Children's Miracle Network are all well conceived, but in order for these marketers to reap the benefits available, each sponsorship must be leveraged.

> Leverage may be defined as the strategic efforts that are designed to support and enhance the sponsorship.

Leverage may be defined as the strategic efforts that are designed to support and enhance the sponsorship. It has been referred to as *collateral support* because it represents activities not specifically included as part of the sponsorship. Thus, it represents an allocation of resources above and beyond the rights fees that are paid to the property owner. *Activation* is another term for this process. Most leveraging actions involve promotion, but other strategic elements may also be involved.

Leveraging activities generally start prior to the beginning of the sponsored event and continue for some time after the conclusion of the event. General Motors had an official involvement with the 2000 Sydney Olympics. The event itself lasted 17 days, whereas the GM leveraging program encompassed some 19 months, starting well before and ending shortly after the actual competition took place. The length of the leveraging program is partially dependent upon the scope of the event being sponsored. It is also a function of the original negotiations, because the sponsorship contract will typically specify the dates during which the sponsor can utilize its official designation and any proprietary trademarks or logos owned by the sponsored property. Although the most obvious critical period for leveraging is the period during the event, the sponsor must not overlook the importance of the pre- and postevent periods.

The pre-event period, especially for major events, is crucial. Ambush marketers will inevitably initiate their efforts prior to the start of an event in the effort to create the perception that they are affiliated with it. Official sponsors must anticipate these activities and initiate their own leveraging plan to combat the ambushers. It is also important to note that not all leveraging activities are initiated with efforts directed toward the final consumer. For example, the sponsor may be seeking to increase its presence on retailer shelves so that subsequent promotions that are directed toward consumers during the event are more effective. Since reallocations of shelf space do not happen instantaneously, the sponsor must initiate its leveraging activities early. Retailers are driven by the bottom line. They need to be convinced that the sponsorship will increase the demand for the sponsor's products and that the increase will translate into additional sales and profits for the retailer.

A License to Spend

The earlier statement that the commitment to a sponsorship is a license to spend more money is based upon the need to allocate additional resources to provide collateral support for the sponsorship. The question becomes, *How much more does a sponsor need to spend?* Unfortunately, there is no uniform answer to the question.

> The commitment to a sponsorship is a license to spend more money.

Some sponsors choose to spend nothing on leveraging activities despite evidence that there is a meaningful relationship between leveraging activities and results.[1] Recent research reported by Performance Research and the IEG indicated that 23 percent of the sponsors they surveyed spent nothing on leveraging activities. The research went on to report that 46 percent matched their rights fees with a comparable amount devoted to leveraging. On average, the typical sponsorship involved some $1.30 being spent on leveraging activities for every dollar spent on rights fees. Figure 7.1 summarizes the results of this study conducted over the period from 2001 through 2004.[2]

While the IEG report indicates that some 7 percent of those interviewed spent at least four times as much on leveraging as they did on rights fees, there are reports of companies greatly exceeding that ratio. Figures as high as 19-to-1 have been reported for premier events. A range of zero to 19 times the amount spent on rights fees is hardly an answer to the question of how much to spend. Industry convention is that the leveraging budget should at least equal the cost of the rights fees.[3] So if a company spends $40 million to

FIGURE 7.1
Leveraging/Spending Ratios

Source: IEG, Inc. Reprinted with permission.

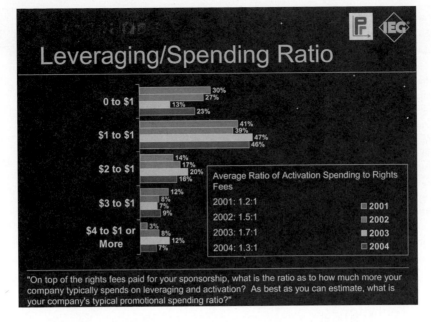

sponsor the World Cup of Soccer, it should be prepared to invest another $40 in leveraging activities. Thus, a $40 million sponsorship evolves into a $80 million sponsorship plan.

> Industry convention is that the leveraging budget should at least equal the cost of the rights fees.

Companies that spend nothing on leveraging activities will likely fail to maximize the potential benefits of their sponsorship simply because consumers will fail to recognize their association with the property. Another problem is that it makes the sponsor vulnerable to ambush marketing efforts. Given that sponsors must leverage, the next relevant question is, *What is the minimum expenditure that the sponsor should consider?* While many experts argue that a three-to-one ratio will produce the maximum value, many will tell you that a one-to-one ratio is the bare minimum. Even at this level of spending, a $40 million sponsorship becomes a $80 million program. Hence, we see the basis for the statement that buying a sponsorship is a license to spend more money. If the sponsorship fails to meet expectations, the first place for the sponsor to look is at itself. Did it do an effective job of leveraging?

> If the sponsorship fails to meet expectations, the first place for the sponsor to look is at itself; did it do an effective job of leveraging?

One note of caution is needed at this point. It is not just about spending money; rather, it is about spending it wisely. The collateral support is just that—support. The leveraging efforts need to focus on the desire to reinforce the awareness of the relationship between the sponsor and the sponsee. When the Wendy's success in its ambushing efforts directed at McDonald's is scrutinized, the finger of blame is often pointed at McDonald's. While McDonald's spent a lot of money advertising during and around the Olympics broadcast, much of the advertising featured its products. Advertising featuring a Big Mac did nothing to reinforce the company's relationship with the Olympics in the minds of consumers.

There are many techniques that can be used to leverage a sponsorship. The next section of this chapter identifies a variety of leveraging techniques that are designed to provide the required support.

LEVERAGING TECHNIQUES 7.1

- Theme-based advertising (general media)
- Advertising during broadcast of event
- Advertising in the event program
- Packaging
- Distribution of free products or premiums
- Provision of prizes
- Point-of-sale display
- Push strategies directed at retailers
- Consumer sales overlay
- Cross-promotion with co-sponsors
- Affinity programs
- Web tie-ins

Leveraging Techniques

There are several approaches to the development of a focused leveraging program. These are summarized in Box 7.1.

Theme-Based Advertising

When utilizing this technique, the objective is to create advertisements that reflect the character of the event being sponsored. If it is soccer, use soccer themes and soccer players. If the event is a concert, use images and sounds that are directly attributable to the performers. Above all, keep it consistent with the target market. The advertising should be placed in electronic and print media that reach consumers who are potential purchasers of the sponsor's products and who are likely to support the event or property being sponsored. Note that theme-based advertising does not need to be broadcast during the event itself. The common theme presented should intensify the relationship between the sponsor and event in such a way that consumers recognize the sponsor and are more favorably predisposed to purchase its products. The decision by adidas to air TV advertisements featuring soccer themes and soccer players before, during, and after the World Cup of Soccer is an example of theme-based advertising. Figure 7.2 provides an example of this type of theme-based advertisement.

Advertising during the Broadcast of the Event

Many sponsored properties are broadcast on free-to-air, premium, or pay-per-view television. In some cases, the commercial time is controlled by the event; this enables organizers to provide sponsors with protection via category exclusivity and the refusal to sell advertising time to competitors of the event's sponsors. However, in most cases the broadcast is controlled by the TV network, which has purchased the rights to the event. In those situations, there may be no protection from ambush marketers airing their advertisements. The sponsor is faced with the same decisions as all other marketers, including ambushers. How much, if any, advertising should be purchased for the broadcast?

Some marketers have chosen to air their typical commercials during the event. A few years ago, McDonald's attempt to leverage its Olympic sponsorship emphasized Big Macs and other products that were readily recognizable by their target markets. It spent a lot of money advertising during the Olympics but did little to reinforce its relationship with the IOC. As discussed earlier in this chapter, that made McDonald's vulnerable to an ambushing attack by Wendy's.

FIGURE 7.2   Example of Theme-Based Advertisement

More recently, McDonald's has modified its leveraging strategy. The commercials aired during the 2004 Olympics stressed the partnership. They also featured sports themes. This approach was much more effective than the company's earlier, more generic strategy.

Advertising in the Event Program

Many events produce and distribute a program. Golf tournaments distribute *pairings sheets* that provide attendees with information on the starting times for the players. *Programs* are sold at sports events; these programs provide information regarding the players, the teams, the leagues, and the event itself. Theatrical productions often provide a *playbill* that provides information regarding the performance and the performers free of charge to each patron. And a charity auction may provide advance information regarding the items to be sold. Virtually all of these materials have two things in common. They acknowledge their sponsors, and they sell advertising space. Another important factor is that attendees read them as they seek information.

When the consumer sees the ad combined with the acknowledgment of the sponsorship in the program and other components such as signage, it serves to reinforce the relationship. The PGA was the organizer for the 2004 Ryder Cup. On its official Web site, the PGA encouraged event sponsors to purchase advertising space in the program by stating that the sponsor's "involvement with the Ryder Cup matches can have even greater impact." The fact that on-course spectators and off-course collectors tend to purchase and keep the program as part of their memorabilia just adds to the value of the sponsors' advertising.[4]

Packaging

When the sponsored property owns recognizable trademarks and logos, a valuable leveraging tool is the incorporation of those symbols on the sponsor's packaging. These symbols can be used legally only with permission from the owner. Sponsors can negotiate the right to use them, which provides a decided advantage over ambush marketers. When used correctly, the consumer will see the association between the two parties. Because this strategy is both effective and inexpensive, it is a common leveraging technique. McDonald's cups and sacks have included the Olympic rings, Coca-Cola cans have incorporated the World Cup logos, and Nature Valley granola bars have included both the PGA and the U.S. National Ski Team logos on their packaging. Snickers (M&M Mars) incorporates the NFL logo and team logos on its specially packaged candy bars.

Distribution of Free Products or Premiums

This strategy may be part of a VIK commitment, or it may simply be an overt effort to leverage the sponsorship. There are two philosophies regarding this strategy. One is to *distribute the sponsor's products* free of charge via a channel of distribution that reaches the target markets. Absopure Water, a sponsor of University of Michigan athletics, passes out free cups of water at Michigan Stadium. It is a strategy that reaches more than 110,000 spectators at each home game. The Nature Valley granola bars are distributed free of charge at PGA shops in airports throughout the United States. This distribution strategy, coupled with the use of the PGA logo on the package, undoubtedly makes some consumers aware of Nature Valley's sponsorship with the PGA.

The second philosophy is the *distribution of premiums* that feature the sponsorship. For example, Chevrolet, a division of General Motors, was a sponsor of the NFL's Indianapolis Colts. As a leveraging strategy, it distributed free posters at the stadium. While these posters may be a part of game-day activity, fans may also take them home to display on their walls. But from a sponsor's perspective, they feature the sponsee while concurrently identifying the sponsor. Therefore, it can be an effective and relatively inexpensive leveraging technique. Hats, T-shirts, water bottles, and the ever-popular bobblehead doll are examples of premiums featuring the sponsors' names and other trademarks that are often distributed free of charge at sporting events.

Provision of Prizes

Event organizers often stage contests where ticket holders, entrants who respond to an advertisement, or those who register on the event Web site can win prizes. The sponsor often provides the prizes for the winners. In this way, the sponsor can leverage its relationship with the event while the event organizers are able to give away prizes at no cost to them. Southwest Airlines is a sponsor of the St. Louis Cardinals major league baseball team. Part of its arrangement with the team is to give free flights to lucky fans who have a winning seat number. Dunkin' Donuts is a sponsor of the Detroit Tigers baseball team. The company has an animated race displayed on the scoreboard. A doughnut, a bagel, and a cup of coffee each represent certain seating sections in the stadium. Fans cheer for their symbol as they race toward the finish line. Why the interest and cheering? Those holding tickets represented by the winner each receive a free doughnut or a $1.00 discount on their next purchase. This not only helps strengthen consumer recognition that Dunkin' Donuts is a sponsor, it also helps gets fans in their stores in the days following the game.

Point-of-Sale Display

While we think of POS display as cardboard posters, the advances in technology have recently provided new opportunities. A key aspect of this type of leveraging is that it will not happen unless retailers accept the presumption that it will help to increase their sales and profits. So part of the task here is to sell retailers on the idea that their willingness to display the sponsor's promotional materials will be mutually beneficial. The effort may also include appeals to the retailers to increase the sponsor's shelf space allocation or display the products and the POS materials in more desirable high-traffic locations within the store. Some of the new high-tech displays include interactive CD-ROM–based equipment. Using this technology, consumers may have the opportunity to simulate driving a race car or steering a snowboard down a mountain.

Whether it is high-tech or low-tech, the objective is the same. For example, adidas uses displays featuring many national soccer and rugby teams in sporting goods stores. Not only does it strengthen consumer recognition, it also creates a competitive advantage for adidas in countries like England (rugby) and Argentina (soccer) where there is great national pride associated with their teams.

Push Strategy for Retailers

Before discussing this concept, let's differentiate between push strategies and pull strategies. They basically refer to the focus of the promotional efforts. With a pull strategy, promotions are aimed at the final consumer. Free samples, discount coupons, and targeted advertising are all designed to influence an individual's purchase behavior. Conversely, push strategies are directed at the trade. In this case, trade refers to the wholesalers and retailers that help facilitate the flow of products from the manufacturer to the consumer.

In using push strategies, the sponsor may agree to reimburse retailers some or all of their expenses for advertising if they agree to feature the sponsor, the event, the products, and the retailer in their advertising. This type of agreement is generally referred to as *cooperative advertising*. The sponsor may agree to pay a retailer for increased shelf space during the leveraging period. The payment of this *slotting allowance* provides an incentive to the retailer while giving the sponsor greater exposure in the market. Another common strategy is a *guarantee of some level of profit for the retailer*. The agreement calls for the retailer to provide a designated space for the sponsor to display its POS materials and products. At the end of the promotional period, the retailer will calculate its profit from the sale of the sponsor's products over the contracted period. If they fail to meet or exceed the promised level, then the sponsor will make up the difference. If the profits exceed the specified amount, then both parties are happy and no further compensation is required.

Consumer Sales Overlays

Simply stated, this often-used strategy provides purchasers of the sponsor's products with an opportunity to purchase tickets to the sponsored event at a discount price. An example is the NBA's Detroit Pistons. Members of the American Automobile Association (AAA) have several opportunities during the season to purchase two tickets for the price of one. In this way, AAA is able to leverage its sponsorship of the popular NBA team and reinforce the public's awareness of that relationship.

Cross-Promotions with Co-Sponsors

A recurring theme throughout this book is the implementation of cross-promotional strategies. As noted earlier, some events have sponsors that can benefit via collaboration and the development of a joint marketing campaign. One recent example involved two sponsors for the U.S. Olympic team: Hilton Hotels and United Airlines. The opportunity to develop packages comprised of air travel and hotel accommodations are obvious. The awarding of bonus points for United Airlines' frequent-flier club and Hilton's frequent-guest program were also part of the joint campaign. For the leveraging to be effective, their promotions needed to include references regarding their sponsorship of the Olympic team.

FIGURE 7.3
Leveraging with Affinity-Based Credit Cards

One of the most unique leveraging programs to date involved collaboration between NASCAR and several of its sponsors. A mobile unit made stops at sponsor Wal-Mart stores during the race week in the 10 cities that hosted that week's race. These stops included premier locations such as Daytona and Indianapolis, two cities rich in motor sports tradition. The tour featured a car display and driving simulators. The activities and show cars were sponsored by a broad array of NASCAR sponsors, including Goodyear, Kodak, Nestlé, XM Satellite Radio, Stacker2, and Kingsford Charcoal. The ability to share the costs combined with the recognition achieved by being associated with *NASCAR on Tour* provided an excellent leveraging platform.[5]

Affinity Programs

Affinity programs have become an important tool in the development of relationship-based marketing. They are most commonly implemented with sponsorships of cause-related marketing campaigns and sports teams. The greatest potential for sponsors has proven to be for financial institutions, especially marketers in the credit, debit, and smart card industries. For example, Standard Bank is a sponsor of several cricket teams in South Africa. Its leveraging strategy includes the issuance of MasterCard credit cards that feature one of those teams, the Kaizer Chiefs. From a cause-related marketing perspective, Bank One issues a Visa card that supports its relationship with St. Jude Children's Research Hospital.

The issuers of these cards typically provide a small contribution to the organization, university, sports federation, or team featured on the card. They also often solicit applications at event venues where the applicants often receive an event-based incentive. For example, they might receive a T-shirt featuring the home team. Figure 7.3 illustrates a solicitation booth for an affinity-based credit card at an MLB stadium.

This technique reinforces the relationship between the sponsor and the sponsee. While doing this, it also helps to create an advantage that allows the sponsorship to improve the marketer's image and sales in the relevant target markets.

Web Tie-Ins

While one of the components sought in a sponsorship contract today is a link to the sponsor from the property's Web site, the sponsor should not ignore the opportunity to acknowledge a sponsorship and use the property's logos on its own Web site. This may or may not include a direct link to the sponsored property. Either way, it simultaneously places the sponsor and the sponsee in front of interested consumers.

The Internet can also be used as part of a direct marketing campaign. For example, the Web site for Vodafone in the United Kingdom incorporates links to the Manchester United soccer team, the Epsom Derby, F1's Team Ferrari, the English cricket team, and the "Life Saver Awards." On the same page, there are direct marketing appeals for Vodafone goods and services for U.K. residents. Figure 7.4 illustrates this component of the Vodafone Web site.

FIGURE 7.4
Vodafone Sponsorship Featuring Web Tie-Ins

Courtesy of Vodafone

An Overview of Leveraging Techniques

The list just covered reflects the major approaches used today in the task of leveraging a sponsorship. While comprehensive, it is by no means complete. There are many other techniques that can be used. Marketers need to be especially aware of push strategies that can be directed toward retailers. Other viable strategies include internal communications with employees, employee participation at the event, public relations opportunities, and efforts designed to build retail traffic.

> **Knowing how to leverage is as important to the sponsee as it is to the sponsor.**

The importance of leveraging is illustrated in the IEG's assessment that "a company will only realize the full value of the sponsored property when it is a central platform around which consumer, trade, employee, and media activities are built."[6] Moreover, knowing how to leverage is as important to the sponsee as it is to the sponsor. An organizer that can provide insight into the leveraging options available to a prospective sponsor is not only selling a sponsorship; it is also selling results based on a program. The survey of sponsors discussed earlier in this chapter indicated that 29 percent of the respondents considered this type of information to be very important.[7]

This section started with the statement that a sponsorship is a license to spend more money. While there is no consensus on how much should be spent, experts agree that it is asking too much to expect a sponsorship to stand alone without collateral support. The task for the sponsor is to decide how much to spend and what strategies to use.

Examples of Leveraging Programs

While the previous section provided many glimpses of leveraging programs, it did not provide any comprehensive examples to illustrate how sponsors often employ multiple approaches in the leveraging of their sponsorships. This section will provide a more comprehensive look at integrated marketing communications strategies designed to support sponsored properties and events.

Sponsor, Office Depot; Property, Zo's Summer Groove

The property is a local festival comprised of music, fine dining, basketball, and entertainment. The event supports organizations that deal with at-risk children. In the event's first six years, more than $2.9 million was raised to support these charitable and social organizations.

Office Depot became the title sponsor in 2003 and immediately announced the introduction of the Office Depot Zo's Summer Groove $50,000 Sweepstakes. Basketball enthusiasts in the area were invited to visit any of the 23 local Office Depot stores and receive free tickets to the Carnival Cruise Lines All-Star Basketball Game. This strategy of including a co-sponsor was designed to increase in-store traffic. At the game, two fans were randomly selected to compete in the contest at the halftime break. They were asked to guess prices of back-to-school items sold at Office Depot, with the winner given the opportunity to make a shot from midcourt for the $50,000 prize.

Sponsor, General Motors; Property, 1996 Olympics (Atlanta)

The property was the Olympics, one known for excellence and the spirit of fair play. It was held in the United States, the home country of General Motors. GM's sponsorship was not part of the TOP program; rather, it was a second-tier sponsorship that involved some $5 million in rights fees.

Since GM was not a TOP sponsor, it did not receive as many benefits as a top-level sponsor. There was no category exclusivity, and the right to use Olympic trademarks and logos was limited. There was basic advertising during the broadcast, and there were automobiles that officials were allowed to use. Additionally, the company introduced a 1996 Buick Olympic Regal automobile that was emblazoned with the Olympic logo.[8]

Sponsor, Visa; Property, National Football League

The NFL is the prime sports property in the United States. Television rights have sold for record amounts as TV ratings continue to be high. The culmination of the NFL season is the Super Bowl. The annual event will be broadcast to a global TV audience and draw close to 100 million viewers in the United States alone.

Visa is actively involved in an array of sports events across the world. This sports presence is exemplified by its sponsorship of the NFL. The leveraging campaign includes advertising during the regular season, the playoffs, and the Super Bowl game. Some of the ads are football-themed; others are more traditional appeals to consumers.

Visa and its member banks issue affinity cards sporting the logo of the cardholder's favorite team. In one promotion, anyone who used his or her Visa card at a supermarket was automatically entered in a sweepstakes that featured a free trip to the Super Bowl as the grand prize; other prizes were Visa gift cards with $500 in credit preloaded. Print advertising featuring Visa, the NFL, and the sweepstakes included a freestanding insert in major newspapers. The supermarket presence was enhanced by a POS display. A similar sweepstakes involved a group of sporting goods stores. A third contest was a strategic alliance with DirecTV, a satellite programming delivery service with rights to broadcast NFL games (sold for approximately $250 per season). This contest featured prizes such as a Super Bowl trip, Visa gift cards, and NFL jackets to winners who qualified by signing up for automatic bill payment. Additional support was provided both online and in the monthly statements mailed to DirecTV subscribers. Yet another contest was directed toward consumers who rode mass transit in New York City. Customers who paid for their MetroCard with their Visa were entered into a contest for a Super Bowl trip. The final leveraging activities included posters, player appearances, and discounts on officially licensed NFL merchandise.[9]

FIGURE 7.5
Leveraging a PGA
Sponsorship

Sponsor, Motorola; Property, National Football League

Motorola has a long history of marketing consumer electronics; more recently, it has moved into wireless communications. The company's sponsorship of the NFL's regular season was reported to cost some $20 million.[10]

Motorola's leveraging campaign emphasized TV advertising that featured NFL themes. There were advertisements that ran on the various networks during the regular season. In addition, advertising was also broadcast during the Super Bowl game. The company also staged a "watch, call, and win" promotion that featured the top prize of a trip to the Super Bowl. Finally, Motorola furnished the NFL with headsets for the coaches; these headsets prominently featured the Motorola brand name, which received significant TV exposure during shots of the activities on the sidelines.

Sponsor, Best Western International; Property, NASCAR

Best Western is the world's largest hotel chain, with some 4,100 hotels in 80 countries. It entered an agreement to become NASCAR's first-ever "official hotel." The sponsorship that began in 2004 is in force for a term of three years.

The planned leveraging activities for Best Western include a variety of promotional activities, contests, on-site hospitality, cross-promotions with co-sponsors, special NASCAR room rates, race ticket access, and the development of the travel industry's first affinity program created for NASCAR fans. The affinity card will provide its holders with a variety of NASCAR-based incentives, rewards, and merchandise. This sponsorship is viewed as a good fit as research indicates that NASCAR fans travel more than nonfans. It is also believed that fans will respond favorably to a contest that offers some lucky people the opportunity to meet driver Michael Waltrip while attending the NASCAR race of their choice.[11]

Sponsor, Nature Valley; Property, PGA Tour

Nature Valley's primary line is in the more-nutritious snack-food industry. Its granola bar is recognized as the official natural energy bar for the PGA tour. The company's leveraging was relatively simple. It involved the use of traditional ads in golf-oriented print media, and the PGA logo was prominently displayed on the product's packaging. Free samples of the product were made available at PGA retail shops, many of which are located at airports in the United States. It is believed that there is a great deal of similarity between golfers, air travelers, and purchasers of nutritious snack foods. Figure 7.5 provides an example of this leveraging effort.

Overview of the Examples

It is evident that leverage is an essential element of any sponsorship program. The array of examples and the comprehensive list of leveraging techniques provide evidence that there in no single way to implement a leveraging program. An important decision that the sponsor must make is whether the leveraging program should be developed in-house or whether outside agencies should play a role. The answer depends on the expertise in-house in regard to sponsorships in general, the sponsee in particular, and the market segments targeted by both the sponsor and the sponsee. That decision is often referred to as the *make-buy decision*.

> There in no single way to implement a leveraging program.

The Make-Buy Decision

According to the 2004 study by Performance Research and the IEG, 43 percent of the sponsors developed and implemented their own integrated marketing communications plan for the activization of their sponsorship program. This approach may be viable for some sponsors, but it is questionable for others. Large corporations with experience in sponsorship may have the expertise to develop (or make) their own leveraging program, whereas small companies may find this to be a difficult task.

When the decision is made to seek outside help with the process, the sponsor has a number of options. The most logical source, and the most often used, is an advertising agency. Advertising agencies understand the media; they understand target markets; they can help the sponsor make optimal use of its budget; and they can help place supporting ads in both broadcast and print media. The second most frequently used outside source is a public relations agency. It is likely that the sponsor has existing relationships with both an advertising agency and a public relations agency.

There are additional outside agencies from which the sponsor can seek valuable advice. These include the sponsee, an independent consultant, and the sponsorship agency/broker that sold it the sponsorship rights. In regard to independent consulting organizations, several have emerged within this industry. Figure 7.6 summarizes the research regarding sponsors' use of outside agencies in the task of developing leveraging programs.

FIGURE 7.6
Agency Use for Leveraging Support

Source: IEG, Inc. Reprinted with permission.

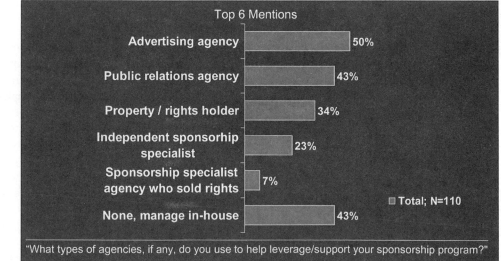

It is not unusual for the sponsor to plan some of the leveraging program while seeking insight from outside experts for other parts of the program. And since no single agency or expert knows everything, the sponsor may well call on two or more sources to assist in the development of an integrated marketing communications plan built around its sponsorship platform.

One of the larger companies from which sponsors can seek outside advice is Octagon Marketing. The consulting firm has considerable expertise in a variety of sports, including tennis, sailing, and rugby. Furthermore, it has a global presence, with offices in 60 cities representing 24 countries and each continent across the world. As evidence that even large multinational corporations can use outside expertise, IBM has recently expanded its relationship with Octagon. Octagon formulated the leveraging strategy for IBM's sponsorship of the French Open (tennis), and the agency is reevaluating IBM's current portfolio of sponsorships, including Wimbledon, and identifying new opportunities across Europe to strengthen the company's portfolio.[12] Similarly, Vodafone has retained the services of the GEM group to help develop the PR component of its sponsorship of Manchester United of the English Premier League. According to a GEM spokesperson, "the range of assets secured by Vodafone in their latest sponsorship deal with Manchester United are very exciting and we look forward to developing and implementing a global PR program to leverage these assets."[13]

| **Closing Capsule** | The closing capsule for this chapter begins much like the closing capsule for the previous chapter. If you are going to invest in sponsorship, you have to leverage it. Remember the statement that you either hit consumers over their heads with your sponsorship message, or you just should not buy into sponsorship at all. |

Leveraging is based on the acknowledgment that sponsorship is not a stand-alone promotional tool. Rather, it is one component of an integrated marketing communications plan than blends the sponsorship with coordinated decisions in the areas of advertising, personal selling, sales promotion, and public relations. These elements provide collateral support for the sponsorship with the primary objective of reinforcing awareness of the relationship between the sponsor and the sponsee in the consumer's mind. Done effectively, it will help the sponsor achieve its goals and attain an acceptable return on its sponsorship investment.

While leveraging focuses on promotion, other strategic initiatives can be utilized. For example, new themed products may be introduced. As part of its leveraging strategy, adidas developed a new rugby ball to support its relationship with the New Zealand Rugby Football Union. New channels of distribution might be used; consider a company that uses direct marketing via the Internet to sell its event-related clothing. It may well be that this channel is viable because a link to the sponsor's Web site is found on the sponsee's home page. In this way, promotional material supporting the sponsorship reaches consumers who otherwise would not have been aware of the relationship, much less considered purchasing the sponsor's products. The leveraging effort may incorporate special prices to fans and patrons of the sponsored property. Clearly, each element of the sponsor's marketing mix can play an instrumental role in its leveraging efforts.

Just as there are many ways to ambush, there are many ways to leverage. While ambush marketing will diminish the effectiveness and value of a sponsorship, leveraging is designed to strengthen it. It is important for all parties involved to understand the principles of leveraging. It is this knowledge that will help in the attainment of their goals.

Review Questions

1. What is meant by the statement that "buying a sponsorship is a license to spend"?

2. Why is theme-based advertising considered better than general advertising in the task of leveraging a sponsorship?

3. Identify 10 leveraging techniques.

4. Why do experts believe that leveraging is the most effective measure that can be taken to battle the efforts of ambush marketers?

5. What is meant by cross-promotion? Go to the IOC Web site and identify two sponsors that could benefit from a cross-promotion strategy. Give a brief explanation of one specific tactic they could employ.

6. Why is the Internet becoming more important for leveraging efforts? Identify a major event in your area; identify one prominent sponsor. Go to the event Web site; to what extent is the sponsor present on the Web site. Go to the sponsor's Web site. To what extent is the event noted on the sponsor's Web site?

7. Why is there no correct answer to the question, How much should be spent on leveraging activities?

8. Assume that your university has just signed a new contract to bring in Nokia as a sponsor of the school's athletic programs. Recommend three specific leveraging activities Nokia could use to strengthen awareness of that sponsorship among members of a key target market.

Endnotes

1. P. Quester and B. Thompson, "Advertising and Promotion Leverage on Arts Sponsorship Effectiveness," *Journal of Advertising Research* 41, no. 1 (January–February 2001), pp. 33–47.

2. IEG, "2004 IEG/Performance Research Study Highlights What Sponsors Want," 2004, www.performanceresearch.com/ieg_sponsor_survey.htm (accessed October 13, 2005).

3. Ibid.

4. "The Official 35th Ryder Cup Matches Journal," 2004, www.pga.rydercup/news_journal.html (accessed May 5, 2004).

5. H. Cassidy, "NASCAR, Wal-Mart Go Mobile: Women's Soccer Goes to Market," *Brandweek* 44, no. 24 (2003), p. 16.

6. *IEG's Complete Guide to Sponsorship: Everything You Wanted to Know about Sponsorship* (Chicago: IEG, Inc, 1999), pp. 1–42.

7. IEG, "2004 IEG/Performance Research Study Highlights What Sponsors Want."

8. S. Gelsi, "GM Leverages Olympic Link with Ring-Emblazoned Buick Regal, *Brandweek* 36, no. 37 (October 2, 1995), p. 8.

9. T. Lofton, "Visa Aims for the Uprights," *Brandweek* 40, no. 34 (July 1, 2000), p. 4.

10. T. Lofton, "Motorola Sets Watch-and-Win Promo Super Bowl Buy to Leverage NFL Tie," *Brandweek* 40, no. 34 (September 13, 1999), p. 4.

11. "Best Western to Become Official Hotel of NASCAR," November 3, 2003, www.sponsorship.com/scontent/4678.asp (accessed October 15, 2005).

12. D. Barrand, "IBM Hires Octagon for Sponsor Strategy," June 19, 2003, www.sportbusiness.com/news/index?news_item_id=151534 (accessed October 13, 2005).

13. C. Britcher, "Vodafone's GEM of a Deal," June 29, 2004, www.sportbusiness.com/news/index?newsItem_id=154993 (accessed October 13, 2005).

CHAPTER EIGHT

Developing and Selling the Sponsorship Proposal

Learning Objectives

- Learn what to do before attempting to sell.
- Experience the process of developing a proposal.
- Understand how negotiations often proceed.

Once the property owner has decided that new sponsors are needed, the next efforts are directed toward a series of steps designed to sell the plan to the prospective sponsor. The steps are classified into three categories: preliminary actions, proposal development, and selling the sponsorship.

Preliminary actions involve basic research that is used to gain insight into the identification of potential sponsors and key aspects about their business and customers. It provides the basis for the development of a comprehensive written sponsorship proposal that will be structured with a particular prospect in mind. The final step is that of meeting with the decision makers and selling the sponsorship. If done correctly, this series of steps will maximize the likelihood of converting a prospect into a sponsor.

Preliminary Actions

The initial task is that of *prospecting*. The objective of prospecting is to identify organizations that represent potential sponsors. This may be accomplished by exploring the newspapers, magazines, and the Internet to see which companies are sponsoring similar properties. Business and trade publications often provide insight into corporate plans, and this insight might provide a hint as to a marketer's receptiveness to the idea of sponsoring various properties and events. Some industries are more actively involved in sponsorship, so companies in those industries may be better prospects. Prospecting may be done via cold calls or direct mailings. Though conversion rates from the latter types of contacts are low, they can still be cost effective, especially for small grassroots types of events and organizations.

Once the prospects have been identified, the task turns to that of *gathering information about the prospects and their target markets*. The rationale behind this activity is that this information is needed for the development of an effective sponsorship proposal. Stated another way, it has been argued that sponsorships need to be *data driven*.[1] That need is addressed with this data collection process.

Sponsorships need to be data driven.

Effective marketing begins with an understanding of the needs of those in the marketplace. When the efforts involve one organization attempting to sell goods and services to another organization, the purchase decisions tend to be evaluated more intensely than when the targeted buyer is an individual consumer. Companies are unlikely to commit large sums of money and other resources based on a hunch or otherwise emotional decision. Therefore, the need for information has never been greater. Fortunately, the information has never been more readily available than it is today.

The sponsorship market today is witnessing a significant increase in demand; however, the supply of opportunities is growing even faster. As a result of this increase, prospective sponsors have more opportunities from which they can select. Since most sponsorships today focus on the bottom line, efforts to sell them must emphasize their ability to help the sponsor achieve its marketing objectives. It must be understood that the commitment of resources for a sponsorship is an investment that could alternatively be put to use in many different ways. Thus, the ability to help the sponsor achieve its objectives will enhance the ability to maximize the return on that investment.

> It is much easier to sell a high ROI than it is to sell a sign at a local stadium.

The idea of a data-driven sponsorship involves two key considerations. First, successful marketing is based upon the ability to help a customer resolve a problem. Thus, an effort to sell a sponsorship is greatly enhanced when its potential to resolve a specific problem is evident. To accomplish this, the sales efforts must exhibit an understanding of the prospect's likely marketing objectives. Only then can the sponsee do a good job of tailoring the proposal to address the needs of the prospect.

The second aspect of a data-driven sponsorship requires knowledge of the prospect's target markets. Research must be undertaken to identify the demographic and lifestyle characteristics of those target markets. An understanding of purchase behavior on the part of the consumers is also beneficial. Much of this information is readily available from secondary data sources, so the research does not generally require primary data collection such as consumer surveys. A key consideration for sponsorship is the match between the markets of the sponsee and the prospective sponsor. The ability to document this match cannot be overemphasized. It is this congruence and the resultant strategic linkage that allows the sponsorship to create a relationship where both entities prosper.

Once these preliminary actions have been completed, the task of developing a written proposal can proceed. The knowledge gained through these preliminary actions and the familiarity demonstrated in the proposal should serve to enhance the receptivity on the part of the prospect.[2]

The Sponsorship Proposal

The sponsorship proposal must be viewed from several perspectives. First, the proposal represents an effort to link the prospect with the event or property that is seeking a sponsorship commitment. As such, it may represent an effort to either acquire a new sponsor or to re-sign an existing sponsor to a new contract. Second, the proposal is a sales tool designed to convince the prospect that a mutually beneficial relationship will result from agreeing to its terms. Third, it provides a basis for negotiation. The prospect will review the proposal and assess its potential. In this regard, the document provides information that prospects can compare to other proposals and existing contracts. It is important to remember that many prospects receive hundreds, if not thousands, of sponsorship proposals each year. Finally, it provides a measure of the sponsee's understanding of the prospect's needs. A sponsorship proposal should not be developed with a one-size-fits-all mentality; rather, it should be tailored to the needs of the prospect. So to develop an attractive proposal, the property owner must have a sound understanding of the prospect's business, markets, and likely sponsorship objectives.

> The proposal is a sales tool designed to convince the prospect that a mutually beneficial relationship will result.

Once this is understood, it is time to incorporate the insight gained through the preliminary actions into an effective data-driven proposal. The following pages will identify the basic elements of a sponsorship proposal.

Introduction

The initial section of the sponsorship proposal should be thought of as a written handshake. Such greetings are replete with pleasantries but offer little substance. Still, they play an important role in establishing interest and a rapport. It projects a first impression. A good one can help open doors, whereas a bad one can lead to a situation where the proposal is given little consideration by the decision makers.

This introduction should not include specifics regarding the proposal beyond the identification of the event or property and a basic description. If there is a cause-related marketing overlay, the beneficiaries should be identified. For many properties, the owner does not manage day-to-day operations. In those cases, the introduction should identify the organization that will be managing the event. Specify the date(s) during which the event will be staged. Provide a broad overview of media coverage. Then move on to the specifics of the proposal.

History of the Event

Prospects may look at the past as a window to the future. Because of this, the proposal may benefit from the inclusion of an overview of the event's life. The intent is to create and reinforce the perception that it has a solid past and a bright future.

When was the event first staged? If it is a new event, when was it first conceived? When was the first event of its type staged? How has the title changed over the years? Who have the participants been? Have any particularly noteworthy teams or individuals been involved? For any cause-related overlay, what charities or organizations have been involved and how much money has been donated to them over the years?

Since sponsors are interested in reaching customers, the history should include an overview of the event's attendance, especially in recent years. If there is a history of radio or TV coverage, the prospective sponsor would want to know the past ratings for the event.

Finally, this section of the proposal should contain basic historical financial data. Although the property owner will be reluctant to disclose sensitive information, the prospect will use financial performance as a measure of future viability.[3] This aspect of the proposal is more important when the objective is to sign a sponsor for an extended period of time. Basic information regarding revenues and costs will allow the prospect to visualize the trend regarding the sponsee's performance over time.

Plan Components

In this section of the proposal, the sponsee begins to tell the prospect exactly what the property can do for it. It addresses the question of what benefits will be provided. In many cases, the plan components can be customized to match the needs of the prospect. Generic, *boilerplate proposals* are less effective in the task of converting prospects into sponsors; therefore, the property owner should make every effort to tailor the proposal to address the

POSSIBLE PLAN COMPONENTS (BENEFITS) FOR SPONSORS

8.1

- Category exclusivity
- Signage
- Rights to use event trademarks and logos
- Distribution rights
- Hospitality areas
- Complimentary advertising (TV and printed event program)
- Free tickets
- Right to purchase additional tickets
- Link on event website
- Inclusion in event promotions
- Access to property's mailing list/database
- Right of first refusal

set of objectives that the prospect will seek to achieve via the sponsorship.[4] Research has documented which components are most important to sponsors in general; however, when creating a proposal for a prospect, the property owner must understand that what is critically important to one sponsor may be only moderately important to another.

Boilerplate proposals are less effective in the task of converting prospects into sponsors.

Basically, this section addresses the problem-solving dimension of the sponsorship. More specifically, it delineates what benefits can be provided to the prospective sponsor. If the objectives of the prospect are understood, then the components of the sponsorship should represent the tools that will help facilitate the achievement of those objectives. Box 8.1 provides a listing of the components that were originally discussed in Chapter 4.

The property owner must carefully select the array of components it will offer. While each component should provide some benefits, the prospect will also see each as a cost. To justify the cost, the prospect must be able to envision the benefits in terms of a return on investment. For instance, the granting of distribution rights to a tire manufacturer that sponsors a motor sports event may have little value. Conversely, that same right for the marketer of a sports beverage such as Gatorade could be viewed as a valuable opportunity to cash in on its sponsorship.

The proposal should also state the dates during which the specified components will be in force. For example, when does the official designation begin and end? For what period of time will category exclusivity be granted; for how long will the signs remain up at the event venue? What is the latest date at which the sponsor can exercise its right of first refusal? Answers to these questions will assist the prospect in the evaluation of the proposed sponsorship's ability to accomplish the anticipated goals and objectives.

If the prospective sponsor's primary objective is the entertainment of clients and employees, then hospitality areas, free tickets, and the right to purchase additional tickets would be considered important components. If the objective is to increase sales, then distribution rights and the ability to use the event's trademarks and logos in advertising and packaging might be beneficial. To increase the awareness of a new product or upon entering a new geographic market, components such as signage, a link on the event's Web site, and complimentary advertising are valuable components. A sponsor will have one or more key objectives that it will seek to achieve via its involvement with a property or an event. It is mutually beneficial if the sponsee can determine the prospect's objectives and include only those components that provide the benefits that specifically address those objectives. Not only will the prospect appreciate the effort made to address its position, but it also increases the likelihood that the sponsorship will be successful. It is this success that leads to long-term relationships such as what we have seen with Coca-Cola and the Olympics.

Value Enhancements

There are several ways in which the sponsee can assist sponsors as they seek to maximize the return on their investment. These enhancements are represented by information that can be provided by the sponsee, actions taken by the sponsee, and opportunities for the sponsor. Specifically, the proposal can document leveraging opportunities that exist within the event itself; it can also identify potential cross-promotion efforts with other sponsors. The prospect would respond favorably to any listing of efforts that will be taken by the property owner in an effort to discourage ambush marketing. If the event plans to engage in any postevent research that will document the effectiveness of the sponsorship, those efforts should be delineated at this point.

Other potential enhancements include a postevent fulfillment report. This report provides documentation that the sponsee met all of the contractual obligations due to the sponsor. It might include answers to the following questions:

- How many signs were displayed?
- Where were they displayed?
- How large was the free ad that was published in the program?
- On what page was the free ad?
- When did the sponsor's link first appear on the event's Web site?
- How many free tickets were provided?
- When were public address announcements made to acknowledge the sponsor?
- Was category exclusivity honored?
- Did the actual number of spectators and TV viewers match projections?

If a fulfillment report will be provided, the proposal should identify the questions it will answer and the date on which the sponsor should expect to receive it.

Beyond the leveraging opportunities within the control of the event itself, the sponsor can benefit from ideas about other leveraging opportunities. This is especially true for marketers that are not experienced in the task of implementing a sponsorship program. If the event has arranged for sponsors to have priority access to media advertising such as the TV broadcast or local billboards, they should be informed of this availability. Not only is it an incentive to sponsor, but it is also a disincentive to not sponsor. Even when the media are not controlled, information regarding leveraging strategies is well received by prospects and sponsors. Although the proposal itself may not outline specific leveraging recommendations, the offer of a workshop for those that sign on can be a valuable marketing tool.

Some properties such as NASCAR are fortunate to have fans who are very loyal to the sponsors of their events, teams, and drivers. Any research that documents loyalty of this type provides objective evidence that the proposed sponsorship can be an effective tool. While care must be taken not to overwhelm the prospect with mountains of data in the

FIGURE 8.1
NASCAR Vehicle
with Sponsors' Decals

proposal, basic insight can be passed along with a promise to provide more information as the need arises. A NASCAR vehicle with its sponsors' decals is shown in Figure 8.1.

All of these services are designed to enhance the value of a sponsorship. When the property owner intends to provide one or more of these services, that intention should be conveyed succinctly in the proposal. Once again, the emphasis is on meeting the needs of the prospect and helping to assure that its objectives will be achieved and that an adequate return on investment will be attained. These value-enhancing services are categorized in the following list.

Value-Enhancing Services

Information provided by the sponsee
- Postevent research
- Fan loyalty research

Actions taken by the sponsee
- Anti-ambush initiatives
- Fulfillment report

Opportunities for the sponsor
- Cross-promotion opportunities
- Leveraging opportunities within the event
- Leveraging opportunities beyond the event

Terms

To this point in the proposal, the emphasis has been on the benefits provided to the sponsor and the value associated with those benefits. We cannot forget, however, that the proposal is a tool designed to help sell the prospect on the idea of signing a sponsorship contract. And for every sales situation, there are terms that need to be discussed. It is at this point in the proposal that timelines and financial commitments are specified.

Regarding financial commitment, the most basic decision is how much to charge the sponsor. Chapter 5 provided a discussion of the task of determining a price that reflects the value of the sponsorship being offered. Using that information as a basis, the property owner must calculate a single number to quote the prospect. The proposal should also indicate any opportunities to fulfill all or a portion of the financial commitment using VIK. When accepting goods and services in lieu of cash, the property owner must specify how the value is calculated. Since this process will be delineated in any subsequent contract, it is logical to note the valuation process in the proposal itself.

The next financial term to consider is the timing of the payments. This is particularly true for events that are either expensive or for which the contract is for a lengthy time frame. For smaller local events, full payment is often required upon the signing of the contract. In fact, it is common that no contract will be required, so payment is made when the commitment to become a sponsor is made. But for larger events and those that encompass more than one year, a schedule of payments should be included. This schedule should include both the date and the amount due for each scheduled payment.

> For smaller local events, full payment is often required upon the signing of the contract.

A sponsorship proposal is not an open invitation with an infinite amount of time to determine its merits. As such, there is a need to specify the date on which the offer will expire. This deadline will require the prospect to make a decision or at least initiate the negotiation process.

At this point, the prospect knows the cost, has an explanation of the benefits, and has a deadline for taking action. Thus, there is a basis for accepting or rejecting the proposal. Of course, every decision is not so clear; in those cases, the proposal serves as a starting point for discussion and negotiation.

Executive Summary

The proposal has the potential to be a lengthy document. When that is the case, the inclusion of an executive summary should be considered. Not everyone involved in the decision will take the time necessary to read the entire proposal. An executive summary will cover the key aspects of the proposal in a few short paragraphs. There will be little elaboration; rather, the most important points will simply be delineated. This summary may be placed at either the beginning or end of the proposal. Although the end may seem to be the most logical place to summarize the document, it may be more accessible and more likely to be read by busy executives and decision makers if placed at the beginning.

The proposal is now complete, so it should be distributed to the prospect(s). An overview of the components of a typical sponsorship proposal is provided in Box 8.2.

Now that there is an understanding of how to develop a sponsorship proposal, it must be acknowledged that there are exceptions to every rule. Many companies receive hundreds, if not thousands, of solicitations for sponsorship each year.[5] These larger companies often employ an in-house group whose job it is to evaluate each proposal and select only those with the most merit for funding. Poorly conceived sponsorships, or even those with a poorly developed proposal, are quickly eliminated by those engaged in the evaluation process.

> Larger companies often employ an in-house group whose job it is to evaluate each proposal.

ELEMENTS OF A SPONSORSHIP PROPOSAL   8.2

- Introduction
- History of the event
- Plan components
- Value enhancements
- Terms
- Executive summary

It has been reported that less than 10 percent of the proposals submitted to prospects are given serious consideration and that less than 1 percent ultimately receive funding from the prospect.[6] Two important points can be inferred from these statistics. First, companies have many sponsorship opportunities and will only select those that best meet their needs. Second, the proposal is not typically a deal-clincher; rather, it is a door opener. The 10 percent that are given serious consideration may well be determined on the basis of the proposal. But the 1 percent that are selected are generally done so on the basis of subsequent direct communications between the property owner and the prospect.

In an effort to streamline the screening of a multitude of proposals, several companies have started to require that all proposals submitted conform to a standardized format. When this is the case, the property owner has no choice except to comply with the prospect's demands. The common aspects of all proposals mean that the screener knows exactly where to look for key considerations. It also means that all pertinent information, from the prospect's perspective, is included while trivial or irrelevant information is excluded. Coors Beer is an example of a company that has implemented a policy of standardization. An overview of the elements included in its format is provided in Box 8.3.

With the first two steps (preliminary actions and proposal development) completed, it is now time to move on to the critical third step, that of selling the sponsorship. It represents the effort to either convert a prospect into a sponsor or sign an existing sponsor to a new contract. These are key issues in marketing today—customer acquisition and customer retention. Of course, if a property owner can retain its current sponsors, then there is less of a need to incur the expenses associated with the task of acquiring new sponsors. But regardless of whether the focus is on acquisition or retention, there will still be a need to sell the sponsorship.

Selling the Sponsorship

Proposals will typically be subjected to intense scrutiny prior to any final decision by the prospect. Many companies employ systematic evaluation procedures in order to objectively compare one proposal to another. The vast majority of the proposals never progress beyond this evaluation stage as the prospects reject those that are deemed unacceptable. Those that do survive this weeding-out process are not all funded. Remember the earlier statistic that only 10 percent of the proposals submitted to prospective sponsors are given serious consideration. It is this 10 percent that survived the initial evaluation. The next statistic was more compelling in that only 1 percent of the proposals originally submitted receive funding. When a property owner seeks to sell

REQUIRED COMPONENTS OF THE STANDARD SPONSORSHIP PROPOSAL SUBMITTED TO COORS BEER

8.3

- Terms
- Rationale (fit within IMC plan)
- Event demographics (market)
- How it works
- What Coors receives
- Cost (with renewal and exclusivity)
- Insurance
- Other issues
- Uniqueness
- Geographic scope
- Help for the brand
- Spin-offs and outreach opportunities
- Suitability to support major consumer promotion
- Continuity prospects
- Cost effectiveness and plausibility

sponsorships, its goal is to have its proposals included within that small group of successful conversions. In other words, selling activities are designed to convert a prospect into a customer—in this situation, a sponsor.

> Only 10 percent of the proposals submitted to prospective sponsors are given serious consideration.

Negotiating the Deal

Every negotiation begins with an offer. Whether the organization is the prospective sponsor or the sponsee, the offer serves as a point from which the two parties will begin their negotiations. A property owner must strive to establish a price for the package of benefits that reflects their value in the eyes of the prospective sponsor. Yet, no matter how hard the seller tries, the prospect will likely issue a counteroffer. That the proposal was not rejected outright indicates that it is being given serious consideration. At this point, the key question is, How far apart are the original offer and the counteroffer? This disparity will be the first hint at how difficult the negotiation process will be.

Since negotiations are almost inevitable, both parties should come to the table fully aware of their positions. What do I need; what can I provide? What are the sponsorship objectives; what components will help to achieve those objectives? It is clear that each party must know a lot about the other. The lack of information will put the uninformed party at a decided disadvantage.

The prospect may ask for additional benefits or a lower price. The property owner may offer benefits that were not included in the original proposal as a way of overcoming price objections, or the property owner may exchange one component for another when the prospect indicates that the proposal isn't quite what it was looking for. The terms of payment may be a point of negotiation. For instance, the prospect may seek to change a cash-only sponsorship into one where part of the commitment can be satisfied with VIK. Or there may be a request to change the way that the value of the VIK is calculated.

Representatives of the property owner must continue to reinforce the idea that the prospect is getting an ideal product at an appropriate price. They need to close the deal. There are a number of closing techniques used by professional salespeople. Four of the most commonly used techniques are the added inducement close, the standing room only (SRO) close, the balance sheet approach, and the alternative decision approach.[7]

The *added inducement close* is where the salesperson provides a new benefit as a negotiation point. For example, the number of free tickets might be increased or a free ad that was not originally included in the proposal may be added to the array of components offered to the prospect. This technique can be use to overcome price objections, especially when the objection is trivial or insincere.

The *standing room only close* is commonly used in both consumer marketing and business-to-business marketing. It is based on the premise that there are only so many sponsorships available for the property under consideration, they are in demand, and if the prospect doesn't buy it today, someone else may buy it tomorrow. Remember that one aspect of the proposal was a deadline to accept. The negotiation process may provide some extra time to make the decision, but it should never be an open-ended offer.

Another technique is the *balance sheet approach*. In face-to-face discussions, the buyer and seller attempt to itemize the pros and cons associated with the sponsorship. A pro could be any asset such as a free ad or signage at the venue. A con would be a shortcoming such as the absence of category exclusivity or the increase in price from the previous contract. Once the balance sheet is formulated, it allows both parties to consider how a perceived shortcoming can be overcome via trade-offs between the two parties.

The *alternative decision approach* might be used to negotiate from one level of sponsorship to another. If the price for the official sponsor designation is too high, perhaps the prospect would consider signing at a lower level such as a marketing partner (FIFA designations), which is available at a lower price, though offering fewer benefits. Conversely, if the prospect wants more benefits, perhaps it is willing to consider moving up to a higher, more expensive category that better meets its needs. In some cases, two or more options are presented to the prospect simultaneously, and the effort to close the sale is simply a question of which option the prospect would prefer to buy. The question might be, "Do you prefer to be an official sponsor or a marketing partner?"

At some point, either an agreement will be reached or the parties will have to resign themselves to the fact that a consensus will not be attained. If an agreement does result from the negotiations, a contract will need to be developed, and it will have to incorporate the changes resulting from the negotiation process. Once the contract has been signed, the prospect has been converted. The property has achieved its goal of selling the sponsorship.

> Right away, the sponsee is working to sell the next contract, even if the renewal period is years away.

The next task involves customer satisfaction. What needs to be done to satisfy the sponsor? These actions are critical in the task of customer retention. So right away, the sponsee is working to sell the next contract, even if the renewal period is years away. Large events often have employees who are classified as *customer relationship managers*. It is their job to communicate with sponsors, determine their level of satisfaction, and seek to resolve any conflicts, concerns, or dissatisfaction on the part of the sponsor. Above all, it is imperative to remember that it is far more cost effective to take the steps required to keep a current sponsor satisfied than it is to acquire a new sponsor to replace one that is dissatisfied and opts to drop out.

Closing Capsule

Events and property owners know what they have to offer to their prospects. The difficulty lies in the identification of prospects and the determination of what they really want. A sponsorship should represent a relationship where both parties win. To achieve this type of mutually beneficial sponsorship, it is important for each party to understand the other.

For the sponsee to fully understand the position of the prospective sponsor, some research will be required. This is the essence of a data-driven sponsorship. Most critical is an understanding of the prospect's target markets along with its likely objectives and marketing strategies. It is this understanding that allows for the development of a written sponsorship proposal that matches the prospect's needs.

So-called boilerplate proposals do not work. The implication is that each proposal must be customized for each prospect. The typical proposal consists of an introduction, a historical account of the event, the plan components, value enhancements, terms (time and money), and an executive summary. Some companies require all submissions to utilize a standardized format. Therefore, it is incumbent upon the sponsee to determine any submission requirements because those that fail to comply with the company's standards may be discarded without any further evaluation.

Sponsorship proposals will be scrutinized by the prospects as they seek to identify those that best meet their specific needs. Many companies utilize an evaluation tool or matrix that facilitates the comparison of all proposals on a common, objective basis. This evaluation process is covered at length in the following chapter. Most proposals will not survive this initial screening; far more proposals are rejected than are accepted. Even those that do survive the screening process are not automatically funded. They are subjected to additional scrutiny. If interest still exists, the sponsee and the prospect move on to the negotiation stage.

Negotiation generally starts with the offer that was delineated in the proposal and the counteroffer by the prospect. The task then becomes one of closing the gap while keeping both parties happy. At this point, the job of selling the sponsorship is just like any other business-to-business sales encounter. The seller will attempt to show how the sponsorship will benefit the prospect. Efforts to overcome objections will focus on typical closing techniques. Once the prospect has been converted into a sponsor, then the emphasis becomes one of assuring satisfaction. In today's environment, which features relationship marketing, the emphasis must be on customer retention. Only then will we see relationships like the one between the Olympics and Coca-Cola–88 years and still counting.[8]

Review Questions

1. What is meant by the statement that "sponsorships should be data driven"?
2. What is prospecting?
3. Why don't boilerplate proposals work?
4. What are the components of a typical sponsorship proposal?
5. Why do companies such as Coors specify a standardized format for the submission of sponsorship proposals?
6. Discuss the concept of value enhancement as it relates to sponsorships.
7. Why does virtually every sponsorship contract involve negotiation?
8. Why do customer relationship managers focus their efforts on sponsor retention?

Endnotes

1. D. Morris and R. Irwin, "The Data-Driven Approach to Sponsor Acquisition," *Sport Marketing Quarterly* 5, no. 2 (1996), pp. 7–10.

2. J. Kuzma, W. Shanklin, and J. McCally, "Number One Principle for Sports Events Seeking Corporate Sponsors: Meet Benefactor's Objectives," *Sport Marketing Quarterly* 2, no. 3 (1993), pp. 27–32.

3. G. Macnow, "Sports Tie-Ins Help Firms Score Big, *Nation's Business,* September 1989, pp. 36–39.

4. L. Ukman, "Back to Basics," *IEG Sponsorship Report,* December 4, 1995, p. 2.

5. C. Shelton, "Funding Strategies for Women's Sports, *Journal of Physical Education, Recreation and Dance* 62, no. 3 (1991), pp. 51–54.

6. Morris and Irwin, "The Data-Driven Approach to Sponsor Acquisition."

7. H. Dodge and S. Fullerton, *Professional Selling,* 8th ed. (Mason, OH: Thompson Custom Publishing, 2004), pp. 7–13.

8. Coca-Cola is signed with the IOC as a TOP sponsor through 2020.

CHAPTER NINE

Pre-event Evaluation

Learning Objectives

- Learn why pre-event scrutiny has increased.
- Learn when these evaluations are needed.
- Develop an evaluation procedure.
- Apply the evaluation criteria in a matrix form.
- Learn how the results are used by a prospective sponsor.
- Understand why the process is important to sponsees.

A number of factors have resulted in an increased emphasis on the assessment of potential sponsorship opportunities *prior to* making the decision to sponsor, or not to sponsor, a particular event or property. In other words, before committing resources to any sponsorship, the marketer needs an objective evaluation of how the sponsorship will help it achieve its stated objectives. This perspective reflects the acknowledgment that in today's environment there is more risk associated with any sponsorship expenditure. Factors that have led to increased scrutiny include

- Increased emphasis on return on investment.
- Increased costs associated with sponsorships.
- Increased number of sponsorship opportunities available to the marketer.
- The growth of sponsorship opportunities beyond the sports domain.
- Better descriptions of the sponsor's and the sponsee's target markets.

> The prospective sponsor engages in this evaluation process in order to identify potentially beneficial sponsorship opportunities.

Although there is a tendency to view pre-event evaluation as the sole domain of the potential sponsor, it is also a valuable tool for the sponsee. The prospective sponsor engages in this evaluation process in order to identify potentially beneficial sponsorship opportunities while eliminating those that are less likely to contribute to the achievement of the marketer's goals. On the other hand, the sponsee should also engage in pre-event evaluation in an effort to assure a better fit between the needs of the prospective sponsor and the plan components provided in the sponsorship plan. By understanding the prospect's goals and expectations, the event or property can create a sponsorship proposal that is more closely aligned with the needs of the prospective sponsor. The result should be a proposal that is viewed more favorably by the prospect. This matching process makes the task of selling the sponsorship much easier as both parties have a realistic perspective in regard to the benefits that they can expect to derive from the proposed partnership. It should also result in a higher retention rate because a satisfied sponsor is far more likely to renew the sponsorship upon the expiration of the current agreement. Prior to looking at the evaluation process itself, we will first examine the factors that have increased the need to engage in pre-event evaluation.

Factors Leading to Increased Emphasis on Assessment

Increased Emphasis on Return on the Sponsorship Investment

As noted in Chapter 3, the primary motivation for a marketer to commit significant resources to a sponsorship program today is the belief that the marketer will achieve important benefits as a result. The implication of this focus is that sponsors will weigh the costs associated with any sponsorship program against the benefits that they would anticipate receiving from that program. The investment will be calculated; the benefits will be estimated; and the decision to sponsor or not to sponsor will be based upon the projected return on investment. Pre-event evaluation reflects an effort to estimate the value of the benefits provided in the sponsorship agreement.

> Sponsors weigh the costs associated with any sponsorship program against the benefits.

Increased Cost Associated with Sponsorship

Two factors have fueled the dramatic increase in the total costs associated with many sponsorship programs. First are the fees paid to the sponsee. From a broad perspective, the past 20 years have witnessed a significant upward trend in virtually every aspect of promotion associated with sports events. The cost for a 30-second advertisement on the broadcast of the NFL's Super Bowl increased from about $600,000 in 1988 to some $2.4 million in 2006. Some stadium naming rights deals have recently reached $10 million per year. Similarly, the cost of sponsoring the World Cup of Soccer went from $17.5 million in 1994 to some $40 million in 2006. Involvement in sports is expensive. This inflation has led some companies to move away from sports and into other categories such as the arts or local fairs and festivals. This is particularly true for sponsorship endeavors. It has increased the emphasis on the assessment of the value of the benefits derived by virtue of the sponsorship program.

The second factor is the cost associated with leveraging activities. Sponsorships are most effective when the relationship between the sponsor and the sponsee is reinforced with collateral marketing efforts. Also, there is often a need to counter ambush marketing efforts by the competition. As noted earlier, many experts in sports marketing believe that every dollar spent on sponsorship rights must be matched with at least one dollar to be spent on leveraging activities. The net effect is that a $60 million sponsorship of the Olympics becomes at least a $120 million investment. It may even be higher; in fact, many marketers feel that a leveraging ratio of up to three-to-one should be considered.

It is evident that marketers must consider the total cost associated with a sponsorship program. This includes both the fees paid to the sponsee and the cost of leveraging activities undertaken in support of the sponsorship. As these costs have continued to escalate, marketers have begun to stress the idea that sponsorship opportunities should be evaluated prior to making a sponsorship commitment, not just upon the conclusion of the program.

> Marketers must consider the total cost associated with a sponsorship program

Increased Number of Sponsorship Opportunities

In today's environment, more properties, events, and causes have recognized the role that sponsors can play in contributing to the revenue stream. Major events have exhibited a propensity to increase the number of sponsors signed on at each level; consider the increase from 10 to 15 in the number of "official sponsors" for the World Cup of Soccer. Organizers of events that had not previously accepted sponsors have begun to reevaluate that decision, and many have reversed that philosophy; the Rose Bowl's decision to sign a presenting sponsor (AT&T) prior to the 1999 game provided a new opportunity for a sponsor to align itself with a prestigious event. Opportunities beyond the sports industry have likewise increased. Approximately one-third of the sponsorship money and VIK invested today is directed into nonsports opportunities such as Ameriquest Mortgage's sponsorship of the Rolling Stones' 2005–06 "A Bigger Bang" World Tour and Qantas Airline's role as the "Official Airline" of the Sydney Gay and Lesbian Mardi Gras.

> Marketers need to select sponsorship opportunities that enhance their position within their target markets.

This dramatic increase in the number of sponsorship opportunities has created new promotional options for marketers. It has provided an array of sponsorships with a broad range of prices. Similarly, the increase has allowed marketers to reach more narrowly defined target markets—small geographic, demographic, or lifestyle-based segments—as well as huge mass markets. This increase in the number of choices has also incorporated an element of risk; marketers need to select sponsorship opportunities that enhance their position within their target markets. Consequently, there is a greater need for today's marketer to evaluate prospective sponsorship programs prior to committing significant resources in an effort to maximize the likelihood that the selected opportunity will be productive and to ensure that it will lead to the achievement of the various goals sought by the sponsor.

Growth in the Number of Sponsorship Opportunities beyond the Sports Domain

As briefly noted in the previous section, marketers today have a wide selection of sponsorship opportunities beyond the sports industry available for their consideration. These opportunities, earlier identified in Chapter 3, include

- *Cause-related marketing* endeavors such as the American Express sponsorship of the Muscular Dystrophy Association.
- *Entertainment, tours, and attractions* such as Ameriquest Mortgage's relationship with the Rolling Stones concert tour and Kodak's sponsorship of the Taronga Zoo in Sydney, Australia.
- *Festivals, fairs, and annual events,* exemplified by Scotiabank's sponsorship of the Stratford (Canada) Festival, Coca-Cola's sponsorship of the Illinois State Fair, and J2O's title sponsorship of the annual London Comedy Festival.
- *Arts* such as DaimlerChrysler's sponsorship of the Vincent Van Gogh art exhibit at the Detroit Institute of Arts.

The proliferation of these nonsports opportunities has provided potential sponsors with better opportunities to match the property or event to the sponsor's target markets. Given such opportunities, the potential sponsor will need to objectively evaluate the target market for the property under consideration. The target market for the Rugby World Cup is quite different from that of the London Philharmonic Orchestra. So whereas a beer company such as Foster's may be a good fit for the Rugby World Cup, it would likely find a similar relationship with the London Philharmonic to be ineffective. Conversely, a financial services provider such as Aviva might find the opposite to be the case. In reality, both of the aforementioned sponsorships were in place for the 2003 events.

Better Descriptions of the Sponsor's and the Sponsee's Target Markets

An indisputable fact in today's marketing environment is that markets are getting larger, but target markets continue to get smaller. The number of potential purchasers in most product categories is steadily increasing. The world's population is growing and becoming more affluent, thus adding potential customers to the market. Many companies have increased their efforts to include new international markets, a strategy that has also increased the overall size of their markets. But while the markets are growing, most firms' target markets are not. In fact, they are getting smaller. At first glance, this might seem to have negative consequences for the marketer, but this is not necessarily the case. Many marketers have flourished because of their ability to target small homogeneous market segments.

Marketers today have more information about consumers than ever before. Consumers have access to more media that focus on specific demographic and lifestyle groups. In New Zealand, there is the Rugby Channel broadcasting a variety of rugby programming 24/7. There is the Golf Channel, Speedvision, and the recently announced Tennis Channel. And there is an extensive array of TV channels that target specific audiences while not focusing on sports. Nickelodeon reaches children, Spike TV is directed toward men, Lifetime Network airs women's programming, and MTV strives to reach Generation Y. Beyond television there are many other media that marketers can use to reach even smaller, more well-defined target markets. These include magazines, radio, the Internet, and direct mail. And of course they include sponsorship opportunities. It is this combination of better information about consumers and more narrowly focused media that has led to smaller target markets. This in turn has led to one of two marketing philosophies: the strategy of niche marketing and that of multisegment marketing.

From a sponsorship perspective, *niche marketing* requires a potential sponsor to focus on properties and events that appeal to the same narrowly defined segment of the market that it has chosen to target in its efforts to sell its own products. Implicit within this strategy is the belief that expensive, broad-based sponsorships are not cost effective. They either reach consumers who are not part of the sponsor's target market, or they reach many different segments with an undifferentiated strategy. The marketer must know the market segments to which the event will appeal and select only those sponsorship opportunities that reach its target market.

Multisegment marketing requires that the marketer tailor its strategy for each unique target market that it seeks to reach. All elements of the marketing mix—price, product, promotion, and distribution—are subject to being modified to better appeal to each segment. For example, the Coca-Cola created Tab to appeal to weight conscious women, whereas Diet Coke (Coca-Cola Light) was initially conceived in an effort to sell low-calorie beverages to men. As a result, it was difficult to appeal to both segments with the same promotional strategy. In a similar context, in order to create an effective sponsorship strategy, a company utilizing such a multisegment approach would be better served to select different properties or events, each of which appeals to and reaches a specific target market rather than investing in a single event or property that reaches the mass market.

The implication of this discussion is that smaller target markets are more narrowly defined and this will require marketers to better understand both the characteristics of their target markets and the market segments to whom the potential sponsored event or property will appeal. This requires the potential sponsor to gather more information prior to investing promotional resources in any sponsorship program.

When Are Pre-event Evaluations Needed?

When *existing contracts expire,* the sponsor will need to reassess the sponsorship prior to making a decision to renew or to terminate the relationship. Although much of this insight will emanate from the postevent evaluation, the systematic pre-event evaluation has a role as well.

The sponsee may propose a new contract that differs significantly from the one that is expiring. Fees may have increased or decreased, sponsorship components may have been added or deleted, or the number of sponsors may have been changed. The sponsor or the sponsee may have redefined its target markets. The prestige or the venue of the sponsored property or event may differ from that when the previous contract was signed. The sponsor's marketing objectives may have changed. Any of these modifications reflect a change in the level of risk associated with a sponsorship, and it is imperative for the sponsor to reevaluate the fit between itself and the sponsee prior to committing future resources.

New opportunities also dictate a need to engage in pre-event evaluation. These new opportunities may result from the emergence of a new event. In this case, there is no history to rely on as a source of information. An example would be the recent emergence of the women's professional soccer league in the United States, the WUSA. The league initiated a search for sponsors prior to the start of competition. Prospective sponsors needed to look at the property in such a way so as to guide their sponsorship decision. Unfortunately for WUSA, the inability to secure sponsors is deemed to be one of the primary reasons the league ceased to operate after the 2003 season, although there was speculation regarding the reemergence of WUSA for the 2005 season. It is likely that this return was predicated upon the ability to attract new sponsors. The inability to achieve this goal has resulted in the continued hiatus for the league. Another emerging event is the World Baseball Classic that made its debut in 2006. Sponsors had the opportunity to forge a relationship with the organizers, yet the lack of history for the event made such an alliance quite risky.

In other cases, an *established property or event has decided to initiate a sponsorship program.* Many of these events or properties have been in existence for many years but are only now deciding to take advantage of the revenue stream associated with sponsorship. The Rose Bowl game has been contested between two of the top American college football teams since 1902, but it was not until the 1999 that the game introduced its first presenting sponsor, AT&T.

Other new opportunities become available when *existing sponsors drop out.* A second look at the Rose Bowl reveals that AT&T chose not to renew its sponsorship when the four-year contract expired. The decision opened up an opportunity for a new sponsor, Sony, to replace the previous sponsor. Sony used the exposure as part of its promotional efforts to support the rollout of the new PlayStation 2 game console. The relationship lasted only one year, and Sony was subsequently replaced by Citigroup (Citibank) beginning with the 2004 event. The uncertainty as to why sponsors were terminating their relationships with the event gave prospective sponsors even more reason to engage in the pre-event evaluation process. Other examples include recent decisions by IBM and UPS to not renew their agreements with the Olympic Games, citing both costs (some $60 million per four-year cycle) and changes in strategic direction. The decision by IBM to terminate its sponsorship opened the door for a new information technology company, China's Lenovo Computers, to step in as a new TOP sponsor starting with the 2006 Winter Games.

A *property may increase the number of sponsors allowed.* For example, it was noted earlier that the World Cup of Soccer increased its number of "official sponsors" from 10 in 1994 to 15 in 2006. Thus, five new sponsors were needed to fill the gap. Prospective sponsors needed to evaluate the potential effectiveness of a sponsorship, and existing sponsors needed to reevaluate the sponsorship to determine whether on not the increased number of sponsors would diminish the effectiveness of the sponsorships, especially in light of the substantial increase in the fees charged for the right to be a sponsor.

Finally, a marketer may have only recently made the *decision to seek sponsorship opportunities.* This decision may represent the marketer's first endeavor into the sponsorship environment, it may represent a change in focus such as moving from sporting events to the arts, or it may simply result from the marketer's satisfaction with recent sponsorship programs leading it to seek out additional opportunities.

> Marketers have a wide array of sponsorship opportunities available to them, and they must be able to differentiate among them.

Regardless of the situation faced by the prospective sponsor, the reasons for pre-event evaluation remain the same. Marketers have a wide array of sponsorship opportunities available to them, and they must be able to differentiate among them. Companies such as Visa International are inundated with far more sponsorships proposals than they could ever fund, so they must select the best opportunities while passing on those deemed unlikely to provide adequate results. In most cases today, that means to identify those that will generate the maximum return on the sponsorship investment.

Despite this evaluation process, risk cannot be totally eliminated. The goal of this process is to avoid making bad decisions. These bad decisions come in two forms. The marketer may select a property that ultimately fails to deliver an adequate ROI. Conversely, the marketer may deem an opportunity to be inadequate when in reality it would have been a good investment. These types of opportunity costs represent the focus of pre-event evaluation. The marketer must seek to identify the good opportunities and eliminate the bad ones while acknowledging that the process is imperfect and that the risk of making the wrong decision regarding an opportunity exists. So the ultimate goal is to reduce the risk associated with the sponsorship selection process.

Evaluation by the Potential Sponsor

The decision to invest in a sponsorship is driven by the contributions that the sponsorship can make in helping the marketer achieve a variety of objectives. To assess the opportunities available to it, the marketer must delineate criteria that will facilitate a systematic, objective evaluation of each sponsorship opportunity under consideration. And of course there is a need to establish a set of objectives to be achieved upon the selection of the events and properties deemed most appropriate to sponsor. As such, there are six steps in the evaluation process designed to provide guidance to the potential sponsor:

- Identify the corporate marketing objectives.
- Delineate and prioritize specific objectives to be achieved via sponsorship.
- Identify a relevant set of evaluation criteria.
- Assign a weight to each criterion in the resultant evaluation model.
- Rate each alternative on each evaluation criterion.
- Select appropriate opportunities and reject those that fail to meet the standards established in the screening process.[1]

Each of these steps is discussed from the potential sponsor's perspective on the following pages.

Identify the Corporate Marketing Objectives

The initial step is the identification of the broad corporate objectives as articulated by the potential sponsor. This assessment focuses primarily upon the marketer's objectives, although it does initiate some consideration of the various aspects of the proposed sponsorship plan. There are three key issues in this step of the process: the marketing objectives, the communications objectives, and the budgetary considerations that direct the firm's allocation of marketing resources.

Corporate marketing objectives focus on future performance. The decision as to the direction to take is balanced by the firm's allocation of resources directed toward the attainment of the stated objectives. Thus, in the task of pre-event evaluation, it is essential for the marketer to delineate the broad set of objectives being sought by the firm. These objectives are broadly stated and not specific to any sponsorship opportunity. Rather, they reflect targeted outcomes that may be achieved via the development of effective marketing strategies. The implemented strategy may or may not ultimately include sponsorship as a component; that decision may be based upon the evaluation of the firm's objectives and whether or not one or more of the alternative sponsorships available to the marketer provide benefits that cannot be matched by any other strategic initiatives, such as increased advertising, lower prices, improvements in product quality, increased distribution, and other initiatives aimed at enhancing customer satisfaction.

It is important to emphasize that this initial step involves the identification of corporate objectives, not specific brand or product goals. It is also important to remember that not all of these objectives can be obtained via sponsorships. For example, the marketer may want to reduce manufacturing costs or to speed up the distribution process in the supply chain. It may seek to introduce new technology or enter new target markets. Each of these may be an important corporate objective, but in most cases there may be *little* that sponsorship can do to help the corporation achieve them.

Within the context of this evaluation, it is important to identify the role that marketing communications will play in the development of marketing strategy directed toward achieving the firm's objectives. *What are the corporation's communications objectives?* A fundamental element of every marketing strategy is an integrated marketing communications plan. This element of marketing strategy focuses on the development of a promotional strategy where each of the components complements the other elements of the promotional mix. Historically, the promotional mix has been deemed to consist of advertising, personal selling, sales promotion, and public relations.

> No single element of the promotional mix will typically lead to the achievement of all of the firm's communications goals.

Recently, many marketers have included sponsorship as a fifth element of the promotional mix. It is important to note that no single element of the promotional mix will typically lead to the achievement of all of the firm's communications goals. This includes sponsorship. Thus, the marketer must coordinate the relevant components of the promotional mix in order to use an integrated marketing communications plan that will facilitate the achievement of the firm's goals. And of course the marketer must still incorporate its integrated marketing communications plan as part of its marketing mix. The promotional strategy must work in harmony with the marketer's product, pricing, and distribution strategies. While acknowledging that all elements must be aligned in the development of marketing strategy, this aspect of the pre-event evaluation process will look solely at the firm's communications objectives.

From a broad perspective, the self-assessment begins by identifying the objectives for the overall communications strategy. Typical communications objectives include

- Increased awareness.
- Enhanced consumer perception.
- Stronger brand loyalty.
- Increased sales.
- Positive public relations.

CATEGORIZATION OF SPONSORSHIP OBJECTIVES

9.1

Corporation-Related Objectives
- Overcome advertising restrictions
- Cut through advertising clutter
- Reach small segments
- Attain positive public relations and enhance company image
- Improve relations with intermediaries
- Enhance community involvement
- Emphasize social responsibility
- Portray company as a good corporate citizen
- Emphasize philanthropic activities
- Capitalize on hospitality opportunity
- Enhance general public awareness
- Enhance employee morale
- Develop corporate philanthropy

Brand/Product-Related Objectives
- Drive sales and market share
- Increase distribution
- Block competition
- Shape consumer attitudes within the target market
- Increase brand's visibility in the marketplace
- Increase brand and product awareness in target markets

Each objective should be delineated in the corporate marketing objectives. The communications objectives will be the more directed subset of its stated corporate-based marketing goals for which the promotional mix plays the key role in the marketer's efforts. Moreover, the marketer must acknowledge that it does not have unlimited resources to devote to its strategic initiatives. So it must face reality and *develop a budget for its promotional activities*. What level of resources can be devoted to promotion? Within that budget, how much can be directed into sponsorship endeavors? Once the budget has been developed, the marketer can move on to the next step, that of delineating and prioritizing specific objectives associated with the firm's sponsorship program.

Delineate and Prioritize the Specific Objectives to Be Achieved via Sponsorship

The second step involves the identification of specific objectives that the marketer will seek to achieve through its selected sponsorships. Once they have been determined, it is appropriate to rank them in order of importance. Clearly, some objectives will be more important than others, so they should be prioritized. A series of typical sponsorship objectives was discussed in Chapter 4. At this point, however, it may be appropriate to further categorize the objectives as either corporation-related or brand/product-related. Box 9.1 summarizes these objectives.

The marketer will identify the specific objectives that it will seek to achieve with the selection and implementation of the most appropriate sponsorship opportunities and the

PRE-EVENT EVALUATION CONSIDERATIONS   9.2

- Budget considerations
- Event management
- Positioning/image issues
- Target market considerations
- Integrated marketing communications issues
- Competition considerations
- Strategic issues

corresponding leveraging programs. Some properties and events may be effective in the task of achieving certain objectives but not others. It is this reality that creates the need for pre-event evaluation. Typically, a varied array of sponsorship opportunities are available to the marketer. If they all provided the same characteristics, then the marketer would simply select the least expensive. In reality, it is not so simple.

> Typically, a varied array of sponsorship opportunities are available to the marketer.

Because each sponsorship will not produce the same results, the prospective sponsor must prioritize its set of objectives. It should rank order the objectives from first to last, reflecting the relative importance of each in the entire set. This prioritization is essential for the completion of the subsequent steps of the pre-event evaluation process. The marketer will then have a better idea of what it wants to achieve with the sponsorship program; so the ultimate task is to select a sponsorship opportunity based upon its congruence with these objectives and the priorities established.

> The ultimate task is to select a sponsorship opportunity based upon its congruence with these objectives and the priorities established.

Identify a Relevant Set of Evaluation Criteria

Step three begins the actual process of evaluating the available opportunities. Each must be subjected to scrutiny using a systematic process. It is this process that allows each alternative to be compared to all others. This third step is where the pre-event evaluation process begins to take shape.

The question now becomes one of identifying the criteria that will be used to assess the array of alternatives from which the prospective sponsor will select. The process begins by identifying *broad categories of evaluation criteria*. Once these categories have been specified, the next phase is to *break each category down into a set of specific criteria* that will facilitate the measurement process. The ultimate goal is to evaluate the fit between the marketer and each property or event under consideration. Given this progression and goal, the prospect must be confident that the selected criteria will serve to differentiate between the good and poor opportunities before progressing to the next step. One of the more comprehensive models was developed in the early 1990s and can still serve as a template to guide the process today.[2] A summary of the seven broad categories included in that model is provided in Box 9.2.

As seen in Box 9.2, a variety of issues may be relevant to this process. The prospective sponsor might opt to use each of the seven broad categories, or it might deem some of them

IEG'S SPONSORSHIP CONSIDERATIONS   **9.3**

- Image compatibility
- Audience composition
- Ability to incent retailers
- Ability to leverage
- Media
- Exclusivity
- Product showcase
- Ability to impact consumer sales
- Efficiency
- Measurability
- Continuity/ability to extend
- Ease of administration
- Rights and benefits granted by sponsee

irrelevant from their perspective. Another concern is whether or not the list in Box 9.2 is collectively exhaustive. There might be other important issues not included in this list that could be used to assist in the decision-making process.

One of the foremost organizations involved in sports marketing today is the Chicago-based International Events Group. In an effort to identify relevant evaluation criteria, the IEG has posed an important question: How do companies decide what to sponsor? In responding to its own question, the group has identified 13 "typical sponsorship criteria."[3] According to the IEG, potential sponsors should utilize the specific criteria as a guide in the development of an evaluation model to be used to assess available opportunities. The IEG does not necessarily advocate the use of all 13 of the criteria, and neither does it reject the idea that other criteria not on the list might be incorporated into the final evaluation model. In the group's words, prospective "sponsors should use them as a guide to designing their own matrix for sponsorship selection—adding, deleting and refining points to dovetail with your (the sponsor's) specific objectives."[4] Of particular note in the preceding quote is the reference to the evaluation matrix. This is a critical issue that relates specifically to the implementation of evaluation process. This matrix concept will be explored more fully in the discussion of step four. Before doing so, however, it is important to recognize the 13 evaluation criteria advocated by the IEG. These considerations are summarized in Box 9.3.

Regardless of the source of the final issues that will be utilized, it is imperative that each criterion be directly related to the requisite fit between the prospective sponsor and the property or event under consideration. Once this initial selection process is completed, the task is directed toward the designation of specific criteria that comprise each broad category. For example, if the selected category is the ability to leverage, the specific criteria used to assess it might be as proposed in Box 9.4.

The identification of specific criteria that reflect each broad category to be used in the assessment process represents the final task in the third step. The criteria must be objective, and the parties involved should not underestimate the critical nature of this aspect of the process. There are no standard answers to the two common questions: How many broad categories should be used? How many specific components are used to evaluate each category? The answer: Use all that are relevant and necessary. The more that are used,

EXAMPLE OF PRE-EVENT MEASUREMENT CRITERIA

9.4

Broad Category
- Ability to leverage

Specific Criteria
- Opportunities for product sampling and display
- Opportunity for cross-promotion with co-sponsors
- Ability to integrate sponsorship with current promotions
- Access to key individuals for promotion (e.g., players)
- Timing fills a void
- Seasonal impact
- Does the event control the media broadcast

the more complicated the process becomes. The fewer that are used, the more difficult it is for the evaluation process to differentiate between the good and the bad sponsorship opportunities. The key then is to find the appropriate balance when developing the final set of criteria while continuing to emphasize the ability to discriminate.

Assign Weights to Each Criterion in the Evaluation Model

The fourth step refines the process to the point that the evaluation process can begin. To progress to this point, a weight must be assigned to each element of the evaluation model. The initial task involves the *determination of the aggregate sum of the weights to be utilized* in the actual measurement process. Although any number of points can be used, normal convention leads most marketers to employ a 100-point model. Regardless of the aggregate total used, the next task is to *allocate those points to the broad categories* in the model such that the allocation reflects the relative importance of each category.

Consider a simple model that uses three broad categories in the evaluation process: budget considerations, target market considerations, and event management. The model in this example has been developed so as to employ a 100-point base. The task thus becomes one of allocating the 100 points to the three categories in such a way that the allocation will characterize the comparative importance of each category in the final decision to consider or not consider the sponsorship opportunity under scrutiny. If target market considerations represent the most important of the three categories, then it should have the most points allocated to it. It is also appropriate to assume that if one category is twice as important as a second category, then two times as many points should be allocated to it. While this process can be cumbersome, it is essential that the allocation represent the practical importance of each category. Thus, if target market considerations are twice as important as budget considerations and if budget considerations are three times as important as event management, then the final allocation to the three broad categories will be

- Target market considerations (60).
- Budget considerations (30).
- Event management (10).

Even though it was not specified in the aforementioned comparison, the final weighting indicates that target market considerations are six times as important as is event management.

THE QUANTITATIVE ALLOCATION PROCESS   9.5

The allocation can be calculated algebraically. This process is applicable regardless of the number of categories used in the evaluation model.

Start by creating a ranking of all elements from least to most important. Assign the value of 1x to the least important. Then compare the least important to the next higher category on the list and assign a relative value to the second category. In the previous example, event management was the least important, so it is assigned a value of 1x. The next most important category is budget considerations; it is assigned a value of 3x because it is three times as important as is event management. The process continues by comparing the second category on the list to the third. In the example, target market considerations were deemed to be twice as important as budget considerations. To reflect this relationship, the target market category is assigned a value of 6x. This value is derived by multiplying the value of the lower category (3x) by the comparative importance of the higher category (2). Once the value for the most important criterion has been determined, the precise allocation can be calculated.

The key issues are the summation of the assigned algebraic values and the total points to be allocated in the model. In this case we have

- Event management = 1x
- Budget considerations = 3x
- Target market considerations = 6x
- Total points to be allocated = 100

The resultant solution is

$$1x + 3x + 6x = 100$$
$$10x = 100$$
$$x = 10$$

Thus,

$$\text{Event management (1x)} = 10$$
$$\text{Budget considerations (3x)} = 30$$
$$\text{Target market considerations (6x)} = 60$$

This allocation may be done using quantitative measures, or it may be done qualitatively using a totally subjective process. Although the qualitative approach is easier to implement, the quantitative approach is generally preferred because it maintains the perceived balance among the evaluation categories. The quantitative approach to pre-event evaluation is demonstrated in Box 9.5.

Though not illustrated in this example, it is important to note that some categories have only marginal importance, and the weights assigned to them will reflect this fact. Also note that categories with equal importance will have equal weights.

Step four continues by *reallocating the weights assigned to each of the broad categories to the specific elements within each category*. The mechanics of this process are identical to those employed in the process of allocating points to each broad category. The only significant difference is that the sum of the weights to be allocated is not the aggregate value (100 in the example); rather, it is that portion of the points allocated to the respective categories. In the example, the category of "target market considerations" was allocated 60 points, so the next task is the allocation of those 60 points to the array of specific criteria that have been selected to evaluate the target market considerations component. Consider the example presented in Box 9.6.

Having identified the five elements that comprise the target market considerations category, the evaluation process continues by reallocating the points assigned to the category, 60 in this case, to the five criteria based upon the relative importance of each in the

TARGET MARKET CONSIDERATIONS   9.6

- Geographic media coverage
- International coverage
- National coverage
- Demographic fit
- Size

evaluation process. This is accomplished by reapplying the methods used in the initial task of allocating weights to the broad categories. For the sake of illustration, consider the following hypothetical allocation shown in Table 9.1.

TABLE 9.1
Target Market Considerations (60)

Consideration	Weight
Geographic media coverage	(10)
International coverage	(2)
National coverage	(8)
Demographic fit	(30)
Size	(10)

It is important to remember that these allocations do not represent the performance ratings for the criteria; rather, they reflect the measure of importance associated with each criterion in the evaluation process. The assignment of performance ratings is accomplished in the next step.

With the model now developed, it can be used to assess sponsorship opportunities in a systematic manner. The process assures that each opportunity is subjected to an identical assessment, thereby facilitating the objective comparison of all sponsorship opportunities under consideration.

> The process assures that each opportunity is subjected to an identical assessment.

The model should be periodically scrutinized because some modifications over time are inevitable. Broad categories in the model may be deleted; new categories may be added; weights for the broad categories may be adjusted; and weights for specific criteria within each category may be changed to reflect new priorities and evolving levels of importance.

A final consideration is that there is no standard model that will be utilized by all potential sponsors and sponsees. Different measures may be included, and different weights may be assigned by any two evaluators. The key point is that the model represents the potential sponsor's decision process and that the evaluation results will assist that potential sponsor in identifying those sponsorship opportunities that best meet its needs.

Rate Each Opportunity on Each Criterion

The process continues to the fifth step of the pre-event evaluation process. At the conclusion of step five, the potential sponsor will have a single numeric value that will be used to assess the viability of each potential sponsorship opportunity.

First *an appropriate rating scale must be selected*. The scale will be anchored by polar adjectives that reflect positive and negative evaluation results. An example of these polar

TABLE 9.2 **The Pre-event Evaluation Matrix**

Source: From R. Irwin and M. Asimakopoulos, "An Approach to the Evaluation and Selection of Sport Sponsorship Proposals," *Sport Marketing Quarterly* 1, no. 2 (1992), pp. 43–51.

Criteria	wt	−4	−3	−2	−1	0	+1	+2	+3	+4	Total
BUDGET CONSIDERATIONS											
Affordability											
Cost effectiveness											
Tax benefits											
EVENT MANAGEMENT											
Event profile											
Organizing committee											
Guarantees											
Legal status											
Government position											
Athletes' cooperation											
Governing body status											
Sport agency profile											
POSITIONING/IMAGE											
Product-sport image											
Sport-product relation											
Sport-service relation											
Image–target market fit											
TARGETING OF MARKET											
Extended media coverage											
International coverage											
National coverage											
Local coverage											
Immediate audience											
Demographic fit											
Size											
Fan association strength											
INTEGRATED COMMUNICATIONS											
Extended audience											
Demographics fit											
Size											
Signage opportunities											
Public relations/publicity											

Criteria	wt	−4	−3	−2	−1	0	+1	+2	+3	+4	Total
Hospitality accommodation											
Community leader presence											
Customer presence											
Staff sport knowledge											
Sales promotions											
Promotional licensing											
Complementary advertising											
Personal sales											
Retail sales at event											
New account opportunities											
COMPETITION CONSIDERATION											
Competition's interest											
Ambush market avoidance											
STRATEGIES											
Level of involvement											
Title sponsor											
Major sponsor											
Co-sponsor											
In-kind supplier											
Exclusivity											
Long-term involvement											
Once-off											
Type of sponsorship											
Established											
New											
Team											
League/championship											
Event											
Facility											
GRAND TOTAL											

adjectives is "extremely strong" and "extremely weak." Although any number of rating points may be designated, the measurement scale should have enough points to assure discrimination, but few enough points so that the differences from point to point are meaningful. One of the most commonly employed scales consists of seven points. Such a scale could consist of points defined as extremely strong, strong, somewhat strong, average, somewhat weak, weak, and extremely weak. From a practical standpoint, it is not mandatory that each rating point be assigned a verbal descriptor; however, the practice does facilitate the rating process. It is important to note that any set of polar adjectives can be used. Instead of "extremely strong" and "extremely weak," the model might use "good" and "bad" or "very acceptable" and "totally unacceptable." The key stipulation is that the same set be used for each evaluation undertaken.

Once the number of points has been determined, the next task is to specify the precise numeric scale to be used. For the 7-point scale described above, there are two numeric scales that are commonly applied. First is a scale from 1 to 7, with 4 representing the midpoint. The second is a scale from a negative 3 to a positive 3 with a midpoint of 0. In operationalizing the scale, it makes no difference which extreme value is assigned to which polar adjective. But from a practical perspective, it is suggested that higher values be associated with better evaluations. Therefore, when using a 7-point scale (1 to 7), it is recommended that the most positive rating (e.g., extremely strong) be assigned a value of 7.

At this point, it is appropriate to revisit the evaluation matrix concept as endorsed by the IEG and introduced earlier in this chapter. Table 9.2 illustrates this concept as it is used to implement the pre-event evaluation process. The matrix presented in Table 9.2 indicates that the evaluation will focus on seven broad categories. These categories, shown in uppercase letters, were initially identified in Box 9.2. They are budget considerations, event management, positioning/image, targeting of the market, integrated marketing communications, competition considerations, and strategies. Listed under each of the headings for the broad categories are the specific criteria that comprise each category. For example, the budget considerations category includes three specific criteria: affordability, cost effectiveness, and tax benefits. There are eight criteria listed for event management and four listed for positioning/image. The matrix continues with the listing of all relevant criteria within the remaining categories. It is evident that the process is comprehensive. The reality is that many issues are important when considering a significant investment in a sponsorship program.

The second key point in Table 9.2 is that the evaluator has chosen a 9-point scale with a range of −4 to +4 with a midpoint of 0. It would be logical to assume that a negative value is associated with a weakness and a positive value a strength.

Focusing on these two considerations, it can be seen how the concept of a matrix approach is created. Along the left margin, the evaluation criteria are delineated. Along the top margin, the measurement scale is indicated. With the grid lines superimposed to indicate each unique cell, the resultant matrix can be visualized. In addition to the measurement scale along the top margin, the matrix includes two additional columns. The column to the far left allows the evaluator to enter the designated weight associated with each criterion; the one at the far right provides a space to enter the outcome derived from the evaluation process.

With the matrix now developed, the process of evaluation can be completed. The key action in step five is the *assignment of a rating to each of the criteria* using the scale decided upon during the development of the evaluation matrix. Table 9.3 illustrates this process using the "budget consideration" category found in Table 9.2. For the purpose of illustration, the budget considerations category has been assigned a weight of 20 and the weights have been assigned to each criterion as noted in the table. Further illustrating this process, the rating for each criterion is indicated by an *x* at the appropriate point on each corresponding rating scale. For example, the "Affordability" criterion was assigned a rating of 1.

TABLE 9.3 **Illustration of the Criteria Rating Process**

Category/Criterion	wt	−4	−3	−2	0	1	2	3	4	Total
BUDGET CONSIDERATIONS	(20)									
Affordability	8					x				8
Cost effectiveness	10							x		30
Tax benefits	2			x						−4

An intermediate assessment can be achieved by calculating the subtotal associated with each category. In the example in Table 9.3, the overall rating derived for budget considerations is 34 (8 + 30 − 4). This subtotal can be compared to the maximum possible aggregate value for the category. This maximum value is calculated by multiplying the sum of the weights for the category (20) times the value associated with the best outcome for each criterion (4). Alternatively stated, a perfect score on each criterion in the budget considerations category would have resulted in an aggregate value of 80 for that category. The evaluator may want to compare the outcome (34 in this case) to the 80 potential points when assessing the potential effectiveness of the sponsorship opportunity under scrutiny. Whether or not this intermediate assessment is performed, the evaluation process continues with the rating of all criteria in the model.

Once the rating process is completed, the viability of the sponsorship is summarized by the aggregate value derived by *summing the results associated with the rating of each criterion*. Again, it may be important to compare the final summation to the maximum possible rating. For the example illustrated in the comprehensive matrix illustrated in Table 9.2, the maximum rating is 400 (100 × 4). With the calculation of the grand total, the assessment of the opportunity may now proceed. Therefore, the task now becomes one of *applying the results in such a way so as to reduce the risk* associated with accepting and rejecting sponsorship opportunities. This task represents the sixth and final step of the pre-event evaluation process. Figure 9.1 illustrates the series of steps starting with the identification of corporate marketing objectives and ending with the actual evaluation of each of the potential sponsorships.

Applications by the Potential Sponsor

Once the rating process has been completed, the potential sponsor will typically utilize the results in one of two ways: (1) the comparison of alternative opportunities to each other, or (2) the comparison of individual opportunities to an established benchmark.

Comparison of Alternative Opportunities

When the marketer has several potential sponsorship opportunities under consideration, the summary value allows for the direct comparison of one opportunity to another. Not only can a hierarchy from best to worst be established, but the potential sponsor can discern a measure of how much more potential one alternative has in comparison to the other alternatives. It is obvious that higher values are associated with greater potential; the extent of the difference can provide a relative measure of the superiority of one opportunity over another.

The marketer may be seeking to identify the single best opportunity available to it. Conversely, it may be seeking to identify an array of acceptable alternatives to consider. The marketer may have budgetary constraints, so it is seeking the one best or the optimal combination of sponsorships that fits within its budget. Finally, the goal may simply be to identify the worst alternatives and eliminate them from further consideration.

FIGURE 9.1
The Pre-event
Evaluation Process

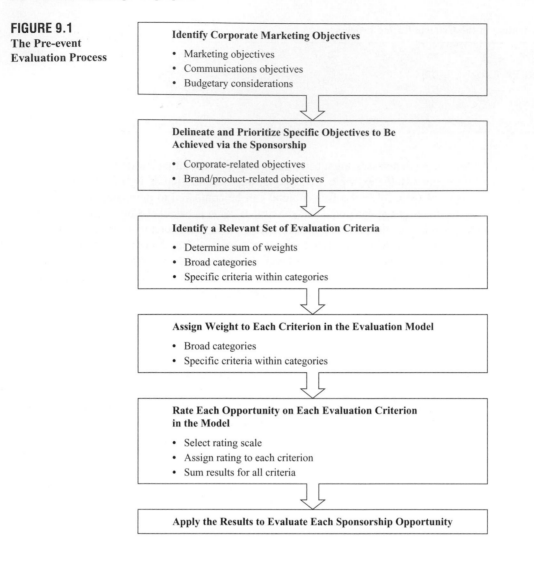

Identify Corporate Marketing Objectives

• Marketing objectives
• Communications objectives
• Budgetary considerations

Delineate and Prioritize Specific Objectives to Be Achieved via the Sponsorship

• Corporate-related objectives
• Brand/product-related objectives

Identify a Relevant Set of Evaluation Criteria

• Determine sum of weights
• Broad categories
• Specific criteria within categories

Assign Weight to Each Criterion in the Evaluation Model

• Broad categories
• Specific criteria within categories

Rate Each Opportunity on Each Evaluation Criterion in the Model

• Select rating scale
• Assign rating to each criterion
• Sum results for all criteria

Apply the Results to Evaluate Each Sponsorship Opportunity

This evaluation process may result in the marketer's selection of specific sponsorships in which it will invest. Alternatively, it may simply identify and lead to the elimination of those that are projected to be poor fits and poor investments. After the elimination process, those alternatives that survive are often subjected to additional scrutiny within the organization. This subsequent assessment often involves an informal discussion of each opportunity's merits as viewed by the decision makers within the potential sponsoring firm. Sponsorship selection is not simply a matter of mathematical comparison.

> Sponsorship selection is not simply a matter of mathematical comparison.

It is important to note that the aforementioned approach is often referred to as a *compensatory model* as it allows strong performance in some areas to offset weak performance in other areas. That the same outcome (grand total) can be achieved in many different ways is characteristic of this type of compensatory model, the *weighted additive model*.[5] In other cases, the prospective sponsor may require a satisfactory rating in one or

TABLE 9.4
Hypothetical Results of the Pre-event Evaluation Process

Event/Property	Rank	Total Points (max = 400)
A	1	311
B	2	306
C	3	205
Benchmark	X	200
D	4	179
E	5	104
F	6	62
G	7	−43
H	8	−222

more specified categories before proceeding with the evaluation. For instance, the evaluator may require a satisfactory rating on the "cost effectiveness" criterion. If it is not achieved, the evaluation will be terminated. Other positive aspects are not allowed to compensate for an unsatisfactory outcome on one or more criteria or categories deemed critical by the prospective sponsor.[6]

Benchmarking

When benchmarking, the marketer is comparing the overall rating of each event or property to a specified standard. The benchmark value would represent the minimum value for an alternative to receive any consideration for funding. That value might simply represent management's expectations. Alternatively, it may be derived from previous successful (or unsuccessful) sponsorships undertaken by the marketer.

When the results of the pre-event evaluation are judged against benchmarks, it is essential that the benchmark value reflect the scale being used. The minimum acceptable value is much higher when using a 1 to 9 scale than it is when using a −4 to +4 scale. When different scales have been applied, the benchmark values must be adjusted so as to be directly comparable to the results attained in the evaluation process. It is also important to note that the benchmark value may need to be adjusted periodically. As sponsorship becomes more oriented toward return on investment, we should anticipate that benchmark values will rise. Therefore, it is recommended that marketers evaluate their criteria on an annual basis and adjust the weights and the resultant benchmarks when appropriate.

Table 9.4 provides a hypothetical example of the results of the pre-event evaluation of multiple opportunities. It includes a benchmark to facilitate the decision-making process. It also demonstrates how the process provides data that are superior to a simple ranking process. From the table, it can be seen that of the three alternatives that exceeded the prospect's benchmark, alternative A is only slightly better than alternative B, which is far superior to alternative C.

Sponsee Applications

While this process is extremely valuable to the potential sponsor, the sponsee would be wise to consider it when developing sponsorship proposals and attempting to sell those proposals to prospects. It is impossible for the sponsee to duplicate each potential sponsor's evaluation model, but it should make an effort to anticipate the key considerations they may have when making investment decisions.

Foremost within this task is the anticipation of sponsor priorities. These will likely be predicated upon the objectives to be sought by the prospect. When these have been identified, it will allow the sponsee to tailor the sponsorship proposal to better meet the needs of the prospect. Finally, it will allow the sponsee to establish a price based upon the perceived value of the sponsorship. A sponsorship that is projected to provide only marginal value to a particular sponsor may need to be offered at a lower price. Conversely, one that is anticipated to provide superior benefits to a sponsor may be able to command a premium price. So in situations where price can be adjusted, it should be considered. Of course, there are situations where a property or event has multiple sponsors at the same level. In those cases, there will be little or no opportunity to modify the proposal because all sponsors will be granted the same rights and benefits at an established, uniform price. Whether such modifications can be made or not, the sponsee would be well advised to consider how the potential sponsor will view the opportunity prior to delivering the sponsorship proposal. This knowledge will assist the sponsee in the development of a sales strategy that will increase the likelihood of converting the prospect into a sponsor.

Closing Capsule

Marketers today have recognized the need to evaluate sponsorship opportunities prior to investing significant resources. A recent report by the IEG documents this upward trend. According to the IEG survey results, 29 percent of the companies responding indicated that they spent a minimum of $5,000 on "predecision analysis" on each alternative under consideration in 2002; 23 percent committed that level of resources to the evaluation process in 2001.[7] Clearly, more potential sponsors are engaging in meaningful pre-event evaluation than ever before.

The purpose of this evaluation process is to assess the viability of each opportunity as it relates to the achievement of the marketer's objectives. Companies may create their own assessment tools or they can hire independent research companies that specialize in this task. For example, Performance Research, a subsidiary of ZenithOptimedia, offers a service whereby it applies a "sponsorship selection model" to assist in the task of reducing the risk associated with the sponsorship decision.[8]

Sponsorship can be risky, and this risk has led to a greater emphasis on the pre-event evaluation process. Among the factors that contribute to this risk are an increased emphasis on return on sponsorship investment, the increased costs associated with sponsorships, the increased number of sponsorship opportunities available to the marketer, the increased availability of sponsorship opportunities beyond the sports domain, and richer definitions of target markets. These have induced marketers to seek a better fit between their target markets and those of the sponsored event or property.

In general, pre-event evaluations are appropriate whenever the marketer is considering making a new sponsorship investment. This includes upon the expiration of existing contracts and the availability of new opportunities. These new opportunities may have emerged because of a property or event's decision to seek sponsors for the first time, their decision to add a number of new sponsors to their existing base, or their need to replace one or more sponsors that have terminated their relationship with the sponsee. Finally, it may be that the marketer has only now decided to add sponsorship to its integrated marketing communications plan.

The evaluation process undertaken by the potential sponsor includes both qualitative and quantitative aspects. The result sought is an objective, systematic process designed to facilitate the evaluation and comparison of sponsorship opportunities available to the marketer.

The process consists of six steps. These steps are the identification of corporate marketing objectives, the delineation and prioritization of objectives sought to be achieved via sponsorship, the identification of a relevant set of evaluation criteria, the assignment of weights to each criterion in the model, the rating of each opportunity using the resultant evaluation model, and the determination of the viability of each alternative in the task of achieving the objectives sought by the sponsor.

Prospective sponsors can use the results of the evaluation process to identify opportunities and to reject those that fail to meet the marketer's standards. The evaluation process may involve a simple comparison of the alternatives, or it may involve the comparison to a benchmark that has been established by the marketer.

The sponsee should also consider models of this type when developing proposals for its prospects. A better understanding of the prospect and its priorities will allow the sponsee to create a sponsorship plan that better meets the needs of its prospects, and it will help in the process of determining the optimal price to charge. This process—by both the prospective sponsor and the sponsee—helps assure that the resultant partnership is mutually beneficial, thus nurturing a long-term relationship between the two organizations.

Review Questions

1. What factors have led to an increased need for potential sponsors to engage in pre-event evaluation?
2. How can sponsorship be used as part of a niche marketing strategy by a sponsor?
3. Under what specific circumstances are pre-event evaluations needed?
4. How does pre-event evaluation reduce the risk associated with the selection of sponsorship opportunities?
5. Identify and briefly discuss the six steps of the pre-event evaluation process.
6. How does sponsorship fit with the concept of an integrated marketing communications plan?
7. What is the derivation of the term *evaluation matrix?*
8. Identify the two categories of sponsorship objectives. List several specific objectives in each category.
9. List several of the pre-event evaluation categories identified in the text.
10. Explain how pre-event evaluation is partially qualitative and partially quantitative.
11. Why do many experts recommend a 7-point scale for rating each of the criteria in the evaluation model?
12. How can the results of the evaluation be used by the prospective sponsor?
13. How can sponsees utilize the concept of the evaluation matrix in the process of developing a sponsorship proposal?

Endnotes

1. Adapted from R. Irwin and M. Asimakopoulos, "An Approach to the Evaluation and Selection of Sport Sponsorship Proposals," *Sport Marketing Quarterly* 1, no. 2 (1992), pp. 43–51.
2. Ibid.
3. *IEG's Complete Guide to Sponsorship: Everything You Wanted to Know about Sponsorship* (Chicago: IEG, Inc., 1999), pp. 15–17.

4. Ibid., p. 15.

5. D. Hawkins, R. Best, and K. Coney, *Consumer Behavior: Building Marketing Strategy* (New York: McGraw-Hill/Irwin, 2004).

6. H. Heneman, D. Schwab, J. Fossum, and L. Dyer, *Personal/Human Resource Management: A Diagnostic Approach* (Homewood, IL: Irwin Publishing, 1988).

7. *IEG Sponsorship Report,* March 11, 2002.

8. "Sponsorship Products and Services," 2004, www.sponsorship.com/products.htm (accessed October 13, 2005).

CHAPTER TEN

Postevent Evaluation

Learning Objectives

- Learn how ROI objectives have led to postevent evaluation.
- Distinguish between cross-sectional and longitudinal research.
- Identify problems associated with the lack of a standard measure.
- Learn how qualitative assessments are made.
- Be able to calculate measures of market response.
- Learn the methodology used by a major service provider.
- Note efforts being made to improve the measurement process.
- Understand the need for a postevent fulfillment report.

The evolution of sponsorship from its initial focus on ego gratification to the more contemporary emphasis on the bottom line has been a driving force in the perceived need to measure the results. As spending on sponsorship has continued to grow at a dramatic pace, sponsors have begun to demand greater accountability.[1] According to a former brand manager at Kraft General Foods, companies "are spending too much money to ignore." Similarly, the national director of sponsorships and promotions for AT&T argued that "sponsorships are no different than a direct mail piece or an ad campaign in that you have to look at the effectiveness."[2] As a result, companies have expressed a need for increased scrutiny of sponsorships across the board.

> "Sponsorships are no different than a direct mail piece or an ad campaign in that you have to look at the effectiveness."

Despite this apparent call for additional postevent evaluation, many sponsors have been reluctant to increase the level of funding devoted to this type of assessment. The oft-cited 2004 Performance Research/IEG study indicated that 84 percent of the sponsors surveyed devoted a sum equal to no more than 1 percent of the rights fees to postevent evaluation. In other words, for every 100 dollars spent on rights fees, most sponsors spent one dollar or less on postevent evaluation. On the other hand, there has been an increased level of importance placed on having that service and the accompanying report provided by the property owner. The percentage of sponsors indicating that this component was *very important* to them increased from 45 percent in the 2002 study to some 57 percent in 2004.[3]

Sponsorship Accountability

By now, we understand that sponsorship activities are undertaken with specific objectives in mind. To fully understand the effectiveness of any sponsorship, the results must be measured. The sponsor is well aware of the rights fees paid to the sponsee; however, to objectively assess the return on investment, there must be a quantitative measure of its performance. Sponsorship is a relatively recent phenomenon, and the ideas of measurement and evaluation are even newer. Prior to the late 1980s, most sponsorships were the responsibility of the public relations or the corporate affairs staff.[4] But that was when sponsorship was primarily based upon ego or philanthropic motivations. The movement toward decisions based upon ROI has changed the pattern of responsibility. The question of whether or not the sponsorship expenditure can be justified has emphasized the need for marketing research. Consider the following scenario that highlights this newfound priority.

Guinness Brewery operates in the European market where sponsorship has exhibited the greatest growth of all marketing sectors.[5] Given that sponsorship costs were increasing dramatically, the firm's marketing staff began to understand that sufficient resources needed to be devoted to a stream of research initiated prior to the sponsorship decision and continued long after the conclusion of the event. The property under consideration by Guinness was the Rugby World Cup. According to Guinness brand managers, research into the event began three years prior to the tournament competition. The initial research efforts focused on the evaluation of the appropriateness of the event as a platform for delivering "relevant and motivating messages" to Guinness' target market. Once the fit was deemed satisfactory, the next research endeavor involved the determination of the budget—one that included both the rights fees and the cost of the leveraging program. Finally, there was a need to conduct research that measured the impact that the sponsorship had on the marketplace. Did it change brand awareness? Did it increase the likelihood that consumers would purchase Guinness? Although questions such as these may be difficult to answer, they will inevitably be asked. Thus, it is important that the sponsorship managers anticipate questions of this type and plan to implement procedures that will allow the questions to be answered.

Lack of a Standard Measure

It has been argued that the measurement and evaluation of the impact of a sponsorship is the most difficult task in sponsorship because no standard measurement process has been endorsed within the industry.[6] Techniques such as cost-per-thousand (CPM) that are commonly used in advertising simply are not appropriate for sponsorship. Yet sponsors continue to clamor for greater accountability. Until some standard process is agreed upon, marketers will continue to apply an array of acceptable techniques. Some argue that no single measure will ever emerge as an industry standard because the reasons for sponsoring events vary significantly. No single approach can capture the performance of any sponsorship in regard to the entire array of potential objectives.

One standard that is generally agreed upon is that longitudinal research is superior to cross-sectional research. The implication is that longitudinal research that tracks performance over time provides better information than does cross sectional research that simply provides a snapshot of the environment at a single point in time.[7] While the snapshot may tell you where the sponsorship is, it will not tell you how much it has achieved. Research that documents the level of sales at the end of the sponsorship period may show a nice picture of where the firm is; however, it provides no insight as to whether this result represents an adequate return on the sponsor's investment. Despite this assertion, some research efforts today continue to look solely at snapshots.

> While the snapshot may tell you where the sponsorship is, it will not tell you how much it has achieved.

It is evident that most efforts are based on a quantitative foundation. Despite the advantages of *results-based measures,* some sponsors continue to use qualitative assessments when analyzing the viability of the sponsorships in which they have invested their resources.

Current Practices

There are three broad categories for the measurement of sponsorship results: qualitative assessment, measures of market response, and media equivalencies. *Qualitative assessments* are subjective and are often based upon the opinions of a small number of executives and managers within the sponsoring firm. In general, *measures of market response* represent longitudinal, quantitative studies, whereas *media equivalencies* fall into the cross-sectional category.

> Market response often requires both a pre- and a postevent measurement of some marketing variable that is reflected in the sponsor's objectives.

Market response often requires both a pre- and a postevent measurement of some marketing metric that is reflected in the sponsor's objectives. Marketing researchers typically refer to this methodology as a before-and-after design. The label emanates from the fact that the variable under scrutiny (i.e., sales) is measured *before* the event; then the strategy is implemented; then the same variable is measured *after* the event. Conversely, media equivalencies are an assessment of the sponsorship's performance during the staging and the broadcast of the event; thus, the measurement represents a snapshot of the environment at the time of the broadcast. There are a variety of metrics that can represent objectives and therefore be subjected to scrutiny. The most common methods for postevent evaluation are identified in the list below and discussed on the following pages.

Postevent Evaluation Methods

Qualitative assessments
Market response
- Change in sales
- Impact on trade participation
- Change in consumer attitudes
Media equivalencies
- Comparable value
- Share

Qualitative Assessments

Qualitative assessment often utilizes the judgment of executives or other experts. They may use postevent measurements, but the absence of pre-event measurements makes it difficult to assure an accurate assessment. For instance, the sponsor may measure consumer attitudes about its brand after the event. Attitudes may be positive; but because there was no pre-event measurement, it is impossible to say how much the sponsorship contributed in the effort to improve the company's image in the marketplace. As a result, the evaluation is generally one of conjecture; do we think that the sponsorship had a positive impact?

Other qualitative assessments have little to do with ROI. For example, AT&T looks at the high-impact, emotional appeal of the Olympic Games. From a qualitative perspective, AT&T believes that the prestigious nature of the sponsorship contributes to the firm's image in the marketplace.[8] Another example is upscale marketer Cartier. The company tracks its mentions arising from sponsorship activities in a variety of media.

It makes a qualitative assessment of the prestige of any publication in which the sponsorship is acknowledged. More *value* is placed on a mention in *Town & Country* magazine than one in *People* magazine.[9] The prestige is the key point of differentiation as Cartier undoubtedly perceives a better fit between the *Town & Country* readers and its own target market.

Market Response

The three measures that reflect market response are the determination of the change in the level of sales, the impact that the sponsorship has on participation by the trade, and changes in attitudes on the part of consumers. As noted earlier, these measures are generally deemed to be more accurate when the before-and-after methodology is employed; however, there are acceptable variations to this measurement process. Regardless of the methodology used, it typically attempts to determine where the sponsor was prior to the start of the program and where it is once it is completed. The different ways in which these assessments can be implemented are described on the following pages.

Change in Sales

Marketers fully expect that each sponsorship in which they are involved will ultimately result in an increase in sales. While it is conceivable that sales will remain the same or even decline, such results are both unexpected and unlikely. Therefore, the question that needs to be answered should be, *How much did sales increase as a result of the sponsorship?* Other sponsors may take the measurement process one step further and attempt to measure the precise impact that the estimated increase in sales had on profitability.

The most common approach is to implement the simple *before-and-after (pre/post) methodology*. For example, a sponsor might measure average weekly sales for some predetermined period prior to the staging of the event. Then the measurement process is repeated upon the completion of the event. Any increase may then be attributed to the sponsorship program. If the sponsored event takes place over an extended period of time, then an intermediate measure of the average sales during the course of the event may also be appropriate. For example, the Olympic Games and the Wimbledon Tennis Tournament each last approximately two weeks. The three measurements provide an estimate of the short-term sales increase that occurred during the event and the residual increase that the marketer was able to sustain for some period after the event has been completed. Care should be taken to recognize the timing and to understand the potential impact of the leveraging campaign. This recognition is an acknowledgment that the entire increase in sales cannot be attributed to the sponsorship alone, especially when the leveraging campaign takes place over a period of months or years.

Other ways to implement this evaluation process are available to the sponsor. For example, *same-period sales can be compared*. This might involve measuring sales over a two- or three-month period that encompasses the sponsorship and then comparing the results with those from the same period in the previous year. Increases that are documented for the sponsorship period are attributed to the program.

If an event has a regional focus, then *sales in that region can be compared to the level of sales in the rest of the market*. If sales increase by 20 percent in the geographic area where the sponsorship is implemented while the rest of the market experiences only a 2 percent increase, then the estimated impact of the sponsorship was an 18 percent increase.

Another approach is to *tie sales directly to the sponsored event*. Many sponsors of a variety of events from the arts to sports provide discount coupons for their products. These coupons are often printed on the backs of tickets, distributed in the event program, passed out at the event venue, or mailed in the envelope with the tickets. Effectiveness is then measured by counting the number of coupons that are redeemed.[10] An example is a college football team that was sponsored by a local restaurant. The restaurant gave a 15 percent discount to anyone who presented his or her game ticket. The effectiveness of the sponsorship was measured by counting the number of people who redeemed their ticket for the discount.

The following examples provide additional insight into the implementation of a sales-oriented evaluation. Corn dogs are a typical food offering at many local fairs and festivals in the United States. In an effort to reach its target market, Sara Lee's State Fair Foods sponsored a number of events that fell into this category. Sales in the markets where sponsored events were staged were compared with those in a group of similar markets where no event or sponsorship program took place. The results documented a 25 percent increase in sales in those markets with sponsored events. This compared to a 3.5 percent increase in the control group of markets where no event took place. Just as dramatic was the measurement that indicated that sales were still up some 15.5 percent in the sponsorship markets a full six months after the sponsored events ended.[11]

> Sales in the markets where sponsored events were staged were compared with those in a group of similar markets where no event or sponsorship program took place.

The fast and accurate availability of retail sales data generated by UPC scanners has provided both richness and flexibility to the measurement process. One of Colgate-Palmolive's noteworthy sponsorships is the cause-related Starlight Foundation, an organization that grants the wishes of seriously and terminally ill children. While the philanthropic aspect of this sponsorship might be enough to justify the firm's investment, Colgate-Palmolive still wants to measure the return on its sponsorship investment. The sponsorship and its leveraging program include coupons that are distributed in freestanding inserts in many local newspapers. The coupons are bar-coded, thus they are easily tracked by the scanners. This additional information provides the aforementioned richness to the data. Using these scanner data, Colgate-Palmolive compares the average weekly sales for the three weeks following the distribution of the sponsorship-related coupons with the average weekly sales for the six months preceding the coupon drop. This allows the sponsor to estimate the net impact of the sponsorship.

Many sponsors would stop at this point; however, Colgate takes it a step further in an effort to assign an accurate value to its estimate of ROI. The company takes the net increase in sales and multiplies it by the product's profit margin in order to estimate the incremental profit. Then it subtracts the cost of the sponsorship program. The net result of this series of calculations is the determination of the true incremental profit associated with the sponsorship.[12] With these measures, the ROI can be calculated. Table 10.1 illustrates a hypothetical application for this type of methodology.

TABLE 10.1
Example of ROI
Determination

Average weekly sales for 6 months preceding coupon drop	$6,000,000
Average weekly sales for 3 weeks following coupon drop	8,150,000
Average weekly increase	2,150,000
Net sales increase associated with sponsorship (3 weeks)	6,450,000
Profit margin (30%)	1,950,000
Cost of sponsorship program (including leveraging costs)	1,250,000
Incremental profit	700,000
ROI (700,000/1,250,000)	56%

FIGURE 10.1
Example of Common Channel of Distribution

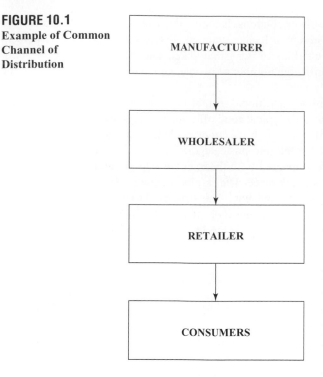

MANUFACTURER

WHOLESALER

RETAILER

CONSUMERS

The last example in this category will document the results for a cause-related marketing sponsorship. The fast-food chain Jack in the Box invested a small sum in its sponsorship of the "Save the Earth Foundation." Recent criticisms of the fast-food industry and of multinational corporations destroying rain forests in order to create grazing lands for the cattle needed to supply the chains with beef may have contributed to the chain's perceived need to enhance its image through this type of relationship. Yet the ultimate objective was to increase sales. The key element of the sponsorship was the opportunity for the restaurant's customers to receive a discount coupon book in exchange for a one dollar donation to the Save the Earth Foundation. A total of 35,000 books were *sold,* with the proceeds going to the foundation. Management had projected a coupon redemption rate of about 3 percent; however, tracking of the coupons revealed an actual redemption rate of 26 percent. This result equated to incremental sales of some $300,000.[13] Results like these illustrate why many marketers are seriously exploring sponsorship opportunities outside of the sports domain.

Impact on Trade Participation

It may be important at this time to clarify what is meant by the term *trade*. When marketers speak of the trade, they are referring to the wholesalers and retailers that participate in the channel of distribution. As a consequence of their location between the manufacturer and the consumers, they are also referred to as *intermediaries*. An illustration of one of the most common forms of the channel of distribution in the consumer market is illustrated in Figure 10.1.

Trade participation may consider several different variables. The most commonly employed are shelf space, their willingness to display point-of-sale (POS) promotions such as posters, the willingness to engage in cooperative advertising, and the percentage of intermediaries in the affected market that agree to stock the sponsor's products.

Marlboro cigarettes sponsored a national darts tournament in the United Kingdom. Since darts are a common activity in pubs in the U.K., it was believed that the effectiveness of the sponsorship could be assessed by determining the number of additional pubs that decided to sell their cigarettes during the course of the sponsorship program.[14]

Listerine mouthwash sponsored the Taste of Chicago Festival in an effort to increase shelf space and the trade's willingness to engage in cooperative advertising with Listerine and its parent company Warner-Lambert. One measure also involved POS displays. In the local Chicago market, the number of displays in local retail stores was 112 percent higher than what Listerine was able to attain in the rest of the United States. Furthermore, retailer participation in cooperative advertising reached the highest level in the history of the brand.[15] It is safe to assume that the marketer believed that the $20,000 sponsorship fee was a sound investment.

A similar objective was articulated by Kraft General Foods for its sponsorship of a NASCAR race team by its Country Time Lemonade brand. One leveraging component of the sponsorship was a mobile race car simulator that was moved from one location to another so as to coincide with upcoming races. In an effort to appeal to their target market, fans were allowed to take a "ride" in the simulator by providing a proof of purchase for a Country Time product. The results were compelling. Not only was a substantial increase in sales recorded,

TABLE 10.2
Measurement Using Before-and-After Design

Premeasurement	20%
Exposure to sponsorship	Yes
Postmeasurement	45%
Impact of sponsorship	+25%

but the sponsorship was also credited with an average increase of 40 case displays in the retail stores located in those cities where the simulator was available to the fans.

Change in Consumer Attitudes

In general, this approach to assessing the impact of a sponsorship requires the measurement of consumer attitudes both prior to and upon the completion of the sponsored event. The consideration under scrutiny will typically be some measure of favorability. Examples include the overall image of the sponsor, attitudes about its role in society, the self-reported likelihood of purchasing the sponsor's products, and whether or not the sponsor's products are superior to those of its competitors.

When utilizing the before-and-after design methodology to make this assessment, the existing attitude within the market must be measured prior to the start of the sponsorship program. For example, what percentage of the target market indicates that they anticipate purchasing the sponsor's product in the foreseeable future? This process does not incorporate the future sponsorship; in other words, consumers are unaware of the impending relationship between the marketer and the property. Once the premeasurement process is completed, management will establish its objectives relative to the attitude in question. The sponsorship and its accompanying leveraging program are then implemented. Upon completion of the program, the attitude under scrutiny is again measured. This postmeasurement allows for the determination of the impact of the sponsorship. For example, if the premeasurement indicated that 20 percent of those surveyed planned to purchase the sponsor's product and the postmeasurement of that phenomenon was 45 percent, then the estimate of the impact of the sponsorship is easily determined. In this case, the purchase intent increased by 25 percent. Now the question is, *How did actual performance compare to the stated sponsorship objectives?* The results of this before-and-after design are illustrated in Table 10.2. But it is important to realize that there are several other experimental research designs that can be used to estimate the impact of a change in marketing strategy.

A variation of this technique is the after-only design with a control group. With this design, no premeasurements are taken; rather, two groups are designated. One group, known as the *experimental group,* is exposed to the sponsorship. A second group, the *control group,* is not exposed to the sponsorship. This often involves two geographic areas. For example, consumers in Memphis may be made aware of the sponsorship of a professional golf tournament while those in New Orleans are not exposed to a either the sponsorship or the corresponding leveraging activities. At the end of the sponsorship period, both groups are subjected to the measurement process and the results are compared. The difference in the postmeasurements is attributed to the sponsorship. Table 10.3 provides an example of this evaluation method.

Lloyd's Bank used this approach to assess its sponsorship of theatrical programming in the United Kingdom. One objective of the Lloyd's Bank Theatre Challenge was to improve the bank's image within the consumer market. When the attitudes of the experimental group were

TABLE 10.3
Measurement Using After-Only with Control Group Design

	Memphis	New Orleans
Premeasurement	No	No
Exposed to sponsorship	Yes	No
Postmeasurement	36%	25%
Difference		+11%

compared with those of the control group, the results indicated that the sponsorship was effective in the task of improving consumer perceptions. The measures of the rating of "Lloyd's as a place to bank," the perception as to whether or not it was "keeping up with the times," attitudes regarding "friendliness," and perceptions of the bank's "accessibility" were some 30 percent higher in the group exposed to the sponsorship.[16] It is likely that management at Lloyd's deemed this result to be quite good and considered the sponsorship to be a success.

Media Equivalencies

One of the most commonly used approaches to postevent evaluation is that of calculating media equivalencies. The basic premise is that sponsorship provides opportunities for exposure in a number of different media. Without the sponsorship, these opportunities might not exist; and if they did, they would come with a cost associated with them. For example, the signage at the venue may be visible to fans watching the event on TV. Consider signage on race cars and how much exposure the lead car creates for its sponsors. Undoubtedly, this element of exposure is the primary consideration when calculating the equivalent value that was generated for the sponsor.

> The basic premise is that sponsorship provides opportunities for exposure in a number of different media.

Figure 10.2 shows how a sponsor can achieve meaningful exposure when the race car in which it has a sponsorship stake is contending for the lead and shown on TV for an extended period of time.

While TV exposure is the most common variable that is subjected to the measurement process, there may be other considerations as well. For instance, it is reasonable to assume that having the sponsor's name mentioned during the broadcast has value. Additional value may be associated with the exposure of the signage and public address announcements to spectators at the event itself. Any complimentary advertisements in the event's published program can be translated into an equivalent media value. Some incremental value may also emanate from news reports, video replays, acknowledgments on the scoreboard, postevent interviews with participants, and press releases.

When considering the use of media equivalencies, the measurement may look solely at the total time during which the sponsor's logo appeared on the screen during the TV broadcast. This approach does provide some fundamental insight into the effectiveness of the sponsorship. The more common application for media equivalencies is that of determining comparable value. Using the comparable value approach, the focus is on the economic value of the exposure. Simply stated, how much would it have cost the sponsor to have purchased the same level of exposure attained by virtue of the sponsorship?

FIGURE 10.2
Exposure for NASCAR Sponsors

The two variations of media equivalencies discussed on the following pages are *comparable value* and *share*. These techniques address the questions of how much exposure the sponsor received, the value of that exposure, and the comparison of the sponsor's results to those of other sponsors of the same event. The measures also facilitate the comparison of the results from one event to the results of other events that the marketer sponsors.

Comparable Value

While there are several companies that provide the service of calculating the comparable value of a sponsor's exposure, Joyce Julius & Associates is at the forefront of this emerging industry. The concept was developed when Ms. Julius was employed by Domino's Pizza. Management at Domino's wondered what they were gaining from the company's sponsorship of an Indy car race team. When an objective answer to that question could not be formulated, Julius decided that there was a need to develop a methodology by which the economic value of the sponsorship could be determined.[17] It was readily apparent that this service would be valuable to many sponsors; this realization precipitated her break from Domino's and the founding of Joyce Julius & Associates. Today, the firm calculates what it refers to as *exposure value* for its clients and publishes some of the results in the *Sponsor's Report*. A sample of this report is available at www.joycejulius.com. While the firm's focus is arguably still on motor sports, recent reports have looked at horse racing, venue naming rights, and product placements in motion pictures.

> The fundamental premise of media equivalencies is that sponsors receive exposure and this exposure has commercial value.

The fundamental premise of media equivalencies is that sponsors receive exposure and this exposure has commercial value. The objective of the comparable value methodology is to assign a single estimate to the monetary value of that exposure.

To illustrate this methodology, the focus will be on the basic evaluation model used by Joyce Julius & Associates in its effort to estimate the value of the exposure received during the TV broadcast of a sponsored event. However, it must be acknowledged that several other service providers employ variations of this methodology. In fact, even Joyce Julius & Associates has developed new procedures in an effort to ameliorate the concerns of critics of the comparable value approach. Some of these improvements will be discussed later in this chapter.

Using the basic method for this calculation, the emphasis is on two components. The most important component is the determination of the exact amount of time that a sponsor's brand name, trademarks, and logos appeared in a readable form for the TV viewers. The second component is the number of times that the sponsor's name was mentioned during the course of the broadcast.

First, let's consider the value associated with the exposure of the sponsor's brand, trademarks, and logos. In a recent NASCAR race, Goodyear images appeared on viewers' screens for a total of 18 minutes and 43 seconds (18:43). While this is a key statistic, it fails to capture the concept of value. The task then is to answer this question: How much would it have cost Goodyear to have purchased an equivalent level of exposure during the broadcast? This question is best answered by determining the cost of purchasing that amount of advertising time for the broadcast. To make this determination, the cost of a 30-second advertisement is used as the basis. For this particular NASCAR race, the cost of a 30-second cell was $4,260. This translates into a cost of $142 per second. The aggregate exposure was 1,123 seconds, thereby creating some $159,466 in value.

The second component is the number of mentions garnered by the sponsor during the broadcast. Thus, there must now be a value assigned to the five times that the Goodyear brand was verbally acknowledged during the course of the telecast. While some people may deem this element of the estimate to be somewhat subjective, the Joyce Julius & Associates'

TABLE 10.4
Example of Calculation of Exposure Value

Exposure time	1,123 seconds	Exposure value	$159,466
Broadcast mentions	5 times	Exposure value	7,100
Total exposure (comparable) value			$166,566

methodology places a value of 10 seconds for each mention; therefore, the five mentions are deemed to be comparable to 50 seconds of exposure. A value for this component may now be developed by multiplying the number of seconds associated with it (50) by the cost per second of a purchased advertisement ($142). The result in this example is $7,100. With the calculations for both components completed, the comparable value for the sponsor's exposure may now be estimated by summing the results. It is estimated that Goodyear received $166,566 in exposure value from its sponsorship during the broadcast. Table 10.4 summarizes these results.

With this estimate in hand, the sponsor may now compare its results to its costs and determine the sponsorship's ROI. A comparison to other sponsors may also be valuable; how did Goodyear perform relative to the array of event sponsors? It may also be productive to compare the results from different events. All of this information may be helpful in making the determination as to whether or not the investment was a sound one. It is especially crucial when it is time to consider the renewal of an existing contract and to objectively evaluate the costs associated with the sponsorship program.

There is a temptation to simply compare the cost of the sponsorship rights to the comparable value generated by it. Unfortunately, this procedure is short-sighted. Critics will argue that 30 seconds of exposure is not equivalent to a 30-second advertisement. Viewers only see a logo; they are not presented with other meaningful visual images or informative narratives that are designed to persuade them to purchase the sponsor's product. It is also understood that the sponsor will generally spend additional money to leverage the sponsorship. A one million dollar sponsorship will ultimately cost far more than the initial rights fees. As a result, the industry standard is that a sponsorship should produce $3 in comparable value for every $1 spent on rights fees.[18] Thus, to be considered successful using this measure, a one million dollar sponsorship should produce a minimum of $3 million in equivalent exposure value.

> The industry standard is that a sponsorship should produce $3 in comparable value for every $1 spent on rights fees.

An example of an application beyond sports that employed media equivalencies was that of the Office of Tourism of the state of Louisiana. In an effort to reach one of its target markets, the Office of Tourism sponsored the International Jazz Festival in Montreal, Canada. There is a cultural link between the French Canadians of the Quebec province and the French heritage of the state of Louisiana. And of course there is the jazz for which New Orleans is renowned. Louisiana spent $250,000 on rights fees and was optimistic that it could attain a 4:1 ratio of comparable exposure value to the cost of its investment. When the results were tabulated, the $8,000,000 in exposure value resulted in a 32:1 ratio. The state was quick to renew its sponsorship for the following year. According to a Louisiana official, "the return was so big we couldn't pass up" the opportunity to renew the sponsorship.[19]

Share

The calculation of the share statistic is similar to the approach used to determine a firm's market share. However, the variable under scrutiny in this case is not sales; rather, it is the

TABLE 10.5
Share of Exposure Time

Source: Joyce Julius & Associates, *Sponsor's Report* 18, no. 2 (2002).

Event:	NASCAR Subway 400
Venue:	North Carolina Speedway, Rockingham, NC
Date:	February 24
Broadcast:	Live, U.S. national, 4 hours, Fox free-to-air TV
Total sponsor exposure:	5 hours, 34 minutes, 26 seconds (20,066 seconds)
Total exposure time for Ford:	17 minutes, 17 seconds (1,037 seconds)
Ford's share of exposure time:	(1,037/20,666 = .052), or 5.2%

comparison of the level of exposure attained by one sponsor vis-à-vis the other sponsors associated with the event. This technique is valuable when an event has many sponsors, when the costs of being associated with an event vary significantly, and when the event is broadcast to the consumer market. Motor sports represent the perfect scenario for the measurement of a sponsor's share.

Each race team will typically have a primary sponsor. The fees paid to a top team can be substantially more than those paid for a similar association with a lesser team. In addition to this disparity, each team will have a myriad of sponsors that paid lower fees for a less prominent relationship with the team, the driver, and the car.

Share is calculated upon the completion of the event's broadcast. To make this determination, management must first specify the unit of measurement to be used as the basis. One measure is simply that of exposure. That is to say, they calculate share as a percentage of the aggregate exposure time gained by all of the sponsors associated with the event. To calculate share using this basis, there must first be a measurement of the total on-air exposure gained by the event's sponsor base. Next is the determination of the exposure time gained by the sponsor performing the evaluation. Finally, share is calculated by dividing the sponsor's exposure time by the aggregate exposure time. The result is the sponsor's share of exposure. In this case, share is simply the percentage of the total exposure time that was gained by the sponsor. Consider the recent example from NASCAR that is presented in Table 10.5.

The results indicate that Ford received approximately 5.2 percent of all the exposure time attained by the (204) sponsors that were affiliated with the event. This measure can be compared to other sponsors at the same level. For example, data from the NASCAR race indicated that Chevrolet and Dodge, two of Ford's direct competitors in the retail automotive market, gained 3.6 and 3.8 shares respectively.

A second example from the motor sports category involves Formula 1 racing. For the 2003 season, share was calculated for each of the team sponsors. In this case, the "team level" was the only sponsorship category considered in the calculation. While Ferrari may have been the dominant team in the racing competition, when the focus was shifted to exposure, the winner was BMW Williams F1. The BMW team secured a share of exposure of some 23 percent.[20] According to a spokesperson for S-Comm, the research company that performed the analysis, the results indicate that the race team was better able to convert media coverage of the team into meaningful exposure for the sponsor.

The two examples illustrate two different applications for the same technique. The NASCAR study included all sponsors at all levels of involvement. This would allow minor sponsors to compare their results to those of midlevel or major sponsors. Of course such an assessment must also take the cost of the sponsorships into consideration. The Formula 1 example looks only at the sponsors of the teams that participated in a particular series of events. Thus, it facilitates only the comparison of the team sponsors.

While the simple share of exposure is adequate for some sponsors, others choose to calculate their share of the aggregate exposure value attained by the array of relevant sponsors.

TABLE 10.6
Share of
Exposure Value

Event:	NASCAR Subway 400
Venue:	North Carolina Speedway, Rockingham, NC
Date:	February 24
Broadcast:	Live, U.S. national, 4 hours, Fox free-to-air TV
Total sponsor exposure value:	$104,791,380
Total exposure value for Ford:	6,005,975
Ford's share of exposure value:	6,005,975/104,791,380 = .057, or 5.7%

A reexamination of the NASCAR example illustrates this type of evaluation. Table 10.6 delineates the sponsor's performance on this criterion.

These results indicate that Ford received a 5.2 percent share of exposure time while gaining a 5.7 percent share of the exposure value attributed to the 204 sponsors that were associated with the event. The difference may cause one to question why the disparity exists. It is important to remember that the Joyce Julius methodology incorporates more than simple exposure into the equation for the calculation of exposure value. It is evident that the Ford sponsorship produced additional value by virtue of being mentioned more often during the broadcast than did the typical sponsorship. When alternative methods that use several different variables are used to calculate exposure value, even more variation is possible. Still, each of the share statistics can provide valuable insight into the postevent assessment process.

Overview of Concerns Surrounding Postevent Evaluation

Undoubtedly there will be many who will argue that the list of measurement techniques discussed on the preceding pages is not complete. When an event is broadcast on TV, the viewer ratings provide a measure of the sponsorship's reach. It affords the opportunity to use the cost-per-thousand (CPM) measure that is commonly applied when considering the effectiveness of a program's ability to reach consumers. But realistically, the CPM statistic is a measure of the vehicle's ability to reach consumers; it fails to capture the essence of the sponsorship's effectiveness. Simply looking at the ratings is also insufficient. TV ratings are an aggregate measure, and it is likely that not all viewers are part of the sponsor's target market. What is more problematic, TV ratings do not provide any information regarding the extent to which the sponsor gained exposure during the broadcast. In general, it is believed that measures of reach derived from TV ratings figures are overstated and inadequate in the sponsor's efforts to measure *results*.[21]

Another common measure is sponsor recognition. Consumers are surveyed upon the completion of the event and asked to identify the sponsors. While the postmeasurement provides some insight, the result is more meaningful when a premeasurement has been taken. The premeasurement is particularly relevant for large, upscale events where the leveraging campaign is initiated well before the event itself is staged. This not only tells the sponsor how effective it has been in communicating its relationship with the sponsee, but it can also potentially identify competitors that have implemented effective ambushing campaigns. Perhaps the biggest shortcoming of this method is that recognition does not necessarily translate into positive behavior from the sponsor's perspective. Even though the consumers are aware that Coca-Cola is a sponsor of the Olympics, this awareness does not always make those consumers any more likely to purchase Coca-Cola products.

> Even though the consumers are aware that Coca-Cola is a sponsor of the Olympics, this awareness does not always make those consumers any more likely to purchase Coca-Cola products.

Qualitative assessments may be viable when the sponsor has a realistic perspective of what the property has to offer. Perhaps the event's prestige and its perceived impact on the sponsor's image are sufficient. In other cases, the sponsorship may be considered effective because it excludes the opportunity for a competitor to be involved. It may be difficult to quantify the impact that hospitality opportunities and the entertainment of employees have, so management may rely on intuition. Marketers new to the field of sponsorship may apply qualitative assessments simply because they have failed to consider ROI as a required element of their sponsorships. In such cases, quantitative objectives are not established and the measurement process is not implemented in a timely manner. Finally, not all sponsors have fully embraced the concept of ROI as the primary motivation for this type of investment. Some sponsors still view ego-oriented or philanthropic objectives as a sound basis for their involvement. If that is the case, quantitative assessments will likely give way to assessments of a qualitative nature. As a rule of thumb, however, qualitative measures should be used to augment the more objective measures designed to evaluate a sponsorship's ROI. It is rare that qualitative measures can answer all of the questions germane to the postevent evaluation process.

Media equivalencies have been used to measure ROI for some 20 years. Several companies provide this type of measurement service to an array of clients that are allocating significant resources to sponsor a variety of properties. The most common criticism is that simple exposure is not truly equivalent to nor does it have the emotional impact of a comparable amount of time devoted to focused advertising. Joyce Julius recognizes this and has attempted to allay the concerns of this methodology's critics by specifying a three-to-one ratio goal of exposure value to expenditures on rights fees.

Another concern is that the array of service providers utilizes different formulas for making this calculation. For example, whereas industry giant Joyce Julius & Associates uses *sponsor mentions* in computing exposure value, its European counterpart S-Comm does not incorporate that component. As a result, the two companies could evaluate the same broadcast yet develop estimates that differ significantly. It has been reported that "every agency makes its own adaptations. A formula of how to measure the exposure value can vary between 5 and 50 percent." In fact, the values are so dubious that Heineken looks toward the lower numbers generated as more realistic estimates.[22]

> A formula of how to measure the exposure value can vary between 5 and 50 percent.

The next concern is the definition of what constitutes a measurable image. How clearly must it be seen? How much clutter can be present? Is there a minimum time that the image must be viewable? Finally, the most commonly used measures incorporate only the exposure gained during the TV broadcast. Obviously, additional value is derived from international broadcasts, replays, news coverage, publicity, Internet images, POS display, and exposure via cross-marketing efforts with co-sponsors. Clearly, media equivalencies can provide important information that allows the sponsorship's ROI to be estimated in an objective manner. But even these measures are viewed as inadequate by many marketers. It is encouraging to note that the measures of media equivalent value continue to be refined in an effort to allay the concerns of their critics. However, the absence of a uniform approach to the measurement of this phenomenon will continue to create discontent and controversy.

> Measures of media equivalent value continue to be refined in an effort to allay the concerns of their critics.

Finally, there are the measures of market response. Since these are specifically designed to evaluate changes in the marketplace, they can be tied directly to the sponsor's objectives. The result is that a precise estimate of ROI can be determined, and this estimate may allow the sponsor to compare its own performance to that of its competition in the same or similar events. It also allows the marketer to compare results across its sponsorship portfolio. Which events and what type of properties allow the marketer to maximize its ROI? But these quantitative measures are not without their critics as well. Effective use of market response measures is dependent upon two key factors. First, the sponsor needs to establish measurable objectives on some key marketing metric prior to the inception of the sponsorship. How much of an increase in sales is anticipated? How many new retailers will decide to sell the sponsor's products? Second, the measurement techniques should be defined prior to the implementation of the sponsorship. In other words, How will the changes in the market be measured? As many marketers have discovered, these measurement methodologies may be difficult to operationalize.

Yet another valid concern relates to the inability to isolate the precise level of market response that can be attributed explicitly to the sponsorship itself. Presumably the sponsor has leveraged its sponsorship with an effective integrated marketing communications plan. If so, the question becomes one of how much of the change can be attributed to the sponsorship and how much should be attributed to the leveraging program. But since the leveraging efforts are an outgrowth of the sponsorship itself, some will argue that there is no need to dissect the components. Therefore, the entire increase may be attributed to the sponsorship.

> Postevent evaluation is essential if the sponsor wants to determine whether or not any sponsorship was a sound investment.

Despite the problems outlined on the preceding pages, postevent evaluation is essential if the sponsor wants to determine whether or not any sponsorship was a sound investment. It is this insight that provides guidance when making the decision to renew or to terminate a relationship with a property or event. The problem is that there is no consensus as to how to perform the measurement process. Because of this absence of a standard measurement, we continue to see new and improved procedures developed. Service providers continue to develop customized methods for their clients that want to be certain that the process relates specifically to their sponsorship goals. So while there may be no consensus as to how postevent measurement should be performed, there is general agreement that it is indeed necessary.

New and Improved Measures

Recognition Grade

This procedure represents an effort by Joyce Julius & Associates to refine the methodology used to calculate exposure value. Remember that one of the criticisms regarding the traditional methodology concerned the definition of what constituted *clear* exposure. Many critics believe that estimates derived via the traditional approach are unrealistically high.[23] Whereas the traditional methodology simply put all "clear and in-focus on-screen time" into a single category, the *recognition grade methodology* takes other considerations into account. According to the firm's promotional materials, this approach includes issues such as the visibility of the identity within the particular camera angle, the amount of sponsor clutter surrounding the brand's name or logo, and the integration/activization level during the particular segment. As a result, company spokespersons state that the methodology considers individual circumstances such as close-ups, unique views, and wide-angle shots. The recognition grade scale is outlined in Table 10.7.

TABLE 10.7
**Joyce Julius &
Associates,
Recognition Grade
Scale**

Source: "Sponsors Report,"
www.joycejulius.com/spon-
sors_report.htm (accessed
March 18, 2006). Reprinted
with permission of Joyce Julius
& Associates, Inc.

Category	% of Value	Characteristics
1	100	Complete name/logo dominance during segment; identity occupies 70–100% of screen
2	70	Name/logo shares segment with up to three other sponsors; identity occupies 50–70% of screen
3	50	Name/logo shares segment with up to 10 other sponsors; identity occupies 20–50% of the screen
4	30	Name/logo shares segment with large sums of sponsors; identity occupies 5–20% of screen
5	10	Name/logo surrounded by clutter; identity occupies less than 5% of the screen

With the recognition grade, exposure that is deemed to be less than ideal and consequently classified as either category 2, 3, 4, or 5 is discounted. It has value, but not as much as the totally unobstructed view of those exposure occurrences that fall into category 1.

NTIV Analysis

The NTIV report is a bit of a paradox. The acronym stands for *National Television Impression Value*. But its analysis goes far beyond television. This methodology is also a proprietary process that was developed by Joyce Julius & Associates. While it also focuses on exposure, it seeks to incorporate additional sources such as radio coverage, the print media, event venue exposure, displays, cross-marketing endeavors, and exposure in the areas in close proximity to the event venue.

The statistical objective is to determine the number of *gross impressions* attained via the array of exposure outlets. It considers the live attendance and those fans' exposure to signage and announcements. Away from the venue, NTIV incorporates the TV ratings, the circulation of the print media publications in which the sponsor's name is referenced, the number of listeners for the radio programs where the sponsor is noted, and the estimated reach of cross-marketing efforts with co-sponsors. Once the number of gross impressions in each category is estimated, those values are multiplied by a measure that reflects the estimated cost of a single impression in the corresponding medium. For example, for the calculation of exposure value from national TV, the estimated number of gross impressions is multiplied by the average cost of advertising during televised sports programming on the major TV networks over the past 12 months on a per viewer basis. An example of the derivation of an NTIV estimate is shown in Table 10.8.

It can be seen that the NTIV value expands the scope of the original estimate. A calculation for the exposure value from the TV broadcast is reflected in the first line of Table 10.8. But it is important to note that even this calculation differs from the traditional approach to the calculation of comparable value. Still, if this measure is used to estimate the value of exposure during the broadcast, it is evident that the incorporation of the additional elements more than

TABLE 10.8
NTIV Estimate

Source: "Exposure Summary,"
2004, www.joycejulius.com/
samplerepors/NTIV%20method-
ology%20Sample.pdf (accessed
July 13, 2004). Reprinted with
permission of Joyce Julius &
Associates, Inc.

Section	Exposure Time	Number of Mentions, Ads/Articles	Impressions	Value
National TV	4:25:35	399	16,493,160	$6,062,510.00
TV news program	NTIV	264	15,788,000	231,767.64
Event site	NTIV	NTIV	73,678,020	1,081.593.33
Cross-marketing	NTIV	NTIV	206,875,682	3,036,935.01
Internet	NTIV	57	82,025,611	1,204,135.97
Print media	NTIV	693	195,848,123	2,875,050.44
Total	4:25:35		590,708,596	$14,491,992.39

doubled the estimated value for this sponsor (which was a title sponsor for a PGA tournament). It can be argued that this is a more realistic perspective of the sponsorship environment, especially when TV is not the key factor in gaining exposure. A more precise description of the calculation procedures can be found on the Joyce Julius & Associates Web site.

Spindex Media Evaluation System

S-Comm characterizes itself as a leading research and evaluation consultancy working solely in the area of sports marketing. Its *Spindex Media Evaluation System* incorporates all sports programming in its market, including free-to-air and cable/satellite. It requires the sponsor's logo to be 100 percent visible to the TV audience in order to be considered as exposure. Essentially, S-Comm determines *media equivalent cost* much the same way that Joyce Julius determines *exposure value*. One key difference is that the firm applies a *Spindex value* based upon its insight regarding the marketplace. This adjusted value is what the firm provides as a measurement to determine ROI. S-Comm also breaks down and reports the location germane to the visibility of the logo. For instance, exposure for Volvo in conjunction with its sponsorship of the European PGA championship included exposure from signage, electronic symbols on the scoreboards, the caddies' clothing, the interview backdrop, and on the tee boxes (among other locations). So not only does the sponsor receive an estimate of its sponsorship value, but it also receives feedback that might facilitate the improvement of the level of exposure in subsequent broadcasts by allowing for the negotiation of more advantageous signage locations for future events.

Sponsorship Scorecard

Research giant A. C. Nielsen has launched a new service that became available to clients in 2004 after first testing the technique in April 2004. The first major client for this service was the NFL which began to use the Nielsen methodology at the beginning of the 2005 season. The company positions *Sponsorship Scorecard* as a "natural progression for sports clients who have asked Nielsen to help develop a more effective tool for measuring sponsorships." Although details are still sketchy, the service is purported to determine value acquired from in-stadium signage, live broadcast promotions, and audio mentions. The service will be delivered to its subscribers via the Internet.[24]

SPORTSi

TNSSport recently introduced a high-tech component into the process of calculating comparable values. The most important aspect of the calculation remains the same; it is still the total time during which the sponsor's brand, trademarks, or logo are in a viewable form for those watching the event on TV. In this regard, the *SPORTSi methodology* is similar to those of its predecessors in the field of service providers that offer the determination of exposure value as part of their assortment of services. But in this case, exposure is monitored electronically rather than by a human observer. Ironically, this service simply represents a new application for an existing software product, so it is not new technology per se.

> Image recognition software does not change all parts of the equation, but it adds "strength, credibility, and a new standard to the measurement of brand exposure."

The recognition software was originally developed to scan business documents and glean key bits of information. Technologically speaking, the software can be trained as to what to look for. In its new application, it is trained to look for identifiers such as trademarks and logos that are related to event sponsors. Exposure data can be extracted with virtually no human input or interaction. Because of the electronic nature of the surveillance, the level of accuracy is enhanced and the resultant estimates should be more accurate. According to a company spokesperson, the image recognition software does not change all parts of the equation, but it adds "strength, credibility, and a new standard to the measurement of brand exposure."[25] The firm also touts the richness of the resultant data. Instead of a single aggregate measure, the broadcast can be broken down into segments so that the sponsor has a better idea of when its exposure peaked. Was it at the beginning of the broadcast or at the end when viewer intensity was at its peak? The answer to this question can provide insight beyond what the aggregate measure of exposure value provides. Therefore, it should help sponsors and prospective sponsors make better decisions.

Sponsee Accountability

To this point, the discussion has focused on the performance of the sponsorship itself. There is considerable risk with sponsorships because the results cannot be predetermined. There is no way to eliminate that risk, so postevent measurement is used to evaluate performance. But not all elements of sponsorship are so difficult to assess. As costs continue to escalate, sponsors have begun to demand greater accountability on the part of the sponsee. The result has been an increased emphasis on postevent compliance reports from the sponsee. The 2004 Performance Research/IEG study indicated that 57 percent of the sponsors surveyed deemed *postevent fulfillment* reports to be very important. This is up from the 45 percent that expressed a similar view only two years earlier.[26]

> The 2004 Performance Research/IEG study indicated that 57 percent of the sponsors surveyed deemed postevent fulfillment reports to be very important.

Sponsorship fulfillment or compliance reports were introduced in an earlier chapter. It should be recalled from that discussion that these reports document the actions taken by the sponsee on behalf of the sponsor. They allow the sponsor to verify that all of the promised components were provided. If the sponsee promised four signs, the compliance report documents their existence. Some organizations go so far as to provide tangible documentation to their sponsors. For example, the Cleveland Cavaliers of the NBA provide copies of advertisements and media affidavits to their sponsors.[27] The more comprehensive reports can also provide a basis for calculating ROI by including attendance figures and estimates of the number of *impressions* generated by sponsorship components such as signage, public address announcements at the event venue, and identification on the backs of tickets.

It is recommended that sponsors include their demand for this report in their original negotiations. By having the sponsee contractually obligated to provide the report, there is less likelihood that the sponsor will be shortchanged during the sponsorship period. In other words, it helps assure that the sponsor receives everything to which it is entitled. This compliance should help make the sponsorship more effective.

Closing Capsule

The keys to evaluating the effectiveness of a sponsorship lay in the delineation of measurable sponsorship objectives prior to initiating the process, then measuring the results upon its completion. Far too many companies fail to implement the appropriate procedures and are left speculating as to whether or not they achieved a satisfactory return on their sponsorship investment.

While there is a growing emphasis on postevent measurement, there is no universally agreed upon method for its implementation. Some techniques have been adaptations of tools used to measure the impact of advertising. Other methods employ traditional experimental designs from marketing research; these include the before-and-after design as well as the after-only design with a control group. Other measurement models that were not discussed in this chapter may also be used in the assessment process.

There are three broad categories of postevent evaluation. Qualitative assessment relies on subjective evaluations. Measures of market response attempt to isolate the changes that occur in consumer attitudes, sales, and participation by the trade over the course of the sponsorship. Media equivalencies are estimates of the comparable value of a sponsor's exposure in terms of the cost of purchasing an equivalent level of advertising during the broadcast. Each technique has its advocates while each technique also has its critics.

> **Marketers have continued to stress the need to develop better measurement tools.**

Sponsors have begun to expand the scope of their evaluations in an effort to relate the results to their bottom line. These measures are important in the task of making decisions regarding the renewal of sponsorship contracts that are set to expire. As a result, marketers have continued to stress the need to develop better measurement tools. Companies such as Joyce Julius & Associates, S-Comm, and A. C. Nielsen have all recently introduced new, and ostensibly improved, methodologies.

It is evident that marketers are emphasizing postevent measurement more than ever before. They are also demanding greater accountability from the sponsee itself. More sponsors have begun to demand postevent fulfillment reports that document that all of the benefits to which they were contractually entitled were actually provided.

As more emphasis has been directed toward sponsorship ROI, there has been an increased emphasis on the measurement of results. More attention is being paid to the sponsee as well. Only when we understand the performance of a sponsorship can we make an informed decision regarding expenditures for future sponsorship opportunities. Sponsorships are expensive; postevent evaluation is the final step in the process to make certain that the marketer does not allocate precious resources to unproductive sponsorships. It isn't easy, but it is a necessary step in the sponsorship process.

Review Questions

1. Why has postevent evaluation become more important to sponsors over the past few years?
2. What is meant by the statement that postevent evaluation lacks a standard measure?
3. Why does the absence of a standard measure create controversy?
4. What is the major weakness of cross-sectional research in the task of assessing the impact of a sponsorship?
5. What are the three broad categories for postevent evaluation?
6. Explain the concept of media equivalencies.
7. Why do some sponsors calculate share as a means of determining effectiveness?
8. Why do firms seek a three-to-one ratio of exposure value-to-costs rather than simply seeking to recover their costs (one-to-one ratio)?
9. How has the implementation of the recognition grade methodology by Joyce Julius & Associates improved the postevent evaluation process?
10. Think about sponsorships with which you are familiar. Identify one where you think its effectiveness is best judged using qualitative assessments. Identify a second where market response is the best tool. Finally, identify a third where media equivalencies represent the best mode of postevent evaluation. Briefly explain your reasoning for these three choices.

Endnotes

1. G. Levin, "Sponsors Put Pressure on for Accountability," *Advertising Age,* 1994, pp. S1, S4.

2. Ibid.

3. IEG, "2004 IEG/Performance Research Study Highlights What Sponsors Want," 2004, www.performanceresearch.com/ieg_sponsor_survey.htm (accessed October 13, 2005).

4. A. Kolah, "No Accounting for Sponsorship," March 5, 1999, www.mad.co.uk (accessed November 17, 1999).

5. S. Bentley, "On the Ball," *Marketing Week,* November 1999, special report.

6. Kolah, "No Accounting for Sponsorship."

7. Ibid.

8. Levin, "Sponsors Put Pressure on for Accountability."

9. *IEG's Complete Guide to Sponsorship: Everything You Wanted to Know about Sponsorship* (Chicago: IEG, Inc., 1999), p. 27.

10. L. Ukman, "Evaluating ROI of a Sponsorship Program," *Marketing News* 30, no. 18 (August 26, 1996), pp. 5, 16.

11. Ibid.

12. Levin, "Sponsors Put Pressure on for Accountability."

13. *IEG's Complete Guide to Sponsorship,* p. 32.

14. Kolah, "No Accounting for Sponsorship."

15. Ukman, "Evaluating ROI of a Sponsorship Program."

16. Ukman, "Evaluating ROI of a Sponsorship Program."

17. SMQ Profile/Interview, *Sport Marketing Quarterly* 7, no. 2 (1998), pp. 6–7.

18. Levin, "Sponsors Put Pressure on for Accountability."

19. "Canadian Festival Sponsorship Yields 32-to-1 Return for Louisiana Tourism," *IEG Sponsorship Report* 19, no. 8 (April 24, 2000), pp. 1–2.

20. C. Britcher, "F1's Sponsor Exposure Race," January 9, 2004, www.sportbusiness.com/news/index?news_item_id=153488 (accessed October 13, 2005).

21. "The Media Value Problem," *SportBusiness,* March 2004, pp. 13–14.

22. Ibid.

23. Ibid., pp. 12–13.

24. C. Britcher, "Nielsen Expands Sports Arm," April 23, 2004, www.sportbusiness.com/news/index?news_item_id=154348 (accessed March 18, 2006).

25. "Are New Tools Made to Measure?" *SportBusiness International,* November 2004, p. 22.

26. IEG, "2004 IEG/Performance Research Study Highlights What Sponsors Want."

27. L. Komoroski and H. Bremond, "Sponsor Accountability: Designing and Utilizing an Evaluation System, *Sport Marketing Quarterly* 5, no. 2 (1996), pp. 35–39.

A Comprehensive Sponsorship Example

The following example incorporates many of the sponsorship considerations that have been discussed in the chapters that address this important marketing resource. Answer the questions that follow the description to see how well you learned many of these concepts. But be forewarned, some of the information provided is irrelevant for the questions asked.

THE SPONSORSHIP SCENARIO

Consider the following scenario where Coca-Cola was the official sponsor of a recent Indy car race. The sponsorship fee paid by Coca-Cola was $250,000 in cash. Additionally, it was required to provide an assortment of drinks, including bottled water and sport drinks, to participants and officials. The total value of this requirement was approximately $90,000 (at retail). The contract provided Coca-Cola with the right of first refusal for next year's race and guaranteed that the cost for renewing the sponsorship would not increase even though it is anticipated that new sponsors would be required to make a financial commitment totaling $400,000 for next year's race. The total number of sponsors will remain unchanged at six; however, category exclusivity is not provided.

In an effort to tie its product to the event and discourage ambush marketing, Coke purchased 19 30-second spots during the race broadcast; each spot was filled with an ad for a Coke product and each ad noted the company's affiliation with the race. There were a total of 166 commercials by 59 different companies aired during the broadcast; each 30-second spot cost the advertiser $60,000. Additionally, each of the six sponsors received a free one-page ad in the official program that was sold at the race site. Coca-Cola purchased two additional pages at the prevailing rate of $18,000 per page. In addition to the advertising that Coca-Cola purchased for the race, it spent another $210,000 on activities directed toward the trade; the intent was to strengthen its tie with the race and to induce retailers to stock more Coca-Cola products. In the absence of the sponsorship, these "trade" promotions would not have taken place.

During the live broadcast, Coca-Cola trademarks appeared on TV for a total of 885 seconds. In an effort to ambush Coca-Cola, competitor Pepsi-Cola purchased a total of 14 advertising spots during the broadcast. Ironically, despite not being an official sponsor (and perhaps because one of the drivers is related to a Pepsi executive), Pepsi-Cola was mentioned by the announcers two times during the broadcast. This delighted Pepsi executives. Coca-Cola fared even better with nine mentions during the race and one more during the interview with the winning driver.

1. How much did Coca-Cola spend leveraging its sponsorship?
2. What was their total financial commitment to the sponsee?
3. Given today's standards, did Coke do an adequate job leveraging their sponsorship? Support your answer.
4. What is the estimated value of the exposure gained by Coca-Cola during the broadcast? (Use the Joyce Julius & Associates measurement model.)
5. Given the data above, was the decision to be a sponsor a good one? Explain the reasons for your answer.
6. Besides exposure, what other factors (not necessarily mentioned above) might provide additional value to Coca-Cola?

Case Study: College Bowl Game Media Impact and Brand Awareness

THE BACKGROUND

Joyce Julius & Associates was contracted by a corporation* to determine the generated media value, and resulting brand affinity, stemming from its event title sponsorship of a 2004 college bowl game. The bowl game has been in existence for several decades, is located near a major metropolitan area, and enjoys broadcast television coverage.

*The actual name of the corporation referenced in this case study has been withheld due to the proprietary nature of the research.

Source: Reprinted with permission of Joyce Julius & Associates, Inc. www.joycejulius.com. Accessed 3/19/06.

THE CHALLENGE

Leading up to the game, the corporation worked extensively with the broadcasting network to maximize in-broadcast exposure, while also increasing its promotional campaign through traditional advertising. The corporation wanted to measure the exposure resulting from its aforementioned adjustments in an effort to ensure maximum impact during future events. Additionally, after more than five years as the event's title sponsor, the corporation had a desire to measure its name recognition in conjunction with the event, as well as the purchase intent of fans attending the game.

THE METHOD

Joyce Julius categorized the corporation's exposure into the following components:

- National event telecast
- Television news/highlights
- Internet
- Print media
- On-site impact
- Promotions

The bowl game telecast was monitored for in-broadcast on-screen time and verbal references of the corporation. For television news/highlights, Internet, and print media, searches were conducted for mentions of the corporation two months prior and one month following the event. On-site impact took into account the corporation's identity stemming from merchandise, printed materials, and on-site signage. All promotions—backed by the corporation, bowl committee, or broadcasting network—were also measured for exposure.

Additionally, Joyce Julius personnel administered a 20-question on-site survey during the day of the game on behalf of the corporation. A combination of qualitative and quantitative questions comprised the survey.

THE RESULTS

The Joyce Julius Media Impact Analysis revealed a 213% increase in overall television exposure compared to the previous year's broadcast, with the bulk of the increase resulting directly from the network's usage of digital graphics containing the corporation's logo. The new graphics package also contributed in collecting some $600,000 of "bonus" exposure monitored during telecasts of six additional bowl games.

Promotions, such as television, print, and radio advertising, along with cross promotions featuring other brands and conducted by the bowl game, led to a 66.5% increase in exposure value over the previous year. Exposure reaped from national television advertising was a catalyst in the growth, rising nearly 50%.

In terms of fan perception, more than 70% of surveyed attendees expressed positive feelings toward the corporation due to its sponsorship while 37% would consider purchasing products from the corporation. Additionally, just 11% were able to successfully name the game's previous title sponsor, indicating a very strong name recognition level between the corporation and the bowl game.

CHAPTER ELEVEN

Sponsorship Foundation and Failure

Learning Objectives

- See the statistics on sponsors' perceptions of effectiveness.
- Identify the essential elements of the sponsorship foundation.
- Learn different bases for deeming a sponsorship to be a failure.
- Learn the many reasons why sponsorships fail.
- Learn from actual cases where sponsors dropped out.

Information developed using the techniques illustrated in the preceding chapter is used to assess the extent to which the sponsorship met the sponsor's expectations. Was it deemed to be a success or a failure? To help in this assessment, sponsors are demanding more information from the sponsee. Unfortunately, that information is not always forthcoming. The study by Performance Research and the IEG that has been cited in previous chapters reported a discouraging statistic: Only 33 percent of the marketers surveyed indicated that the properties they sponsored were meeting their expectations regarding the provision of pertinent information.[1] Therefore, sponsors must have a clear understanding of the assessment tools that are available to them. Whether the information is provided by the sponsor, the sponsee, or an independent research organization, one reality is clearly evident: Many sponsorships are characterized as failures. Were the expectations too high, or did the sponsorships fail to deliver results that represented legitimate goals? Regardless of the answer, the reality is that many sponsors are disappointed with the results.

Marketers have many tools available to utilize in their efforts to attain their goals. Sponsorship is one of those tools, but there is considerable uncertainty as to how to effectively utilize and support it. If a sponsorship fails to deliver the anticipated results, questions will be raised as to why the objectives were not attained. In the earlier chapter on leveraging, it was stated that the evaluation of that failure must start with an assessment of the sponsor's own actions. Was the sponsorship sufficiently supported with a focused leveraging program? Are there any other areas where the sponsor was remiss in its understanding and implementation of the sponsorship program?

> Only 33 percent of the marketers surveyed indicated that the properties they sponsored were meeting their expectations regarding the provision of pertinent information.

The second focal point will likely be the sponsor's competitors. What strategies did they employ in an effort to neutralize any competitive disadvantage faced by virtue of the sponsorship? Was there piracy, ambush marketing, significant increases in their promotional efforts, or other changes in marketing strategy, such as a price decrease or slotting allowances paid in an effort to increase retail shelf space? The sponsor cannot expect its competitors to sit idly by while it reaps the benefits of the sponsorship. As the earlier statement from the Qantas Airlines executive indicated, to not attempt to neutralize a competitor's advantage would be unprofessional.

The third focal point is the property that was sponsored. Did the property owner provide all of the benefits that were promised; did it meet its own expectations in regard to media exposure and attendance? Was the event the target of ambush efforts? There are many issues specific to the property or event that could adversely affect the performance of the sponsorship.

> In order to understand failure, there must first be an understanding of the basis for a sound sponsorship foundation.

In order to understand failure, there must first be an understanding of the basis for a sound sponsorship foundation. If the foundation is weak, it jeopardizes anything built around it. Like a house, a weak foundation can cause all the good work done around it to crumble. It is this weakness that leads to the perception that the sponsorship has underperformed. Although many of these aspects of the sponsorship foundation should have been addressed prior to signing any contract, it represents a logical point to start the assessment of the failure.

The Sponsorship Foundation

The sponsorship foundation represents the fundamental requirements that lead to the effective use of sponsorship in the pursuit of a firm's communications goals. They are basic concepts, and the failure to adequately address them will increase the likelihood that the results will be unacceptable. So if a sponsorship fails, these are the first points that should be examined. Was each of these requirements understood and addressed? These requirements are delineated in Box 11.1 and discussed on the following pages.

THE SPONSORSHIP FOUNDATION   11.1

Every sponsorship should be

- Defined
- An appropriately selected communications medium
- Objective-led
- Integrated
- Effectively screened
- Contracted
- A long-term commitment
- Protected from ambush
- Leveraged
- Evaluated

Source: D. Arthur, D. Scott, and T. Wood, "A Conceptual Model of the Corporate Decision-Making Process of Sponsorship Acquisition," *Journal of Sport Management* 13, no. 3 (1995), pp. 223–33.

Fundamental Requirements for Effective Sponsorship

Sponsorship Should Be Defined

Many organizations fail to understand the concept of sponsorship; thus the perception of sponsorship can vary significantly from one organization to another. If the organization does not understand the concept, it will probably not take the appropriate steps to implement the sponsorship. Sponsorship is not simply the act of advertising in the various media as many companies believe. It is imperative to understand that sponsorship is represented by a *direct association with an event or property* in a manner whereby the marketer can use it to achieve an array of corporate, marketing, and communications objectives.[2] Only when the marketer fully understands the scope of sponsorship can it develop an appropriate set of objectives. And without an appropriate set of objectives, the perception of failure is likely to persist.

Sponsorship Should Be an Appropriately Selected Communications Medium

Marketers have many tools available when developing their integrated marketing communications plan. Sponsorship is not always the best tool to use. So the key consideration is whether or not the sponsorship in question represents an effective use of resources.

The second consideration is how well it fits with the other elements of the marketing strategy. A sponsorship should have a meaningful effect on the market in its own right, but it should also have a synergistic impact on the firm's advertising, sales, public relations, and sales promotion efforts. Thus, the basic question is, Does this sponsorship make sense? In turn, this question suggests several others:

- Can the firm use the sponsorship to reach its target markets effectively and efficiently?[3]
- Does the market have an emotional attachment to help build a personality for the brand?[4]
- Will the sponsorship provide the media coverage sought by the sponsor?[5]
- Can the sponsorship be used to implement a positioning strategy?[6]

Sponsorship Should Be Objective Led

The objectives of any sponsorship should be specified prior to the consideration and selection of any proposal. Do not look at the sponsorship and ask what can be achieved; rather, look at the objectives and ask how the proposed sponsorship can help achieve them. The short-run performance is easy to measure, but the marketer must also incorporate long-term goals and objectives.

> Do not look at the sponsorship and ask what can be achieved; rather, look at the objectives and ask how the proposed sponsorship can help achieve them.

Companies have many goals and objectives that they are seeking to accomplish at any one time. This complexity makes it difficult to isolate the precise impact of any particular sponsorship program. But whether the assessment is directed toward the evaluation of opportunities presented by a potential sponsorship or the measurement of performance upon the conclusion of a program, the question of the appropriateness of the sponsor's objectives must be addressed. Success is built on the foundation of clearly articulated objectives that are appropriate for sponsorship activities; the absence of these objectives is a fundamental cause of dissatisfaction with the results.

> A sponsorship is destined to fail if a set of unattainable objectives is specified.

Not only do objectives need to be formulated, but they must also be reasonable. In other words, they must be achievable. A sponsorship is destined to fail if a set of unattainable

SPONSORSHIP INTEGRATION   11.2

Objectives lead to strategic initiatives in the following areas:

- Target market selection
- Price
- Product
- Distribution (place)
- Promotion
  - Advertising
  - Sales
  - Sales promotion
  - Public relations
  - Sponsorship

objectives is specified. Realistically, the sponsorship doesn't fail in these situations; the failure is a result of the sponsor's lack of understanding as to what can reasonably be accomplished. Still, the perception will be that the sponsorship failed. And as marketers have been told for many years, *perception is reality*.

Sponsorship Should Be Integrated

It is time to revisit a statement made much earlier in this book and touched on earlier in the section of this chapter that addressed the appropriate selection of sponsorship opportunities: *Sponsorship is not a stand-alone technique.* The implication is that sponsorship works in concert with a number of strategic initiatives implemented by the marketer. This includes both the promotional mix and its integration within the marketing mix. Some examples may help to clarify this point.

Efforts to enhance shelf space are more effective when salespeople are increasing their contacts and efforts to persuade retailers that more shelf space is warranted. The retailers might be inclined to respond more favorably if they believe the sponsorship will increase the demand for the sponsor's products. Thus, the combined effect of the sponsorship and the efforts by the salespeople should result in higher levels of sales for both the retailer and the sponsor.

If the objective is to increase the trial rate for a new consumer product, then the sponsorship would be more effective when supported by traditional advertising and sales promotion (such as free samples and discount coupons). Throughout this book, there has been an ongoing reference to the concept of an integrated marketing communications plan. Promotion is most effective when the elements of the IMC plan complement each other. Failure to do so will result in a less than optimal use of resources that could ultimately be the reason that the objectives for the sponsorship were not achieved.

Even when a sound marketing communications plan is developed, there is still a need to further integrate it within a cohesive marketing mix. The promotional strategy must blend, not conflict, with the product strategy, the pricing strategy, and the distribution strategy. And of course this overall strategy must be directed toward the appropriate target market. If any element of this strategy is inconsistent with the others, the chances of the strategy being effective are reduced. So prior to signing a sponsorship contract, the prospect must consider how it fits into and complements the entire realm of strategic initiatives. Box 11.2 provides an overview of the interaction of the elements of the typical marketing strategy.

One weakness of sponsorship is that decisions to enter into such relationships are often made without coordination among a disparate group of departments within the organization.[7] If companies would make an effort to coordinate the sponsorship goals with those of the organization as a whole, then perhaps this suboptimization could be avoided.[8] Some analysts have suggested that, as a means of assuring a sponsorship's fit, firms should designate a single functional area within the organization to bear the ultimate responsibility for making most, if not all, sponsorship-related decisions.[9] Marketers such as AT&T and Citibank have done just that. Although this will not guarantee that every sponsorship will be successful, it should increase the probability of success. And in those cases where a sponsorship fails to deliver what was expected of it, the reasons for its shortcomings should be easier to determine.

Sponsorship Should Be Effectively Screened

Prior to making any sponsorship commitment, the opportunity should be evaluated in order to objectively assess the fit. Many companies perform this task themselves by applying tools such as the pre-event evaluation matrix discussed in Chapter 9. Others hire outside consultants to perform this screening task. This process is purposely designed to identify only the best opportunities for a prospective sponsor, but it does not guarantee success.

Failure could result from the absence of clearly stated sponsorship objectives. If these are missing or misstated, then the pre-event evaluation process will be misdirected. Even if an appropriate set of objectives has been established, there are two major mistakes that could lead to an overly optimistic evaluation. The evaluation could place the wrong weights on the characteristics of the sponsorship. In other words, too much emphasis could be placed on one category while too little is placed on another.

Even when the weights are appropriately allocated in the pre-event evaluation matrix, an accurate assessment is still dependent upon the validity of the ratings assigned to each element. Recall from Chapter 9 that ratings were assigned to each element of the model. If an overly optimistic rating is assigned to a factor such as *opportunity for cross-promotion with co-sponsors,* then that aspect of the sponsorship will likely fail to deliver the anticipated results. While this may be portrayed as sponsorship failure, the reality may be that the screening process failed. What is obvious is that the importance of developing an accurate screening process cannot be overstated.

Sponsorship Should Be Contracted

A written contract will help assure that there are no surprises in the provision of the benefits granted by the sponsee. All terms and conditions are established in a legally binding contract. There are no questions as to exactly what benefits the sponsor is entitled to receive, thus, the likelihood of any misunderstanding or the lack of compliance on the part of the sponsee is minimized. In those cases where the promised benefits and components are not provided, the likelihood of achieving the stated objectives is adversely affected. In such situations, the written contract can serve as a point of reference in any effort to resolve the conflict between the sponsor and the sponsee.[10]

> A written contract will help assure that there are no surprises in the provision of the benefits granted by the sponsee.

Any effort to determine the reasons for the failure of a sponsorship to achieve its goals should include the verification that the sponsor received all of the program benefits to which it was entitled. This is the rationale for seeking a fulfillment report at key points during the course of the sponsorship period and upon the conclusion of the event.

Sponsorship Should Be a Long-Term Commitment

As noted earlier in this book, it is generally believed that the effectiveness of any sponsorship is enhanced when the sponsor and the sponsee maintain an extended relationship. Too often, sponsors are unrealistic regarding the potential impact of *once-off* sponsorships. Although these short-term opportunities may create immediate awareness, they offer little in the area of long-term image enhancement.[11] So while it may have been effective when Sony used a one-year sponsorship with the Rose Bowl as a way of creating awareness for its new PlayStation 2, it is doubtful that many people today remember that Sony ever sponsored that event. If the consumers quickly forget about the relationship between the sponsor and the sponsee, any hope of realizing future benefits is unrealistic. Therefore, sponsors must fully understand the constraints imposed by a sponsorship with a short time horizon. Too often, unrealistic expectations lead to results that are deemed to be unacceptable. Thus, the perception on the part of management is that the sponsorship failed. The reality is that the failure might be the result of management's delineation of objectives that simply were not attainable in a short-term relationship.

> The benefits of sponsorship may start to accrue during the first year but not become fully realized until the third year.

One opinion is that the benefits of sponsorship may start to accrue during the first year but not become fully realized until the third year.[12] Consider Ford Motor Company's sponsorship for the Australian Tennis Open. A key measure that was monitored by Ford was the Australian public's awareness of the relationship. Upon the completion of year one, only 12 percent of those surveyed correctly acknowledged Ford's sponsorship. Year two saw a modest increase to 14 percent, whereas the statistic for the third year was 20 percent.[13]

The lesson to be learned here is that the sponsor should not doom its own sponsorship to failure by focusing solely on the short run. And if the decision is made to enter into a short-term agreement, the sponsor must recognize the inherent weaknesses and not impose unrealistic goals for the sponsorship to accomplish.

Sponsorship Should Be Protected from Ambush

Initiatives can be undertaken by both the sponsor and the sponsee to protect the sponsorship from ambush marketing efforts. In most cases, ambush marketing is perfectly legal, although some new legal restrictions have been enacted in the past few years. Existing laws designed to protect intellectual property rights such as trademarks and logos have long been in place. A number of methods that can be used by the parties to discourage ambush marketing were discussed in Chapter 6.

> Much of the onus is on the sponsor itself to understand the environment in which it operates and to implement strategies that will protect it.

The decision to use sponsorship as a stand-alone promotional tool opens the sponsor up to ambush marketing attacks. The failure to understand the protections that are offered in different countries means that the sponsor is not fully utilizing the laws to its advantage. Likewise, the failure to understand the inherent risks associated with different countries makes the sponsor more vulnerable to ambushers. As can be seen, much of the onus is on the sponsor itself to understand the environment in which it operates and to implement strategies that will protect it. It is also essential that the contract specify any actions to be taken by the sponsee in an effort to discourage ambush marketing directed at the event and its sponsors. And as we learned earlier, one key consideration is that of leveraging.

Sponsorship Should Be Leveraged

Consider the following statements: to be effective, sponsorship must be supported by other marketing efforts,[14] and companies that want to succeed will have to leverage, leverage, and leverage some more.[15] This leveraging process reflects the sponsor's efforts to integrate the sponsorship with the other elements of the promotional strategy. Effective leveraging helps reinforce the nature of the relationship between the sponsor and the sponsee. Poorly executed leveraging or its complete absence will make it virtually impossible for the sponsorship to produce the results sought by the sponsor.

Sponsees should provide leveraging opportunities, and sponsors should take advantage of them. Independent efforts by the sponsor should also be utilized, as the sponsee cannot possibly control all of the media and marketing channels that the sponsor may want to incorporate within its leveraging efforts.

> The failure of a sponsorship has both financial and emotional consequences.

While there are many causes of sponsorship failure, the absence of a well-executed leveraging plan is a deficiency that greatly hinders any chance for success. Yet it is one aspect of the sponsorship that is easily controlled. Leveraging can be an expensive proposition; however, the failure of a sponsorship has both financial and emotional consequences. It is both expensive and embarrassing. When a prospect is evaluating proposals and the rights fees to be paid to the property owner, it must consider the entire cost of the program. Thus, the sponsorship budget should include both the sponsorship fees and the anticipated cost for activating an effective leveraging plan. The prospect should not commit to any sponsorship unless it can afford to support it at a reasonable level. To do so is simply courting failure.

Sponsorship Should Be Evaluated

It is impossible to know if a sponsorship was a success or a failure if the results are not evaluated upon the conclusion of the sponsorship-related activities. Measurable goals should have been developed and performance needs to be evaluated. With the results documented, an objective evaluation can be undertaken. In the absence of goals and the measurement of performance, the assessment of the sponsorship can become too subjective.

The key measurement criteria were presented in Chapter 10. Sponsors and sponsees should be aware of the various evaluation techniques. Eventually, management will want to see the results so that it can calculate the ROI. Therefore, prior to the decision to commit to any sponsorship, the basis for calculating its ROI should be defined.

Other Reasons for Sponsorship Failure

Clearly, a weak foundation is one factor that can, and often does, lead to failure; but it is not the only factor. Although taking precautions to perform the 10 tasks associated with building a sound foundation will improve the likelihood for success, it does not guarantee it.

Another concern is that the concept of failure may differ in the eyes of the sponsor and the sponsee. For the sponsor, it is based upon the comparison of the anticipated results to the actual results. Did the sponsorship deliver an adequate ROI? For the sponsee, success is often measured by one simple consideration: Did the sponsor renew its commitment for the next cycle? So perhaps the better question is, Why did the sponsor elect to terminate its relationship with the event or property owner? Some potential answers to that question are discussed on the following pages.

Decrease in Market Value

If a perceived decrease in the value of a sponsorship is not matched with a comparable decrease in the rights fees, then the sponsor will generally view the sponsorship as over-priced. For example, there could be a loss of prestige for the event or perhaps the number of attendees has been on a downward trend. Lower TV ratings mean that the sponsor is reaching fewer consumers; the lower reach translates into lower value. New events or new pricing policies on the part of existing events may also impact the market value for a sponsorship. Regardless of the reason, a lower value will cause the sponsor to reconsider the viability of the sponsorship. When the price paid for the sponsorship exceeds the value received from it, the result will likely be that the sponsor will choose not to renew the contract. According to some definitions, this represents a failure for the sponsorship.

Cost Becomes Prohibitive

Even when the event or property delivers value comparable to the price it charges, the opportunity may be priced beyond the budget of some potential sponsors. As events become more popular, the cost for sponsoring them may escalate very quickly. A sponsor may look at the cost and simply decide that it is no longer affordable, especially when combined with the cost of leveraging efforts.

Even when the sponsor has the resources to renew its relationship, the cost may drive it away from the event and to alternative promotional vehicles. Xerox looked at the $55 million price tag for the Athens Olympics and announced its intention to terminate that relationship at the end of the contract in 2004. It had become difficult to justify the expense. So even though Xerox had been a TOP sponsor since 1994, it made the decision to divert those resources into other customer initiatives.[16] The same scenario will confront the 15 official sponsors of the 2006 World Cup of Soccer. The sponsorship fees are expected to rise dramatically for the 2010 competition; consequently, current sponsors will have to make a decision regarding the economic viability of a continued relationship with the event. In planning for the inevitable attrition, FIFA anticipates the retention of only six sponsors for the cycle that encompasses the 2010 competition.

Change in Corporate Direction

Marketing strategies are dynamic. Target markets change; marketers seek to create a new image. Corporate mergers and divestitures constantly change the character of the large multinational corporations that actively invest in sponsorship opportunities. Under these circumstances, it is not unusual for the sponsor to decide that another course of action is more appropriate. This might involve a movement from one sponsored property to another. As discussed earlier, some companies have opted to change categories while still investing in sponsored properties. For instance, there may be a movement away from sports properties to other categories such as the arts or cause-related marketing endeavors. Of course, the marketer may simply opt to move from one property to another within the same category. If the changing demographics of the market suggest that such changes would be prudent, the sponsor might move from basketball to tennis or from a theatrical production to a local symphony orchestra.

It is also conceivable that the sponsorship will be abandoned in favor of more traditional promotions. Instead of allocating large sums of money to sponsor an event or property, the decision may be made to redirect those resources to traditional media such as television and magazines. Or perhaps the resources will be used to support an increased presence of sales-people. In many cases, this change comes after a long affiliation with a property. The aforementioned example of Xerox's decision to terminate its relationship with the IOC after 10 years as a TOP sponsor was, in part, predicated upon a change in corporate direction.

Another example is Isuzu's decision to end its seven-year association with the Celebrity Golf Challenge. According to Isuzu's vice president of marketing, the sponsorship was effective for those seven years, but the decision not to renew was "predicated solely on a change in direction" that was being designed to create a new image for Isuzu in the marketplace.[17]

Property Hopping

This phenomenon involves a sponsor that exhibits a pattern of repeatedly moving from one short-term commitment to another. The idea may be to reach a diverse array of consumers, or it may revolve around the desire to keep the marketer's name in front of the public by continuing to invest in properties throughout the year. The marketer may sponsor a university sports team in the fall, an art exhibit in the winter, a home and garden show in the spring, and a golf tournament in the summer. Then the next year, it may decide to sponsor a completely different set of properties.

> Short-term tactics that take precedence over long-term results should be reconsidered.

It has already been established that short-term programs offer limited value to the sponsor. Therefore, the concern is that the sponsor is not allowing itself the time needed to establish the relationship and derive the potential benefits associated with that relationship. Short-term tactics that take precedence over long-term results should be reconsidered.

Property hopping is typically associated with sponsors that have little experience in developing leveraging campaigns and focusing on long-term relationships. In some cases, this inexperience results in unsatisfactory performance. As a consequence, the marketer moves on to another property in search of a more positive outcome. Unfortunately, the initial failure is often followed by another failure, a cycle that continues until the firm learns how to fully activate its sponsorship. Or in some cases, the inexperienced sponsor that tires of this pattern of failure will hire an independent consulting firm to develop a sponsorship strategy for it. Companies such as Octagon and Performance Research are two such service providers.

Timing Considerations

Events are not always staged the same time every year. In most cases, sponsors have little input as to when an event will be staged. As a consequence, the dates for an event may suddenly conflict with other strategic initiatives on the part of the sponsor. It may be sponsoring other events, or the change may not coincide with seasonal considerations that the sponsor has. Discontinuation of a sponsorship under these circumstances is not always a sign of failure or dissatisfaction with past results. Rather, it is a reflection of the belief that it would not produce the required results in the future.

Failure to Understand What Is Not Received

The IEG refers to this as *due diligence overlooked*.[18] Sponsors generally believe that they have a good understanding of what is included in their contract; however, this does not imply that they necessarily know what is *not* included. Earlier, there was a discussion on the merits of having a written contract that specifies exactly what is included. For example, if a contract includes category exclusivity, how broad is that protection? If a sponsor believes it has broad protection for its entire product assortment only to discover that one of its competitors is on board in some official capacity, it may well decide not to renew the sponsorship.

Greenwashing

It is not uncommon for companies to sponsor organizations, events, and charities that have an environmental or other CRM focus. In the marketing literature, we speak of *green marketing*.

Examples include Shoebox Greeting Cards (a division of Hallmark Cards), a company that produces cards on recycled paper. Starkist Tuna has engaged in green marketing by implementing and promoting a policy that they now fish for tuna in areas where the risk to dolphins is minimized. It has been shown that green marketing is well received by many consumers; in fact, research has indicated that these market segments are often willing to pay a premium to purchase *environmentally friendly* products. It is only logical that sponsorship of a variety of these causes, organizations, events, and charities could be an important component of a green marketing strategy.

> Don't sponsor green unless you are green.

But in the words of the IEG, "don't sponsor green unless you are green."[19] Consumers and investigative news reports continue to scrutinize cause-related marketing initiatives. The sincerity of the marketer is often questioned. Is it truly an effort to be a good corporate citizen, or is it simply a public relations ploy? Any goodwill that was generated can quickly disappear when the sponsor's motivations are called into question. Even in those cases where the sponsor's intentions are good, the negative publicity may drive it away from future relations with the sponsored property. So it is logical to assume that the insincere sponsor that is guilty of greenwashing will quickly be exposed, thus rendering its sponsorship investment worthless. The natural consequence of this is a decision to terminate the relationship between the sponsor and the sponsee and to label it as a failure.

Overreliance on Small Sponsorships

Although a marketer can sponsor several smaller events for the cost of a single, high-profile event, brand equity is best enhanced via relationships with large, prestigious properties. Smaller, grassroots sponsorships can play an important role in local geographic markets; however, the money invested typically does not provide the returns generated by large properties such as the NFL or the Olympics. It should be noted that there is minimal turnover in the array of sponsors for the prime properties, but smaller events and organizations are often faced with the task of replacing dissatisfied sponsors and property hoppers on an annual basis.

Failure to Sell Internally

Sponsorship is often heartily endorsed by those involved in marketing. But to be effective, the value of the sponsorship must be recognized by others within the organization, both up and down the organizational chart. Since different functional areas have different goals, this sales task can be quite difficult. Whereas marketers view sponsorship as a way to reach customers, others may see it as an expenditure that limits their ability to use the money in other ways, such as R&D or funding a pension account for retirees. Each constituency within the sponsoring organization must buy into the idea that the sponsorship will provide organization-wide benefits and that the marketers will not be the only beneficiaries.

> The value of the sponsorship must be recognized by others within the organization, both up and down the organizational chart.

In looking down the organizational chart, salespeople who interact with intermediaries must believe that the sponsorship will benefit them. Otherwise, their efforts will fail to incorporate the sponsorship in the task of acquiring space on the retailers' shelves. It is also their enthusiasm that encourages retailers to incorporate some aspects of the sponsorship such as point-of-sale display and cooperative advertising in the retailers' marketing strategy. Line workers in manufacturing facilities must recognize how the achievement of the sponsorship goals will help provide job security and a better work environment; otherwise, it is likely that questions regarding the sponsors' priorities will be raised by the employees and their union representatives. It is evident that the failure to sell the sponsorship internally throughout the organization will lead to a poorer perception of the actual results and general dissatisfaction.

Failure to Deliver Sought Results

In recent years, sponsors have sought accountability on the part of property owners. The reality that sponsors are seeking a tangible return on their investment has struck a chord. Chapter 10 provided insight into how this ROI could be measured and compared to the sponsor's objectives. When there is a gap between the targeted and the actual results, questions will be raised as to why the sponsorship failed to deliver.

> When there is a gap between the targeted and the actual results, questions will be raised as to why the sponsorship failed to deliver.

Competition always seeks to neutralize any competitive advantage held by an adversary. If the sponsorship is viewed as such, then the sponsor should anticipate a response by its competitors. It may come in the form of piracy or ambush marketing, but most likely it will be through an effort by a competitor to enhance its own position by adjusting its marketing strategy accordingly. In this respect, it is no different from any other competitive advantage. If a company has patent rights, a competitor might seek new technology that will eliminate the advantage. If a retailer's advantage is predicated upon location, a competitor may seek to neutralize it by implementing an aggressive pricing policy. If competition can neutralize an advantage held by virtue of a sponsorship, then the sponsorship will likely be deemed a failure and abandoned as a consequence.

Overview of Failure

Regardless of the reasons, and irrespective of the appropriateness of the objectives, sponsorships characterized as failures are not likely to be renewed. It is easy for a sponsor to rationalize such a termination if it sees benefits accruing to the sponsee while failing to realize the benefits that it had anticipated for itself. This outcome defeats the goal of establishing a win–win relationship between the parties and hastens the demise of a relationship deemed to be one-sided.

> Sponsors should attempt to determine why a sponsorship failed and learn from the experience.

Clearly, there are many reasons sponsorships are not renewed. What is not always so evident is who was at fault. Was it the sponsor, the sponsee, or the result of effective competitive efforts? Sponsors should attempt to determine why a sponsorship failed and learn from the experience. As sponsors move up the learning curve, future failure becomes less likely. Of course, it can be a hard and expensive lesson to learn. The reasons for sponsorship failure are restated in Box 11.3.

REASONS FOR SPONSORSHIP FAILURE

11.3

- Poor sponsorship foundation
- Decrease in market value
- Cost becomes prohibitive
- Change in corporate direction
- Property hopping
- Timing considerations
- Failure to understand what is not received
- Greenwashing
- Overreliance on small sponsorships
- Failure to sell internally
- Failure to deliver sought results

Examples of Sponsorship Failure

- **Xerox** terminated its TOP sponsorship with the **International Olympic Committee** upon the completion of the 2004 Olympic Games in Athens. It had been associated with the IOC for 40 years and became a TOP sponsor in 1994. According to a spokesperson at Xerox, the company decided to redirect those resources into "other customer-facing initiatives."[20]

- **Travelex** is a large European-based foreign exchange company. It chose to abruptly end its sponsorship of the **Toyota Formula One Racing Team.** The contract stipulated a five-year commitment; however, Travelex chose to end it after only two years. The company cited Formula One's lack of a global audience, a glaring deficiency for a company that decided to establish a brand identity in the United States. This change in corporate direction led the company to seek alternatives that would facilitate its American initiatives.[21] Reportedly, these alternatives may or may not include sponsorships.

- **Siemens** also cut its ties with Formula One racing, specifically, the **McLaren Mercedes F1 Team.** Company executives expressed a concern that the image of Formula One racing was not consistent with the overall corporate image that Siemens had attempted to develop and nurture.[22] The company did continue other sponsorships deemed to be consistent with that image, such as its partnership with the Real Madrid soccer team.

- **Saturn,** a division of General Motors, severed its relationship with the **Saturn Cycling Team** after some 12 years. The primary goal when the sponsorship was signed in 1992 was to create awareness for the fledgling car brand. Overall, the sponsor had only good things to say about the relationship. Even as the decision was announced, Saturn was praised for its contributions to cycling. So why was it a failure? Again, the decision not to renew was not predicated upon dissatisfaction; rather, it was based on the sponsor's decision to pursue a new marketing strategy. The change was reflected in an effort to focus on individual products rather than the Saturn brand; thus, sponsorship was considered to be a less effective tool than the other alternatives available to the automotive marketer.[23]

- **UPS** used its sponsorship of the **IOC** to increase its visibility and consumer awareness in markets outside of the United States. It ended a six-year sponsorship that was punctuated with some contentious overtones. There was considerable concern expressed over the Sydney Organizing Committee's decision to allow a UPS competitor, TNT, to have an official role in

FIGURE 11.1
IBM and the IOC

the 2000 Olympic Games. According to a UPS spokesman, the sponsorship was "built on a business strategy and a business objective . . . they've changed over time."[24]

- The **Amulet Group's** sponsorship of the **Manchester City Football (soccer) Club** in the England fell apart after the first year of a three-year contract when the company was placed in bankruptcy.[25] This is similar to the demise of **Enron's** stadium naming rights deal for the home field of Major League Baseball's **Houston Astros.**

- **IBM** terminated its relationship with the **IOC** after the Sydney Games. While IBM was a TOP sponsor, it provided the IOC with much of the information technology required to stage the games. The 38-year relationship ended when IBM opted not to sign the eight-year extension it was offered. The wedge that drove the two apart was the inability to agree on the compensation due to IBM for the products and services it provided; in other words, what was the value of their VIK? Signage that leveraged that sponsorship is shown in Figure 11.1.

- The **United States Postal Service (USPS)** ended its often criticized relationship with **Lance Armstrong and the U.S. Pro Cycling Team** at the end of 2004. Despite Armstrong's five consecutive Tour de France championships, many could not rationalize the USPS decision to spend $25 million for a five-year sponsorship that generally involved races staged outside of the United States. Critics argued that there was no logical relationship between the two. A postevent evaluation of the sponsorship also indicated that Lance Armstrong did not deliver. Despite high levels of TV exposure for the USPS, the estimated payoff on the $25 million investment was some $698,000 in additional sales.[26]

- One of the most widely recognized sponsorships in the United States featured **R. J. Reynolds Tobacco Company (RJR)** and **NASCAR.** The primary competition in NASCAR had long been the Winston Cup series of races; Winston is RJR's flagship brand. The relationship began in 1971 after new U.S. laws prohibiting the advertising of cigarettes on TV were enacted. More recently, new laws that limit the ability of Winston to leverage its sponsorship have also taken effect. The economic conditions in 2003 and 2004 also caused the marketer to reconsider making such a sizable investment.[27]

- Women's sports have often endured a great deal of difficulty in the efforts to secure sponsors. While great headway has been made, this problem continues to plague many women's sports. The Professional Women's Bowling Association (PWBA) folded after the 2003 season because of the loss of sponsors for the association and its tournaments. Even the Ladies Professional Golf Association has not been immune to that problem. The **LPGA** lost **Welch's** as the title sponsor of the Tucson Open after a 15-year association. It was reported that the event was in search of a sponsor; however, if one could not be secured in time, the event would be dropped from the 2005 LPGA schedule.[28]

- The list of failures could go on and on to the point that any reader might begin to question the wisdom of sponsorship. However, the last that will be identified takes us away from the monster deals that are associated with sports.

- **Ford Motor Company** had a sponsorship that provided naming rights for the **Ford International Jazz Festival.** In the absence of the $250,000 in rights fees paid by Ford and the inability to sign a new sponsor, it was announced that the 2004 festival would be the last. While no reason was given for the decision, the inability of the festival to quickly attract a new sponsor would seem to imply that the property did not produce results commensurate with its price.

Closing Capsule

Despite the best efforts of the prospect to evaluate every sponsorship proposal and select only those with the greatest potential, many sponsorships still fail to deliver the results that are expected of them. In an effort to assure the success of a sponsorship, a sound foundation is required. One key element of this foundation is the specification of objectives sought from the implementation of the sponsorship program. The absence of these objectives will make it difficult to assess the success (or failure) of any sponsorship.

Failure is difficult to define. Some view it strictly as the inability of the sponsorship to deliver the anticipated results. Others consider it a failure whenever the sponsor decides not to renew its contract; yet there are numerous examples where the relationship was mutually beneficial, but new conditions caused the sponsor to move in a different direction.

There are many examples of failure, several of which are discussed in this chapter. The failures include an array of properties from sports to the arts. In general, the major sports events have little trouble securing new sponsors to replace those that drop out. Unfortunately, minor events and properties have considerably more difficulty in the recruiting process. The result is that these minor events and properties often find themselves in jeopardy of being canceled due to the lack of resources.

> Minor events and properties often find themselves in jeopardy of being cancelled due to the lack of resources.

The high incidence of failure underscores the need to establish a sound foundation. Prospective sponsors should always be selective when making decisions as to which properties they will target for investment. Success is a function of a sound foundation and appropriate measures being taken by the sponsor and the sponsee. Objectives are essential, as is postevent evaluation. Only when both are present can an objective assessment of the sponsorship's performance be made. And that assessment is a key consideration in the sponsor's decision to renew or terminate a sponsorship.

Review Questions

1. What is meant by the statement that "sponsorship should be integrated"?
2. Why is it important to establish sponsorship objectives early in the process?
3. Why is it difficult to define *sponsorship failure?*
4. Identify 10 reasons why sponsorships fail.
5. What is the basis for the statement that "sponsorship should be a long-term commitment"?

6. What is the importance of selling a sponsorship internally?

7. Identify a sponsorship that you would deem a failure. What is the basis for your selection? Why do you think it failed?

Endnotes

1. IEG, "2004 IEG/Performance Research Study Highlights What Sponsors Want," 2004, www.performanceresearch.com/ieg_sponsor_survey.htm (accessed October 13, 2005).

2. D. Sandler and D. Shani, "Olympic Sponsorship versus 'Ambush' Marketing: Who Gets the Gold?" *Journal of Advertising Research,* August–September 1989, pp. 9–14.

3. C. Brooks, *Sports Marketing: Competitive Business Strategies for Sports* (Englewood Cliffs, NJ: Prentice Hall, 1994).

4. A. Tobin, "The Business of Sponsorship," *Australian Leisure Management,* December–January 1998, pp. 35–36.

5. N. Lough, "Factors Affecting Corporate Sponsorship of Women's Sport," *Sport Marketing Quarterly* 5, no. 2 (1996), pp. 11–19.

6. B. Pritchard, *Complex Marketing Made Simple* (Sydney: Milner Books, 1995).

7. K. Parker, "Sponsorship: The Research Contribution," *European Journal of Marketing,* 25, no. 11 (1991), pp. 22–30.

8. D. Howard and J. Crompton, *Financing Sport* (Morgantown, WV: Fitness Information Technology, 1995).

9. D. Thwaites and A. Carruthers, "Sport Sponsorship Motivation and Applications: The Case of Rugby Union," *paper presented at the 4th European Congress on Sport Management,* 1996, Montpellier, France.

10. D. Healy, *Sport and the Law* (Sydney, Australia: University of New South Wales Press, 1996).

11. S. Sleight, *Sponsorship: What It Is and How to Use It* (Maidenhead: McGraw-Hill, 1989).

12. Ibid.

13. M. Kiely, "Sponsorship: It's a Buyers' Market," *Marketing,* February 1993, pp. 9–12.

14. Parker, *Sponsorship.*

15. Bradley, "Selling the Games," *Australian Magazine,* March 15–16, 1997, pp. 20–23, 33–34.

16. M. Kleinman, "Xerox Winds up £30M Olympics Deal," *Marketing,* October 16, 2003, p. 4.

17. L. Brockington, "Isuzu Drops Tourney Sponsorship," *Sports Business Journal,* September 21–27, 1998, p. 3.

18. *IEG's Complete Guide to Sponsorship: Everything You Wanted to Know about Sponsorship* (Chicago: IEG, Inc., 1999), p. 38.

19. Ibid.

20. Kleinman, "Xerox Winds up £30M Olympics Deal."

21. "Travelex Terminates £7M Toyota F1 Sponsorship," *Marketing Week,* October 2, 2003, p. 12.

22. "Siemens Set to Drop £10M Tie-up with F1," *Marketing Week,* October 23, 2003, p. 14.

23. "Saturn Ends 12-Year Cycling Sponsorship: After More than a Decade on Two Wheels, Saturn Seeks a Change in Marketing Strategy," September 18, 2003, www.sponsorship.com/news/Content/4460.asp (accessed October 13, 2005).

24. UPS Withdraws as Olympic Sponsor, December 21, 2000, www.espn.go.com/oly/news/2000/1221/966279.html (accessed October 13, 2005).

25. B. Bold, "Amulet Collapse Ends Man City Sponsorship, *Marketing,* June 5, 2003, p. 5.

26. S. Callahan, "USPS to Break with U.S. Cycling Team," *BtoB,* May 3, 2004, p. 5.

27. "Tobacco Company Considering Ending Its NASCAR Sponsorship," February 5, 2003, www.sportsline.com/autoracing/story/6170665 (accessed October 13, 2005).

28. C. Britcher, "LPGA Event Loses Sponsor," June 11, 2004, www.sportbusiness.com/news/ index?news_item_id=154842 (accessed October 13, 2005).

CHAPTER TWELVE

Endorsements

Learning Objectives

- Revisit the concept of matching.
- Learn why athletes are valuable endorsers.
- Delineate the selection process.
- Learn how Q Scores are used by marketers.
- Identify the five prominent problems with celebrity endorsers.
- Learn how good personalities can still present problems.

One common strategy in today's marketing environment involves the use of celebrity endorsements. While the use of athletes to promote a product is not a new phenomenon, it has certainly gained momentum in recent years. Golfers Jesper Parnevik and Tiger Woods recently signed endorsement contracts with Upper Deck, one of the primary marketers of collectible trading cards. As part of their agreements, Parnevik wears the Upper Deck logo on his hat and Woods has granted the company the exclusive right to produce and market all of his autographed memorabilia.

Of course, endorsements deals are not the sole province of athletes. There have been many endorsements by other well-known individuals such as entertainers and politicians. While these individuals are instrumental in the marketing of sports events and sporting goods, they may also serve a key role in the marketing of consumer products and business-to-business products. Examples include the use of Jon Bon Jovi to endorse Duracell batteries, Bob Dole to promote Pepsi-Cola, David Beckham to promote the game of soccer (football), Michael Jordan and Larry Bird to promote McDonald's, Sarah Ferguson to promote Weight Watchers, and Arnold Palmer to promote handheld dictation equipment for Lanier Worldwide.

> The use of celebrities in a marketer's communications strategy can contribute to greater brand recognition and can create a positive perception in regard to the endorsed product.

It is believed that the use of celebrities in a marketer's communications strategy can contribute to greater brand recognition and can create a positive perception in regard to the endorsed product. Foremost, however, is the belief that the celebrity endorser will be instrumental in the task of persuading the consumer to purchase the product initially and in inducing a higher degree of brand loyalty once the initial purchase has taken place. The endorser with a solid image can transfer that image to the product, thereby helping to create and maintain an aura of credibility for the marketer and its products. At a minimum, the endorser can help cut through the competition's advertising clutter so as to attract and maintain the consumers' attention in the effort to gain market share.

The Matching Process

An *endorsement* involves a payment to a spokesperson who will recommend and encourage the purchase of a marketer's product. The key distinction between an endorsement and a conventional advertisement is that with the former, a celebrity spokesperson is employed to promote the product in a more proactive manner. Rather than an anonymous actor, a celebrity is used in ways that consumers recognize the spokesperson and develop an association between him or her and the product being endorsed. For an endorsement to be effective, there must be a match between the endorser and the marketer. As stated by Reed Bergman, the president of Impact Sports, "the essential element between any partnership is the balancing of needs."[1]

For the relationship between the marketer and the endorser to flourish, there must also be a match with the target market. The marketer must deliver a product sought by the target market, and the endorser must be able to exert some influence on members of that target market and their purchase decisions. If any of these matches is absent, the endorsement is less likely to be effective. This kind of relationship is exemplified in a recent statement about the endorsement power of Tiger Woods. According to Dean Bonham, president of the sports marketing firm the Bonham Group, Tiger "has that ability to get the masses out there to buy clubs, play golf, and buy merchandise. He's fueling the Internet and pumping up TV ratings."[2] This is the result of sound matching between the marketer, the endorser, and the target market.

Endorsement Applications

The use of celebrity endorsements in conventional advertising and other forms of promotion is typically implemented via one of three endorsement modes. Determining the appropriate mode is generally a matter of assessing the nature of the relationship between the product and the celebrity endorser. Of course, the marketer must keep in mind the extent to which members of the target market will understand that relationship and be influenced by it. Properly implemented, the marketer can develop a sustainable competitive advantage that its competition will find difficult to neutralize.

The initial application is characterized by the statement that "*I use it, so should you.*" Nike has effectively used this strategy in its efforts to make headway in the golf equipment market. Tiger Woods's endorsement of Nike golf balls allowed the company to quickly attain a meaningful share of that market. Nike has continued this strategy with Woods's and New Zealand golfer Michael Campbell's endorsements of the company's golf clubs.

This strategy is also appropriate when the product being endorsed is not sports-related. For example, American Express has long used celebrities to endorse its credit cards. At the end of each TV advertisement, the viewer sees that the endorser has been a "member" with an American Express card for some extended period of time. It reinforces the key issue that "I have an American Express card, so should you." Similarly, the aforementioned endorsement by Jon Bon Jovi was implemented by showing footage of the band in concert and indicating that when in concert, the band used Duracell batteries in their wireless microphones. Figure 12.1 illustrates the "I use it, so should you" endorsement strategy. It features former and current NFL All-Star quarterbacks Archie, Peyton, and Eli Manning in an advertisement for milk.

The NBA 2004 Rookie-of-the-Year LeBron James recently signed a four-year, $5 million contract to endorse the chewing-gum brands of Cadbury Schweppes. James constantly chews gum while playing basketball, and he once pronounced his love for the marketer's Bubblicious bubble gum. But the deal doesn't stop there. Not only will James appear in print and TV advertising, but the company has introduced a new LeBron-inspired flavor. There is also a belief that his endorsement will be a crucial component in Cadbury

FIGURE 12.1
Peyton, Archie, and Eli Manning—We Drink Milk, So Should You

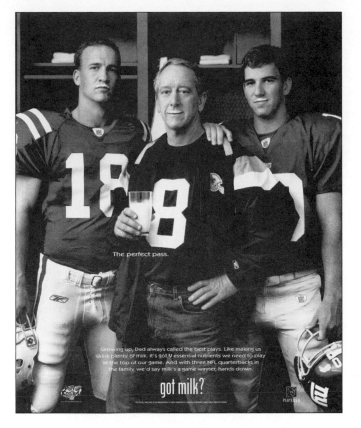

Schweppes' introduction of a new "sports gum." It is easy to see that the "I use it, so should you" appeal is both common and effective.

A second application is based upon the ability to portray the endorser as an expert within the product category such that members of the target market view the individual as a viable source of information. This mode is represented by the argument that "*I am an expert, and I think that you would be smart use this product.*" Note that it does not indicate that the endorser actually uses the product; rather, the endorser attempts to convey the message that it would be wise for members of the target market to use it. For example, few consumers would think that the typical Formula One or NASCAR vehicle would use the same engine lubricants or fuels that consumers use in their cars, but the professional drivers would certainly be viewed as experts within their domain. Thus, any endorsement by well-known drivers such as Michael Schumacher or Dale Earnhardt Jr. would benefit from their perceived expert status. As an example, consider A.J. Petty (of NASCAR fame) and his endorsement of the famous motor lubricant STP. Consumers did not know if he used it or not, but they respected his opinion. It is this respect as an expert that will induce many members of the target market to purchase the product. An example in a nonsports setting could be a doctor's endorsement for a pain reliever or a musician's endorsement for stereo components such as audio speakers. Within their domains, they are perceived to be experts whose opinions are well respected among certain groups of consumers. There is perhaps no person who is perceived as move of an expert in the field of air travel than Sir Richard Branson, president of Virgin Atlantic. His endorsement of Samsonite luggage certainly conveys the message that as an expert, he thinks that you would be wise to use the product that he is recommending.

The final application is more basic and does not emphasize any strong relationship between the endorser and the product. The marketer does not attempt to portray the endorser as either a user of the product or an expert on the product category. This endorsement application is characterized by the belief that "*I think its cool, so you should use it.*"

FIGURE 12.2
Sir Richard Branson
of Virgin Atlantic
Airways—I'm an
Expert in the Field of
Air Travel, and I
Think You Should
Use Samsonite
Luggage

Marketers using this strategy see the endorser as a way to get attention, by cutting through the clutter of advertising in today's marketplace. The strategy may also be used to reposition a brand or a product. Tiger Woods tells consumers that the Buick brand of automobile is cool, and he suggests that consumers give Buick some consideration in the purchase process. Woods is not an automotive expert, nor is he seen driving around in his own personal Buick; but the endorsement strategy may induce others to purchase a Buick. If so, the strategy has been effective. The advertisement featured in Figure 12.3 seeks to capitalize on the strategy where athletes neither purport to use the product nor provide expert opinions about the merits of the product. The effectiveness of the ad is based upon the consumers' ability to recognize Jeff Gordon, who projects the "it's cool" image to wear Tag Heuer watches.

Athletes as Endorsers

It has been stated that "great athletes, because of their prominence in our society, tend to play many different roles. They are not viewed simply as sports entertainers, but are often expected to engender strong values and morals that conform to societal and cultural norms."[3] This premise has been severely strained over the past few years as more athletes across the globe have found themselves on the wrong side of the law. Thus, the task for the marketer is to identify those athletes who possess the qualities that society embraces and who are unlikely to stray from that lifestyle. While that process is considerably more difficult today, marketers that can identify and sign these athletes can reap considerable rewards.

Legal and moral transgressions do not represent the only risk for marketers that opt to utilize athletes in endorsement roles. A second concern that may greatly diminish the value of an endorsement deal is the health of the athlete. This may include illness or injury. NBA star

FIGURE 12.3
Jeff Gordon—Tag Heuer Watches are Cool, So You Should Buy One

Magic Johnson saw a significant drop in his endorsement power when he was diagnosed as HIV positive and forced to retire. Similarly, dual sport (National Football League and Major League Baseball) star Bo Jackson saw his lucrative endorsement world crash when he sustained a career-ending hip injury. Some athletes have been able to sustain a viable endorsement agenda after retirement, but those cases are exceptions. Such an opportunity depends upon the athlete's ability to continue to influence the target market. Golfer Arnold Palmer has continued to flourish in this role, and there is little doubt that recently retired Michael Jordan will continue to have a significant role in the endorsement arena for years to come.

Factors Favoring the Use of Athletes as Endorsers

Athletes seek endorsement contracts that generate significant income, and marketers seek athletes who can favorably impact their own position in terms of perception and revenues. For the athlete, there are several issues that directly influence their earnings potential. First, their accomplishments represent a key factor in the selection process. The more they have accomplished, the greater potential they have in a marketing role. Second, any athlete who has an enduring personality and whose persona is always associated with a sport may earn a place in the elite club those who have ongoing endorsement potential. Third, an athlete who participates in an international sport has more endorsement opportunities outside of his or her sport and home country.[4] That is to say that professional tennis players and Olympic athletes have greater earnings potential than an American baseball player or a player on an Australian Rules Football team. Still, all of these points would be irrelevant were it not for the evidence that the use of athletes as product spokespersons works.

A HISTORY OF MARKETING THROUGH CHAMPIONS

12.1

The roster reads like a Who's Who of Sports.

Babe Ruth is there. So are Jackie Robinson, Michael Jordan, Bronko Nagurski, Walter Payton, and John Elway.

Bruce Jenner, Mary Lou Retton, Billy Mills, and Babe Didrikson Zaharias also have captured a coveted spot on the Wheaties box.

Jack Armstrong, the fictitious All-American boy, set the standard as the first athlete on the Wheaties box in 1934. Those who followed were chosen because they excelled in sports and captured the heart and soul of America.

The same year Armstrong appeared on the box, Wheaties honored baseball great Lou Gehrig.

Since then, hundreds of athletes have been put on the orange cardboard pedestal as General Mills Inc. created its own Hall of Fame to promote Wheaties, one of the stalwarts in its line of Big G cereals.

"Most athletes look at this as a great honor," said company spokeswoman Pam Becker.

That was the case for decathlon gold medalist Dan O'Brien, who was pictured on the Wheaties box following the 1996 Olympics. "This is one of my dreams," O'Brien said.

Forward Karyn Bye of the 1998 U.S. women's hockey team that won the gold in Nagano, Japan also was thrilled.

"I know I'm going to drive into a gas station and somebody is going to say, 'Hey, you're on the Wheaties box!'" Bye said. "And I'm going to say, 'I know it. Do you believe it?'" Some of the athletes also have made commercials and personal appearances on behalf of Wheaties.

In the early years, the athletes appeared on the back of the box. The first on the front was Olympic pole vaulter and fitness crusader Bob Richards, a two-time gold medal winner who was a Wheaties spokesman for 12 years, beginning in 1958.

Wheaties, which began picturing athletes on its boxes 10 years after the cereal was introduced, is celebrating its 75th anniversary this year. General Mills decided to honor the public's top 10 favorites by reissuing their original boxes. Earlier this year, Wheaties boxes included a ballot listing 75 of the hundreds of possible choices plus a spot for write-in votes.

Wheaties' association with sports began in 1933, when it began sponsoring broadcasts of Minneapolis Millers baseball games. Later that year, the advertising slogan "The Breakfast of Champions" was created by advertising executive Knox Reeves for a large signboard at the ballpark.

Wheaties' baseball broadcasts were expanded to other teams and eventually were heard on 95 stations around the country. At one of those stations, WHO in Des Moines, Iowa, a young broadcaster named Ronald "Dutch" Reagan entered a contest for Wheaties broadcasters. He won a trip to Hollywood, all expenses paid, and never returned.

Athlete testimonials were a key part of the broadcast package. In addition to Gehrig, Ruth, and Robinson, baseball greats Joe DiMaggio, Stan Musial, Ted Williams, Yogi Berra, Mickey Mantle, and Johnny Bench spoke for Wheaties. In 1939, 46 of the 51 players chosen for the Major League All-Star Game endorsed the cereal.

Despite the success of the sports advertising, Wheaties changed course in the early 1950s and began using the Lone Ranger and Mickey Mouse Club to capture more of the children's market. In the process, it lost some adults.

"Sales dropped more than 10 percent in one year," Becker said.

The company resurrected its sports and physical fitness marketing strategy, hiring Richards as its main spokesman and establishing the Wheaties Sports Federation to support and promote fitness. It stuck with sports as it expanded the cereal line to include Crispy Wheaties 'n Raisins and Honey Frosted Wheaties.

The strategy continues to work, Becker said. The company received tens of thousands of ballots after the boxes with the 75th anniversary ballots, which were due last month, hit the shelves January 1, she said.

All this for a cereal that began as an accident.

In 1921, a health clinician in Minneapolis was mixing a batch of bran gruel for his patients when he spilled some of the mix on a hot stove, where it crackled and sizzled into a crisp flake.

He took the crisped gruel to the folks at General Mills' predecessor, Washburn Crosby Co. Head miller George Cormack then began testing wheat varieties to create a stronger flake that wouldn't turn into dust inside a cereal box.

A contest was held among company employees and their families to rename the new cereal, which was introduced in 1924 as Washburn's Gold Medal Whole Wheat Flakes. Wheaties was the winning entry and the cereal was renamed in 1925.

—

Source: Karren Mills, Associated Press; from *Marketing News*, March 15, 1999, p. 12. Reprinted by permission of the Associated Press.

Basic evidence of the effectiveness might be inferred from the increased use of the strategy. Studies indicate that the presence of athlete endorsements in print advertisements has trended upward since the 1920s. However, that actual percentage in general readership magazines is still quite low. Endorsement ads appear in sports-related magazines such as *Sports Illustrated* and *New Zealand Sport* with greater frequency. Presumably, this is due to the closer fit between the endorser and the each magazine's target market. This fit should make the athlete endorser more effective. This raises the question as to whether or not there is evidence that these marketing efforts actually work.

> Recent studies support the belief that endorsements provided by athletes do provide positive results for the marketer.

Recent studies support the belief that endorsements provided by athletes do provide positive results for the marketer. However, in one study the results varied significantly from one athlete to another. For example, the percentage of sample members who correctly identified Michael Jordan's relationship with Nike was 73 percent. Conversely, only 7.6 percent correctly associated Gabriela Sabatini with Yamaha.[5] The authors of that study also stated a belief that recognition rates would be better when the endorsement addresses sport-related products rather than mainstream consumer products like watches and fast-food restaurants. Thus, it would be argued that Michael Jordan's endorsement of Nike is likely to be more effective than his endorsement for Hanes underwear. Similarly, Serena Williams's endorsement of Nike should produce better results than will her endorsement of Wrigley's Doublemint gum. Box 12.1 sketches the history of people who have appeared on Wheaties boxes.

From a different perspective, a recent study documented a positive relationship between a firm's stock price and the announcement that the firm has signed a contract with a celebrity endorser.[6] The implication is that investors tend to view these relationships in a positive way and anticipate increases in market value. Thus, it appears that consumers, marketers, and investors all recognize the potential benefits that the celebrity spokesperson can provide.

Factors Impacting Endorsement Effectiveness

A number of factors have been identified as potentially impacting the effectiveness of an endorsement campaign. These factors primarily relate specifically to the endorser; however, others relate to the fit among the endorser, the product, and the market. Another factor involves the long-term sustainability of an endorsement program. Each of these factors is described on the following pages.

Endorser Is a High Achiever

There is a correlation between the effectiveness of an athlete in an endorsement role and what the athlete has achieved throughout his or her career. This is true even if the athlete has retired. Award-winning entertainers have more marketing power than do character actors who perform in minor roles, and winning politicians generally have more impact than perpetual losers. From a strict impact perspective, the marketer is generally best served when able to secure the services of a high achiever. Of course, a high-achieving endorser will be paid higher fees, so impact must be weighed against cost to arrive at a true measure of effectiveness. It is noteworthy that many marketers feel that it is better to retain a single high achiever rather than several less expensive, lower-profile endorsers. From a sports perspective–local, regional, national, and global—there will be a limited number of high achievers available. Unfortunately, in addition to being more expensive, these high achievers may limit the number of endorsement deals in which they will participate at any given time. They may also have existing contracts with competitors that preclude their ability to endorse the marketer's product. Simply stated, high achievers may be difficult to sign.

Endorser Has Believability/Credibility

Motive is an issue in regard to believability. Why is the celebrity endorsing the product? Is it because it truly is perceived to be superior, thus worthy of endorsement? Or is it because one marketer outbid another for the celebrity's support? Two recent issues concerning Tiger Woods come to mind in this regard. His switch from Titleist to Nike raised some eyebrows, even to the point where his competitors spoke of Tiger's performance with "inferior equipment." From a different perspective, when Woods's five-year contract with Rolex watches expired, he signed a new contract with competitor Tag Heuer. Questions were raised as to the motive for the switch, with many critics offering the belief that it was because Tag Heuer offered a more lucrative deal, not because they produce a superior watch.

> If BMW pays someone to endorse its cars, it doesn't want to see that individual in advertisements for Porsche.

For an endorser to be effective, the target market must believe that the spokesperson is sincere. This requires an assessment of the character and past activities of the endorser. It also dictates that the marketer should identify potential conflicts and contractually limit the spokesperson's ability to endorse other brands within the same product category. In other words, if BMW pays someone to endorse its cars, it doesn't want to see that individual in advertisements for Porsche. Conflicts such as these make it difficult for the consumer to accept any claim of product superiority made on behalf of the marketer.

Endorser Is Known

People in the target market must be familiar with the celebrity endorser. In light of this reality, marketers have historically selected high-profile athletes from major sports to serve as their spokespersons. It is believed that these individuals are more effective in the marketer's task of achieving the objectives tied to an endorsement program.

If it is a face and name with which the consumer is not familiar, the endorser might as well be an aspiring actor. In sports, this creates problems for athletes who participate in secondary events. The Olympic gold medalist in women's ice skating may be well known; but her gold medal–winning teammate in snowboarding may be comparatively unknown. This might explain why Sarah Hughes has endorsement contracts (including Wheaties Cereal and Campbell's Soup) while few opportunities exist for her gold medal–winning teammate Kelly Clark. Interestingly, because she is well known and an acknowledged achiever, silver medalist skater Michelle Kwan has signed an array of contracts, the most notable being Disney. It is a reality that fewer female athletes are known by the general public, which has meant fewer endorsement opportunities for women. However, the recent growth in women's sports—soccer, golf, and basketball, in particular—is leading to more and better contracts for women athletes. For example, in 2003 Nike signed its first female golfer, Grace Park of Korea. But many people look to Nike's 2005 signing of Michelle Wie to represent a major breakthrough in the endorsement environment for female athletes.

Endorser Is Likable/Popular/Admired

Emotion plays a key role in celebrity endorsements. This emotion is based upon the extent to which a consumer likes or dislikes the spokesperson. From a sports perspective, one would anticipate that local athletes would be viewed favorably while arch rivals would be looked upon with considerable disdain. Reebok has recently suffered significant losses in market share to adidas and Nike in key Asian markets. To counter this trend, Reebok signed the very recognizable and admired Yao Ming to an endorsement contract. It is hoped that his popularity in China will provide Reebok with a sustainable competitive advantage that will be difficult for competitors to neutralize.

The athlete's personality also plays a key role, as reflected by comments made to and reported in the press. Serena Williams recently mocked the French citizens in a TV interview saying they'd rather drink wine and make clothes. She said this while speaking with a "French accent." Even with all the positives regarding her, there were few endorsement opportunities in the French market. Similarly, U.S. baseball star Barry Bonds has achieved much in his career but has not achieved any real measure of likability outside of his home market. In the words of Kathleen Hessert, president of Sports Media Challenge, "why would a company align itself with a person who's not likable? Barry Bonds hasn't made himself likable yet."[7] Such public disdain could in fact result in situations whereby the consumer chooses not to purchase a product because of the endorser. It is evident then that marketers must assess many dimensions in selecting celebrity endorsers, and consideration must be given to the extent to which the potential endorser is viewed favorably by members of the target market.

> Why would a company align itself with a person who's not likable?

There are also geographic considerations to address in this regard. An endorsement using cricket player Shane Warne may be effective in Australia but suffer due to his relative anonymity in the United States[8] just as the effective Campbell's Soup campaign that uses NFL player Donovan McNabb in the United States would not be effective in Australia. Similarly, an endorsement by NHL player Claude Lemieux may work in Montreal, Denver, or Dallas where he is revered for his tenacity while playing hockey for the local teams, but it would be counterproductive in Detroit where he is reviled because of his reputation for questionable behavior on the ice. The issue for the marketer is that different geographic areas may require different spokespersons as no one person may be able to sufficiently enthuse consumers in all of the company's geographic markets.

Endorser Is Recognizable

Celebrities are often featured in TV advertisements and print media in their capacity as product endorsers. The extent to which celebrities are easily identified plays a meaningful role in determining the potential impact of the endorsements and the corresponding testimonials. An easily recognizable face is desirable, but an easily recognizable name is essential. Throughout the world, most sports fans and virtually all soccer fans recognize David Beckham. A recent survey by *SportBusiness International* identified Beckham as the athlete who delivered the "best return on endorsement investment in 2003—from a global perspective."[9] Consequently, he is featured in a variety of advertisements for an array of products throughout the world. In some cases, his exposure may be limited to certain geographic areas; for example, his endorsement deal with Meiji Seiku is primarily limited to Japan. Conversely, his endorsement deal with adidas has global dimensions. Table 12.1 summarizes the results of the aforementioned study.

In most cases, however, the target market is not global; thus, the marketer can attempt to sign a celebrity who is easily recognized in a more limited geographic area. Examples include rugby union player Jonah Lomu in New Zealand or Tonga; another is ice hockey player Dominick Hasek in the Czech Republic. Though there is a relationship between recognizability and achievement, it varies significantly among the set of athletes available for product endorsements. For instance, tennis player Anna Kournikova is quite recognizable despite a modest level of achievement, whereas her fellow competitor Justine Henin-Hardenne has accomplished much more but is far less recognizable outside of her home country of Belgium.

Two other factors that affect recognizability are media exposure and visibility during an event. Players who often appear on TV or who are the focus of media reports are more

TABLE 12.1
Global Value of Select Athlete Endorsements

Reprinted by permission of www.sportsbusiness.com.

Who delivered the best return on endorsement investment in 2003 from a global perspective?	
Athlete	**% of Respondents**
David Beckham	36.7%
Jonny Wilkinson	20.1
Michael Schumacher	9.8
Tiger Woods	8.6
LeBron James	7.4
Annika Sorenstam	5.6
Lance Armstrong	5.6
Venus and Serena Williams	2.7
Sachin Tendulkar	1.8
Peyton Manning	1.5
Alex Rodriguez	0.3

recognizable. Visibility at a venue is a function of fan proximity and view-obstructing equipment and uniforms. Golf fans get a close look at the participants both at the course and on TV. As a result of this intimacy, many professional golfers are easily recognized by members of the general public. Unlike players in contact sports, there is no protective headgear to obstruct the view of the players. This may be a problem for athletes in sports such as American football and ice hockey.

> The ideal situation will result when the endorser has both a recognizable face and a recognizable name.

In some cases, the name is recognizable even when the face is not. Such was the case when 7Up employed Olympic champion Jackie Joyner-Kersee as a spokesperson. When the TV commercial was produced, her name was superimposed as a graphic in the video. The result was that 7Up was able to capitalize on her notoriety even though her face was not readily identifiable by the target market. In other words, many consumers recognized her name but not her face. This lack of recognition forced the marketers to adapt their advertising accordingly. It is evident that the ideal situation will result when the endorser has both a recognizable face and a recognizable name.

Endorser Provides Ease of Recall

As marketers emphasize promotions that the consumer is able to remember, they focus on finding spokespersons who they can count on to secure a place in the consumer's memory. It is important that there be a discernable relationship between the endorser and the product. In the retail environment, a celebrity endorser may not be exhibited on all point-of-sale displays. But even when a likeness of the endorser is not visible, a properly executed program will cause the consumer who sees the product to recall the association with the endorser. In other words, when done correctly, the consumer will see the product and the celebrity endorser will come to mind. If not, much of the marketer's endorsement effort is wasted. Clearly, high achievers may be easier to recall, but achievements alone may not be sufficient to generate the desired results from the endorsement campaign. Achievement needs to be combined with a meaningful frequency for exposing the target market to the endorsement message. In other words, consumers need to see and hear the spokesperson more than once in order to confirm the relationship between the endorser and the marketer's product.

Endorser Is Congruent with Target Market

For an endorser to be effective in the task of influencing purchase behavior, noteworthy similarities between the spokesperson and the target market must be evident. In some cases, this may be represented by similarities in demographics or lifestyle. For instance, NBA star Allen Iverson is said to have great "street credibility" that makes him an ideal spokesperson for Reebok in its efforts to reach the young, male, African American segment. In many cases, however, it is not the similarity of the endorser and the target market that is crucial. Rather, it is the endorser's impact on a target market and the extent to which that target market represents the focus of the marketer's efforts. For example, Tony Hawk participates in a sport (X Games skateboarding) that appeals primarily to a young (8–18) male segment. So even though Hawk himself does not fall into that demographic category, he is a solid fit for the marketer seeking to reach that group. Quiksilver and Hot Wheels (toy cars) are examples of brands endorsed by Hawk. A relatively young African American golfer, Tiger Woods, finds that his greatest appeal is among middle-aged and older white males. Many of his endorsements reflect this fact, as evidenced by his contracts with Buick automobiles and Tag Heuer watches. Clearly, the marketer must first identify the target market then select a celebrity endorser who is relevant to it. Otherwise, the endorsement program will not be as effective as it could be.

Endorser Is Physically Attractive

Recent research has shown that the physical attractiveness of the endorser can have a positive impact on some key considerations that are important to marketers. A recent study reported that there was a strong correlation between the attractiveness of the endorser and the overall evaluation of the advertisement.[10] This relationship has paid dividends for athletes who are attractive but who have yet to achieve any real measure of success in their chosen sport. Perhaps the most noteworthy in this regard is Anna Kournikova.

A second positive correlation of which marketers will take note is that the respondent's perception of the product itself is related to the attractiveness of the endorser. In other words, a more attractive spokesperson contributes to a better perception of the product. Ironically, even though attractive endorsers contributed to a more favorable perception of both the advertisement and the product being advertised, endorser attractiveness did not have a meaningful impact on the consumers' willingness to purchase the product. The implication of this finding is that attractiveness may be a consideration for the marketer, but it is an insufficient factor in its own right. It can, however, provide synergy when coupled with other more important factors such as being a high achiever or having believability.

Continuity Prospects

As with sponsorship programs, endorsement campaigns tend to be more effective when there is an ongoing, long-term relationship. Contracts that call for a single endorsement or otherwise short-term relationship may be effective when the marketer wants to exploit a current newsworthy event. For example, it is common for the Most Valuable Player in the NFL's Super Bowl to walk off the field saying he is going to Disneyland. In this way, Disney takes advantage of the spontaneity and the immediate recognition of the sports celebrity. However, most endorsement contracts will run for several years. LeBron James's contract with Nike is for 10 years, and Reebok has a "lifetime contract" with Allen Iverson.

There is risk involved for both parties in a long-term contract. The athlete may lose his or her market appeal such that the benefits to the marketer are diminished. Conversely, the athlete may be locked into a contract that provides less than market value in later years after the athlete's accomplishments have significantly increased. Interestingly, NBA star Kobe Bryant can be highlighted in both of these scenarios. Bryant's contract with adidas was deemed inadequate, so the player paid the marketer $8 million to be released from his contract. Shortly thereafter, Bryant signed a new seven-year, $40 million contract with Nike. In the aftermath of Bryant's sexual assault charges, some have questioned whether or not Nike will receive adequate value over the life of the contract. If not, it is conceivable that Nike would opt to terminate the contract on the basis of the omnipresent morals clause. In another example, David Beckham endorses U.K. department store Marks & Spencer. When he was transferred from his U.K.-based team, Manchester United, to the Spain-based Real Madrid team, Marks & Spencer executives immediately indicated a need to renegotiate his contract. Their belief was that Beckham had lost some of his influence in the U.K. market. The bottom line is that marketers need to seek long-term contracts with celebrity endorsers, but they must also recognize the risks involved.

Selection Process

As documented earlier, there are numerous potential pitfalls of which the marketer must be aware. Thus, there are some basic guidelines that must direct the process of evaluating and selecting effective endorsers. Endorsers must be

- Trustworthy.
- Recognizable (by the target audience).
- Affordable.
- At little risk for negative publicity.
- Appropriately matched to target audience.[11]

Of course the process is complicated by the fact that there is some risk involved in these assessments. For instance, until his indictment on criminal sexual conduct charges, few people associated the risk of negative publicity to NBA star Kobe Bryant. To a lesser extent, cheating charges directed at baseball star Sammy Sosa have also raised some questions regarding his future endorsement opportunities. The second element of risk is that there may be several athletes with comparable value to the marketer. The decision to select one athlete over another opens the marketer up to criticism if the selected endorser engages in unacceptable behavior or if he or she simply fails to produce the results sought by the marketer. Many endorsement contracts cover a multiyear period and may result in nonproductive payments continuing to be paid to the ineffective endorser.

In the selection process, the marketer must remember to maintain a set of options. There is not just one celebrity who can fill the role, so the marketer must assess the alternatives. If one celebrity is too expensive or has a contract that precludes a relationship with the marketer, who else could provide the benefits and attributes sought in an endorser? Also, many endorsers expect to be well compensated. The marketer should understand that it may well be better to pay a large sum to a "star" as opposed to a lesser amount for a less prominent individual. As one market researcher said in regard to the use of endorsers lacking star quality, "you might as well have your sister or your nephew be the spokesperson."[12] In other words, stars provide benefits that lower-performing individuals cannot provide, and the marketer must be prepared to pay if it is seeking a high-profile star to represent the company.

Once the list of alternative spokespersons and a potential budget have been developed, the selection process can continue. A key step is the delineation of a set of values that are characteristic of the company; these values should also reflect the personality and lifestyle of the prospective endorser. Remember that there should be a fit between the company and the endorser. The next step is to look at measures of effectiveness. Rather than developing

Q SCORES

An important and readily available tool for marketers considering the use of celebrity endorsers are Q scores. These scores are calculated by Marketing Evaluations, Inc. The list of celebrities scored includes athletes, entertainers, and other well-known individuals such as news broadcasters. These scores are used as measures that help assess each celebrity's potential as a paid endorser. Among the factors considered in the process are recognizability and likability.

Q scores typically fall in a range between 0 and 60, though higher values are possible. Higher ratings reflect greater potential marketing power. A marketer seeking to decide between soccer player David Beckham, basketball player Yao Ming, Formula 1 driver Michael Schumacher, and actor Tom Cruise can use the Q scores as one of the objective measures in the task of deciding who, if anyone, to offer a contract to. Still, it is important to note that these scores represent only a portion of the evaluation process and should not be used as the sole measure of suitability. Furthermore, since the measures reflect market power, they can be used to negotiate a reasonable contract with the celebrity.

It is also important to note that Q scores are typically reported for the population at large. However, ratings can be generated for a variety of market segments. For example, a company considering using Tony Hawk (Extreme Sports skateboarder) as a spokesperson is primarily interested in his marketing power for younger consumers. The firm may also be focusing on males. It would find that the highest Q scores are in evidence when assessing the younger (< 35) male segments and thus represent a far better match for Mountain Dew than for Liz Claiborne clothing. Below is a list of celebrities and their approximate (2002) Q scores.

Tiger Woods	50–55
Barry Bonds	20–30
Brandi Chastain	10–20
Michael Jordan	40–50
Bill Cosby	40–50
Mel Gibson	44–57
Julia Roberts	33–36
Sarah Hughes	31–36
Marion Jones	31–36

Source: Information provided courtesy of Marketing Evaluations, Inc. See www.qscores.com.

the measurement process itself, the marketer may rely upon information from an outside provider. One of the most common quantitative measures available to marketers is the *Q score;* this measure assesses potential by measuring the recognizability and likability of celebrities under consideration (see Box 12.2 for an explanation of Q scores). Alternatively, a marketer can create its own measurement tool in an effort to objectively compare one prospective endorser to another. An example of such a measurement process is presented in Tables 12.2 and 12.3.

By examining the process outlined in Table 12.2, it can be seen how a marketer can objectively evaluate a potential endorser. This evaluation can help the marketer decide whether or not to consider the prospect to be a viable candidate as a spokesperson. In that regard, it represents a screening process. Those prospects who fail to achieve adequate results are eliminated from further consideration.

Table 12.3 provides an example of the preliminary evaluation process. The results shown in Table 12.3 indicate that the prospect Michael Campbell has the potential to be an effective spokesperson for Sony. The marketer may have a benchmark indicating specific values that merit further consideration. For example, perhaps any aggregate measure exceeding 3.5 will result in progressing to the next step in the evaluation process. Alternatively, perhaps the marketer is evaluating several prospects and will advance only

TABLE 12.2
Model for Preliminary Evaluation of Prospective Endorsers

Step 1: Select a company, brand, or product to be endorsed.
Step 2: Identify the target market to be reached with the endorser.
Step 3: Identify a potential celebrity endorser.
Step 4: Select a series of criteria deemed relevant in the matching and selection process.
Step 5: Assign a weight to each criterion based upon the relative importance in identifying effective endorsers.
Step 6: Evaluate the prospect on each criterion on an appropriate scale (e.g., 1 to 5, with 1 = poor and 5 = excellent).
Step 7: Multiply the weight for each criterion by the prospect's rating on that criterion.
Step 8: Sum the results.
Step 9: Use the sum to evaluate potential effectiveness of the prospect or to compare one prospect to another.
Step 10: Make decision to continue the evaluation process or to eliminate the prospect from further consideration.

the top few to the next stage regardless of the exact values resulting from the preliminary assessment process.

The next step is the qualitative assessment of each prospect who attains acceptable results in the preliminary evaluation process. Examine the media for negative publicity. What positions and statements in regard to controversial issues has the prospect articulated? With which groups is the prospect associated; are there any controversial or extremist groups? Is the celebrity already overexposed to the point that his or her endorsement is trivialized? What is the geographic scope of the public's familiarity with the prospect? How much time is likely remaining in the celebrity's career? Are there any health problems that might jeopardize the prospect's long-term effectiveness?[13] Again, the goal in this step is to make a decision based upon an objective evaluation of each prospective endorser, even if there is only one prospect under consideration.

The final step is to get the contract signed. This means that both the endorser and the marketer view the potential relationship as mutually beneficial. The marketer must often deal with agents who are paid to negotiate lucrative contracts for their clients. It must also be recognized that celebrities often face time constraints, so the timing of photo shoots and appearances must reflect this. Don't expect a premier soccer player to agree to personal appearances during the World Cup competition. These issues–inflexibility in terms of time, dealing indirectly through agents, and prolonged negotiations over compensation—often make this final step an arduous, time-consuming process. Yet it is this final step that finally allows the marketer to begin to implement an appropriate promotional strategy that incorporates celebrity endorsements.

TABLE 12.3
An Example of the Preliminary Evaluation Process

Product: Sony Plasma TV
Potential endorser: Michael Campbell (New Zealand golf pro)
Target market: High-income males in the United States

Criterion	Weight	Rating (1–5)	W*R
1. Achiever	.2	3	.6
2. Known	.2	2	.4
3. Likable	.1	4	.4
4. Credible	.2	5	1.0
5. Congruence/target market	.3	4	1.2
Overall assessment	1.0	x	3.6

Problems with Celebrity Endorsers

Despite all of the positive aspects of celebrity endorsements, there are a number of potential pitfalls of which that the marketer must be aware. Most endorsement contracts today have a morals clause that will allow the marketer to unilaterally terminate an endorsement contract with a celebrity who behaves in ways that are deemed unacceptable and potentially damaging to the reputation of the marketer. Hertz Car Rental Company terminated its contract with O.J. Simpson in the wake of his indictment for murder. Other noteworthy athletes who have seen their endorsement contracts rescinded are (boxer) Mike Tyson, (tennis pro) Jennifer Capriati, and (golfer) John Daly.

> Most endorsement contracts today have a morals clause that will allow the marketer to unilaterally terminate an endorsement contract with a celebrity who behaves in ways that are deemed unacceptable.

Ironically, there has been some discussion of the premise that "bad" sells. The National Basketball Association has seen the growth in popularity of some of its "bad boys," such as Allen Iverson. Still, there is a limit at which even the bad-boy image becomes counterproductive. The following summary provides the profiles of five troublesome celebrity spokespersons.[14]

The Criminal

The moment a spokesperson is involved in criminal activity, the marketer must rethink the relationship and the associated marketing communications strategy. Even when actions do not result in criminal charges, they may still have a detrimental impact on the public's perception of the individual spokesperson, and that perception could be transferred to any marketer with which that individual has an endorsement contract. In the past few years, more instances regarding murder, domestic abuse, gambling, sexual misconduct, and substance abuse among celebrity endorsers have been reported, and many of these transgressions have resulted in the termination of endorsement contracts. A study performed by *Advertising Age* indicated that the sexual assault charges filed against Kobe Bryant in 2003 resulted in 22 percent of the respondents saying that a Bryant endorsement would make them less likely to purchase the endorsed brands and products.[15] It is important to note that this negative impact was in evidence prior to any actions by the judiciary system. Similar issues caused Pepsi-Cola to terminate its endorsement relationship with pop singer Michael Jackson in the aftermath of the 1993 allegations of sexual abuse of a minor and his acknowledged addiction to prescription pain-killing drugs.

The Prima Donna

The celebrity is often the focus of attention. As a result, it may be difficult for the endorser to accept a secondary role. It may be a blow to the celebrity's ego when faced with the reality that he or she is not the key consideration in the relationship; rather, it is the marketer and its brands and products that are most important. Even though the celebrity is being paid, he or she may find it difficult to accept being the secondary focus. There are also celebrities who present problems regarding scheduling and the fulfillment of other obligations, such as promotional appearances on behalf of the marketer. Some celebrities may also use their appearances and their position to promote themselves. This concern must be weighed against the potential benefits offered by the potential prima donna celebrity.

The Fading Star

Celebrities in all categories are aware that their fame may be short lived. Athletes lose their skills, actors find themselves in less demand because of rising stars, and politicians are replaced. The best endorsement relationships tend to be long-term ones; however, the celebrity of today may not project the same image in the future. Some stars have continued to shine even after their prowess on the athletic field or in the entertainment industry has faded. An example is golfer Arnold Palmer, who is still highly respected by consumers and viewed as a viable spokesperson for companies such as Callaway Golf, Pennzoil, and Lanier Worldwide. Still, the fading star can present a dilemma for the marketer, be it facing the question of whether or not to offer the spokesperson a new contract or in the task of estimating the financial value of the endorser to the company when the decision to continue the relationship has already been made.

The Lightning Rod

This individual speaks out or supports causes that are subject to considerable scrutiny and criticism. The concern in this case is that a significant portion of the population may be offended by the statements or positions taken. If this happens, it is likely that pressure will be applied in an effort to persuade the marketer to drop the controversial spokesperson. The most significant impact is often achieved by the critics by way of a boycott of any products endorsed by the controversial endorser. Although this problem is more likely to occur with outspoken entertainers and politicians, it is still a consideration for the marketer considering the use of an athlete in an endorsement role.

The Tongue-Tied

Remember, the endorser is a spokesperson for the marketer. As such, the endorser's communications skills are an important asset for the marketer. This may not be relevant for scripted TV advertisements or photo shoots for print ads, but it can be vitally important when the endorser is seen or heard making impromptu comments in casual environments. Speaking in a casual conversation, even though still in the role of endorser, the person may not be doing what he or she does best. As a result, we often witness rambling monologues replete with clichés. Because of this, the marketer must consider the different ways in which the celebrity will be asked to represent the company and its products. How much will be scripted and controlled? How much will be spontaneous?

Overview

A recent article in *Executive Update Online* captures the essence of some of these potential problems with celebrity spokespersons. See Box 12.3 for a reprint of this article.

Other Potential Problems

Ambush Marketing

From an endorsement perspective, ambush marketing occurs when a celebrity's name or likeness is used without the legal right to do so. It could reasonably be argued that this crosses the boundary beyond ambush marketing and should be characterized as piracy. The marketer engaged in this tactic is attempting to convey the idea that the celebrity endorses the product. Two examples of this are Rio Ferdinand (Manchester United Soccer), whose name has been used to promote a company (BAE Systems) in the defense system industry, and NBA player Yao Ming, who sued Coca-Cola over what

CELEBRITY PR HORROR STORIES 12.3

Many associations have shared the pain of finding a spokesperson on the front page of *USA Today* under less-than-desirable circumstances. When your board of directors asks you to find a celebrity spokesperson, here are some incidents to help you counsel against haste:

- "I'm inconsolable at the present time. I was a very good friend of Jordan; he was probably the greatest basketball player this country has ever seen. We will never see his likes again."—Mariah Carey on CNN after a *USA Today* reporter asked her to comment on the death of King Hussein of Jordan (not Michael Jordan). According to one account, Carey was then led away by her security entourage in a state of "confusion."

- "Smoking kills. If you're killed, you've lost a very important part of your life."—Brooke Shields, during an interview to become spokesperson for a federal antismoking campaign.

- "Tell him not to serve fried chicken next year. Got it? Or collard greens or whatever in the hell they serve."—Fuzzy Zoeller, referring to Tiger Woods after Woods won the 1997 Masters Golf Tournament. Zoeller, also a professional golfer, was forced to make a public apology to Woods and the African American community.

- Actress Cybill Shepard was a spokesperson for the beef industry until she revealed that she generally avoided red meat.

- Pepsi-Cola had a series of debacles with three tarnished celebrities: Mike Tyson, Madonna, and Michael Jackson.

- O.J. Simpson was a spokesman for Hertz until . . . well, you know the rest.

Source: C. Stenrud, "Celebrity PR Horror Stories," *Executive Update Online,* August 2001, www.gwsae.org/ExecutiveUpdate/2001/August/celebrity.htm (accessed September 18, 2003). Reprinted with permission by The American Society of Association Executives.

he perceived to be the unauthorized use of his photo. Yao has an endorsement contract with Pepsi-Cola and Coca-Cola has a contract with the Chinese National Basketball team, of which Yao is a member. It was Coca-Cola's contention that its contract with the Chinese team allows it to use likenesses of players on the team in its promotions and packaging. Of course Pepsi's position was that Coca-Cola was guilty of ambush marketing. In a last-minute settlement before going to trial, Coca-Cola acknowledged that it had used Yao's image without advance consent and that its assertion that the relationship with the Chinese National team gave it the right to do so was incorrect. The company then issued an apology for its actions.[16]

Other ambush efforts are not so overt. Paul Hogan (Crocodile Dundee) successfully sued a shoe manufacturer. The actor's argument was that the use of the movie's famous knife scene in commercials falsely implied Hogan's endorsement of the company's shoes. Clearly companies recognize the potential benefits that may be derived from the use of a celebrity's name and likeness in their promotions, and some are willing to push such use to the point of being unethical or illegal. In such cases, it is generally the endorser, not the marketer, who must pursue legal remedies to eliminate those instances where his or her name or likeness is being used without permission.

Costs

Without fail, every high-profile, high-value endorsement contract that is signed is met with the argument that the high cost will be passed along to the consumer in the form of higher prices. Nike's recent signing of the young basketball phenom LeBron James to a lucrative ($90 million) contract has met with such criticism. From time to time, dissenting voices from within the equipment industry highlight this concern. John Hillerich of H&B, the manufacturer of PowerBilt golf clubs, is quoted as saying: "I had to make a decision. Spend millions to have name players use my clubs, or spend that money to improve my product. I chose the latter, and I'm glad I did because PowerBilt clubs today are superior to the ones that won all those pro tournaments. I've also been able to keep my prices down."[17]

Consumers use an endorsement as a testimonial of quality.

While this is a difficult argument to win, the marketer can use the concept of economies of scale to defend its actions. To the extent that the endorsement creates additional demand, it serves to drive down average costs. The result may be lower prices rather than higher ones. Additionally, it might be argued that consumers use an endorsement as a testimonial of quality, thus, there is added peace of mind when buying a product endorsed by a well-known celebrity. Consider Nike again. Tiger Woods's endorsement may be valuable to the average golfer in assessing the quality of Nike products. Additionally, there is little doubt that Tiger's endorsement was a key factor in Nike's quick success in attaining a sizable market share upon its recent entry into the golf ball market. Higher market share equates to higher levels of production and the resultant economies of scale.

Misrepresentation of Use

This issue is particularly relevant for athletes endorsing a brand of athletic equipment. Professional golfers endorse a variety of brands of clubs. Tennis players are paid to endorse rackets produced by several competitors. They appear in their competitive arenas with the appropriate brand in hand; thus, it reflects the "I use it, so should you" mode of endorsement. But some argue that the brand name is where the similarity between what they are using and what they are selling to the everyday player ends. After Juan Carlos Ferrero won the 2003 French Open, equipment manufacturer Prince issued a press release that Ferrero had used a "Triple Threat Graphite Mid" to win the tournament. In reality, he used a custom-modified racket that had been cosmetically treated so as to look like the racket in question. It is so common in tennis that it is referred to as a "paint job."[18] Manufacturers justify this as a way to recover the $350,000 to $1 million per year paid to top pros to endorse and help create demand for new models. Similarly, it is common knowledge that golfers often order special weights, balances, and grips not available to the everyday buyer. Finally, some players do not use the brands they endorse. Though he has long endorsed Nike, Tiger Woods has often used a Titleist driver. His contract, like many others, requires him to make his "best effort" to use the products that he endorses, but it does not mandate such use as an absolute condition. Thus, the marketer must be prepared for complaints about misrepresentation.

In some cases, the players may be contractually required to use the marketers' brands. After the 2006 Olympics, one hockey player's equipment did not get back to him in time to resume his NHL season. In order to play, he was forced to borrow hockey sticks from one of his teammates. Unfortunately, the sticks were not the same brand that he was paid to endorse and required to use. In a good faith effort to honor his contract, he obscured the logo by taping over it. One sport that relies heavily upon player endorsements is golf. Club, shoe, and ball manufacturers have a vested interest in assuring that their spokespersons use their products when competing. But how can this use be verified? One way is to rely on information provided by the Darrell Survey. This service performs an inventory of each golfer's equipment at the start of many tournaments across the world. Box 12.4 provides an overview of the Darrell Survey.

Endorsement Conflicts

There are occasions when an athlete endorses one brand of product while the governing body involved with the athlete's sport endorses another brand. This is similar to the conflict regarding Yao Ming's endorsement of Pepsi while the Chinese national basketball team was

THE DARRELL SURVEY 12.4

Many professional golfers are compensated in exchange for their agreement to use a certain marketer's equipment during competition. Additionally, these marketers see great public relations value associated with high levels of usage on the professional tours. How can a marketer ensure that there is compliance with endorsement contracts—that the golfers whom they pay to use their clubs, golf balls, gloves, shoes, and other equipment are actually using those products? How can a marketer document that a high percentage of the players on each tour or the winner of an event is using their equipment? The answer is, the Darrell Survey.

The Darrell Survey Company is a marketing research company that collects data regarding brand usage on each to the major professional golf tours in the world. As each golfer approaches the first tee on the tournament's opening day of a PGA, LPGA, Senior PGA (Champions Tour), Nationwide, PGA of Japan, or certain premier amateur events, he or she is met by a representative of the Darrell Survey. Data are collected on the brands of irons, woods, wedges, putters, balls, gloves, shoes, shafts, spikes, grips, bags, and visors being used by each golfer. Data are collected via direct observation in order to assure their accuracy.

According to the representatives of the company, such information is vital in the manufacturers' efforts to verify compliance of the golfers whom they pay to endorse or use their equipment. Additional uses of the information include the measurement of market share, assisting in the development of sales strategies, gaining insight into the competition, and assisting in the creation of effective advertising messages.

Consider the statistics reported in regard to the 2003 Greater Hartford Open. The number of golfers using the following brands of equipment was as follows:

Balls		Drivers		Irons		Wedges		Putters	
Titleist	92	TaylorMade	53	Titleist	31	Titleist	119	Titleist	69
Callaway	30	Titleist	39	TaylorMade	28	Cleveland	107	Odyssey	30
Nike	15	Callaway	38	Cleveland	26	TaylorMade	29	TaylorMade	20

Source: C. Monarrez, "The Darrell Survey: Sir May I Check Your Bag?" *Detroit Free Press,* August 1, 2003, pp. 1D, 8D. Also see www.darrellsurvey.com.

sponsored by Coca-Cola. This dilemma surfaced in earnest during the 1992 Summer Olympics. The U.S. basketball team was sponsored by Reebok, whereas many of the players endorsed, and typically wore, clothing and shoes from other manufacturers. The most notable was Michael Jordan, who had enjoyed a long-standing endorsement relationship with Nike. When he and the other players mounted the victory stand to claim their gold medals, many had the American flag draped over their shoulders. It was not just a show of patriotism; it was also an effort to obscure the Reebok logos that adorned their Olympic clothing. More recently, Belgian tennis player Kim Clijsters indicated that she would not participate in the 2004 Olympic Games in Athens if not allowed to wear Fila apparel. She endorses Fila, but the Belgian Olympic team was sponsored by adidas. According to Clijsters, "It seems normal that I respect my contract and do not play in another outfit; it has nothing to do with money." Issues such as this have led many to question the decision to allow professional athletes to compete in such prestigious events. Ironically, few question it on the basis of their right to display their skills; rather, they express concerns about these types of conflicts and the athletes' reluctance to fully embrace the sponsors that commit significant resources to the national teams and their governing organizations.

Conflicts with Sport Regulatory Bodies

There have been a few instances where athletes have endorsed products that fail to meet the specifications deemed acceptable by a governing body. Ten-pin bowling has regulations regarding the weight and the coefficient of friction for any bowling ball. Golf has established specifications for the velocity of golf balls and the coefficient of restitution (COR) for drivers. Bowlers seek higher friction in order to hook the ball more and get better pin action (and higher scores). Golfers seek a higher COR so that they hit the ball further. The controversy surfaces when a respected athlete endorses a product that fails to conform to specifications established by the various regulatory bodies. Such was the case with Arnold Palmer's endorsement of the rule-violating Callaway ERC II driver. His contention that it would be good for the average golfer was met with considerable criticism by the USGA and by many within the golf media. It seemed to make no difference that the other key regulatory body, the Royal & Ancient (R&A), declared it acceptable. The lesson here is that the endorser and the marketer must anticipate that potential conflicts of this type might surface, and they should anticipate the need to develop an appropriate strategy to counter the criticisms. One alternative is to abandon the endorsement. Another more drastic alternative for the marketer is the decision to abandon marketing efforts for the product in question.

Amateur Status

There have been a number of recent signings of young athletes. A shoe company recently signed soccer star Freddy Adu when he was only 14 years old; another signed a very young basketball player with a talent for shooting free throws. Though the payments for young athletes such as these have typically been directed into trust accounts, questions have been raised as to whether or not such deals move the youngsters into the professional category, thereby negating their amateur status. With Olympic amateur athletes such as Carl Lewis earning a significant income from endorsements, the issue of amateurism is not clear. Both the endorser, through appropriate representation, and the marketer must have a clear understanding of the consequences of signing any endorsement contract.

Unwholesome Nonsports Products

Celebrities have been used to endorse an array of products that are subject to intense public criticism. When it is the athlete in this role, criticism is often pointed toward concerns that many of the athlete's most impressionable fans are children. We have seen players and former players endorse candy bars, tobacco products, alcoholic beverages, and casinos.

In response to such criticisms, many sports organizations have imposed their own regulations that prevent questionable endorsements by current players. For example, in the United States, active professional players cannot appear in advertisements for beer. Once they retire, however, that restriction is no longer in place. As a result, Americans see a number of retired athletes in beer commercials. In the face of such regulations, marketers either have to look outside the realm of the athletic arena for endorsers or look to retired athletes who still have marketing appeal.

Overexposure

There are questions raised regarding athletes who endorse a wide array of products. If an athlete endorses say 20 products, does it hinder the consumers' ability to recognize the association thereby negating any perceived market power? If so, should athletes limit the number of endorsement contracts they sign? Of course, this raises questions regarding compensation. The argument might be that since an athlete has voluntarily, or contractually, agreed to limit his or her endorsement deals, he or she may expect to command greater compensation for the selected contracts. The marketer should consider the athlete's level of exposure when negotiating the compensation to be earned by the endorser.

Closing Capsule

It has been stated that "the public backlash against the on- and off-field transgressions of pro athletes is causing marketers of athletic products to rethink the role of sports stars in their marketing campaigns."[19] Despite this concern, the use of athletes in endorsement roles continues to gain in popularity. It is viewed as a way to cut through promotional clutter to help marketers achieve their strategic goals.

The selection process is not easy, and the marketer must be prepared to pay a premium for a top-level sports star. The ultimate selection decision is guided by a review of factors such as what the athlete has achieved, how much the consumer can believe what the athlete says, and how easily recognized the athlete is. There are a number of potential problems; foremost are the instances of legal and moral transgressions on the part of the athlete. As a result, virtually every endorsement contract signed today has a morals clause that allows the marketer to cancel the contract. Marketers must weigh the advantages against the disadvantages. Given the compensation provided in several recent high-profile signings, it is apparent that marketers still see this strategy as both viable and valuable.

Review Questions

1. What are the three basic applications for the use of celebrity endorsers?
2. Explain the Darrell Survey.
3. How can a marketer use the Darrell Survey to assist in strategy development?
4. What are the five key selection criteria for prospective endorsers?
5. Select a prospective endorser and a product (or company). Create a model and complete a quantitative assessment of the prospect. Is there a good fit between the prospect and the product?
6. What are the primary uses for Q scores?
7. Briefly discuss the five categories of problem endorsers.
8. What is the morals clause that is typically included in endorsement contracts?
9. Look through several magazines and identify three endorsement ads with each ad adhering to a different mode of endorsement. For example, find one ad that employs the "I use it, so should you" strategy.
10. Select three celebrities and three products; create three different magazine ads, one for each of the three endorsement modes.

Endnotes

1. L. Petrecca, "Bergman Matches Ballplayers, Marketers," *Advertising Age,* May 15, 2000, p. 26.
2. D. Rovell, "Tiger Worth Every Penny of That $100 Mil," *ESPN Golf Online,* September 20, 2000, http://espn.go.com/golfonline/tours/s/rovell/0920woods.html (accessed October 13, 2005).
3. M. Jones and D. Schumann, "The Strategic Use of Celebrity Athlete Endorsers in *Sports Illustrated:* A Historical Perspective," *Sport Marketing Quarterly* 9, no. 2 (2002), pp. 65–76.
4. Ibid.
5. D. Stotlar, F. Veltri, and R. Vishwanathan, "Recognition of Athlete-Endorsed Sports Products," *Sport Marketing Quarterly* 7, no. 1 (1998), pp. 48–56.
6. K. Farrell, G. Karels, K. Monfort, and C. McClatchey, "Celebrity Performance and Endorsement Value: A Case of Tiger Woods," *Managerial Finance* 26, no. 7 (2000), pp. 1–15.
7. M. Hyman, "The Trouble with Barry," *BusinessWeek,* October 15, 2001, p. 100.
8. Shane Warne is a popular Australian cricket player.

9. "Athlete Endorsement: Who Has Delivered the Best Return on Endorsement Investment in 2003—from a Global Perspective?" 2003, www.sportbusiness.com/poll/poll-results?poll_id=850 (accessed October 13, 2005).

10. M. Shank and L. Langmeyer, "Maximizing the Impact of Athletes as Endorsers: Exploring Athlete Attractiveness," *AMA Sports Marketing SIG Proceedings,* August 1999.

11. A. Miciak and W. Shanklin, "Choosing Celebrity Endorsers," *Marketing Management* 3, no. 3 (1994), pp. 51–59.

12. C. Stenrud, "Celebrity PR Horror Stories," *Executive Update Online,* August 2001, www.gwsae.org/ExecutiveUpdate/2001/August/celebrity.htm (accessed October 13, 2005).

13. Ibid.

14. Ibid.

15. D. Barrand, "Jordan Still Top of the Market," October 28, 2003, www.sportbusiness.com/news/index?region=global&page%5no=1&news_item_id=152926 (accessed October 13, 2005).

16. D. Barrand, "Yao and Coke Resolve Image Row," October 20, 2003, www.sportbusiness.com/news/?news_item_id=152825 (accessed October 13, 2005).

17. J. Hillerich IV, "Product List," www.powerbilt.com/hrtg/hllrch.cfm (accessed September 24, 2003).

18. S. Walker, "That Same Old Racket," *The Wall Street Journal,* June 27, 2003, p. W6.

19. J. Stevens, A. Lathrop, and C. Brandish, "Who Is Your Hero?" *Sport Marketing Quarterly* 12, no. 2 (2003), pp. 103–10.

CHAPTER THIRTEEN

Venue Naming Rights

Learning Objectives

- See the history of this special form of sponsorship.
- Learn how various groups benefit from the practice.
- Delineate the components of a venue naming rights plan.
- Identify the key drivers for success.
- Learn how to calculate the value of a naming rights contract.
- See examples from sports and beyond sports.
- Learn how to evaluate the impact—the results.
- Identify problems and concerns associated with the practice.
- Learn where the growth potential lies in the twenty-first century.

The concept of *venue naming rights* is best described as a special case of sponsorship whereby the sponsor pays to have its name attached to a facility for a specified period of time. We most often think of this activity within the domain of sports venues. More so, within the sports domain, many initially viewed it as an American phenomenon. But both of these generalizations have changed over the past few years.

The most noteworthy naming rights contracts have been sports-related; however, there are numerous examples from outside the world of sports. Recent deals involving the performing arts put this type of venue high on the list of many prospective sponsors. But other types of facilities, including shopping malls, museums, convention centers, public schools, and hospitals, have secured naming rights agreements with a variety of corporate partners.

The practice is also becoming more commonplace outside of the United States. Recent examples include the new Allianz Arena in Germany in 2005, Reebok Stadium in England, and the renamed Telstra Stadium in Australia in 2004.

> Corporate sponsors view venue naming rights as a strategic initiative that will aid in the achievement of corporate business objectives.

The key point is that corporate sponsors view venue naming rights as a strategic initiative that will aid in the achievement of corporate business objectives. Seldom is the activity implemented solely for philanthropic reasons. It is safe to assume that the motivation for a corporate sponsor to enter into a venue naming rights contract has evolved much the same way that sponsorship in general has changed. Initially, the motivation for a firm to attach its name to a noteworthy building seemed to be *ego gratification*. Then *philanthropic motives* became important. Finally, we saw the migration toward *ROI motives*. Undoubtedly, ROI is the driving force behind the practice today.

History of Naming Rights

Compared to most business practices, venue naming rights have a relatively short history. Despite the recent applications of the practice, there is some disagreement as to when it was first employed. This absence of a consensus is likely based upon the reprioritization of the objectives germane to the practice. There are several early examples of philanthropic initiatives that resulted in the attachment of the benefactors' names to the facilities. Health care and higher education facilities were at the forefront of this phenomenon. Many readers of this text likely attend a college or university that operates under the name of a major contributor. In that regard, maybe naming rights are not all that new. What is new, however, is the business orientation of those entities that view the resources devoted to venue naming rights as both an investment and a promotional tool. It is this evolution that has redirected the focus to sports venues.

It is widely believed that the first sports venue naming rights contract that involved a corporate entity was in Buffalo, New York, where Rich Products Corporation committed $1.5 million for the right to have the football stadium for the NFL's Buffalo Bills called Rich Stadium. This contract signed in 1973 was valid for 25 years.[1]

The recognition of the opportunities to use sports as a marketing tool for mainstream products, in combination with the growing global economy, has resulted in more such contracts. But these contracts have required a much larger commitment of resources on the part of the corporate sponsor. A quick look at the United States reveals that only about 30 percent of the professional teams played in a *sponsored venue* in 1997. That number had surged to some 70 percent by 2002.[2]

Early contracts involved high-profile venues in high-profile sports. Today, these relationships include minor league sports such as AutoZone Park, for the Memphis Redbirds of the International Baseball League, and Value City Arena, the home court of the Ohio State University basketball teams. The rapid escalation of prices for major sports venues has been one motivation for corporations to seek less expensive alternatives.

The concept of venue naming rights is no longer just an American phenomenon. But the deals outside of the United States have generally been less expensive. So while the history of venue naming rights is relatively short, its continued growth indicates that we can expect the strategy to persist far into the future.

Benefits

A properly executed naming rights contract should provide benefits to a number of key groups. It is reasonable to presume that benefits accrue to the fans, the community at large, the sponsor, and the resident organization. If the facility is a sports venue not owned by the team that plays there (the resident organization), it is still reasonable to assume that the team benefits from the relationship between the sponsor and the facility. Of course, in many cases the venue and team are owned by the same corporate entity.

> It is reasonable to presume that benefits accrue to the fans, the community at large, the sponsor, and the resident organization.

Benefits for the Fans

Revenues derived from naming rights deals are often used to renovate existing facilities or to help in the construction of a new state-of-the-art facility. This can provide better seating and better amenities for those in attendance, benefits that help make the fans' experience *more enjoyable*. Among the potential upgrades that benefit the fans are high-quality video equipment and improved restroom facilities.

One potential benefit is often viewed with considerable skepticism. The staging of an event or the fielding of a sports team can be an expensive proposition. If funds from the sponsorship are used to defray these costs, then it is conceivable that ticket prices will be more reasonable. Clearly, if the *fan pays less,* then she or he has derived a benefit.

The extra resources can be used to bring in premier performers. In sports, this may involve a star player. For a museum, it could allow an exhibition by a renowned artist. For a performing arts center, this individual could be a famous performer. In all of these examples, the fans benefit from an enhanced entertainment scenario. In essence, the venue is facilitating the *improvement of the product* that it provides for its target markets.

Another somewhat controversial issue is when sports teams seek to have a new stadium built while threatening to move away if their demand is not met. There are numerous examples of this strategy. The NFL's Baltimore Colts moved to Indianapolis when the team's request for a new stadium was rejected. Conversely, the threat of a move was one factor that contributed to the decision to build a new stadium for MLB's Seattle Mariners. If the revenues from naming rights allow a community to *retain its team,* the fans benefit.

Benefits for the Community at Large

The aforementioned retention of the local team not only benefits the fans, but it also contributes to the well-being of the community at large. The building of a new facility or the renovation of an existing one *provides jobs* for local tradespersons. This translates into increased purchasing power for the community and increased tax collections by a number of government entities.

Increased entertainment options translate into *higher levels of tourism*. Fans from out of town come in to be entertained. In addition to the money paid for tickets and parking, these fans rent cars, buy gasoline, eat at local restaurants, rent hotel rooms, and shop at local stores. Many local businesses, particularly those in the services industry, will benefit accordingly.

The typical sports stadium built today will cost between $300 million and $650 million to construct. A reality of sports economics is that the construction of virtually every one of these new stadia will involve some use of the taxpayers' money. If some of those construction costs can be defrayed by the sponsor's contribution, then *the burden on the taxpayers can be reduced*.

Benefits for the Resident Organization

In sports, we think of the resident organization as the team that plays its games at the sponsored venue. In some cases, the same entity owns both the team and the facility in which the team plays its home games. Alternatively, many stadia and arenas are owned by municipal authorities that lease the facilities to the teams. Beyond the world of sports, we see naming rights conveyed by museums, university structures, and performing arts centers.[3] Yet each of these facilities has one or more resident organizations that can benefit from the cash infusion emanating from a venue naming rights deal.

Each of these resident organizations will derive the same basic benefit that is associated with naming rights; that benefit is a *new revenue stream* that provides discretionary resources. It enables sports teams to recruit high-profile athletes who improve team performance and attract more fans. For nonsports organizations, the funds can be used to enhance the services that they provide to the public. This could be a high-profile art exhibit, new medical services, a renowned university scholar, or a popular musical performer. This can provide an *enhanced level of prestige for the resident organization*.

The revenue is often used to partially fund the construction of new facilities. New amenities and luxury suites make association with the venue more desirable; as a result, more *corporations are interested in becoming involved in a more traditional sponsorship capacity*. This generates additional revenue that allows the owners of the facility to build and maintain structures and better fulfill the mission of their organization.

Benefits for the Sponsor

As with any sponsorship, the company with the naming rights for any facility will seek tangible benefits in exchange for its investment. The implication of this goal is that companies should carefully evaluate the options available to them and enter into the agreements that best fit their needs. Many of the benefits sought by the sponsor are identical to those discussed in Chapter 4. Among them are increased awareness, an improved image, a sustainable competitive advantage, hospitality opportunities, and increased sales.

Increased awareness is a result of the ongoing publicity and the repeated mentions that are received in the media within the targeted geographic region. The *improved image* can be attributed to the perception that the firm is making a positive contribution to the community, the fans, and the venue's resident organization. The image is particularly enhanced when citizens believe that the facility adds prestige to the community or that the sponsor's resources are being used to *improve the team or other resident organization that uses the facility. A sustainable competitive advantage* may be gained because the sponsor's competitors cannot duplicate this strategy. The sponsor may capitalize on *hospitality opportunities* and entertain a variety of individuals who are important to the firm. Finally, *increased sales* should result from the combined effects of the aforementioned benefits. Increased awareness, an improved image, hospitality opportunities, and a sustainable competitive advantage should all contribute to increased levels of sales.

In order to attain these benefits, care must be taken in the negotiation process to ensure that the naming rights are supplemented with an array of components that will facilitate the achievement of the firm's goals. The marketer must evaluate the fit with its target markets as well as the fit within its existing sponsorship portfolio. Leveraging opportunities must be explored, and consideration must be given to the ways in which the naming rights sponsorship can be integrated with the other elements of the firm's integrated marketing communications plan.

> The marketer must evaluate the fit with its target markets as well as the fit within its existing sponsorship portfolio.

To reiterate an ongoing theme of the first half of this book, the decision to invest should be predicated upon a set of established objectives. Prospective sponsors must consider the array of components that will augment their naming rights and increase the likelihood that their business objectives will be achieved. These components are the subject of the next section of this chapter.

Plan Components

It was stated earlier that venue naming rights are a special case of sponsorship. It is not uncommon to see the term *stadium sponsor* or *building sponsor* used to describe the holder of these rights. And much the same way that sponsorship deals include an array of components or benefits for the sponsor, the holder of venue naming rights today expects to receive far more than simply the right to attach its name to a building. Because of the complexity of today's contracts, many of the negotiations are handled

COMPONENTS AVAILABLE TO HOLDERS OF VENUE NAMING RIGHTS

13.1

- Signage
- Logos—on uniforms and in concession areas
- Advertising—broadcast and printed programs
- Designation for leveraging purposes
- Category exclusivity
- Recognition on PA announcements and on scoreboard
- Hospitality
- Complimentary tickets
- Web presence on venue site
- Distribution rights
- Other marketing initiatives

by agencies that specialize in this service. Envision is one of these consulting organizations. The venue seeks to maximize its revenues, while the sponsor wants to maximize the potential impact of the association by securing the plan components that will facilitate the achievement of its objectives. The list of relevant components is outlined in Box 13.1; examples are given and each of the listed components is discussed on the following pages.

Signage

It is logical to assume that the marketer with venue naming rights would expect a significant amount of on-site signage to further reinforce the relationship. Conspicuous signage at the main entrance is likely insufficient in the sponsor's eyes. Depending upon the configuration of the facility and the events that take place there, additional signage is likely to be placed in areas that are easily seen by both the TV audience and those attending the event. For the TV audience, the solution might also include computer-generated *virtual* signage.

As an example of traditional signage, consider the home of Major League Baseball's Detroit Tigers, which is named Comerica Park after a regional bank. The bank's name is prominently displayed throughout the stadium: on signage located outside the main entrance, on each team's dugout, on the scoreboard, on rotating signage behind home plate, along the upper-deck railing, on the outfield walls, in the main concourse, and on trashcans.[4] Figure 13.1 illustrates signage of this type.

Logos

Additional signage may also be visible in the concession areas. This is often combined with the marketer's logos on cups and napkins. Worker uniforms often display the logo as well.

As rights holders have sought new and effective ways to reinforce their relationship with the venue and its resident organization, some have sought to have their logos appear on the participants' uniforms. While this may have little effect on the fans in attendance, it would most assuredly increase the sponsor's level of exposure during TV broadcasts and news reports. Comerica Bank's request for this benefit was rejected because MLB prohibits this type of commercial presence.

FIGURE 13.1 Venue Naming Rights Based Signage

Advertising—Broadcast and Printed Programs

An extremely important component of many recent contracts is the inclusion of a predetermined level of advertising. It is easy to understand that these sponsors often receive recognition and free advertising space in the event's printed program. However, many of the negotiations today seek a number of advertising spots to be included for the sponsor during the radio or television broadcast.

This concept is very similar to what we see with many traditional sponsorship contracts. An example discussed in an earlier chapter is the Nextel sponsorship of the NASCAR race series. Nextel's title sponsorship includes a substantial number of advertising spots during the live TV broadcasts. Similarly, the naming rights contract for Comerica Park includes approximately 12 advertising spots during the radio and TV broadcast of each Detroit Tigers baseball game. A similar contract was signed by Citizens Bank for the naming rights of the new (2004) baseball stadium in Philadelphia. The total contract is for $95 million over 25 years. However, the advertising time that is stipulated in the contract cannot be classified as complimentary. Of the $95 million committed by Citizens Bank, $57.5 million was designated for the naming rights and the remaining $37.5 million will be devoted to advertising on the baseball team's radio and TV broadcast over the life of the contract.[5] Table 13.1 summarizes the Citizens Bank contract.

The advertising should be incorporated as part of an integrated marketing communications plan. Companies with naming rights should use these opportunities to leverage their sponsorship of the facility. Likewise, the sponsorship should be consistent with the firm's marketing strategy and represent a synergistic component for its array of promotional activities.

Designation for Leveraging Purposes

Every sponsor should implement a leveraging plan that strengthens consumer awareness of its relationship with the property. Companies with venue naming rights often seek to be

> Venues that offer their naming rights sponsor a presence on their Web site are providing them with valuable access to a potentially important market segment.

Venues that are not noted for sports also maintain Web sites. Consumers visit these sites to check the schedule of events, to buy tickets, and to get directions. Venues that offer their naming rights sponsor a presence on their Web site are providing them with valuable access to a potentially important market segment.

Distribution Rights

Many companies try to extend their venue naming rights into an opportunity to sell their products to those in attendance. A key consideration for the Pepsi Center in Denver and Miller Park in Milwaukee is the pouring rights for their beverages at the respective stadia. Comerica Park in Detroit has three ATMs located within the stadium; to no one's surprise, these ATMs belong to Comerica Bank. In addition to distribution rights, the sponsor will likely seek to bundle it with category exclusivity, thereby locking its competition out of the facility.

> A key consideration for the Pepsi Center in Denver and Miller Park in Milwaukee is the pouring rights for their beverages at the respective stadia.

Not all companies that maintain the naming rights for a venue sell products that are readily sold at the event. Examples include the American Airlines Center in Miami, Allianz Arena in Germany, and Aussie Stadium in Sydney, Australia (named after Aussie Home Loans). However, they can still use their access to fans for other marketing initiatives.

Other Marketing Initiatives

This category includes the ability to take orders, accept applications, showcase products, and engage in giveaway promotions. When thinking about this category, it is important to remember that many of the recent naming rights contracts have not involved sports facilities.

Within the sports environment, consumers can order cellular phone service at U.S. Cellular Field in Chicago or apply for an Arizona Diamondbacks affinity Visa credit card at Chase Field in Phoenix. At the Toyota Center in Houston, the automaker has taken the opportunity to showcase some of its vehicles. In fact, one area in the Houston venue has been designated the Tundra Zone, in which Toyota customers are entertained and the Toyota Tundra vehicle is displayed. The final example of a marketing initiative concerns the decision to give items to those in attendance. The giveaway could be a sample of the sponsor's product, but it is more likely to be a promotional item that displays the sponsor's name and logo. These items could be posters, caps, bobblehead dolls, refrigerator magnets, or other small items that are likely to be taken home and kept by a meaningful portion of the fans. One component of Comerica Bank's contract provides it with four promotional giveaway opportunities over the course of each baseball season.

Key Success Drivers

Several studies have attempted to identify the key factors that are characteristic of a successful naming rights relationship with a venue of any type. The results indicated that the closeness of the fit between the venue's target markets and the sponsor's target markets is the most influential driver of the sponsorship's success. In the earlier chapters on sponsorship, this fit was referred to as a strategic linkage. Next is the opportunity to leverage. The third

KEY SUCCESS DRIVERS 13.2

- Target market fit (strategic linkage)
- Ability to leverage
- Integration within IMC plan
- Multipurpose facilities
  - Multiple sports
  - Various types of events

consideration is the ability to incorporate the relationship with the other promotional efforts that comprise the firm's integrated marketing communications plan. The fourth driver is the only real departure from the results that would have been expected for traditional sponsorships. Naming rights appear to be more effective when the venue can be used for a variety of purposes. Box 13.2 provides a brief overview of the key drivers for the success of a venue naming rights sponsorship.

Target Market Fit

It is difficult to envision that a facility has its own target market. What is easy to understand is that the primary resident organization of the facility will target the segments that best represent its perception of its customer base. Sports such as rugby, basketball, tennis, and cricket have target markets that differ significantly. Likewise, a concert venue that features a symphony orchestra has a far different target market than does a venue that features contemporary music acts.

Throughout the earlier chapters of this text, there was an emphasis on the fit or the strategic linkage between the sponsored property and the sponsor. Coors Field represents an excellent match as the target markets for baseball and beer are very similar in many respects. Conversely, it would be less effective for Coors to become involved with a venue that features opera and classical music.

> Coors Field represents an excellent match as the target markets for baseball and beer are very similar.

Ability to Leverage

Leveraging is an essential element of any successful naming rights plan. The naming of a "venue capitalizes on the media that surrounds sports" and the other events that take place in the venue.[7] Sponsors should exploit the resultant publicity by developing a corresponding leveraging program; otherwise there will be a diminished ability to capitalize on the relationship. One key issue that must be taken into account is the sponsor's ability to devote sufficient resources for the required leveraging plan.

Prior to investing in a naming rights deal, the potential sponsor must consider how it will implement a leveraging plan. What types of promotions can be used to reinforce the relationship in the target market's mind. It is important to remember that leveraging is undertaken in an effort to assure that consumers recognize the relationship. Done correctly, it allows the marketer to capitalize on the goodwill that is created and to impact the bottom line in a positive manner.

Integration within IMC Plan

This form of sponsorship can serve as a central point in the firm's marketing platform.[8] It is important to understand that the emphasis at this point is not on the development of the leveraging strategy; rather, the marketer's goal is to assess the extent to which the naming rights sponsorship and its attendant leveraging program are consistent with the existing elements of the firm's promotional strategy. The concept of integration should not be underestimated. Does the sponsorship represent a good fit with their target markets, and does it complement the current and planned components of their integrated marketing communications plan?

Multipurpose Facilities

Firms today typically direct their efforts toward a number of unique target markets. These efforts will occur over the course of the entire year. One concern about naming rights is that venues with a single resident organization as a tenant may have a comparatively narrow focus. Although it may be effective in reaching some of the sponsor's target markets, it may completely fail to reach others. Another criticism is that a single-purpose facility may be in use for only a few months each year. For example, if an NFL team is a stadium's only tenant, then the stadium will typically be used a total of 10 times over a period of five months. As a consequence, companies are often urged to seek out opportunities where the facilities will be used for a variety of events over the entire year.[9]

In some cases, this will involve two or more sports. Philips Arena in Atlanta is the home of both an NHL team and an NBA team. Qualcomm Stadium in San Diego played host to an NFL team and a MLB team until the San Diego Padres moved into the new Petco Park at the inception of the 2004 baseball season. The combination of football and baseball was generally viewed as a good opportunity for the sponsor because it means the stadium is in use for about nine months each year. Unfortunately, in the United States, these multipurpose stadia are giving way to ones dedicated to a particular sport. And this trend away from multisport stadia is evident across the globe. For instance, where rugby and cricket were often staged in the same stadium, many communities have begun to recognize the need for two separate facilities.

Another variation of the multipurpose facility is one that stages an eclectic array of events. This array of events may or may not include sports. Ford Field is the home of the NFL's Detroit Lions. The facility is also used to stage concerts for entertainers who can fill the 65,000 seats. A recent concert featured rap artist Eminem. This multiple use allowed Ford to reach two different groups of fans, and the Eminem concert also put the Ford name in the news during the summer when football is not on most fans' minds.

Value Determination

As the cost of naming rights continues to escalate, potential sponsors have begun to question the value received from having their brand name attached to a building. It is a very difficult question to answer. As a result, a number of consulting firms that seek to help answer this question have emerged throughout the world. In the absence of this expert advice, the prospective sponsor needs to gain an understanding of the criteria that provide value in this type of relationship. A number of these value-adding criteria are listed in Box 13.3 and discussed on the following pages. While the emphasis in this discussion is on sports facilities, many of the points are also relevant for facilities that do not feature a sports team as their primary resident.

VALUE-ADDING CRITERIA FOR VENUE NAMING RIGHTS

13.3

- Plan components
- Income demographics of the fans
- Size of the population
- Geographic location
- New opportunity (facility or team)
- Potential backlash
- Enduring (endeared) resident organization
- Attendance
- Sport popularity
- Team record (quality associated with tenant)

Source: E. Neils, "Brand Value Plays a Role in Stadium Naming Rights," 2002, www.absolutebrand.com/research/brandvalue.asp (accessed October 13, 2005).

Plan Components

Sponsors should anticipate paying for category exclusivity, signage, advertising, and distribution rights when they are included as part of the contract. Other components also add value. When considering the cost, the prospective sponsor needs to balance it against the benefits that should result from the bundle of components that the contract provides.

Income Demographics of the Fans

The events that are staged in any venue will appeal to identifiable socioeconomic groups. Consideration should not focus solely on those who attend the events, but those who watch on TV or listen on the radio must be also taken into account. The key point is to see if any generalizations can be drawn about the fans and verify that they represent a desirable target market for the prospective sponsor. This assessment should take us back to one of the drivers for success: *Is there a sound match between the target markets for the venue and those of the sponsor?*

Size of the Population

There is a positive correlation between the size of the population of the area served by the venues and the fees paid for the naming rights.[10] It is logical to assume that such a fee structure is justifiable because *greater reach translates into greater value*. Simply stated, the sponsor's name reaches more consumers. Traditional measures of promotion effectiveness lead us to acknowledge that larger populations will result in more gross impressions, and the number of impressions influences the value of any promotional effort. Given this, a naming rights strategy may actually be more cost effective than traditional advertising. This translates into additional value for the sponsor.

Geographic Location

Prices of many products vary across different geographic locations. This is especially true when international alternatives are being considered. Venue naming rights are no different in this regard. For example, it is generally acknowledged that the rights fees for comparable facilities will be higher in Germany than in the United Kingdom. Venue operators need to understand the impact that this disparity has on the value of their naming rights.

The media and consumers in some markets are more receptive to calling a structure by a corporate name. Others may be quicker to acknowledge the goodwill that the sponsor has sought to create. This openness and acknowledgment create value for the organization that holds the naming rights to facilities in these responsive geographic markets.

New Opportunity

This category includes the construction of a new facility or an expansion team moving into an existing venue that has no corporate sponsor. When considering the construction of a new facility, it might simply involve the move of an existing local team from an obsolete facility into a new state-of-the-art facility in the same market. Alternatively, such a move might involve a team relocating from one city to another. A great deal of consumer enthusiasm and higher levels of attendance inevitably accompany such endeavors. Both of these factors make stadium naming rights attractive, especially in the short run. This attractiveness provides value that is often translated in to higher rights fees being charged.

Potential Backlash

Rather than providing value, the potential consumer backlash that is associated with an unpopular decision to attach a corporate name to a facility will diminish the value associated with the rights. This is particularly true of sports arenas with a long history of tradition. These stadia hold a special place in the hearts and minds of many fans. Any effort to rename one of these stadia would be criticized by the fans and the media. Moreover, many members of the media are reluctant to recognize a facility by its corporate identification. When Candlestick Park was renamed 3Com Park, many fans and media representatives still referred to it as Candlestick Park or by its more acceptable nickname, the Stick. One can only imagine the consumer backlash if there was any attempt to rename Fenway Park, Wrigley Field, or Old Trafford.

> Many members of the media are reluctant to recognize a facility by its corporate identification.

Although the backlash is undoubtedly more severe when an existing facility is renamed, new stadia are not immune to this criticism. The New York Yankees have tentative plans for a new stadium that would open for the 2009 season. There will be some indignation if the new stadium is not called Yankee Stadium. Any potential corporate sponsor must recognize that there could be considerable consumer and media resentment to what they perceive to be a departure from the team's heritage.

Enduring Resident Organization

This category is a bit of a paradox. There are positive effects for the association with a long-standing resident such as a sports team or a symphony orchestra. Conversely, there are potential negative ramifications from the aforementioned consumer backlash and resistance to change. Still, some marketers emphasize the benefits that are attributed to the association with a popular team and hope that the resentment is a short-term phenomenon. The positives can easily outweigh the negatives, especially when the team is moving into a new facility. There is no doubt that there is more value when associating with teams that have a long history of success.

Attendance

Fans in the seats translate into *reach*. Higher levels of reach mean that the sponsor's name is exposed to more spectators. In addition, the fans in attendance are also exposed to any leveraging efforts that take place within the venue. Thus, there is an obvious correlation between the number drawn to a facility and the fees charged for the naming rights for that facility.[11]

Sport Popularity

While this is related to attendance, the popularity of a sport also translates into more TV viewers, more coverage in the local and national media, and more informal conversation among the fans. Venues that feature popular sports provide more value and can command higher rights fees from their sponsors. In the United States, the National Football League is at the pinnacle of popularity for professional sports. Major League Baseball seems to be recovering from the public's discontent over the players' strike in 1994. As a result of the increased popularity, a number of new naming rights contracts have been signed. The bottom line is that there is a strong belief that the popularity of the sport played by the primary resident will have a direct impact on the value of the sponsorship.

Team Record

In general, there is a correlation between the home team's record and game attendance. Championship-caliber teams fill their venues, while the teams at the bottom struggle to attract fans to the stadium. Good teams also appear on TV more often. The net result is that the quality of the resident team translates into value for the sponsor.

One major concern regarding this assertion is that high quality is virtually impossible to sustain over an extended period. In the 1995–96 NBA season, the Chicago Bulls won almost 88 percent of their games. The players' skills, primarily those of Michael Jordan, put the team on TV as often as the NBA contract would allow. This resulted in additional exposure for United Airlines because the team played its home games in the United Center. Few would deny that having a championship team as the arena's primary resident organization provides considerable value for the marketer. Conversely, in the 2000–01 season, the Bulls won only 18 percent of their games and rarely appeared on national TV. The reduced exposure meant that United Airlines did not receive as much value from its sponsorship during the season when the team played poorly.

Naming rights today often cover a period of 20 to 30 years. It would be unwise for a sponsor to assume that any team will be good throughout the entire term of these lengthy contracts. There may be more certainly when considering amateur sports such as college football and college basketball. There is also more consistency with a number of international teams. As a result, more marketers are looking to university sports and venues outside of the United States for naming rights opportunities. Another key point is that the sponsor must seek to capitalize on the opportunities when the team is playing well. The sponsor's leveraging program might be more intensive with more promotions designed to take advantage of the situation.

Overview of Value

There are many factors that influence the value of naming rights for a sponsor. It has been stated that the determination of the price to charge for these rights is still a combination of art and science. However, as new mathematical models are developed to generate estimates of value, the process is becoming more scientific.

> The determination of the price to charge for venue naming rights is still a combination of art and science.

It is becoming far more commonplace for consulting organizations to be involved in the valuation process. Companies like Envision, SFX Sports Group, and Sport+Markt are three examples. It has been reported that Sport+Markt was central to the determination of

TABLE 13.2
Naming Rights
Terms for Selected
Sports Venues

Venue	Location	Tenants	Total Fees (millions)	Years	$ per Year (millions)
Air Canada Centre	Toronto, Canada	NBA, NHL	$30	20	$1.5
Philips Arena	Atlanta, GA	NBA, NHL	180	20	9.0
Pepsi Center	Denver, CO	NBA, NHL	68	20	3.4
Comerica Park	Detroit, MI	MLB	66	30	2.2
FedEx Field	Washington, DC	NFL	205	27	7.6
Molson Centre	Montreal, Canada	NHL	21	20	1.05
Bank of America Stadium	Charlotte, NC	NFL	140	20	7.0
Safeco Field	Seattle, WA	MLB	80	20	4.0
General Motors Place	Vancouver, Canada	NHL	18.5	20	0.93
Staples Center	Los Angeles, CA	NBA, NHL	100	20	5.0
Allianz Arena	Munich, Germany	Bayern, TSV	110	15	7.3
Petco Park	San Diego, CA	MLB	60	22	2.7
Reliant Stadium	Houston, TX	NFL	300	30	10.0
ANZ Stadium	Brisbane, Australia	NRL	27	10	2.7
U.S. Cellular Park	Chicago, IL	MLB	68	23	2.96
Citizens Bank Park	Philadelphia, PA	MLB	57.5	25	2.3
Jaguar Arena	Coventry, England	Premier	13	12	1.1

the price to be charged to Allianz for the right to attach its name to the stadium outside of Munich, Germany. Sport+Markt states that its evaluation model "can provide site owners and sponsors with a reliable and objective measurement against which the real value of the naming rights can be established."[12] This trend toward quantification will continue to persist for the foreseeable future.

Sports Examples

Numerous examples of naming rights are worthy of mention. The list provided in Table 13.2 focuses on sports venues. Most are in the United States, but several others are cited to facilitate the comparison of recent contracts. Readers are encouraged to review the list and consider the large variation in the prices paid by the naming rights sponsors. Then consider the value-adding criteria that were delineated in the previous section; it can be seen that many of those factors are influencing the final price. For instance, a quick review of the list shows that new contracts involving NFL teams commanded higher prices than those where Major League Baseball is played. Arenas that feature both an NHL team and an NBA team generally have higher values than those that host only an NHL team. Though the disparity appears to be shrinking, arenas in the United States still tend to be priced higher than comparable facilities elsewhere. Finally, the more recent deals are characterized by higher values, which reflect the rising cost of all forms of sports sponsorship.

Beyond the World of Sports

As has been noted throughout this book, many sponsors have begun to explore options beyond the world of sports. The IEG has identified an array of such naming deals, showing that there are numerous opportunities in addition to professional sports venues that are appropriate for this special form of sponsorship. Table 13.3 provides an overview.

TABLE 13.3
**Naming Rights
Beyond Pro Sports**

Source: L. Ukman, "Naming
Rights: Not Just for Stadiums
Anymore," February 21, 2002,
www.sponsorship.com/learn/
namingrights.asp (accessed
October 13, 2005).

Venue	Location	Contract Specifics/Comments
Verizon Ampitheater	Irvine, CA	Selected over sports opportunity
Touchstone Energy Convention Center	St. Paul, MN	10-year title sponsorship
Mattel Children's Hospital	Los Angeles, CA	Goodwill; good fit with target market
Discover Mills (shopping mall)	Atlanta, GA	Target market consistency
General Motors Center for African Art	Detroit, MI	Hometown of General Motors
American Airlines Theatre	New York, NY	10 years; $8.5 million total
Comcast Arena (University of Maryland)	College Park, MD	10 years; $25 million total
Eastman Kodak Theater	Hollywood, CA	20 year deal; home of Academy Awards

Measuring the Results

Measurement of the impact of naming rights is a relatively new phenomenon. As a result, the measurement tools are still in the developmental stages. The techniques currently employed are similar to those used to assess the impact of advertising and traditional sponsorships. With this in mind, it is important to acknowledge that the ultimate objective of most promotional efforts is to increase sales, and many sponsorships are measured against this benchmark. In general, there are quantifiable measurements and qualitative assessments.

From one quantitative perspective, exposure from the mass media, to signage at the venue, and from promotional items that feature the sponsor's logo can easily be measured. Yet the *qualitative aspects* of a naming rights relationship can have as much value as exposure.[13] Of course, it is much more difficult to attach a monetary value to these qualitative assessments.

> The qualitative aspects of a naming rights relationship can have as much value as exposure.

When a sponsor has distribution rights at a venue, it can track the sales that are generated on-site. For instance, Pepsi-Cola can document its sales that take place at the Pepsi Center. This provides a partial measure of impact, but it fails to capture any sales that were influenced by the sponsorship that took place away from the venue.

Another common approach is to utilize a *consumer survey* to measure awareness. If we accept the premise that awareness of the sponsorship improves the image of the company and that this improved image has a positive impact on sales, then it is easy to rationalize using measures of awareness as a means of assessing the effectiveness of a naming rights deal. On the other hand, it can be argued that awareness does not always translate into sales. Knowing that Allianz is the sponsor of the new stadium in Germany may not motivate many soccer fans to buy new insurance policies from them.

A recent study in Germany found that only 26 percent of the consumers who expressed an interest in watching soccer on TV were aware of the Allianz association with the stadium. The study, the results of which are shown in Table 13.4, took a broad look at several marketers with venue naming rights in Germany. There is no doubt that some of the sponsors were disappointed with the results.

As the measurement process evolves, there will be more effort to assess the direct impact on sales. This is beginning to happen in the United States, but most European efforts are still confined to measures of awareness.[14] In the United States, a study assessing awareness was recently completed by Performance Research. The results were more compelling than those

TABLE 13.4
Unprompted Awareness of Naming Rights Sponsors in Germany

Source: M. Glendinning and J. Knapple, "The Name Game: Gunners for Hire," *Sport Business International,* May 2004, p. 46.

Sponsor	% Identifying Sponsor
AOL	56%
Allianz	26
Volkswagen	14
Bayer	11
Gottlieb Daimler	8
AWD	6
GEW RheinEnergie	4

in the German study. A telephone survey of sports fans in 14 major cities found that as many as 90 percent of the residents in cities with a stadium bearing a sponsor's name were able to correctly identify that sponsor.[15] More important, 35 percent of those interviewed indicated that this relationship had a "positive effect" on their opinion of the sponsor. An overview of the results of the Performance Research study is presented in Table 13.5.

The personal benefits cited in the Performance Research study were *lower taxes, more sports opportunities,* and *lower ticket prices.* The impact of attitudes such as these is difficult to place a value on. Consequently, there is still considerable emphasis placed on qualitative assessments.

Finally, measures of *media equivalencies* can be employed. Comerica Bank tracks its publicity and media coverage emanating from Comerica Park because it is relatively easy to attach a value to it.[16] Consultants for the Delta Center track the number and the quality of the *impressions* that are attained by virtue of the sponsorship. Joyce Julius & Associates has added the calculation of the exposure value gained by a naming rights sponsor to the assortment of services that it provides to its clients. This procedure is almost identical to the process that was discussed in regard to postevent evaluation for traditional sponsorships. The objective is to measure the sponsor's exposure during any TV broadcast originating from a sponsored venue and to attach a value to that exposure.

Box 13.4 shows a press release from Joyce Julius & Associates. It documents the value attained by the *St. Petersburg Times* (newspaper) in an arena bearing its name during the broadcast of a game during the 2004 NHL Stanley Cup finals. A look at the bottom line shows that the sponsor received some $817,200 in exposure value.

Problems, Concerns, and Criticisms

As with every element of marketing strategy, the concept of venue naming rights is not devoid of critics. There are a number of commonly articulated problems, concerns, and criticisms surrounding this strategic initiative. The most common are identified in Box 13.5 and discussed on the following pages.

TABLE 13.5
Attitudes Regarding Naming Rights in the United States

Source: E. Neils, "Brand Value Plays a Role in Stadium Naming Rights," 2002, www.absolutebrand.net/research/brandvalue.asp (accessed October 13, 2005).

Sample: Sports Fans in 14 Major U.S. Cities	
Correctly identifying naming rights sponsor	(almost) 90%
Report "positive effect" on sponsor's image	35
Report facility adds to community in a favorable way	61
Believe they personally benefit	20

JOYCE JULIUS & ASSOCIATES PRESS RELEASE 13.4

Ann Arbor, MI, May 26, 2004
Joyce Julius & Associates

Tampa Arena Sponsor Benefits from ESPN's Stanley Cup Telecast

Game one coverage of the **2004 Stanley Cup Finals** on **ESPN** Tuesday night saw the entitlement sponsor of the Tampa Arena, the **St. Petersburg Times**, garner more than $800,000 of in-broadcast exposure value.

According to research conducted by **Joyce Julius & Associates**—which has specialized in documentation and analysis received by corporate sponsors since 1985—the St. Petersburg Times' logos appeared clear and in-focus for **11 minutes, 17 seconds** (11:17), while the St. Petersburg Times Forum was **also mentioned once** by the ESPN crew.

To determine a value for the in-broadcast exposure, Joyce Julius & Associates applies its proprietary **Recognition Grade®** methodology to each instance of on-screen exposure—which takes into consideration such items as **logo size, brand clutter, and integration activation into the program**—and then compares the result with the estimated advertising rate for the telecast in question. Recognition Grades are not predetermined or dependent upon the type of source under consideration. This methodology insures an accurate measurement, taking each individual circumstance during the telecast into consideration (i.e., close-ups, unique handheld camera angles, wide-angle shots).

St. Petersburg Times Exposure

Source	On-Screen Time	RG Value
Center-ice logos	5:32	$399,200
End-board sign	5:18	343,200
Mention (1)	N/A	40,000
Graphics	0:22	26,400
Marquee sign	0:02	5,600
Side-board sign	0:01	2,000
Second-deck sign	0:02	800
Total: (1 mention)	11:17	$817,200

Source: Reprinted with permission of Joyce Julius & Associates, Inc.

Perhaps the most commonly mentioned concern is the *cost* associated with premium properties. In recent months, several contracts have exceeded the $7 million per year mark, with one reaching $10 million. Contracts signed in recent years reflect the steep upward trend in the fees paid for the right to associate a corporate name with a public facility. As with most sponsorships today, marketers view the financial commitment as an investment. With costs escalating so rapidly, questions are being raised as to whether or not an acceptable ROI can be achieved.

Fans have often been critical of these deals; they may label team or venue owners as greedy. As a result, there may be considerable *reluctance on the part of the public* to embrace the facility's corporate identity. It is especially problematic when an existing facility is renamed. This reluctance will likely prevent venerable old stadia such as Yankee Stadium or Old Trafford, the home of Manchester United, from ever selling their naming rights to a corporate sponsor.

In addition to public resistance, there is often *resistance on the part of the media*. The media's complaint is that the sponsor is getting the equivalent to advertising without paying for it. As a result, some facilities are identified by nicknames which allows the announcers to avoid using the corporate identity. Prior to the recent merger of Bank One and J. P. Morgan Chase Bank, the MLB stadium in Phoenix was known as Bank One Ballpark. It was

NEGATIVE ASPECTS OF VENUE NAMING RIGHTS

13.5

- Costs
- Public resistance
- Media resistance
- Difficult to measure impact
- Sponsor transition
- Arena obsolescence
- Lack of consistency in quality of product
- Limited number of sports opportunities
- Team mobility
- Sponsorship clutter

reported that Bank One Ballpark lost a lot of exposure value because many announcers opted to refer to it as "the BOB." In some international broadcasts, the announcers are directed to refrain from using the official name; as a result, they often refer to it by its geographic location. The result is that Toyota Stadium may alternatively be referred to as the rugby pitch in Sydney. These adaptations deprive the sponsors of some of the recognition for which they have paid.

> Bank One Ballpark lost a lot of exposure value because many announcers opted to refer to it as "the BOB."

It is *difficult to measure the impact* of this type of sponsorship. This makes it difficult to quantify the results, which in turn creates problems when attempting to justify the investment. While marketers are quick to acknowledge the potential benefits of naming rights, those benefits might not be so evident to others within the sponsoring organization.

The term *sponsor transition* refers to a situation in which changes occur in the sponsoring organization that render the existing venue name obsolete. Corporate mergers fall into this category. As a result of a corporate acquisition, the First Union Center in Philadelphia is now known as the Wachovia Center. As noted earlier, Bank One was recently acquired by J. P. Morgan Chase & Company, so the Bank One Ballpark has changed its name to Chase Field. This lack of continuity causes disruptions in the effectiveness of the sponsorship.

Even more disconcerting are the changes dictated by a sponsor's failure to honor the terms of its agreement. Bankruptcy has precipitated the need for the Savvis Center in St. Louis, Enron Field in Houston and Pro Players Park in Miami to explore new naming options. Enron Field became Minute Maid Park as a result of Enron's legal and financial problems. The ultimate irony regarding Enron is that the Houston team paid the company some $2 million to terminate the agreement.[17]

Many existing arenas throughout the world are old, and they do not offer the amenities and the luxury suites that are common in the newest facilities. This *arena obsolescence* means that the teams that reside there often seek new venues, even to the point of threatening to move to another city. When new facilities are built, existing venues are abandoned. This leaves marketers with naming rights to the old facility in an unenviable position. They may be given the option to transfer their rights to the new facility, undoubtedly at a higher cost. Or they may have no option as the rights may be sold to another marketer. This happened in Washington, DC, where the USAir Arena was abandoned in favor of the new MCI Center.

Whether the facility hosts sports, art exhibits, or the performing arts, one potential problem is the *lack of consistency in the quality of the product* from year to year. Sports teams that compete for a championship one year may suffer a significant decline in quality the next year. Museums that bring in high-profile exhibits one year may have trouble attracting comparable exhibits the next year; performing arts centers that feature popular plays one season may find it difficult to match that quality the next season. The result of this variability is unpredictable attendance that causes the value attained by the naming rights sponsor to fluctuate significantly from year to year.

Particularly in the American market, the *number of opportunities in professional sports is limited*. Most stadia have long-term contracts that have reduced the number of available venues to a small number. That set is reduced even more when those venues that are not amenable to signing a naming rights sponsor are excluded from the list.

Teams move for a variety of reasons, but most of these reasons are economic in nature. A team that sees itself mired in an unattractive stadium lacking modern amenities is likely to move. Cities recruit teams with attractive offers that include a new facility. When such moves take place, the existing naming rights contract for the abandoned facility becomes virtually worthless. This concern has led many sponsors to include an *escape clause* in their contracts. If the primary resident organization moves, the contract is voided.

In sports, teams typically have an array of sponsors. Many of these sponsors have signage throughout the venue, free advertising, recognition on the scoreboard, and acknowledgment via public address announcements. This exposure competes with the naming rights sponsor's exposure for the fans' attention. The *sponsorship clutter* can diminish the value of the naming rights.

Growth Opportunities

The major sports venue opportunities in the United States are almost exhausted. Some 70 percent of those facilities have existing naming rights contracts. Most of these contracts have at least 10 years remaining, with many extending much further into the future. For example, the Ford Field contract is not set to expire until 2042. Of the 30 percent of the venues without such contracts, some have not and will not actively pursue a primary sponsor. Naming rights for some venerable old facilities are simply not for sale. This limitation forces prospective sponsors to seek new and different opportunities.

> Naming rights for some venerable old facilities are simply not for sale.

There may still be some opportunities in *the professional sports environment in the United States*. It has been reported that the Palace of Auburn Hills, the home of the Detroit Pistons, has explored new naming rights opportunities. Some expiring contracts will not be renewed, thus opening opportunities for replacements. Other opportunities will arise when new facilities are constructed. As noted earlier, in many cases the existing sponsor does not have right of first refusal on the new facility. Still other opportunities surface when the naming rights sponsor defaults because of legal or financial constraints. Perhaps the most noteworthy example is Enron Field; the well-documented problems of the venue's original sponsor opened the door for a new sponsor. As noted earlier, the facility is now known as Minute Maid Park. MCI has also filed for bankruptcy protection, so it is conceivable that the operators of the MCI Center will be entertaining prospective sponsors to replace them.

A second growth area is in *the nonsports environment*. Table 13.3 listed recent naming rights contracts for museums, performing arts centers, shopping malls, convention centers, and health care facilities. More marketers will move toward grassroots sponsorships as they seek to enhance their image within their defined target markets.

Secondary sports facilities are also getting the attention of today's marketers as well. Minor league teams in various sports typically play in cities where there are no major league facilities, thus providing new opportunities for marketers. Examples include the Compuware Arena, where the Plymouth Whalers of the Ontario Hockey League play their home games, and AutoZone Park, the home the Memphis Redbirds, a minor league baseball team. Similarly, some marketers are exploring the prospect of entering into naming rights deals with universities. Perhaps the most noteworthy example involves Ohio State University; its basketball teams play their games in the Value City Arena.

Finally, there are tremendous opportunities *outside of the United States*. Telstra Stadium in Australia, Allianz Arena in Germany, Reebok Stadium in England, the Molson Centre in Canada, and Westpac Park in New Zealand are recent examples of this phenomenon. Look for emerging opportunities in the Premier League in Europe; Super 14 Rugby in Australia, New Zealand, and South Africa; and soccer stadia in South America. Sport+Markt has applied its valuation model and determined that the naming rights for the stadium that features the Premier League's Arsenal Soccer Team could approach the $10 million per year mark, thereby putting it in the same financial category as Allianz Arena.[18] Many of the existing facilities are old. As new ones are built to replace them, the resistance to naming rights will diminish and marketers will look to capitalize on these opportunities.

As companies become more convinced that venue naming rights are an effective form of sponsorship, marketers will seek new opportunities. The wide variety of options that exist covers a broad spectrum of facilities and a wide range of prices. This means that companies ranging from moderately sized local marketers to large multinational corporations are becoming involved. This breadth of opportunities combined with the multitude of prospective sponsors will continue to provide the impetus for growth.

Brokers and Consultants

The use of brokers to negotiate naming rights contracts has become more commonplace in recent years. Throughout this chapter, it has been emphasized that this type of sponsorship is comparatively new. As a result, neither the venue operators nor the prospective sponsors have much experience in determining the market value of the naming rights for a particular facility. The brokers have this experience. Some will work on the sponsor's behalf; others will work for the venue operators. The key is to reach an agreement whereby both parties believe that they will benefit from the relationship.

These brokers have gained their experience by working in a variety of sports marketing capacities over the years. Many have specialized in traditional sponsorship and have applied that knowledge to naming rights. As experience has been gained, some consultants have developed mathematical models to aid in the task of setting a price based upon the anticipated value for the sponsor. Perhaps the most noteworthy of these brokers and consultants are Envision, Octagon, Sportacus, Sport+Markt, and the SFX Sports Group. Each of these organizations has an international presence. To better understand the scope of these organizations' activities, you should check their Web sites. The URL for each is provided in Appendix A.

Closing Capsule

Venue naming rights represent a special form of sponsorship that involves the identification of a facility by its sponsor's name. The most noteworthy contracts have involved sports facilities in the United States; however, this is changing. Recent deals have been consummated for a number of nonsports venues; likewise, the practice is becoming far more common in markets outside of the United States. Marketers across the globe are beginning to recognize the potential of this form of sponsorship in their efforts to achieve their business objectives.

Properly executed, venue naming rights provide benefits to the fans, the community, the sponsor, and the resident organization. That resident might be a sports team, a performing arts group, a museum, or a health care facility (among others).

Like traditional sponsorship, naming rights contracts provide an array of components. No longer is it simply an opportunity to affix a corporation's name to a building. This set of components is extensive and includes elements such as signage, broadcast advertising, category exclusivity, and hospitality. With this sampling of components, the similarity to traditional sponsorship is easily recognized. Another similarity is that the relationship must be leveraged in order to fully reap the potential benefits available to the sponsor.

Research has identified four key drivers for success. Those are the congruence between the target markets of the facility and those of the sponsor, the ability to leverage, the extent to which the sponsorship can complement the sponsor's integrated marketing communications plan, and the ability to reach a variety of market segments with a venue that is used for a number of different types of events.

One of the common concerns about sponsorship in general is the difficulty in determining its value prior to the signing of a contract. There are a number of dimensions that directly impact the perceived value of any naming rights deal. Foremost is the array of components that are included, but value is influenced by factors such as the population base, the quality of the team or service that resides in the facility, the number of patrons who visit the facility, and the public's attitude about the facility's primary tenant. Some consulting firms have developed mathematical models in an effort to determine a fair market price, but there is still a qualitative assessment that most marketers will consider prior to signing a contract.

The typical contract for a sports venue in the United States is hovering around $3 million per year, but that number is escalating. Recent contracts have approached $10 million. Less expensive deals can still be found; many of these involve second-tier or amateur sports, nonsports venues, or facilities outside of the United States. Numerous opportunities now exist in European, Australian, and Asian markets as the practice is becoming more widely accepted in those areas of the world.

Measuring the results is a major problem. This concern is often articulated in regard to efforts to calculate the ROI of any investment in a venue naming rights contract. The most common approaches for measuring the results are consumer awareness surveys and a form of media equivalencies. Third-party consulting firms such as Joyce Julius & Associates, A. C. Nielsen, and Performance Research are actively involved in these types of evaluations. One concern in regard to measurement is the inability to accurately estimate the impact that the sponsorship has on sales and the bottom line.

Beyond the costs and the measurement problems, there are several other perceived negative aspects of venue naming rights. These include public resistance, media resistance, facility obsolescence, and clutter. Because of the uncertainties regarding the value and the effectiveness of this type of sponsorship, more organizations are employing consulting firms and brokers to assist in the negotiation process. Their role is to reduce the risk on the part of both participants, the venue operators and the naming rights sponsor. If done correctly, both parties will benefit as the marketer uses this special form of sponsorship as an integral part of its marketing strategy.

Review Questions

1. Why do you think that most venue naming rights deals have involved sports facilities?
2. What four groups should derive benefits from a properly executed naming rights deal?
3. What are the primary benefits for the naming rights sponsor?
4. Identify a sports venue in your area (one with a corporation owning the naming rights); evaluate the fit between the sponsor and the most common target market for the venue.
5. Identify a nonsports venue in your area (one with a corporation owning the naming rights); evaluate the fit between the sponsor and the most common target market for the venue.
6. What is meant by the statement that "venue naming rights are not simply an opportunity for a corporation to attach its name to a building"?
7. Why is it essential for a marketer to leverage its venue naming rights sponsorship?
8. What are the four key drivers for the success of venue naming rights? Which do you think is most important? Why?
9. There are several value-adding dimensions for naming rights contracts. Which do you think are most important for a sports venue? Which do you think are most important for a nonsports venue?
10. What are the most common methods used to assess the impact of a naming rights contract?
11. What are the major negative aspects of a venue naming rights relationship?

Endnotes

1. T. DeSchriver and P. Jenson, "What's in a Name? Price Variation in Facility Naming Rights," *Eastern Economic Journal* 29, no. 3 (Summer 2003), p. 359.
2. J. Karolefski, "The Sport of Naming," May 13, 2002, www.brandchanel.com/start1.asp (accessed October 13, 2005).
3. L. Ukman, "Naming Rights: Not Just for Stadiums Anymore," February 21, 2002, www.sponsorship.com/learn/namingrights.asp (accessed October 13, 2005).
4. B. Yerak, "Comerica V-P Keeps Bank's Image in Forefront at Park," *Detroit News*, April 30, 2000, p. B1, B3.
5. "Citizens Bank Pays Phillies $95 Million," June 17, 2003, www.espn.go.com/mlb/2003/0617/1569181.html (accessed October 13, 2005).
6. Yerak, "Comerica V-P Keeps Bank's Image in Forefront at Park."
7. J. Karolefski, 2002, "The Sport of Naming," May 13, 2002, www.brandchanel.com (accessed October 13, 2005).
8. D. Lippe, "Inside the Stadium Name-Rights Business," October 28, 2002, www.adage.com/news.cms?newsld=36406 (accessed October 13, 2005).
9. Ibid.
10. DeSchriver and Jenson, "What's in a Name?"
11. E. Neils, "Brand Value Plays a Role in Stadium Naming Rights," 2002, www.absolutebrand.com/research/brandvalue.asp (accessed October 13, 2005).
12. C. Britcher, "Europe Warms to Stadia Deals," April 27, 2004, www.sportbusiness.com/news/index?region=global&news_item_id=154365 (accessed October 13, 2005).
13. M. Glendinning and J. Knapple, "The Name Game: Gunners for Hire," *SportBusiness International,* May 2004, p. 46.
14. H. Zastrow, "Bundesliga Boom," *SportBusiness International,* May 2004, p. 47.
15. Neils, "Brand Value Plays a Role in Stadium Naming Rights."
16. B. Yerak, "Market Gurus Are Examining the Value of Naming Rights," *Detroit News,* April 30, 2000, p. B3.
17. D. Lippe, "Inside the Stadium Name-Rights Business," October 28, 2002, www.adage.com/news.cms?newsld=36406 (accessed October 13, 2005).
18. D. Smith, "Gunners' Naming Rights Could Be Europe's Biggest," August 9, 2004, www.sportbusiness.com/news/index?region=global&news_item_id=155368 (accessed October 13, 2005).

CHAPTER FOURTEEN

Licensing

Learning Objectives

- Learn the history of licensing.
- Delineate the array of licensable intellectual properties.
- Learn how to file for a trademark.
- See how compensation is determined.
- Learn the importance of compliance reviews.
- Identify the benefits for the licensor and the licensee.
- Learn about infringement and market surveillance.
- Be able to develop a licensing plan.
- Learn the three key growth strategies for licensing.

Licensing may be defined as the right to use proprietary and intellectual properties for designated marketing activities. But from a practical standpoint, *licensing* is best characterized as a *value-adding process* that provides revenue-generating opportunities via the conveyance of the right to use another organization's intellectual properties for commercial purposes. These properties include trademarks such as brand names, slogans, and logos that have been protected by the various governmental and regulatory entities that control this facet of business operations. Only when the intellectual properties have been duly registered can the organization claim sole ownership.

With a licensing agreement, the owner allows another organization to utilize contractually agreed upon intellectual properties in its marketing efforts. Such use may occur in advertising and other promotional efforts, but it generally involves the manufacture of products that bear the image of the intellectual properties. This was earlier referred to as a value-adding process; the logic of this characterization is very evident. Consider Fruit of the Loom, a large manufacturer of undergarments for men and women. A quick check at your local store will reveal that its standard T-shirt retails for approximately $4. But when a Detroit Red Wings team logo is affixed to that same shirt, the price climbs a healthy 300 percent to $16. Clearly, the logo added value to the shirt.

> A quick check at your local store will reveal that the standard T-shirt retails for approximately $4, but when a Detroit Red Wings team logo is affixed to that same shirt, the price climbs a healthy 300 percent to $16.

Historical Perspective

The earliest acknowledged licensing agreement is believed to have been undertaken in England in the 1770s. However, the relationship between Saintbury Chemical Fluid and a British countess would be best characterized as an endorsement by today's definitions.

TABLE 14.1
Chronology of
Licensing in Sports

Year	Sports Entity
1963	National Football League
1967	Major League Baseball
1973	UCLA
1976	NCAA
1979	National Hockey League
1981	National Basketball Association
1985	U.S. Olympic Committee

Modern licensing can trace its roots to the entertainment industry in the 1930s when Walt Disney conveyed the rights to use its array of intellectual properties to marketers of consumer products. The subsequent success tied to the sale of products featuring Mickey Mouse and Donald Duck led to other companies granting the rights to use their trademarked icons; that list included Bugs Bunny, Shirley Temple, and Little Orphan Annie.

Television is credited for the tremendous increase in licensing contracts in the 1950s. The new mass medium reached a growing market and made characters such as Superman, Howdy Doody, and Hopalong Cassidy household names. In this era of licensing, many children took their lunch to school in a lunchbox bearing the likeness of one of TV's popular characters. This widespread recognition is still an essential element of successful licensing programs today.

Sports became a key participant in the 1960s. With the NFL leading the way, professional sports were the key driver. A decade later, college sports began to take advantage of these emerging opportunities. UCLA, fresh on the heels of an unprecedented run of championship basketball seasons, initiated its licensing program in 1973. Today, top universities earn in the neighborhood of $4 million per year from the sale of officially licensed merchandise bearing their logos and other trademarks. They are even compensated when their university or its name appears in a motion picture. Table 14.1 provides a chronology of the entry of major sports entities in the United States into the licensing industry.

Key Concepts

To fully comprehend the licensing environment, it is important to understand the key concepts. These include the participants in the licensing agreement and the types of intellectual properties for which licensing rights are commonly granted.

The Participants

In this context, *participants* refers to the two parties for whom the licensing contract is legally binding: the licensor and the licensee. The *licensor* is the owner of the properties that are designated in the contract. It is the licensor that is granting the right to use its intellectual properties to a second party. The party to whom the rights are granted is the licensee. The *licensee* does not own the properties in question; rather, it is given permission to use them for specified marketing activities.

An example of the licensor–licensee relationship should help clarify the distinction between the two participants. The University of Michigan owns a number of registered trademarks. Among them are

- University of Michigan
- **M** (the Block M)
- Michigan Wolverines
- The Big House (Michigan Stadium)

These trademarks cannot be legally used without the express permission of the university. When permission is granted, the University of Michigan is the licensor.

The university has granted permission to use specific trademarks to Nike. As the licensee in this agreement, Nike is allowed to manufacture and market an array of sporting goods and apparel that incorporate one or more of the university's trademarks. Both Nike and the University of Michigan have garnered significant revenues as a result of this relationship.

The Intellectual Properties

From a broad perspective, *intellectual properties* are intangible assets for which an organization can claim ownership. The list below identifies a variety of properties that fall into this category. These intellectual properties include, but are not limited to, the following:

- Name
- Logo
- Slogan
- Symbol
- Likeness

The essential criterion for the right to claim ownership is that the organization has taken all of the appropriate steps to legally protect its properties, thereby allowing it to prevent others from using those properties without its permission. This process can lead to the designation of these properties as *registered trademarks*. These trademarks are generally identified with the ™ or ® symbols as a means of communicating their protected status. The process of protecting intellectual properties is discussed later in this chapter.

A *name* can refer to an individual or an organization. Neither "Tiger Woods" nor the "Hard Rock Café" can be used for any commercial effort without the permission of the namesake. A *logo* is a graphic representation that is associated with the property owner. While the word *Ohio* represents an American state and can't be protected in general, the distinctive way that it is written allows this image to be excluded from the public domain. The "script Ohio" at the Ohio State University is an example of how ownership of a commonly used term or expression can still be claimed when certain conditions are met. Another example that falls into this category is a letter of the alphabet; the University of Michigan has trademarked its widely recognized Block M.

> The "script Ohio" at the Ohio State University is an example of how ownership of a commonly used term or expression can still be claimed when certain conditions are met.

Many organizations have *slogans* associated with them. Nike's "just do it" is one of the most noteworthy slogans in sports. Another example is the trademark that was granted to coach Pat Riley when he had the (unfulfilled) expectation that his Los Angeles Lakers team was about to "threepeat" as the NBA champions. A *symbol* is similar to a logo; however, the logo may be words and graphics. Conversely, a symbol is generally deemed to consist solely of a graphic representation. The Nike "swoosh" and the University of North Carolina's depiction of a "tar heel" are two well-recognized examples. Others include the IOC's "Olympic Rings" and McDonald's "golden arches." Finally, a *likeness* may be a photograph or other representation of an individual. An example from an earlier chapter highlighted the unauthorized use of Yao Ming's photograph on packaging for Coca-Cola in China.

The Financial Perspective

Licensed merchandise sales in the United States in 2003 were estimated at some $110 billion. These sales produced a net payment of some $5.8 billion to the owners of the trademarks and the related intellectual properties. The industry exhibited incredible growth from 1970 through 2000, but that growth has stalled in recent years. Consider the fact that the sales of licensed merchandise in North America in 1982 accounted for only $13.6 billion. Given those results, it can be seen that sales grew by more than 800 percent over the period from 1982 to 2003.[1]

> Licensed merchandise sales in the United States in 2003 were estimated at some $110 billion.

The growth in sales has resulted in a financial windfall for many sports organizations and universities. As licensors, they receive a percentage of the revenue generated by the sale of licensed merchandise bearing their logos and other trademarks. This compensation is typically referred to as a *royalty*. While the prevailing royalty rate today hovers around the 8 percent mark, it will generally fall within the range of 6 to 10 percent. To better understand the financial impact this can have, consider the two top universities in terms of revenue in the 2005 fiscal year: the University of North Carolina and the University of Michigan. Each earned approximately $3.5 million in royalties from their licensees. Most of this revenue is directed toward the provision of benefits for the general student body. For example, at the University of North Carolina, 75 percent of the income is designated for scholarships and financial aid.[2]

While the application of sports-oriented trademarks is perhaps the most visible form of licensing as well as the fastest-growing category, its royalties comprise only 13.9 percent of the industry total. This figure makes it the fourth-largest category in the industry. The dominant category is represented by characters in entertainment, TV, and movies; this category commands a 43 percent share of the market. Table 14.2 provides an overview of the industry and the royalties paid to members in each of the nine categories in 2003.

TABLE 14.2   Estimated Licensing Revenue by Category (2003)

Source: "LIMA Sponsored Harvard/Yale Statistical Study Released: U.S. Royalty Revenues Reach $5.8 Billion," 2004, www.licensing.org (accessed June 8, 2004). From: Annual Licensing Industry Statistical Survey, International Licensing Industry Merchandisers' Association. Reprinted with permission.

Rank	Category	Example	Royalties ($ million)
1	Characters (entertainment/TV/movies)	James Bond	$2,502
2	Trademarks/Brands	Coca-Cola	1,060
3	Fashion	FUBU	848
4	Sports (leagues/teams/individuals)	NFL	807
5	Collegiate	Notre Dame	203
6	Art	*Stock Market* (Nieman)	167
7	Music	*Born in the USA* (Springsteen)	113
8	Publishing	*My Life* (Clinton)	43
9	Non-profits (museums/charities)	Smithsonian Institute	40
10	Others	Computer clipart	22
	Industry total		**$5,805**

Establishing and Maintaining Ownership

A marketer must take a series of steps to protect its intellectual properties from unauthorized use by outside organizations. The exact process differs from one country to another, so the marketer needs to identify the steps relevant to its situation and the level of protection provided. For the sake of illustration, the focus here will be on the process in the United States.

The initial step is not part of the official process; however, it is a critical action on the part of the firm seeking to protect its names, symbols, and logos. It involves the *identification of terms and images that merit ownership* and that are likely to gain protected status from the government. To *ensure that there are no conflicts,* the marketer can search the database of existing trademarks that have previously been registered by going to the Web site of the United States Patent and Trademark Office (USPTO), www.uspto.gov. Alternatively, an attorney who specializes in trademarks can be retained to perform the search.

The next step is to *file the application.* The application fee is $375, and it must be accompanied by sample items that reflect examples of how the trademark will be used by the organization. At this point, the USPTO will perform its own search to verify that there is no conflict. Then there will be a determination as to whether or not a word, phrase, or symbol qualifies for protection. If a term is too generic, the application will be denied. For example, in the aftermath of the events of September 11, an application for a trademark on the phrase "let's roll" was rejected.

> In the aftermath of the events of September 11, an application for a trademark on the phrase "let's roll" was rejected.

Once the government has deemed the application to be viable, the *proposed trademark is made available for scrutiny by lawyers, companies, and the public in its "notice of publication."* It remains accessible for 30 days during which objections can be raised. It is possible that the USPTO will request more information from the applicant. At this point, the *application will be approved or rejected.* If accepted, then the applicant can claim exclusive rights to the trademark for a period of 10 years.

Six years after ownership has been established, the trademark owner must *file an interim review.* The purpose of this review is to assure that the trademark is still actively used by the organization. This report must include samples of products, packaging, or promotional items that demonstrate its active status. The failure to file this report or the inability to sufficiently document the continued use of the trademark puts the organization in jeopardy of losing its exclusive rights. When this happens, the trademark is returned to the public domain, thereby allowing others to use it. If the organization can document continued use, the protection is continued through the end of the 10-year period.

At the end of the initial 10 years, the trademark owner must *refile* in order for protection to be extended for another period. If the application is not refiled, the trademark is deemed to be abandoned and it returns to the public domain.

These steps are outlined in Box 14.1. Readers are also encouraged to visit www.uspto.gov for more insight into this process.

While every country has its own rules and procedures, many are very similar to those of the United States. Additionally, marketers can seek international protection by filing an application with the World Intellectual Property Organization (WIPO). The latest guidelines are designated in the Madrid Protocol Guide. To learn more about WIPO, the Madrid Protocol, and the process of gaining international protection, visit www.wipo.int/madrid/en/general/index.htm.

ESTABLISHING AND MAINTAINING A TRADEMARK

14.1

- Identify words and images that merit protection
- Search existing trademarks for potential conflicts
- File the application with the appropriate government agency
- Proposed trademark is placed under scrutiny in "notice of publication"
- Application approved (or rejected)
- Interim review filed after six years
- Refile for protection after 10 years

Types of Agreements

When considering a licensing contract, both parties need to determine the scope of the agreement. In other words, how broad are the rights that will be granted to the licensee? This discussion concerns the specific products for which licensing rights will be granted, the issue of exclusivity, and the geographic scope.

Specific Products for Which Licensing Rights Will Be Granted

A common strategy is to grant the right to use the organization's trademarks on a single *product item*. When this situation occurs, the licensee's rights are limited to the one item that was originally submitted with the application. In many cases, this is all that the licensee seeks. For instance, if the only item a firm manufactures is a baseball hat or a teddy bear, then there is obviously only one product germane to its contract. Still, the agreement should specify this limitation to guard against the licensee's attempt to extend its rights to any new products that the licensee later introduces to the market. Even a firm that has a diverse array of products may seek to acquire rights to incorporate the licensor's logo on only one of its items.

A second strategy is to convey rights for a *product line*. Marketers will recognize a product line as an array of related product items. For example, instead of producing only baseball hats, the marketer might produce a deep line of headwear. This could include baseball hats, bucket hats, do-rags, and winter ski hats. Another product line could be an array of shirts; a third line could be footwear; and a fourth might include sports equipment such as golf balls, soccer balls, rugby balls, and basketballs. Large multinational corporations such as Nike and adidas are recognized as having the capability of producing a multitude of product lines. When the contract limits the rights to one or more specific product lines, the licensee is prohibited from using the licensor's trademarks on other lines that it produces. If adidas is granted permission to use an organization's logos solely on its headwear, then it is precluded from using those logos on its line of shirts. In fact, it is likely that the licensor has granted the rights to use its logos on a line of shirts to another manufacturer such as Antigua or Nike.

On rare occasion, a licensee might acquire the rights to use the licensor's trademarks on an entire *product assortment*. This type of agreement provides unrestricted rights to use the logos for any and all items that the licensee sells. When rights of this breadth are granted, the contract should address both the current product assortment and future additions to it. Care should be taken to assure that future additions do not infringe upon the rights of other licensees.

FIGURE 14.1
NHL's Red Wings
Trademark

Exclusivity

Contracts can be classified as either exclusive or nonexclusive. From a practical stand-point, it addresses the question of whether licensees will be in direct competition with each other. When an *exclusive contract* for a product item, line, or assortment is granted, those rights are granted to a single company. Nike has the exclusive rights to produce bas-ketballs for several colleges throughout the United States. For those universities, Nike has no direct competition in the basketball market. Conversely, the contract for Detroit Red Wings jerseys is *nonexclusive*. At one time, officially licensed jerseys bore the brands of Koho, Nike, Starter, and CCM and featured the Red Wings' famous trademark, the "winged wheel" (see Figure 14.1).

Geographic Scope

A license may be valid in a limited *regional* area. This stipulation is especially relevant in countries with large landmasses and populations. The licensor may deem it appropriate to issue multiple licenses but to limit the applicability of each to a confined geographic area. For example, a license may permit the sale of logo merchandise produced by a single licensee in the organization's local market. This allows local marketers to participate on a limited basis, especially when they do not have the manufacturing, distribution, or finan-cial capacity to compete with large national and international marketers.

A regional license is not necessarily limited to a portion of one country. Rather, it can reflect an opportunity to penetrate much larger regions. For example, one licensee could be granted rights for North America; another could be given a license for Europe; still an-other could be granted the rights to the South Pacific region.

Finally, the decision may be to grant a license that encompasses the *global market*. Contracts of this type will be granted to large multinational marketers that have brand equity and a distribution network that make it viable for a single company to reach consumers throughout the world. The adidas contracts with the New Zealand All Blacks and the 2004 U.S. Track and Field Olympic team are examples of this broadest type of rights. Once again, however, the issues of exclusivity and the products for which the rights are granted impact the nature of the opportunities presented to the licensee.

Compensation

For a licensing agreement to be mutually beneficial, the merchandise must generate adequate sales. The licensee benefits by virtue of its revenue exceeding the cost of goods sold (COGS). These costs include outlays for the manufacture of licensed products (or the cost of purchasing the products from an independent supplier). Also included are the marketing costs such as promotion and distribution that can be directly attributed to the products. And of course the compensation paid to the licensor must be taken into account.

The compensation to the licensor takes two basic forms: a fixed fee and a royalty. The *fixed fee* would be considered an initial rights fee. It represents an up-front payment made to the licensor. While this may cover the initial cost of evaluating and approving the application, it represents an amount that the licensor is guaranteed regardless of the level of sales or the future financial health of the licensee. Thus, it reduces the risk borne by the licensor. In most cases, this fixed fee can simply be considered a "signing bonus." But in others, deferral of the initial royalty payments is used to offset this initial payment. For example, if the initial payment is $10,000, the licensee's first $10,000 in royalty obligations is forgiven. After that point, all royalties are paid per the terms of the contract.

> In most cases, the fixed fee can simply be considered a "signing bonus."

The largest portion of the licensor's revenue is derived from *royalty payments*. This compensation is similar to a salesperson's commission in that the licensor receives a set percentage of the total revenue earned by the licensee in its marketing of the organization's "official" merchandise. It is important to note that this revenue figure does not necessarily represent the aggregate sum paid by consumers. When the licensee sells to an intermediary, royalties are based upon the amount paid directly to the licensee. For example, if Nike sells a shirt to a retailer such as Foot Locker for $15 and Foot Locker in turn sells it to a consumer for $25, the royalties due are based upon the $15 earned by Nike. If Nike sells that same shirt directly to a consumer through a company-owned store or its Web site for $25, the royalty is based upon the $25 figure. Note that in both cases the royalties are calculated on the basis of the amount of money paid directly to Nike.

While the royalty fees are subject to negotiation, the typical rate hovers around the 8 percent mark. The percentage will often depend on which brand has more equity and is the better driver of sales. If the licensor is extremely popular, thereby translating into high levels of demand for the licensee's products, the licensor might be able to negotiate a larger percentage of the revenue.

Another consideration is that royalties may not be based upon a fixed percentage; rather, they might be subject to a sliding scale. As sales increase, the royalty rate may change at designated levels. For instance, the rate might be 8 percent on the first $1,000,000 and 10 percent on sales exceeding that mark. What is constant in the relationship is that the licensor earns a portion of the revenue by simply granting another organization the right to use its trademarks.

The fixed fee and the royalties constitute the aggregate payment made to the licensor. Another component of many licensing contracts is a *guaranteed minimum payment*. If the compensation earned from the sales fails to reach the minimum level that is guaranteed, the licensee must make up the difference. The NBA imposes this guarantee on its licensees. This precautionary step will assure the licensor of attaining what it deems to be a satisfactory return from the relationship.

In summary, the licensor earns income based on the initial fee payment and the royalties derived from sales. In some cases, guaranteed minimum payments must be enforced. Regardless, the licensor needs to verify that it has been paid everything that it is owed. This takes us to the issue of compliance.

Compliance Reviews

It has been reported that the underpayment of royalties due to the licensor is a common occurrence. Whether resulting from intentional efforts to misrepresent the amount due or simply miscalculations by the licensee, these underpayments may represent as much as 50 percent of the amount due to the licensor. Given today's level of sales, a 50 percent shortage could easily translate into hundreds of thousands of dollars.[3] In light of this, more licensors have begun to demand compliance reviews. For this demand to be enforceable, this stipulation must be included in the original contract.

> Underpayments may represent as much as 50 percent of the amount due to the licensor.

Compliance reviews require the licensees to document the level of sales and the resultant royalties that are due. While the data may be self-reported, it is not unusual for the licensor to demand access to the licensee's accounting records.[4] These reviews should be initiated within the first year of the contract and repeated as often as deemed necessary. Without them, there is no way licensors can be certain that they are receiving all the payments they are due.

Benefits

If done correctly, the licensor and the licensee should find the relationship to be mutually beneficial. The parties provide each other with opportunities that could not be as easily exploited in the absence of the partnership.

Benefits for the Licensor

The most obvious benefit for the licensor is the *revenue stream*. The fees paid by the licensee can represent a substantial level of income that might not otherwise be available. Consider that the University of North Carolina recently earned some $3.5 million in licensing revenues during a single year. A second benefit is that the agreement provides the opportunity for the licensor to attain this revenue with *no significant investment*. The licensee bears the risk associated with the manufacture, distribution, and marketing of officially licensed products.

Inevitably, the array of products bearing the trademarks of the licensor will include many that are outside of its core business. Therefore, the licensor is able to ensure that products beyond its areas of expertise are available for consumers. This *broader product assortment* allows the licensor to reach market segments that might otherwise be ignored. A university's core activity is the education of students, not the manufacture and marketing of clothing. But many universities throughout the world have licensing agreements that allow manufacturers to produce a wide range of clothing that bears their trademarks and logos. From a nonsports perspective, even companies such as Coca-Cola, Budweiser, and Caterpillar have entered into such agreements with clothing manufacturers. It is important to note that there are a multitude of licensing agreements that do not involve clothing. As an example, consider a recent agreement whereby Ohio State University licensed the right to use its "buckeye" trademark to a restaurateur who opened the Buckeye Hall of Fame Café. Likewise, Harley-Davidson has an agreement that allows Ford Motor Company to use the motorcycle company's name on a model of its popular F150 pickup truck.

> A university's core activity is the education of students, not the manufacture and marketing of clothing.

Licensed products *create awareness and interest* by virtue of their presence in the marketplace. Greater distribution of a large variety of products means that the licensor's trademarks and logos are seen by many consumers throughout the world. The NBA has made officially licensed merchandise available through an authorized dealer network that spans the globe.

Firms that seek to enter into an agreement as a licensee will seek approval from the licensors that present them with the best marketing opportunities. The approval process will generally require the prospect to submit exact replicas of the products that they are seeking to manufacture and sell. This process allows the trademark owner to select only those that meet specific standards. Combined with continued scrutiny of those products, the licensor has the opportunity to *control the standards of quality* for the products bearing its "name."

The approval process also allows the licensor to *control the array of products* that feature its trademarks and logos. By selecting only products it deems appropriate, the organization can also *protect its image* in the marketplace. Eastern Michigan University has the Eagle as its mascot. An entrepreneur approached the university with an application to use the Eagle trademark on a product that the school's marketing staff deemed inappropriate and a likely detriment to its image. As a consequence of this assessment, the prospect's application to market an Eagle brand condom was rejected.

Benefits for the Licensee

There are four key benefits attained by the licensee. Foremost is the ability to *capitalize on the licensor's brand equity*. Generally, the trademarks of the licensor are better known and more valuable than are those of the licensee. A T-shirt manufacturer may be relatively unknown, but as soon as the Olympic Rings are printed on the shirt, awareness and demand are created. It may also provide access to channels of distribution that were not previously available to the licensee. Retailers that are not anxious to sell the licensee's traditional products and brand may become far more receptive to stocking those same products when they feature a popular logo.

Even when both the licensee and the licensor are well respected, the licensee will still benefit from its partner's brand equity. As an example, consider the relationship between Duke University and Nike. While Nike is well known, the ability to incorporate a Duke trademark or logo on its products can stimulate additional demand, especially within the geographic area in close proximity to the university.

A second key consideration is the ability to *capitalize on short-term phenomena*. In sports, the greatest opportunity involves the period immediately following a championship season. The market is flooded with licensed products in the aftermath of a college claiming a national crown. The University of Florida won the NCAA basketball title in 2006; the University of Texas claimed the football championship by winning the title game in the

BENEFITS OF LICENSING

Benefits for Licensor
- New revenue stream
- Distribution without significant investment
- Broader product mix
- Creation of customer awareness and interest
- Control standards of quality
- Control array of available products
- Protect image

Benefits for Licensee
- Capitalize on licensor's brand equity
- Capitalize on short-term phenomena
- Achieve economies of scale
- Reach new price points

2006 Rose Bowl Game presented by Citi. Both wins were punctuated by championship T-shirts and hats made available to consumers only minutes after the games were completed. This phenomenon is not limited to college sports; licensees also seek to capitalize on the accomplishments of professional teams.

The third noteworthy benefit involves the ability to *capitalize on economies of scale.* On an individual basis, many of the production runs would be quite small. But when the manufacturing process involves many licensors, the aggregate production becomes comparatively large. By purchasing in larger quantities, better utilizing its plant and equipment, and running an uninterrupted production line, the manufacturer will see the average cost of producing each item go down.

Finally, the licensee can benefit by attaining a higher level of profit because of the *new price point* that is reached by virtue of the addition of a popular logo. Earlier, it was noted that licensing is a value-adding process. One outcome from licensing is that the pricing flexibility results in higher profit margins. While there are some additional costs, namely added production costs and royalties paid, these are more than offset by the higher prices consumers are willing to pay.

Box 14.2 summarizes the key benefits that accrue to the licensor and the licensee in this type of mutually beneficial relationship.

Selection Criteria

Owners of desirable intellectual properties are likely to receive many applications from prospective licensees. Some will be accepted; many will be rejected. Each of these owners will establish its own selection criteria for the task of determining its future partners. One objective will be the selection of partners that will maximize the royalties paid to the licensor. There will also be a verification that the prospect's proposal, if accepted, will not be in conflict with other licensing contracts that are in effect for the trademark owner. Another aspect of the selection process is the assurance that the proposed products are consistent with the licensor's objectives and image in the market.

OHIO STATE LICENSEE SELECTION CRITERIA   14.3

- Quality
- Marketability
- Liability
- Appropriateness to university's goals and mission
- Method of distribution
- Availability of similar product
- Price point

Source: "Licensing Program Criteria," *Ohio State Trademark and Licensing Services,* 2004, www.buckeyeplates.osu.edu/criteria.html (accessed October 14, 2005). Reprinted with permission of The University of Ohio Trademark and Licensing Services.

As an example, consider the criteria used by Ohio State University. The Trademark and Licensing Service Office at the university states that each submission will be evaluated by the Ohio State Licensing Advisory Group. This entity is comprised of both on-campus and off-campus representatives. Furthermore, the policy stipulates that applications must be accompanied by a representative non–Ohio State sample of each product specified in the application. These samples provide information that addresses some of the key criteria in the selection process. The primary criteria used by Ohio State University are listed in Box 14.3.

Infringement

Earlier, there was a discussion on the prevalence of underpayments by legitimate licensees. While this is a major concern, more problematic is the *unauthorized use of an organization's trademarks and logos* by companies that illegally incorporate them on products that they sell. Obviously, there is no intention to provide compensation to the owners of those trademarks. Many of those guilty of infringement are small local entrepreneurs. While these individuals are nuisances, they are not the most significant concern.

> It is quite likely that the knockoffs do not reach the standards of quality demanded of legitimate licensees.

Of greater concern are the large-scale counterfeiters. Not only is the trademark owner deprived of revenue, but it is quite likely that the knockoffs do not reach the standards of quality demanded of legitimate licensees. Many of these large counterfeiters are located in Asia and Eastern Europe; however, their merchandise may be sold throughout the world.

Another potential concern is not really an infringement as it has been defined; rather, it is a conflict between similar trademarks. There is often a fine line that marks the difference between protected trademarks. These similarities are allowed when the granting agency believes that the organizations are substantially different and the consumer will not be confused. For instance, the USPTO has granted many trademarks bearing the letters "ABA." Does a shirt bearing an ABA logo represent the American Billiards Association, the American Bar Association, the American Basketball Association, or the Academy of Business Administration?

While there is little that can be done to prevent the type of conflict described in the preceding paragraph, efforts can be made to reduce the level of intentional infringement directed toward a trademark owner. Obviously, infringement is more common when the trademarks are well known, valuable, and difficult to attain the rights to. The implication is that there are more counterfeiters using the Olympic logos than there are illegally copying the trademarks owned by a minor league hockey team such as the Pensacola Ice Pilots. Still, every organization that owns valuable trademarks should actively engage in market surveillance.

Market Surveillance

Market surveillance involves the policing of the marketplace in an effort to locate counterfeit merchandise as well as other trademark infringements, to take appropriate measures to end the infringement, to remove any illegal products, and to discourage such efforts in the future. Surveillance should involve traditional retail outlets as well as vendors that set up in temporary facilities. In some cases, there are efforts to sell the illegal merchandise in public places such as bowling alleys and the workplace where market surveillance is impractical. When violations are discovered, employees of the affected organization should directly contact the manufacturers and the sellers of any illegal products. Legal cease-and-desist orders can be imposed in an effort to discourage future illegal efforts. Furthermore, laws in most countries allow the confiscation and disposal of the knockoffs. Since law enforcement for this type of crime is passive at best, much of the onus of tracking down offenders is placed on the trademark owners.

> Law enforcement for trademark infringement is passive at best.

Infringement, Surveillance, and Remedies

Numerous examples can be used to illustrate the occurrence of trademark infringement. The following situations are meant to demonstrate the magnitude of the problem, how market surveillance can reduce its detrimental impact, and the remedies that the trademark owners may have in their efforts to address the issue.

The Gay Olympics featured gay and lesbian athletes engaged in an array of sports competitions. However, the word *Olympics* is a registered trademark owned by the IOC. Although the organization has authorized the use of the word in conjunction with the staging of other events, such as the Special Olympics, it did not give its permission to the organizers of the Gay Olympics. To protect its intellectual property rights, the IOC insisted that the unauthorized use of its trademark be terminated. The organizers had no real option other than agree. As a result, the competition's name has been changed to the Gay Games.

Another example involving the IOC concerned the unauthorized reproduction of its Olympic Rings logo. Prior to the 2002 Winter Olympics in Salt Lake City, an ingenious farmer cut a replica of the rings into his cornfield and charged people $5 to walk through the maze. The Salt Lake Olympic Committee demanded that he either mow it down or pay a fee of $10,000 for the right to maintain it.[5]

Ohio State University engaged in market surveillance and identified a man whose company was producing and selling T-shirts with nonlicensed depictions of Ohio State trademarks. Adding to the university's disdain was the nature of some of these depictions. In one, the representation was of Brutus Buckeye, OSU's registered mascot, in a sexually explicit pose with a woman dressed as a University of Michigan cheerleader. Under the rules established by the State of Ohio's anticounterfeiting law, the man was arrested and the illegal merchandise and the equipment used to produce it were confiscated.[6]

> It appears that the search and seizure method is discouraging these illegal entrepreneurs.

During the day of the traditional Army–Navy football game in 2002, representatives of the Collegiate Licensing Company policed the stadium and the surrounding area in an effort to protect the property rights of the two military academies. The result was that some 500 items were seized from 10 vendors. The same action in the previous year had resulted in the seizure of approximately 4,500 items.[7] Given this information, it appears that the search and seizure method is discouraging these illegal entrepreneurs.

In recent years, the Detroit Red Wings have had an impressive record, including three Stanley Cup Championships in the NHL. The playoff environment raises the excitement level and leads to greater interest in the purchase of logo merchandise. Knowing this, many entrepreneurs produce their own merchandise bearing one of the many Red Wing logos. This illegal merchandise is sold from private cars and at small temporary facilities set up on many street corners. To protect itself and its authorized licensees, the team engages in a market surveillance program. College interns drive the streets in search of illegal products. Once the violators are identified, team officials contact them and take steps to discourage such unauthorized activities in the future.

Technology can be placed under scrutiny as well. Consider the Web site for the Universal Nude College Girls. Its URL attracted the attention of the Collegiate Licensing Company and one of its clients, the University of North Carolina. The contention was that the domain name UNCGirls.com infringed upon the university's "UNC" trademark. The court agreed, issued a cease-and-desist order, and awarded the university $325,521 for damages and legal fees. Furthermore, the potential sale of the domain name was blocked and ownership of UNCGirls.com was transferred to the university.[8]

The NCAA sued Coors Beer in regard to alleged infringements of trademarks used in conjunction with the NCAA's annual college basketball championship tournament. Even though the back of each ticket indicates that it cannot be used as a sweepstakes prize without the permission of the NCAA, Coors chose to offer them in its "Coors Light Tourney Time Sweepstakes." The NCAA advised Coors that it needed to eliminate the tickets from its promotion because it created the misconception that the brewer was officially associated with the NCAA. Furthermore, Coors was instructed to refrain from using phrases *similar* to other NCAA trademarks such as "March Madness" and "Final Four." The final remedy was the threat to deny admission to any fan holding a ticket won in any unauthorized promotion.[9]

Three other examples have global implications. FIFA informed Nike that it was to cease its use of "USA2003" in its promotions involving the U.S. women's national soccer team. Nike was accused of engaging in unfair competition by using advertising that might create the false impression that it was sponsoring FIFA-related events.[10] In what might otherwise be considered an ambush marketing effort, FIFA contends that the use of the confusing trademarks moves it into the piracy category.

The New Zealand All Blacks have initiated legal action aimed at ending the unauthorized use of the "All Blacks" trademark by a Welsh rugby team. Every rugby fan in the world recognizes the famous trademark. The New Zealand Rugby Football Union (NZRFU) wants to protect its brand equity and prohibit anyone from using the "All Blacks" trademark without its permission.[11]

The final example involves a proactive effort to discourage both ambush marketing efforts and trademark infringement surrounding the 2008 Summer Olympics in Beijing. One of the IOC's chief concerns about China as an Olympic venue was its history of the counterfeiting of intellectual properties. To allay these concerns, new laws designed to protect intellectual property rights were established in 2001. Threatened with severe penalties, including jail time, potential violators are likely to reconsider any effort that infringes upon the "trademarks, logos, patents, and other creative works related to the Games."[12]

Developing a Licensing Plan

On the preceding pages, the discussion offered insight into the process of developing a licensing plan. Box 14.4 pulls all of that information together and summarizes the process.

Box 14.4 introduces one new consideration, performance review. This step is necessary at the end of each contract; however, it would be prudent to subject each licensee to scrutiny during the course of the agreement. *Performance review* involves financial considerations as well as the key elements in the task of compliance review. Foremost in many licensors' minds is the question of financial performance. Did payments meet expectations? Are there growth opportunities that will facilitate improved financial performance in the future? Are there other prospective licensees that could provide better results over the next contract period?

The second aspect concerns the licensee's performance in the production and marketing of its products. Did the firm adhere to the restrictions regarding the products it was authorized to sell? Were the quality standards sufficient? Did the licensee have an acceptable presence in the retail market? Was the product readily available to the target market? Did the licensee sufficiently leverage the relationship?

DEVELOPING A LICENSING PLAN — 14.4

- Identify licensable property
  - Uniqueness
  - Value
- Establish fee structure
  - Initial fee
  - Royalty structure
  - Guaranteed minimums
- Establish the selection criteria
- Establish the type of agreement
  - Exclusivity
  - Geographic scope
  - Product range
- Engage in compliance review
  - Underpayment
  - Adherence to product guidelines
- Market surveillance
  - Find counterfeits
- Performance review
  - Renewal criteria
  - Financial performance
  - Production and marketing

THE UNIVERSITY OF MICHIGAN TRADEMARKS & LICENSING PROGRAM

14.5

Welcome to the University of Michigan Trademark Licensing!

The University of Michigan enjoys a rich heritage, national acclaim and a prestigious reputation as an outstanding public institution of higher education, research, public service and sports. The growth of the University, its alumni base, and the national attention received by its athletic programs have produced strong demand for products that display the trademarks, logos, and symbols associated with the University. The University's Licensing Program was developed in response to this demand for UM merchandise.

Who will need a license?

Any manufacturer of products bearing the marks of the university must be licensed before offering the product for sale. All retail outlets are responsible for insuring that the merchandise they sell is licensed.

What products may be licensed?

The University has the authority to approve or disapprove any product submitted. No product using the University's marks may be reproduced without approval of a representative of the University of Michigan Licensing Program.

Who is responsible for the University's Licensing Program?

On the University of Michigan campus, the person responsible for the licensing program is:

Manager of Trademark Licensing
University of Michigan
1000 S. State Street
Ann Arbor, MI 48109-2201

For information on how to become a licensee and produce University of Michigan merchandise, contact:
The Collegiate Licensing Company

What qualifies as a University of Michigan trademark?

A trademark is any name, word, symbol, or device used to identify the goodwill and/or services of the University of Michigan. They include, but are not limited to artwork and/or graphic representations.

The Athletic Department was one of the first to establish a comprehensive licensing program of University logotypes in 1980 when both state and federal registrations were obtained on all pertinent designs and marks. The original purpose was to protect and control the use of all marks and to insure the image of the University would not be damaged. To this end, the Collegiate Licensing Company was hired to assist us in enforcing all licensing agreements and policing the national marketplace.

All use of Michigan's marks must be submitted to our licensing director for review and to insure the standards of the University are met. **This approval includes all agencies of the University.** University departments, schools, and official student groups are exempt from licensing fees, but must (1) complete a licensing form, (2) obtain approval of the use of any registered mark, and (3) present a signed University licensing form to a screen printer or manufacturer before ordering.

Forms and approvals can be obtained from The Athletic Department.

Source: www.umich.edu. Reprinted with permission of the University of Michigan.

Answers to these questions are crucial in the task of determining whether or not the contract with a particular licensee should be renewed. Denial of an application for renewal will strain relationships with rejected partners, but the focus must be on the future. The New Zealand All Blacks' decision to move away from New Zealand–based Canterbury Clothing to adidas was not an indictment of Canterbury's past performance; rather, it was predicated upon the brand equity, the international presence, and the enhanced revenue stream that adidas was able to offer.

Boxes 14.5 and 14.6 detail some of the licensing stipulations at the University of Michigan and the University of North Carolina. In general, the information presented on the universities' Web sites identifies specific trademarks, application procedures, and payment schedules. A more comprehensive look at the University of North Carolina's policies

LICENSING BASICS, UNC–CH LICENSING OFFICE

14.6

What Are UNC–CH trademarks?

A UNC–CH trademark is any mark, logo, symbol, nickname, letter(s), word, or derivative that can be associated with UNC–Chapel Hill and can be distinguished from other institutions or entities. Some examples of UNC–CH trademarks are *UNC, Carolina, Tar Heels, The Old Well,* and *The Strutting Ram.*

Where Does the Licensing Revenue Go?

75% to scholarships and student aid; 25% to UNC–CH athletics.

Who Needs to Be Licensed?

Anyone that uses the name or marks of the University of North Carolina at Chapel Hill for a commercial purpose. Manufacturers of products with UNC–CH marks on them are required to pay an 8 percent royalty on the wholesale price of the item.

UNC–CH trademark use in advertisements, motion pictures, etc. also requires licensing approval and a payment of a licensing fee.

License applications are available from the Collegiate Licensing Company at (770)-956-0520. UNC–CH trademark use in the traditional news media are not subject to licensing fees.

Source: www.licensing.unc.edu/New/General/WelcomeGen.htm. Reprinted with permission of the University of North Carolina Trademarks & Licensing Committee.

is presented in Appendix B in this book. Also noteworthy, each of the universities' Web sites clearly indicates their involvement of the Collegiate Licensing Company (CLC). Most major universities are aligned with the CLC; for more information, go to the CLC's Web site (www.clc.com). It is also likely that your university has a trademark licensing office and that similar information is available on its Web site.

Examples of Licensing Contracts

Table 14.3 provides a brief list of a sample of recent licensing contracts. Some have expired; some are in their initial contract period; others have been extended one or more times. Several of the examples were discussed earlier in this chapter.

TABLE 14.3 **Examples of Recent Licensing Contracts**

Licensee	Licensee	Products
National Hockey League	The Hockey Company	Sticks, helmets, jerseys
European Rugby Cup, Ltd.	Re:Activ	Branded merchandise, staff uniforms
Major League Baseball	Majestic	Uniforms and replicas
National Hockey League	Callaway	Golf balls, bags, putters
CART	Mattel	Toy cars
Ohio State University	Buckeye Hall of Fame Café	Restaurant
University of Michigan	Nike	Shoes, apparel, sports equipment

Growth Strategies

Given the financial implications surrounding the sale of licensed merchandise, there is little wonder as to why both the licensee and the licensor seek strategies that will result in increased sales. Three of the more common growth strategies are described in this section. They are new target markets, new up-market products, and more traditional advertising.

New Target Markets

In the sports category, there has been an increased emphasis on a number of demographic segments. Perhaps the most lucrative has been the *female consumers*. Attend a sports event today and you are almost as likely to see a female fan wearing logo merchandise as you are to see a male fan wearing a team jersey or a hat. A recent study reported that 43 percent of the NFL's fan base is female, but it wasn't until 1997 that a line of NFL-licensed apparel was created for the female segment. Now the NBA, MLB, and the WNBA also have product lines designed specifically for women.[13]

> A recent study reported that 43 percent of the NFL's fan base is female.

A second segment is that of *children*. Kids today are among the most ardent sports fans, and they idolize the star players. That admiration translates into a demand for licensed merchandise. The NBA and MLB also see the emphasis on kids as a way to reach new fans. The NBA sees the game of basketball as the number one participation sport among 8- to 14-year-old girls in the United States. This has led the league to enter into an agreement with Mattel for NBA-themed Barbie dolls. This example also demonstrates that sports-oriented licensing deals do not always involve clothing.[14]

Hispanics have become more interested in sports in general, but in baseball and soccer in particular. Again, many sports marketers have developed products and directed promotions for this increasingly important target market.

Finally, the industry has witnessed increased opportunities in *international* markets. As sports like basketball have been exported to countries such as France and Australia, new markets have emerged. Similarly, MLB has initiated its own marketing efforts in Mexico.[15] International sports are also making headway in North America. Rugby already has a foothold, and the International Cricket Council is exploring opportunities to penetrate the American market. As these sports gain in popularity, the sale of licensed merchandise associated with them will grow.

New Up-Market Products

Historically, trademark licensing rights have been conveyed to marketers of relatively inexpensive consumer products. Today, we are witnessing a dramatic increase in the marketing of more expensive, upscale products that feature a licensor's trademarks. Recent product introductions of this type include contact lenses, coffins, and sport utility vehicles. These more expensive products result in high levels of revenue for the licensee. As a result, the licensor's royalty collections increase in relation to the revenues realized by the licensee.

> Today, we are witnessing a dramatic increase in the marketing of more expensive, upscale products that feature a licensor's trademarks.

More Traditional Advertising

This strategy can be equated to the task of leveraging. In general, the responsibility for most of the promotional efforts lies with the licensee. Done correctly, advertising will reinforce the relationship between the two parties. It is also essential to increase the advertising budget when new market segments are being targeted. Advertising will not sell products that consumers do not want, but it can be used to inform them about the array of products available and where they can be purchased. This increased awareness will help the firm grow sales—as long as the licensee is marketing products that are relevant to the target markets being reached.

Advertising is also important in the effort to achieve greater penetration within the currently acknowledged important target markets. The objective is to have current customers purchase even more. Although white males have long represented the most lucrative market, other groups have been recognized for their receptivity to licensed products and the market potential that this produces. In particular, the strategy of increased levels of advertising has been effective in both the African American and Hispanic segments.[16]

Closing Capsule

Licensing is best characterized as a value-adding process that provides revenue-generating opportunities via the conveyance of the right to use another organization's intellectual property for commercial purposes. These properties include a variety of trademarks, brand names, and logos. The licensor is the owner of the intellectual properties and provides limited rights for licensees to use these properties in their commercial endeavors. When properly conceived, the relationship is mutually beneficial with both the licensor and the licensee deriving substantial benefits.

> Licensing is best characterized as a value-adding process that provides revenue-generating opportunities.

There are a variety of intellectual properties, but to be eligible for licensing, a property must be registered with appropriate agencies. It is this registration process that provides ownership for the organization. The financial consequences of trademark licensing are enormous. Professional sports organizations earn millions of dollars in compensation from licensees. The top American universities are approaching the $4 million per year mark. Box 14.7 lists the top 10 American universities in terms of licensing revenue for fiscal year 2005. A list of the top 50 can be found on the Collegiate Licensing Company's Web site (www.clc.com).

TOP 10 AMERICAN UNIVERSITIES—LICENSING REVENUE FOR 2004–2005 FISCAL YEAR — 14.7

1. The University of North Carolina
2. The University of Michigan
3. The University of Texas at Austin
4. University of Georgia
5. The University of Oklahoma
6. University of Notre Dame
7. University of Tennesee Knoxville
8. University of Florida
9. Louisiana State University
10. The University of Alabama

Source: "The Collegiate Licensing Company," *News Releases,* 2005, www.clc.com/clcweb/publishing.nsf/Content/Rankings+Archive%3A+ 2000–2005 (accessed April 12, 2006). Reprinted with permission of the Collegiate Licensing Company.

Each country has its own requirements for applying for and receiving sole rights to a registered trademark. International protection can be sought through the World Intellectual Property Organization.

When considering the initiation of a licensing program, the organization must first determine the viability and the earning capability of its trademarks. Prospective licensees often approach the owner with unsolicited offers. When the decision to grant a license is made, the parties will negotiate many factors. Important decisions involve the type of agreement; these decisions include the products that the licensee is allowed to use for its own marketing efforts, the geographic scope of the agreement, and the issue of exclusivity.

There are many documented cases of licensors being significantly underpaid. To ensure that they are not being shortchanged in the royalties due, most licensors have begun to demand compliance reports.

In addition to the new revenue stream, the licensor benefits from the ability to put products in the retail market without making any significant investment, particularly when the manufacture and marketing of such products fall outside of the licensor's core competencies. The licensee derives significant benefits from the relationship as well. It can capitalize on the licensor's brand equity and on short-term phenomena that cause spikes in the demand for certain products. Also, by combining production for similar products for several licensors, the licensees can attain economies of scale that drive the average cost per item down. These lower costs, when combined with higher prices that consumers are willing to pay, can add significantly to the licensee's bottom line.

One of the major concerns is trademark infringement. Most owners of valuable intellectual properties regularly engage in market surveillance in an effort to ensure that the market is free of counterfeit products that feature their trademarks without the authorization to do so. When unauthorized use is detected, the trademark owner or its representatives will generally confront the offenders. Cease-and-desist orders will be issued. Counterfeit items can be confiscated and destroyed with no compensation provided to the offender.

> Counterfeit items can be confiscated and destroyed with no compensation provided to the offender.

Licensing activities grew rapidly in the latter part of the twentieth century, but this growth has slowed dramatically in recent years. Still, it is imperative that licensors and licensees pursue strategies aimed at growth. Among the most common growth strategies are the designation of new target markets, the introduction of new up-market products, and the use of more traditional advertising aimed at leveraging the relationship.

Many organizations have significantly benefited from licensing. In fact, many trademark owners are simultaneously involved with hundreds of licensees. But it is still important for each licensing contract to be consistent with each organization's mission and marketing capabilities. Figure 14.2 illustrates a page from the game-day program for an East Coast Hockey League game. It features players and emphasizes that fans should recognize officially licensed merchandise. Furthermore, it reaches out to potential manufacturers and retailers that might like to become involved in this business sector. Clearly, the emphases are on preventing counterfeiting and the growth of the industry. It is imperative that licensors and licensees seek new opportunities in the future if the industry is to reestablish its momentum in the twenty-first century.

FIGURE 14.2
ECHL Program Page
Featuring Licensing

Review Questions

1. Why is licensing considered to be a value-adding process?
2. What does the term *intellectual property right* mean?
3. Think of a name or slogan you would consider using for a new sports team. Go to the USPTO Web site and see if there are any conflicts that might preclude the use of your idea.
4. What are the trade-offs for the licensor and the licensee when the contract has an exclusivity provision?

5. What decisions does the licensor have to make when establishing the type of agreement to be signed?

6. What types of compensation decisions have to be made when a licensing contract is being written?

7. What is a compliance review? Why are they so common today?

8. What are the key benefits for the licensor?

9. What are the key benefits for the licensee?

10. How can a licensee benefit from economies of scale?

11. What is the concept of trademark infringement?

12. What is market surveillance? What is the purpose of this activity?

13. Go to the CLC Web site (www.clc.com); see if your university is affiliated with them.

14. Go to your university's Web site; see if you can find guidelines for the licensing of intellectual properties that they own.

15. Describe the key growth strategies in the licensed merchandise industry.

Endnotes

1. "LIMA Sponsored Harvard/Yale Statistical Study Released: U.S. Royalty Revenues Reach $5.8 Billion," 2004, www.licensing.org (accessed June 8, 2004).

2. "Trademark Licensing Revenue Sets New UNC Record," *News*, September 25, 2002, www.unc.edu/news/archives/sep02/license092502.htm (accessed October 14, 2005).

3. T. Harrison, "Solutions to Recurring Errors in Reporting Royalty Payments," *The Licensing Book*, no. 7, (1985), pp. 10–12.

4. D. Irwin, "Financial Benefits of Trademark Licensing," *Sport Business: Operational and Theoretical Aspects,* ed. Peter J. Graham (Dubuque, IA: William C. Brown Communications Co., 1984), pp. 115–20.

5. "Farmer Contends He Was Given OK," September 6, 2002, www.espn.go.com (accessed October 14, 2005).

6. "Counterfeit T-Shirts Seized, Seller Arrested," *Ohio State News,* November 3, 1998, www.osu.edu/osu/newsrel/archive/98-11-03_arrest_made_in_counterfeiting_case.html (accessed October 14, 2005).

7. "Counterfeit Army–Navy Merchandise Confiscated," *News Releases,* December 10, 2002, www.clc.com/Pages/home2.html (accessed October 14, 2005).

8. "UNC Wins Federal Case against Pornographic Web Site," *News*, September 16, 2002, www.unc.edu/news/newsrel/archives/sep02/uncgirls091602.htm (accessed October 14, 2005).

9. "NCAA Accuses Coors of Trademark Infringement," November 28, 2001, www.espn.go.com (accessed September 25, 2002).

10. D. Barrand, "Nike and FIFA Head for Court," September 25, 2003, www.sportbusiness.com/news/?news_item_id=152582 (accessed October 13, 2005).

11. C. Britcher, "All Blacks Trade Mark Row," May 1, 2003, www.sportbusiness.com/news/index?region&page5fno=3&news_item_id=151074 (accessed October 13, 2005).

12. J. Swanwick, "Beijing Bans Commercial Use of Olympic Symbols," November 2, 2001, www.sportbusiness.com/news/?news_item_id=116062 (accessed October 13, 2005).

13. C. Levitt and D. Stankevich, "Making the Market," *Discount Merchandiser* 38, no. 6 (June 1998), pp. 77–80.

14. Ibid.

15. Ibid.

16. D. Hirshberg, "Reaching Out," *Sporting Goods Business* 27, no. 8 (August 1994), pp. 86–87.

The Marketing of Sports

Part Three provides a comprehensive perspective of the application of specific strategies and tactics within the domains that are characterized by the marketing of sports products. As such, our focus now shifts to the marketing strategies used within the product-focused and the sports-dominant domains of the sports marketing environment. Marketing strategy has historically been viewed as the combination of a target market and a corresponding marketing mix. Chapter 15 will examine the target marketing issues by delineating the market segmentation process. Chapters 16 through 19 each cover one of the variables within the marketing mix. These are product, distribution (place), price, and promotion.

CHAPTER FIFTEEN

Segmentation of the Sports Market

Learning Objectives

- Revisit the concept of market segmentation.
- Examine a model used to segment the sports fan market.
- Learn how to segment the general participation market.
- Apply segmentation principles to a single sport.

Our emphasis to this point has been on the practice of marketing through sports. This discussion encompassed both the mainstream strategies and the domain-focused strategies that are used to market nonsports products. Now the emphasis will shift to the strategies that are used in the marketing of a variety of sports products. As such, we will now scrutinize the two categories of strategies that were earlier designated as product-focused or sports-dominant. It marks a good time to reconsider the basic philosophy that underscores the majority of today's marketing efforts. In this regard, the marketing of sports products has much in common with the strategic initiatives that are utilized in the marketing of clothing, cars, and fast food. One basic premise is that markets must be segmented on some relevant basis and that organizations must then designate the most viable segments as target markets. The mass market is simply too large and too diverse for any single marketing strategy to be effective.

> The marketing of sports has much in common with the strategic initiatives that are utilized in the marketing of clothing, cars, and fast food.

In July 2004, an article in *Growth Strategies,* a popular business publication, declared that "the mass market is dead."[1] At the same time, a *BusinessWeek* cover story lamented "the vanishing mass market."[2] The implication is that marketing efforts designed to appeal to everyone tend to be ineffective. An analogy would be one-size-fits-all clothing, where no single piece of attire actually fits everyone well. As a result, mass marketing has given way to the use of *differentiated strategies* specifically tailored to the characteristics of the selected target markets. An understanding of this philosophy by sports marketers will lead to the implementation of differentiated strategies that are superior to mass marketing efforts.

The rationale and procedures for market segmentation were introduced in Chapter 2. Implementation of a number of segmentation strategies was also discussed within the context of marketing nonsports products using a sports platform. Whether this type of marketing strategy emphasizes traditional strategic initiatives or a partnership that integrates traditional sponsorship, venue naming rights, endorsements, or licensing, it should now be evident that effective marketing is the result of developing strategies and tactics that are consistent with the firm's target markets.

Just as market segmentation is a key strategic element in the marketing of nonsports products, it is equally important in the task of marketing sports products. Whether the objective is to sell tickets to events, to increase participation, or to increase the level of sales for a variety of sporting goods and apparel, marketing efforts are enhanced when effective segmentation strategies are implemented. Thus, the focus will now shift to the marketing of sports products. In essence, we are now focusing on *sports consumption*.

In the same manner that automotive marketers develop different models of cars and tailor their strategies to be consistent with each of their target markets, those involved in the sports industry must adopt differentiated strategies. At the same time, marketers must understand that this does not always mean that the product is altered. Differentiated strategies may also rely on modifications to the firm's distribution, pricing, or promotional strategies in ways that are relevant and meaningful to each target market.

Before proceeding to the discussion of specific strategies, it is imperative that we fully understand the principles of market segmentation. So we will begin with a quick review and a reminder that market segmentation and target market selection were covered in detail in Chapter 2.

Segmentation Review—The Consumer Market

Market segmentation was earlier defined as the process whereby the mass market is subdivided into a number of smaller, more homogeneous groups of consumers. The designation of these groups must be based upon one or more relevant characteristics that are common among the consumers within each individual segment. The most common bases for these characteristics are demographics, geographics, psychographics, and product-related variables.

Marketers select target markets from the array of segments that are identified. Implicit within this procedure is that marketers may decide to ignore some segments. This decision may be based upon many factors. A segment may simply not be deemed viable as a target. It may be too small; it may be difficult to reach with promotional efforts; or it may be loyal to a competitor. Of course, it may simply represent a group that is not likely to purchase the marketer's product. For example, when did you last see a marketing effort for an expensive sports car directed toward the low-income segment? Needless to say, the low-income segment is not one of Ferrari's target markets.

Once the target markets have been selected, the task then becomes one of developing strategic initiatives that capitalize upon the opportunities presented by each target market. Each may require a different product configuration; they may be more likely to be exposed to certain media; they may have different ideas as to what represents an appropriate price; and they may patronize different types of retailers. In other words, the product, promotion, price, and distribution (place) strategies must be tailored to each target market. This set of four strategic variables was earlier referred to as the *marketing mix*.

> The product, promotion, price, and distribution (place) strategies must be tailored to each target market.

This chapter is designed to explain how market segmentation is applied in a sports setting. First, it will identify a number of examples within the spectator sports market; then the focus will shift to the participation market.

TABLE 15.1
Examples of
Demographic
Segmentation

Demographic	Entity	Market Segment (target)
Gender	Major League Baseball	Ladies (Day)
Age	X Games	18–24-year-olds
Income	National Basketball Development League	Less affluent
Ethnicity	Major League Baseball	Latino

Segmentation of the Spectator Sports Market

The four broad bases that were earlier identified as potentially relevant segmentation criteria are each appropriate when seeking to develop an effective strategy for the segmentation of the spectator sports market. The following discussion illustrates how sports marketers have effectively used demographics, geographics, psychographics, and product-related variables to segment their respective markets.

Demographic Segmentation

As is the case with nonsports products, perhaps the easiest basis to apply is that of demographic variables. Table 15.1 identifies a few such examples.

There are numerous examples of gender-based segmentation. An early strategy used by Major League Baseball was *Ladies Day*. Admitting women at a reduced rate was viewed as a way of increasing both attendance and interest on the part of female fans of all ages. More recently, the NFL created a new strategy designed to teach women the fundamentals of football. Sounding like a college course, Football 101 invites women to the stadium to learn the basics of the game. The belief is that a better understanding of the game will lead to a new group of enthusiastic fans. The Indianapolis Colts offered a follow-up session, Colts 201. It can be noted that the advertisement specifically targets women, and each of the participants shown in the ad is female. This promotion is illustrated in Figure 15.1. In recognizing the increased size and significance of the female segment, the NFL and the NHL were both quick to add products designed for women to their lines of licensed merchandise. These include new products, new colors, new designs, and new sizes.[3]

The organizers of the X Games initiated their marketing efforts by targeting the male segment, but recent efforts have been made to increase the appeal of the X Games among female consumers. New events and more female competitors are viewed as initiatives that will be favorably received by the female segment.

Regardless of gender, the X Games continue to focus on a younger segment. It has been reported that extreme sports' "hardcore audience lies in the 18- to 24-year-old age bracket."[4] Age has long been considered a relevant variable for segmenting the spectator market for golf. Historically, the prime target market was comprised of older consumers. However, new young stars such as Tiger Woods and Michelle Wie have provided opportunities for those who market golf tournaments to reach out to a younger segment. This younger segment also tends to be less affluent than the traditional golf fan.

Income is often used as a means of defining segments in the professional sports market. Many minor leagues and their teams develop promotional appeals that feature lower ticket prices in an effort to attract fans who might not be able to afford tickets for the top-level sports teams. The Toledo Mud Hens of baseball's International League ran an advertising campaign that emphasized the affordability of their tickets. More recently, the National Basketball Development League (NBDL) was founded. While tickets for an NBA

FIGURE 15.1
Colts 201 Program
for Female Fans

game can easily reach the $70 to $100 level, the NBDL has tickets for as little as $5 and a top price of $35.[5]

> **Because of its size and growth, sports marketers tend to view the Hispanic segment in a very favorable way.**

Ethnicity is also a key consideration. The NBA has attempted to reach Chinese consumers with a Chinese language Web site. Not only does this have international implications, but the initiative has also been instrumental in the league's efforts to appeal to those with a Chinese heritage living in the United States. The Hispanic segment has also been intensely pursued in recent years. Because of its size and growth, sports marketers tend to view the Hispanic segment in a very favorable way.[6] Among the efforts to reach this group is the San Diego Padres' decision to simultaneously broadcast their games in English and Spanish. Major League Baseball's official Web site (MLB.com) has a Spanish version available. Several teams have sought to capitalize on the large number of Latino players on professional teams. For example, the Toronto Blue Jays' schedule features a Latin theme night with promotional prices and ethnic-based entertainment. Exhibition games have been played in Latin American countries such as Mexico, Venezuela, and the Dominican Republic.[7] Major League Baseball even went so far as to schedule some of the Expos' "home games" in Puerto Rico during the team's last two seasons in Montreal. Looking at future opportunities for other sports, it has been stated that Major League Soccer (MLS) teams could greatly benefit by featuring strategies that are designed to appeal to the sport's avid fans in the Hispanic segment.[8]

Geographic Segmentation

The second broad basis for market segmentation is geographics. The aforementioned efforts to play games in foreign countries represent geographic-based segmentation. The NBA has sought to increase its acceptance in Europe by participating in events such as the recent McDonald's Cup exhibition played in France. Major League Baseball has played regular season games in Japan. The National Football League has created a European League in an effort to extend the reach of gridiron football into areas that have a strong affinity for a different type of football, namely soccer. An aggressive strategy by the National Hockey League involved the location of teams in warm-weather locations in an effort to broaden the game's appeal. It started with the trade of hockey icon Wayne Gretzky to the Los Angeles Kings. Soon, new or relocated franchises appeared in warm-weather locations such as California, Texas, Arizona, Florida, Georgia, Tennessee, and North Carolina.

> The National Football League has created a European League in an effort to extend the reach of gridiron football.

Psychographics (Lifestyle)

Many consumer products have provided evidence that psychographics can be used effectively in the segmentation process. Because of the relationship between lifestyle and consumer behavior, knowledge of a segment's dominant lifestyle leads to a better understanding of consumers' preferences and purchase decisions. While demographic and geographic segmentation strategies have been effectively implemented in the sports industry, new initiatives based upon lifestyles have come to the forefront. Teams, leagues, and specific sports have used a variety of lifestyle characteristics to define market segments and target markets. In addition to these efforts, lifestyle has emerged as an important criterion in the efforts to segment the market of sports fans in general. Table 15.2 provides a set of examples that illustrate how lifestyle has been used at each level.

At the team level, the WNBA's Los Angeles Sparks have recognized the market power and the interest in basketball among consumers within the gay and lesbian community. In acknowledging this group, the team has aggressively marketed themselves, particularly to the lesbian segment. The team's initial effort involved a pep rally at a gay bar in West Hollywood.[9] Even though the strategy was considered risky by many people, the effort was deemed "classic target marketing" by WNBA president Val Ackerman. It should also be noted that many marketers tend to view sexual orientation as a demographic variable rather than a lifestyle, but regardless of the designation, this segment is very important to today's marketers.

Major League Baseball has developed products and promotions aimed at reaching consumers who are active on the Internet.[10] This includes Web sites designed to provide information, sell tickets, and facilitate direct interaction through chat rooms. The league and its teams have also developed a network by which both audio and video can be streamed to fans worldwide, so long as they are wired to the Web.

The sport of rugby acknowledges many different segments, including some that are defined primarily on the basis of fan lifestyles. Like many sports, one key segment for rugby is the *sociables*. The sociables may watch the game, but their primary objective is to have a few

TABLE 15.2
Examples of Psychographic Segmentation

Level	Specific Entity	Market Segment (Target)
Team	Los Angeles Sparks (WNBA)	Gay and lesbian
League	Major League Baseball	Internet users (Generation X)
Sport	Rugby	Sociables
Sports fans	Spectator sports	Players (of the sport)

beers and spend time with their friends.[11] Many readers will recall friends or acquaintances who started the day at a tailgate party and never made it to the game itself. The game provided a forum that satisfied the fans' need for a social experience. In America, we can see this phenomenon on any given Saturday when the local college football team is playing a home game. These sociable fans eat, drink, and have fun. Undoubtedly, this segment is an important part of the American college football market as well as a variety of other popular sports worldwide.

Finally, there have been a limited number of efforts to categorize sports fans in general. At this level, the focal point is not a specific team, league, or sport; rather, it is an effort to categorize fans irrespective of their preference for a particular sport. In other words, there is a common lifestyle that contributes to an individual's decision to watch a golf tournament, a basketball game, the Olympics, a yacht race, or any other sports event. One example delineated in Table 15.2 involves spectator sports and the *player* segment. The underlying assumption for this segment is that individuals who play a sport are more likely to be fans when others play the sport. Golfers are more likely to attend or watch a golf tournament on TV. People who either play or once played soccer are more inclined to be soccer fans. Understanding this phenomenon, many marketers have intensified their efforts to increase the number of players with a long-term objective of increasing the number of fans for their particular sport.

Product-Related Variables

The final category for segmentation of the consumer market is that of product-related variables. In Chapter 2, the three criteria that were identified for this basis were the level of use, the degree of brand loyalty, and the benefits sought by the consumer.

Virtually every sport will segment on the basis of *level of use*. The most important segment may be the season ticket holder. These fans often receive perks that the more casual fans do not receive. The Detroit Lions distributed a Christmas ornament to season ticket holders. The Detroit Red Wings invited their season ticket holders to a gala celebration after the team won the Stanley Cup championship. The Detroit Tigers included the opportunity for their season ticket holders to purchase tickets for the 2005 All-Star baseball game played in Detroit.

Regarding brand *loyalty,* the best example relates to the consumer's decision to continue to purchase tickets over time. Even when the team struggles to win, these fans maintain their relationship with the team. Such loyalty gives fans in this segment the first opportunity to select new (better) seats prior to the start of each new season.

Spectators attend a sports event for many different reasons, so marketers stress a broad array of *benefits*. Earlier, there was a discussion of the sociable segment. The primary benefit sought by this group is the opportunity to socialize with their friends. Benefits sought by other segments include being entertained by talented athletes whom the fans admire. Businesspeople may attend primarily for the benefit of entertaining customers in an effort to increase future sales.

Regardless of the basis used to segment the market, the objective is the same. Segmentation allows the marketer to tailor a strategy specifically for each target market. This customization should lead to enhanced customer satisfaction. And as with all marketing efforts, satisfied customers are more likely to remain loyal to the marketer.

Segmenting the Fan Market—A Broad Perspective

In recent years, a limited number of studies have focused on the delineation of segments of sports fans in general. Early segmentation studies emphasized demographics and geographics, but more recently the studies have begun to stress psychographics and product-related variables. One study identified six attributes as keys in the designation of six segments of sports fans: involvement, participation, social needs, identification, appreciation of sport, and sex appeal.[12] The following list delineates the six segments of sports fans that were identified in this study; each segment is discussed on the following pages.

- Players
- Patriots
- Appreciators
- Socialites
- Friends
- Voyeurs

Players

The underlying assumption with this segment is that individuals who play a sport are more likely to enjoy watching others play. These fans' own participation may be quite competitive. Players understand the skills required of the athletes that they watch, and they are highly involved with the sport. Their passionate intensity leads them to seek information about their chosen sport. Members of this segment often invest considerable time and money in sports in general and their favorite sports in particular. Golf, soccer, rugby, tennis, and bowling are sports where the fan base is comprised largely of players.

Patriots

Individuals in this segment view sports as a means of establishing community and national pride. They follow "their" team and cherish each win, especially one over a hated rival. Involvement may be high. Patriots follow their team on TV, on the Internet, and in the print media. This segment also views sports as one way in which social needs can be fulfilled.

National Olympic teams evoke a strong sense of patriotism worldwide. Olympic medal counts serve as a measure that patriots view as a source of pride. In addition to the Olympics, there are many sports that are primarily played at national levels. For example, the most noteworthy cricket matches generally pit the national team of one country versus the national team of another country. A test match between India and England promotes a sense of euphoria among fans of the winning team. These same emotions are expressed when the New Zealand and Australian rugby teams compete. The Ryder Cup and the various World Cup events featuring soccer, rugby, and cricket also evoke an intense sense of patriotism.

While the emphasis is often on national pride, patriotism can exist at lower levels. Residents of one city may view a win over a team from another city as a source of civic pride. Boston versus New York City; Sydney versus Melbourne; Madrid versus Barcelona; and Beijing versus Hong Kong are examples of *municipal rivalries* that result in strong patriotic emotions.

Appreciators

Those in the appreciator segment admire the skills of the participants. They are drawn by the talent and by the aesthetic qualities exhibited in the sport and by those who play it. Appreciators also admire hard work, teamwork, and achievement. These fans may be drawn to individual sports such as golf as well as team sports such as basketball. The focus is not necessarily on winning or losing; rather, it is the opportunity to witness excellence that draws the appreciator to the TV or event venue.

Socialites

For socialites, sports provide one way in which fans can interact with their friends. Decisions as to which events to attend are significantly influenced by the individual's reference groups. Members of this segment are not necessarily knowledgeable of the rules or the competitors for the sport that they are "watching." In many cases, it is the alternative entertainment or activities at the venue rather than the sport itself that attracts these fans. Essentially, the sport satisfies a social need. At the end of the game, the socialites may not even know the final score. Furthermore, they may not care what the score was or which team won.

Any event or sport is likely to have a segment of socialite fans. The Super Bowl and the finals of the World Cup of Soccer are prestigious events and places for socialites to be seen. Lower-level sports such as minor league baseball are also good candidates for this segment, especially for younger fans seeking a comfortable place to get together. Tickets are inexpensive and readily available. This segment represents an important source of revenue for the sports marketer; therefore, its impact cannot be ignored.

Friends

The primary motivation for a friend's attendance is to provide support for friends and family members who are participants in the event. The key consideration for this segment is the relationship with the participants. These fans may have a basic understanding of the sport, but there is little or no involvement beyond the effort to follow the exploits of those who are close to them.

The typical high school sport draws primarily from two groups. Relatives of the participants are often vocal supporters of the team. The other primary group of attendees is comprised of classmates of the team members. Both of these groups fall into the "friends" segment. This segment is also important for amateur recreational sports such as softball, soccer, and basketball. In cases like these, the sport itself may be irrelevant to the fans. The objective of attending is to support people that the fans know and care about.

Voyeurs

For this segment, the most important aspect is sex appeal. It is not the sport per se that the voyeur finds exciting; rather, it is the physical attractiveness of the participants. In many cases, voyeurs are not fans of the sport as much as they are fans of an attractive participant.

A specific athlete may exude sex appeal. Many people watch a women's tennis tournament to see attractive players such as Anna Kournikova play. Beach volleyball features athletes in skimpy attire. Male athletes may perform their sport while wearing revealing uniforms. An athlete may simply be attractive. Some will argue that voyeurs are fans for the wrong reasons. Still, they watch sports, especially on TV, and their motivations often form the basis for efforts to market sports events that possess an element of sexuality.

An Overview

The six segments discussed above represent an effort to isolate homogeneous groups within the heterogeneous sports fan market. Table 15.3 summarizes each segment's tendencies

TABLE 15.3 **Segmentation of the Sports Fan Market**

Source: J. Watson and A. Rich, "From Players to Voyeurs: A Six-Category Typology of Sports Fans," unpublished manuscript, December 30, 2000.

	SEGMENT					
Criterion	**Player**	**Patriot**	**Appreciator**	**Socialite**	**Friend**	**Voyeur**
Level of involvement	High	Medium/high	Medium	Medium	Various	Low
Level of participation	Competitive	Various	None or social	None or social	Various	Various
Social needs	Low	Medium	Low	High	High	Low
Level of identification	Medium	High	Low	Low	Various	Low
Appreciation of talent	High	Medium	High	Low	Various	Low
Sex appeal	N/A	N/A	N/A	N/A	N/A	High

relative to the six criteria that were used in the segmentation process. By reviewing the table, the most important criteria for each group can be identified. For instance, sociability is the most important consideration for the friends segment, whereas sex appeal is the only criterion of note for the voyeur group.

While the six-segment model represents one effort to place fans into homogeneous groups, it is not the only tool available to sports marketers. One recent concept that has surged to the forefront is the *old school–new school dichotomy*.[13] *Old school fans* place a high priority on work ethic, player integrity, and fundamental skills. These fans favor sports that feature players who acknowledge their positions as role models. Conversely, *new school fans* favor "*street cred.*" To gain this credibility with fans on the street, the sport, team, or player needs to project a more rebellious demeanor. There is a flamboyant, anti-establishment mentality among new school fans. Leagues and teams often develop separate promotional campaigns in an effort to appeal to both the old school and new school segments.

Sports marketers need to assess their own environments and implement the segmentation strategies that they deem most appropriate. There is not one model for segmentation that should be used by all sports organizations. In fact, it is not uncommon for an organization to simultaneously utilize two or more approaches to segment its market. For example, a team may use demographic segmentation and develop a strategy for the female segment. Concurrent with this strategy, the team might also tailor an effort to reach old school fans while also targeting the socialite segment.

> The marketing of a spectator sports has much in common with the marketing of cars, fast food, and clothes; it is governed by one simple rule: one size does not fit everyone.

The preceding discussion highlighted the need for sports marketers to effectively segment their markets in order to better understand the fans' motivations for attending an event or watching it on TV. It is also essential to understand that market segmentation is seldom based upon a single dimension. Several criteria may be used to define the segments within any mass market. Regardless of the methods or variables used, segmentation is critical to the process of selecting target markets. And selection of target markets is required prior to the development and implementation of the organization's marketing strategy. In this regard, the marketing of a spectator sports has much in common with the marketing of cars, fast food, and clothes; it is governed by one simple rule: one size does not fit everyone.

The Participation Market

Rather that watch, participants play. The participation market represents an enormous level of consumer spending, and as with every other large market, it is quite diverse. Participants engage in a variety of activities. The popularity of a broad array of such activities was earlier illustrated in Chapter 1. In addition to the breadth of these activities, the motivations for participating can vary significantly. There are three broad reasons individuals choose to participate: personal improvement, appreciation of the sport, and the facilitation of social interaction.[14] It is this heterogeneity that again provides the rationale for segmenting the market into smaller, more homogeneous groups.

The same bases that were used for segmenting the spectator market—namely, demographics, geographics, psychographics, and product-related variables—can be used to segment the participation market. In this market, there are two levels for which segmentation can be implemented. The broader level of aggregation involves the general participation market. Such efforts generally address two questions regarding participation: who and why? At this broader level, there is no effort to analyze the markets for individual sports.

FIVE PARTICIPATION SEGMENTS   15.1

- Excitement-seeking competitors
- Getaway actives
- Fitness-driven
- Health-conscious sociables
- Unstressed and unmotivated

Source: B. Bryant, "Built for Excitement," *American Demographics* 9, no. 3 (1987), pp. 38–42.

The second level reflects greater specificity in that the effort involves the desire to identify the various segments for a particular sport. For example, one recent study identified five segments of golfers. The following overview of the two types of segmentation levels may provide a better understanding of how such efforts have been implemented and how segmentation can lead to more effective strategies for those involved in the marketing of participation sports.

Segmentation of the Aggregate Participation Market

Remember that segmentation of the participation market generally addresses the questions of who is playing and why they choose to do so. In an effort to answer these questions, five categories of participants have been designated. These five segments are listed in Box 15.1.

Excitement-seeking competitors are prone to engage in risky activities. The majority are male; they are relatively young; and they are usually single. Extreme sports, snowboarding, and activities such as bungy jumping appeal to members of this group. The *getaway actives* are vacation prone. For this segment that is evenly divided between men and women, a primary motivation is based upon social objectives. They want to have fun with their family and friends. Activities that appeal to members of this group include skiing, golf, camping, and hiking.

The third segment consists of individuals who are *fitness driven*. College graduates and women dominate this group. They tend to engage in activities that require strength and stamina; thus, the activities can be stressful. Running, aerobics, martial arts, and weight lifting are viable options for this segment. The fourth segment, *health-conscious sociables,* seeks activities that foster good health. Their chosen activities are not as risky or stressful as those undertaken by the more-active segments. The average age is higher, and about two-thirds of the members of this segment are women. Walking, light cardiovascular exercising, and some of the slower-paced martial arts attract this health-conscious group. They are also more prone to consider purchasing food products that are consistent with their goal of staying healthy.

The final group is the *unstressed and unmotivated*. There is no dominant demographic group, though they tend to be somewhat older. Members of this segment are not inclined to engage in any meaningful recreational activities. Their preference is to remain inactive; therefore, there are few physical activities that appeal to them. There is also very little that marketers can do to alter their passive mind-set.

When marketers that provide facilities and equipment to tennis players have a better understanding of who is playing and why they are playing, they can implement more effective marketing strategies.

While benefits will be secured by marketers that segment the aggregate participation market, there is little doubt that the greatest opportunities exist for marketers of specific sports and other recreational activities. For instance, when marketers that provide facilities and equipment to tennis players have a better understanding of who is playing and why they are playing, they can implement more effective marketing strategies. Thus, we now turn our attention to the process of segmenting the participant market for specific activities.

A Comprehensive Example—The Golfer Market

A recent study used the skill of golfers as the basic criterion for developing five unique segments. The five are competitors, players, sociables, aspirers, and casuals. Competitors are the most skilled golfers while casuals tend to post the highest scores. The resultant groupings documented several meaningful differences across the five segments. Among the differences were the reasons for playing golf, how often they play, what they buy, where they buy, and their inclination to take golf vacations.[15] Box 15.2 provides a comprehensive overview of each of the five segments of golfers.

A review of Box 15.2 illustrates the insight that marketers can gain via the process of segmenting the market and engaging in meaningful marketing research. Clearly, the marketers of any participation sport or other recreational activity can benefit from the acquisition of information such as this. Tennis, skiing, skateboarding, bowling, hunting, and circuit training are but a few examples of sports for which marketers should undertake segmentation in an effort to develop more effective strategic initiatives customized for the designated target market.

Other Less Comprehensive Applications

Not all efforts are as detailed as that of the golf market. Some use a single demographic variable in an effort to distinguish among the participants. Yet even these comparatively simple approaches can provide important information to the marketers. For example, gender has been used to segment the golf market.[16] The growth of the female segment has even resulted in new magazines such as *Golf for Women* and induced *Golf Digest* to incorporate an "Extra for Women" section for the magazine's 100,000 female subscribers.[17] When the *Golf Digest* strategy was reevaluated, the publishers made the decision to acquire the publication rights to *Golf for Women*. It was felt that the initial "extra" section did little to excite female golfers. The acquisition was an acknowledgment that any superior targeting required a significant and meaningful change in the publisher's product strategy and that the change needed to specifically address issues germane to female golfers. Figure 15.2 illustrates the cover of a recent issue of *Golf for Women*.

FIGURE 15.2
Cover of *Golf for Women* Magazine

ATTRIBUTES OF FIVE SEGMENTS OF GOLFERS   15.2

Competitors—Handicap Lower than 10 (18.6%)
- Play for competitive edge
- Most likely to play in leagues
- Early adopters (e.g., lob wedge)
- Indicate they love the game
- Practice most frequently
- Own more golf clothing
- Purchase most golf balls

Players—Handicap 10 to 14 (25.7%)
- Practice a lot (but less than competitors)
- Purchase from custom club makers
- Like competition
- Exercise and companionship are important
- Most likely to take out-of-state golf vacation

Sociables—Handicap 15 to 18 (17.8%)
- Purchase from off-price retailers
- Often play with family
- Play for sociability
- Most likely to take winter vacation incorporating golf in a warm destination

Aspirers—Handicap 19 to 25 (18.4%)
- Love to play; hate to practice
- Most inclined segment to use golf for business purposes
- Golf shows represent important sources of information
- Want to get better, but not competitive
- Sociability is unimportant

Casuals—Handicap 26 or higher (19.5%)
- More women in this segment
- Own least golf clothing
- Recreation is most important factor for playing
- Exercise and companionship are moderately important
- Play less than other segments
- Do not practice
- Purchase fewest golf balls
- Most likely to shop in course pro shop
- Least likely to take a golf vacation

Another key demographic is age. A segment of consumers over the age of 55 has become fixated with fitness.[18] As a result, this segment has become an important target market for those companies that sell exercise equipment and memberships to health clubs.

While more detailed segmentation using a number of criteria may yield better information, clearly, even a little information is helpful. Segmentation using a single variable can provide insight that can be used to identify behavioral tendencies and marketing opportunities.

It is worth noting that many activities in the sports and leisure market are not participation sports. However, many of these leisure activities directly compete with the marketers of participation sports for a share of the consumer's discretionary income. On a more positive note, many of these activities complement the participation market. In this regard, a key market to consider is that of vacation and travel. By recognizing the synergy between participation and travel, it was understood that each industry could benefit from the segmentation of the travel market. One study that focused on the Australian market identified six "travel" segments. These segments are physical challenge seekers, family vacationers, culture and entertainment seekers, nature tourists, escape and relax vacationers, and indifferent travelers.[19] The names of the six segments should provide some insight into the types of activities that would appeal to each. Undoubtedly, information gleaned from this segmentation process will help marketers make better decisions. As noted at the beginning of this chapter, in this regard the marketing of sports is no different from the marketing of most consumer products.

Closing Capsule

Throughout the first half of this book, the importance of market segmentation was continuously stressed. Marketers of many nonsports products choose to use a sports platform for their efforts because sports provide a linkage to many of their current and prospective customers. Just as market segmentation is an essential component of a firm's marketing strategy when it is marketing through sports, it is equally important when the objective involves the marketing of sports products.

While there may be a tendency to speak of the market for spectator sports, there should be an acknowledgment that the aggregate market is large and diverse. The same is true for the markets for participation sports and the wide array of other sports products such as sporting goods, apparel, and athletic shoes.

The reality of marketing today is that segmentation is an essential step in the development of effective marketing strategies. When the mass market is redefined on the basis of smaller, more homogeneous segments, marketers can customize their strategies in an effort to appeal to members of each targeted segment. When done correctly, such differentiated strategies will be more effective than a single mass marketing effort.

In the marketing of spectator sports, the objective may be to sell tickets to new fans, to increase sales to current fans, or to secure renewal orders from season ticket holders. It may also reflect an effort to increase the number of fans who watch a sport or event on television. Marketers of participation sports seek to enhance consumer interest in a variety of sports, recreation, and leisure activities. Similarly, marketers of sporting goods and apparel implement strategies that are designed to sell more equipment to participants and a variety of clothing products to both participants and fans.

While early segmentation strategies emphasized demographic and geographic variables, the recent emphasis has been on applications involving psychographics and product-related variables. Despite this reprioritization, even basic segmentation that uses a single demographic variable can significantly enhance the marketer's effectiveness. For instance, the NFL has effectively used gender as a basis for developing new products and promotions that target female fans.

From a broad perspective, the spectator market is comprised of six distinct segments. These fans may be players, patriots, appreciators, socialites, friends, or voyeurs. More recently, marketers have also begun to draw distinctions between old school and new school fans. Any sport may well appeal to more than one segment, so it is imperative that marketers understand who is watching and why they watch a particular sport or attend a particular event.

When the focus shifts to participation sports, the same type of heterogeneous market exists. One study identified five segments of participants; these are the excitement-seeking competitors, getaway actives, fitness driven, health-conscious sociables, and the unstressed and unmotivated. Clearly, the segments are defined primarily on the basis of lifestyles and the benefits sought by those who choose to participate. An assessment of these five groups also isolates a number of demographic considerations. So even though the group assignments are not based upon demographics, considerable insight regarding age and gender is evident. Whether the effort involves the marketing of golf or bungy jumping, information of this type should lead to the implementation of more effective strategic initiatives. Similarly, efforts to sell equipment such as snowboards or apparel such as officially licensed NBA jerseys should be based on an acknowledgment that the mass market is vanishing and that segmentation, coupled with effective selection of target markets, will help the marketer achieve its goals. Just as one size of an NBA jersey will not fit every fan, undifferentiated strategies aimed at the mass market tend to be ineffective. Sports marketers must recognize the three key steps for developing a differentiated marketing strategy: segment the market, select target markets, and customize a marketing mix for each target market. By doing so, the likelihood of success is greatly enhanced.

> Just as one size of an NBA jersey will not fit every fan, undifferentiated strategies aimed at the mass market tend to be ineffective.

Marketing books generally stress the two key components of marketing strategy. They are a target market and a corresponding marketing mix. Now that we have a clear understanding of the process of segmentation and the selection of target markets, we can turn our attention to the marketing mix. The next four chapters each focus on one of the variables in the marketing mix. Upon the completion of Chapters 16 through 19, there should be a better understanding of how sports marketers make decisions regarding their product, promotion, pricing, and distribution (place) initiatives. We will then be better equipped to coordinate the target market and marketing mix decisions in such a way that more effective strategies are the result.

Review Questions

1. Why is segmentation deemed to be a crucial element for success in sports marketing?
2. Which bases for segmentation are likely to be more effective in the marketing of sports? Why?
3. Look at the Web site for any professional sports team. What segments can you identify from the information presented in the Web site?
4. Select a sport and identify (from the six segments of sports fans) the segment that you think is most important to that sport. Explain your reasoning.
5. Consider the last sporting event that you attended. Using Table 15.3, try to determine which fan segment you fall into.
6. Briefly describe the five segments of sports participants.

7. How can segmentation of the participants for a particular sport such as tennis assist in marketing efforts?

8. How would you describe old school fans? Select an athlete that fits with the old school mentality; explain why you feel the athlete represents the old school group. Find an advertisement or Internet page for a sport, a team, or an event that features an old school philosophy.

9. How would you describe new school fans? Select an athlete that fits with the new school mentality; explain why you feel the athlete represents the new school group. Find an advertisement or Internet page for a sport, a team, or an event that features a new school philosophy.

10. Why has the magazine *Golf for Women* been so successful?

11. What are the three steps for the implementation of a differentiated marketing strategy?

Endnotes

1. "The Mass Market Is Dead," *Growth Strategies* 967 (July 2004), p. 1.

2. A. Bianco, T. Lowry, R. Berner, and M. Arndt, "The Vanishing Mass Market," *BusinessWeek,* July 12, 2004, p. 60.

3. S. Shore, "NHL, NFL Design Products for Women Fans, *Advertising Age,* August 26, 1996, p. 8.

4. M. Bidinost, "Xtreme Culture: Young and Lifestyle-Savvy," *Sportsau.com*, 1999, pp. 24–25.

5. M. McCarthy, "Basketball League Shoots for Less Affluent Fan," November 19, 2001, www.usa-today.com/money/general/2001/11/19/nbdl.htm (accessed October 14, 2005).

6. L. McCarthy, "Marketing Sport to Hispanic Consumers, *Sport Marketing Quarterly* 7, no. 4 (1998), pp. 19–24.

7. L. Petrecca, "MLB Turns Up Spotlight on Its Latino Ballplayers," *Advertising Age,* March 20, 2000, p. 8.

8. McCarthy, "Marketing Sport to Hispanic Consumers."

9. W. Drehs, "A Coming-Out Party for Professional Sports," May 21, 2001, www.espn.go.com/page2/s/drehs/010524.html (accessed October 14, 2005).

10. Petrecca, "MLB Turns up Spotlight on Its Latino Ballplayers."

11. J. Watson and A. Rich, "From Players to Voyeurs: A Six-Category Typology of Sports Fans," unpublished manuscript, December 30, 2000.

12. Ibid.

13. D. Aiken and A. Sukhdial, "Explaining the Old School Concept: Adding Definition to a "New" Market Segmentation Dimension," *Sport Marketing Quarterly,* 13, no. 2, (2004), pp. 73–81.

14. G. Milne, W. Sutton, and M. McDonald, "Niche Analysis: A Strategic Measurement Tool for Sports Marketers," *Sport Marketing Quarterly* 5, no. 3 (1996), pp. 15–22.

15. S. Fullerton and H. Dodge, "An Application of Market Segmentation in a Sports Marketing Arena: We All Can't Be Greg Norman," *Sport Marketing Quarterly* 4, no. 3 (1995), pp. 43–47.

16. J. Collier, "On the Upswing," *Detroit Free Press,* September 13, 2004, pp. C1, C5.

17. J. Hodges, "Women's Role Drives New 'Golf Digest' Effort," *Advertising Age* 67, no. 8 (February 19, 1996), p. 34.

18. C. Kucinski, "55-Up Crowd Becomes Fitness-Fixated," *Ann Arbor News Free Weekly,* August 16, 2001, pp. 1, 6.

19. C. Lang and J. O'Leary, "Motivation, Perception, and Preference: A Multi-Segmentation Approach of the Australian Nature Travel Market," *Journal of Travel and Tourism Marketing* 6, no. 3–4 (1997), pp. 159–80.

Product Decisions in Sports Marketing

Learning Objectives

- Review basic product concepts.
- Define the three categories of sports products.
- Distinguish between spectator sports' core and peripheral products.
- Establish guidelines for changing the core product.
- Identify strategic initiatives for each of the three product categories.

It is now time to shift our attention to the set of strategic initiatives that are designed to capitalize on the opportunities presented by each designated target market. Regarding this set of initiatives, many people tend to have a far too narrow perspective of marketing. Foremost in the minds of many outside observers is the belief that advertising and marketing are synonymous. This belief is incorrect; advertising is but one of the tools available to marketers. By recalling our earlier discussion of the marketing mix, we understand that marketing involves a comprehensive set of decisions that are used in an organization's efforts to appeal to its target markets.

Another reality is that poor products can seldom be sold solely on the basis of good advertising. To succeed, marketers must focus on customer needs. Therefore, one key initiative for the marketer is the development of an appropriate product strategy directed toward the satisfaction of those needs while remembering that product decisions represent just one of the components in a marketing plan. As with every other industry, the efforts to sell sports products must incorporate a marketing mix whereby the four controllable variables work in harmony with each other.

Sports marketers have historically used a variety of promotional tools to sell tickets and other products. In addition to TV, radio, and print advertising, a number of game-day promotions are used by most professional and many amateur teams. Postgame concerts, postgame fireworks, autograph opportunities, on-field activities for kids, and a variety of giveaways featuring items such as bobblehead dolls, thundersticks, towels, caps, and other sport-related items are examples of typical promotions used by the marketers of spectator sports. Later in this chapter, we will see how promotions of this type often represent components of a sports marketer's product strategy. Table 16.1 summarizes the game-day promotions used by a Major League Baseball team during the 2005 season. It is noteworthy that the team featured marketing promotions for 31 of their 81 scheduled home games.

Our assessment of the marketing mix will begin with the product variable. You should recall from Chapter 2 the earlier designation of the four strategic domains within the sports marketing environment. Two of these domains feature the marketing of sports products. The product-focused domain involves the use of traditional strategies to create demand for

TABLE 16.1
**MLB Select Team
Game-Day
Promotions**

Source: "Promotions &
Giveaways," 2005,
http://losangeles.dodgers.mlb.
com/NASApp/mlb/la/schedule/
promotion.jsp (accessed
October 14, 2005).

Date	Promotion/Giveaway	Sponsor(s)	Eligible Fan
April 2	Magnet schedule	AltaDena Dairy	All attending
April 3	Magnet schedule	AltaDena Dairy	All attending
April 12	Magnet schedule	AltaDena Dairy	All attending
April 13	Schedule poster	N/A	All attending
April 15	Jackie Robinson figure	N/A	All attending
April 17	LA Cap Night	Farmer John	All attending
April 27	Fleece blanket	Toyota	All attending
April 30	Cinco de Mayo fireworks	Bank of America	All attending
May 1	Autograph Day 1	N/A	Kids 14 and under
May 13	Rally towel	76 and Auto Club	All attending
May 15	Photo Day	N/A	All attending
May 16	dodgers.com T-shirt	Kragen	All attending
May 30	Trading cards	N/A	All attending
June 1	Bobblehead 1	Bosley	All attending
June 3	Wooden nesting dolls	N/A	Kids 14 and under
June 4	Hollywood stars	N/A	TBD
June 12	Beach towel	Carl's Jr.	All attending
June 27	Sandy Koufax figure	N/A	All attending
July 2	Autograph Day 2	N/A	Kids 14 and under
July 3	Independence Day fireworks	Farmer John	All attending
Aug. 12	Lunch bag	Farmer John	Kids 14 and under
Aug. 14	Autograph Day 3	N/A	Kids 14 and under
Aug. 26	Trading cards	N/A	All attending
Aug. 27	Viva Los Angeles	Toyota & Coca-Cola	All attending
Aug. 28	1955 World Series team	N/A	All attending
Sept. 9	School binder	N/A	Kids 14 and under
Sept. 10	Rally towel	Adelphia	All attending
Sept. 23	LA Light Show fireworks	N/A	All attending
Sept. 24	Team photo	N/A	All attending
Sept. 25	Fan Appreciation Day	Farmer John	All attending
Sept. 29	Bobblehead 2	N/A	All attending

sports products, whereas the sports-dominant domain features sports products in a sponsorship environment. Since the emphasis of this text has now shifted to marketing efforts for sports products, it is these two domains that represent the primary focus of our discussions regarding the development of sports marketing strategy.

This chapter will delineate a number of key product concepts. It will address issues relevant for products in general and sports products in particular. Furthermore, it will identify a number of strategic initiatives that have been implemented within the product-focused and sports-dominant domains.

The Product Variable

Products are comprised of an array of attributes and features. One unfortunate reality is that there is no uniform acknowledgment of exactly what constitutes a product. Still, it is an essential strategic component of every organization's marketing mix. The product represents what marketers are attempting to sell to their customers.

Many textbooks seek to draw a distinction between products and services. In line with this reasoning, automobiles, televisions, and golf balls represent tangible products, whereas auto financing, TV repair, and golf lessons are intangible services. Other books distinguish between goods and services while stressing that both tangible goods and intangible services comprise the product environment. For the duration of this book, both goods and services will be deemed to be products. Typical goods offered by sports marketers include skis, soccer balls, and tennis rackets. Among the services offered for sale are skiing lessons, admission to a World Cup of Soccer match, and court-time at a local tennis club.

Since the inclusion of both goods and services is appropriate for the product variable, any definition should be broad enough to incorporate both. In line with this, a *product* can be defined as a good, service, or idea that can satisfy the needs of consumers.

> A product can be defined as a good, service, or idea that can satisfy the needs of consumers.

Though we now have a clear definition of a product, it is important to further classify the concepts and the strategic considerations associated with product decisions. This assessment begins with a brief overview of several basic product concepts.

Basic Product Concepts

Many products are marketed on the basis of the primary benefit that they provide to those who purchase them. This *primary benefit has been designated the augmented product*. In an example from the marketing of nonsports products, the augmented product for an automobile is transportation. For a television, it is likely that entertainment is the augmented product; and the primary benefit derived from a haircut for the majority of consumers is improved appearance.

Marketers generally emphasize the augmented product in the development of their strategies; however, two considerations must be kept in mind. First, different segments may view the augmented product differently. For toothpaste, one segment may value cavity prevention, whereas another segment is seeking whiter teeth. So even though consumers may focus on the augmented product, marketers must use differentiated strategies tailored to the primary benefit sought by each segment.

The second key consideration is that products are seldom purchased solely on the basis of the augmented product. While transportation may represent the fundamental benefit derived from the purchase of a car, the astute automotive marketer understands that there is an array of additional benefits that add value and influence the final purchase decision. Consumers may consider the security provided by a warranty, the low-interest financing, the prestige of the brand name, the fuel efficiency, and the safety record of the vehicle in selecting one car over another. Though marketers have applied a number of terms to represent these benefits and features, one of the more descriptive terms is *ancillary components*. It is these ancillary components that comprise a set of product attributes that consumers view as supplements to the augmented product. These attributes provide benefits and value to the consumer. The augmented product and the corresponding array of ancillary components make up the *total product*. Marketers must consider consumer needs and how the total product compares with competitive offerings in their efforts to create consumer preference and demand.

Most organizations today are involved in the marketing of a number of products. This array is typically referred to as the *product assortment*. Every marketer should periodically engage in an evaluation of the appropriateness of its assortment. Although marketers of sports products tend to sell a relatively narrow assortment, this periodic evaluation is still necessary. Upon the completion of this assessment, decisions can be made regarding recommended changes in the product assortment that is available for customers to buy.

In some cases, the best decision is to *maintain the status quo*. The product assortment is deemed appropriate and no changes are required. It is important to note, however, that

PRODUCT ASSORTMENT DECISIONS   16.1

- Maintain status quo (no product changes)
- Modify existing products
- Product extension
- Introduce new products beyond current product assortment
- Delete existing products

even though the product assortment is unchanged, other elements of the marketing strategy may be adjusted. For example, the organization's pricing, promotion, and distribution strategies may be changed in an effort to improve the marketability and the profitability of the existing products. Each year, professional teams will weigh the impact of a change in ticket prices. Did salaries increase; was performance better; will fans pay more to attend? Answers to questions such as these directly impact the marketer's decision as to raise, maintain, or lower ticket prices.

A second option is to *maintain the existing product assortment but to make modifications to those products* so as to better appeal to consumers. Spectator sports such as professional basketball have changed their rules without changing the basic game; marketers of apparel have introduced new colors in their efforts to better appeal to female fans.

The third option is *product extension*. Implementation of this strategy adds choices that do not represent a radical departure from the organization's existing product strategy. The National Basketball League recently introduced two new product extensions. The Women's National Basketball Association and the National Basketball Developmental League represent two new options for basketball fans. Yet both are based upon the NBA game itself.

A fourth option is to *introduce new products that represent a significant departure from anything that is currently part of the organization's product assortment.* Nike's recent decision to become involved with rugby required the company to introduce a line of sporting goods and apparel that differed substantially from anything it had previously offered. The NFL's decision to create the NFL Network for cable and satellite TV subscribers provided a sports product that is far different from simply selling tickets to a football game.

Finally, *product deletion* is sometimes the optimal decision. Products are evaluated on the basis current performance and future opportunities. When products become a financial burden to the organization, they are often eliminated from the assortment. The recent abandonment of the XFL is an example of a recent deletion decision for a sports product. A brief overview of the decisions that result from the systematic evaluation of any organization's product assortment is presented in Box 16.1.

Sports Products

Earlier in this text, the concept of sports products was introduced. Now that we have gained greater insight into the sports market, it is time to expand the scope of our discussion regarding product decisions. This will begin with the delineation of the three broad categories of sports products in the consumer market. They are identified in Box 16.2 and discussed on the following pages.

BROAD CATEGORIES OF SPORTS PRODUCTS | 16.2

- Spectator sports
- Participation sports
- Sporting goods, apparel, athletic shoes, and sports-related products

Spectator Sports

From college sports to minor league sports to the highest level of professional sports and for international events such as the Olympics, one key marketing objective is that of selling tickets. Yet it is not only those who purchase tickets to a game or event who are important; sports marketers also work to increase viewership and listenership on a variety of broadcast media. This includes television options such as free-to-air TV, premium cable and satellite networks, pay-per-view for special events, enhanced access to a sport's broadcasts (such as DirecTV's NFL Sunday Ticket), and devoted networks such as the Rugby Channel and the Golf Channel that are dedicated to an array of events and programming germane to a single sport. Other media include radio and audio/video streaming on the Internet.

With this in mind, we might look at the spectator sports product from two perspectives. Marketers sell access to events; that access may legitimately be viewed as the product. However, this access has no value without the competition on the field of play. Thus, it is the game or event that represents the product in the spectator sports market.

> Marketers have sought to refine their sports much the way that Coca-Cola has attempted to modify, improve, and add to its product lines.

Recognizing that the value is generated by the sports event, marketers have sought to refine their sports much the way that Coca-Cola has attempted to modify, improve, and add to its product lines in its efforts to enhance consumer preference, satisfaction, and repeat patronage. In the spectator sports domain, such changes include modifications to the rules in ways that impact how the game is played or the competition takes place. Examples of how such changes have been implemented and guidelines regarding any significant modifications are discussed in the "Strategic Initiatives" section later in this chapter.

Participation Sports

The category of participation sports rightfully includes an array of activities that might not normally be perceived as sports. While we readily recognize organized soccer leagues, golf, and tennis as participation sports, other activities that may be done on an individual basis are not always acknowledged as sports. The absence of competition that identifies a winner and loser may be the basis for this reluctance. Individuals who jog around the neighborhood or who lift free weights at home or at the health club are not typically characterized as athletes. There is yet another tier of activities that represent participation and competition although even the most liberal definition does not permit them to be classified as sports. The most recent addition to this category is poker. Even sports networks such as Fox Sports and ESPN have begun to broadcast poker tournaments. Other activities such as darts, fishing, and billiards are also noteworthy from a participation perspective.

The array of activities should cause the reader to recall the earlier assertion that individuals participate in activities such as these for one of three reasons. They seek personal improvement, they appreciate the sport, or they seek social interaction. Marketers must recognize the array of activities, the various market segments that comprise the participation environment, and the motives that drive individuals to participate.

> Marketing's role is to increase the number of participants and the frequency in which current participants choose to engage in a specific activity.

In many cases, marketing's role is to increase the number of participants and the frequency in which current participants choose to engage in a specific activity. For example, the marketer may want to attract new golfers while at the same time induce current golfers to play even more. The primary benefit to these marketers is that increased participation keeps facilities such as golf courses, tennis clubs, swimming pools, and health clubs busy. A secondary benefit is that it creates demand for more sports equipment and apparel. This leads us to the third and final category of sports products.

Sporting Goods, Apparel, Athletic Shoes, and Sports-Related Products

The final category of sports products is somewhat more difficult to define. While sporting goods such as snowboards, apparel such as skiwear, and athletic shoes are easy to understand, the final component, sports-related products, is very diverse. It includes sports souvenirs, publications, lessons, and a diverse assortment of products that can be purchased at event venues.

The market for this final category of sports products is enormous. Many individuals participate in a variety of sports on a casual basis. They may swim or do aerobics when they can fit these activities into their schedules. They might join their friends in a quickly planned game of football at a local park. Consumers might take advantage of some spare time to go to the driving range or sneak in a quick round of golf. Marketers also understand that much of the participation is based upon organized, regularly scheduled competition. Golf, bowling, softball, and soccer each have millions of players who participate in regular leagues and tournaments. One result of all of this participation is a demand for sporting goods.

Sporting goods include tangible products specific to a participation sport or activity. These products may be sold to casual participants as well as those who take part in organized activities. The 55 million Americans who participate in bowling create a demand for bowling equipment. Golfers throughout the world have fueled a tremendous increase in the sale of clubs, balls, bags, and gloves.

Apparel is clothing that falls into one of two categories. First and foremost, it may be purchased to facilitate participation. The annual start of a new season for many sports creates demand for new uniforms. Style changes may induce golfers to abandon last year's clothing in favor of new styles so that they look good on the golf course. The second category is based on the acknowledgment that sports apparel can be fashionable within certain market segments. These buyers may be fans who wear clothing that features the logos of teams they support. Others may buy the same apparel, not because they support the team, but because the clothing is in vogue among their contemporaries. Understanding the importance of these segments, marketers have begun to broaden the scope of the distribution network that sells apparel.

The third component of this category is *athletic shoes*. These were once primarily devoted to the participant market, but this has changed significantly since the advent of Nike's Air Jordan shoes. Today, athletic shoes are an integral part of almost everyone's wardrobe. For participants, there are designs deemed appropriate for specific activities such as racket sports, basketball, running, walking, and cross-training. No longer are

SPORTS PRODUCTS   16.3

Spectator Sports
- Tickets for attendance
- Viewership and listenership on electronic media

Participation Sports
- Organized participation (leagues and tournaments)
- Casual participation
- Access to public and private athletic facilities

Sporting Goods, Apparel, Athletic Shoes, and Sports-Related Products
- Sports equipment (skis, golf clubs, and soccer balls)
- Sports apparel (hunting clothing, swimwear, and team uniforms)
- Athletic shoes
- Sports-related products (souvenirs, lessons, and refreshments)

athletic shoes combined into the generic category of tennis shoes. From a fashion perspective, there are various styles that feature different colors and materials. For both the participant and fashion markets, athlete endorsement is an essential element of the marketing strategy. High performers such as LeBron James, David Beckham, and Venus Williams have followed in the footsteps of Michael Jordan as highly paid celebrity endorsers of the athletic shoes offered by companies such as Nike, adidas, and Reebok.

> No longer are athletic shoes combined into the generic category of tennis shoes.

The final component consists of a broad array of *sports-related products*. These include souvenirs that may be purchased at event venues as well as a number of other official retailers. Consumers often purchase sports magazines. These may feature sports in general, but many focus on a single sport or even a specific team. Lessons to improve one's skill at sports like tennis or golf fit best within this category as well. But the broadest set of products in this category is comprised of venue-specific products. While these products are not tied to a sport per se, they are purchased by spectators in attendance. So while many might be reluctant to classify beer as a sports product, it represents an important revenue stream for teams and stadium operators. Other beverages, food, game-day programs, and souvenirs also fall into this category.

These three broad categories summarize the array of sports products sold in the consumer market. Sports marketers must understand which products are important to their target markets and develop a product strategy that meets those needs. Furthermore, the product strategy must be consistent with the other elements of the marketing mix. Only then can the sports marketer take advantage of the opportunities that exist. Box 16.3 provides an overview of the sports products that are important to today's marketers.

Earlier in this text, the sports marketing environment was broken down into four domains. The two characterized by the marketing of sports products are the product-focused and sports-dominant domains. Before our discussion progresses to the implementation of marketing strategy, there is a need to assure that there is an understanding of these two domains. A brief overview of the overall sports marketing environment follows. A more comprehensive discussion can be found in Chapter 2.

Sports Marketing Domains

Nonsports products are often marketed using a sports platform. The *mainstream domain* is represented by the marketing of nonsports products and the use of traditional marketing initiatives that incorporate a sports component. McDonald's use of a soccer theme in its advertising is an example of a marketing effort within the mainstream domain. *Domain-focused* strategies emphasize nonsports products and some type of sponsorship involvement. An example is Coca-Cola's sponsorship of the Olympic Games. These two domains were the emphases in Chapters 3 through 14.

Of primary interest to us now are the domains where the objective is the marketing of one of the many types of sports products identified in Box 16.3. Product-focused strategies represent an effort to create demand for sports products using traditional target market selection and the development of a corresponding marketing mix. Examples include the use of newspaper advertising in a team's attempt to sell season tickets, a retailer's use of end-of-the-season sale pricing to clear its inventory of snowboards, and the use of the Internet to sign up members for a new health club.

The *sports-dominant* domain emphasizes an official sponsorship-based relationship with a sport or athlete in the effort to sell sports products. It is important to recall that we earlier identified four types of sponsorship: traditional, venue naming rights, licensing, and endorsements. One example of a sports-dominant strategy is the sale of athletic shoes that feature the endorsement of a well-known athlete. Another is the use of Tiger Woods in advertising that encourages African American kids to consider playing golf. Many companies use licensing agreements to gain a competitive advantage over their rivals. Nike uses its rights to incorporate many universities' logos on products as a way of selling sports equipment, apparel, and shoes. Clearly, endorsements and licensing represent the bulk of the strategies in the sports-dominant domain; however, traditional sponsorship and venue naming rights can be used under certain circumstances.

Strategic Initiatives

With the review of the four domains of the sports marketing environment complete, it is now time to look at specific strategic initiatives and guidelines. This will be achieved by looking at the three basic categories of sports products and by examining how marketers have sought to influence the demand for these goods and services.

Spectator Sports

When the term *sports marketing* is mentioned, the task that immediately comes to mind for most people is that of selling tickets to sports events. In a less elegant way of stating it, the job of sports marketers is perceived by many outside observers to be one of "putting bums in the seats." The reality is that most students who are seeking a career in sports marketing are intent on working in this capacity for one of the major professional teams in their geographic area.

Marketing strategy can play a key role in the effort to attract fans, and one required element of that marketing strategy is the organization's set of decisions regarding its array of products. Marketers of spectator sports often modify their product in an effort to attract new fans and to encourage current fans to attend more often. In other words, marketers of spectator sports will tweak their product in order to put more fans in the seats.

These marketing efforts tend to fall within the product-focused domain. In this domain, product decisions tend to be viewed as the most important aspect of the marketing mix. This brings us to the key question: Just what product are marketers of spectator sports really selling?

Modifications to the spectator sports product can take two forms. The more dramatic is a change in the core product. The *core product* has been defined as the game itself, that is, whatever takes place on the field of play, including the manner in which it is conducted, the style and strategy employed, and the interpretation of understood laws, rules, regulations, and historical precedents.[1]

> The core product has been defined as the game itself, that is, whatever takes place on the field of play.

Many sports organizations have changed the rules or instructed game officials to enforce the rules in different ways. As noted earlier in this chapter, such changes are generally implemented in an effort to make the game more appealing to the fans. Changes are often designed to enhance competition, to increase scoring, or to speed up the pace of the game. A brief description of some of the changes in the core product of several sports illustrates strategic initiatives of this type.

NASCAR is one of the most popular spectator sports in America. Despite NASCAR's excellent relationship with fans, several significant changes were implemented at the start of the 2004 season. These changes have had a direct impact on the manner in which key competitions take place. For example, the overall champion is the winner of the Nextel Cup. In some seasons prior to the change in the rule, that winner was determined well before the final race was completed. Now drivers compete for the majority of the season in order to qualify for the "Chase for the Cup." Only the top 10 drivers qualify for a competition that takes place over the final 10 races to determine the overall champion. Another change involved the undesirable situation where a race was completed under the caution flag. To reduce the likelihood of this occurrence, NASCAR implemented the "green-white-checkered finish" rule. The change provides for an extra lap to be run when it provides a reasonable assurance that the race will be completed at full speed under a green flag condition. In general, despite some trepidation on the part of NASCAR officials, the rules changes have been well received by the fans and the drivers.

Americans have been slow to embrace soccer. They often voice concerns about low scores and what is perceived to be a lack of action. Indoor soccer was viewed as one solution. A smaller playing surface, boards that keep the ball in play, and more goals being scored were seen as changes to the core product that would help overcome the major objections voiced by Americans.

In the aftermath of the labor strife that resulted in the suspension of play for the entire 2004–05 season, the National Hockey League developed several new rules that were designed to appeal to the fans. One of these changes addresses tie games. For several years now, a five-minute sudden death period with only four skaters per team has been used to open up the ice and to assure that fewer games ended with a tied score. The change that began with the 2005–06 season involves those games that remain tied after the overtime period. Those games are now determined with a "shoot-out" during which each team designates three players to take penalty shots. The team that makes the most penalty shots is declared the winner. Other changes were designed to open up the game, to provide talented players more opportunities, and to increase scoring. These include the removal of the center red line as a limitation to long breakaway passes, more stringent enforcement of holding and obstruction rules, and limitations on the size of the goaltenders' equipment. The belief is that the new rules will excite existing fans, attract new fans, and help the league recover from the loss of an entire season.

Many years ago, the NBA adopted a 24-second shot clock in an effort to add to the action and generate higher scores. More recently, the league added a three-point shot. The rationale was that it gave trailing teams a better chance to catch up. It was also believed that the extra value of the long shot would cause the defense to spread out and that this adjustment would open up the play under the basket.

Major League Baseball long struggled with the fact that very few pitchers were also good hitters. The result was that pitchers almost always batted last and were generally considered an easy out. The American League implemented the designated hitter (DH) rule that allows a regular hitter to be inserted into the batting order. Having a better-hitting player bat in the pitcher's place is credited with increasing the offensive output of American League teams.

Rugby has leagues and competitions with rules that differ significantly from the original Rugby Union code. International Sevens has fewer players and higher scores. Rugby League and Rugby Union are more similar; however, Rugby Union has more players, different rules regarding possession, different point values for scores, and bonus points in the standings for scoring four or more times (or what rugby refers to as a try).

Guidelines for Changing the Core Product

Caution must be exercised when modifications to the core product are being considered. Changes that are deemed frivolous or that do not otherwise represent improvements to the sport put the organization at risk of alienating its most loyal fans. For example, MLB has many old school fans who still view the designated hitter rule as a diminishment to the heritage and the integrity of the game. Substantive changes in the way that any sport is played will be scrutinized by fans. Therefore, sports organizations and marketers must consider a set of guidelines when contemplating changes in the way a game is played on the field or in the arena.[2]

> Caution must be exercised when modifications to the core product are being considered.

Changes to the core product should have positive economic consequences. Changes that are made to enhance the nature of competition or to reward skilled players should result in greater enthusiasm on the part of the fans. With this enthusiasm, the sport should anticipate higher attendance and better TV ratings. Higher attendance results in increased ticket revenue. Improved TV ratings should result in higher rights fees being paid by the organization that broadcasts the events on TV, radio, and via video streaming on the Internet. With this in mind, such changes are often made when attendance is sagging or when there is a need for positive public relations. MLB's designated hitter rule was introduced in the midst of a significant downturn in attendance. And as just noted, the NHL introduced a litany of rules changes in the aftermath of the cancellation of the entire 2004–05 season. Not only were the changes designed as an effort to reenergize hockey fans, but they also represented a proactive effort to head off the potential negative public relations that were anticipated in the aftermath of labor negotiations during which fans and the media were critical of both the players and the team owners.

If positive economic results are not likely to materialize, then any planned changes should be reconsidered. That is not to say that they should be abandoned; however, they need to be designed so that fans view them in a positive light. Many fans are traditionalists who view any change as undesirable.

Core changes should not be made on the basis of implications for the media. One complaint often articulated is that the media, especially television, seem to dictate the flow of the game. Whether they are at the venue or watching on TV, fans need to be the focus. College basketball in the United States has a "media time-out" in each four-minute segment of play. Fans in attendance often complain about an excessive number of TV time-outs during NFL games.

As NFL games began to routinely exceed the three hours that were allocated for the typical TV broadcast, rules were changed regarding clock stoppage. The result was that there were fewer prolonged stoppages of the clock and games were completed in a slightly shorter time frame. So while we say that changes should not be made for the media, it is obvious that this caveat is routinely ignored. The key is to position such changes as benefits for the fans.

Tradition is a major consideration in changing sport's core product. In some cases, it is a break from tradition that is the basis for new leagues. Indoor soccer, arena football, and Hong Kong Sevens (rugby) are comparatively new sports that represent dramatic departures from their traditional counterparts. Generally, these sports will not compete head-to-head with the traditional league on which they are based. For instance, the arena football season starts immediately after the NFL's season ends.

> Dramatic changes that significantly alter the way a game is played may be disdained by a sport's most avid fans.

It is also important to understand that tradition is often the basis for resisting change. Dramatic changes that significantly alter the way a game is played may be disdained by a sport's most avid fans. Even though some fans may view it as an improvement, care must be taken to understand how any change to the core product will impact the fans' perception of the sport. In Major League Baseball, the National League has refused to adopt the designated hitter rule that is used in the American League. As a result, teams that are competing for the same championship do so using different sets of rules.

As these examples show, there is often a reluctance to change the core product and break from tradition. In such cases, the sports marketers reject change out of the fear of alienating their existing fans. However, emerging leagues often use dramatic changes as a way of differentiating their sport from the original version. These marketers attempt to capitalize on the strengths of a sport and implement changes that overcome its perceived weaknesses. Often the focus is on increasing the intensity of the action and the level of scoring. These two attributes can be emphasized in promotions aimed at new target markets.

Core changes are often based upon the emergence of competition and its impact on the status quo. Many professional leagues long existed in a business environment that could best be described as a monopoly. Although they have had to compete with alternative forms of entertainment, there was typically no direct competition. In fact, many sports still fit this description. As a consequence, few changes in the core product were made.

More recently, changes in rules have originated with emerging leagues. In the United States, the NFL has endured a constant barrage of entries into the professional football market. From the American Football League (AFL) in the 1960s, the World Football League (WFL) of the 1970s, the United States Football League (USFL) of the 1980s, the Arena Football League (AFL) of the 1990s, to the XFL and its extreme version of football in the 2000s, each new league entered with a focus on different rules designed to produce a more exciting, higher-scoring style of football. Other sports such as basketball, hockey, and rugby have similarly endured the emergence of upstart competitors that stressed rules changes designed to appeal to their target markets.

> Each new league entered with a focus on different rules designed to produce a more exciting, higher-scoring style of football.

When these new leagues prove to be a threat or when fans become enamored with the new rules, the original league may likewise opt to invoke similar changes. The two-point conversion in the NFL and the three-point shot in the NBA were popular in the upstart leagues. And though each of the fledgling competitive leagues eventually failed, they did have a meaningful impact on the way that the games are played today.

Core alterations will not overcome poor quality. Many of the new leagues have given rise to subsequent changes in the core product of the traditional sports on which they are based. The NFL has adopted the two-point conversion that was used by its fledgling imitators, including the WFL and the USFL. The NBA now features the three-point shot that was originally implemented by the American Basketball Association (ABA). So it is apparent that fans can embrace changes. But these changes alone will not be enough to overcome poor quality on the field of play.

The XFL offered an "extreme" form of football that featured significant changes from the way the traditional game of football is played. New rules, fan involvement, and sexy cheerleaders were not enough. Though the league opened with a strong personality (WWE's Vince McMahon) as its leader and a national TV contract, it suffered from declining TV ratings as fans perceived it to be a low-quality imitation of football. Within two years, the league ceased operations.

> Instead of changing the core, consider changes to the peripheral product.

Instead of changing the core, consider changes to the peripheral product. This approach represents the second way in which the spectator sports product can be altered in an effort to better appeal to one or more of the organization's target markets. The *peripheral product* represents the elements surrounding a game or event over which the organization can exercise a reasonable level of control. In this regard, the peripheral product can be considered the ancillary components of the spectator sports product. While the game or event is central to the marketing effort, other factors such as the entertainment during intermission, postgame activities, and the distribution of free items can be used to encourage attendance. These peripheral products tend to be more important to teams that are neither winning nor filling their stadia or arenas. They are also important to minor league sports that simply don't have the quality of play that is characteristic of the top leagues.

As an example, consider the marketing efforts of three midwestern U.S. minor league baseball teams: the Lansing Lugnuts, the Michigan Battlecats, and the West Michigan Whitecaps. Most of their marketing efforts are directed toward kids. Special promotions between innings, giveaways, and carousels provide entertainment beyond the games themselves. To quote the owner of the West Michigan Whitecaps, "in minor league ball, marketing is everything." In fact, it was minor league baseball that introduced night games in 1929.[3] What was originally a novelty for the Kansas City Monarchs of the old Negro League is now the standard practice in MLB.

> "In minor league ball, marketing is everything."

Modifications and new peripheral products represent relatively easy approaches to appealing to new target markets. MLB has seen the use of Ferris wheels, batting cages,

FIGURE 16.1
**Kids Getting
Instruction at an
MLB Stadium**

pitching radar guns, and on-field opportunities as strategies for attracting young fans in the hope of developing long-term relationships with this demographic segment. Figure 16.1 illustrates a promotion where kids were able to get instruction from MLB players on the field prior to the start of a regular game.

In an effort to strengthen relationships by providing more avid fans with more information, sports leagues and events have used wireless technology to provide video feeds to fans in the stands. This video may originate from the venue where the fan is in attendance such that the fan gains access to replays, statistics, and other stadium services such as concessions.[4] Similar technology known as Ref!Link has been well received at a number of rugby grounds in the United Kingdom. This technology provides fans with the opportunity to listen to the discussions involving referees and other game officials.[5] The Professional Golfers Association (PGA) has tested its "virtual caddy system" for television viewers. This system provides information and "virtual graphic enhancements" designed to increase both the knowledge and the enjoyment of the viewers.[6]

Each of these peripheral products is designed to make attending or watching a game more enjoyable. Some provide greater depth for the avid fan; others are designed to provide alternative entertainment for the less dedicated fan. The need to develop multiple strategies is based upon the recognition that different target markets respond differently to the organization's marketing efforts.

To this point, product strategy has been approached from the standpoint of modifying existing products. It would be shortsighted not to consider a market development strategy whereby existing sports are simply exported to a new market. One noteworthy initiative involves cricket, which is extremely popular in countries such as England, India, Australia, New Zealand, and the islands of the West Indies. The sport also has a meaningful participation base in the United States, where there are more than 500 active cricket clubs.[7] Building on this foundation, the International Cricket Council (ICC) has announced plans to establish the American Pro Cricket tournament. Eight teams will play a quicker variation of the game that is designed to be completed in three hours instead of the four or five days required for a regular test cricket match.[8] It is evident that this market development strategy also involves a significant change in cricket's core product. Conversely, efforts to achieve greater interest in rugby in the United States involve no meaningful changes in the way the game is played. Similarly, while originally billed as baseball's equivalent to a world cup competition, the initial World Baseball Classic in 2006 has been viewed as a way to open new markets to the traditional game of baseball by capitalizing upon the patriotic segments of sports fans across the world. With growing globalization of business, culture, and lifestyle, more sports marketers are attempting to capitalize on opportunities to export their sports to new international markets.

> The initial World Baseball Classic in 2006 has been viewed as a way to open new markets to the traditional game of baseball by capitalizing upon the patriotic segments of sports fans across the world.

Participation Sports

Much of the effort to market participation sports falls within the product-focused domain of the sports marketing environment. Efforts to increase the number of individuals who engage in sports such as golf and tennis often rely on the development of a traditional marketing mix to support the sports product. To attract more golfers, marketers must consider how to promote the sport or a specific golf course, where to locate facilities, and the optimal pricing strategy. They must also identify the target markets that represent reasonable growth opportunities. Figure 16.2 illustrates a traditional promotional effort aimed at African American kids in golf's effort to appeal to a target market that has emerged as a result of Tiger Woods's dominance of professional golf even though the promotion itself does not directly reference the prominent golfer.

Other efforts fall within the sports-dominant domain. Such efforts generally involve direct endorsements by star athletes who are widely recognized by the public. In essence, they are encouraging others to play their sport.

Earlier in this chapter, it was indicated that marketing's role in regard to participation sports is to attract new participants and to increase the frequency of the activity among current participants. The benefit to facilities managers is clearly evident. If there are more people engaged in racket sports, then there is greater demand for court time. If more

FIGURE 16.2
Golf in the Hood

people are working out, then fitness clubs can sell more memberships. Yet not all increases in participation result in greater reliance on such facilities.

Some participation activities tend to be more casual than others. For instance, joggers often use public facilities for running. This may be a street, a bike path, or tracks at public institutions such as parks and schools. But as participation increases, it creates opportunities for marketers. How can we get them away from running in the street and into the comfort of a climate controlled facility featuring a cushioned running track?

Increases in participation also directly influence the level of sales in the other two categories of sports products. With increased participation, the demand for equipment and apparel related to the sport also rises. New surfers don't use private facilities, but they do purchase new equipment and apparel. Improved bowlers buy new high-performance bowling balls. People who run more frequently than they did in the past add to the array of shoes and running clothes that they own in an effort to be better preferred for a variety of running conditions.

In regard to spectator sports, it was earlier noted that one of the key market segments is that of the "players." People who play a sport are more inclined to be a fan of that sport. The most likely attendee of a golf tournament is an individual who plays golf. By increasing the number of people who play golf, marketers are increasing the size of an important target market from which they can draw fans to golf events. Consider some of the recent strategic initiatives aimed at increasing participation levels for golf.

> By increasing the number of people who play golf, marketers are increasing the size of an important target market from which they can draw fans to golf events.

An earlier example featured "golf in the hood." The poster that featured a young black golfer was directly aimed at African American kids. The sport, which has historically been associated with older, higher-income, white males, is seeking to capitalize on the fame of the most recognizable African American golfer in the history of the sport, namely Tiger Woods. The segment, which was largely ignored in the past, is now viewed as one that is characterized as having high growth potential.

Another effort by the golf industry to reach kids does not take ethnicity into account. The World Golf Foundation instituted a program known as "the First Tee." According to the organization's Web site, the focus of the First Tee is "to give young people of all backgrounds the opportunity to develop, through golf and character education, life-enhancing values such as honesty, integrity, and sportsmanship."[9] While the organization's mission involves character development, it would be naïve to ignore the potential impact that the program has on bringing new golfers into the sport.

Not all marketing efforts are directed toward kids. It is generally acknowledged that women represent a key growth segment in the golf market. Not only does the industry want to recruit more female golfers, it also wants to retain those who currently participate in the sport. Retention has been a major weakness in recent marketing efforts directed toward women by the golf industry. Ladies beginner leagues have been formed. These leagues allow women of comparable ability to play and to improve while not being intimidated by more skilled golfers. It also allows course operators to engage in organized activities designed to improve their skills. This may involve discounted lessons, free workshops, or an evaluation of their equipment.

> Retention has been a major weakness in recent marketing efforts directed toward women by the golf industry.

Regardless of gender, the golf industry has begun to consider segments with different levels of ability. For less skilled golfers, courses can be set up easier with tee and hole locations that reduce the frustrations often associated with the game. For more talented golfers, a more challenging set of tees will test their ability. Some courses have moved away from the traditional three-tee (blue, white, and red) standard and have established up to five tee areas for each hole. Golfers can select the tees that best match their skills. Some courses have even begun to implement policies that use a player's skill (as measured by his or her official handicap) as the basis for determining which tees can be used by any individual golfer. In other words, a 36-handicap golfer would not be allowed to play from the back tees. Not only would playing the course at its longest frustrate the high-handicap golfer, but it also slows the pace of play and builds frustration among the faster-playing, more talented golfers in the groups following the high handicapper. By making the sport more enjoyable to golfers of varying playing ability, they are more likely to come back and play again.

While the examples to this point have focused on golf, similar strategies can be utilized for many participation sports. Kids enjoy 10-pin bowling, but they often grow frustrated by their futile efforts to knock down any pins. To eliminate "gutter balls" and increase the enjoyment for these kids, bowling proprietors have introduced "bumper bowling." The bumpers keep the ball out of the gutters; kids' scores go up and they want to play again and again. Bowling has also sought to appeal to teenagers and young adults with "cosmic bowling." Shoes and bowling balls that glow under the ultraviolet lighting, reduced over-all lighting, and popular music being played all add to the bowling experience. Cosmic bowling is often offered late on Friday and Saturday evenings to make it attractive to this younger target market. Other efforts have included themed leagues with shorter seasons. These include a NASCAR league with NASCAR merchandise provided to participants and Las Vegas leagues where members have an opportunity to win a trip to Las Vegas at the end of the season. Using techniques such as these, bowling has been able to maintain its position as one of the top participation sports in the United States.

Efforts to increase participation in many sports often involve the establishment of competitive amateur leagues. These leagues may be established by professional sports organizations, management of sports facilities, educational institutions, or municipal governments. While educational institutions and municipal governments may be encouraging healthier lifestyles, the objective of professional sports organizations is to increase consumer involvement with a goal of increasing their own fan base. Managers of sports facilities view participants as a revenue stream—the impact of increased participation represents greater profit potential. Common recreational leagues include those in golf, soccer, tennis, rugby, bowling, basketball, and softball.

In the United States, rugby is considered a niche sport. In an effort to achieve greater penetration in the U.S. market, USA Rugby is seeking to develop greater participation among American college students. The organization recently announced a plan to establish programs at up to 30 universities. By getting more participants, it will also help to increase the talent pool of American players. Likewise, USA Rugby has noted that many high schools have dropped wrestling from their array of competitive sports; the organization has characterized this development as an opportunity to achieve greater penetration of rugby in the high school market.[10]

NFL International has developed a flag football program for Chinese school children.

In an interesting strategy designed to reach the massive Chinese market, NFL International has developed a flag football program for Chinese school children. Referred to as "Olive Ball" because of the shape of the ball, increased participation faced several significant hurdles. There is a lack of Asian players in the NFL; this variety of football does not have Olympic status; and there is a cultural aversion to violent sports.[11] Consequently, the effort to introduce American-style football to China has begun with a noncontact version played by kids. The increased participation has already had a positive impact. China fielded its first national flag football team and competed in the NFL Reebok Flag Football World Championship in 2004. Another outgrowth of the increased penetration of American-style football is that the Shanghai Media Group has signed a contract to broadcast the Super Bowl in China through 2009. It has also led to the increased demand for football apparel with Nike now exploring the long-term potential of the Chinese market.

Fitness centers often provide free introductory memberships to individuals. Lasting only one to four weeks, the idea is to impress these consumers enough during their introductory period so that they will sign a long-term commitment for membership. Marketers understand that trial is often the key to adoption. In a similar strategy designed to increase trials, the Michigan Professional Golfers Association instituted a program that featured an alliance with teaching professionals and a major retailer of golf equipment. The trial process included three discounted lessons with one of the many teaching pros who participated in the program. Upon the completion of their lessons, participants received a discount coupon that they could use to purchase equipment and apparel for playing their new sport.

> Marketers understand that trial is often the key to adoption.

One last intriguing example also involved golf. Building a new course can be very costly, especially in locations where land is either scarce or expensive. Such is the case in the Cayman Islands. Yet tourists often like to play golf. In a compromise of sorts, a new type of course was built. The developer wanted a course that required typical skills and the use of all of the clubs in the golfer's bag. The major limitation was that it could not take up the vast area required of a traditional championship course. The result was the construction of a course that was about half as long as a regular course. To make it more realistic, a new ball was developed. Called the "half ball" or "Cayman ball," it only flies about half the distance of a regular golf ball. Thus, a 185-yard hole becomes equivalent to a 370-yard par four hole. Hazards that are 125 yards down the fairway suddenly come into play. The innovation provided golfers with an opportunity to participate where it might otherwise have been virtually impossible or cost prohibitive. The concept has also proven popular in Japan, another land-starved country with high costs associated with the acquisition of real estate. The need to develop this new ball takes us to the final category of sports products.

Sporting Goods, Apparel, Athletic Shoes, and Sports-Related Products

Much of the demand for products in this final category is a direct outgrowth for the demand for spectator and participation sports. Still, marketers cannot ignore the fact that some segments purchase their products for reasons not specifically related to being either a sports spectator or a sports participant. Many of these products are sold at sports venues, but much is sold through traditional retail outlets. As a result of this variability, some of the marketing efforts fall within the product-focused domain and others can be characterized as sports-dominant strategies. In other cases, the products are not what one would generally consider sports products; rather, they are nonsports products sold at a sports venue. Thus, one might consider products such as beer and peanuts that are sold at a stadium to fall within the domain-focused category. Alternatively, when no official sponsorship is in force with the team or venue, the strategy might be classified as an effort within the mainstream domain. Regardless of its official marketing designation, these types of products are sold at every venue and events at all levels of the sports event pyramid. While the sale of such

EXAMPLES OF SPORTING GOODS, APPAREL, ATHLETIC SHOES, AND SPORTS-RELATED PRODUCTS

16.4

Sporting Goods
- Participant-oriented
  - Organized
  - Casual

Apparel
- Participants
- Fans
- Fashion

Athletic Shoes
- Participant
- Fashion

Sports-Related Products
- Venue-specific
  - Souvenirs
  - Programs
  - Food and beverages
  - Peripheral products featuring alternative entertainment
- General
  - Magazines
    - General
    - Sport-specific
- General electronic media
- Sports-oriented Web site access

products is important to venue operators, it represents a relatively small fraction of the total sales associated with this final category of sports products.

Box 16.4 illustrates the four subcategories and a few examples that fall into this final broad category of sports products.

Sporting goods may appear to change little over time, but the other variables of the marketing mix must be adjusted as changes occur in the marketing environment. Still, there are opportunities to modify the product itself. Many sports have a strong link to technology. Marketers introduce new models of their products that incorporate this new technology in order to gain a competitive advantage. Tennis rackets with a bigger sweet spot, golf clubs that allow the player to hit the ball farther, and skis that provide greater turning ability are some examples. Even skateboards have seen a new entry into the market; the new version is said to simulate the feel that one would experience while snowboarding.

Other opportunities exist when new sports enter a market. A few years ago, snowboards and in-line skates were virtually nonexistent. Then they surfaced as products for very small

FIGURE 16.3
The XFL Football

market niches; finally they evolved into products that were sought by a significant number of participants. Efforts to popularize new sports in foreign markets also provide opportunities to introduce new sporting goods. Nike is attempting to capitalize on efforts to bring rugby to the United States as well as the aforementioned effort to introduce American-style football to China.

Finally, new sports often use slightly different equipment. In some cases, the changes are cosmetic; for example, the XFL simply used a different color football, see Figure 16.3. As a result, many informal games of football were seen using the distinctive red and black ball. In other cases, the changes are more fundamental. The significant growth in women's basketball led to the sale of basketballs that are slightly smaller and lighter than the ones used by male players. Likewise, the growth in the number of female participants in softball has led manufacturers to introduce new headgear that accommodates ponytails and new chest protectors that better coincide with the female catcher's anatomy.

Perhaps the most significant changes for sports-related products fall within the *apparel* category. Not only are they subject to style changes, but new emphases on emerging target markets often accelerate changes in existing products as well as the introduction of new products. Another key influence is the decision by a popular team to change colors, logos, and the style of their uniforms. Such changes are important when fans are favorably predisposed to purchasing and wearing their favorite team's licensed apparel. Finally, participation rates also influence the demand for clothing products.

One noteworthy change that has impacted pro teams, college teams, and recreational players is the trend toward long, baggy basketball shorts. The old, tight shorts are obsolete. Conversely, some recreational sports have seen a retro movement. For example, many of the shirts ordered for today's bowling teams bear a strong resemblance to those worn 40 or 50 years ago. Tennis wear is strongly influenced by what the top professionals are wearing, especially the female market. Fashion trendsetters like Serena Williams have fundamentally changed tennis apparel, especially among young female recreational players.

> Changing the looks and logos is one of the most dangerous things to do in sports.

Many professional teams have changed uniform designs. While such changes may represent new marketing opportunities, there is also an element of risk for the marketer. According to one representative of the Collegiate Licensing Company, "changing the looks and logos is one of the most dangerous things to do in sports. Sports is a business that is steeped in tradition. Fans identify with a look or logo. If not done properly, it can be a major mistake." The NFL's Tampa Bay Buccaneers recently changed the color of their jerseys, the color of their helmets, and their primary "pirate" logo. The new image paid off with a substantial increase in sales. In the NBA, Michael Jordan's return from retirement featured a change in his uniform number. Many fans hurried to buy the new (number 45) Michael Jordan jersey. Other recent uniform changes in the NBA involved the Denver Nuggets and the Detroit Pistons.

New target markets also drive demand. Licensed merchandise targeting women has seen new sizes, designs, and colors introduced. New teams located in new cities are met with considerable excitement in the community; MLB's Washington Nationals began play in the 2005 season and are a good example of this phenomenon. New fans also come forward when the team is winning. These fans often exhibit their newfound enthusiasm by purchasing and wearing the team's logo merchandise. College basketball teams that make unexpected runs in the NCAA championship tournament invariably experience a significant upturn in the sale of apparel bearing university logos. For example, Oakland University's unexpected success in gaining entry to the 2005 NCAA tournament reportedly allowed the university to sell more apparel in three days than it had sold in the previous 12 months. New players also create opportunities. Whether the player is a newly acquired veteran such as Real Madrid's acquisition of David Beckham or a newly signed, much heralded rookie such as the NBA's LeBron James, fans often rush to be the first to own this new apparel.

> Oakland University's unexpected success in gaining entry to the 2005 NCAA tournament reportedly allowed the university to sell more apparel in three days than it had sold in the previous 12 months.

The marketing of apparel tends to be more effective when certain guidelines are followed. These guidelines are to

- Design sports apparel to fit a variety of silhouettes.
- Design and merchandise complete outfits.
- Actively market apparel to women.
- Promote sports apparel as a lifestyle product.
- Use advertising portraying men, women, and kids wearing apparel in casual situations.[12]

The third subcategory, *athletic shoes,* continues to grow. Much of this growth is the result of athlete endorsements. Many well-known athletes in a variety of sports have been used as spokespersons to encourage consumers to purchase their style of shoes. Manufacturers have also introduced a variety of new models. Specially designed shoes are used to target participants of specific sports. The industry that has long been criticized for pricing shoes beyond the reach of many consumers has recently seen the introduction of new, low-priced models. In an effort to capitalize on the retro trend, Reebok recently introduced a "classic" style of shoe that was promoted in advertisements featuring popular entertainers such as Queen Latifah and Samuel L. Jackson. The celebrity endorsements were considered key factors in Reebok's effort to reach younger black consumers.[13]

Finally, sports marketers have to consider strategies to sell an array of *sports-related products*. The New York Yankees and the Real Madrid soccer team have their own television networks. Teams often operate their own merchandise stores. While these stores feature apparel, they often sell a broad assortment of souvenirs. These include balls, books, autographed photos, and videos. These teams also sell a variety of nonsports products at their games. Products such as food, beverages, programs, and alternative entertainment like the Ferris wheel at Detroit's Comerica Park are but a few examples.

Other products that fall into this category involve various media. Many TV networks feature sports without focusing on a single sport or event. ESPN's recent initiatives have involved two high-definition options. Since they are not selling viewership for a single spectator sport, these marketing efforts fall within this final category of sports products. Magazines that are broadly based, as well as some that specialize in a particular sport, have also emerged in today's market. It is also appropriate to place these magazines in this final grouping of sports products. Similarly, there has been an explosion in the number of Web sites that feature sports news and require a subscription fee to be paid in order for the consumer to have access to the controlled portions of the site. ESPN's "Insider" pages at the espn.com Web site are one example of this trend.

Closing Capsule

It should now be evident that the sports product encompasses a broad spectrum of goods and services. No longer should you look at sports marketing as simply the task of selling tickets and putting fans in the seats. While building attendance at spectator sports is one key dimension of sports marketing, other marketers in this industry focus on establishing demand for participation sports and the final category of sports products that includes sporting goods, apparel, athletic shoes, and a variety of other sports-related products.

> No longer should you look at sports marketing as simply the task of selling tickets and putting fans in the seats.

The second key point is that sports marketing is much like any other industry in that the products offered to consumers comprise only one component of the organization's marketing strategy. Of paramount importance are the target markets that are designated by the organization. Then, for each target market, the organization must develop a corresponding marketing mix whereby the decisions made regarding price, promotion, and distribution work in harmony with the product in the effort to appeal to each target market. The implication is that sports marketers must use a differentiated strategy and develop marketing mixes that effectively impact each target market. In short, it is important to remember the earlier assertion that marketing strategy is like clothing; one size does not fit everyone.

Just as sports marketers have to continually assess their promotion, pricing, and distribution strategies, they must also consider modifications to their product strategy. New sports products are added; existing products are modified; products that have lost their economic viability are abandoned. Although this may sound easy, every product decision incorporates an element of risk.

Marketers of spectator sports make important decisions regarding both their core and peripheral products. When changing the core product, marketers alter the nature of the competition. Rules changes and new interpretations are often implemented in an effort to make the sport more appealing to fans. Of course, the risk is that these changes will not be universally accepted and that some fans will feel that the sport has been compromised. Thus, the consequences of any changes must be considered. This need to look to the future has led to the development of a set of guidelines regarding alterations to the core product.

In many cases, peripheral products represent a less risky approach to altering the spectator sports environment. These include alternative entertainment such as postgame concerts and promotions where products such as posters, caps, and bobblehead dolls are given to those in attendance.

For participation sports, one key objective is that of increasing the number of people who play the sport while also increasing the frequency with which current participants engage in the sport. The number of participants directly impacts the use of facilities designed to accommodate them. By increasing the number of racquetball players and how often they play, the effect is an increased demand for court time at private and public facilities. Marketers of participation sports have reached out to new target markets; they have organized new leagues and tournaments in an effort to increase participation. New geographic markets also represent opportunities for marketers of participation sports. Efforts to introduce football into the Chinese market mirror similar attempts to better penetrate the American market with rugby.

It should also be understood that increased participation directly influences sales in the other two broad categories of sports products. Since a sport's best fans are often those individuals who also play it, increasing the number of players has the potential of adding to the fan base of the spectator sport. Participants also purchase more sporting goods, apparel, athletic shoes, and a variety of other sports-related products such as souvenirs and sport-related magazines.

> Of particular note is the female segment, which continues to grow with higher participation rates and more women attending spectator sports events.

Sporting goods, apparel, and athletic shoes have grown as a result of appeals to new target markets. Of particular note is the female segment, which continues to grow with higher participation rates and more women attending spectator sports events. Sporting goods often change as a result of new technology. Apparel changes result from new styles being introduced and teams changing their logos or the color of their uniforms. There has been considerable expansion in the number of styles and the range of prices for shoes. Marketing efforts for sporting goods, apparel, and athletic shoes often feature endorsements by one or more of the sport's high-performing athletes.

This final category of sports products encompasses an array of sports-related products. Some of these products are purchased at a sports venue; examples include souvenirs and game-day programs. For products such as food and beverages, it may be a stretch to refer to them as sports products. Whether they truly fit this category or not, they represent an important stream of revenue for teams and venue operators.

> An organization can have a great product, but if it fails to develop distribution, pricing, and promotional strategies that are consistent with its product strategy and the target market, then the marketer is not fully capitalizing on the opportunities that exist.

The last two chapters have focused on two key components of marketing strategy: target marketing and product strategies. We will now continue to develop our understanding of how the remaining variables of the marketing mix are integrated with these two key components. An organization can have a great product, but if it fails to develop distribution, pricing, and promotional strategies that are consistent with its product strategy and the target market, then the marketer is not fully capitalizing on the opportunities that exist. Our discussion of marketing mix decisions will now shift to the distribution variable.

Review Questions

1. What is a product?
2. What is the augmented product? The ancillary components? The total product?
3. Discuss the following statement: "Marketing and advertising are synonymous."
4. What are the three broad categories of sports products?
5. What is the core product for spectator sports?
6. Briefly discuss the six guidelines for changing the core product.
7. What is the peripheral product? Why is it an important component of the sports marketer's product strategy?
8. Thinking about your favorite spectator sport, what changes in the core product do you recall? Do you think that these changes have been effective?
9. If you were to recommend changes to the core product and the peripheral product of the most popular sport in your country, what would they be?
10. What are the five potential decisions that result from a sports marketer's systematic assessment of its product assortment?

11. Review the examples given for strategies designed to increase participation in golf. Which do you think was the best strategy? Explain your reasoning.

12. What are the five basic guidelines for the marketing of sports apparel?

Endnotes

1. W. Sutton and I. Parrett, "Marketing the Core Product in Professional Team Sports in the United States," *Sport Marketing Quarterly* 1, no. 2 (1992), pp. 7–19.

2. Ibid.

3. G. Hunter, "Marketing Is the Name of the Game," *Detroit News,* August 10, 1997, pp. 1C, 3C.

4. T. Neff, "Bane of the Blind Referee," *Clear Channel,* August 1, 2002.

5. C. Britcher, "Understanding Referees," *SportBusiness International,* November 2004, p. 22.

6. D. Barrand, "Sportvision Wins Virtual Deal," October 29, 2003, www.sportbusiness.com/news/news/index?news_item_id=152962 (accessed October 13, 2005).

7. C. Britcher, "Cricket to Push into U.S.," March 26, 2004, www.sportbusiness.com/news/ index?news_item_id=154142 (accessed October 13, 2005).

8. C. Britcher, "U.S. Cricket League Unveiled," June 25, 2004, www.sportbusiness.com/news/index?news_item_id=154979 (accessed October 13, 2005).

9. "The First Tee," www.thefirsttee.org/Club/Scripts/Home/home.asp (accessed October 14, 2005).

10. J. Swanwick, "This Time It's Serious," *SportBusiness International,* October 2003, p. 30.

11. A. Chozick, "Chinese Fans Get Ready for Some 'Olive Ball,'" *The Wall Street Journal,* February 2, 2005, pp. B1, B3.

12. D. Fowler, "The Attributes Sought in Sports Apparel: A Ranking," *Journal of Marketing Theory and Practice,* Fall 1999, pp. 81–88.

13. A. Wong, "Back to the 'Classics': Old Shoes Give Reebok New Life," *The Wall Street Journal,* August 9, 2001, p. B1.

CHAPTER SEVENTEEN

Distribution Decisions in Sports Marketing

Learning Objectives

- Identify key venue and ticket issues for live audiences.
- Learn options for reaching media-based audiences.
- Learn how global strategies are spurring growth.
- Identify the different types of participation facilities.
- Review principles of distribution for sports merchandise.

The second component of the marketing mix we will examine involves the wide array of decisions that define the organization's distribution strategy. The previous chapter highlighted product decisions, and those strategies must be supported with a viable distribution network or else they are likely to fail. There is an often-quoted line from the motion picture *Field of Dreams:* "If you build it, he will come." Unfortunately, sports marketing is not that simple. And it is made even more difficult by the varied array of sports products for which marketers must develop appropriate distribution strategies.

Upon the completion of this chapter, readers should have a better understanding of the strategies and tools that marketers use to make spectator sports, participation sports, sporting goods, clothing, athletic shoes, and sports-related products more readily available to their target markets. This chapter will integrate distribution principles from traditional marketing with strategies specific to the sports marketing industry. Our discussion will begin with an examination of the market for spectator sports.

Spectator Sports

The marketing of spectator sports primarily involves two tasks: (1) attracting more fans to an event and (2) increasing the number of fans who witness the event via some electronic medium. For the live audience, the key decisions concern where special events should be staged, in which cities teams should be located, where a stadium should be located within a local community, the capacity of the venue, and the timing of the event or sports season. In addition, decisions concerning the distribution of tickets must also be made. While the traditional box office remains an important component of the ticket distribution strategy, a number of technology-based options have come to the forefront.

> One should never understate the value of the live audience; however, the growth of the rights fees paid by broadcasters has caused sports marketers to focus more attention on the distribution of video, audio, and text to fans.

One should never understate the value of the live audience; however, the growth of the rights fees paid by broadcasters has caused sports marketers to focus more attention on the distribution of video, audio, and text to fans who are not actually in attendance at the event venue. Advances in technology have created more distribution opportunities for today's sports marketers. The original broadcast medium of radio serves as an example of this phenomenon. The industry started the electronic dissemination of sports events via AM radio. Today, the options include FM radio, audio streaming on the Internet, and satellite delivery of the original signal to a special type of radio receiver. These distribution strategies will be discussed, but the initial focus will be on strategies designed to put fans in the seats.

Live Audience

When referring to the *live audience*, the focus is on those spectators who are attending the event in person. Not only do they provide a significant stream of revenue to the marketer, but they also contribute an emotional asset. They cheer, whistle, and boo when things that they cannot control occur during the course of competition. These spectators also purchase a variety of sports-related products such as refreshments and souvenirs at the event. They also serve as a visual prop for video broadcasts. No organizer wants TV viewers at home to see the event being contested in a venue dominated by empty seats. As a result, marketers of spectator sports must make distribution decisions that are designed to support their product and increase the number of spectators in attendance at the event venue. A key consideration in this regard concerns the venue at which these events and competitions will take place.

Venue Issues

For special events such as the Super Bowl, various all-star games, national championships such as the NCAA's Final Four in college basketball, and international events like the Olympic Games and the various World Cup competitions, a critical decision is the *location of the competition*. Cities often declare themselves to be candidates for an event and compete with other cities vying for the right to host that event. The International Olympic Committee (IOC) recently selected the location of the 2012 Olympic Games from five candidate cities; the five cities with this high aspiration were London, Madrid, Moscow, New York City, and Paris. Each city engaged in an aggressive marketing campaign designed to highlight its strengths in an effort to convince the IOC to select it for the 2012 games. Ultimately, the IOC selected London as the host city. In essence, the decision regarding the host city represents a distribution decision. Each city had a vested interest and sought to engage in promotional activities designed to influence the IOC's decision. Figure 17.1 illustrates one of the promotional efforts used by Beijing in its successful marketing efforts aimed at being selected to host the 2008 Summer Olympic Games.

Olympic candidate cities seek both the prestige associated with the staging of the prestigious event and the economic impact that will result from the influx of fans from all over the world. Prior to making its decision, the IOC evaluates each candidate city on several criteria. One key criterion is each city's infrastructure. Does the city have the actual venues required to stage the competition? If not, is the city willing to commit the resources required to build new facilities prior to the event? Is there adequate public transportation? Is there an adequate facility to house the athletes? Are there enough hotel rooms to accommodate the fans and the media? If the answer to any of these questions is no, the likelihood of being awarded the right to stage the event is greatly diminished, if not completely eliminated. These same questions must be addressed for any major competition

FIGURE 17.1
Promotional Effort by the Beijing Organizing Committee for the Olympic Games

that routinely moves from one location to another, not just the Olympics. In an unusual solution to a shortage of hotel rooms, the NFL accepted Jacksonville's bid to host the 2005 Super Bowl based upon the city's plan to use leased cruise ships docked on a nearby river as temporary lodging for visitors.[1] While decisions in regard to special events such as the Super Bowl and the Olympics are important components of the spectator sports environment, more common issues involve the location of professional teams.

One fundamental distribution decision is that of determining *which city or cities deserve a franchise in one of the many professional leagues*. New leagues are founded and numerous franchises are awarded to some of the aspiring cities. Existing leagues expand and cities compete for these new franchises. Leagues often use expansion as a means of achieving broader geographic coverage. The NHL's most recent expansions primarily involved warm-weather cities where hockey had yet to gain a foothold. Similarly, Rugby Union's expansion of the Super 12 to the Super 14 beginning in 2006 included the awarding of a franchise to the city of Perth. Officials hope that the first team in Western Australia will help the game grow by adding to its fan base.

> Leagues often use expansion as a means of achieving broader geographic coverage.

Existing leagues are often faced with the need to relocate an existing team to a new location. These leagues must consider the ability that each candidate city has in adding to the sport's fan base and attracting spectators to the stadium or arena.

Another venue-related issue involves the *construction of new stadia and arenas*. When cities are selected for new or relocated franchises, a common requirement is the construction of a new facility. In the case of an existing franchise, an old, obsolete structure that had been used by the local team may be replaced by a new state-of-the-art facility. When these construction decisions are made, a key issue involves the precise *location* within the geographic area. Because of the impact on jobs and the increased demand for services provided by local restaurants, bars, hotels, and parking lots, different parts of the community often vie for construction to take place in their neighborhood. Conversely, because of traffic and the strain on local resources, some communities lobby against having it built in their area. But new stadia are inevitable, and several key questions must be answered. Will it be located in the central business district or in a suburban location? The trend toward the suburbs in the United States seems to be giving way to a movement back to downtown locations. New facilities such as San Diego's Petco Park, San Francisco's SBC Park, and the FedEx Forum in Memphis are examples. Such construction is often supported with public tax monies as a component of a downtown revitalization plan.

In the United States, the majority of the major professional teams play in new facilities. Some of the teams that don't have new venues play in old but venerable stadia steeped in tradition. Fans would oppose any effort to replace historic facilities like Boston's Fenway Park or Chicago's Wrigley Field with new stadia. In Detroit, the move from Tiger Stadium was condemned by many fans who saw it as an abandonment of the team's heritage. Five years after the move to a new ballpark, Tiger Stadium still stands as local officials seek proposals on how to use it to create a positive impact on the community and the neighborhood economy. Meanwhile, many local bars, restaurants, and parking lots around the old stadium have been forced to close because of a lack of customers.

With the American professional marketplace creating fewer opportunities for stadium designers and construction companies, the focus has begun to shift to two significant growth markets. There are a number of opportunities in the global market as new stadia proposals are surfacing in Europe, Asia, the South Pacific, Canada, and Mexico. At the same time, colleges and universities are seen as the next growth area for new facilities in the American market. Clearly, there are many groups that have a vested interest in these location decisions. Local politicians, citizens, fans, and players all exert considerable influence on those who ultimately make these decisions.

It is apparent that venue location is also a key strategic component of a team or league's distribution strategy. It must serve the target market and possess an infrastructure that adequately addresses traffic and parking issues. When assessing the reasons for low attendance at the home games of the NBA's New York Nets and the NHL's New Jersey Devils, much of the blame was directed toward the location of the arena in which the two teams play. It was described as an old, "antiseptic" arena with poor highway access, no access via public transportation, and inadequate parking. As a consequence, officials of the two teams began to lobby for a new, more conveniently located arena.[2]

Any new arena should also provide good sightlines so that those in attendance have an unobstructed view of the action. Other considerations include the number and location of luxury suites available and how to accommodate the members of the TV, radio, and print media who broadcast or report the action that takes place within the venue. But as important as these venue decisions are, they are not the only ones that the marketer of spectator sports faces.

For many years, the construction of stadia emphasized multipurpose facilities. In the United States, old stadia such as Philadelphia's Veterans Stadium and Cincinnati's Riverfront Stadium could be adapted for both football and baseball. Each of these stadia has been demolished and replaced within the past three years. Internationally, many facilities could be used for cricket, rugby, and Aussie rules football. While the obvious advantage was the cost savings, such facilities were not without their critics. The configuration often resulted in unusual dimensions or sightlines that were not focused directly on the action. In light of these shortcomings, *most new stadia are being built with a single sport in mind.*[3] Although the facilities may be used for other events such as concerts, most stadia today are constructed with a specific focus. Consequently, it is not unusual for a city to have two or more stadia and arenas within its borders. When this is the case, the facilities are often built side-by-side in order to take advantage of an area's infrastructure. The cluster of facilities that includes Philadelphia's Citizens Bank Park for Major League Baseball, its Lincoln Financial Field that is home to the NFL's Eagles, and the Wachovia Center that plays host to the city's NBA and NHL teams illustrates this phenomenon. Clearly, the trend today is the construction of stadia designed to maximize the fan's enjoyment of a specific sport.

> The trend today is the construction of stadia designed to maximize the fan's enjoyment of a specific sport.

Another decision concerns the *capacity of the facility*. How many spectators should it seat? The larger the stadium, the higher the construction costs. But smaller facilities may represent an opportunity cost in that the demand for seats may exceed the supply. The task is one of providing adequate seating to accommodate fans while keeping seating scarce enough to encourage season ticket and advance ticket sales. In this regard, new stadia for football and baseball have tended to feature lower capacities. This phenomenon is especially prevalent in baseball, where teams have moved from multipurpose stadia to ones built expressly for the sport. The typical capacity of a new baseball stadium is approximately 40,000, whereas the old facilities would generally seat in excess of 50,000 spectators. NFL teams have another capacity-related issue to consider when conceptualizing a new stadium. With the NFL's TV contract, the blackout rule prohibits any team's home game from being broadcast in its local market if it is not sold out at least 72 hours prior to the scheduled start. The desire to allow local fans to watch their team on TV was one factor that led the Detroit Lions to move from the 80,000-seat Pontiac Silverdome to the new 65,000-seat Ford Field.

> With the NFL's TV contract, the blackout rule prohibits any team's home game from being broadcast in its local market if it is not sold out at least 72 hours prior to the scheduled start.

The final consideration for the live audience involves the *timing of the event*. This includes dates and times. Some schedules are fairly well established with a league's season beginning and ending around the same dates each year. Other special events are more varied. Some leagues play their annual all-star games during the course of the regular season; others stage theirs at the end of the season. Other competitions such as the Olympic Games and the World Cup of Soccer are subject to considerably more fluctuation. Even the weather can be a consideration. Weather seasons differ in the Northern and Southern Hemispheres. The 2000 Summer Olympics in Sydney, Australia, that began on September 15 actually saw its opening ceremonies take place at the end of the Australian winter. The dates were selected more on the basis of tradition than on the season of the year.

In other cases, competitions are scheduled in an effort to limit conflicts with other events that attract similar target markets. Some spectator sports have also begun to alter their schedules in regard to the time of day. Most spectator sports are scheduled during the evenings on Monday through Friday, whereas there is a mix between day and night for events staged on Saturday and Sunday. In one effort to boost attendance, the Sydney Turf Club moved its regularly scheduled Wednesday races to Sunday. The move paid off with significant increases in attendance and wagering.

As seen in the preceding discussion, marketers of spectator sports have a significant set of issues to consider in their efforts to maximize their live audience. Box 17.1 provides an overview of the set of decisions that form the basis for their distribution strategy.

Tickets

The event itself is the product for the marketer of spectator sports, and access to it must be controlled by a ticket distribution strategy that is effective in reaching the organization's

VENUE-RELATED DISTRIBUTION DECISIONS   17.1

Event Decisions
- Which city—location of events and teams

Stadium Decisions
- Where to locate within the selected city
- Is a new facility needed?
  - Single-purpose or multipurpose
  - Seating capacity

Timing Decisions
- Traditional timeframe or scheduling flexibility
  - Time or year
  - Days of week
  - Time of day
  - Coordinated with other types of events

target markets. Recent advances in technology have greatly enhanced the ability to make the purchase of tickets more convenient for fans, regardless of how far they are from the event venue. Today's fans have many options beyond the traditional box office.

Despite these technological advances, marketers cannot abandon the *box office*. Fans may walk up and purchase advance tickets for a future date or tickets for an event scheduled for later that same day. The box office also serves as a will-call point where tickets that are prepurchased can be collected. From the fans' perspective, there are two major limitations associated with purchasing tickets at the traditional box office. Many fans who attend an event do not live in close proximity to the venue. Thus, it is impractical for them to go to the box office in person. Second are the hours of operation. The box office may be open when most fans themselves are working. Other common hours of operation are those immediately preceding another event at the venue. Going to the box office at that time might entail significant traffic and require the ticket purchaser to pay the prevailing rate for event parking. Both of these barriers represent disincentives for fans to purchase advance tickets at the venue itself. Still, for games and events that do not typically sell out, the box office is essential for *walk-up sales*.

In addition to personal service at the box office, most venues will take *phone orders*. Tickets purchased via the phone can be delivered to the fan, or they can be collected at a will-call location. Again, the box office's hours must be taken into consideration. It should be noted that this service is often outsourced, so the ticket buyer may not actually be speaking to anyone at the box office. Yet another concern for the buyers is that the phone call may not be toll-free, so some fans may worry about running up a large phone bill while waiting on hold prior to being served by a representative of the box office. The venue may opt to add a toll-free number for the convenience of the customer. The added cost for these transactions may be added to the cost of the tickets in the form of a service fee. However, dealing directly with the box office is still generally the lowest-cost alternative for the ticket buyer.

The last few years have seen the emergence of *ticket retailers and brokers* such as Ticketmaster and Ticketek. These intermediaries are authorized to sell tickets on behalf of the event organizers. They often have facilities in a number of retail stores where consumers can check availability, compare seats, and purchase tickets. These retailers and brokers may also accept orders over the phone and through their Web sites. Purchasers pay the face value of the tickets plus additional fees. Typical fees include an order-processing fee that is imposed on each transaction and a convenience fee that is added to the price of each ticket. One recent Ticketmaster transaction for two NBA tickets included a $3.90 processing fee and $10 in convenience charges. So while sellers of this type greatly enhance the sports marketer's ability to reach potential ticket buyers, some complaints regarding excessive fees are inevitable.

Another type of retailer that has emerged is the one that *buys tickets and attempts to resell them at a profit*. Other similar organizations work more as an *agent or broker* in an effort to bring buyers and sellers together. For example, Stubhub will broker the sale of one's excess or otherwise unused tickets to fans who are seeking access to the specific events. In many cases, these organizations are not working on behalf of the event organizers. Under these circumstances, they are generally classified as unauthorized sellers, and fans are often warned of potential dangers while being discouraged from purchasing tickets from them. As such, these ticket sources are not part of the event's distribution strategy, but they do impact the market. Their presence has caused many events to impose limits on the quantity of tickets that can be purchased in any single transaction. Additionally, some of the authorized sellers on the Internet require the purchaser to input a specific entry in an effort to eliminate automated purchases that are made by these unauthorized brokers and resellers who often seek to acquire a significant number of tickets for the express purpose of reselling them at a profit. The terms *scalper* and *tout* are commonly used to designate these unauthorized sellers.

Each of the aforementioned types of sellers has discovered the opportunities presented by the Internet. Teams, leagues, event organizers, and sports organizations typically incorporate a *ticket link* on their Web site. An array of authorized retailers, as well as many unauthorized resellers, have also added Internet sales to their more traditional walk-up and telephone options. Not only can tickets be delivered to or collected at a will-call location by the purchaser, but they can also be printed using the ticket holder's own computer and printer. As with today's printed tickets, self-printed tickets are bar-coded. Holders seeking admission will have their tickets scanned in order to assure that no duplicates have been reproduced in an effort to defraud the event or the purchaser.

> Teams, leagues, event organizers, and sports organizations typically incorporate a ticket link on their Web site.

Several teams and events have recently added an Internet-based service for season ticket holders who want to redistribute their own tickets. The original purchaser can enter a user ID and password to transfer ownership of tickets to another person. The recipient receives an e-mail specifying the event, the date, and the seats that he or she is now entitled to use. This e-mail also incorporates a bar code. The original tickets are voided, and entrance will be granted only to the recipient who uses the e-mail as a surrogate ticket; thus, any effort to use the original ticket to gain entrance to the event will be denied. It can reasonably be argued that this strategy is not actually part of the marketer's distribution strategy. However, by facilitating the transfer of ownership, the marketer reduces the number of empty seats associated with *no-shows* and brings in more fans who may pay for parking and purchase other products such as souvenirs and refreshments at the venue.

Box 17.2 provides a summary of the types of outlets used to sell and distribute tickets. Event organizers must implement the strategies that are most effective in the task of reaching their own target markets. It is evident that purchasers have far more options today than they

TICKET DISTRIBUTION OPTIONS 17.2

- Venue box office
  - Walk-up
  - Phone
- Authorized retailers or agents/brokers
- Unauthorized resellers and brokers
- Internet
- E-mail transfer

had in previous years. The effect is that the added convenience of the expanded distribution network provides marketers with more opportunities to sell tickets.

With the discussion of decisions concerning the live audience and the distribution of tickets now complete, the focus will shift to those fans who witness a game through electronic media. This category of fans is best characterized as *media-based*.

Media-Based Fans

Advertisers continue to seek better vehicles for reaching their target markets. Sports fans continue to grow in number, and they represent a number of demographic segments that marketers find attractive. But a key consideration for sports marketers is the rights fees paid by the various media organizations. If a sport or event can increase its media-based audience, then it can command higher fees from the broadcast media.

Increasing the media-based audience also has a positive impact on both public relations and the live audience. For example, viewers who watched a game on TV last night are likely to discuss it during informal conversations during work and leisure time. The ability to provide the fan with access to game broadcasts is viewed favorably by the local fans and news media. To the extent that this enthusiasm adds to the level of interest, then more of these media-based fans will eventually find their way to the venue as part of the live audience. Among the broadcast media available to sports marketers are television, radio, and the Internet. Two emerging options are cellular phones and smart watches. Each of these five media will be discussed on the following pages.

Television

The most prominent medium for the transmission of the spectator sport product is still television. Yet TV itself has undergone a dramatic transformation over the past 30 years. Many years ago, the dominant delivery mode for TV signals was *free-to-air TV*. This generally included a small number of local affiliates of national networks, an educational channel, and one or two small-budget independent channels. As such, there were few options for sports properties that sought to have their events broadcast to either a local or national audience, and there was certainly no meaningful way to broadcast a live or recorded event to an international audience. As a result, most sports broadcasts were limited to weekend slots within their own local or national markets.

In the United States, early sports broadcasts on free-to-air network TV included *Friday Night at the Fights,* the Saturday afternoon broadcast of MLB's *Game of the Week,* and the NFL's *Monday Night Football.* In Canada, the Canadian Broadcasting Corporation has long been recognized for its Saturday night broadcast of the NHL's *Hockey Night in Canada.* From these examples, it is apparent that there were some early efforts to move sports into prime time.

The 1970s saw the emergence of cable TV within the mass market. This has been followed up by new technology that delivers TV signals to the viewer's home via satellite. The key change that emanated from these delivery systems is the fragmentation of the viewing audience. Consumers had more channels to choose from, and many of the stations began to focus on programming that appealed to more narrowly defined target markets. It was often stated that television had begun to move from broadcasting to *narrowcasting*. However, in some international markets, even subscribers to cable and satellite TV still have a limited number of channels to watch.

In 1979, the industry witnessed the emergence of ESPN, the first dedicated national sports network. Newer networks such as Fox Sports and Sky Sports are now important members of this genre of TV networks. A key point for networks of this type is that they would be characterized as *general sports networks*. Rather than featuring a single sport, they include a wide variety of sports competitions, sports news, and sports-oriented entertainment such as motion pictures. As such, they have provided opportunities for broadcasts of niche sports such as college lacrosse as well as alternative outlets for prime-time broadcasts of more popular sports such as football and basketball. Their success has produced significant revenues, thereby allowing them to pay the higher rights fees that are commanded by the major sports leagues and events.

As the broadcasting capacity continued to expand, more networks aimed at specific target markets were founded. Some of these networks focus on fans of specific sports. Their broadcast content tends to feature a single sport, often 24/7. One of the early entries in this *specific sport network* category was The Golf Channel. Another prominent network is the Speed Channel, which features motor sports. More recent entries to this category are the Rugby Channel in New Zealand, the Fox Soccer Channel, and the Tennis Channel. These networks attract a relatively small number of viewers, but the low ratings are offset by the fact that they attract avid fans of a specific sport. Programming that has no chance of appearing on major networks can take advantage of the opportunities presented by these niche marketers. The success of these specific sport networks has led to the establishment of networks by prominent leagues. Examples in the United States include NBA TV Daily and the NFL Total Access Network. More recently, it was announced that Major League Baseball plans to launch its own Baseball Channel.[4]

> Programming that has no chance of appearing on major networks can take advantage of the opportunities presented by these niche marketers.

Satellite and cable delivery systems have also given rise to programming that is best characterized as a *sports tier*. Virtually every game in the major sports is broadcast somewhere, if only to the local markets represented by the competing teams. Moreover, the signal is available for any company that is willing to pay for the right to redistribute it. This allows viewers access to broadcasts of a large number of games that are available on the sports tier to which they subscribe. In the United States, fans have access to the NFL's Sunday Ticket, MLB's Extra Innings, NHL's Center Ice, the NBA League Pass, and other tiers that provide access to a large number of college football games, college basketball games, Barclay's English Premier League games, and MLS soccer games. Clearly, the avid fan of any particular sport has an overwhelming supply of games available for viewing. The cable and satellite providers must pay a fee for the broadcast rights, and they generally sell season-long programming to subscribers. Typical charges to viewers range from about $69 for less popular programming such as MLS's Direct Kick to $299 for Barclay's English Premier League soccer. Figure 17.2 illustrates a promotion used by DIRECTV in its efforts to sell subscriptions to the NFL Sunday Ticket tier.

Recently, the television industry has begun to see the establishment of networks that emphasize programming germane to a single team. These *team-dedicated networks* can be

FIGURE 17.2
DIRECTV Promotion for NFL Tier

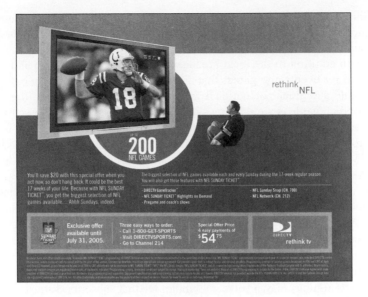

effective in large metropolitan markets or where teams have a large regional, national, or international fan base. Two examples are the YES Network and the Manchester United Network. The YES Network features live broadcasts of games, replays of recent games, replays of classic games from the past, news, and talk shows that focus on MLB's New York Yankees. The Manchester United Network features programming involving the world-famous soccer team. Although these networks do not necessarily feature a single team 24/7, such a focus does represent a significant portion of their broadcasting content.

The final category of TV programming is *pay-per-view (PPV)*. The PPV era began in earnest in 1980 with the championship boxing match between Sugar Ray Leonard and Roberto Durand. Viewers paid $15 for access to this broadcast. Boxing has continued to be at the forefront of this medium. More recently, a 49-second fight between Mike Tyson and Clifford Etienne drew more than 100,000 PPV buys at $24.95 per subscriber.[5] Another sport that generates significant revenues from PPV is wrestling. Although pay-per-view is currently confined to a limited number of special events, there is a growing concern that major events may move in that direction. Instead of free-to-air TV, events such as the Olympics, the finals of the World Cup of Soccer, and the Super Bowl may be moved to the PPV format. Concerns such as these have led some countries to pass laws that forbid the removal of key sports events from free-to-air TV. For example, Australia's *antisiphoning law* requires events that are special to Australia citizens to be broadcast on free-to-air TV. As a result, events such as the Australian Open will remain available at no charge to all Australian viewers.

> Although pay-per-view is currently confined to a limited number of special events, there is a growing concern that major events may move in that direction.

Clearly, there are many TV options available for viewers and broadcasters. However, TV is not the only electronic medium available for the broadcast of the spectator sports product.

Radio

AM radio has long been and remains the primary carrier of games involving local professional and college teams. To use the TV terminology, such broadcasts represent free-to-air radio. Virtually every professional team has a contract to air its games over local AM radio. As broadcasts signals have gotten stronger, the effective range within which listeners can hear the broadcast has increased substantially. When teams are seeking a broadcast partner, they often limit their negotiations to those stations that have the most powerful transmission signals. A weak broadcast signal simply does not reach the maximum potential number of media-based fans.

In addition to the local broadcasts, many stations pick up and rebroadcast the audio feed for events and games that do not involve local teams. In essence, this strategy can create a regional or national radio broadcast. For example, the NFL's Monday Night Football game is aired over a syndicate of radio stations that essentially provides national coverage for each game. These local stations pay for the rights to rebroadcast the signals from a syndicated source as well as the right to originate broadcasts for local teams. While FM radio represents an option, most sports programming on free-to-air radio remains on AM stations.

One format that has grown significantly in the past three years is *satellite radio*. These audio signals are transmitted via satellite and can be received by subscribers who pay for the service. At the forefront of this trend are two providers: XM and Sirius. They provide many audio options for subscribers. The typical package includes classic rock, classical music, rap, show tunes, jazz, talk radio, soul, and country music. More recently, the providers began to include sports programming. Much like a sports tier on TV, access to sports stations may involve a premium fee that subscribers must pay.

> Given the technological superiority of satellite radio over traditional AM and FM signals, the future of sports broadcasting will likely involve more emphasis on this new transmission alternative.

The major advantage of satellite radio is that the signal does not fade as the listener's car moves from one city to another. The format has proven popular enough that it is now offered in a more traditional type of radio. No longer is the signal available only to those listening in a motor vehicle. At last report, Sirius had 1.1 million subscribers and XM subscribers exceeded 3.3 million in number.[6] Prominent Sirius broadcast rights in the sports product category include Wimbledon, an all-NFL station, the English Premier League, the NBA, the U.S. Formula One Radio Network, and the NHL. XM also owns some valuable broadcast rights, including almost every game played in Major League Baseball, select NASCAR races, college basketball and football games of three prominent conferences, and NFL games. It also announced the 2005 launch of a Spanish-language sports station in an effort to reach the Hispanic segment. Given the technological superiority of satellite radio over traditional AM and FM signals, the future of sports broadcasting will likely involve more emphasis on this new transmission alternative.

Internet

The growth of the Internet will continue to provide new opportunities to the marketers of spectator sports. Increased bandwidth and the resultant increase in transmission speed have made audio and video streaming more practical. This has given fans all over the world the opportunity to watch or listen to games involving their favorite teams, no matter how far they are from the event itself.

Some of the programming may be free. For example, games that originate on free-to-air radio are often available on the radio station's Web site. Other programming requires a subscription fee. Some of the major sports leagues make it available on a one-game, monthly, or season-long basis. Examples include broadcasts of MLB and NBA games that are available through any Internet service provider (ISP). In other cases, one ISP will pay for the exclusive right to broadcast an event or league's games, thereby gaining a monopoly on those sports products. An example of this arrangement is T-Online's contract that provides it with the exclusive right to broadcast soccer games played by German first-division teams. Sports marketing on the Internet will be covered more extensively Chapter 21.

Cellular Phones

It may be difficult to believe, but cell phones have been hailed as the next broadcast medium to emerge for the distribution of sports programming and information.[7] Globally, cell phones have achieved high levels of penetration, especially among younger consumers who are also more likely to be sports fans.[8] Some kids and young adults seem to never be far from their cell phone.

> Cell phones have been viewed as the ultimate medium for one-to-one marketing.

The fact that new phones have a screen, color video capability, and text capability means that they are a potential broadcast medium. AT&T Wireless capitalized on this opportunity by transmitting text messages to its subscribers during the 2004 Olympics in Athens. By 2005, cellular providers were including video transmissions featuring sports highlights to the tiny screens as one of the services available to cellular subscribers. Look for advances in technology that will be used to reach the 200 million cellular phone subscribers in China as well as the growing European market.[9] And while the emphasis seems to be on mass markets, cell phones have been viewed as the ultimate medium for one-to-one marketing. Each cellular customer can select his or her own content. Marketers often refer to this as *mass customization*.

Smart Watches

While this category may still be viewed as a novelty, Microsoft has developed a new *smart watch* that can deliver the latest news, scores, and statistics to those wearing it. Microsoft's strategic alliance with ESPN provides coverage only in North America, but the marketer has its sights set on the global market. According to a Microsoft spokesperson, "the MSN Direct service is currently designed to broadcast text and graphics. That said, the possibilities for MSN Direct are boundless."[10] Can the transmission of video be a component of the next generation of smart watches? Stay tuned for future developments.

There are many options for reaching media-based fans. Box 17.3 provides an overview of the options available to sports marketers.

Market Development Strategies

One of the growth strategies often employed by mainstream marketers is that of market development. Implementation of this strategy involves no new products; rather, it is achieved by entering new markets with the organization's existing product assortment. In other words, one or more new target markets are designated with the objective of establishing interest and demand for existing products. An example outside of the sports environment is the growth that Coca-Cola has achieved via its entry into emerging international markets such as China and Vietnam. Similar opportunities exist for sports marketers.

The designation of any defined segment as a new target market represents the initial step of a market development strategy. For example, when the golf industry designated the female segment as a target, the effort involved selling the traditional game of golf to a new market: women.

Other efforts at market development involve entry into a new country. Whether the objective is to attract more fans for the live audience or to increase the number of media-based fans, international expansion is a viable strategy. Even though the marketer may be exporting a mature product, it represents a new option for members of these new target markets. For example, the game of rugby is now being aggressively marketed in parts of the United States. While fans in Australia, England, France, New Zealand, and South Africa are familiar with the intricacies of one of their favorite sports, the marketers' first

OPTIONS FOR REACHING MEDIA-BASED FANS 17.3

- TV
  - Free-to-air
  - General sports networks
  - Specific sport networks
  - Sports tier option
  - Team-dedicated networks
  - Pay-per-view
- Radio
  - Free-to-air
  - Satellite
- Internet
  - General radio
  - Sport specific audio and video streaming
- Cellular phones
- Smart watches

task in the United States is to create awareness and interest in a game about which most Americans know very little. Without this interest, members of this new target market are unlikely to either attend a game or take advantage of any of the electronic media to watch or listen to the game.

> Whether the objective is to attract more fans for the live audience or to increase the number of media-based fans, international expansion is a viable strategy.

The saturation of domestic markets has caused many sports marketers to focus on international markets. Furthermore, the emergence of global media such as the Internet, satellite TV, and satellite radio have provided access to international markets that were previously inaccessible. Consequently, many spectator sports have grown via market development strategies that have involved entry into one or more new markets.

When the decision to implement a market development strategy has been made, there are several specific ways in which it can be implemented. To illustrate these techniques, several examples are delineated on the following pages. Some of these examples have already been implemented; others are under consideration for future efforts. These include efforts designed to increase the live audience as well as the media-based audience.

Global Competition

Opportunities to compete in new international locations represent viable options for many spectator sports. It is particularly applicable for special events and for sports that are contested in a series of competitions held in different locations.

Many of the special events are staged regularly, but the location changes each time. Quite often, efforts to grow a sport are represented by staging an established tournament in a new location. In other cases, new tournaments are developed with the purpose of showcasing the sport and encouraging international participation. The Olympics may be the ultimate global competition. The NBA formed its first American Dream Team and won the gold medal at the 1992 games in Barcelona. As a result of this international exposure, the NBA has gained a foothold in Europe and Australia and is now seeing an influx of international players. Future strategies under consideration by the NBA include teams holding their preseason camps in Europe and the possibility of locating a team in Europe by 2010.[11]

The NHL has sought to emulate the NBA's strategy and success. Starting with the 1998 Olympic Games in Nagano, NHL officials began a practice of actually shutting down the league for a time and allowing players to represent their countries in the Olympic tournament. The NHL commissioner indicated that the league's long-term goal was to increase exposure to the sport and to add to the fan base.

Other examples of global competition include efforts in the 1990s to stage professional tennis tournaments in China. And while soccer has already achieved a measure of success in the American market, FIFA has begun to consider holding the Soccer World Club Championship in the United States in an effort to further enhance fan interest. This would represent a continuation of FIFA's effort that began by staging the 1994 World Cup of Soccer in nine American cities.

NASCAR recently founded a new organization that will focus on building interest in stock car racing in Mexico. These efforts include the initial NASCAR Busch Series race in Mexico City in 2005 and the launch of Desafio Corona, the country's first national stock car series. In addition to NASCAR Mexico, the organization also launched NASCAR Canada. As a result of these efforts, NASCAR now has a strong and unified presence across North America.[12]

Recently, there have been discussions regarding modifications to the Ryder Cup golf competition. Until 1979, the tournament featured a team from the United States against a combined team from Great Britain and Ireland. Beginning with the 1979 event, it became the Americans against the Europeans. The European team has included players such as Seve Ballesteros, a Spaniard who had previously been ineligible to play. Now there is talk of expanding the European team to include the rest of the world. With highly ranked golfers from countries such as South Africa, Fiji, Australia, Japan, and Argentina, many see this as a logical move. The international participants would create a global interest and fuel an increase in the live audience as well as the media-based audience. Undoubtedly, the tournament venues would ultimately include golf courses in countries outside of the United States and Europe.

The Middle East is seen as a fertile ground for growth. With high per capita income, countries like the UAE, Qatar, Oman, and Saudi Arabia have emerged as opportunities. With the recent political changes in Iraq, sports marketers are interested in exploring future opportunities there. The Middle East has recently hosted its first Formula One Grand Prix, a European PGA Tour event, a WTA tennis tournament, and World Superbikes. The power and wealth of countries in this region of the world are simply too large to ignore.

In some cases, completely new international competitions are established with the growth objective in mind. The inaugural A1 Grand Prix was positioned as the World Cup of Motorsport. Based in the United Arab Emirates, the competition took place in 2005 and 2006 at several racing venues across the globe. The inaugural World Baseball Classic was played in 2006. This competition, won by Japan, was also positioned as a "World Cup" event with games being played in the United States, Latin America, and Asia. Figure 17.3 illustrates one of the promotions used in this effort to broaden the interest in baseball.

While new international competitions represent the most common market development strategy, other approaches to growth can also be effective. A few examples will illustrate these additional strategies.

Established leagues may choose to expand by locating a new team in a new country. For instance, the aforementioned example of the NBA's consideration of locating an expansion team in Europe is one potential market development strategy. MLB has reportedly considered

FIGURE 17.3
2006 World Baseball Classic Promotion

both Mexico and Puerto Rico for future teams, even though baseball's earlier entries into the Canadian market produced mixed results. There has been some measure of success in Toronto, but the Montreal team suffered from fan apathy; as a result of the low attendance, the Montreal team was moved to Washington, DC, at the start of the 2005 season. Super 12 Rugby considered locating one of its two new franchises that began play in the new Super 14 in Japan. Representatives from Argentina and a combined Pacific Island consortium of Fiji, Tonga, and Samoa were also given some consideration.

Another approach is the creation of an entire new league. For example, the NFL has established NFL Europe. Not only does the league appeal to American expatriates living abroad, but it has also been effective in attracting new European fans. The primary countries involved are Germany, the Netherlands, and Scotland.

Established leagues may opt to schedule games in countries beyond their current borders. These may be exhibition games or part of the regular season schedule. The former Montreal Expos played 22 of their "home" games in Puerto Rico during the 2004 season. MLB has often scheduled exhibition games in Mexico. The league also opened the 2004 baseball season with games played in Japan, and recent discussions have addressed the possibility of MLB scheduling a limited number of games in Italy. The NHL once opened its season with two games in Japan in what was a precursor to the 1998 Olympics and the initial participation of NHL players on their countries' Olympic teams. Similar consideration is also being given to staging an actual NFL game at the new Wembley Stadium in London as well as playing a game in China prior to the 2008 Olympics in Beijing. Another sign that China has gained importance as a sports market is the NBA's decision to stage of its first China Games in 2004. The event featured two teams, the Sacramento Kings and the Houston Rockets, playing preseason games in Beijing and Shanghai.[13] Clearly, the NBA was attempting to capitalize on the presence of its own Chinese superstar, Yao Ming, on the Houston team.

> The former Montreal Expos played 22 of their "home" games in Puerto Rico during the 2004 season.

Secondary competitions are often staged abroad. Part of the NBA's strategy has involved these types of events. The McDonald's Open in Japan featured an NBA team in a round-robin tournament against some of the best teams from Europe. Similarly, the two organizations have established "Basketball without Borders," an effort that features local tournaments and NBA-themed attractions staged in Asia, Latin America, and Europe.[14] Events such as these tend to be sporadically scheduled, but they do represent an opportunity for a sport to gain exposure and to develop interest in new international markets.

Global Media

There have also been numerous efforts to raise the profile of a sport by attracting new media-based fans in new international markets. The proliferation of global media such as the Internet, satellite TV, and satellite radio are fueling this growth strategy. Despite the problems associated with events being staged several time zones away from the target audience, more live events are being broadcast than ever before. Prime properties are finding their way to the commercial airwaves.

Setanta Sports broadcasts Super 14 Rugby to North America. Soccer has found its way to sports networks such as the Fox Soccer Channel and a number of PPV outlets. Residents of Mexico can watch the Premier League live. The American Sports Network is now operating as a premium service in the United Kingdom. In 2003, the network aired more than 250 baseball games, 200 basketball games, 200 ice hockey games, 85 college football games, and some NASCAR events.

The Euro 2004 soccer tournament and the NFL's 2006 Super Bowl were broadcast in more than 200 countries. In 2004, the Super Bowl was broadcast live in China for the first time. The NFL also recently signed a contract with DIRECTV Latin America that grants the satellite service provider with exclusive distribution rights to the NFL Sunday Ticket sport tier in Mexico, Brazil, Columbia, and Chile. The NBA has partnered with Alhurra Television to broadcast a top NBA match-up each week in the Middle East. Even individual teams have started to explore the possibilities that these global media present. The Real Madrid Soccer Club recently entered into a joint venture for the launch of a new interactive TV program; *Realmadrid Life* will be broadcast on free-to-air TV in China, Hong Kong, South Korea, Thailand, Vietnam, Indonesia, Malaysia, and Singapore.[15]

> The Euro 2004 soccer tournament and the NFL's 2006 Super Bowl were broadcast in more than 200 countries.

Every league is seeking growth. And while many efforts are directed toward the live audience, there is also considerable emphasis on the media-based markets. The key word that appeared many times on the previous pages is *opportunity*. Leagues and sports constantly seek to take advantage of opportunities that expansion into new countries provides. Not only can they increase both the live and the media-based audiences, but expansion of this type also favorably impacts the sale of sporting goods and licensed merchandise. Clearly, sports marketing encompasses far more than just selling tickets.

Participation Sports

When marketers create demand for participation sports, they concurrently create demand for the facilities where the participation will take place. As such, the typical distribution decisions concern the number of facilities and their location within a geographic market. An inadequate number means that existing facilities are crowded and that not all of the aspiring participants can be served. Conversely, overbuilding means that facilities are underutilized. To address this excess capacity, marketers of these facilities often engage in expensive promotions and aggressive price discounting in an effort to build market share. In addition to competition from other marketers of participation facilities, the market is also often influenced by the presence of publicly owned facilities.

While the emphasis of this discussion is on facilities constructed expressly for the purpose of attracting participants, it will also address open-access properties. *Dedicated facilities* include golf courses, gyms, swimming pools, and tennis courts. These facilities may be privately owned, or they may be publicly owned and operated by some government entity. *Open-access facilities* include lakes for fishing, fields for hunting, paths for biking, and facilities for skateboarding. Some of these activities are regulated through licensing; some have small user fees attached; others have completely unrestricted access. In some cases, facilities not designed for participation activities are adapted to meet the needs of the aspiring participant.

Dedicated Facilities

The most common type of dedicated facility is built and managed for the express purpose of providing a venue that meets the needs of those who want to participate in a specific activity. Construction is generally a function of supply and demand. It is also influenced by the distance that people are willing to travel to use these resources. For example, some golf courses draw customers from a limited geographic area; others draw from a wider region; and others attract golfers from all over the country or even the world. The Old Course at St. Andrews and Pebble Beach are two examples of renowned golf courses to which participants travel great distances for the chance to test their golfing skills.

Operators of privately owned facilities are generally in the business to earn a profit. They are also in competition with others who provide similar services. The task is to balance the capacity to provide services to participants with the number of people who choose to engage in a specific activity. Typical of this genre of providers are those who provide facilities for golf, tennis, bowling, swimming, downhill skiing, skating, and general exercise.

> The task is to balance the capacity to provide services to participants with the number of people who choose to engage in a specific activity.

The golf market provides an excellent example of a distribution system that has become unbalanced. Throughout the 1990s, developers were excited by the increase in the number of golfers and their frequency of play. New courses were built so that the anticipated growth in play could be accommodated without straining the system. Many of these new courses were up-market, high-daily-fee courses that were open to the general public. Unfortunately, a struggling economy and declining demand have tempered this enthusiasm. As a result, there are more golf courses than the market can support. Operators have found themselves in a battle for market share that is marked by lower fees being charged in an effort to attract golfers. Other courses have simply closed; many have been transformed into housing developments.

Today, there is a growth market for exercise facilities. One of the fastest-growing franchises in the United States is Curves. This service provider has designated the female segment as its target market, but it is not without meaningful competition. Gold's Gyms, Bally Fitness Centers, and Powerhouse Gyms all provide a similar set of services for consumers. In the future, care must be taken not to overbuild or these providers may find themselves in a situation similar to what golf course operators are facing today.

Some service providers are now finding themselves in competition with the employers of consumers who reside in their target markets. Employers recognize the benefits of having healthy, physically fit employees. The most common type of facility provided by employers in their efforts to maintain a healthier workforce is a gymnasium. These employer-owned gyms undoubtedly take some customers away from commercial enterprises that offer many of the same services and benefits for a fee.

Still other dedicated facilities are publicly owned and open to certain groups of citizens. Universities often provide an array of facilities to students, faculty, and staff. Government entities also maintain a variety of facilities such as golf courses, swimming pools, basketball courts, skateboarding venues, gymnasiums, and tennis courts. Residents may be able to use the facilities for free or at a discounted rate. Nonresidents may also be allowed to use facilities for a fee. The result is that these publicly owned facilities are in direct competition with those that are privately owned and operated.

Open-Access Facilities

Many recreation sites are readily accessible to the general public, and many of these open-access venues provide opportunities for people to participate in regulated activities. In

DISTRIBUTION OPTIONS FOR THE PARTICIPATION MARKET

17.4

Dedicated Facilities
- Private
  - Commercial
  - Employer provided
- Public
  - Government
  - Universities

Open-Access Facilities
- Licensed activities
- Unrestricted access
- Public adaptation

some cases, the privilege of participating is contingent upon obtaining a license. For example, while anyone may be allowed to enter a field or woods without express permission, they cannot hunt ducks or deer without the appropriate license. These licensing fees represent revenues for the government, but they are also used to control the number of participants and the anticipated harvest of the area's wildlife. Other activities typically regulated by a government agency are fishing and boating. Licensing often is required when natural resources are being used or depleted. Open-access facilities of this type are also in direct competition with many privately owned operations where consumers pay the owner for the right to hunt, fish, or boat on private property.

Other open-access facilities are generally available to anyone who chooses to use them. Bike paths, tennis courts at the local park, and tracks for running or walking are widely available for anyone to use. The use of these facilities is generally free of charge, yet they impact the supply of facilities designed to provide such services.

Finally, there are facilities that were not designed for participation sports, but the public adapts them to meet their needs. Public roads are used for walking and running. Shopping malls are used, especially by senior citizens, as venues for walking. In fact, some malls open their doors and coffee shops to accommodate these participants' hours before the regular stores open for daily operations.

Clearly, the distribution system for participation sports is quite diverse. Marketers must pay attention to supply and demand, and they must also consider trends that will impact participation in the future. The ultimate task is to provide the level of service that is needed in the marketplace while recognizing that there are many sources of competition. Box 17.4 summarizes the types of organizations that comprise the distribution network for the provision of services that satisfy the needs of the participation market.

Sporting Goods, Apparel, Athletic Shoes, and Sports-Related Products

The final category of sports products is the eclectic combination of sporting goods, apparel, athletic shoes, and sports-related products. Other than the sports-related products, the distribution system for this category of sports products is largely based upon general retailing principles. The first decision concerns the availability of the products in any geographic region. From the marketer's perspective, this involves the level of exposure.

Some manufacturers might opt for *intensive distribution*. With this level of exposure, the product is sold at a large percentage of the appropriate retail outlets within the area. Nike might seek intensive distribution in an effort to make its shoes, apparel, and sporting goods easily attainable by every member of its target markets. The term *appropriate outlets* refers to retailers that would typically include those types of products as part of their regular assortment of goods. Nike does not want to sell its shoes in a 24-hour convenience store, but it does desire a presence at general merchandise retailers as well as specialty stores such as Foot Locker that feature in athletic footwear.

When the distribution objective is to make the product scarcer, the marketer often seeks to establish *selective distribution*. Wieder does not want its exercise equipment sold in every retail store that sells sporting goods. This scarcity is consistent with a strategy designed to project a more prestigious image. It also helps retailers maintain prices that produce acceptable profit margins while reinforcing the consumer's perception of being a source of high-quality, premium products. So while you might find Wieder products at a sports specialty store, you are unlikely to find them at a discount retailer such as Kmart, Wal-Mart, or Carrefours.

The ultimate level of scarcity is when the manufacturer implements an *exclusive distribution* policy; that is, it limits the availability of a product to a single source within a specific geographic area. In this final category of sports products, exclusive distribution generally is not a viable option. However, it could be appropriate in situations where the products are very expensive or customized to meet the exact needs of the customers.

Another distribution decision concerns the question of using direct response marketing (DRM). Efforts of this type fall into the category of *nonstore retailing*. The marketer uses a variety of techniques to reach consumers and provides a means by which consumers can provide feedback. The most common types of DRM efforts involve catalogs, direct mail, TV advertisements, infomercials, magazine advertisements, and the Internet. Many marketers use a combination of these techniques. Catalogs and other direct mail efforts may originate with the manufacturer, an authorized retailer, a team, a league, or some other sports organization.

Many DRM efforts also incorporate the marketer's URL. For example, the same products offered in many of the catalogs distributed by MLB teams are also available at the MLB.com Web site. The Internet has become a powerful sales tool that allows the marketer to interact directly with the buyer. Magazine advertisements achieve the same objective by including a postcard that encourages and facilitates the consumer's response. Infomercials and TV ads provide toll-free numbers for the consumer to call to place an order.

It can be argued that the alternatives presented in the direct response category are not truly distribution decisions. Rather, they are promotion decisions that allow the marketer to sell directly to the consumer. Again, efforts can originate with a manufacturer, retailer, league, team, or sports organization such as FIFA and the IOC. These techniques allow the organization to reach potential customers who may not have easy access to a retailer that sells the products they want to buy.

The final area for discussion is the sports-related products that are sold at the venue. Team officials and stadium operators must still consider the distribution aspect of their marketing strategy. They must determine the optimal number of service facilities and where they should be located within the stadium or arena. The answers to these questions often depend upon the size of the facility and the anticipated number of fans in attendance. A new trend involves waitstaff service for concessions for customers sitting in the more expensive "premium" seats at the venue. Another question involves the use of vendors who walk around the venue to sell their products. By bringing the products to the spectators, purchases are more convenient and the fan does not risk missing key action while waiting to make a purchase at a concession stand. Some stadium operators do not allow beer to be sold by these vendors. This policy helps assure that the consumers are of legal drinking age, and it also helps control the level of consumption.

Closing Capsule

"If you build it, he will come." The reality is that sports marketers need to do more than simply develop good products. They must also develop distribution strategies that make the products available to their target markets. Distribution is one of the elements of the marketing mix, and it must be coordinated with the organization's product, pricing, and promotion strategies that are designed to appeal to key target markets. This coordination is required for all three categories of sports products.

For spectator sports, the marketer must be concerned with the dual objective of increasing both the live audience and the media-based audience. For the live audience, there are several key issues that must be considered. In what city or community should the event be staged? Is a new stadium or arena required? Where within the selected locale should any new venue be constructed; how many fans should it accommodate; and when should the event be held?

Marketers of spectator sports must also develop a network for the sale and distribution of tickets. There are many options other than the traditional box office; among them are authorized retailers and agents such as Ticketmaster. The Internet has also emerged as an important tool in the distribution of tickets. Marketers of spectator sports must also be cognizant of the sale of tickets by unauthorized resellers. In regard to these unauthorized sales, the task of the distribution system is to limit their ability to acquire large supplies of desirable tickets for popular events. Otherwise these institutional buyers can quickly exhaust the supply of tickets thereby making it difficult for individuals to secure the tickets they desire. In some cases, the only option for the consumer is to pay the higher prices demanded by the scalpers who control the inventory of tickets.

> Institutional buyers can quickly exhaust the supply of tickets thereby making it difficult for individuals to secure the tickets they desire.

While it is important for marketers of spectator sports to put fans in the seats, many of today's efforts are devoted to increasing the number of media-based fans. They drive up TV ratings; they purchase licensed merchandise; and they carry on informal conversations about the team, sport, or event. In short, they are major economic contributors to the marketers of spectator sports.

These media-based fans can still be reached most effectively with TV. This includes free-to-air, cable, and satellite delivery services. The spectator sports product takes the form of regular programming on traditional TV stations, general sports networks, specific sport networks, sports tiers, stations that focus on a single team, and pay-per-view. Other electronic media that should readily come to mind are radio and the Internet. More recently, technological advances have led to the use of cellular phones and smart watches as media for the transmission of text and video images regarding the results from various sports events.

Much of the recent growth in spectator sports has been achieved via the implementation of market development strategies. While this can be implemented by targeting new demographic or lifestyle segments, the greatest growth seems to have occurred when marketers designated a new geographic area as a target market. For sports marketers, this strategy often involves entry into a new country. They may stage a competition in a country in which such an event is uncommon. NASCAR's race in Mexico City is an example of this strategy. Established leagues such as MLB and the NHL have scheduled both exhibition and regular season games outside of their Canadian and American base. New leagues such as the NFL Europe have been established. Secondary competition can be staged in a targeted country; an example is the NBA-sanctioned basketball tournament that was held in Japan. There have also been numerous efforts to penetrate new international markets via one or more of the available broadcast media.

For participation sports, distribution decisions are also important. Marketers neither want to overbuild nor underbuild, so they must constantly reassess the nature of supply and demand within their markets. Much of the participation takes place at dedicated facilities such as golf courses and gyms. Some open-access facilities are also used for activities such as hunting and boating. In many cases, these activities require a license to be issued by some regulatory agency.

The final category of sports products is comprised of sporting goods, apparel, athletic shoes, and sports-related products. In general, basic retailing principles apply when developing an appropriate distribution strategy. Where will the product be sold? How many stores in a given market will be allowed to sell it? What type of store shall be used? For the sports-related products sold at the venue, the marketer must consider the number of service facilities that will sell the products. There will likely be more facilities selling food and beverages than there will be selling licensed clothing. Venue operators must also consider the use of vendors who walk around the stands and bring the product to the customer rather than forcing them to leave their seat and risk missing some of the action. These vendors undoubtedly increase the level of sales at every sports event in which they are allowed to operate.

We have now addressed target marketing decisions, product strategies, and distribution strategies. This takes us to the next decision area in the marketing mix, namely, the organization's pricing strategy. This aspect of marketing strategy will be explored in the next chapter.

Review Questions

1. When speaking of spectator sports, what is meant by the terms *live audience* and *media-based audience?*

2. Why is increased attention being focused on the media-based audience?

3. Why do cities bid to host special events such as the Summer Olympics?

4. Why is the traditional box office still important to marketers of spectator sports?

5. In addition to the traditional box office, what other outlets can the marketer incorporate into its ticket distribution network?

6. Briefly describe each medium that represents an opportunity to attract a media-based fan.

7. What does the term *narrowcasting* mean?

8. In regard to television, what is a sports tier?

9. Explain the antisiphoning law? Identify four events in your country that you would protect using such a law.

10. How has the NBA used market development strategies to grow its sport and the league's stature?

11. Identify the most popular sport in your country. What market development strategies would you recommend if they were to attempt to increase their fan base?

12. How can the media be used to implement a market development strategy for a spectator sport?

13. What are the key distribution decisions regarding the marketing of participation sports?

14. Give five examples of dedicated participation facilities close to your school. Do not list more than one facility for any single sport or activity.

15. What are the primary reasons for requiring a license for activities such as deer hunting?

16. What are the key distribution decisions in the marketing of sporting goods, apparel, athletic shoes, and sports-related products?

17. What is meant by direct response marketing? Develop an argument that it is more of a promotion strategy than it is a distribution strategy.

Endnotes

1. A. Carrns, "For Super Bowl XXXIX, a River of Logistics," *The Wall Street Journal,* January 31, 2005, pp. B1, B3.

2. K. Whiteside, "Wins Can't Lure Jersey Fans," March 5, 2003, www.usatoday.com/sports/2003-03-05-cover-new-jersey_x.htm (accessed March 6, 2003).

3. E. Robertson, "It's Where You Play That Counts," *Fortune,* July 21, 1997, pp. 54–57.

4. B. Wilner, "Major League Baseball Plans Television Network," *SportBusiness International,* October 2004, p. 6.

5. D. Barrand, "Tyson Still a PPV Winner," February 27, 2003, www.sportbusiness.com/news/index?news_item_id=15025 (accessed October 14, 2005).

6. Associated Press, "Sirius Properties: Wimbledon, Howard Stern," April 6, 2005, www.sports.espn.go.com/sports/tennis/news/story?id=2031486 (accessed October 14, 2005).

7. S. McKee, "Big Events on Tiny Screens," *The Wall Street Journal,* August 20, 2004, p. A8.

8. "Sports Business," aired on Comcast Sports Network, March 30, 2005.

9. M. Luer, "Clarity Comes to Asia," *SportBusiness International,* October 2003, p. 26.

10. C. Britcher, "What Score Is It?" *SportBusiness International,* November 2004, p. 21.

11. D. Barrand, "NBA Looking to Include Europe," October 9, 2003, www.sportbusiness.com/news/index?news_item_id=152747 (accessed October 13, 2005).

12. D. Smith, "NASCAR Extends to Mexico," August 6, 2004, www.sportbusiness.com/news/index?news_item_id=155357 (accessed October 14, 2005).

13. D. Smith, "McDonald's and NBA in Lifestyle Partnership," April 26, 2005, www.sportbusiness.com/news/index?news_item_id=157329 (accessed October 13, 2005).

14. Ibid

15. D. Smith, "Real Launches Interactive Asian Show," April 26, 2005, www.sportbusiness.com/news/index?news_item_id=157341 (accessed October 13, 2005).

CHAPTER EIGHTEEN

Pricing Decisions in Sports Marketing

Learning Objectives

- Learn the basic factors that influence pricing decisions.
- Learn pricing strategies for the three categories of sports products.
- Be able to apply general pricing strategies to sports products.
- Learn variations in pricing for the live audience.
- Be introduced to the controversial policy of Permanent Seat Licenses (PSLs).

The sports marketer has selected a target market and developed a product strategy that is designed to satisfy those customers' wants and needs. The distribution strategy that most effectively gets those products to the market has also been conceived. One of the next tasks in the development of the organization's marketing strategy is to establish a pricing strategy that is consistent with the target market, product, and distribution strategies that the sports marketer plans to implement. These strategic initiatives should be integrated in such a way that they complement each other. This integration should have a synergistic effect that helps the organization achieve its marketing goals. Strategies that conflict with each other simply are not as effective. For example, the sale of lower-quality sporting goods at a discount retailer using a premium pricing strategy would be ineffective.

This chapter will address the pricing decisions that confront the sports marketer. It begins with an overview of key pricing considerations that are relevant in any industry. Then the focus will shift to applications in the sports marketing industry. The emphasis of this discussion will be on spectator sports; however, pricing decisions for participation sports as well as the third category of sports products (i.e., sporting goods, apparel, athletic shoes, and sports-related products) will also be addressed.

Fundamental Pricing Concepts

There are many fundamental principles that must be understood as the marketer seeks to develop its optimal pricing strategy. Regardless of the industry in which the marketer operates, these principles apply. Whether the objective is to sell sports products or consumer electronics, there should be an understanding of the definition of price, the market's typical reaction to price changes, the factors that influence the price decision, and the various approaches for determining the final price that will be charged to members of the target market.

Definition of Price

Price can be defined as what the buyer gives up in the exchange process. For most formal transactions, price is defined as the amount of money that the buyer pays to gain rightful ownership of the product being offered for sale. To many people, price is perceived as a measure of value. If the potential buyer thinks that the price being asked exceeds the value provided by the product, then the purchase is unlikely. Conversely, a consumer surplus exists when the perceived value is greater than the asking price. Such a surplus increases the likelihood that the product will be purchased.

> **Price can be defined as what the buyer gives up in the exchange process.**

The comparison of price and value will also occur in informal transactions where the price is not stated in terms of some monetary unit; rather, the price in expressed in terms of *barter*. In situations such as this, it is likely that neither party is a business entity. An example of this type of exchange could be your two tickets to an upcoming football game for your friend's sports marketing textbook.

Reaction to Price Changes

The market's response to price changes is generally measured by determining the price elasticity of demand. From an economics perspective, *price elasticity* is a measure that reflects the change in the level of demand in response to a change in price. Almost without fail, a price increase will result in a corresponding decrease in demand. But if price is raised by 10 percent, how large will the corresponding decrease in demand be? Will it be 5 percent, 10 percent, 15 percent, or some other level? The answer to this question is important to every marketer.

From a practical perspective, price elasticity is a measure of the market's responsiveness to a price change. Prices can go up or down. The key question concerns how strongly the market will react to the change. Depending upon that reaction, a market will be characterized as possessing either an elastic or inelastic demand curve.

Most products are characterized by an *elastic demand curve*. When this market condition exists, a change in price will result in a significant change in demand. For the marketer, the important implication of this market condition is that there is an inverse relationship between price and total revenue. If the price is increased, total revenue will decline. Conversely, a decrease in price will result in a substantial increase in demand that will more than compensate for the reduction in revenue generated by each item sold. Table 18.1 illustrates an elastic state in the marketplace. Assume that the marketer's original price was $15; then note the changes in revenue associated with a price increase to $22.50 and a price reduction to $10.

As noted earlier, most products are characterized by an elastic demand curve. Table 18.1 illustrates the danger of raising prices in this type of market. Demand will decline as the market seeks substitute products or simply cuts its level of consumption. As a result, the total revenue generated at the new higher price will be lower. Of course, the total costs incurred by the marketer will also decline because of the elimination of a portion of the total variable costs. Therefore, the marketer must weigh the reduction in revenue against the resultant reduction in costs.

A quick decision based solely upon the information in Table 18.1 might be to lower prices because of the reality that the higher level of demand coupled with the new price will provide the marketer with additional revenue. But marketers are not in business to

TABLE 18.1
**Example of an
Elastic Demand
Curve**

Price	Demand (units sold)	Total Revenue
$10.00	1,000	$10,000
15.00	600	9,000
22.50	360	8,100

TABLE 18.2
Example of an Inelastic Demand Curve

Price	Demand (units sold)	Total Revenue
$10.00	1,000	$10,000
15.00	900	13,500
22.50	800	18,000

maximize revenues; rather, the typical goal is to maximize profits. With higher levels of production, the marketer will incur additional costs. Therefore, the key question concerns the extent to which the additional revenue exceeds the added costs. In other words, what happens to profits as the price that is charged to buyers is manipulated?

> Marketers are not in business to maximize revenues.

For most marketers, an inelastic demand curve is the preferred market condition. *Inelasticity of demand* is characterized by markets that are not as responsive to price changes. This may occur with a product that has achieved a high degree of brand loyalty or one for which there are no acceptable substitutes. Consider how consumers responded to the higher gasoline prices that marked 2005. The price of gasoline increased by approximately 40 percent over the first four months of the year. Although many people reduced their consumption by driving less or purchasing more fuel-efficient vehicles, few people reduced their consumption at a rate commensurate with the 40 percent increase in price. As a result, the total revenues for those selling petroleum products increased. With an inelastic demand curve, there is a direct relationship between price and total revenue. Increased prices produce higher revenues, whereas a price reduction will result in a corresponding decrease in total revenue. Other products where price inelasticity is likely to exist are cigarettes and prescription drugs. Table 18.2 illustrates a situation where an inelastic demand pattern exists. Once more, assume that the marketer has an established price of $15, then note what happens to total revenue in response to a price increase and a price reduction.

Mainstream marketers often attempt to create a differential advantage for their products. With such an advantage, some buyers will exhibit a higher degree of brand loyalty, perhaps even brand insistence. As a result, the marketers may achieve their desired goal of creating an inelastic demand curve. For sports marketers, an inelastic demand curve means that they have greater flexibility in making their pricing decisions.

Two key factors that influence the elasticity of demand are the availability of substitutes and the extent to which purchasers can simply forgo the purchase of a specific product irrespective of the availability of substitutes.

Substitute Products

Substitute products are goods and services that satisfy the same wants and needs as the marketer's product. The availability of substitute products allows the buyer to simply shift from one product to another when market conditions become unfavorable. For example, when the mad cow scare drove up the price of beef, many consumers simply shifted to pork, lamb, poultry, or seafood. There are many acceptable substitutes for beef. Conversely, when the price of gasoline surged, consumers had nowhere to turn. There is no acceptable substitute for the fuel that powers most vehicles. Although consumers did reduce their consumption of gasoline, their expenditures for this necessary product still tended to increase. Applying what was learned on the previous pages, we can conclude that the demand for beef is elastic whereas the demand for gasoline is inelastic.

For spectator sports, there are a number of substitute products. Not only are there other spectator sports events, but for the consumer who is simply seeking entertainment, available substitutes include theater, motion pictures, and sports on TV. Minor league baseball teams often promote their lower prices in an effort to attract fans who might view MLB as too expensive and seek substitute entertainment alternatives.

Buyers' Willingness to Forgo the Purchase of a Specific Product

The second issue that impacts elasticity is the buyers' willingness to give up the purchase and consumption of the product. In some cases, an unwillingness to cease consumption relates more to brand loyalty than it does a product category. For example, if the price of motorcycles goes up, then many potential customers will seek a less expensive alternative or simply drop out of the market. However, with prestigious brands such as Harley-Davidson, not only are potential buyers unwilling to give up on their plan to purchase a new motorcycle, these aspiring Harley owners are unlikely to waiver from their brand of choice. Even higher prices may not dissuade the buyer from purchasing a new Harley.

> The NFL's Green Bay Packers sell out every game and have a waiting list of some 67,000 people seeking season tickets.

In most markets, tickets for spectator sports are likely to exhibit an elastic demand curve. Teams address this reality by offering tickets at different price levels. Fans have the choice of moving to more distant seats that can be purchased at a lower price. Teams that typically sell out have more flexibility because demand exceeds supply. For example, the NFL's Green Bay Packers sell out every game and have a waiting list of some 67,000 people seeking season tickets. Price increases might reduce demand, but demand still exceeds the supply of available seats. The luxury boxes that are part of virtually every new stadium or arena likely possess an inelastic demand curve. There are a limited number of suites available, there are few substitutes, and the typical purchaser is a corporation that views a suite as an investment through which it can entertain customers, prospects, and employees. The resultant increases in sales and employee morale make the corporation unwilling to forgo the purchase of the suite unless its price becomes prohibitive. The corporation will weigh the price against the anticipated benefits.

Buyers' Ability to Forgo the Purchase of a Specific Product

In some cases, a product is an absolute necessity. When this is the case, the consumer may seek alternatives in the form of substitute products. If substitutes are not available, the consumer has little choice except to pay the higher price for the product. Prescription drugs often fall into this category. If the price of a diabetic's insulin is increased, the absence of any acceptable substitute forces the patient to pay more for the drug. Not buying it simply is not a viable option for the consumer.

Sports products are seldom classified as necessities. The purchase of tickets to a sports event, a membership in a health club, new inline skates, a new Real Madrid team shirt, a new pair of running shoes, or a beer at the stadium can hardly be classified as essential products. Given this, sports marketers must carefully consider the potential impact of any new pricing strategy.

Factors that Influence Price

An array of factors directly impact the prices asked by the marketer. These factors typically lie beyond the control of the marketer; however, the optimal pricing strategy will take these factors into account. Box 18.1 provides a list of many of these influences, and a brief discussion of each follows.

FACTORS THAT INFLUENCE PRICE   18.1

- Situational influences
- Costs
- Competition
- Supply and demand
- Marketing objectives
- Legal considerations
- Consumer perceptions
- Marketing mix consistency

Situational influences are represented by unusual circumstances that tend to impact consumer behavior. They may result in a consumer's decision to make a purchase that he or she would not make under normal circumstances. In many cases, these purchases are unplanned. A husband who has angered his wife might purchase a card and flowers to ameliorate the situation and say "I'm sorry." If it's cold at a sports event, a fan might deviate from the normal practice of drinking a beer in favor of a cup of coffee. Or someone might purchase a sweatshirt at the stadium in an effort to keep warm when he or she had no prior intention to make that type of purchase. While such factors can influence consumption, they have little impact on the prices established by the marketer.

In sports, an important situational influence on prices is the team's performance. Winning creates demand. Although sports marketers would be reluctant to raise their prices during the course of a season, winning certainly affects a team's ticket pricing decision for any postseason playoff games as well as the following season. Winning teams have far more flexibility and often raise prices. Teams that are losing during the course of the season often utilize promotional pricing as a strategy for selling tickets. The hope is that lower prices will attract more fans. Another situational factor is a team's move to a new stadium. Such a transition is typically associated with a price increase of 10 to 25 percent.

> Another situational factor is a team's move to a new stadium; such a transition is typically associated with a price increase of 10 to 25 percent.

For any business, prices are influenced by the *costs* incurred. Higher prices often reflect a need to offset higher costs. In the marketing of goods, the primary cost is that of manufacturing or purchasing the goods from a supplier. For services, the salaries paid to those who provide those services represent the key cost. Other costs include marketing expenses, taxes, insurance, and other fees imposed on the product.

In the marketing of sporting goods, apparel, athletic shoes, and sports-related products, the marketer's focus is on the cost of goods sold. For participation sports, the cost of building and maintaining the facility, the cost of equipment, salaries paid to employees, utilities, insurance, and taxes must be taken into account. These costs can vary significantly from one location to another; this often results in large deviations for the prices charged for the same services in different geographic regions. For spectator sports, the majority of the cost incurred is typically the salaries paid to players. The total team payroll for MLB's Boston Red Sox in 2004 was $127,298,500, and their average ticket price was $44.56. Compare that to the $27,528,500 payroll and average ticket price of $16.86 for the Milwaukee Brewers.[1]

In most industries, marketers must monitor the prices charged by their direct *competition*. When consumers are searching for a place to purchase gasoline, they often seek the lowest price. Many retailers of consumer electronics offer a price-matching policy. They will meet the price for any identical item advertised by one of their local competitors. To reduce the consumer's reliance on price as the determining factor, marketers attempt to differentiate their products from those sold by their competitors.

In spectator sports, few cities have more than one team in any league. Therefore, it could be argued that they have no direct competition. However, fans can change their behavior and start attending sports events with lower prices. For instance, the average price of an NBA ticket for the Los Angeles Lakers in 2004 was $75.40. When considering entertainment options, a fan might be enticed to purchase tickets for MLB's Los Angeles Angels because of the average ticket price of $17.36.

The construction of new facilities is one factor that has led to increased levels of competition in the participation market. Too often, this battle for market share is based upon the establishment of bargain prices. To avoid erosion of market share, much like many retailers of nonsports products, others targeting the same market segments often match the competition's lower prices. This is especially true when the consumers cannot discern any meaningful differences between the marketers and their products. On the other hand, if a provider can impart the perception that it has superior facilities and services in comparison to its competition, then perhaps the consumer will be willing to pay more for access to the enhanced level of services. The implication of this effort is that the product strategy and the promotional strategy are used to support the pricing decision. It further demonstrates the need to coordinate all elements of the marketing mix.

The basic economic principle of *supply and demand* also has a significant role in the setting of prices. More specifically, it is the relationship between the two that is important. If supply exceeds demand, prices tend to gravitate downward. When automobile manufacturers build up large inventories of unsold cars, they typically offer rebates and other discounts that effectively lower the final price paid by consumers. When demand exceeds supply, there are two typical responses. The price is often raised in an effort to bring supply and demand into equilibrium. The higher prices will drive down demand, but ideally only to the point where supply is exhausted. The entire supply is sold at the higher price. The second response is to increase supply. In many cases, more units can be manufactured or acquired in an effort to meet the excess demand. In spectator sports, increasing the supply is difficult. The capacity of most stadia is finite, although some have been able to increase their capacity via stadium expansion during the off-season. In other cases, teams have supplemented the supply by adding temporary seats or by selling standing-room-only tickets.

> Teams have supplemented the supply by adding temporary seats or by selling standing-room-only tickets.

For other categories of sports products, higher demand will typically translate into higher prices. For example, during a league's playoffs, the demand for licensed apparel for teams with a chance to win the championship will increase. One could argue that the increase is due to a situational influence that induces consumer behavior. It is at this time that the demand for these products is at its peak. Interest in the team will wane after the team is eliminated from contention or after the passage of some significant time. This translates into diminished levels of demand to which marketers inevitably respond by lowering prices in an effort to liquidate their supply.

Another factor that exerts considerable influence on the final pricing decision is the set of *marketing objectives* established by the organization. Does the organization want to convey a prestige image and target an affluent segment? Does it prefer to pursue the mass market, a strategy that calls for a moderate- or low-price strategy? What are the market share objectives; is the organization seeking to build, maintain, or reduce its market share? The answers to questions such as these will help the marketer establish its final price.

Outside of the sports industry, Rolex seeks to maintain a high level of prestige for its watches while giving little consideration to market share. These factors lead to a high price. Conversely, the providers of long-distance telephone service find themselves in an environment marked by battles for market share. Since there is little to differentiate the services from the various providers, these battles generally entail lower prices.

Within the sports industry, several NBA teams provide seats at the floor level. The Detroit Pistons recently added eight seats, four next to each team's bench, that are priced at $2,500 each. Undoubtedly, part of the appeal of these seats is ego driven rather than value based. A similar situation involves the sale of authenticated autographed memorabilia. With such memorabilia available only in small quantities, the authentication process assures the buyers that they are receiving a legitimate product rather than a counterfeit. The overt decision to limit supplies indicates that the marketers of these products are not striving for high market penetration; consequently, these products are sold at a premium price.

Many industries must adhere to a myriad of *legal considerations* when establishing their prices. While most industries are market driven, some regulations will restrict the price-setting flexibility in other industries. This may come in the form of cost increases such as tariffs on imported goods. Import restrictions may constrict the supply of some products, thereby exerting upward pressure on prices. Utility companies are often highly regulated and price increases must be approved by a governmental agency.

> Many cities and countries have laws that expressly prohibit the scalping of tickets at prices above the face value.

In spectator sports, there are a number of legal issues that impact prices. Many cities and countries have laws that expressly prohibit the scalping of tickets at prices above the face value shown on the ticket. Not only does this affect the individuals whom these laws are targeting, but it also poses questions regarding the legality of teams selling their own tickets for more than the face value. Officials of MLB's Chicago Cubs found themselves in a court of law when they acknowledged the sale of tickets that had been returned to them. Their "Premium Ticket Service" was a subsidiary of the Cubs' team, and it sold the highly sought tickets at inflated prices. Another legal decision concerns parking. These service providers are generally licensed by local governments. In some cities, the prices are regulated and not allowed to deviate from the established price.

Consumer perceptions play an important role in the marketer's pricing strategy. Perception relates specifically to the consumer's attitudes and beliefs about a product. Perception does not always coincide with reality. When this discrepancy is the case, the consumer's perception may well override reality. A product may be high quality, but if the consumer believes it to be of it is of lesser quality, that perception will influence the individual's purchase behavior. Products perceived to be inferior are difficult to sell at premium prices. Negative consumer perceptions of cars manufactured in Korea have been a significant barrier to sales. As a result, the Korean manufacturers have offered extended warranties in an effort to dispel consumer perceptions. Still, the Korean cars are priced lower than those of their Japanese competitors, who benefit from the perception that they produce superior vehicles.

In sports, some leagues have a perceptual advantage over others. In fact, some sports are perceived as a superior product in comparison to other sports. For sporting goods, many brands work hard to instill the image of superiority over their competition. Titleist has long held such an advantage over other manufacturers of golf balls. This advantage has allowed Titleist to charge a premium price. Competitors such as Nike continue to use advertising and endorsements by top golfers in an effort to neutralize that advantage. After all, if Nike is good enough for Tiger Woods, surely it is good enough for the recreational golfer.

Finally, every marketer has to develop a pricing strategy that is *consistent with the other elements of the marketing mix*. Prestige products and brands are not sold through discount retailers. Product alternatives that involve a high level of customer service must offset those costs with higher prices. Marketers advertise on TV programs and in magazines that reach their target markets. Regardless of the industry, the pricing strategy must fit with the target market, product, distribution, and promotional strategies.

Consider the luxury suites that were previously discussed. The suites sell for high prices. There is little advertising done in the effort to sell them; rather, salespeople call on corporate customers identified as prospective buyers. The product includes the suite itself, early access to the venue, private toilets, video monitors, and food and beverage service. These suites are present in every new arena, though the number in each venue is limited. In this example of a sports marketing endeavor, the elements of the marketing strategy are consistent.

> **Marketers cannot focus on a single factor when they seek to set their price.**

The previous discussion delineated eight factors that influence the pricing decision, but some overlap is obvious. For example, it is impossible to separate marketing objectives from consumer perceptions. Situational factors influence demand. Likewise, supply and demand is intricately tied to the competition. The implication is that marketers cannot focus on a single factor when they seek to set their price; they must consider the impact of the entire set of factors. Only when these are taken into account can the marketer implement an effective pricing strategy.

General Implementation Strategies

Marketers should determine the impact of each of the aforementioned considerations and incorporate that insight into the process of making their pricing decisions. This insight can be gained through marketing research that assesses buyer behavior and motivations. Only when all of the pertinent information has been evaluated can the marketer make an informed decision that will result in the implementation of a pricing strategy that will lead to the achievement of the organization's marketing goals. We will start by looking at general pricing strategies. This will include a number of examples from the sports marketing environment.

Cost-plus is a pricing strategy whereby the buyer pays all of the costs associated with a product along with a fee for the seller. This policy is often used for the development of new products. For example, if Boeing signs a contract with a government agency to develop a new, high-tech military airplane, the agreement often calls for the buyer to pay all of the costs associated with the design and manufacture of the new airplane plus a fee to compensate Boeing for its time and effort. In sports, this approach can be used for the pricing of a new stadium. The final price charged to the buyer includes design and construction costs plus a fee that is stipulated in the contract.

Markup pricing is commonly used in the retailing environment. To implement this strategy, the marketer simply starts with the cost of an item as the base and adds a specified percentage of that cost to determine the final price. If the retailer's policy is to markup its products 50 percent, then an item with a $10 cost will be priced at $15. The percentage by which a product will be marked up varies significantly from product to product and from retailer to retailer. For example, the markup for licensed apparel at the souvenir shop at the stadium is likely to be far higher than the markup for a similar product at a discount retailer.

Promotional pricing is used to provide additional value to the consumer. It may be implemented by putting a product on sale. An alternative to offering a discount is to bundle the product with additional items. For example, a person might be able to purchase four tickets to an MLB game and get four hot dogs, four soft drinks, and a game program as part of the bundle.

A strategy that has gained popularity over the past few years is that of *bidding*. With this process, the item is not offered at any predetermined price. It is offered to the public in some form of auction and is sold to the highest bidder. This approach has commonly been used for artwork, estates, classic cars, and antiques. Today, auctions are much more common. Consumers have become familiar with eBay and have learned the intricacies of auctions. Public TV uses auctions to raise funds to pay for operations and programming; local radio stations use the same approach to raise money for charitable causes.

Sports products are often used for the aforementioned cause-related marketing efforts. Individuals often use eBay to sell tickets to major events. Some teams have even placed items for auction on their own Web sites; examples of these items include apparel and equipment used by players during an actual competition. Bidding works well when the supply is very low, perhaps only one item, and the seller is uncertain as to what the highest bidder is willing to pay.

> Some teams have placed items for auction on their own Web sites.

One of the newer strategies is *yield management*. This approach is generally associated with the airline industry, but it has been applied throughout the travel and hospitality industries. With this approach, various prices are used in an effort to fully utilize the marketer's facility. Airline companies will drop prices as a flight that is not fully booked gets closer to its departure date. They often substantially discount those flights in the period immediately preceding its scheduled departure. The philosophy is that they earn more using a discount rate than they do from an empty seat. The key is to not lower prices too soon as they attempt to sell the flight out at the higher initial prices. Airlines and hotels often use third parties such as priceline.com and hotels.com as outlets for selling their deeply discounted services.

It could be argued that marketers of spectator sports use a yield management strategy when games are not typically sold out. Prior to the start of the season, advance tickets are sold at or near the list price. As game day approaches, the team will attempt to fill some empty seats by offering substantial discounts. Occasionally, the team will distribute complimentary tickets, effectively dropping the price to zero. Whether the ticket holders paid full price, a discounted price, or nothing, these spectators still fill the stands. Not only do they look good on TV, but they also pay to park and purchase a variety of sports-related products at the venue.

> Whether the ticket holders paid full price, a discounted price, or nothing, these spectators still fill the stands.

Target return pricing is used when the marketer has a firm understanding of its costs and a reliable sales forecast. With target return pricing, the marketer seeks to attain a specified return on its investment (ROI). An automotive manufacturer that sells a special model with a known maximum level of production can use target return pricing to assure an acceptable ROI for that vehicle. In sports, this approach can be applied for special events that have a high probability of selling out. The marketer can estimate its fixed and total costs as well as the number of fans who will purchase tickets. By having a targeted ROI, the marketer can then determine the price that will lead to the achievement of its profit goal.

The preceding discussion has provided fundamental insight into the general approaches for implementing any organization's pricing strategy. They are applicable in a variety of industries. Some are viable in the sports industry; others are more applicable outside of the sports marketing environment. We will now turn our attention to pricing applications for sports products.

Pricing Applications for Sports Products

Now that there is a better understanding of the pricing policies available to marketers in any industry, we need to take a more detailed look at how they are implemented in the sports marketing environment. The remainder of this chapter examines pricing tactics for all three categories of sports products.

Spectator Sports

Of the three categories of sports products, the pricing decisions regarding spectator sports are undoubtedly the most scrutinized. The industry has been criticized for pricing its tickets beyond the reach of the everyday fan, yet many games are still played before capacity crowds.[2] Whether the venues are full or not, the organization must carefully develop its pricing strategy. There are many target markets to be considered, and the factors that are important to one segment may be unimportant to another. Furthermore, the situational influences can have a dramatic impact on the demand for tickets. Because of this disparity, marketers do not have one specific pricing strategy that will work in all cases.

> The industry has been criticized for pricing its tickets beyond the reach of the everyday fan.

Although there are some general pricing policies that are used, the implementation of specific tactics varies significantly from league to league and from team to team. The following section will address the general policies while noting several specific pricing applications in the marketing of spectator sports.

For team sports that compete over the course of a multigame season, one of the most important segments is the *season ticket* holder. Each year, efforts must be made to attain a high renewal rate from existing season ticket holders while also recruiting new buyers. These buyers will receive tickets for the same seat for each game played at the team's home venue.

It is evident that there are different target markets of season ticket buyers. Perhaps the most noteworthy distinction is between corporate customers and individual consumers. Other strategic issues are important, perhaps even more so than the price. Preferred seating, early admission, and opportunities to participate in events designed to strengthen the relationship between the season ticket holder and the team are common components of the overall marketing strategy.

For season tickets, one pricing strategy is to charge the full face value for each ticket. Other teams substantially discount tickets when they are purchased in a season-long block. An infield box seat for the Atlanta Braves for the 2006 season was priced at $32 to $35 per game. With 81 home games (plus two exhibition games), the effective value of a season ticket was $2,735. But rather than being charged full price, purchasers of season tickets received a discount, paying only $2,241. Conversely, the NFL's Chicago Bears played 10 home games (also including two exhibition games). In one seating area, the face value of each ticket was $70; therefore, the season ticket price of $700 provided no savings. One likely reason for these divergent strategies is that the Bears will sell out all of their games, whereas the Braves will have unsold tickets for most, if not all, of theirs. It is also more likely that season ticket holders for the Bears' games will attend each of the regular season games, but holders of Braves' season tickets are very unlikely to attend all 81 of the regularly scheduled games (plus the two exhibition games).

A popular variation of the season ticket plan is the *partial season ticket* plan. In MLB, buyers can choose from a variety of packages that include a specified number of games. One team provides the following set of alternatives: the full season (81 games), the half season (40 games), and a quarter season (20 games). For the partial season plans, the same seat is sold to multiple buyers. The obvious constraint is that there can be no conflict; the team cannot sell tickets entitling more than one person to the same seat for any given game. Partial season ticket buyers generally have the same seat for each game, but the plans are staggered so as to avoid any conflict. In essence, four quarter-season ticket holders collectively own that seat for 80 games; only opening day is excluded. It is analogous to four people sharing a single season ticket. This reduces the overall price for any one buyer while providing some of the same benefits that are provided to the purchasers of full season tickets. It is not unusual for these partial season ticket buyers to receive small discounts as well. For instance, a ticket for an infield box seat at a Detroit Tigers game has a face value of $35; however, purchasers of the quarter-season plan pay the discounted price of $32 each. This translates into a $60 savings for each seat over the course of the partial season.

> For the partial season plans, the same seat is sold to multiple buyers.

Another strategy used by virtually every marketer of spectator sports is that of *price tiering*. This strategy is an acknowledgment that the various target markets create different price points for the organization to take into account. Implementation simply involves the sale of tickets for different seating locations in the venue at different prices. It will take into account those customers who are relatively insensitive to price; these buyers will pay top prices for the best seats. Seats farther from the action sell for a lower price. For events that do not generally sell out, the team will often offer inexpensive seats for those who will not or cannot pay the prices required for the best seats. The result can be a myriad of different price tiers. An example of this phenomenon is the Atlanta Braves. For weekend games during the 2005 season, the team had 12 seating alternatives that comprised 10 price tiers ranging from the top level of $53 to a low of $1. The array of pricing alternatives is shown in Box 18.2.

A comparatively recent innovation in ticketing involves *variable pricing*.[3] This strategy is implemented by selling a seat for different prices depending upon timing or the opponent. The rationale for the differentials is based upon the anticipated level of demand. For example, Ohio State University charges more for games against a national power such as the University of Michigan than it does for a less famous opponent such as Miami of Ohio. At the University of Texas, tickets for the game against the University of Houston sold for $40, whereas tickets to the game against the national power and archrival team from the University of Oklahoma had a face value of $60.[4]

More common is a variable pricing strategy based on timing. Many MLB teams charge more for weekend games than for weekday games; this is one of the variables that the Colorado Rockies use to designate each of their games as either a premium, value, or classic game. The St. Louis Cardinals' tickets are $3 higher from May 23 through September 11. In each case, the reality is that some games are more appealing or more convenient for the fans. It is these games where demand is likely to increase, which provides the team with the opportunity to enhance its revenue by charging higher prices.

Value pricing is a philosophy common to discount retailers. In addition to low prices, the marketer must support this strategy with promotions that portray the team or event as a bargain when compared to the alternatives. Many minor league teams emphasize this aspect of their marketing strategy. A look at the prices of tickets for MLB and minor league baseball games documents this difference. According to the most recent "Team Marketing Report," the average price for a ticket to an MLB game in 2005 was $21.17; the average for

ATLANTA BRAVES 2005 PRICING TIERS — 18.2

Single Ticket, Saturday Game
- Dugout — $53
- Lexus — 37
- Field — 35
- Terrace — 35
- Lexus pavilion — 29
- Terrace reserved — 27
- Field pavilion — 23
- Terrace pavilion — 23
- Upper reserved — 11
- Upper pavilion — 5
- Skyline — 1

Source: "Braves," 2005, www.ticketmaster.com/event/0E003A269C69AFE6 (accessed April 30, 2005).

minor league baseball was $6.01.[5] Minor league hockey in Canada and the United States uses a similar strategy to differentiate itself in a positive way from the National Hockey League.

Teams often use *promotional pricing* to increase demand for games that are unlikely to fill the arenas and stadia to capacity. MLB's Minnesota Twins provided two children's tickets for free when two adult tickets were purchased. This promotion represented an overt effort to appeal to families by making the price less of a barrier. In Toronto, the health scare associated with SARS was keeping fans away from the Blue Jays' MLB games. By offering select tickets for $1, the team was able to attract more spectators to the stadium. The strategy was also designed to promote the city of Toronto as a safe city for tourists to visit.[6]

The Toronto Convention and Visitors Association also teamed with other organizations using a pricing strategy known as *bundling*. This particular promotion included one night in a Toronto hotel, two tickets to a Blue Jays game, two tickets to a top theatrical production, and dinner for two at an upscale restaurant. The price for this bundle was far less than if the consumer had purchased all four components separately. Most often, bundling does not involve outside organizations. The Grand Slam Ticket Pack of MLB's Atlanta Braves provides four game tickets, four hot dogs, four Coca-Colas, four Braves bucket caps, one game program, and parking at prices as low as $59.

Another variation of promotional pricing is the *cross-promotion discount*. This generally involves a sponsor that is associated with the discount. The Atlanta Braves have Coca-Cola Tuesdays and McDonald's Outfield Advantage on Wednesdays. Both promotions provide the opportunity to purchase a ticket in a specified seating area and receive a second ticket free. The Detroit Tigers entered into a cross-promotion with the Bowling Centers Association. Coupons were distributed at bowling facilities; these allowed consumers to purchase up to four upper-box tickets at half price. A classic example of cross-promotion involved the Houston Astros and Coca-Cola. The team plays at Minute Maid Park. Not coincidentally, Minute Maid is a brand owned by Coca-Cola. The promotion required fans to bring two labels from select Coca-Cola products to the box office to qualify for the special offer that allowed them to purchase four mezzanine tickets, four hot dogs, four Coca-Colas, and two caps for $55. Without the labels, the same array of products would have cost $122.

Another strategy requires purchasers of season tickets to make a *qualifying payment* that gives them the right to purchase their tickets. This payment is not deemed to be part of the ticket price, yet it makes a meaningful contribution to the team's revenues. This strategy has emerged in both professional sports and collegiate sports. One term commonly applied to this qualifying payment is *permanent seat license (PSL)*. Others refer to it as a *personal seat license*. Regardless of the designation, it is evident that PSLs are most relevant when the stadium routinely sells out. In professional sports, the Chicago Bears recently instituted a PSL fee. The onetime fee varies according to seat location, and only the least desirable seats are exempt from this qualifying payment. The distinction between personal seat licenses and permanent seat licenses will be clarified in Chapter 22 when our attention turns to the controversial issues within the realm of sports marketing.

Universities have been quick to adopt this strategy for their football games. Some refer to it as a PSL; others position it as a donation to the athletic program. The University of Tennessee requires an annual donation ranging between $500 and $1,000 per seat in addition to the price of the tickets. The University of Michigan's required donations range from $125 to $500 per seat per year. Most major college football programs have instituted some sort of qualifying payment, especially for the more desirable seats.[7]

> The University of Tennessee requires an annual donation ranging between $500 and $1,000 per seat in addition to the price of the tickets.

In a relatively new pricing strategy, Ticketmaster used the *bidding* process to determine who could purchase VIP tickets to a boxing match between Lennox Lewis and Kirk Johnson. The top 150 bidders received the package that included tickets for two ringside seats. A spokesperson for the venue indicated that it allowed the promoters to establish prices that coincided with what the consumers were "ultimately willing to pay."[8]

It is evident that marketers of spectator sports have a large number of pricing strategies that they can implement for the live audience. Box 18.3 provides an overview of these strategies.

As with the live audience, marketers must also consider many factors when setting prices for the media-based audience. How much should be charged for a PPV event or for video streaming on the Internet? What fees should be charged to broadcasters for the rights to distribute audio and video signals to their media-based audiences?

Setting the price for a spectator sports product is an essential step in the development of a marketing strategy. To this point, the focus has been solely upon spectator sports. But there are two other categories of sports products for which pricing strategies must be developed. Our discussion will now continue with an examination of the strategies used to develop the optimal pricing strategy for participation sports.

Participation Sports

The fees charged for membership and utilization of participation facilities are based on many factors, consequently there is no single pricing strategy that meets the needs of all service providers. The following section will consider the implementation of pricing strategies for an array of participation sports. It will emphasize the golf industry, as there are numerous examples that illustrate how marketers in this industry establish and adjust their prices. Though the emphasis is on golf, these practices are applicable for operators of facilities that address the needs of participants of other sports and activities. Some of these other applications will also be discussed.

In highly competitive markets, a key consideration is *supply and demand*. High supply coupled with low demand serves to drive prices down. Earlier in this book, there was an acknowledgment that there is an overabundance of golf courses in many geographic areas. The high supply as measured by the ability to accommodate golfers exceeds the demand for

PRICING APPLICATIONS FOR SPECTATOR SPORTS

18.3

- Season ticket
  - Full season
  - Partial season
- Price tiering
- Variable pricing
  - Timing
  - Opponent
- Value pricing
- Promotional pricing
  - Discounting
  - Bundling
  - Cross-promotion
- Qualifying payment
  - PSL
  - Donation
- Bidding

the available tee times. This imbalance has driven down prices, even at many of the up-market courses that have historically charged higher prices to their customers. In the United States, this same imbalance has been evident in 10-pin bowling. While many bowling facilities are closing, others operate well below their capacities to provide their services. In other countries, this type of bowling is new, so there are relatively few establishments. As such, demand exceeds supply thereby exerting upward pressure on prices.

A second strategy is to base the price on the *level of service* provided. Marketers often use added service as a means of attaining a differential advantage over their competition. Golf courses that charge premium prices often have attendants who assist players with their clubs prior to and upon completion of their round of golf. The price may also include a power cart or a caddy. Another service is the inclusion of the use of practice facilities such as a driving range and a putting green. Golf courses that offer few or no services beyond the basic golf course cannot command the higher prices.

Gymnasiums also give strong consideration to the level of service that they provide when determining their pricing strategy. Service takes into account issues such as the size of the facility, its comfort, the array of exercise equipment provided, the availability of trainers and consultants, security, the ease of parking, the use of personal lockers, and the privacy provided in changing rooms and showers. Some marketers provide only the most basic set of services; others seek to be perceived as a full-service provider. The costs associated with providing the enhanced services will drive prices up; however, consumers who associate added value with these services are willing to pay the higher prices.

For establishing pricing differentials, some participation sports facilities use an approach similar to that of the *variable pricing* strategy used by many marketers of spectator sports. Using this strategy, the service provider establishes different prices for the same service. The differentials are generally based upon some issue related to timing. The use of the same facility may be higher on weekends than from Monday through Friday. Similarly, prices for facilities that can be used any time of the day are often higher in the evening than they are in the morning or afternoon. The lower prices are intended to even out the demand over the various time frames. Since most people work during the day, Monday through Friday, they are limited in terms of when they can engage in a specific activity. Others are more flexible with their schedule, so marketers employ lower prices to encourage them to use the facilities during nonpeak periods.

Golf courses use special twilight rates to encourage golfers to start late and play until darkness forces them to quit. Using a similar strategy, operators of bowling facilities often have "night-owl" bowling. This allows participants to bowl at a substantially discounted rate late at night when the facility would normally find it difficult to attract customers.

> Golf courses use special twilight rates to encourage golfers to start late and play until darkness forces them to quit.

In addition to using the time of day and day of the week as pricing factors, some facilities establish different prices during different seasons of the year. Many gymnasiums experience a significant seasonal component in their demand. Because a variety of outdoor options are available, such as walking, running, and bicycling, gymnasiums often experience a significant decline in demand during the summer. To encourage people to use these facilities during the off-season, many gyms offer special prices. Many golf courses have lower rates in early spring and late fall; their highest prices are charged during the peak golf season. Of course, there is considerable variability as to when the discounted rates begin and end. The golf season in North Dakota or England is far shorter than the season in Hawaii or Singapore. In fact, golf is viewed as a yearlong activity in many locales.

Another form of variable pricing is based upon *individual considerations* rather than timing. For example, many facilities are operated as private or semiprivate clubs, though these clubs may accept nonmembers as occasional participants. Members may use the facility at no additional fee beyond the cost of their annual membership, or they may be charged a participation fee each time they use the facility. Nonmembers will be charged a fee that generally exceeds that paid by members.

The New Zealand golf market is dominated by courses that allow individuals to pay a yearly membership for unlimited access. When they play their home course, no additional fee is required. When they play another course, they are required to pay a rate reserved for "affiliated members." Guests of members may pay yet a different price. Finally, those with no New Zealand course affiliation pay much higher rates. The New Zealand Golf Association recognizes that many tourists view golf in New Zealand as a bargain. The variable pricing policy is one way of generating more revenue for local clubs while insulating residents from the higher prices. The pricing strategy for Formosa Auckland Country Club is shown in Table 18.3. It indicates that daily greens fees range from $0 to $125.

Sporting Goods, Apparel, Athletic Shoes, and Sports-Related Products

As noted earlier in this chapter, products in this category are generally distributed and sold through some type of retail environment. These retailers may be traditional brick-and-mortar retailers, virtual retailers on the Internet, or direct response marketers such as those seen on TV home shopping networks, in infomercials, in catalogs, and in traditional advertising. Also important are the retail storefronts that sell a variety of sports-related products at the event venues. As such, price determination is generally based upon fundamental retailing principles.

A key point of differentiation is the way in which value is added to many of these products. For apparel, the inclusion of the licensed trademarks of a fan's favorite team adds value that provides greater pricing flexibility for the marketer. For sporting goods

TABLE 18.3
Variable Pricing Policy of Formosa Auckland (New Zealand) Country Club

(18 Holes, no cart, priced in New Zealand dollars)

Source: "Formosa Auckland Country Club," 2005, www.formosa.co.nz/golf_intro.htm (accessed October 14, 2005). Reprinted with permission of Formosa Auckland Country Club.

Player's Status	Greens Fees
Member	$0
Member's guest	55
NZGA-affiliated member	65
Nonaffiliated golfer	125

and athletic shoes, endorsements by popular, high-performing athletes may add value that commands higher prices.

Service is not a key component of most products in this category. Furthermore, the vast majority of these marketers are retailers that simply purchase their products from suppliers and, in turn, resell them to their customers. While these retailers do need to consider the cost of maintaining a storefront and the labor to staff it, the primary outlay is paid for the acquisition of the products that they will resell. This was earlier defined as the cost of goods sold (COGS). Given this, the most popular form of pricing is the *markup* method, which involves taking the cost and adding a desired margin to arrive at the final price. This may sound simple, but the marketer must take care in determining the optimal percentage to be added. If it is too high, the unfavorable price will reduce demand to the point that the marketer has excess inventory. Conversely, if it is set too low, the marketer incurs an opportunity cost because of the lower profit margin.

> **At the venue, consumers are less sensitive to pricing.**

The markup rate can vary significantly from one product to another. For example, teams generate greater profits (measured as a percentage of the selling price) for beer than they do for a team T-shirt. Still, these markups are higher than those of traditional retailers because the fan has few alternatives. At the venue, consumers are less sensitive to pricing. Applying what was learned earlier, demand in this environment is less elastic or perhaps even inelastic. Consumers will often pay as much for a single beer at a sports event as they would for a six-pack of the same beer at the supermarket. Markups on special souvenirs such as those designating a championship are also candidates for higher markup percentages. Conversely, the merchandise of the nonwinners may be sold at sharply lower prices, perhaps even deeply discounted, especially toward the end of the season. Even winning teams have season-ending sales in an effort to liquidate their excess inventory.

Closing Capsule

Marketers in all industries must strive to develop pricing strategies that are consistent with the other components of their marketing mix. Price has many definitions, but it represents what the buyer gives up in the exchange process. A key consideration in establishing price is the elasticity of demand. This is a measure of the market's response to changes in prices. Marketers often attempt to establish a differential advantage over their competitors in an effort to minimize the market's reaction to price increases. Such inelastic demand curves are more plausible when there are no substitute products that fulfill the same need or when the consumer is simply unwilling or unable to forgo the purchase of a particular product.

> **Marketers often attempt to establish a differential advantage over their competitors in an effort to minimize the market's reaction to price increases.**

There are many factors that have a direct impact on the prices that can be charged. These include situational factors, costs, competitive actions, supply and demand, the organization's marketing objectives, legal considerations, consumer perceptions, and the need for the pricing strategy to be consistent with the other elements of the marketing mix. Once these factors have been evaluated, the marketer must decide upon the general pricing strategy to be employed. The most common of these strategies are cost-plus, markup, promotional pricing, yield management, and target return pricing. By understanding the factors that impact pricing and the general strategies used to determine final prices, the sports marketer can implement its own pricing strategy. There is no single strategy that is applicable in all cases.

Price is perhaps the most commonly criticized aspect of the strategies employed by marketers of spectator sports. The most common accusation is that sports are being priced beyond the reach of the typical sports fan. The most common pricing strategies for spectator sports are the season ticket plans, partial season plans, price tiering, variable pricing, promotional pricing, qualifying payments, and bidding.

For participation sports, the emphasis is on supply and demand, the level of service provided, the viability of a variable pricing policy, the use of memberships, and other individual characteristics. The marketers of participation sports must also take the costs associated with providing their services into consideration when establishing their prices.

The final category of sports products is represented by goods that are normally sold through a retail environment. The most commonly used approach for determining final prices is the traditional markup method. The retailer simply takes the cost of a product and adds the desired profit margin to arrive at the final price. The markup rate can vary significantly, so the marketer must take care to neither overprice nor underprice its products. Finally, once a season or event is over, the price is often subject to markdowns in an effort to convert excess inventory into cash.

With the pricing strategy now established, the marketer's attention turns to the fourth and final element of the marketing mix. The promotional strategy will address the most effective ways in which the marketer can communicate with its target markets. Specifically, the need is to develop the promotional mix, or what was identified earlier in this text as the integrated marketing communications plan.

Review Questions

1. Define price.
2. What is meant by elastic and inelastic demand? Why is it an important consideration for marketers?
3. How do substitute products play a role when making pricing decisions?
4. What are the eight factors that influence price? Which do you think is the most important in the marketing of spectator sports?
5. What are the five general implementation strategies discussed in this chapter? Which do you think is most appropriate for determining the prices for spectator sports, participation facilities, and sporting goods?
6. Why is the price of spectator sports subject to so much scrutiny and criticism?
7. Go to the Team Marketing Report Web site. Find the most recent Fan Cost Index (FCI) values for the four major sports in the United States. How have the prices changed in recent years?
8. Explain how an MLB team's sale of one half-season and two quarter-season tickets is equivalent to selling one season ticket.
9. What is price tiering in spectator sports?
10. What is variable pricing, and why has it become so popular for spectator sports?

11. What are the two types of qualifying payments that can be used by marketers of spectator sports? Under what circumstances are they most viable? Why are they subjected to so much criticism?

12. Explain the concept of bundling.

13. Select one of the athletic teams at your university. Select a target market; then develop a bundling strategy for appealing to your selected target. What would you include? What price would you charge?

14. Select a local facility for participation sports in your community. Assess the level of service that it provides and compare it to the price of membership.

15. How is variable pricing used to even out demand for participation facilities?

16. Why is the markup method the most popular approach for determining the prices for sporting goods, apparel, shoes, and sports-related products?

17. Why is demand for items sold at a sports venue less elastic (or even inelastic) than for the same goods sold at a local retailer?

Endnotes

1. "Team Marketing Report," 2005, www.teammarketing.com/fci.cfm (accessed July 6, 2005).

2. D. Smith, "Fans Turned Off by High Prices," October 25, 2004, www.sportbusiness.com/news/index?news_item_id=15597 (accessed October 13, 2005); and E. Swift, "Hey Fans: Sit on It!" *Sports Illustrated,* May 15, 2000, pp. 71–85.

3. G. Foster, S. Greyser, and B. Walsh, *The Business of Sports* (Mason, OH: Thomson South-Western, 2006), p. 298.

4. D. Rovell, "Sports Fans Feel Pinch in Seat (Prices)," June 21, 2002, www.espn.go.com/sportsbusiness/s/2002/0621/1397693.html (accessed October 14, 2005).

5. "Team Marketing Report."

6. C. Britcher, "SARS Prompts $1 Ticket Offer," April 28, 2003, www.sportbusiness.com/news/index?news_item_id=1510511 (accessed October 13, 2005).

7. D. Lederman, "Schools Making Fans Give More to Keep Best Seats," *USA Today,* August 25, 2004, pp. 1A, 4A.

8. C. Britcher, "Bid Up for Ringside Seats," May 1, 2003, www.sportbusiness.com/news/index?news_item_id=151106 (accessed October 13, 2005).

CHAPTER NINETEEN

Developing a Promotional Strategy for the Marketing of Sports Products

Learning Objectives

- Review the principles of communications and promotion.
- Learn why components of an IMC plan must fit together.
- Evaluate the role of sponsorship in marketers' IMC plans.
- Consider the inclusion of direct response marketing.
- Learn how each component of the IMC has been applied.
- Understand the role that brand equity plays in marketing.
- Learn how marketers can take advantage of cross-promotion.
- Learn how the NBA has integrated the elements of IMC.

In any industry, *promotion* can be characterized as an effort to communicate with one or more of the organization's target markets. The short-run goals of these promotional efforts can vary significantly; but in the long run, the ultimate goal is generally one of increasing sales. Every marketer must develop a promotional strategy that is focused on a variety of objectives. The specific strategy will be influenced by the product being sold, the target markets, the distribution strategy, the pricing strategy, and the marketer's short-term objectives. The communications efforts may also reflect the personality of those charged with the task of developing the promotional strategy. As a consequence, there is no standard model that can be applied by all marketers. In fact, even competitors within the same industry will use far different promotion strategies in their efforts to sell the same products to identical target markets.

When the earlier discussion in this text focused on the marketing of products through sports, it introduced the concept of the promotional mix. Historically, this component of the organization's marketing mix was deemed to consist of advertising, personal selling, sales promotion, and public relations (publicity). More recently, many marketers have begun to support the inclusion of sponsorship within the promotional mix. Still others have indicated a belief that direct response marketing should likewise be included. Although our focus has shifted to the marketing of sports products, our initial point of emphasis remains the same; marketers of sports products must develop a comprehensive promotional strategy as an essential part of their overall marketing strategy.

The second point of emphasis is that the promotional mix constitutes the set of tools the organization can use in its efforts to communicate with its target markets. Instead of applying the term *promotional mix,* marketers now speak of the *integrated marketing communications (IMC) plan.* The term itself conveys the underlying premise that the elements used to communicate with the various groups should be coordinated in such a way that they complement each other as the marketer strives to attain its goals.

> The elements used to communicate with the various groups should be coordinated in such a way that they complement each other as the marketer strives to attain its goals.

Finally, the organization's integrated marketing communications plan must be consistent with the other elements of the marketing strategy. In other words, it needs to support the marketer's strategies regarding its product offerings, the methods for distributing those products, and pricing. It should also reach the desired target markets while conveying the desired message. The overriding theme of the last few chapters has been one of integration. The terms *consistency* and *synergy* were also commonly used to characterize marketing strategy. Stated another way, the elements of the IMC plan must fit together; the overall promotional strategy must fit with the other elements of the marketing mix; and the marketing mix must fit with the characteristics of the target market. Only then will all of the strategic elements work in harmony and increase the likelihood that the organization will achieve its marketing goals.

We have now reached the point in this text where we are ready to consider the final basic element of our marketing strategy. As such, the emphasis of this chapter will be on the development of an integrated marketing communications plan in an effort to sell sports products. The discussion will delineate several fundamental principles of promotion as well as numerous examples of how the various components of an IMC plan have been implemented within the sports marketing environment.

Principles of Promotion

Regardless of the industry, there are several basic principles that must be understood by those charged with the task of developing the organization's promotional strategy. Since the basic objective of any promotion is to convey a message, this review will begin with a brief overview of the communications process.

The Communications Process

Whether we are talking about marketing or any other effort to communicate with an individual or group of individuals, the basic communication process is relevant. This textbook represents the author's effort to communicate with the readers; as such, these fundamental elements of the communications process needed to be considered.

Every effort to communicate begins with a sender and ends with a receiver. Figure 19.1 not only verifies these initial and terminal points, but it also identifies the role of encoding and decoding as well as the need to select an appropriate medium for transmitting the message.

The *sender* is the source of the message. In marketing, the source is the organization that is attempting to influence another's behavior. It represents the point of origination for the message to be conveyed.

FIGURE 19.1
The Basic Communications Process

Encoding represents the sender's choice of words, expressions, and symbols used to denote the intended message. An understanding of the targeted receiver of the message is essential in this step. The sender must use vocabulary and images that are readily understood by those in the target audience. Not only must they be understood, but the message must also reflect the sender's intent. Words have different connotations in different countries, even in different parts of the same country. Americans wait in a line, whereas residents of Australia wait in a queue. To some people, dinner is the evening meal; to others it is the afternoon meal. Colors convey different meanings in different cultures; even certain numbers have special significance in different parts of the world. The point is that the sender must take care to use words and images that reflect the intended message.

The *medium* represents the mechanism used to transmit the encoded message. Traditional media such as television, radio, magazines, newspapers, and billboards should readily come to mind. Telephones have long been used to deliver telemarketing messages, but recent changes in the laws that regulate this activity have placed significant limitations on their viability as a marketing communications medium.

More recently, marketers have looked at opportunities presented by venue signage, including scoreboards. Patches on participants' uniforms might also be viewed as a medium. A recent report on TV even went so far as to report on a firm that was considering the use of temporary tattoos on players. One medium that has emerged as an effective and cost-efficient approach for delivering messages is the Internet. All of these media are regularly used in marketing efforts for sports products as well as the mainstream and domain-focused efforts where nonsports products are sold using sports as a marketing platform.

Once it has selected the medium, the marketer needs to decide how to best use the choices available within that medium in the effort to reach its target market. The marketer might opt to use TV because it reaches large audiences, but there must still be a decision as to which TV programs to use. Should the advertisement be broadcast during the evening news or an afternoon soap opera? The two programs likely reach quite different audiences. The same is true for every other mass medium.

Magazines, newspapers, and radio programs reach well-defined demographic markets. And like TV, the alternatives in each media category often reach different market segments. No matter how effective the sender has been in the encoding process, the failure to utilize the correct tools for the transmission of the message will hinder the sender's ability to achieve its communications goals.

As the message is transmitted via the selected medium, the next step is that of *decoding*. This represents the interpretation of the message by those receiving the message. If the message was correctly conceived and encoded, the interpretation will more closely coincide with the sender's intent. Otherwise, it may lead to confusion or a misunderstanding that will adversely impact the sender's ability to communicate the desired message.

> If the message was correctly conceived and encoded, the interpretation will more closely coincide with the sender's intent.

Finally, there is the *receiver*. Whether it is an individual or a group of individuals, the receiver is the targeted audience. Even if the message is decoded correctly, it will only be effective if the medium reaches those for whom it was intended. It should be evident that the communications task is twofold. The marketer must (1) develop an effective message and (2) deliver it to the correct audience. Failure to accomplish either of these two tasks is enough to render the message totally ineffective.

Any discussion of the communications process would be incomplete if it did not include the concepts of noise and feedback. *Noise* is any barrier that hinders the communications process and threatens the ability of the message to be correctly interpreted by the receiver.

FIGURE 19.2
Comprehensive
Model of the
Communications
Process

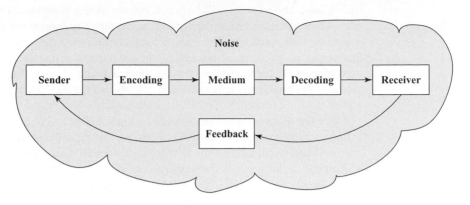

Clutter in the form of excessive advertising on TV, advertising pages in a magazine, or signs in the stadium means that there are too many messages competing for the receivers' attention. Often, the result is that the receiver simply does not devote the time or effort needed to see, hear, or decode the message. Noise can also be a physical distraction. A telephone call or a family member's request for help in the kitchen might cause the intended receiver to miss a message completely. Remote controls for TVs represent a barrier as many viewers *zip* from one channel to another when the commercials begin. To few people's surprise, this zipping behavior is more common among male viewers than it is for female viewers.

In an effort to gauge the effectiveness of any communications effort, marketers assess *feedback*. In essence, feedback represents a transformation in the communications process whereby the channel is reversed. The initial receiver becomes the sender and the original sender becomes the receiver. Another way of explaining it is that feedback represents the flow of information in the opposite direction. Feedback is far easier to measure when interpersonal media such as personal selling or the telephone are used. These media also provide the sender with the opportunity to clarify any ambiguities and correct any misinterpretations of the original message. The ultimate level of feedback is the recognition that the receiver has behaved in the manner sought by the sender. This could be a request for additional information, or the receiver might place an order. Of course, the receiver also seeks feedback from the sender. This continuous loop of communications represents an interactive process that characterizes a dialog between the parties.

Having added feedback and noise to the environment, we should now reconceptualize the communications process. The new model resulting from these additions is depicted in Figure 19.2.

Now that there is a better understanding of the process, let's consider the objectives of any message. At this point, we are not speaking of marketing goals such as increased sales or changes in attitudes; rather, we are talking about communications objectives. The ultimate marketing goal may be to influence the receiver's purchase behavior, and the attainment of this goal is more likely when the message achieves a specific series of communications goals. This communications principle is referred to as the AIDA concept.

AIDA Concept

The AIDA model is a hierarchy of the following four basic communications objectives, starting with the most fundamental task and ending with the most important: *a*ttention, *i*nterest, *d*esire, and *a*ction (hence the acronym AIDA). As marketers seek to develop the most effective IMC plan, they must consider how their messages and each element of their promotional strategy fit within the AIDA model.

To be effective, any effort to communicate with another party must first gain the *attention* of the intended receiver. If the receiver's attention cannot be gained, there is little chance the message will have any impact on that individual's future behavior. In the sale of both sports and nonsports products, the use of endorsements by popular athletes can overcome clutter and open the lines of communication between the sender and the receiver. Depending upon the target market, images of attractive models, kids, and animals can be used to gain the attention of the target audience. Other creative strategies include the incorporation of popular music in radio and TV ads and the use of large headlines in ads where a print medium is used.

Once the receivers' attention has been gained, the next goal of the marketer's communications effort is to develop *interest* on the part of those receivers, that is, to arouse their curiosity and instill in them the belief that the sender's message may be relevant to them. This interest is what allows the sender to overcome noise while holding the attention gained earlier in the communications effort. The initial part of any message must give the receivers the sense that it is appropriate for them; otherwise they will simply tune it out. They may change channels, flip pages, or simply put up perceptual barriers that hinder effective communication. The encoding is crucial because the words and images used by the sender impact the receivers' comprehension of the message. If the receiver does not understand the message, it will be difficult to hold that individual's interest. The message at this point may begin to address the features of the product as well as the benefits derived by the consumer.

The third objective is desire. The concept of *desire* relates to the receivers' conviction that the product has value for them and represents a superior option when compared with other alternatives in the marketplace. If successful in creating such desire, the marketer has developed a differential advantage. The marketer has then gained the receivers' attention, developed an interest, and convinced them to behave in certain manner; most often, this sought behavior is the purchase of one of the marketer's products.

Finally, the marketer's communications efforts should facilitate action. From the perspective of the sender, *action* represents the initiation of the desired behavior. The receiver might seek additional information, place an order, or go to the store to purchase the product. Not all messages are developed with the purchase of a product as the primary marketing objective. The action sought might be a cancer screening for individuals, a change in attitude regarding a controversial company, or more fan involvement on the part of the crowd at a sports event.

The various components of the IMC plan have different capabilities and applications in respect to the achievement of the various communications objectives that comprise the AIDA concept. The practicality of any of these IMC components is also influenced by the size of the target audience, the characteristics of that audience, the action being sought by the marketer, and the resources available to devote to promotional activities. The components of an integrated marketing communications plan were identified earlier in Chapter 3. They are advertising, personal selling, sales promotion, public relations, and sponsorship. To ensure a sound understanding of the IMC plan prior to the discussion of how the components have been applied in the marketing of sports products, we will next briefly discuss each of these components. We will also consider the inclusion of a sixth component, direct response marketing, within the integrated marketing communications plan.

Components of the Integrated Marketing Communications Plan

Regardless of the industry in which the marketer operates, the same basic set of promotional tools is available for the efforts to communicate with the intended receivers. In general, these intended receivers represent the organization's target markets.

Advertising was earlier defined as a paid, nonpersonal form of communication that is generally disseminated via one or more of the mass media. These media include electronic broadcast media such as TV and radio, print media such as newspapers and magazines, and placement media such as billboards, signage at public venues, and signage on public transportation vehicles. The key consideration is that while mass media are employed, marketers will use advertising selectively in their efforts to more effectively reach a narrowly defined target market. The proliferation of options that can be used to reach specific demographic and lifestyle segments within each media category has enhanced these targeting efforts.

> Marketers will use advertising selectively in their efforts to more effectively reach a narrowly defined target market.

At this time, it is appropriate to draw a distinction between a medium and a vehicle. A medium was earlier defined as the mechanism used to transmit a message. These are broad categories such as TV, magazines, and radio. The *vehicle* represents a specific option within the selected medium. For example, TV is a medium; *60 Minutes* is a vehicle. Magazines are a medium; *Sports Illustrated* is a vehicle. Each medium has a variety of vehicles that appeal to different market segments. By selecting the appropriate vehicle, the marketer increases the likelihood that its message will reach the intended target audience. Though advertising can be expensive, it can be used effectively, especially when the goals of the communication efforts are to create awareness and interest on the part of those target markets.

Personal selling is the antithesis of advertising. Instead of being a mass communications tool, personal selling is a paid form of direct interaction between a selling entity and a prospective buyer. It can be the essence of one-to-one marketing in that it is designed to influence an individual's purchase behavior. The primary strength of personal selling is the feedback that facilitates two-way interaction. A second strength is that the message can be adapted or otherwise modified on the basis of that feedback. A third strength is that more persuasive messages intended to create desire on the part of the receiver can be delivered. Finally, the salesperson can initiate action as the message is being delivered. The marketer does not need to wait for the prospective buyer to respond at some later time and face the possibility that the action being sought will be delayed, reconsidered, or rejected. Personal selling is a key promotional tool in the business-to-business market, in the task of influencing the demand for expensive or high-tech products, and in the marketing of consumer services such as insurance and custom tailoring.

Sales promotion is an eclectic category that incorporates a wide array of promotional tools. These tools generally represent direct inducements designed to encourage a particular response. Although the response being sought is often the purchase of a product, other responses are the trial use or consumption of a product and the seeking of additional information about the marketer or its products. Among the most popular types of sales promotion are discount coupons, free samples, point-of-sale displays, contests, rebates, trade shows, and specialty advertising. Some of these sales promotion tools are most appropriate for the marketing of consumer convenience goods, but they can be used outside of the mass merchandising environment. As with advertising, these promotions represent a paid form of mass communication; as such, the marketer must carefully select the tools to be used as well as the methods for their distribution so as not to waste resources by communicating with individuals who are not part of the target market. Otherwise, the marketer is unlikely to create the desire that will induce action on the part of the receiver.

Public relations (PR) efforts are not generally aimed directly at the marketing objective of increasing sales. A common goal is one of garnering positive publicity in the local media. Similarly, the marketer may seek to counter negative PR that has been disseminated by local, national, and international media. In this regard, public relations can be defined as a nonpersonal form of communication designed to influence the attitudes and opinions of various groups of stakeholders. This may include consumers, investors, investment counselors, government officials, employees, and the general public. Since publicity cannot be controlled, not all PR efforts are productive in the marketer's quest

REVISED COMPONENTS OF AN IMC PLAN   19.1

- Advertising
- Personal selling
- Sales promotion
- Public relations
- Sponsorship
- Direct response marketing

to generate positive publicity; however, the absence of control also adds the element of credibility in the eyes of the various stakeholder groups. Though publicity is free, organizations will devote significant resources to the PR budget with the express goal of gaining favorable publicity.

> Though publicity is free, organizations will devote significant resources to the PR budget.

Sponsorship is the fifth component of today's IMC plans. Earlier in this book, sponsorship was characterized as the relationship between a marketer and a property that requires the marketer to pay a cash or in-kind fee for access to the exploitable commercial potential associated with the property. More often than not, this relationship involves the association of a nonsports product or organization with a sports property such as an event, a team, a sports venue, or a participant. Louis Vuitton's involvement with the America's Cup Sailing Regatta is but one example. Still, there are opportunities for sports products to maintain a sponsorship relationship with other sports properties. There are also opportunities for sports properties to become involved in sponsoring a vast array of nonsports properties such as tours by popular entertainers, local festivals, the arts, and charitable causes. One recent sponsorship endeavor involved the NFL's involvement with fund-raising for the Hurricane Katrina Relief Fund after the devastating storm all but obliterated New Orleans in 2005.

Direct response marketing (DRM) represents an effort to communicate with the target audience in a manner such that the receivers can immediately initiate action upon receiving the message. DRM is best characterized as a paid form of mass communications. What distinguishes it from traditional advertising is the mechanism that encourages and facilitates an immediate response by the receiver. DRM can use traditional broadcast media such as TV commercials and infomercials. It can use print media such as magazines and newspapers. Direct mail that uses catalogs, coupons, and DVDs is also an important medium. With more consumers connected to the Internet, the World Wide Web has also emerged as an effective DRM medium. Telemarketing is still an option, though many consumers tend to be alienated by a medium that they view as an intrusion to their daily lives. New laws that restrict when consumers can be called, new "do not call" registries, voice mail, call screening, and caller ID technology have all placed barriers in front of today's telemarketers.

Box 19.1 provides a summary of the six components of an integrated marketing communications plan. It is important to understand that an effective IMC plan does not require activity in each of the components. That is to say, the marketer may opt to employ only some of these activities; perhaps only advertising, sales promotion, and PR will be used. While there is no universal agreement that all six activities belong, there is agreement that any marketer's promotional efforts must fit together in such a manner that they are complementary rather than contradictory. This integration greatly enhances the likelihood that the marketer will achieve both sets of goals: its communications goals and its marketing goals.

> An effective IMC plan does not require activity in each of the components.

Implementation of Promotional Strategy in Sports Marketing

Each of the aforementioned components of an IMC plan has been effectively employed in the marketing of sports products. To illustrate these applications, we will take another look at each of the six components. Each example is meant to document one of the key components individually, but keep in mind that the marketer will seek to integrate these components into a comprehensive promotional strategy. The emphasis will again be on spectator sports, the live audience in particular; however, a number of examples will also be drawn from the marketing of participation sports as well as the category of products, which includes sporting goods, apparel, athletic shoes, and sports-related products. It is important to understand that these examples represent only a portion of each of the highlighted organization's integrated marketing communications plan. Our examination will start with the most readily recognized component of any promotional strategy, advertising.

Advertising

The most readily available form of promotion is advertising. When incorporating this component into the IMC plan, the marketer must take care regarding the selection of the media to be used as well as the vehicles within each medium. Clearly, the medium selected has a significant impact on the message that can be developed and delivered to the target audience. Conventional TV and radio commercials have significant time constraints. Can an effective message be conveyed in a 15- or 30-second block of time? Furthermore, radio precludes the use of any visual component; the message relies completely on words. Every medium presents some communications opportunities for the marketer, yet each has its own limitations. It should be apparent that media selection is greatly influenced by the nature of the message the marketer intends to send.

Perhaps even more important than the media selection decision is the one of determining which vehicles to use. Recall that a vehicle is a specific tool within each of the media that can be used for the transmission of information. For example, if the selected medium is newspapers, vehicles options may include the *Wall Street Journal, USA Today,* the *New York Times,* the *New Zealand Herald,* the *International Herald,* and the *London Times.* There are local, regional, national, and international newspapers within the set of vehicles available today. The selection of the vehicle is one of the key factors that determine the cost of the ad. More important, the vehicle provides the opportunity to reach the target audience while minimizing waste coverage. If a vehicle reaches a large number of people who are not part of the organization's target market, then resources are being wasted.

Applications of Advertising for Sports Products

You could likely cite advertisements for each of the three categories of sports products. And while you may not recall the vehicle, you will likely remember the medium. That there is recall of a specific advertisement implies that a relevant message was delivered using a vehicle that reached some members of the organization's target market. Perhaps you will recall some of the following examples.

Anyone who watched the 2005 Masters Golf Tournament will likely remember the fantastic chip shot made by Tiger Woods as he rallied to win one of golf's most prestigious events. The ball hesitated on the lip of the cup for a dramatic pause prior to falling in. Readily visible to the viewers was the Nike logo imprinted on the ball. Within three weeks, that famous shot was the primary component of a creative message used in Nike ads designed to sell its newest golf ball. The vehicles selected were The Golf Channel and the TV network that was airing the weekly PGA tournament. Retailer demand for the new ball was so high that Nike sold out of its anticipated production before the ball ever made it to the consumer market.

Many other marketers of sporting goods also rely on celebrity endorsements as a way of generating interest in their products. Consider some of the following examples. Commercials and print ads for adidas feature the New Zealand All Blacks in an effort to sell the company's new shoes and rugby balls in that geographic market. Signage on NASCAR vehicles promotes many different products, some of which relate directly to motor sports. A person watching a telecast of drag racing would likely see decals for Crane cams, Holley carburetors, Edelbrock manifolds, Hooker headers, Goodyear tires, and STP; and a viewer who actually participates in such competition may see these products as having the potential of improving their own performance on race day or during an impromptu competition Endorsements are also critical in the task of influencing consumers to purchase specific brands and styles of athletic shoes and apparel. Reebok's use of Venus Williams has been evident in a number of advertising vehicles that reached women in general and tennis enthusiasts in particular. While some of these examples reflect sponsorship involvement, we should recall that sponsorships are typically leveraged through the use of traditional advertising.

Not all efforts involve endorsements. Many marketers use traditional advertising to differentiate their products from those of their competition. Others use it to help perpetuate the image that they are seeking within the market. Prior to the World Cup of Soccer, Nike placed images of its "swoosh" logo and "Just Do It" trademark on public transportation vehicles in Lisbon, Portugal. Both the city and the country are widely recognized for the fervor of their soccer fans.

> Prior to the World Cup of Soccer, Nike placed images of its "swoosh" logo and "Just Do It" trademark on public transportation vehicles in Lisbon, Portugal.

Advertising is also used for the marketing of participation sports. A popular medium and vehicle is the local newspaper. Depending upon the season, ads that feature venues for skiing, skating, softball, soccer, and bowling are common. These generally represent an effort by one service provider to attract participants to a particular facility. In general, the broadcast media are too expensive for many of these operators, although some new, inexpensive opportunities for local TV advertising have emerged on local cable systems. Operators of year-round participation facilities also tend to rely on the local print media; some also view billboards as a viable option as they reach consumers who are physically within the specified geographic borders of the market. Tennis, racquetball, and squash clubs have used these media, as have operators of fitness centers such as Powerhouse and Gold's Gym.

Other advertising is done to influence primary demand rather than selective demand. For example, some advertising is designed to increase the number of golfers rather than to induce them to play at a particular course. Clearly, this strategy can be used to raise the level of participation in any sport or activity, not just golf. In many cases, such advertising is aired during a TV broadcast of the particular sport. For instance, commercials touting the fun and social aspects of 10-pin bowling are often aired during the broadcast of Professional Bowlers Association events. These commercials may use recognizable professional bowlers to help deliver a message, or they may rely on actors who are placed in the roles of recreational bowlers. Every participation sport with professional competitions that are broadcast on TV has this option for delivering its message to a receptive target market.

Advertising is a key component of the IMC plan in the marketing of spectator sports. This includes efforts designed to attract fans to the venue or to get them to witness it via some broadcast medium. In other words, advertising is used to increase both the live audience and the media-based audience. In many cases, the marketers of spectator sports are granted a predetermined amount of advertising time as part of the rights package that is sold to the broadcasters. These commercials are typically aired during the broadcast of the event. They may be designed to attract fans to the venue at a later date, or they may inform the viewer of future broadcasts in an effort to increase the size of the media-based audience. The NBA has a creative theme that positions its sport as "fan-tastic." The obvious double association of fans and a fantastic game is designed to attract larger audiences. Many ads of this type feature star players from the sport being advertised.

> Advertising is used to increase both the live audience and the media-based audience.

Local professional teams use a variety of media to reach their local markets; these include TV, radio, newspapers, billboards, and the Internet. When using broadcast media, it is important to select vehicles that emphasize the local geographic area while reaching an audience that fits the marketer's definition of its own target market.

Signage at the venue is seen by fans who attend a game in person, watch it on TV, or access a broadcast via video streaming on the Internet. Signs often promote upcoming games or identify the media through which these games can be viewed or heard. Special events are promoted, as are events that will take place in the same facility or those that will be staged at another venue by the same organization. This type of promotion is referred to as cross-promotion, a strategy that will be discussed in more depth later in this chapter. Venue signage can be a permanent display, an electronic sign such as one generated on the scoreboard, or a virtual sign.

Relatively new to this mix is *virtual signage*. These signs are not seen by spectators at the stadium; rather, they are computer-generated and seen only by the TV viewers. The major advantages of virtual signage are that new signs take little time to construct, the viewable images can be changed many times throughout the broadcast, and the signage can be altered for different geographic markets. They are applicable for any sport, but they may be even more valuable in the broadcast of sports such as rugby and soccer that have few, if any, breaks during the course of play. Many of these virtual signs are used for advertising nonsports products, but others promote future attendance and viewership.

Signage is also found on the participants' uniforms. MLB's St. Louis Cardinals had patches on their uniforms that promoted the last season at Busch Stadium during 2005. Part of the intent was to create nostalgia that would induce a casual fan to attend one last game. The 2005 Detroit Tigers' uniforms included a patch that called the fans' attention to the 2005 MLB All-Star Game played in the team's home stadium.

A few more examples highlight the application of advertising in the marketing of spectator sports. Women's soccer has been a difficult sell in the United States. The WUSA league's operations went into a hiatus upon the completion of the 2003 season. In an effort to revitalize interest, marketers for the league developed a "Keep the WUSA Dream Alive" campaign. Its execution involved a variety of media, including the league's Web site (www.wusa.com).[1] The National Hockey League used the broadcast of its 2003 All-Star game to deliver TV advertising that supported the league's effort to increase attendance for teams that were struggling to attract fans.[2] The National Thoroughbred Racing Association engaged in a new, well-funded advertising campaign designed to raise horse racing's "profile and popularity using a nationwide branding campaign and increased television coverage."[3] The advertisements aired over the weeks that coincided with the lead-up to and the staging of racing's Triple Crown events in May and June. Advertisements for the X Games were broadcast on ESPN and MTV in an effort to reach the core fans of extreme sports and alert them to the upcoming broadcasts.

Clearly, advertising plays a key role in the promotional strategy of today's marketers of sports products. But it is only one of the components of an IMC plan that can be used by these marketers. Our examination of the application of promotional efforts on the part of these marketers will now continue with a look at personal selling.

Personal Selling

The primary applications of personal selling in the marketing of sports products involve the business-to-business market. The expense associated with sales activities makes personal selling impractical for most consumer-oriented marketing endeavors. Still, it can play a role in the IMC plan of a marketer of consumer products; for instance, some sales that take place in a retail environment have a strong emphasis on personal selling. Efforts to sustain relationships with existing customers also use sales representatives, but these individuals are generally inside salespeople who use the telephone as their primary communications medium. Consider the following examples.

Applications of Personal Selling for Sports Products

In the field of spectator sports, personal selling plays a key role in the marketing efforts for the luxury suites that are now available in virtually every new major stadium and arena built throughout the world. These suites can be very expensive, with annual fees at some venues exceeding $500,000. Prices like these not only support the cost of personal selling efforts, but they also confirm the need for direct interaction with the prospect. Creating desire and stimulating action on the part of the prospect often requires an immediate response to a question or an objection. While the efforts to sell luxury suites may be supported with traditional advertising and the Internet, it is likely that these forms of communication will ultimately redirect the prospective buyer to a salesperson.

> Creating desire and stimulating action on the part of the prospect often requires an immediate response to a question or objection.

Telemarketing is used by most teams' sales forces in their efforts to attain renewals from their current season ticket base. Team officials view this type of interpersonal communication as an effective way to maintain and strengthen the relationship with this key customer group. For instance, such communication enables the season ticket holder to address the opportunity to move to better seats without moving to a higher-priced tier. It also provides the organization with the ability to talk to the ticket holder about *trading up*. This action involves the ticket holder's decision to purchase better seats in a more expensive tier. Trading up also refers to the decision of a partial-season ticket holder to purchase a more extensive ticketing package. For instance, the salesperson might encourage a half-season ticket holder to move up to a full season. Even if the buyer does not change price tiers, the selection of seats available to the full-season ticket buyer is generally superior to those reserved for partial-season ticket buyers. The salesperson has the opportunity to explain this option as well as any additional benefits that are granted to purchasers of season tickets.

In the marketing of participation sports, some facilities offer a free trial period membership to attract prospective customers. Once these individuals have experienced the services at the facility, a salesperson will undoubtedly attempt to convert that trial membership into one with a longer duration. Bally Fitness Centers have drop boxes in many locations where consumers can enter their contact information for a chance to "win" a two-week trial membership. Once these trial members go through an initial indoctrination, the salesperson will discuss the merits of upgrading to a contract that covers an extended period.

For customized products, the role of the salesperson is valuable for both the buyer and the seller. Sporting goods often require custom fitting, with the salesperson serving as a problem solver. Products such as skis, bowling equipment, and exercise equipment better fit the needs of the buyer when the marketer is able to assess those needs, suggest the appropriate products, and modify those products so that they provide a perfect fit. In some cases, the products are actually custom made. Many golfers now seek the services of a custom club fitter. By interacting with the golfer, the fitter can adjust the clubs to precisely match the golfer's stature, swing, and capabilities. This communications process should reduce the likelihood that the golfer will spend a considerable sum of money for clubs that simply do not satisfy his or her needs.

For other products that are sold through normal retail channels, the salesperson provides a modest amount of information to consumers. More important is the interaction between the manufacturer's salespeople and the employees of retail institutions who ultimately make the decisions as to which products will be sold at their stores. It is these retail buyers, not the consumers, who attract direct attention from the marketer's sales force. Products such as basic sporting goods, apparel, and athletic shoes fall into this category; however, advertising is likely to be the dominant component of the IMC plan for these products when the focus of the communications effort is on final consumers. From this example, we should further see how the components of any integrated marketing communications plan must work together in the effort to achieve the organization's communications and marketing goals. Advertising and personal selling are the two most visible components of the promotional strategy, but several other tools are available. We will now turn our attention to the third component of the IMC plan, sales promotion.

Sales Promotion

Marketers in every industry have continued to expand their use of sales promotion in an effort to provide direct inducements and stimulate immediate action on the part of the prospective buyer. In this regard, the marketing of sports products is no different. In spectator sports, many of these promotions were discussed in terms of extensions beyond the core product, which was earlier defined as the game the way it is played on the field of competition. In the previous chapter, the practices of promotional pricing and bundling were introduced. We can now see how the marketing mix is integrated in ways such that each decision or strategy complements the others. But for now, the discussion will address the use of sales promotion in the marketing of sports products.

Applications of Sales Promotion for Sports Products

Coupons are a popular form of sales promotion in the United States. Marketers of spectator sports use coupons as a means of providing discounts to select consumers. They may be sent through the mail, printed off the Internet, distributed at the venue, passed out door to door, or provided by local retailers. Most coupons specify an expiration date; this shortened validity period is designed to induce a quick response by the consumer. Failure to use them promptly will cause the coupons to lose their value. Some MLB teams provide a coupon for two free tickets to individuals who coordinated the purchase of group tickets. This promotion allows the group leader to attend another game at a later date without being burdened by the tasks of organizing and controlling a group of individuals.

Coupons are also used by marketers of participation sports, sporting goods, apparel, and athletic shoes. Once more, the period during which they are valid tends to be limited. The primary benefit to the buyer is that the coupon provides additional value. It may be a fixed monetary discount, a percentage discount, or a free gift that is given to anyone who makes a purchase within the specified time frame. For participation sports, a major focus is on discounts. But quite often, these discounts require more than one participant. Memberships

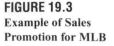

FIGURE 19.3
**Example of Sales
Promotion for MLB**

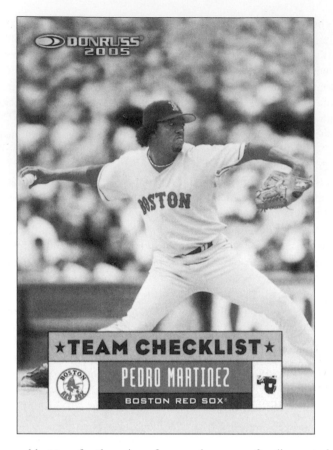

sold at two for the price of one and coupons for discounted prices for foursomes at a local golf course are two examples of this strategy.

Premiums that represent free items to be given to fans are also popular. Again, the question of whether this is part of the promotional strategy or the product strategy might be raised. Regardless of the answer, it represents a component of the overall marketing strategy. Popular giveaways are bobblehead dolls, caps, posters, magnetized schedules, inexpensive sporting goods, and souvenirs. Secondary sports such as those played in the minor leagues often emphasize the use of premiums in their IMC plans. Many major league teams have also used premiums in their efforts to develop a comprehensive IMC plan. Promotions of this type are often directed toward kids in an effort to nurture relationships with future paying fans. So not only does it build current demand, but it establishes a foundation for building future demand. Figure 19.3 illustrates one of the free trading cards that were distributed on opening day of the 2005 MLB season at each stadium. This promotion was important to MLB, but it also represented an approach for each of the four major marketers of baseball trading cards to get samples of their products into the hands of more than a million baseball fans in a span of a few days.

The distribution of the cards brings us to another popular form of sales promotion, *free samples*. This tactic is designed to stimulate trial, which was earlier acknowledged as a common precursor to adoption and purchase. The aforementioned example highlighting the provision of free, limited access to a participation facility can also be put into this category. The complimentary access provides a risk-free opportunity for the prospective member to evaluate the facility. The success of the strategy of using these free samples and trial memberships is typically measured by the conversion rate. How many prospects are converted into buyers?

The Internet has created new opportunities to provide specific information to potential ticket buyers through *virtual tours*. The Web site for the NBA's Memphis Grizzlies provides a virtual tour of the FedEx Forum where the team plays its home games. Many teams, including MLB's Colorado Rockies, allow the prospective ticket buyer to click on a section of the stadium or arena where the event will take place and get a virtual view from the seats available for purchase there. This practice is becoming common as more ticket buyers are shifting away from traditional retail options to the virtual box office.

Trade shows are used to gain direct access to potential buyers. Some of these shows are limited to retail buyers and require an invitation for admission, but others allow individual consumers to attend. Marketers set up displays designed to attract the attention of those in attendance while exhibiting their products for all to see. The annual PGA show is specifically for buyers from retail operations and the media. The emphasis is on new equipment that the manufacturers want the retailers to sell. The media's presence is designed to foster good public relations with an objective of gaining favorable publicity in the local, national, and international media.

Other trade shows focus on consumers. Attendance usually requires the payment of a modest admission fee by the consumer. Many local communities host an annual golf exposition. Consumers can see the new products; in fact, they often get a chance to try them out. *Contests* are used to attract prospective buyers. In addition to new equipment, many service providers also have a presence at these trade shows. Among the goods and services promoted and sold at these events shows are golf lessons, self-improvement DVDs, tee time services, and housing developments. New courses may have representatives there in an effort to create awareness of their new options for golfers. Whatever the product, these trade shows reach an eager segment of the golf participation market. They are also an appropriate promotional vehicle for a wide array of participation sports and other recreational activities. For example, some communities will play host to an annual boat show or perhaps a camper and RV show.

Many teams and manufacturers of sporting goods have *camps,* many of which emphasize the development of skills among young players. Alternatively, they may be fantasy camps that allow older fans to interact with current and former players in a camp setting. Examples include Nike's annual basketball camps for aspiring athletes and the 2006 Boston Red Sox Fantasy Camp that was limited to participants over the age of 29 who were willing to pay $3,695 for this nine-day endeavor.[4] While the attendees enjoy the participatory aspects of these camps, the marketers will seek to strengthen relationships with them with an eye toward future sales opportunities. Box 19.2 provides an overview of the Red Sox Fantasy Camp.

Public Relations

The least controllable aspect of any marketing communications effort is the publicity emanating from the organization's public relations efforts. The marketer will almost always disseminate information with a positive perspective, but not all sources share that same vision. Sources of negative publicity are competitors, consumer protection organizations, the media, and various governmental agencies. Although the publicity cannot be controlled, the public relations effort can be. However, despite all the organization's efforts, the PR may not result in any meaningful publicity from the media. As noted earlier, much of the PR effort may be designed to counter the negative publicity that has been broadcast, printed, or delivered through some other public forum such as speeches and the Internet. Examples of negative publicity on the Internet are the news reports and Web sites that have criticized Nike for its production practices in Vietnam. There was a harsh report on the ESPN Web site and there are numerous "hate Nike" Web sites that are maintained by individuals who continue to condemn Nike in this public forum.

Applications of Public Relations for Sports Products

Most teams have a *fan appreciation day*. This usually involves the local media and season ticket holders. In some instances, the team will invite the local community. It may take

FANTASY CAMP FOR MLB'S BOSTON RED SOX   19.2

Location:	Fort Myers, Florida
Dates:	February 4–12, 2006
Age requirement:	Aged 30 and over
Cost:	$3,695
Components:	

- One or two games daily with instruction from pros
- Game against pros and celebrities
- Red Sox uniform and accessories
- Deluxe hotel accommodations
- Daily continental breakfast in clubhouse
- Opening night reception
- Midweek cigar party
- Closing night awards banquet
- Minimum of four meals and events with the pros
- Autographs
- Participant's likeness on baseball card

place toward the end of the season during regularly scheduled home games, or it may be scheduled as a special event upon the conclusion of the season. The Plymouth Whalers of the Ontario Hockey League invited the general public to their arena. Fans were given a variety of sales promotion items, including posters, media guides, and key chains. The team set up an autograph table at which fans could interact with several team players. They were also allowed to skate on the ice at the arena. The primary objective of this entire day was to enhance the team's image in the eyes of the community and the fans of the team.

Press releases are used to announce awards and the signing of player contracts. Changes in ticket policies or in the schedule are commonly announced through a press release. Personnel changes such as those resulting from player trades and free agent signings are often first made public through this type of communication. New endeavors by major sports organizations are often the subject of news stories. When the NBA announced the formation of the National Basketball Development League, when the NBA announced its financial backing of the WNBA, and when the NFL disclosed plans for NFL Europe, the initial dissemination of the information to the public involved press releases to the national media and reports on the leagues' respective Web sites.

Many teams, leagues, and events are aligned with widely recognized *charities*. Often done in conjunction with a sponsor, the arrangements typically call for a contribution to be made to the charity. It may be a set amount, a portion of revenues, or an established amount to be donated each time that some specific achievement is attained. Perhaps your favorite baseball team commits to make a set donation for each home run that one of its players hits. Periodically throughout the season, the total of these donations will be disclosed using local broadcasts and press releases to the local media. This involvement with the community resonates well with its citizens, even those who are not real sports fans.

Finally, teams and event organizers may provide *free tickets* for a popular event. Quite often, these are provided to local media outlets for use as prizes for their viewers and listeners. The announcers will "tease" the audience with proclamations that the free tickets will be given away soon. While it keeps viewers and listeners tuned in, it also keeps the event or team's name before the public.

Several guidelines are cited as strategies for gaining favorable publicity. Marketers need to learn how to develop press kits, and they must establish and maintain contact with representatives of the media. As easy as it may sound, care needs to be taken when writing a press release. Among the recommendations made is to use an inverted pyramid writing style; simply stated, this technique involves leading with the most important aspects of the communication. Learn how to be interviewed and anticipate tough questions. Finally, learn how to use the Internet as a PR outlet.

Sponsorship

Sponsorship is generally viewed as a promotional tool that involves the marketing of nonsports products through an association with a sports property. However, sponsorship can also be used effectively in the marketing of sports products. In some cases, it is a sponsorship relationship that features two marketers of sports products. The more unusual situation is where a sports product is involved in the sponsorship of a nonsports property. Recall the other four categories of sponsorable properties discussed earlier in this text: local fairs, festivals, and annual events; entertainment tours and attractions; the arts; and causes. Marketers of sports products may find it advantageous to align themselves with one or more of these alternative sponsorship opportunities as they seek to develop an effective IMC plan.

Applications of Sponsorship for Sports Products

One of the more common alliances is that of two sports properties. Sports-related products are often involved in the sponsorship of teams, leagues, organizations, and venues. Nike uses its association with sports programs at major universities as a primary component of its marketing thrust. Among the sponsorships maintained by Nike are those with the University of Oklahoma and Louisiana State University. Other Nike sponsorships include its association with professional teams and events such as the Brazilian soccer team. The array of properties provides the broad exposure that is part of a promotional strategy designed to sell the company's different products. Reebok Stadium in the United Kingdom represents that sports marketer's attempt to use venue naming rights as part of its promotional strategy. Similarly, many sponsors of motor sports teams sell products that fans can use on their own cars as they prepare to participate in local amateur races or to simply add horsepower to their personal vehicles. While they may not be as well known as Nike or Reebok, their sponsorships can provide access to important target markets.

> Nike uses its association with sports programs at major universities as a primary component of its marketing thrust.

A recent NHL initiative was the introduction of NHL skating rinks. The belief was that the NHL brand provided a differential advantage that other ice skating facilities could not match. The value provided by a brand's recognition and its marketability is referred to as *brand equity*. Some may feel that this example is more indicative of a joint venture; however, it has many of the characteristics of a traditional sponsorship or a licensing agreement.

> The PGA issued a press release during the 2005 tour season that announced the organization's aggregate donation to charitable causes had exceeded $1 billion.

FIGURE 19.4
Tackling Men's Health and the NFL

A major sponsorship thrust for professional sports teams and organizations involves cause-related marketing. The team or event's sponsorship provides a mechanism for contributions to worthy charitable causes. The NFL is associated with the United Way; the NBA is aligned with the "Read to Achieve" program; and the PGA is involved with many causes, including St. Jude Children's Hospital. As noted earlier in this text, the NFL is a co-sponsor of a CRM program known as "Tackling Men's Health." To capitalize on this type of sponsorship, the teams, leagues and events will use advertising and PR tools, including press releases and short videos that promote their involvement. In other words, the organization is using its IMC plan to leverage its sponsorship. The videos are usually shown during the TV broadcast of their games and events. For example, the PGA issued a press release during the 2005 tour season that announced the organization's aggregate donation to charitable causes had exceeded $1 billion; announcers on PGA telecasts also called the viewers' attention to this fact. Obviously, sponsorships of this type should be integrated with traditional advertising and a targeted PR effort designed to highlight the involvement of the sports organization with these charities. Figure 19.4 illustrates an ad used to promote the relationship between the NFL and the "Tackling Men's Health" program.

Direct Response Marketing

Better known simply as direct marketing, this strategy has only recently begun to receive mention as a separate component of the IMC plan. Although some practitioners may prefer to classify this activity as a variation of advertising, it does have specific characteristics that serve to distinguish it from traditional advertising. As noted earlier in this chapter, direct response marketing provides a mechanism whereby the receiver can provide immediate feedback to the sender even though most of the marketers' efforts still involve mass communications.

Applications of Direct Response Marketing for Sports Products

Promotional pieces are often sent through the mail. These include letters, brochures, and catalogs. Another type of communications device that has emerged is the DVD. Bowflex has used this method to reach potential buyers who responded to a standard TV advertisement. Each of these different types of promotional vehicles is sent to consumers in the hope of converting some of the prospects into buyers.

TV advertisements often provide a feedback mechanism. Consumers who have their interest piqued by the message can contact the company through methods detailed in the ad. This may be a postal address, a toll-free telephone number, or an Internet address where orders can be processed or additional information can be requested. The most common applications involve expensive sporting goods and licensed apparel that celebrates the achievements of a team or player. When an extended period of time is required to deliver the message, these marketers often resort to *infomercials*. This technique will typically involve the marketer's purchase of 30 minutes of television broadcast time during which they can demonstrate the product, provide testimonials, and use celebrities to endorse the products being sold. This is a popular strategy for many marketers of fitness equipment.

The Internet continues to grow as an increasingly powerful tool within the DRM domain. By accessing the appropriate Web sites, consumers can purchase all three categories of sports products. Teams, leagues, and events all sell tickets on the Web. Participation equipment can be purchased, and time at participation facilities can be booked. Using DRM, manufacturers and retailers offer a wide range of sporting goods, sports apparel, and athletic shoes for sale to individual consumers.

Overview of the IMC Components Available to Sports Marketers

The discussion of the integrated marketing communications plan is almost complete. Each of the six components has been discussed in detail, and examples for each component have been provided. During the course of this discussion, the concept of brand equity was introduced. It can be argued that effective promotion enhances brand equity and that higher levels of brand equity enhance the marketer's promotional efforts. Given the importance of this phenomenon, we should further explore brand equity.

The discussion also delineated situations where two marketers joined together in a single marketing effort. This tactic can work well when only one organization has a high level of brand equity, but it is more effective when each of the partners has widespread brand recognition in the marketplace. This type of co-marketing effort is often referred to as *cross-promotion*. Efforts of this type are commonly used in the marketing of spectator sports. The practice of cross-promotion will be explored later in this chapter.

Brand Equity

Branding has a functional role in that it allows the consumer to identify products that are offered for sale by a particular marketer. Consumers don't buy cola; they buy Pepsi-Cola or Coca-Cola. They don't buy chocolate disks; rather, they ask for M&M's. In this regard, the brand can provide a differential advantage when viewed in a positive manner by consumers because it conveys a message of quality. Can brand equity play a role in sports marketing? Are there teams that sell tickets because of their reputation? Do some participation facilities hold a perceptual advantage vis-à-vis their competitors? Do some marketers of sporting goods, apparel, and athletic shoes sell more products because of brand equity? The answer to each of these questions is a resounding yes!

Teams such as Manchester United, the New Zealand All Blacks, and the New York Yankees all possess high levels of brand equity. Events such as the Olympics and the Super Bowl also possess valuable brand identities. Clearly, promotion has a role in the effort to perpetuate the image of quality, thereby further enhancing the value associated with the brand name.

High levels of brand equity can create opportunities for the introduction of new products that capitalize on the market's perception of the brand. It can also reduce the market's concern about higher prices as the brand loyalty exhibited by fans creates a comparatively inelastic demand curve. Contemporary women's professional basketball debuted in 1996 with the founding of the American Basketball League. The following year marked the initial season of the ABL's direct competitor, the WNBA. Despite being first in the market, the ABL could not overcome the power of the upstart league's association with the powerful NBA. By 1998, the ABL had declared bankruptcy and ceased all operations. The WNBA continues to operate today; undoubtedly, the brand equity provided by the NBA trademark helped to create a differential advantage that attracted better players and more fans.

> High levels of brand equity can create opportunities for the introduction of new products that capitalize on the market's perception of the brand.

Other sports marketers have used their brand equity to extend their reach by applying their brand name to an array of sports products and even some nonsports products. ESPN recently announced the formation of the ESPN Golf School. The brand was an instrumental asset in attracting golfers who saw these lessons as an opportunity to improve their playing skills. And because more highly skilled golfers tend to play more frequently, some advantages will likely accrue to owners and operators of golf courses. There are numerous self-improvement videos that can be purchased by aspiring players, their parents, and youth coaches. In a recent brand extension strategy, ESPN introduced its own version of "Learn Baseball." The video features an ESPN announcer, current players, former players, and current coaches. But perhaps most important, it features the valuable ESPN brand. Another ESPN strategy was ESPN–the Store, an entertainment-based retail store that features licensed merchandise bearing the ESPN trademarks.[5] The network has also used a brand extension strategy to introduce the ESPN SportsZone, a restaurant and sports bar. Similarly, Fox Sports Network has also been involved in the development of sports bars in high-profile locations such as major airports. Each of these restaurants is capitalizing upon the brand equity of their namesakes. And each serves as a means of distributing these networks' sports products that consist of sports broadcasts and logo merchandise. Figure 19.5 illustrates this application of brand equity in the brand extension used by Fox Sports.

FIGURE 19.5
Brand Extension—
The Fox Sports Bar

MLB's Chicago Cubs certainly possess brand equity with significant value. Even when the beleaguered team is enduring a losing season, its fans remain avid supporters and still purchase tickets to its games. When the Cubs are winning, this equity translates into a situation where the demand for tickets outstrips the supply.

It has been suggested that the ability to license a trademark is the ultimate illustration of brand equity.[6] Fans' efforts to identify with a team by purchasing logo merchandise reflect the power of brand equity; an even more compelling measure is when that merchandise is sold outside of the team or event's natural geographic market.[7] The earlier examples of the All Blacks, the Yankees, and Manchester United all possess strong national and international appeal.

In the participation market, there is brand equity of a different derivation. Again focusing on the golf market, the notoriety of certain course designers can attract customers. Avid golfers have favorite courses that they have played, so when on vacation, they may seek courses that were designed by their favorite architect. Even deceased architects still have the power to attract golfers. Most avid golfers readily recognize the names of premier designers such as Donald Ross, Robert Trent Jones, Pete Dye, Arthur Hills, and Jack Nicklaus. An example of the more traditional form of brand equity in the participation market is associated with Gold's Gym. Some participants who move from one city to another or who are seeking a fitness center while away from home for work or vacation specifically search for a Gold's Gym in their temporary location. This loyalty is a manifestation of brand equity.

Sporting goods sold under brand names such as Titleist, Weider, Rollerblades, and Nautilus are highly respected. Apparel such as CCH, Majestic, Champion, and New Era garner this same respect from consumers. Nike, adidas, and New Balance are brands of shoes that are often specifically sought by consumers. Internationally, brands such as Gilbert, Canterbury, Umbro, and Puma evoke strong feelings on the part of consumers. These examples clearly demonstrate that brand equity provides an advantage upon which marketers can seek to capitalize when selling their broad arrays of sports products.

> Internationally, brands such as Gilbert, Canterbury, Umbro, and Puma evoke strong feelings on the part of consumers.

Brand equity specifically relates to the ability of the marketer to consider its brand as an asset, one that provides value to the marketer. It is apparent that brand equity can play an important role for marketers of all three categories of sports products. It contributes to brand loyalty and provides opportunities for the marketer to branch out with new products. In this regard, it creates opportunities for the owner of the brand and obstacles for its competitors. It is imperative that marketers protect, enhance, and capitalize on any brand equity that they have been able to develop.

Cross-Promotion

A common strategy employed by many marketers is *cross-promotion*. This occurs when there is common ownership or when two or more independent marketers join forces to develop a promotional strategy that provides each entity with tangible benefits.[8] It may involve cooperative advertising, with both organizations, products, or brands appearing in a traditional advertisement. With spectator sports, cross-promotions often target the fans in attendance. This can be done by placing advertisements in the event program, by making public address announcements, via venue signage, by distributing discount coupons, or by distributing free premiums that feature the partner.

FIGURE 19.6
Cross-Promotion—
College and NHL
Hockey

At the Joe Louis Arena, an NHL venue, there is an annual competition that features several national powers in college ice hockey. In an effort to attract fans to those college games, marketers distributed premiums at some of the NHL games played there. One premium was a coffee mug that featured the theme "College Hockey at the Joe." On the NHL game days, public address announcements and ads in the game programs encouraged fans to attend the college games. One ticket package included tickets to four college games and two hard-to-get tickets for NHL games. Figure 19.6 illustrates part of this cross-promotion campaign.

In many cases, the partner property may be some other type of entertainment event. The Memphis Grizzlies sent an e-mail to subscribers alerting them to the opportunity to purchase tickets for a Destiny's Child concert two days prior to the tickets being offered for sale to the general public. In a similar strategy, the Detroit Pistons distributed discount coupons to a Steven Wright concert during the last game of the 2004–05 season. The partner event was to be staged at a music venue owned by the same organization, Palace Entertainment, that owns the basketball team.

Not all cross-promotions involve the live audience. Print ads and commercials on broadcast media can be employed. The ESPN Golf School that was mentioned earlier also has a strong cross-promotion component. The endeavor involved ESPN and Nike. Each student received a free Nike driver and a dozen of the popular Nike One golf balls. The cross-promotion effort used publications such as *Golf* magazine to promote the ESPN/Nike alliance. In addition to sharing the costs associated with the program, each company benefited from the other's presence because of the brand equity associated with the partner's brand name.

Effective Promotions—A Case Study of the NBA

One interesting study identified the marketing techniques utilized by NBA teams in their efforts to put fans in the seats. Of the 21 techniques evaluated, 11 would be classified as components of a team's IMC plan. Some of the techniques were broad-based, such as newspaper advertising. Others addressed more specific tactics, such as the promise of a

TABLE 19.1
Ranking of Promotion Techniques Used by NBA Teams (from most important to least important)

Source: Adapted from L. Mawson and E. Coan, "Marketing Techniques Used by NBA Franchises to Promote Home Game Attendance," *Sport Marketing Quarterly* 3, no. 1 (1994), pp. 37–44.

Rank	Promotion Technique
1	Promotional giveaways
2	Promotional strategies
3	Newspaper advertising
4	Direct mail advertising
5	Public relations
6	TV advertising
7	Winning season incentives
8	TV game incentives
9	Radio advertising
10	Promotion of a star player
11	Magazine advertising

winning season. Of the 11 techniques in question, the one deemed most important by the teams' marketing directors was the category of "promotional giveaways." This tactic involves both pricing and product strategies, but it is important to recognize that the giveaways that were earlier classified as sales promotion efforts are typically supported with conventional advertising. At the bottom of the list were the tactics of promoting a star player and using magazine advertising.[9] A summary of the results of this study is presented in Table 19.1.

Of note is that there were meaningful differences in the perceived importance of some of these techniques between teams with low attendance and those with high attendance. For example, the use of newspaper advertising and direct mail were deemed far more important by teams that were struggling to attract fans to their arenas. Other techniques were viewed in a similar manner by both categories of teams. For example, both groups deemed issues such as PR to be relatively important, and both viewed magazine advertising unfavorably. If this study were to be repeated today, the Internet would undoubtedly play a prominent role in the discussion.

> Changes in the market, the media, and the competitive environment require marketers to reevaluate their integrated marketing communications plan on a regular basis.

The study demonstrates that marketers of spectator sports recognize the importance of developing an effective promotional strategy. In addition, it shows that no one strategy fits every marketer's needs. Changes in the market, the media, and the competitive environment require marketers to reevaluate their integrated marketing communications plan on a regular basis.

Closing Capsule

This chapter marks the end of our discussion of the marketing mix. Care should be taken not to construe the order in which these components (product, distribution, pricing, and promotion decisions) were covered as the absolute progression for the marketer's decision-making process. Promotion may well be considered prior to any decisions regarding pricing and distribution strategies are made. Another point that merits repeating is that each of these decisions should reflect the marketer's efforts to appeal to the target markets that have been designated. Under ideal circumstances, the target markets will be selected first; then the corresponding marketing mixes will be developed.

Contemporary marketing practice has seen a dramatic change in the way that the traditional promotional mix is viewed. Until recently, this mix of promotional tools was deemed to consist of advertising, personal selling, sales promotion, and public relations (or publicity). Though not universally endorsed, sponsorship and direct response marketing have been incorporated by some marketers into this array of alternatives. Regardless of the tools chosen, marketers have moved away from the "promotional mix" terminology in favor of the integrated marketing communications plan. There are many options for today's marketers as they attempt to communicate with their target markets. Because they seldom rely on a single mode of communications, these marketers must take care to ensure that a consistent message is being directed toward the target market. This consistency is the hallmark of integration. The promotional strategy consists of many elements that fit together to create an effective communications plan. All marketers, including those selling sports products, would be better served if they kept this basic principle in mind.

> Since they seldom rely on a single mode of communications, today's marketers must take care to ensure that a consistent message is being directed toward the target market.

Effective promotion requires an understanding of the basic principles of communication. The communications process requires the sender to create a message using words, symbols, and expressions that will readily be understood by those receiving the message. A good message will overcome noise while facilitating feedback. Critical to this process is the selection of a medium that will be used to transmit the message to the targeted audience. Messages have both communications goals and marketing goals. Marketing goals may include increased sales, higher market share, and enhanced consumer awareness. Conversely, the typical communications goals are to gain *a*ttention, to create *i*nterest, to stimulate *d*esire, and to induce *a*ction on the part of the target market—known as the AIDA concept, using an acronym derived from the goals.

Once the marketing and communications goals have been defined, the task turns to that of developing the appropriate integrated marketing communications plan. Some promotional tools tend to target the mass audience; examples include advertising and public relations. Marketers are able to narrow their reach by selecting the proper vehicle–one that reaches their own target markets. Personal selling is a form of interpersonal communications that provides the opportunity to establish an interactive dialog. Marketers use sales promotion to stimulate an immediate response by the target audience; examples include free premiums, discount coupons, and trade shows. Public relations efforts may be directed toward several different audiences; however, the two key groups are the media and the consumer market. Like all sponsorship efforts, those where a sports property is the sponsor represent an attempt to benefit by virtue of the association with the sponsee. Finally, there is direct response marketing. Using communications mechanisms such as infomercials, direct mail, and the Internet, the sports marketer attempts to stimulate action by providing a direct link that allows the consumer to seek information or even place an order.

As a marketer's brand becomes more entrenched in a positive manner within the consumer's psyche, it becomes more valuable. It is this brand equity that marketers strive to create and nurture because it can provide many potential benefits. Brand loyalty, an inelastic demand curve, opportunities for brand extensions, and the licensing of trademarks because of the prestige associated with the brand represent four of these opportunities. Not only do marketers seek to capitalize on their own brand equity, they often use cross-promotions to draw benefits from their marketing partners. In many cases, these cross-promotions involve two teams or events that are related in some way; for instance, both may be scheduled at the same venue. Done correctly, cross-promotion can be a powerful tool for today's marketers of sports products.

Our coverage of promotional strategies completes the discussion of the marketing mix. To a great extent, the strategic focus has been on the task of acquiring customers. However, there have been numerous references throughout this text to the concept of relationship marketing. As more marketers have accepted that it is often easier and less expensive to maintain current customers than it is to acquire new ones, the philosophy of relationship marketing has gained a foothold in the development of marketing strategy. A natural ending to the discussion of marketing strategy would be one based upon the premise that a marketing relationship should never end. Our next chapter will focus on this premise by examining relationship marketing within the sports environment.

Review Questions

1. Differentiate between media and vehicles.
2. Why do you think vehicle selection is so important to marketers today?
3. Differentiate between marketing goals and communications goals. Give an example of each type of goal for each of the six elements in the comprehensive IMC plan.
4. Why is feedback an important element of the communications process?
5. Go to the Internet and find a press release for a sports team. What are the communications goals for your example? Are there any apparent marketing goals that can be identified?
6. Explain how one sports marketer can partner with another sports marketer in a sponsorship relationship in its efforts to promote sports products.
7. Explain cross-promotion. How can the Internet be used to implement a cross-promotion campaign?
8. Form a group and explore the promotional efforts that are being used by one of your favorite teams. Which elements of the IMC are they using? Explain how well you think that the team's promotions have been integrated in the execution of its IMC.
9. Why is personal selling the key component of an IMC when the marketing goal is to sell luxury suites? How could advertising be used to support these marketing efforts?
10. Explain brand equity. In your country, which team do you think has the greatest brand equity? How has the team used it to capitalize on marketing opportunities?
11. Find a print ad for a sports marketer. What are the marketing goals and the communications goals that you think the ad is attempting to achieve?

Endnotes

1. C. Britcher, "Just the Ticket for WUSA," February 17, 2004, www.sportbusiness.com/news/index?news_item_id=153784 (accessed October 14, 2005).
2. J. Swanwick, "NHL Plans Sales Boost," January 30, 2003, www.sportbusiness.com/news/index?news_item_id=150024 (accessed October 13, 2005).
3. M. Briones, "And They're Off," *Marketing News,* March 30, 1998, pp. 1, 14.

4. "Boston Red Sox Fantasy Camp," 2005, www.sportsadventures/com/htmls/boston.htm (accessed October 14, 2005).

5. J. Gladden and G. Milne, "Examining the Importance of Brand Equity in Professional Sport," *Sport Marketing Quarterly* 8, no. 1 (1999), pp. 21–29.

6. D. Aaker, *Managing Brand Equity* (New York: Free Press, 1991).

7. W. Sutton, M. McDonald, G. Milne, and J. Cimperman, "Creating and Fostering Brand Equity in Professional Sports," *Sport Marketing Quarterly* 6, no. 1 (1997), pp. 23–32.

8. L. Boone and D. Kurtz, *Contemporary Marketing* (Mason, OH: South-Western, 2006).

9. L. Mawson and E. Coan, "Marketing Techniques Used by NBA Franchises to Promote Home Game Attendance," *Sport Marketing Quarterly* 3, no. 1 (1994), pp. 37–44.

Emerging Issues in Sports Marketing

Part Four examines issues that are important whether the task is one of marketing products through sports or the marketing of sports products. Marketing was once deemed to be the process of acquiring customers; that focus has begun to shift toward customer retention. This model has been referred to as relationship marketing. A second consideration is emerging technology. These advances have impacted each of the decisions in marketing strategy. Not only can technology help marketers acquire new customers, but it plays an important role in many relationship marketing efforts. Finally, we must understand that marketers, especially sports marketers, are under intense scrutiny. Many controversial issues must be addressed. Chapters 20 through 22 outline key issues in each of these three areas—relationship marketing, the role of technology, and controversial issues within the sports marketing industry.

CHAPTER TWENTY

Relationship Marketing in the Business of Sports

Learning Objectives

- Recognize the concept of lifetime customer value.
- Create a focus on retention rather than the acquisition of customers.
- Identify the components of relationship marketing (RM).
- Understand the concept of relative relationship strength.
- Learn how to apply a variety of RM techniques in sports marketing.
- Examine comprehensive RM programs used by today's sports marketers.
- Learn how sports marketers assess the effectiveness of RM programs.
- Develop a set of guidelines for implementing recovery marketing.

Marketing efforts have long been designed with two broad objectives: to attract new customers and to retain existing customers. Though acquisition and retention have both been acknowledged for their roles in driving business, there is little doubt that the primary emphasis of many marketers was long directed toward customer acquisition. When applying this philosophy, the marketer's task was to find a customer, sell a product, and then move on to the search for the next customer. As marketers began to understand the inefficiency of this approach, the discipline evolved; the mode of operation began to shift from being transaction oriented to one that focused on maintaining relationships. With this emerging philosophy, marketers began to recognize customers as valuable assets. Consequently, the emphasis shifted toward the development of strategies designed to enhance customer retention. This shift has allowed many marketers to more effectively capitalize on the potential long-term value that each of their current customers represents.

While a strategy of customer retention is fundamentally superior to one that emphasizes customer acquisition, there is a key financial consideration as well. Strategies designed to enhance retention require the marketer to allocate significant resources in the efforts to foster communications and resolve the customers' problems. Despite these costs, it is commonly understood that the resources required for the acquisition of a new customer far exceed those required to keep an existing customer satisfied. One estimate is that the cost of acquiring a new customer is six times that of taking the required steps to retain an existing customer.[1]

> One estimate is that the cost of acquiring a new customer is six times that of taking the required steps to retain an existing customer.

THE ROLE OF IT IN RELATIONSHIP MARKETING 20.1

- Build customer database
- Collect customer-level data
- Differentiate customers
  - Segments
  - Niches
  - Individuals
- Develop innovative programs

The Foundation of Relationship Marketing

While there are many definitions of *relationship marketing,* perhaps the most appropriate is that it is "an integrated effort to identify, maintain, and build a network with individual consumers and to continuously strengthen the network for the mutual benefit of both parties through interactive, individualized and value-added contracts over a long period of time."[2] The longevity goal reflects the fact that customers are assets, and these assets provide the greatest value when cultivated over time. Only when the customer is retained over an extended period can the marketer reap the full benefits represented by the *lifetime customer value (LCV).*[3]

One of the driving forces that has encouraged greater emphasis on relationship marketing is information technology (IT), which has continued to grow both more powerful and more cost effective. IT has allowed marketers to develop databases to maintain records and details regarding individual customers. An example of details that may be included is information regarding historical purchase behavior: What has the customer bought and how often have these purchases been made? The database may also include personal information such as age or even the customer's birthday. With this type of information, the marketer can differentiate among its customers. This differentiation allows the marketer to identify segments, smaller niches, or even individuals who represent targeted marketing opportunities. By identifying these opportunities, the marketer can develop innovative programs tailored specifically to the characteristics of those target markets.[4] Box 20.1 outlines the role that information technology can play in the development of relationship marketing strategies.

Benefits for the Marketer

For marketers in every industry, there are several potential benefits that can be gained. A key benefit is *loyalty* exhibited by the customer. For a traditional marketer, brand loyalty means that there is less likelihood that the customer will be lured to a competitor, regardless of the competition's marketing efforts. Clearly, such loyalty is important to marketers of sporting goods, apparel, athletic shoes, and facilities for participation sports.

Marketers such as Reebok and Gold's Gym engage in a variety of efforts designed to enhance brand loyalty. Marketers of spectator sports can also derive substantial benefits when they create a strong sense of loyalty among within their fan base. This loyalty may result in a fan's insistence to attend a specific sporting event when alternative entertainment options are available. For instance, the fan may convince friends to attend a football game instead of a basketball game or a concert. Loyalty also comes into play when there are competing franchises that play the same sport in single geographic area. In MLB, this phenomenon is evident in the major markets of Chicago, New York, and Los Angeles. MLB has sought to capitalize on these intramarket rivalries by scheduling regular season games between the two teams within each of these markets. The NBA has a similar situation in New York and Los Angeles, although the league has not altered its scheduling pattern to exploit these rivalries the way that MLB has.

Loyalty has other benefits associated with it. From the most basic perspective, there is a positive impact on revenue. Loyalty brings out fans. It also contributes to the ability to maintain a significant season ticket base, even when the team has not been performing well. MLB's Chicago Cubs have not played in a World Series since 1918, yet the team continues to fill its stadium. Loyalty also translates into an inelastic demand curve. The loyalty of the fans of the Boston Red Sox has allowed the team to routinely sell out its stadium despite the highest ticket prices in the sport.

A second potential benefit is that the ability of the customers to communicate their concerns and complaints to the marketer represents a forum that can facilitate the *resolution of the fans' complaints*. No business is immune to problems. But when a customer believes that the marketer is indifferent, he or she is less likely to remain a customer in the future. The communications mechanism not only provides the basis for problem resolution, but it also demonstrates concern on the part of the marketer. When problems are adequately resolved in the consumer's mind, the likelihood of remaining a customer is greatly enhanced.

Finally, relationship marketing can convey a *sense of belonging*. It transcends loyalty in that the customer views the relationship as an informal partnership, one in which he or she is more than simply a buyer. This can be crucial for sports teams and regularly played sports events. Fans who feel that they are a part of the team attend games; they watch and listen to media broadcasts; they read accounts of their team in magazines and newspapers; and they engage in informal conversations with friends, family, and co-workers.

This sense of belonging also means that the fan is more likely to feel an association with the team or event. One way in which this association is demonstrated is through the purchase of officially licensed products. This includes apparel that the fans wear as well as nonapparel products such as souvenirs and collectible memorabilia. These avid fans are also more likely to engage in BIRGing and CORFing. BIRGing, or *basking in reflected glory*, is when the fan views him- or herself as a part of the team. These fans do not say that their favorite team won the World Cup of Soccer; rather, they declare "we won!" Conversely, CORFing is the act of *cutting off reflected failure*. Their team lost, but the loss can be explained or minimized. A loss may be blamed on an errant official's call or a bad break; or the loss may be minimized, with fans declaring that it was inconsequential. The fans may accept the loss because their team is still in first place, or they may minimize it by referring to the fact that their team is still the defending champion. Box 20.2 illustrates the key benefits that accrue to sports marketers who implement successful relationship marketing programs.

Components of Relationship Marketing

There is no consensus regarding the exact components of any relationship marketing program. Despite this lack of a universal agreement, several factors routinely emerge in the ongoing discussions regarding the implementation of any relationship-based strategy. These include mutual benefit, trust, communications, empathy, bonding, and continuity.

Mutual benefit refers to the fact that both the buyer and the seller gain in what many characterize as a win–win relationship. In any relationship, either social or business, if one entity is perceived to be the sole beneficiary, the viability of the relationship is jeopardized.

POTENTIAL BENEFITS OF RELATIONSHIP MARKETING

20.2

- Loyalty
  - More business
  - Advantage over competing alternatives
  - Advantage over competitors in same sport
- Complaint resolution
  - Image of concern
  - Aids in customer retention
- Sense of belonging
  - Attend more games
  - Watch and listen to broadcast media
  - Read accounts in newspapers and magazines
  - Engage in informal conversations
  - Purchase more licensed merchandise
  - Engage in BIRGing and CORFing behaviors

The disadvantaged partner will seek alternatives that allow for the acquisition of some of the benefits to which it feels entitled. Unlike sports, successful relationships are characterized by two winners, not one winner and one loser.

> Unlike sports, successful relationships are characterized by two winners, not one winner and one loser.

Relationship marketing provides the basis for establishing and maintaining such mutually beneficial partnerships. The buyer gains because the marketer seeks to enhance each customer's overall level of satisfaction. Products are developed to meet the buyer's needs. The seller seeks to enhance quality and resolve any perceived problems on the part of the buyer. Each of these benefits makes the buyer a winner. At the same time, the enhanced satisfaction will lead to greater customer loyalty. As noted earlier in this chapter, satisfied customers are not only less sensitive to pricing, but they are also valuable promotional tools. Their positive word-of-mouth advertising is an informal communications medium that has high credibility in the marketplace. Consumers generally have more faith in the words of a friend, neighbor, family member, or co-worker than they do in any paid form of promotion. These benefits make the marketer a winner too.

In spectator sports, the team and the fan each derive specific benefits from a well-executed relationship marketing strategy. Consider a team's relationship with ongoing purchasers of season tickets. The team benefits by selling more tickets during and after the good seasons, from lower attrition of fans during the bad seasons, and because fans are less concerned about the rising price of tickets. At the same time, the long-standing season ticket buyers benefit from superior seating options, ongoing communications with team representatives, and opportunities to participate in special events such as fan appreciation day and championship celebrations.

Trust is based upon the belief that one party will not attempt to take advantage of the other and that any communications will be truthful. Problems and concerns articulated by the buyers will be sincere, and the seller's answer to any question will be honest. There will be no attempt to deceive the other party. If suspicion exists, it is likely because of one of two weaknesses in the relationship. The relationship may be relatively new; as a result, the parties have not interacted enough to develop the requisite trust. To this end, trust is built over time. When enough positive outcomes have occurred, trust will supersede suspicion. The second weakness is more of a breakdown. The suspicion arises from previous experiences that cause one of the parties to view the other as untrustworthy. The buyer reneges on an agreement to purchase a number of group tickets. The seller assures a fan that the tickets being purchased are the best available, only for the fan to discover that better seats are available when collecting the tickets at the box office on game day. Breakdowns in trust caused by these types of behavior make it difficult to establish or maintain a mutually beneficial relationship.

One professor of sports marketing takes his class to an NHL game each semester. The team's marketing staff will reserve a large number of seats for the class without requiring advance payment, even though the games are routinely sold out. The team officials trust the professor to fulfill the obligation and pay for the tickets. At the same time, the professor trusts the organization to arrange a special tour and presentation for the students. To date, neither the team nor the professor has failed to meet the other's expectations. This has strengthened the level of trust in this relationship.

Empathy refers to the condition whereby each entity in the relationship can view the situation from the other's perspective. This leads to a mutual understanding of any obstacles that threaten a harmonious partnership. Both the buyer and seller must have realistic expectations regarding the options available to resolve any potential conflict. It is difficult, if not impossible, for a problem to be satisfactorily resolved if either of the parties has an unrealistic expectation regarding the other's behavior. Therefore, the absence of empathy will hasten the demise of any relationship.

A partial-season ticket holder for an MLB team may find it difficult to attend each of the games included in the ticket package. When a game is missed, the team could be tempted to provide no recourse for the fan by simply imposing a policy that unused tickets have no value; it is up to the ticket holders to use them. Conversely, the team can implement a policy that reflects the inevitability of a partial-season ticket holder missing one or more of the regularly scheduled games. Such a policy might allow the ticket holder to exchange the unused tickets for tickets on an alternative date. The dates of eligibility might be limited and the seats may not be quite as good, but the fan is not severely impacted by the inability to attend a game. The team understands that the fan will seek an equitable solution that provides comparable value, while the ticket holder understands that the team's solution is limited to available seats and dates. Each can empathize with the other; this empathy allows both parties to compromise a bit as they accept the solutions to each other's potential problem.

Communication is perhaps the most important element of any relationship. This includes both routine communication that creates a type of dialog between the parties as well as issue-specific communication that addresses the resolution of a specific problem or concern. The communication can be achieved through one or more of the various channels that transmit messages from a sender to a receiver. One of the more common channels has long been the telephone. Purchasers of season tickets often have a direct number for an account representative who has the authority to address questions, problems, and special requests. The sports marketer may also initiate communication. Typical appeals are for renewals of season tickets, tickets for special events such as an all-star game, or attendance at fan appreciation events that are not open to the general public.

> Purchasers of season tickets often have a direct number for an account representative who has the authority to address questions, problems, and special requests.

Remembering that the communications process requires a mechanism for feedback, the marketer should seek to make the process interactive. Direct mail can be used, but it is most effective when the fan is provided with some means of establishing direct contact with the team's marketing staff. The Internet has also become a popular medium through which fans can contact team personnel to pose a question or articulate a complaint. The team's response may be posted on a Web-based bulletin board; however, for sensitive issues, the response is more likely to be sent via a personal e-mail. Neither party in the relationship will want to embarrass the other. Public confrontation is not likely to occur until such time that the signs point to the likely demise of the existing relationship.

Bonding refers to the creation of a unified commitment that holds the principals together. Rather than a separate buyer and seller, bonding creates the sense of unity that is sought from the implementation of any relationship marketing program. Bonding should be a natural consequence if both parties have benefited from the relationship, when they trust each other to do the right thing, when they can each view the situation from the other's perspective, and when there is a mechanism that supports interactive communications. To a great extent, bonding creates the aforementioned sense of belonging. It marks the point at which the relationship is truly characteristic of a partnership. Marketers of fashion products have long been effective in creating this type of loyalty and sense of belonging among members of their primary target markets. For example, FUBU (For Us, By Us) was able to make great inroads with the African American target market by virtue of the company's efforts to create a sense of unity. And while bonds such as these are important in the marketing of goods, they are perhaps even more important when the marketer operates within the service industry.

Sports marketers have numerous opportunities to create these bonds. Because of the emotional aspects, the greatest opportunities to create partnerships exist within the spectator sports market. One study attempted to show how a measure of the strength of the bond between a sports team and its fans could be developed. This measure was referred to as the *relative relationship strength*.[5] Box 20.3 outlines the components used to develop

COMPONENTS OF RELATIVE STRENGTH   20.3

- **Core Relationship**
  - Usage
    - Length
    - Intensity
    - Frequency
      - In-person
      - Media-based
  - Fan identification
    - Emotional involvement
      - BIRGing
      - CORFing
    - Personal commitment
    - Loyalty

- **Expanded Relationship**
  - Product Merchandising (DRM)
  - Word-of-mouth

this measure. It is comprised of two primary components: the core relationship and the expanded relationship.

The Core Relationship

The core relationship is based upon various usage and identification levels on the part of the fan. Usage specifically relates to the length of the relationship, the intensity exhibited by the fans, and the frequency of the various modes of contact.

Usage

The initial element of the usage construct, *length of the relationship,* reflects the current duration of the partnership. In spectator sports, this measure reflects how long the individual has been a fan of the team or event. The longer the relationship has been intact, the stronger the bond tends to be. No relationship is completely devoid of problems; however, longtime partners are more likely to amicably resolve those problems than are those whose partnership has been intact for only a short period. In those cases, the pain of separation often exceeds the pain emanating from the problem itself. The empathy between the partners also increases over time and lends itself to problem resolution. In sports, a long-term fan is more likely to forgive a team for its shortcomings while looking to the future.

Intensity refers to the level of commitment that one party has for the other. Indifference leads to the breakdown of a relationship. Enthusiasm serves as a catalyst for problem resolution. Intensity is often correlated with the length of the relationship. As it strengthens over time, the emotional bonds develop and grow. Each partner feels like something important would be lost if the relationship is abandoned.

Frequency of contact basically refers to the number of times in which the fan is a spectator. It considers the nature of that contact by taking into account the situations where the fan is either a member of the live audience or part of the media-based audience. The growth of media options has presented more opportunities for a fan to be part of the media-based audience. In regard to the live audience, more teams today are working with the travel industry in an effort to accommodate individuals and groups of fans who want to attend games away from home. It is evident that sports organizations are seeking to capitalize on the various opportunities to increase the frequency of contact for their fans.

Fan Identification

Fan identification represents the second major component of the core relationship. While usage is generally based upon measurable behaviors, fan identification reflects the emotional side of the fan. To what extent does their emotional involvement influence behaviors such as BIRGing and CORFing? What is their level of personal commitment? How loyal are they to the team? Fan identification is a key consideration because highly identified fans are less likely to terminate a relationship, even during prolonged periods of unsuccessful competition.[6]

Emotional involvement represents the level of psychological attachment that the fan has with the team. The relationship with the team contributes to the fan's psychological well-being. If the team were to move or be dissolved, the fan would experience a sense of loss in his or her life. Fans who are emotionally involved experience highs and lows depending upon the team's performance. In other words, they bask in the reflected glory of their team's success and they cut off the reflected failure when they lose. In this regard, BIRGing and CORFing reflect a bond with the team.

The fans celebrate victories as though they had a role in determining the outcome. They find excuses for losses as a way of reducing the emotional toll of failure. Indifferent fans feel little emotion irrespective of the outcome; they simply view the game as a form of entertainment. Avid fans experience emotional highs and lows that may be more extreme than those experienced by the athletes themselves. The avid fans who view themselves as a part of the team are not only more likely to engage in BIRGing and CORFing, but they are also likely to attend more games and they tend to be less concerned about the price of tickets.[7]

> Indifferent fans feel little emotion irrespective of the outcome; they simply view the game as a form of entertainment.

Personal commitment is also a key part of the fan identification component of the core relationship. Strong commitments contribute to the fan's tendency to devote more time following the team in media reports and learning about the sport. In addition to spending time, highly committed fans also spend money in an effort to follow the team. The willingness to expend their own resources in this manner is indicative of a strong relationship between the fan and the team.

Emotional involvement and personal commitment are also related to the fan's *loyalty*. Even when the team is struggling, some fans refuse to stop buying tickets and terminate their relationship with the team. They continue to attend games, take in games via the various media alternatives, and read about the team's efforts in the print media and on the Internet. Many loyal season ticket holders continue to renew their subscriptions as they have visions of a better future. The mantra of "wait until next year" resonates with these loyal fans.

The Expanded Relationship

Each of the aforementioned elements influences the core relationship between the fan and the team. While this represents the primary component of the relative relationship strength measure, sports marketers must also take the expanded relationship into account. To do so, their attention turns to the fans' response to product merchandising and the propensity to engage in positive word-of-mouth exchanges with other people.

In the context of relationship marketing, the fan responsiveness to *product merchandising* refers to the purchase of licensed merchandise. Of particular interest is the purchase and display of apparel and other products that bear the team's logo. Even fans who seldom attend a game can purchase officially licensed merchandise from retail stores and direct response marketers. Teams that have been successful in nurturing strong relationships with their fans are the ones that sell the most licensed merchandise. Not only do the players get a psychological advantage from seeing so many fans dressed in their team colors, but they also reap the financial rewards associated with increased sales. Increased exposure may increase the level of support and can be effective in reaching young fans who represent the next generation of relationships for the team.

Finally, the relative strength of the relationship is influenced by the fans' behavior regarding *word-of-mouth advertising*. How much do fans talk about the team, the players, the league, and the sport when engaged in informal conversations? Some fans will talk about the last game, player personnel changes, and future expectations. Once more, BIRGing and CORFing activities will take place. As in any industry, positive word-of-mouth advertising can have a profound impact on attitudes and behaviors. It represents an effective and inexpensive form of communication that serves to build the fan base for the team.

It should now be evident that bonding is a key consideration when assessing the strength of any relationship. Marketers implement a variety of strategies that are specifically designed to strengthen that bond. Once established and strengthened, the marketer's next step is to perpetuate that relationship far into the future.

Continuity refers to the general belief that the most valuable relationships represent long-term commitments. Transaction-based marketing tends to view the prospect as a short-term opportunity to sell a product. If the sale can be consummated, profit is earned. Once the transaction is completed, the task shifts to one of converting yet another prospect into a customer. With this mind-set, success is measured by the ability to attract a string of customers over an extended period of time. Conversely, relationship-based marketing recognizes the value that any individual customer represents over time. Once a prospect becomes a customer, the task becomes one of engaging in activities that will increase the likelihood that each new customer will continue to purchase products from the marketer far into the future. Only when customers are viewed as long-term assets will marketers begin to consider the potential sales and profits that can be attributed to each individual customer in the long run. Earlier, this perspective was referred to as lifetime customer value.

> Relationship-based marketing recognizes the value that any individual customer represents over time.

Marketers of virtually every spectator sport seek to maintain long-term relationships with two key target markets: spectators and sponsors. If a fan fails to renew a season ticket, the team must seek to fill that vacancy. While some teams such as the NFL's Green Bay Packers have a season ticket waiting list, this situation is not typical. Teams that are not sold out engage in expensive advertising and personal selling in their efforts to replace dissatisfied former ticket buyers.

Teams also seek to nurture their relationships with sponsors. These sponsors spend large sums of money in order to associate themselves with the team. They also receive a bundle of benefits, including hospitality, venue signage, and free tickets. In some cases, major sponsors may have access to a luxury suite at the venue. In the aftermath of a poor season, a team might need to adjust prices downward or enhance the array of benefits that sponsors receive in order to keep the sponsorship attractive. The team's marketing staff must listen and respond to the sponsors' concerns; otherwise the relationship may well be terminated.

Applications of Relationship Marketing in Sports

With a sound understanding of the principles of relationship marketing, the discussion will now shift to tactics for its implementation. The tactics used by marketers of automobiles, airline services, and submarine sandwiches are also appropriate for marketers of sports products. Box 20.4 delineates a number of commonly used initiatives that have either been applied or have the potential to be incorporated into relationship marketing efforts in the sports industry.

Clubs

Clubs represent an effort to convert an informal relationship between a customer and a marketer into a more formal partnership. By transforming a customer into a member, the bond between the two is strengthened. This strategy is becoming common in the marketing of spectator sports, participation sports, and sporting goods. For spectator sports, membership in some clubs is limited to kids; however, this type of marketing strategy can be applied to other segments or even the entire market in an effort to develop relationships with individual fans. For example, MLB's Toronto Blue Jays have a Silver Jays club that is open to senior citizens. Clubs such as these are generally free of cost for the fan, but occasionally, modest membership fees will be charged.

APPLICATIONS OF RELATIONSHIP MARKETING   20.4

- Clubs
- Serial marketing
- Frequency incentives
- Affinity marketing programs
- Routine periodic communications
  - Traditional
  - E-mail
- Interactive opportunities
- Gifts
- Fan appreciation activities
- Contests
- Logo merchandise
- Direct access/personal representative
- Recognition

One of the sports for which fans in New Zealand are most devoted is cricket. This devotion has led to the formation of the Cricket Fraternity, a club that offers fans the opportunity to belong to "cricket's extended family." Among the benefits of belonging to this club are discounts at local retailers, periodic newsletters, and a video membership card that allows the cardholder to view actual cricket action. While these benefits are inviting, the opportunity to win prizes is perhaps the most appealing aspect of being a club member. By running their membership cards through interactive scanners at the venues that are hosting select cricket matches, members can check to see if they have won a prize.

Benefits such as these make each fan who belongs to the club a winner. But the sport benefits as well. In addition to the nominal fee of $5, each member provides meaningful information that can be used to develop a customer database. With an accurate database intact, these members can easily be contacted, and they represent some of the best opportunities to sell tickets to special events. Fan loyalty, sense of belonging, bonding, and commitment may all be strengthened through the communications efforts common to this type of club membership. Figure 20.1 illustrates a solicitation brochure designed to recruit new members for the Cricket Fraternity.

An example of the use of a club aimed at kids in the spectator sports domain is the Detroit Lions Club. Eligibility is limited to kids under the age of 13. Prospective members complete an application and compose a question about the sport or the team. If the question is used on the affiliated local radio program, the member receives a variety of team merchandise. Of course, the chance of winning encourages the youngster to listen to the Monday night radio program that precedes the broadcast of the Monday Night Football game. In MLB, the Toronto Blue Jays' KidZone represents a similar club for young fans. The applications for clubs of this type request information such as the child's age, birthday, phone number, and e-mail address. The Blue Jays' marketing staff uses applications for their KidZone club to update their database.[8] This information can be valuable as the team seeks to solidify its relationship with the next generation of baseball fans.

In the participation sports domain, the marketing intent may be to create a club that will appeal to many of those who are involved in a particular activity. While the club may

FIGURE 20.1
Club for Cricket Fans

attract some fans of a sport who do not actually participate, the majority of the members will be people who play the game. Of course, it is also important to recall that one of the important segments of sports fans is comprised of "players." Therefore, this type of club reaches individuals who not only participate in the sport, but many are also fans who are part of the important spectator market. One of the more effective clubs of this type involves golf's PGA Tour Partners Club.

For $12 per year, the member receives an official membership card, a gift such as a small box of golf balls, a free video on the rules of the game, a decal for his or her home or car window, a ball marker, and a subscription to a members-only magazine. Members are also tempted by the prospect of being given new products to test. To reinforce the idea of exclusivity, the appeal to a prospective member boldly states that he or she has been "nominated" for membership. All of the gifts and the ongoing communication using the magazine serve to enhance the strength of the relationship between the golf industry and the golfers. It is also designed to strengthen the bond between the fans and the PGA Tour while concurrently encouraging more frequent participation on the part of the club members.

Marketers of sporting goods often form clubs based upon the past purchase of one or more of their products. One such club is Storm Chasers, a group comprised of bowlers who have purchased a Storm (brand) bowling ball. Membership is free, but each person does complete a short application that includes demographic information as well as a modest amount of behavioral data. Members receive an introductory gift, a catalog from which logo merchandise can be ordered, discounts on future purchases, and a newsletter that alerts them to new technology and upcoming new product introductions. By going to the club's Web site at www.stormchasers.net, members can place orders, catch up on bowling news, and get technical assistance on how to best use their equipment.

Serial Marketing

The basic premise of serial marketing is that it keeps the consumer involved with the marketer over some meaningful period of time. This type of promotion has long been

FIGURE 20.2
Example of Serial Marketing

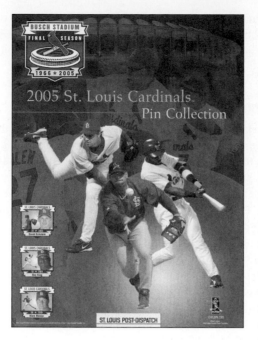

effective in the marketing of consumer products, so it is only logical that it has found its way into the sports product environment. Designed to encourage repeat patronage, serial marketing has a positive effect on customer involvement, thereby producing an increased levels of sales.

Teams may use a variety of giveaways over the course of the season. When these premiums are related, the objective is to instill within the fan the desire to accumulate the entire set. In spectator sports, using the extended product in this manner becomes a key component in the effort to build upon relationships and encourage more frequent attendance. Typical premiums include collector cards featuring team members, an array of bobblehead dolls, and collector pins. Fans may keep these items for an extended period, often for many years. Consequently, this type of serial promotion can be effective in help-

ing to perpetuate a long-term relationship with the fan. In some cases, the items must be purchased. However, they may not all be available at any one time. Typically, the purchases take place over the course of the season, thereby maintaining both interest and involvement on the part of the fan. Figure 20.2 illustrates a promotion involving player pins for MLB's St. Louis Cardinals.

Frequency Incentives

It could reasonably be argued that frequency marketing is a variation of serial marketing in that it is also designed to provide the consumer with rewards over time. Consumers readily understand how airlines use frequency marketing to reward their best customers. As fliers accumulate miles, they begin to receive free air travel. The more they fly in a given year, the more benefits they receive. For example, Northwest Airlines has four levels of members in its frequent-flier program: base, silver elite, gold elite, and platinum elite. Members have been known to take unnecessary flights simply to accumulate enough miles to move up to the next level. Another frequency incentive program with which university students may be familiar is the one used by Subway restaurants. Consumers who fill their cards with 10 stamps benefit by receiving their next sub sandwich for free. The most common benefits to consumers who take advantage of the various frequency marketing efforts are discounts, upgrades, and free products. Marketers of sports products can offer these same benefits.

Some marketers of spectator sports have begun to use frequent attendance cards; when certain thresholds are reached, the bearer can redeem the points for discounted or free merchandise and tickets.[9] For example, the Rugby Football Union (RFU) in England recently launched a fan loyalty reward system using smart card technology. Cardholders will be able to accumulate points that can be redeemed for discounts on RFU products, game tickets, or membership in the England Rugby Supporters Club. Not only does the fan reap the rewards from using the card, but the RFU also receives a small percentage of each transaction. According to one executive, the "card-based membership gives the RFU the chance to build upon a long-lasting and mutually rewarding relationship" that goes beyond attending games."[10] This approach is similar to the affinity marketing programs, which will be discussed next.

Similarly, some marketers of participation sports have begun to offer the opportunity to participate for free once the requisite number of paid visits has been attained. Among the participation sports for which this strategy can be effective are 10-pin bowling, golf, miniature golf, and pool.

Affinity Marketing Programs

When consumers have an affinity for something, it can be inferred that they have an attraction that can serve as the basis for an enduring relationship. We all have an affinity for many organizations that we personally believe provide benefits to society in general. This affinity can be even stronger if we have personally derived some benefit from the organization in the past or if we perceive the opportunity to gain some benefit from it in the foreseeable future. Historically, many affinity marketing programs were focused on charities and universities that consumers supported.

The implementation of an affinity program generally emphasizes benefits that accrue to the individual consumer. For example, the basis for the marketing of many credit cards today is that the cardholder can acquire points that can be redeemed for goods and services. An example of a popular execution of this type of strategy is the use of credit cards that accumulate points for free travel on a specific airline carrier. This tactic differs from the frequency incentives in that the points are not earned by purchasing the marketer's goods and services; rather, they are earned by engaging in a transaction with a participating third party. For the airline-based credit cards, points are not awarded for traveling on that airline; instead, they are awarded for using the card to charge routine purchases of products such as food, clothing, and entertainment.

Regardless of the sponsoring organization, affinity programs capitalize upon consumer sentiments by securing the involvement of individuals who share common interests and activities. The programs provide extra value for consumers, and this value encourages the development of stronger relationships.[11] Once more, the mutually beneficial nature of the relationship is a key to strengthening the bonds and assuring that the partnership does not end prematurely.

One of the most successful affinity programs has been the aforementioned use of targeted credit cards. In the sports marketing environment, the best opportunity to employ this tactic has been within the spectator sports domain. The avid fan may choose to use a credit card that features a favorite team or organization. Examples include virtually every professional sports team as well as organizations such as the United States Olympic Committee. The fan may opt to use the card simply because it incorporates the logo of a favorite sports entity. Another driving force might be the understanding that the featured sports entity will receive a small monetary contribution each time that a purchase is made. The more that is charged to the card, the greater the contribution. In this way, the fan is making an indirect donation that benefits the sports entity. The fan may perceive this as a way of assisting the team or organization in its effort to improve and compete. When viewing him- or herself as a contributor to a team's success, a fan will have no doubt that the relationship is enhanced. Figure 20.3 illustrates an appeal for a credit card from a bank that targeted fans of the NHL's Detroit Red Wings team.

An emerging affinity-based marketing strategy is for the relationship to encompass the fan, the team, and a team sponsor. Total Oil is the primary sponsor for the Watford soccer team in England. As part of an affinity marketing strategy, the sponsor distributed credit cards to the team's season ticket holders and to the team's minor sponsors. Each time the card is used to purchase fuel at one of the 950 Total stations in the United Kingdom, a small contribution will be made to the team. The expectation is that the total contributions over the first two years will be close to $1,000,000 (£500,000).[12]

FIGURE 20.3
An Affinity Credit
Card Solicitation

In addition to the benefits that accrue to the sports organization, the cardholder also gains from this type of relationship marketing program. Although the psychological rewards associated with assisting a team or an organization may be substantial, other more tangible rewards may be required. As the fan uses the credit card, these rewards begin to accumulate. The more the card is used, the more benefits the fan accrues. Included within the set of potential benefits are free or discounted tickets, free or discounted merchandise, and opportunities to engage in social activities with team representatives. Clearly, affinity programs can deliver benefits to the sports entity, the fans, and sponsors. There is little wonder as to why this tactic is one of the fastest-growing activities in marketing today.

Routine Periodic Communications (One-Way)

Marketers in virtually every industry have implemented relationship marketing programs that allow them to transmit information to selected members of their target markets. This may be achieved via electronic communications such as e-mail or by using traditional print media such as brochures, newsletters, and magazines.

Traditional Print Media

The most commonly employed print media involve simple mailings through the postal service. Using an appropriate mailing list, the marketer will send newsletters, brochures, and special offers to its important customers. Marketers featuring any of the various sports products that have been discussed in this text can utilize this tool.

Marketers of spectator sports inform their fans of upcoming special events and promotions. During the off-season, these mailings are used to alert fans of player signings,

FIGURE 20.4
Callaway Golf
Magazine

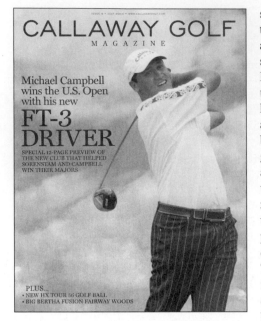

schedules, and opportunities to purchase tickets in advance. Season ticket renewals are generally distributed to the previous season's ticket holders via traditional mail. Marketers of participation sports facilities use newsletters and brochures to delineate healthy activities and diets. Of course, they also send out renewal forms when a membership is about to expire. Some sporting goods companies publish magazines that are sent to known purchasers of their products. For example, *Callaway Golf* magazine contains editorial commentary and testimonials touting the use of the company's new equipment. New technology is discussed and new products are introduced. The magazine is not only designed to reinforce the idea that each of these Callaway owners made a sound purchase decision, but it is also designed to induce the purchase of new equipment while, of course, promoting loyalty to the Callaway brand. Figure 20.4 illustrates a recent cover from the *Callaway Golf* magazine.

E-Mail

With more individuals being connected to the Internet, e-mail has emerged as an inexpensive, yet effective, approach for staying in contact with individual consumers. The source of these communications efforts can be an athlete, a team, a league, a sports organization, an event, management of a participation facility, or a manufacturer of sporting goods, athletic shoes, or apparel.

MLB recently used e-mail as a means of thanking each fan who used the Internet to vote for the all-star teams. Of course, the message also informed the fan as to when and on which TV network the game would be broadcast. The NBA's Memphis Grizzlies use e-mail to reach fans who have signed up for periodic updates through the team's Web site. The typical message summarizes recent results, promotes upcoming games, and outlines special events and other entertainment alternatives. For example, the Grizzlies use this cross-marketing opportunity to offer fans on the team's e-mail list the chance to purchase tickets for special events prior to the tickets being offered for sale to the general public. This benefit allows the team and the fan to take advantage of the mutually beneficial relationship that they maintain.

The major limitation of e-mail is that various filters may now either label it as spam, place in a holding mailbox, or simply discard it as trash. Marketers have begun to request that the addressees place the sender's address on a list of acceptable sources of e-mail communications, thereby increasing the likelihood that the intended recipient will receive it and open it.

Interactive Opportunities

New technologies have created opportunities for marketers to develop programs that allow the fan to become more involved with a sport, event, or team through interactive modes of communication. At the more basic level, the Internet has seen the emergence of chat rooms as a means of reaching individual fans. By signing on at a predetermined time, the fan is able to participate in a conversation or question-and-answer session with a player, coach, or other representative of some sports organization. Another unique approach has been implemented by some venue operators; in some seats, they have installed new technology that allows the spectators to view highlights, review statistics, place an order for concessions, and interact by responding to questions that are being asked and polls that are being taken.

One of the leading sports entities in the application of marketing principles is NASCAR. Thus, it is no surprise that it has been quick to adopt fan-directed interactive technologies. Fans can go to the TrackPass link at NASCAR.com during the course of a race and review video highlights and timely statistics. The organization has even begun to test the use of cards that allow the fans to call a phone number and listen to the radio conversations between a driver and the driver's team.[13] This same audio is available to TrackPass subscribers.

> Fans can go to the TrackPass link at NASCAR.com during the course of a race and review video highlights and timely statistics.

Non–technology-based interactive marketing tactics can also be important. In the aftermath of an interruption of league play because of a contractual dispute, NBA officials had players greet returning fans in the commons areas of the arenas and thank them for their continued support. MLB players often stage instructional sessions on the field prior to a game during which time they interact directly with the kids in attendance. Not only does this type of effort strengthen the kids' and their parents' relationship with MLB, but it is also a good promotional tool for the task of acquiring new fans.

Gifts

Free gifts that are given to fans for a myriad of reasons represent additional, often unanticipated, value to the fan. They provide the sense of partnership that is at the core of relationship marketing. In some cases, the gift may incorporate the organization's trademarks and logos. Another alternative is a voucher or a discount coupon for some sports-related product sold at the venue. They may be distributed to an entire class of fans such as season ticket holders or owners of luxury suites. Conversely, they may be provided to select fans on a situational basis. The NHL's San Jose Sharks use information from a database to identify a small set of customers who receive presents on their birthdays.[14] Gifts of this nature are not the product extensions that are distributed to all fans; rather, they are given to select individuals who continue to engage in a meaningful relationship with the marketer.

In a new technology-based effort, organizers of the Indianapolis 500 sent an interactive CD-ROM postcard to the event's existing accounts. The CD contained vintage video that chronicled the history of the fabled race. It was complete with video, audio, and still photographs. The software also provided a link for the fans to connect online and renew their tickets for the next year's race. Measurement of the level of consumer awareness generated by the marketing effort was facilitated by the fact that the fans' usage of the online components could be tracked and tabulated.[15]

With more database marketing, organizations have increased the amount of information that they maintain for each season ticket buyer. This has provided new opportunities such as giving a gift to a season ticket holder on his or her birthday or when longevity milestones have been reached. Such customized service delivery can be viewed as a value proposition that is tailored expressly for the individual fan. This type of one-to-one marketing is effective in the effort to retain customers by increasing their level of satisfaction and commitment to the marketer. Technology has also meant that some gifts can be sent indirectly via e-mail or the Internet, although regular mail remains an option. If vouchers or coupons are used, they are often redeemed at the venue or in an online retail Web site. Not only does the fan redeem the coupon, but the likelihood that he or she will purchase additional merchandise also exists. The net result is that both the fan and the sports marketer benefit from this type of marketing effort.

Fan Appreciation Activities

Teams often attempt to endear themselves with casual fans, season ticket holders, suite owners, the general public, sponsors, and the media within their local markets. One effective approach continues to be the staging of events positioned as fan appreciation activities. While the majority of these activities focus on the existing fan base that has an underlying relationship with the team, others are directed toward the general market with the objectives of acquiring new fans and generating positive publicity in the local media.

The NHL's Detroit Red Wings have a season ticket base of some 18,000 fans plus 83 owners of luxury suites at their venue, the Joe Louis Arena. Upon their recent winning of the league championship (the Stanley Cup), the team hosted a party at the arena. Among the invited guests were season ticket holders, suite owners, sponsors, and the media. The exclusive nature of the affair along with the guests' ability to see the players and the Stanley Cup trophy provided an opportunity that few people ever have, and it served to reinforce the sense of belonging and partnership with the select fans and other guests.

Teams in the NBA and MLB also stage fan appreciation days late in their regular seasons. Anyone in attendance has the opportunity to win a prize, the most treasured of which is a jersey that was worn that game by one of the team's players. In some cases, the prizes are awarded on the basis of a random selection of seats for that game. In other situations, the fans in attendance must complete an entry blank that solicits information such as the fan's name, address, and e-mail address. Winners and losers alike become part of the team's database that will be used for future promotional efforts. But the hope of winning a star player's jersey means that most fans willingly divulge this personal information.

Teams with a small season ticket base will reach out to the casual fans and to local residents. This approach is particularly useful for minor league sports. While there is a significant focus on customer satisfaction and retention, the team also seeks to reach out and engage in customer acquisition. The end-of-season effort is designed to get people into the arena, have them interact with players and team officials, and distribute remaining items such as posters, press guides, pens, magnets, and key chains. With close-out prices on logo merchandise as an incentive, new and existing customers often purchase products that demonstrate a higher level of involvement with the team. Figure 20.5 illustrates a press release sent to fans via e-mail inviting them to the Fan Appreciation Day for the Ontario Hockey League's Plymouth Whalers.

Contests

While contests may be incorporated as part of the fan appreciation activities, they generally serve as stand-alone activities. Winners can be determined through probability-based selection procedures or they may emerge as victors from some type of competition. Entrants may complete some sort of form to facilitate a random drawing; they may enter via traditional mail; or they may use the organization's Web site as a mode of entry.

FIGURE 20.5   **Fan Appreciation Day Invitation**

Reprinted with permission of Peter Krupsky, Plymouth Whalers.

News Release

Contact: Pete Krupsky
Phone: (734) 927-3269

FOR IMMEDIATE RELEASE
Tuesday, April 5, 2005

PLYMOUTH WHALERS OFFER FAN APPRECIATION DAY APRIL 16

PLYMOUTH TOWNSHIP – After enjoying their best attendance since moving to Plymouth in 1996, the Ontario Hockey League's Plymouth Whalers are holding a Fan Appreciation Day on Saturday, April 16 from 3:00 pm to 6:00 pm at the Compuware Sports Arena.

Activities include:

- Free Open Skating at the Compuware Sports Arena NHL rink from 3:30 pm to 5:30 pm.

- Player Appearance and Autographs.

- Used Equipment Sale – excellent deals can be had all kinds of Whalers' used equipment.

- Discounts from 10 to 50 percent off in a Blow-Out Sale at the Compuware Sports Arena Pro Shop.

- Special Prize Raffles.

- Kids will enjoy interacting with the Plymouth Whalers' energetic mascot, Shooter.

"Our Fan Appreciation open-house is one of the ways we thank our fans for all the support they provide the team each season," said **Rob Murphy,** Plymouth Whalers Director of Corporate Sales and Marketing. "The entire organization appreciates that our fans choose to spend part of their weekends with us from September through March. Our coaches, players and staff build relationships with our fans over the course of the season. The opportunity to say thank you to our fans for their support is an honor for us."

The Whalers – who moved to Plymouth in 1996 – set a single-season attendance mark this season when 109,699 fans attended 34 regular season home dates – an average of 3,324 fans per game. The Whalers' previous high was set in 2002–03, when they drew 108,051 fans over 34 home dates for an average crowd of 3,178.

Season tickets for the 2005–06 season are available and can be purchased at the Compuware Sports Arena Box Office by calling (734) 453-8400. The CSA box office is open Monday through Friday from 9:00 am to 5:00 pm.

Though many contests are open to anyone who completes the required entry form, others are confined to a list of invitees. These invitees generally have some existing relationship with the sports marketer. They may be season ticket holders, frequent ticket buyers, suite owners, or fans who have registered for periodic e-mail updates on the marketer's Web site. As with many relationship marketing endeavors, the completed entry blank includes contact information that can be used to update the organization's

FIGURE 20.6
MLB All-Star Game
Ticket Contest

database. Figure 20.6 illustrates the front and back of an entry form that featured two tickets to the 2005 MLB All-Star game as a prize. Note that the contest features sports organizations and their sponsors. Specifically, it incorporates MLB, the Detroit Tigers, and the four manufacturers of officially licensed baseball trading cards. So not only does this effort enhance the relationship between MLB and its fans, but it also serves to strengthen the bond between MLB and four of its key marketing partners.

Logo Merchandise

While there is little doubt that the sale of licensed merchandise provides substantial revenue to the sports marketer, it also plays a crucial role in the task of developing a stronger sense of identification on the part of the fan. Sports teams, leagues, and organizations have broadened the channels of distribution to make this type of merchandise more readily available to fans. In addition to retail facilities at event venues, officially licensed merchandise can be purchased from traditional brick-and-mortar stores such as specialty stores selling sporting goods and apparel, department stores, and discount retailers. It is also available on the Internet, as many sports marketers now maintain a virtual storefront that makes logo merchandise easily attainable by fans all over the world. Such a retail presence is important for teams with a global presence such as Manchester United and the New Zealand All Blacks.

Some teams even give away logo merchandise in their efforts to foster relationships. In many cases, these gifts are distributed in conjunction with a team sponsor. For example, one MLB team recently gave a bucket hat to every adult who entered the stadium. The hat incorporated the team's logo as well as that of a major sponsor that shared the cost of the promotion (Budweiser Beer). Other giveaways used by MLB are baseball caps and baseball gloves that include the team's logo. Many fans show up at subsequent games with their hats and gloves. These keepsakes are valued both as utilitarian and as souvenirs. The propensity to keep them for extended periods supports the team's belief that the complimentary distribution of inexpensive logo merchandise can be an effective relationship marketing tool.

Direct Access/Personal Representative

This tactic involves the assignment of a contact person for the marketer's best customers. Instead of calling a generic number and filtering through several customer service representatives, the customer has a personal representative who can be reached by mail, telephone, or e-mail. To emphasize the importance of the relationship, the marketer may give the customer a name and a direct phone number to call when questions or problems arise. Season ticket holders who need additional tickets for a game can call their personal representative instead of going through the normal ticketing channels. The representative can also address complaints and is often authorized to take the steps necessary to resolve any perceived problem on the part of these important fans. Resolution of complaints is an essential element for season ticket renewal. It also creates a sense of importance knowing that the team cares enough to listen and respond accordingly. Generally, the fan will be assigned the same person as his or her personal representative as long as that employee continues to work in that capacity for the team. When it is time to renew for next season, the representative will personally discuss options with the fan. On some occasions, better seats become available within the same price range. The opportunity to improve one's seating is favorably received by any ticket holder.

Recognition

Albeit a minor commitment, marketers can benefit by simply acknowledging special occasions for their best customers. Large groups may be recognized with a public address announcement or a message on the scoreboard. Noting a season ticket holder's birthday or anniversary on the scoreboard may suffice.[16] Perhaps a mention during the radio or TV broadcast can be used to mark those special occasions. That these important fans are receiving something that the occasional fan does not get can add to the intensity of the relationship and create an even stronger sense of loyalty among the team's core customers.

Overview of Relationship Marketing in the Sports Marketing Environment

It should now be evident that relationship marketing encompasses all facets of marketing strategy. Each variable of the marketing mix–product, distribution, price, and promotion–must be tailored to address the characteristics of each target market. In addition, there is no single strategy that is right for all marketers. Another key consideration is that there are many tactics that can be employed, and they are not mutually exclusive. For example, fan appreciation activities may incorporate routine periodic communications, contests, and gifts. Serial marketing may involve frequency incentives, e-mail communications, and gifts. The marketer's task is to determine the optimal array of tactics to use to appeal to the desired target market and strengthen the existing relationship.

> **Relationship marketing encompasses all facets of marketing strategy.**

Emerging as an important element in the implementation of an effective relationship marketing program is the ability to develop comprehensive databases that include important information about the marketer's customers. As noted earlier, contests, clubs, and affinity cards often require specific details on entry blanks and application forms. Relevant information is combined with that from other individuals to create a more comprehensive database that can be searched using data-mining techniques. The result is that the available information can be used by the marketer to tailor its relationship marketing effort to market niches or even to individuals. This customized service delivery was earlier characterized as an *individualized value proposition*. This one-to-one marketing is the essence of relationship marketing.

Comprehensive Relationship Marketing Programs

The preceding discussion identified numerous tactics designed to enhance the relationship between the marketers of sports products and the members of their target markets. But any single tactic alone is unlikely to produce the desired result. To be effective, the marketer must integrate a number of relationship-based initiatives. Only with the effective integration of these initiatives will the marketer be able to develop, sustain, and strengthen its ties with its customers. While marketers of all sports products can benefit from relationship marketing, the best opportunities exist for marketers of spectator sports. To illustrate this point, we will examine the comprehensive relationship marketing program that NASCAR has implemented. But as noted earlier, marketers of products other than spectator sports can also benefit from tactics designed to retain existing customers through enhanced brand loyalty. To illustrate this point, we will also review the relationship marketing program used by one of the major marketers of athletic shoes, Reebok. Our examination of comprehensive integrated relationship marketing programs will begin with a look at NASCAR.

Integrated Relationship Marketing Program in Spectator Sports—NASCAR

NASCAR events have experienced sustained growth from two perspectives. First is the noteworthy increase in the size of the fan base; significant growth in both the live audience and the media-based audience has continued over the past few years. Second is the intense loyalty exhibited by these fans. They are loyal to the drivers and their sponsors. While many marketing initiatives have contributed to these phenomena, perhaps none have been more important than those that fall within the domain of relationship marketing. In this regard, NASCAR has focused on product extensions and a comprehensive integrated marketing communications plan in its efforts to appeal to individual fans.

The Lowe's Motor Speedway has an apartment building adjacent to the track; needless to say, this housing option will primarily appeal to the avid NASCAR fan. In an attempt to reach individual fans, NASCAR provides unrivaled access to information on its Web site. Retail operations include the NASCAR Thunder store and NASCAR Café. The organization has also licensed its trademarks to facilitate the establishment of a chain of NASCAR Silicon Motor Speedway Amusement Centers that feature simulators of the powerful NASCAR vehicles.

> NASCAR has focused on product extensions and a comprehensive integrated marketing communications plan in its efforts to appeal to individual fans.

At the forefront of this marketing effort is DAYTONA USA. Daytona is acknowledged by most stock car racing fans as the site of the most famous of all NASCAR races. Visitors to DAYTONA USA, a Disney-like theme park, can experience many of the thrills and the adrenaline rush associated with the Daytona 500 while simultaneously strengthening their bond with NASCAR. Much of the effort is directed toward younger fans while capitalizing on the opportunity to form a stronger relationship with new fans. Visitors access the entertainment complex via a tunnel similar to the actual entrance to the Daytona Raceway infield. A walkway features photos that illustrate the history of the Daytona race; it also includes a number of actual race cars. An interactive exhibit allows visitors to "converse" with eight drivers. They can also compete in Ford's 16-Second Pit Stop Challenge, which tests their ability to refuel and change the tires on an actual car. The Dupont Technology of Speed exhibit is aimed at educating fans about the role of technology in racing. There is the Pepsi Theatre, which has chain-link fencing like at the track, and Gatorade's Victory Lane, where the visitor can see an actual winning car, complete with the scrapes and dents resulting from the perils of competing in a NASCAR race. Finally, the ESPN exhibit allows the visitor to simulate the role of a race announcer. The relationship is further strengthened as the visitor is provided with a recording of his or her foray into the world of broadcasting a NASCAR race.[17] It is noteworthy that NASCAR, by incorporating its sponsors and their trademarks within the program, has used this strategy as a means of enhancing its own relationships with sponsors while concurrently allowing the sponsors to strengthen their relationships with their own customers. Thus, the integrated effort actually encompasses three distinct relationship marketing programs:

- NASCAR with its fans.
- NASCAR with its sponsors.
- NASCAR sponsors with their customers.

Other spectator sports would be well advised to consider developing similar programs in the effort to increase fan involvement and loyalty.

Integrated Relationship Marketing Program in Apparel and Shoes—Reebok

Reebok is generally acknowledged to have been at the forefront of the efforts by sports marketers to target female segments.[18] The company's pioneering efforts also contributed to the decision to implement relationship marketing efforts directed toward both consumers and the retailers who ultimately interact with the consumers. From the consumer perspective, the focus on women incorporated a key demographic consideration, while the creation of new products needed in the emerging aerobics and fitness markets emphasized lifestyles. The ability to enhance relationships with retailers was based upon the prevailing strategy of selling Reebok products through small specialty retail stores. By considering various aspects of the consumer market while working with retailers in the channel of distribution, Reebok was able to "create and establish lasting and relevant bonds and relationships with (our) target specialty retailer and the end consumer."[19]

Efforts to create the bonds that exemplify relationship marketing were key components of Reebok's integrated marketing communications plan. Its advertising featured endorsements by athletes who were well known to the target market. Included in this list was Venus Williams. Advertising was also used to leverage the company's various sponsorships while emphasizing its roots in the runner market. One of these key sponsorships was the U.S. Olympic Track and Field team for the 1996 Summer Olympics in Atlanta. At a grassroots level, sponsorships of university teams and regional running clubs were used to influence local amateur runners. Reebok also sponsored a number of local special events, including running clinics and product exhibits, which served to further enhance the firm's image. At a more basic level, newsletters were sent to individuals known to participate in running activities. In the retail stores, point-of-purchase displays, brochures, and posters were used to reach out to consumers. At the same time, Reebok would continually seek input from retailers. The grassroots involvement and the treatment of retailers as business partners served to further strengthen the relationships.[20] The net result was that Reebok was able to develop and maintain meaningful relationships with consumers and retailers. Box 20.5 provides a brief overview of Reebok's efforts.

REEBOK'S RELATIONSHIP MARKETING PROGRAM

20.5

- Sponsorship
  - 1996 U.S. Olympic Track and Field team
  - Universities
  - Local running clubs
  - Local events
    - Running clinics
    - Product exhibitions
- Endorsements
- Advertising
  - Leveraging of sponsorships
  - Focus on involvement with running
- Sales promotion
  - Newsletters
  - Point-of-purchase display
  - Brochures
  - Posters
- Retailer interaction
- Grassroots involvement
- Seeking of input from retailers
- Inventory management assistance
- Dedicated customer service

Evaluating the Effectiveness of a Relationship Marketing Program

Each of the tactics discussed has some cost associated with it. Like any other marketing initiative, this cost must be offset by some positive return. Just as sponsors have begun to measure the return on their investment upon the completion of a sponsored event, organizations similarly seek to develop an objective measure of the benefits gained from their investment in a relationship marketing program. Despite the importance of this measure, evaluation of the impact of relationship marketing efforts is still relatively rudimentary.

At the most fundamental level, the marketer can simply *track sales* trends. Since the inception or modification of the relationship marketing strategy, have sales increased, remained constant, or decreased? If sales have exhibited an upward trend, how much of that increase can be attributed to the program? There is one primary caveat to this approach. So many intervening variables also influence sales that attributing any change to the relationship marketing program is tenuous at best. A second weakness is that aggregate sales figures fail to distinguish between existing customers and new customers. Still, some information is better than none at all. But ideally this measure will simply be the initial step toward the development of a more precise measure of effectiveness.

A second measurement tool is that of *monitoring complaints*. Complaints are articulated via many approaches. For instance, consumers may write letters, call account representatives, or send e-mails. For the marketing of goods, an effort should also be made to monitor returns.

Many retailers ask why the product is being returned, and this information can help identify persistent problems. So can information gleaned from repair orders. Although these approaches have limited applicability in the marketing of most sports products, they can be useful in measuring customer satisfaction with marketers of sporting goods, apparel, and athletic shoes.

Efforts to measure satisfaction are important because it is difficult for a marketer to maintain a relationship with any individual who is dissatisfied. In a proactive approach to measuring satisfaction, some marketers use *customer satisfaction surveys*. To reach the correct market segment, a marketer can use a database to select a representative sample of fans who will be contacted by regular mail, e-mail, or telephone. The Detroit Tigers recently employed the services of an outside consulting firm to assess the level of satisfaction among season ticket holders during a period in which the season ticket base was dwindling.

> Efforts to measure satisfaction are important because it is difficult for a marketer to maintain a relationship with any individual who is dissatisfied.

Many sports marketers incorporate the Internet in their implementation of relationship marketing strategies. Common components of the Web sites are bulletin boards and chat rooms. These resources provide consumers with the ability to express unsolicited comments. By *monitoring Internet chat rooms and bulletin boards,* the marketer can identify points of contention. Even though the comments are difficult to attribute to an individual consumer or fan, the marketer can gain considerable insight from the feedback. Issues that would serve to diminish the strength of relationships with their customers can be identified. Over time, the intent is to reduce the number of times that a particular complaint or criticism is expressed.

When a Web site is being used, the team, league, event, or organization often directs visitors to other pages that are part of a relationship marketing program. In some cases, access requires a user ID and a password. By requiring this input, the marketer can limit access to the segment and individuals of interest. It could be season ticket holders, club members, or known purchasers of a specific product. The effectiveness of these Internet-based marketing efforts is often measured by *calculating the click-through rate*. More effective components will induce a larger percentage of the visitors to use their mouse to click through to the suggested page. This tool will allow the marketer to adjust its strategy by identifying the components that are most effective. In some cases, the marketer may be delivering a sales offer, providing entry into a contest, seeking applications for an affinity-based credit card, or simply seeking information from members of different segments. Regardless of the strategic purpose, the marketers can derive substantial benefits when they are able to achieve high click-through rates.

Finally, we have seen the development of *customer relationship management (CRM) software* that can be used to glean important and actionable information from existing databases. This process is often referred to as *data mining*. Like a prospector hunting for gold, the objective is to sift through what has been gathered while seeking something of value. It is not gold that will be found; rather, it is valuable information from which the marketer can derive substantial benefits. Recently, the Arena Football League implemented a new CRM program with the stated objective of increasing fan loyalty and boosting league revenues.[21] Additionally, the CRM software available today can analyze the data and produce the metrics that summarize the marketer's performance in the quest to instill that loyalty and increase profits.

> The objective of data mining, like a prospector hunting for gold, is to sift through what has been gathered while seeking something of value.

Recovery Marketing

Marketers can only hope that their strategies are all effective, that nothing will happen to threaten customer retention, and that their efforts to measure the results of their relationship marketing programs are accurate and enlightening. Unfortunately, marketing is not that simple. Problems do occur, and as a consequence, marketers incur a significant risk of losing customers. When something threatens a marketer's ability to retain its customers, the best solution may be the implementation of a recovery marketing strategy.

The most profound negative impact that marketers of spectator sports must counter involves labor issues. Virtually every major sports league across the world has incurred one or more work stoppages due to impasses in labor negotiations. Players unions have authorized strikes and league management has implemented lockouts that have caused the cancellation of games, championship series, and entire seasons. However, not all problems center on issues with the players unions. A star player may suddenly make an unanticipated retirement announcement. A favorite player may leave to sign a contract with another team. Injuries may turn a promising season into one filled with disappointment.

Another issue that is becoming far too common is the case of a player committing legal or ethical breaches of conduct. Recent legal and ethical indiscretions have included sexual misconduct, larceny, the use of performance enhancing drugs, murder, distribution of cocaine, the use of equipment that does not conform to the rules of the game being played, fights with fans, the selling of complimentary tickets for important games, officiating scandals, and allegations of bribery. Seemingly, the list of violations is endless. When behaviors such as these are reported by the media, they adversely impact the fans' perception of the players, the team, and the sport. Whether the problem emanates from labor issues, personnel changes, unanticipated poor performance, or player indiscretions, it has the potential of straining a relationship to the point that fans may abandon it.

> Whether the problem emanates from labor issues, personnel changes, unanticipated poor performance, or player indiscretions, it has the potential of straining a relationship to the point that fans may abandon it.

Two recent situations provide examples of sports marketers that needed to consider the use of recovery marketing in an effort to win back alienated fans who became disenchanted because of unanticipated actions. The NHL's 2004–05 season was canceled because of a lockout arising from the inability of the league and the players union to reach an agreement on a new collective bargaining agreement. Compounding that problem was the decision by the major TV carrier of NHL games (ESPN) to cancel its contract. Fans were angry, and they complained about wealthy owners and rich players compromising the integrity of the game over a dispute about money. In an effort to recover, each team implemented its own version of a recovery marketing program. Most teams reduced the price of tickets; for instance, the Carolina Hurricanes provided reductions of up to 30 percent from the 2003–04 season. Anaheim provided free refreshments and free parking for the first three games to season ticket holders; Columbus offered season ticket holders the opportunity to attend a picnic with the team's coaches. While the teams' efforts were quite varied, it was evident that they all recognized the need to recover from an undesirable situation by engaging in efforts designed to win back the fans.[22]

The second major breakdown in a sports relationship occurred in the 2005 American Grand Prix Formula One race at Indianapolis Speedway. Because of concerns over the safety of their tires, 14 of the 20 driving teams refused to race. Seeing only six cars competing at the start of the first lap, fans threw debris onto the track, demanded refunds, left early, and booed the winners as they stood on the podium. It quickly became evident that most of the spectators were dissatisfied, and it was equally clear that not many of the fans would eagerly purchase tickets to any future Formula One race. This dissatisfaction can be summed up in two quotes from fans who were in attendance:

> I came all the way from South America, from Bolivia, to watch this thing. But for me, this is the last time that I go to Formula One.
>
> I have been to this race every year they've had it here. My brothers and I have followed Formula One since the 70s and have never seen anything as outrageous as this. As far as I'm concerned, if they do have the race here again, I would be questionable about coming here.[23]

The entire fiasco was characterized as a disaster in which the fans got cheated. At various times, the finger of blame was pointed at Michelin for providing the wrong tires for the Indianapolis track, at Team Ferrari for being the only team to oppose changes to the track that would have slowed the cars to a safer speed, and at FIA for refusing to alter the rules to allow the 14 affected race cars to switch to an alternative tire. Many critics indicated that the ordeal could be the death knell for Formula One racing in the United States. Initially, there were questions concerning whether 2005 race would be the last one staged in the United States; however, plans were announced for the race to be held in 2006. But questions remained about the continuation of the event beyond the 2006 date. Will it be the last race in the series to be staged at an American venue? The answer depends, in part, on how effective the organizers have been in the development of their recovery strategy. At the time this book was published, the answer to that question was still unknown.

Procedures for Recovery Marketing in Spectator Sports

Effective relationship marketing will help create an environment in which the fans are more forgiving of the problems incurred by the sports marketer. When there is a meaningful threat of attrition, there is a need to implement a recovery marketing strategy. While there is no guarantee that the fans who are alienated by some unacceptable set of circumstances can be appeased, the lack of action would virtually guarantee that a significant number of disillusioned fans would opt to break off the relationship with the marketer. To reduce the level of fan attrition, the marketer should consider implementing the following five-step approach to recovery marketing.

> While there is no guarantee that the fans who are alienated by some unacceptable set of circumstances can be appeased, the lack of action would virtually guarantee that a significant number of disillusioned fans would opt to break off the relationship.

Foremost in the task of overcoming dissatisfaction is to *apologize to the fans* who see the issue as the failure to deliver a level of service that they deem acceptable. Acknowledge their concerns, and remember that empathy is a key element in maintaining a relationship. The sports marketer must be able to assess the situation from the fans' perspective. Do not blame others because the fans care little about where the fault lies.

The next step is to *make it personal*. Initiate contact by reaching out to fans with direct communications. Letters, phone calls, and e-mails can be important. Respond to their complaints in a timely manner. In the aftermath of the NBA's most recent work stoppage, the Portland Trailblazers had some 300 employees, including the team's head coach, call each of the team's 16,500 season ticket holders. The effort conveyed a personal message to the team's key segment: "We're back in business and we need you!"[24]

Next, the marketer needs to *provide a value-added solution* to the fans' problem. Gifts, discounts, and fan appreciation activities can be effective in this step. Referring back to the NBA's work stoppage, season ticket holders were contacted and informed of the opportunity

FIVE STEPS FOR RECOVERY MARKETING   20.6

- Apologize to the fans
- Make it personal
- Provide a value-added solution
- Offer risk-reducing incentives
- Communicate and follow up

to attend a practice session or a preseason game free of charge. Fans eagerly accepted these opportunities, and the teams benefited from the resultant goodwill. According to the Trailblazers' director of ticket sales, the combination of phoning the season ticket holders and providing value-added solutions "contributed significantly to achieving season ticket renewals that far exceeded . . . expectations."[25]

The fourth step is to *offer risk-reducing incentives* to the fans. Some gifts may be dependent upon the fan's continuation of the relationship. Prices can be held constant or even reduced for season ticket buyers. Teams can make specific guarantees regarding performance. A winning season or making it into league playoffs can be guaranteed. Failure to attain the promised level of performance can be addressed by refunding a portion of the cost of the season tickets. Not only can such guarantees help overcome the problem, but they also create the belief on the part of the fans that the same problem will not arise again in the foreseeable future.

The final step is to *communicate and follow up*. Initiate contact with the fans during this critical step. Assess their attitudes and their level of satisfaction. The goal of this final step is to determine how effective the first four steps have been. However, it is also designed to strengthen the bond between the team and the fans. These five steps are outlined in Box 20.6.

Note that each of the basic elements of relationship marketing has the potential to play a role in the task of recovery marketing. You should recall that these elements are: that the relationship is mutually beneficial; the parties trust each other; they are empathetic, thus able to view the issue from the other's perspective; there is an effort to maintain lines of communication; there is a bond between the fan and the team that is difficult to break; and there is a goal of continuity. In essence, recovery marketing relies upon the same principles of relationship marketing. And since no relationship is devoid of problems, sports marketers must be ready to address them and provide a rationale for the fan to continue to purchase tickets.

Closing Capsule

Marketing is a dynamic process that continues to evolve over time. Recently, that evolution has featured the transition away from transaction-based strategies to relationship-based strategies, now considered by many marketing practitioners to be more effective. Stated another way, customer retention is superior to customer acquisition. Using relationship-based strategies, the marketer seeks to capitalize on the lifetime value that each customer represents. Relationship marketing often focuses on individuals via one-to-one marketing, a strategy that has become more plausible with the recent advances in database management and data-mining capabilities.

When properly implemented, relationship marketing enhances customer loyalty, provides a mechanism for resolving customer complaints, and serves to develop a sense of belonging on the part of the customer. Every industry has the potential to benefit from the implementation of an effective relationship marketing strategy, but perhaps nowhere is that potential greater than it is in the sports industry, especially for marketers of spectator sports.

Marketing relationships have much in common with social relationships. They can develop and endure when each party reaps a benefit from the association, when they know they can trust each other, when they can view any situation from the other's perspective, when there is a bond that would make separation difficult, and when there is effective, interactive communication. The absence of any of these conditions can stress a relationship to a point that its continuity is threatened.

There are a myriad of tactics that can be used as part of an integrated relationship marketing program. From the consumers' perspective, some of the more popular tactics of sports marketers are clubs, frequency incentives, affinity programs, and contests. Marketers should explore the entire set of initiatives at their disposal and implement those that are most appropriate for each target market. No single program meets the needs of every marketer.

Each component of a relationship marketing program requires a commitment of resources. These costs are best viewed as an investment aimed at increasing long-term profitability. When viewed as such, it is only appropriate for the marketer to seek an acceptable return on that investment. The assessment of ROI can be undertaken by tracking changes in sales over time; monitoring complaints, including the reasons why products are deemed unsatisfactory and returned to their point of purchase; administering customer satisfaction surveys; monitoring Internet feedback; calculating Web-based click-through rates; and using customer relationship management software.

> Sports fans can be demanding customers, but they can also be among the most dedicated and loyal customers that a marketer can serve.

Try as they might to avoid them, marketers often encounter problems that place a significant strain on their relationships with customers. In sports, one of the major debilitating occurrences is the cancellation of a scheduled competition. Strikes and lockouts emanating from the inability to secure a collective bargaining agreement between the players union and the owners are inevitably met with great disappointment by the fans. The cancellation of the 2004–05 NHL season created a great deal of fan animosity. When problems such as these arise, the sports marketer often chooses to implement a recovery marketing program. The five steps for this type of strategy are straightforward. They are (1) apologize, (2) make it personal, (3) provide a value-added solution, (4) offer risk-reducing incentives, and (5) maintain a channel of communication that promotes effective feedback. Sports fans can be demanding customers, but they can also be among the most dedicated and loyal customers that a marketer can serve. Every effort should be made to ensure that the relationship between the sports entity and its customers lasts long into the future.

Review Questions

1. Why is relationship marketing considered to be more effective than transaction-based marketing?

2. Explain the concepts of BIRGing and CORFing. Give an example of how you, a family member, or a friend has engaged in each of these actions.

3. Select a professional sports team and explain how you would develop a relationship marketing strategy that provides benefits to the team and to a subset of its most important fans.

4. Explain the role of communications in a relationship-based marketing strategy.

5. Identify your favorite team; then (qualitatively) evaluate the strength of your relationship with the team using the components outlined in Box 20.3.

6. Go to a team's Web site and identify each element of relationship marketing that is incorporated within the team's home page.

7. Why are contests popular with fans and with sports teams?

8. What is meant by the assertion that the tactics available for the development of a relationship marketing program are not "mutually exclusive"? Provide an example to support your answer.

9. Why is it important to evaluate the effectiveness of a relationship marketing program?

10. What elements would you have included in the development of a recovery marketing strategy for Formula One racing in the United States in the aftermath of the problems surrounding the staging of the American Grand Prix in 2005?

Endnotes

1. L. Rosenberg and J. Czepiel, "A Marketing Approach to Customer Retention," *Journal of Consumer Marketing* 1, no. 1 (Spring 1984), pp. 45–51.

2. D. Shani and S. Chalasani, "Exploring Niches Using Relationship Marketing," *Journal of Consumer Marketing* 9, no. 3 (1992), pp. 33–43.

3. M. MacDonald and G. Milne, "A Conceptual Framework for Evaluating Marketing Relationships in Professional Sport Franchises," *Sport Marketing Quarterly* 6, no. 2 (1997), pp. 27–32.

4. Ibid.

5. Ibid.

6. D. Wann and N. Branscombe, "Diehard Fans and Fair Weather Fans: Effects of Identification on BIRGing and CORFing Tendencies," *Journal of Sport and Social Issues* 14 (1990), pp. 103–17.

7. D. Wann and N. Branscombe, "Role of Identification with a Group, Arousal, Categorization Processes, and Self-Esteem in Sports Spectator Aggression," *Human Relations* 45 (1992), pp. 1013–34.

8. D. Shani, "A Framework for Implementing Relationship Marketing in the Sport Industry," *Sport Marketing Quarterly* 6, no. 2 (1997), pp. 9–15.

9. R. Lapio Jr. and M. Speter, "NASCAR: A Lesson in Integrated and Relationship Marketing," *Sport Marketing Quarterly* 9, no. 2 (2000), pp. 85–95.

10. D. Barrand, "RFU Launches Loyalty Scheme," February 7, 2003, www.sportbusiness.com/news/index?news_item_id=150093 (accessed October 13, 2005).

11. L. Boone and D. Kurtz, *Contemporary Marketing* (Mason, OH: South-Western, 2006).

12. C. Britcher, "Watford's Lucrative Reward," November 19, 2003, www.sportbusiness.com/news/index?news_item_id=153145 (accessed October 13, 2005).

13. Lapio and Speter, "NASCAR: A Lesson in Integrated and Relationship Marketing."

14. Shani, "A Framework for Implementing Relationship Marketing."

15. D. Smith, "Indy 500 Getting Serious," June 2, 2005, www.sportbusiness.com/news/index?news_item_id=157682 (accessed October 13, 2005).

16. D. Lewis, unpublished presentation to sports marketing class, June 14, 2005.

17. Lapio and Speter, "NASCAR: A Lesson in Integrated and Relationship Marketing."

18. A. Rohm, "The Creation of Consumer Bonds within Reebok Running," *Sport Marketing Quarterly* 6, no. 2 (1997), pp. 17–25.

19. Ibid.

20. Ibid.

21. C. Britcher, "AFL Agrees New CRM System," April 21, 2004, www.sportbusiness.com/news/index?news_item_id=154328 (accessed October 13, 2005).

22. J. Gerstner, "Wings Strive to Win Fans Back," *Detroit News,* September 26, 2005, pp. D1, D5.

23. Associated Press, "Bewildered Fans Want Restitution," July 2, 2005, www.sports.espn.go.com/rpm/news/story?series=f1&id=208995 (accessed October 14, 2005).

24. R. Burton and D. Howard, "Recovery Strategies for Sports Marketers," *Marketing Management* 9, no. 1 (2000), pp. 42–49.

25. Ibid.

CHAPTER TWENTY-ONE

The Role of Technology in Sports Marketing

Learning Objectives

- Learn the foundation for effective Internet applications.
- Identify the four types of websites in sports marketing.
- Understand methods used by these sites to create a revenue stream.
- See how the WWW can be applied in sports marketing.
- Learn how technology beyond the WWW has a role.

Technology has a tremendous impact in the way that sports marketers develop their strategies. Among the innovations discussed in previous chapters is virtual advertising, a new technology that can be used to reach the target markets for both sports products and non-sports products. New satellite-based technology has allowed marketers of spectator sports to reach a global market with improved video and audio capabilities. Another example cited earlier is the use of a DVD to promote an upcoming race. The list of applications for new technology is extensive. However, many observers enthusiastically look to the Internet and the World Wide Web (WWW) as the innovation that has created the greatest opportunity for sports marketers, especially for those in the spectator sports segment. It has become apparent that the WWW can play a role in every aspect of marketing strategy.

Although this chapter will address several emerging technologies, the primary focus is directed toward the use of the Internet within the sports marketing environment. As such, it will explore the various applications that only a few years ago were just dreams; today they are a reality. Prior to examining these applications, those aspiring to use the WWW as a marketing tool should have a basic framework to follow. We will start by examining the foundation governing the use of the Internet as a marketing tool.

Foundation for Internet Applications

Marketers throughout the world are seeking ways in which they can incorporate emerging technology into their marketing strategies. But no other technology has captured the interest of marketers and consumers the way that the Internet has. With the rapid adoption of this innovation, many millions of consumers already have access to the Web. In addition to the increase in users, the technology has also evolved at a rapid rate. Faster transmission speeds and more secure transmission protocols have been achieved, and these technological advances have been embraced by virtually everyone with Internet access. Even when the Internet is not available in people's homes, there are many alternative sites that provide free access. Schools provide it as part of the educational process; many workers have it available in their offices. Public libraries often provide access for their local residents. In some emerging economies such as Costa Rica, the Internet is available in public locations such as the local post office. In addition to the multitude of free opportunities, Internet cafés provide an inexpensive alternative for consumers. Many restaurants and coffee shops use wireless access as a way of attracting customers. So the rationale behind the use of the Internet as a marketing tool is relatively straightforward. The number of users is enormous and growing every day.

But before the sports marketer can develop an effective Internet-based marketing strategy, several fundamental questions should be answered. These are best summed up in a few words: why, who, what, where, and how?[1] Each of these questions will now be briefly examined.

Why?

A key caveat here is that the marketer should not feel compelled to use the Internet simply because it is available. The technology itself does not assure the marketer of making an impact. The issue is how the technology can be used to create a more effective marketing strategy when integrated with the marketing mix and target market decisions. Will a Web presence enhance the marketer's image? Will it augment other strategic initiatives? Will it drive sales?

Who?

To be effective, an Internet-based strategy must be consistent with the target market. By knowing who will be using the Web site, the marketer can design it so as to be consistent with the users' capabilities. The marketer should be careful to avoid *innovation overload* by not incorporating features and technology that the target market neither understands nor deems relevant. For instance, it does little good to incorporate video streaming on a Web site if the majority of visitors to the site are still using slow dial-up access. So the key issues for this question are

- Who will utilize the site?
- Is it open to everyone?
- Will adults or children use the site?
- What other Web sites will be linked to it?

> The marketer should be careful to avoid *innovation overload* by not incorporating features and technology that the target market neither understands nor deems relevant.

What?

This question concerns the purpose for developing the Web site. Marketers should identify the specific objectives and develop the site with those objectives in mind. Understand that a single page on a Web site cannot accomplish everything that a marketer needs to do in order to be successful. Thus, there are two key issues. What is the core purpose for developing the Web site? What effect will it have on the target market?

Where?

Marketers should consider this to be a two-part question. First, it should address the most likely locations of those who view the Web site. The Web site must be designed to meet the needs of the recreational user at home or the business user at work. Not only might this influence cosmetic issues, but functionality should also be considered. Computers at work are more likely to have better capabilities than many of the personal computers used at home by casual surfers. Home computers are also less likely to be networked with other users and hardware. Issues such as these should be taken into account.

DEVELOPING AN INTERNET PHILOSOPHY   21.1

Why?

Will it enhance the marketer's image?

Will it augment other strategic initiatives?

Will it result in increased demand?

Who?

Who will utilize the site?

Is it open to everyone?

Will it target adults or kids, or both?

What other websites will be linked to it?

What?

What is the site's core purpose?

How will it impact the target market?

Where?

Where will the user gain access to the site?

Where will the site be developed and maintained?

How?

How will the user receive the information?

How will the site be developed?

How will the site be evaluated?

Source: R. Caskey and L. Delpy, "An Examination of Sports Web Sites and the Opinion of Web Employees toward the Use and Viability of the World Wide Web as a Profitable Sports Marketing Tool," *Sport Marketing Quarterly* 8, no. 2 (1999), pp. 13–24.

The second "where" question involves the developer. Specifically, it addresses the hardware and software available and the resources required to maintain it. The server to be used must have adequate storage capacity and the ability to handle traffic. Essentially, the marketer must ultimately decide whether to maintain it in-house or to outsource it to a company that specializes in this type of service.

How?

The question of "how" is actually several important questions. First, how is the information likely to be received? The answer depends on who is receiving the information. However, the basic issue concerns the incoming communications mode. Is it dial-up or a direct connection? The growth of broadband and other high-speed delivery alternatives will continue to provide new opportunities for delivering richer content to the viewer.

How will the site be developed? Will it be done in-house or by an independent contractor? Is the marketer proficient with HTML (hypertext markup language)? Can the site be maintained without outside expertise? Finally, the key question is, How will the site be evaluated? Alternatives include a postdevelopment evaluation by those who created the site, evaluation by peers, and user feedback. Hit rates and click-through rates may also provide quantitative measures of the effectiveness of the Web site. Box 21.1 provides an overview of the five questions central to the development of an effective Web site.

TYPES OF WEBSITES IN THE SPORTS MARKETING ENVIRONMENT

21.2

- Content sites
- Team or league sites
- Commerce sites
- Gambling sites

Source: R. Caskey and L. Delpy, "An Examination of Sports Web Sites and the Opinion of Web Employees toward the Use and Viability of the World Wide Web as a Profitable Sports Marketing Tool," *Sport Marketing Quarterly* 8, no. 2 (1999), pp. 13–24.

Types of Sites in Sports Marketing

Four types of Web sites have been identified within the sports marketing environment, as listed in Box 21.2. Each of these four will be discussed on the following pages.

Content Sites

A content site is one that incorporates a large base of information where users can go to find news, scores, and analysis. These sources are independent from the sports themselves; rather, they use sports as a means of attracting consumers. These sites are generally an extension of some media vehicle. As such, the vehicle can be associated with a general news service such as the *New York Times* newspaper or a sports-oriented vehicle such as the *Sporting News*. Print media companies have been quick to incorporate the WWW into their array of services. Many members of the electronic media have also incorporated a Web component within their product strategy. General news media such as CNN, the BBC, and many local TV channels are a few examples. Similarly, sports networks such as Sky Sports, Fox Sports, Setanta Sports, and ESPN all maintain extensive content Web sites that receive millions of hits each day.

Team or League Sites

These are the official sites of amateur or professional teams and leagues. Within the category of amateur teams and leagues are the Web sites maintained by colleges and universities. Some amateur bowling leagues, soccer leagues, and softball leagues also maintain their own Web sites. Sports associations fall within this category. Association sites would include those for federations with control and oversight of an array of athletic entities and competitions. Among these are well-known organizations such as FIFA, the NCAA, and the IOC as well as less renowned associations such as the United States Bowling Congress (USBC).

Information provided in this type of Web site tends to be sport or event specific. Typical content is player information, statistics, results, schedules, and highlights. Video streaming is often used to provide the visitor with a brief look at action that has recently taken place. These Web sites provide a wealth of information about the particular sport or event that may be of interest to fans and members of the media. As noted in Chapter 17, many of these sites are also serving as virtual box offices and storefronts where fans can purchase tickets and officially licensed merchandise. Given this emphasis on sales, such Web sites could reasonably be placed within the third category, commerce sites.

Commerce Sites

E-commerce is the use of the WWW to provide a virtual retail storefront where visitors can purchase an array of sports products. Included are retailers of general sporting goods, athletic shoes, and sports apparel. Other commerce sites sell officially licensed merchandise; such sites may be maintained by either the licensor or the licensee. In other words, the fan may purchase a New York Yankees cap on the MLB or the Yankees' team Web site, or on the New Era Web site. And the fan also has the option of purchasing a Yankees cap from an independent retail Web site such as Lids.com.

Manufacturers may prefer not to sell directly through the Internet. For example, adidas does not want to sell shoes one pair at a time. Many companies, like adidas, are concerned that individual direct sales might create conflict within the channel of distribution as retailers express their displeasure with the idea of competing directly with the manufacturer. In such cases, rather than selling the product directly to consumers, the manufacturer's Web site will provide information regarding local retailers. By entering an address or a mailing code, the Web site user can view, and even print out, a list of nearby retailers that sell the manufacturer's products. Driving directions may even be provided as a means of facilitating the purchase process.

Gambling Sites

Sports marketers generally attempt to disassociate themselves from the sites that accept wagers on the outcome of sports events. Still, this category has expanded rapidly over the past few years. These sites provide information while attempting to market their services. In essence, they represent a combination of a content site and a commerce site. They are a visible aspect of the sports marketing environment, though many people are reluctant to characterize them as sports marketing Web sites because the service they are selling is not a true sports product. However, they are in fact selling their services by using a sports platform, and selling through sports is deemed to fall within the sports marketing environment. The rapid growth of this genre of Web sites has been acknowledged and led to a recent iGAMING seminar that was staged by SportBusiness International and *iGAMING Business* magazine.[2]

Revenue Streams

Not every Web site is established with a direct link to a revenue-producing activity. For example, components designed to enhance relationships or provide information may not have a specific revenue stream associated with them. Yet they are expected to play a role in the enhancement of brand loyalty, the inducement of visitors to the Web site, and increased levels of customer satisfaction. From a broad marketing perspective, each of these outcomes should contribute to the marketer's financial health. Therefore, a well-designed Web site can still have a positive impact on profitability even when it does not have a direct revenue-producing component.

> The ability to set revenue goals and measure actual results provides a mechanism by which a Web site can be evaluated.

Many Web sites do incorporate components that produce one or more direct revenue streams. The ability to set revenue goals and measure actual results provides a mechanism by which a Web site can be evaluated. It is evident that sports entities are no longer simply developing Web sites as novel afterthoughts. They are a vital component in a sports marketer's strategic arsenal. The following discussion will delineate the revenue-producing aspects of the various types of Web sites within the sports marketing environment.

Revenue Models for Content Sites

There are three basic approaches for the generation of revenue by a content site. These are online advertising (and sponsorship), subscription fees, and e-commerce.

Online Advertising/Sponsorship

Advertising on sports-oriented Web sites has been reported to exceed $7 billion per year.[3] Fans are often passionate, and this passion results in an effort to find more information about the athletes, teams, sports, and events that they support. As the number of hits on content sites has increased, these sites have begun to be recognized as a viable advertising medium. The question that has been difficult to answer concerns the monetary value associated with any advertising space on a particular Web site. Not all Web sites provide equivalent opportunities, so how much should a prospective advertiser be asked to pay? In part, that answer may depend upon the type of advertisement used.

> Advertising on sports-oriented Web sites has been reported to exceed $7 billion per year.

Banner ads often appear as a static component of the Web site. The copy and graphics remain the same for each visitor, as does the location of the ad within the Web site. While the premium position is at the top of the page, other locations are commonly used. Many Web sites now offer the visitor the option of closing or reducing the size of the advertisement, thereby removing it from further view. *Ad badges* are small icons on which the user can click. These hyperlinks will then load a new webpage that provides additional information about the advertiser's products. This strategy is often used as a component for sponsors of a sports property. Because of the low click-through rates on ad badges, banner ads are generally perceived as having higher value. Conversely, a banner ad cannot convey nearly as much information as a hyperlinked ad badge that moves the visitor to a page rich with content on the advertiser and its products.

Specific advertising rates are generally determined in one of three ways. First is the traditional cost-per-thousand (CPM) approach. Also popular is a fee based upon click-through rates (CTR). Finally, the advertiser may be charged a flat rate.

The *cost-per-thousand* method is the most common approach for determining the price to be paid by the advertiser. Using this approach, the marketer will consider the size, type, and location of the ad in addition to the demographic audience reached by the Web site. By considering these criteria, the advertiser will be able to place a value on each 1,000 impressions. For example, the advertiser may agree to pay the operator of the Web site $45 for each 1,000 people who view the Web site. If the advertisement achieved 50,000 impressions, then the cost would be calculated as $2,250 ($45 * 50).

The *click-through* basis sets a value on each time a consumer clicks on the ad badge for the marketer. Viewers who do so are presumed to have some interest in the company or the product being advertised. Visitors to the Web site who do not click through to the advertiser's page impose no financial obligation on the part of the advertiser. Of the 50,000 visitors noted in the previous example, perhaps only 600 clicked through. If the advertiser agreed to pay $2 for each of these visitors, the cost of the advertisement would be $1,200 ($2 * 600). As suggested by this example, click-through rates tend to be quite low, with a rate around 1 percent being the norm.

> Click-through rates tend to be quite low, with a rate around 1 percent being the norm.

The final pricing method is based upon a single *flat rate*. While CPM focuses on traffic and CTR is based upon customer action, the flat-rate method takes neither of these into final consideration. In this case, the price is a fixed sum. Although anticipated traffic and the expected CTR may have been taken into account in the task of establishing the fee, it is unlikely that the rate will be adjusted once it has been established. In this regard, it is much like a TV ad for which the marketer pays an established fee for 30 seconds of advertising time.

Subscription Fees

Many content Web sites provide general information to anyone on a complimentary basis. Yet sports fans often seek access to minute details, rumors, and news reports. This process of *drilling deep* for such detailed information can be done on the Internet, thus representing a significant advantage over traditional print and electronic media. Fans have exhibited a willingness to pay modest subscription fees for this type of access. ESPN's Insider is an example of a relatively inexpensive service of this type. Sportbusiness.com provides basic updates and access to fundamental information to anyone who subscribes to its free service; however, the site offers a more expensive subscription service to those seeking greater detail. ESPN's Insider service costs $40 per year, whereas the comprehensive service from sportbusiness.com is priced at approximately $390 (£199) per year.

E-Commerce

Many content Web sites do not actually sell the products featured on their sites. In other cases, there may be only a limited selection of the featured products. General news organizations are likely to outsource any retailing activities. In such cases, the operator of the content site may process the order and pass along the details to another marketer that will bear the responsibility for fulfilling the order. In some cases, a click on an icon will take the consumer away from the content site that was being viewed and onto one maintained by the marketer that will take the order and arrange shipment of the merchandise. The operator of the original content site is compensated for bringing the buyer and the seller together with some percentage or perhaps a fixed amount for each sale.

Revenue Models for Team and League Sites

There are three primary revenue streams for operators of team and league sites. These include the same type of online advertising/sponsorship model that is commonly associated with content sites. Because of the more narrowly defined content, fan interest gives the marketer the opportunity to charge subscription fees for premium services it provides. This may involve membership to fan clubs, fantasy sports leagues, and access to more details than the casual fan will normally seek. These sites can also incorporate an e-commerce component. From this brief introduction, it is evident that the potential revenue streams for team and league sites mirror those associated with content sites.

Online Advertising/Sponsorship

Many team and league sites sell advertising space to a number of marketers of sports and nonsports products. The aforementioned banner ads and ad badges are commonly employed in the effort to reach specified target markets. Pop-up ads are also used, but many browsers now incorporate guards in their software that greatly limit the effectiveness of this type of ad.

> With a 30-second spot during the TV broadcast priced at $ 2.4 million, marketers that could not afford that level of investment were still able to align themselves with the NFL and the Super Bowl via advertising on the league's Web site.

Not only can teams and leagues generate revenue from outside advertisers, but they can also place their own promotions on the site. Special prices, giveaways, and the upcoming presence of a premier player or team can be strategically placed within the content area. Making space available for sponsors to leverage their relationship with the sports property can also add value that will generate additional revenue from the sponsors. Some marketers have opted to advertise on the Web sites for premier events simply because such a presence is considerably less expensive than the purchase of a 30-second time slot during the actual broadcast of the event. An excellent example of this phenomenon is the tremendous upsurge in advertising generated by the superbowl.com Web site. With a 30-second spot during the TV broadcast priced at $2.4 million, marketers that could not afford that level of investment were still able to align themselves with the NFL and the Super Bowl via advertising on the league's Web site.[4]

Subscription Fees

The various sports entities provide proprietary content that few outside organizations can duplicate. Newsletters from inside sources, audio and video streaming of copyrighted highlights, and direct interaction with participants are a few examples of the opportunities for which consumers will pay subscription fees that provide access for some established term. Typical terms are a month or a year. An example is the Real Madrid soccer team, which charges a subscription fee of either $6 per month or $42 per year for access to its Exclusive Zone. Not only do subscribers gain access that allows them to drill deep into the content about the team, the players, the league, and recent matches, but they also gain access to video streaming of games that is otherwise unavailable to the general public.

E-Commerce

Teams and leagues perform in a retail role by offering the public a variety of products related to their property. Many of the people who visit a team or league site tend to be avid fans, who, as research has shown, are more prone to purchase logo merchandise. Thus, typically the emphasis of e-commerce on these sites is apparel that bears the logos of the property and other affiliated properties. For example, a team may sell not only apparel featuring its own logo but also apparel featuring the logos of league events. A fan visiting the Web site of any NFL team would be able to purchase that team's own products on the site and also find available league-based apparel such as that bearing the Super Bowl logo. At the same time, the league site (NFL.com) will provide links that make team apparel available.

Sporting goods may be sold on team or league Web sites, but the majority of these products would be classified as souvenirs. As with the apparel, these products typically display the logo of one or more of the related sports entities. For example, a soccer ball may have both the Barclay's Premiership League and the Manchester United soccer team's logos imprinted on it. A variety of other souvenirs are also sold; for example, golf balls, beach towels, and stuffed animals may be available on some teams' Web sites.

Revenue Models for Commerce Sites

Commerce sites generate the bulk of their revenue by making goods available for sale to consumers. Today, many of these virtual retailers are simply extensions of traditional brick-and-mortar retailers. Furthermore, the store may be one that specializes in a narrow line of sports products or a general merchandise retailer that includes a line of sports products within its broad product assortment. Or the retailer may not even have a physical storefront for the potential buyer to visit; it might exist only on the Internet. Regardless of the aforementioned considerations, there are three basic revenue streams to consider. They are sales revenue, commissions, and online advertising.

Sales Revenue

Retailers buy merchandise from suppliers and resell it to consumers. In this regard, virtual retailers are no different than their brick-and-mortar counterparts. Revenue is generated with each sale. This revenue must cover the cost-of-goods sold (COGS) and operational costs so as to produce an acceptable profit margin. Because retailers are at risk when they cannot sell at a profit, they must take care to anticipate the demand for their products. Examples of commerce sites that rely extensively on sales revenue include lids.com, nikesoccerworld.com, sportsweb.com, basspro.com, and fogdog.com.

Commissions

Some commerce sites do not fit the strict definition of a retailer. Rather than buying and selling, some organizations serve as a liaison for other marketers. Much like a real estate agent, they attempt to link a buyer with a specific seller. These Web sites may incorporate a mechanism for accepting orders for products that will be provided by a third party. The order is placed; the Web site operator notifies the supplier; and the supplier ships the order directly to the buyer. For serving as the liaison and processing the order, the operator of the commerce site receives a commission. This generally takes the form of a designated percentage of each sale.

Other sites do not take the order; instead, they provide a hyperlink that transfers the consumer to the actual seller's Web site. The order is then completed using the seller's resources. For providing the link, the commerce site receives a commission. It may be calculated as a fixed fee per transaction. This differs from a click-through fee in that the original site is paid only when a purchase is actually made. Yet another compensation option is one based upon a straight commission rate, with larger sales resulting in larger commissions being paid.

Online Advertising/Sponsorship

Large commerce sites may generate enough hits so that other marketers view it as an opportunity to reach one or more of their own target markets. While some of the advertisers will be sports brands that are offered through the site, others will be mainstream marketers seeking to capitalize on strategic alliances. Beer, bottled water, insurance, telecommunications services, and credit card issuers are examples of nonsports industries that advertise on sports-related commerce sites that are not their own.

Revenue Models for Gambling Sites

While we may be reluctant to classify these sites as sports sites, many are directly tied to the sports industry. Most of these sites provide online gaming opportunities, an activity that many observers place within the sports and leisure domain. For instance, a number of TV sports networks now routinely broadcast poker tournaments to an increasingly large viewing audience. Some gambling Web sites provide a virtual "sports book" where visitors can bet on the outcomes of sporting events. Though these sites are difficult to classify and are controversial, they merit discussion within the context of sports Web sites. The three most viable streams of revenue for gambling sites are derived from wagers, subscription fees, and online advertising.

Wagers

The primary source of revenue is the aggregate wagers placed by online gamblers. A reality of gambling is that the odds inevitably favor the house, not the gambler. As a result, in the long run the house will take in more than it pays out. This is true whether it is a casino in Monte Carlo or an online gambling Web site.

Subscriptions

Gambling Web sites require the consumer to register prior to being given access for entry. The information requested involves the gambler's name, age, and credit card information. Once registered, the gambler can login with his or her individual user ID and password. This provides access to a variety of gambling resources, which may include information such as lessons, tips, and news stories. For such access, some gambling Web sites require a subscription fee. Even if the consumer never places a bet, revenue is still generated from the daily, weekly, monthly, or yearly fee.

Online Advertising

Gambling sites have the potential of providing advertisers with a link to key market segments. Though this revenue stream has been slow to materialize, some gambling sites do have a modest amount of independent advertising. For example, citycasino.com provides a link for marketers interested in advertising on the site. Potential advertisers include traditional casinos, broadcast media companies, information services, magazines, and providers of travel services. At this time, however, there is little outside advertising as traditional marketers view the controversial nature of these Web sites as a barrier to effective communication.

Web-Based Objectives

To better understand the objectives of Web-based marketing endeavors, we must refer back to one of the five questions that should be answered in the effort to develop an understanding of the foundation for this genre of marketing. The "why" question concerns the core purpose of the Web site. But the marketer must not overlook that a Web site can be used to achieve multiple objectives. In general, there are two broad categories of objectives germane to Web-based marketing. These objectives may be classified as either communications or operations in nature. Table 21.1 summarizes the results of a recent study that evaluated the relative importance of an array of communications objectives among 328 sports marketing organizations.

Careful scrutiny of Table 21.1 reveals that the eight communications objectives fit into three broad categories: to provide information, to facilitate distribution, and to enhance customer relationship management. In addition to these three objectives, the Web can be used to facilitate day-to-day operations for the sports organization. As such, it reduces the labor intensity of a number of activities, thereby reducing the costs incurred by the sports marketer. Box 21.3 lists the four broad-based Web objectives for those marketers that operate within the sports environment. Each of these objectives will be examined on the following pages.

TABLE 21.1
Communications Objectives for Sports Marketing Websites

Source: M. Brown, "An Analysis of Online Marketing in the Sport Industry: User Activity, Communications Objectives, and Perceived Benefits," *Sport Marketing Quarterly* 12, no. 1 (2003), pp. 48–55.

Order of Importance	Objective
1	Provide information on the organization
2	Create awareness of the organization
3	Project a favorable image of the organization
4	Establish an interactive channel of communication
5	Gain access to previously inaccessible customers
6	Provide an opportunity for customer feedback
7	Sell tickets or other merchandise
8	Generate new leads for sales force follow-up

WEB-BASED OBJECTIVES FOR SPORTS MARKETERS

21.3

- Provide information
- Facilitate distribution
- Enhance customer relationship management
- Facilitate operations

WWW Applications in Sports Marketing

The four categories of Web-based objectives are appropriate for marketers in any industry. But the primary purpose of this chapter is to gain a better understanding of how each is operationalized within the sports marketing industry. This will be accomplished by examining specific examples of Web-based marketing initiatives for each of the categories. This examination will begin with a look at strategies and tactics that involve the transmission of information to one or more key target markets.

Provide Information

Undoubtedly, the initial Web-based marketing initiatives were designed to provide information to sports fans, the media, and the general public. With an almost limitless capacity to store information, the Web possesses a key advantage over traditional media in that it can provide detailed information that is simply not feasible for TV, radio, and newspapers. Many sites even provide search engines that allow the user to hone in on specific content. The Web is not limited by time or geographic borders. Information is available 24/7; the Web does not restrict the user to a specific time frame like television. If you miss a TV broadcast, you may never have another chance to watch the program. The WWW also does not require the user to be present within the community for which information is being sought. A fan of the English rugby team who lives in Japan can access the Web and acquire timely information about the team, its recent matches, its players, and its upcoming schedule.

A recent study of the Australian National Basketball League indicated that there are several informational components commonly incorporated within the Web sites of the league's 10 teams. And to keep each site easy to find, the URL for each team mirrors the team's name. For instance, the URL for the Sydney Kings team is www.sydneykings.com.au. The information content that is commonly provided by these teams is summarized in Table 21.2. It is

TABLE 21.2
Information Provided on NBL Team Web sites

Source: J. Carlson, R. Rosenberger III, and S. Muthaly, "Nothing but Net! A Study of the Information Content in Australian Professional Basketball Websites," *Sport Marketing Quarterly* 12, no. 3 (2003), pp. 184–89.

Information Category	% Using
Player information	100%
Schedule	100
Current team statistics	100
Press releases	90
Upcoming promotions	90
Club history	60
Standings/position	50
Public relations	40
Stadium history	30
Game-day information	20

TABLE 21.3
Examples of
Information-Based
Web sites

Sports Entity	Type	URL
Barry Bonds	Player (MLB)	www.barrybonds.com
Los Angeles Lakers	Team (NBA)	www.nba.com/lakers
F.A. Premier League	League (soccer)	www.premierleague.com
Madison Square Garden	Facility	www.thegarden.com
International Association of Athletics Federations (IAAF)	Association	www.iaaf.org
America's Cup	Event (yachting regatta)	www.americascup.com/en
Fishing	Participation sport	www.takemefishing.org

reasonable to assume that other leagues, teams, and associations are similarly inclined to provide this type of information. Furthermore, the inclusion of each of the listed types of information is likely to become even more common in the foreseeable future.

In today's environment, it is almost essential for every team, league, association, and event to maintain its own Web site. Even individual players have adopted this practice. It is evident that fans want more information about their favorite sports entities than ever before. As noted earlier, the Internet provides the fan with the opportunity to drill deep into the available information and glean details that would otherwise be difficult to attain. Table 21.3 provides a representative sampling of the informational Web sites that are maintained by various of sports entities.

Teams, leagues, and associations commonly use informational sites; however, as shown in Table 21.3, other sports entities find this marketing tool to be beneficial as well. In addition, marketers of sporting goods, apparel, and athletic shoes can provide information such as product reviews and retailer locations in an effort to gain an advantage over their competition. In the participation market, skiers can get weather and ski condition updates from the Web sites maintained by ski resorts.[5] Many sites for golf courses also provide information on weather, short-term forecasts, greens fees, and course difficulty. In the United Kingdom, golfers can access the PGA Web site and download driving directions to any course in the UK.[6] In New Zealand, the NZGA site provides information on courses; it also allows visitors to search for individual golfers' most recently posted scores and their official handicap.[7]

Facilitate Distribution

Earlier in this text, there was a discussion of the virtual box office. Spectators can purchase tickets that are transmitted electronically. Instead of receiving the traditional paper tickets through the regular mail or at the traditional box office, the buyer receives an e-mail confirmation or an electronic facsimile of the tickets that can be printed using a home or office computer. Teams, leagues, events, and venue operators have begun to adopt this application of Web-based marketing. The NHL's Buffalo Sabres recently implemented a program called Tickets@Home that allows fans to purchase and print tickets using their own personal computer. Bar-code technology is used to create a uniquely identifiable ticket that is electronically validated upon its presentation at the arena's entry gate. Similar technology for MLB has fueled online sales that now exceed the volume generated by telephone-based sales. It is believed that the Internet will be used for the purchase of the majority of single-game tickets for baseball in the near future.[8] Expectations are that online ticket sales will represent 10 percent of the tickets sold for sports events in 2006.[9]

Expectations are that online ticket sales will represent 10 percent of the tickets sold for sports events in 2006.

FIGURE 21.1
St. Louis Cardinals'
Prime Seat Club

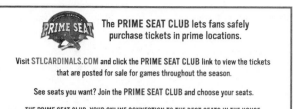

The PRIME SEAT CLUB lets fans safely purchase tickets in prime locations.

Visit STLCARDINALS.COM and click the PRIME SEAT CLUB link to view the tickets that are posted for sale for games throughout the season.

See seats you want? Join the PRIME SEAT CLUB and choose your seats.

THE PRIME SEAT CLUB, YOUR ONLINE CONNECTION TO THE BEST SEATS IN THE HOUSE.

The WWW is also being used to bring buyers and sellers of tickets together. These sites may be affiliated with a team, or they may be independently operated. The St. Louis Cardinals operate a Prime Seat Club on the stlouiscardinals.com Web site.

Season ticket holders can post the seat numbers and the price of the tickets that they wish to sell; club members can browse the availability for specific games and complete the transaction online. The buyer gets tickets that would not normally be available through traditional ticketing channels, and the seller receives a fair price for tickets that might otherwise have gone unused. Figure 21.1 illustrates a mailing that was sent to a list of known ticket buyers in an effort to create awareness of this new distribution option.

Marketers such as tickets.com, ticketek.com, ticketmaster.com, and stubhub.com all sell a variety of tickets through the Internet. In some cases, these service providers have a contractual relationship with the team or event, but in others, they buy and resell desirable tickets. As noted earlier, there is a growing concern that services such as these use technology to horde and sell tickets for sold-out events at inflated prices. Event and sports marketers are seeking to implement safeguards within their Web sites to prevent purchases in excessive quantities, especially through the use of automated purchasing software. The next time you visit a site that sells tickets, you will likely be asked to reenter a short series of partially disguised letters and numbers that are relatively easy for the human eye to decipher, but difficult for the computer to replicate. While this action may be a nuisance, it is done for the benefit of the fans.

The discussion on distribution in Chapter 17 noted the rapid adoption of video and audio streaming technology. Fans who are far away from home can now gain access to live broadcasts. English soccer provides an excellent example of this phenomenon. The number of subscribers to the broadband Internet soccer programming in the United Kingdon increased by more than 150 percent from January 2003 to January 2004.[10] Many marketers of spectator sports have also begun to offer replays of competitions from their archives through this medium. The fan who wants to relive the glory of a walk-off home run or a golden goal from the past may now have that opportunity. For example, it was reported that 1,700 fans paid $3.95 to download the video of the entire MLB game in which Roger Clemens recorded his landmark 300th victory.[11] In addition to the applications for major sports, the Internet provides an opportunity for niche sports to be broadcast on a global basis. Cycling and track and field are two examples of such niche sports that find it difficult to command a meaningful TV presence.[12]

> 1,700 fans paid $3.95 to download the video of the entire MLB game in which Roger Clemens recorded his landmark 300th victory.

Both of the aforementioned applications are becoming more commonplace. For example, during the 2000 National Basketball League in Australia, only half of the teams had enabled their Web sites to process online ticket sales. Today, every team has that capability. Video streaming has become more common as well. MLB.TV provides baseball fans with virtual access to the vast majority of the games played in major league ballparks. Other leagues, associations, and events that have recently begun to offer their sports through the Web are NASCAR, the WNBA, the NBA, the Davis Cup tennis tournament, the NFL, and the FIH Indoor Hockey World Cup. Video and audio streaming are generally associated with team and league Web sites, but they are becoming increasingly available on content Web sites such as ESPN.com.

TABLE 21.4
Relationship Marketing Initiatives Incorporated within NBL Team Web sites

Source: J. Carlson, R. Rosenberger III, and S. Muthaly, "Nothing but Net! A Study of the Information Content in Australian Professional Basketball Web sites," *Sport Marketing Quarterly* 12, no. 3 (2003), pp. 184–89.

Relationship Marketing Initiative	% Using
Fan club	80%
Club sponsors information	60
E-mail subscription to newsletter	50
Bulletin boards	40
Voting polls	30
Chat room	30
Giveaways and prizes	30
Downloads	20
Trivia competition	20

Enhance Customer Relationship Management

As we learned in Chapter 20, relationship marketing represents the recent focus on customer satisfaction and an emphasis on customer retention over customer acquisition. *Customer relationship management* is best characterized as the strategic initiatives that are implemented in the marketer's effort to nurture and sustain relationships with its customers. One of the key components of relationship marketing that was identified earlier in this book is bonding. When a bond is created, the customer perceives a sense of unity or partnership with the marketer. A second key component is communications. Whether it is one-way communication from the seller to the buyer or an interactive dialog between the two parties, the ability of any marketer to retain its customers is greatly enhanced when a meaningful communications mechanism is in place. In this regard, the Internet is an invaluable asset. Table 21.4 summarizes the extent to which Australia's NBL teams reported the incorporation of relationship marketing initiatives within their Web sites.

The ultimate execution of relationship marketing is the development of individualized value propositions for each customer. Also known as one-to-one marketing and mass customization, the objective is to develop product and communications strategies tailored to each individual buyer. Nike has launched an online store that provides this type of personalization through its Nike iD initiative. In addition to providing customized shoes, the online presence creates a positive image among online buyers who comprise a significant portion of Nike's customer base. A similar application was implemented by FanBuzz.com; its CustomFan Solution provides online buyers with the ability to design their own apparel featuring trademarks and logos of a number of sports teams. Style, size, color, and graphics can be specified by the customer when placing the order.[13]

To enhance relationships and strengthen the requisite bonds in foreign countries, many sports marketers have developed versions of their Web sites in languages indigenous to those markets. UEFA has a Korean version of its site; the NBA has a Chinese version; and MLB has a Spanish-language site.

Avid fans like to be associated with their favorite teams. This passion was noted as the basic driving force behind affinity-based credit cards. The Internet has provided a novel new way in which the fan can exhibit his or her relationship with a team. A personal e-mail address that incorporates the team's name will undoubtedly catch the eye of people who communicate via that medium. The NBA now provides this opportunity through NBA.com. An example of this is as follows: fan.name@lakers.com.[14] The NHL's Detroit Red Wings invite fans to visit detroitredwings.com and become a Cyberwing by registering for a Red Wings e-mail account. A typical e-mail address for those fans would be fanname@detroitredwings.com. Figure 21.2 illustrates an advertisement for this service; it is important to note that the ad was placed in a game-day program at the arena where the Red Wings play their home games.

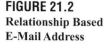

FIGURE 21.2
Relationship Based
E-Mail Address

Many teams use polls to increase their fans' level of involvement. They pose questions regarding team and player performance. Fans can join clubs; they can post messages on bulletin boards, enter Web-based contests, and download screensavers and wallpaper for their personal computers. Teams also use e-mail as a means of routinely communicating with fans. Such communications may be more effective than traditional advertising because of the personalization involved.

A close look at Table 21.4 may have caused some confusion. Included in the list of relationship marketing initiatives was the category of "club sponsors information." In this regard, it is important to understand that not all relationship marketing efforts involve the consumer. In cases such as these, the goal is to strengthen the relationship between the sports property and its sponsors. The demonstration of a win–win partnership will help to accomplish this objective. This explains why a sponsor's recognition on the sports property's Web site—whether a basic description or a hyperlink to the sponsor's site—is a key component in many of today's sponsorship contracts.

Facilitate Operations

The final category of objectives involves the routine activities associated with the business aspects of a sports marketing organization. The site can provide contact information, job postings, a mechanism for applying for a job, information for the media, information on advertising, ticket sales, customer account management capabilities, and ticket exchanges.

The Web can also be used to gather marketing research information. Many of these functions overlap with some of those discussed within the context of the various information, distribution, and customer relationship management applications. This overlap is common; the four categories of Web-based applications should not be presumed to be mutually exclusive.

The following examples provide an overview of how the WWW can be used in an operational capacity by a marketer of sports products.

Marketing Research

The WWW can provide resources for the collection of primary data as well as the acquisition of relevant secondary data. *Primary data* are those data that are collected specifically for some problem at hand. For example, a team may seek to learn why its season ticket renewal rate is disappointingly low. To answer that question, the team may ask season ticket holders from last year, including those who have not yet renewed, to respond to a problem-specific survey. This target population is contacted and asked to go to a specific Web site and complete the survey. The initial contact is often by e-mail, but traditional mail can be used. Some safeguard such as a password will be required in order to be relatively certain that ineligible respondents do not compromise the integrity of the data.

Secondary data are those data that already exist in some form but that might be useful in addressing a particular problem. A sports marketer considering the televising of games in a high-definition format may need to know the percentage of households with a high-definition receiver. Rather than collecting primary data with a survey, the marketer might discover that the answer to that question already exists. Perhaps it can be found by performing a search using one of the popular search engines such as Google. Or the answer may be found by going to a bibliographic database search service such as ABI-Inform. Secondary data sources such as these allow the marketer to use key terms to search a large set of journals, newspapers, and magazines. Perhaps the answer to the question is in *Advertising Age* or the *Wall Street Journal*. If so, there is a high likelihood that the marketer's question will be answered without the time and expense associated with the collection of primary data.

There are several sites that provide access to sports-specific secondary data. Examples include the ESPN Chilton Sports Poll (www.sportspoll.com), which allows marketers to benefit from the wide range of information maintained on its Web site. Sports-specific models that more closely resemble the ABI-Inform bibliographic database search capabilities are the Canada-based www.SIRC.ca site and the U.S.-based www.SBRnet.com.

Account Management

Several teams now provide access to the information in a season ticket holder's account through the Internet. Whether the season ticket buyer is a corporate customer or an individual consumer, this access can be used to accomplish several tasks. While it provides a convenient interface for the buyer, it also reduces the staffing needs for the team. Marketers whose hours of operation tended to reflect the typical workday can now provide a variety of Internet-based services on a 24/7 basis. MLB's Detroit Tigers promote their My Tigers Account program as "convenient, online season ticket management." Using the service, season ticket holders are able to

- Update contact information.
- Verify the status of payments.
- Order extra tickets for individual games.
- Electronically forward tickets to another person.
- Exchange tickets for a future game.
- Renew tickets for the upcoming season.

Database Management

Tickets are ordered. Fan clubs are joined. Contests are entered. Questions are asked. Accounts are managed. All of this, and much more, is done through the Web. The aggregate result of all of this activity is that a multitude of information is transmitted via the Internet, much of which has value for sports marketers. A marketer can use such information to track the individual fan's behavior and relationship with the sports entity. Detailed information allows the marketer to provide customized content to each fan, to routinely contact someone who periodically purchases tickets, to contact a fan when a team that he or she has exhibited an interest in watching is scheduled to play locally, and to implement relationship marketing actions such as the sending of a celebratory greeting and a special offer on the fan's birthday. These examples further illustrate the earlier point that operational applications overlap with the other Web-based objectives of providing information, facilitating distribution, and engaging in CRM activities. With more people connected to the Internet, greater security, and faster transmission speeds, database management applications are likely to become far more commonplace in the near future.

Interoffice Communications

Not only must marketers communicate with fans, but they must also communicate with others within their own organizations. Information may be shared with bona fide users on a secure Web site. Another option is to send pertinent information such as spreadsheets and word-processing documents as e-mail attachments. As greater security becomes assured, more information is being transmitted through these forms of dissemination. The result is that the Web is being used more and more in this type of communications capacity.

Participant Registration

Many events are open to anyone who chooses to participate. Others are limited to individuals who meet established qualification standards of performance. Local triathlons and marathon races are examples of events where aspiring participants can use the Web to register for the competition. Those who fail to meet the event's qualification standards will not be allowed to register. For instance, a marathon race that attracts international participants may impose a standard whereby eligibility is predicated upon having previously met a time requirement in a sanctioned race. The event may also offer eligible participants the option of an online check-in that provides each competitor with a reporting time, location, and a registration number. For example, the World Outgames allowed participants to register on the host organization's Web site at www.Montreal2006.org. The participants enjoy greater convenience, and the event benefits from a reduced level of labor. The reduced reliance on labor may cut the need for volunteers and other officials required to stage the event. Some events have encouraged Internet-based registration by reducing the entry fees for those participants who do so.

> Some events have encouraged Internet-based registration by reducing the entry fees for those participants who do so.

Technology Beyond the Internet and WWW

Although the Internet has been the most revolutionary technological innovation for marketers, it certainly is not the only one that has created new marketing opportunities. Other emerging technologies have allowed marketers to perform many of the same tasks commonly associated with the Internet. Still others have no relationship with the World Wide Web other than the fact that fans and consumers place them all in the same high-tech category. This chapter will conclude with a brief look at some of the ways in which sports marketers have implemented high-tech strategies in an effort to improve service, augment their product offerings, and enhance customer satisfaction. In this regard, we will take a quick look at applications involving mobile technology, virtual imaging, electronic funds transfers, interactive TV, wireless technology, and global positioning systems (GPS).

Mobile Technology

On Comcast Sports Network's *Sports Business* program that aired on March 30, 2005, a primary topic of discussion was the cell phone as a distribution medium. Because some people, especially younger people, seem to never be without their cellular phone, and given the one-to-one marketing opportunities provided by the technology, the cell phone was hailed as "the next broadcast medium." Supporting this premise is a recent report indicating that there will be 2.5 billion mobile handsets in use by the year 2010.[15] Already in the United States, MLB is offering every game through a wireless carrier; audio and video are available to Cingular customers for $9.99 per month.[16]

Instead of a broadcast of the complete event, partial content in the form of video highlights can be provided to the wireless handset. This strategy was used to provide subscribers in India with the highlights of the 2005 Wimbledon Tennis Tournament. In addition to the video highlights, the subscribers could also download the Wimbledon ring tone and the official Wimbledon Java game.

> Mobile devices provide tremendous opportunities for sports marketers to deliver customized content.

If the actual broadcast is more than MLB fans need, for $3.99 per month they can subscribe to a team-specific information service that provides scoring updates toward the end of each game. This mobile service also distributes information on injuries, trades, and other news stories. Subscribers also periodically receive special promotions. Other available products include the ability to download the logo of the fan's favorite team to the screen on their mobile device. Although the emphasis is on cellular phones, other mobile devices provide tremendous opportunities for sports marketers to deliver customized content. Whether the technology is used to provide information or distribute programming, it can play an important role in the efforts to nurture relationships between the fans and their favorite teams.

Virtual Imaging

We've discussed the use of virtual imaging for the insertion of computer-generated signage during live sports broadcasts, but this same technology has a role in enhancing the actual product being delivered to TV viewers. Virtual images can be inserted to provide information. One popular example in motor sports is the superimposition of drivers' names on pit road to let viewers know where each pit crew is stationed. Another is the virtual "first down" line that indicates the point to which a football team needs to advance the ball in order to get a new set of downs. In a novel application, cricket has used the imaging in an attempt to clarify the difficult "leg-before-wicket" (lbw) call. Should the batter be declared out or not? Taking this question a step further, controversial calls will be available on a popular U.K. cricket Web site to see if fans can make the calls more accurately than did the match officials.[17]

Electronic Funds Transfer Technology

Fans attending a sports event may find the purchase of food, beverages, and souvenirs to be a time-consuming process. Rather than wait for service and risk missing some of the action, some fans simply forgo these purchases completely. Both the fan and the marketer lose when this occurs. Part of the slowdown can be attributed to the payment process. Even those who pay cash must wait for the attendant to count the money then count the customer's change. In addition to the lengthy wait, the potential for error is significant. One new program designed to speed the process and its accuracy is Powerpay. Fans acquire a Powerpay tag that is linked to a bank debit card or a traditional credit card. Instead of paying cash, the fan waves the tag in front of a reader and confirms the transaction amount. The team, event, or venue receives the value of the transaction less any applicable merchant fee via a transfer from the fan's bank or credit card company. Because lines are shorter, more products may be sold. And because no money changes hands, transactions will be completed more accurately. Both the fan and the marketer can benefit from this advance in radio frequency identification (RFID) technology.

Interactive TV

Interactive television has not only been viewed as a platform that provides new choices for viewers; it is also seen as an opportunity to enhance the fan's relationship with the televised sport or event. The technology is dependent upon the fans' access to digital TV, but it has been projected that the number of digital TV subscribers will reach 300 million by 2010.[18] Through the interactive format, subscribers can obtain content on demand, record live programming for future viewing, view a variety of games and contests, and even partake in gambling. The marketers of spectator sports are the group most likely to be able to exploit the opportunities offered by interactive TV's anticipated growth.

WiFi Stations

As noted earlier, some marketers of spectator sports offer wireless connections for spectators who have a laptop or other hardware with an Internet interface. Journalists also view the presence of this resource favorably. At sports contests, spectators and members of the media can use the wireless technology for Internet access. Among the benefits of this connectivity are the ability to listen to audio from the broadcast, view video replays that are not shown at the venue, and check real-time statistics. Essentially, the fans and reporters can do anything at the venue that they can do on the Internet at home or in the office.

Global Positioning Systems

As of now, the use GPS is still somewhat of a novelty, but it has the capability of making meaningful contributions to participants in some of the most popular sports and leisure activities. Some golf course operators offer the GPS service as a product extension. Typically installed on the power carts, a GPS system can provide important information to the golfer. Among the most important details are the distances to hazards and the green. With this information, the golfer should feel more confident regarding club selection and his or her upcoming shot. It may even lead to lower scores, which enhances satisfaction and may provide the incentive to play even more. The service is generally included for those who pay to use a power cart; however, some course operators offer it only to those who pay a small additional fee. Regardless of the operator's strategy, GPS can be an intriguing addition to augment its product strategy.

Portable GPS systems are also becoming popular with runners and cyclists. The system can display maps, calculate the distance traveled, and download performance information to the participant's computer. One of the major manufacturers, Garmin, has referred to its portable GPS device as a personal trainer. This technology will become more commonplace as increased levels of adoption will serve to drive prices down.

Closing Capsule

There are many factors driving interest in the Internet on the part of marketers in every industry. More people are connected; international exposure is gained; the Web has become more secure; users have become more diverse; and transmission speeds are much faster. The same factors that appeal to marketers of automobiles and books resonate with the marketers of sports products. In fact, the passion of sports fans may make the Internet especially attractive.

Prior to developing a Web presence, the sports marketer should answer five questions: Why? Who? What? Where? and How? There are four categories of Web sites within the sports marketing environment; they are content sites, team or league sites, commerce sites, and gambling sites. The Web has few practical limitations regarding the amount of information that can be made available; consequently, these sites tend to be quite extensive and offer details that greatly exceed the realistic capabilities of traditional media.

Maintaining a Web site has costs associated with it. Therefore, marketers also look to the Internet for its ability to create one or more streams of revenue. Different types of sites have different capabilities in this regard. Perhaps the most common revenue stream is generated through the sale of advertising space on the sports marketer's Web site to an outside organization. For example, on a recent visit to the ESPN Web site, visitors would have seen advertisements for Dell high-definition TVs, David's sunflower seeds, and Orbitz Travel. The major dilemma for the operator of any Web site is the determination of the fees to be charged to advertisers. In addition to advertising, the most common revenue streams are in the form of subscription fees and e-commerce.

> On a recent visit to the ESPN website, visitors would have seen advertisements for Dell high-definition TVs, David's sunflower seeds, and Orbitz Travel.

In general, there are four broad-based applications involved with the sports marketer's use of the Internet. They are to provide information, facilitate distribution, enhance customer relationship management, and facilitate routine operations requisite to the management of the organization. These operational aspects include marketing research, account management, database management, interoffice communications, and the registration of participants for events such as a local marathon.

Other emerging technologies are also assuming roles in the execution of sports marketing strategies. Mobile technology offers many opportunities to reach fans with customized content. Virtual imaging and electronic funds transfers are among the myriad of technological advances that can also be used by today's and tomorrow's sports marketers. There is no doubt that tomorrow's sports marketers will need to be more attuned to modern technology. Without that knowledge, others will leave them behind. And this is not a race that they can afford to lose.

Review Questions

1. What are the five questions that should be answered as the marketer seeks to develop a foundation for the use of the Internet in its sports marketing efforts?

2. Why might the Internet be more effective for sports marketers than it is for marketers of consumer goods such as automobiles?

3. What are the four types of Web sites used by sports marketers? Go to the Internet and find one site for each category.

4. What is the click-through rate? How can the price of Internet-based advertising be determined on the basis of the CTR?

5. Go to the Internet and find three sports sites that incorporate a subscription fee for access to part or all of their Web site content. List each Web site, the cost, the term, and what the subscription fee entitles the subscriber to access.

6. What are the four broad Web-based applications for sports marketers?

7. Find the Web site for your favorite sports team. Compare the information included in that site to the categories listed in Table 21.2. Repeat that assessment using Table 21.4.

8. How can the WWW be used as a marketing research tool? What do you think its limitations are in regard to the collection of primary data?

9. Why is mobile technology becoming more important to sports marketers?

Endnotes

1. A. Gillentine, "Developing an Internet Philosophy," S*port Marketing Quarterly* 12, no. 1 (2003), pp. 63–64.

2. T. Farthing, "Sign Up Now for iGAMING Seminar," May 30, 2003, www.sportbusiness.com/news/index?news_item_id=151373 (accessed October 13, 2005).

3. J. Carlson, R. Rosenberger III, and S. Muthaly, "Nothing but Net! A Study of the Information Content in Australian Professional Basketball Web sites," *Sport Marketing Quarterly* 12, no. 3 (2003), pp. 184–89.

4. J. Swanwick, "Super Bowl's Online Boom," *SportBusiness International*, December–January 2004, p. 10.

5. L. Kahle and C. Meeske, "Sports Marketing and the Internet: It's a Whole New Ball Game," *Sport Marketing Quarterly* 8, no. 2 (1999), pp. 9–12.

6. C. Britcher, "PGA Drives RAC Deal," July 8, 2003, www.sportbusiness.com/news/index?news_item_id=151753 (accessed October 13, 2005).

7. "Fuji Xerox New Zealand Golf Network," 2004, www.golf.co.nz (accessed October 13, 2005).

8. D. Barrand, "Online Ticket Sales Boost for MLB," November 25, 2003, www.sportbusiness.com/news/index?news_item_id=153193 (accessed October 13, 2005).

9. M. Brown, "An Analysis of Online Marketing in the Sport Industry: User Activity, Communications Objectives, and Perceived Benefits," *Sport Marketing Quarterly* 12, no. 1 (2003), pp. 48–55.

10. C. Britcher, "Premium Subs Soar," February 19, 2004, www.sportbusiness.com/news/?news_item_id=153836 (accessed October 13, 2005).

11. D. Barrand, "Clemens Good for MLB.com," June 19, 2003, www.sportbusiness.com/news/index?news_item_id=151531 (accessed October 13, 2005).

12. Kahle and Meeske, "Sports Marketing and the Internet."

13. L. Evans, "FanBuzz.com Launches Mass Customization Capability," *Sporting Goods Business* 34, no. 1 (2001), p. 16.

14. B. Spoonemore, "Case Study: NBA Gives Fans a 'Place' They Can Call Their Own," *Revolution,* March 2001, p. 36.

15. "Going Deeper into the Mobile Opportunity," *SportBusiness International,* May 2005, p. 6.

16. "Listen Up . . . the MLB Goes Mobile," *SportBusiness International,* May 2005, p. 30.

17. D. Smith, "Cricket Fans to Sit in Judgment," July 5, 2005, www.sportbusiness.com/index/index?news_item_id=157912 (accessed October 13, 2005).

18. C. Barnes, *Interactive TV: The Opportunities for Sport* (London: SportBusiness International, 2005).

Controversial Issues in Sports Marketing

Learning Objectives

- Learn about criticisms regarding target market decisions.
- Identify controversies regarding product decisions.
- Identify controversies regarding distribution decisions.
- Identify controversies regarding pricing decisions.
- Identify controversies regarding promotion decisions.
- Learn about broad-based controversies in sports marketing.

As evidenced by the discussion in the preceding chapters, there are numerous criticisms that are routinely directed toward the sports industry. Yet the examples that were noted primarily expressed concerns regarding unacceptable behaviors on the part of athletes. A second common area for criticism is the reasoning behind unpopular personnel decisions. In this regard, fans will raise questions as to whether or not a team, league, or event has taken the appropriate steps to assure that competition at the highest possible level will take place. There has been an increased emphasis on fair competition, especially as it relates to the athletes' use of performance enhancing drugs or illegal equipment. But it should be evident that criticisms of this type are directed at the sport or event; they do not specifically address perceived indiscretions on the part of those involved either in the marketing of sports products or the marketing of nonsports products through sports.

The strategic initiatives of sports marketers have long been a focal point of criticism voiced by consumers, consumer advocacy groups, fans, and the media. As in every other industry, questions have been raised regarding the propriety of the decisions regarding target marketing, product strategies, distribution decisions, pricing policies, and promotional practices. These questions and concerns involve the marketing of sports products as well as the practices employed in the marketing of nonsports products using a sports platform. It is important to understand that these criticisms generally represent perceived breaches of ethical conduct, not violations of legal statutes. But at the same time, vocal fans and consumers often have many sympathetic listeners who can impact the legal environment through legislative changes. Continued misconduct often leads to the implementation of new laws designed to mandate acceptable behavior on the part of sports marketers.

Controversy, like ethics, is a subjective assessment. What is perfectly acceptable to one person may be deemed totally inappropriate by another. Behavior that raises no concerns among members of one segment may anger members of another segment. Judgments of behavior may vary significantly from one country to another. The sports market is not a homogeneous set of individuals who respond the same way when targeted by a marketer's efforts. Participants and fans are becoming more diverse as many sports are making headway into new markets and as the broadcast media send their signals to viewers and listeners around the world. As a result of this heterogeneity, it is difficult for sports marketers to always "do the right thing" in the eyes of outside observers. For example, some segments of society feel that it is inappropriate to target the gay and lesbian community. Yet others believe that the failure to acknowledge this viable segment is both unethical and unwise. Given the diversity of opinion such as this, it is evident that any organization involved in sports marketing will ultimately be a target of vocal critics in the marketplace.

> Any organization involved in sports marketing will ultimately be a target of vocal critics in the marketplace.

The objective of this chapter is to provide a comprehensive overview of the controversial issues within the sports marketing environment. Many of these issues were identified in earlier chapters. Notwithstanding, criticisms deserve specific coverage in a single chapter so that aspiring sports marketers can have a concise reference and a better understanding of the criticism that they may encounter. The following pages represent an effort to categorize complaints relative to the decision areas germane to the development of a comprehensive marketing strategy.

Controversial Issues in Sports Marketing

In addition to the controversies involving target market and marketing mix decisions, there are a number of controversial issues that do not neatly fit into one of these micromarketing decision areas. These broad-based criticisms tend to reflect complaints about the general behavior of sports marketers. In such cases, they encompass a wide range of decision areas. Our discussion of controversial issues will be based upon the delineation of criticisms in each of the five elements of marketing strategy, and it will also include examples of the broad-based criticisms that encompass the general practice of sports marketing. The discussion will begin with the examination of issues regarding target marketing decisions.

Target Marketing Controversies

As discussed earlier in this text, target markets represent specific segments of consumers at which marketers direct their efforts. Over the years, sports marketers have exhibited a tendency to expand the scope of their efforts to encompass new target markets, thereby reaching out to more consumers. While the targeting of some groups has led to outspoken criticism, the most pronounced controversy has emanated from exclusionary policies that adversely impact specific demographic groups. Comparatively few of these criticisms have been directed toward marketers of spectator sports; rather, they most often surface when assessing the strategies of those companies involved in the marketing of memberships to participation sports facilities. The other major concern involves the marketer's decision to target kids. This complaint is often directed toward companies selling athletic shoes and apparel products.

Exclusionary Membership Policies

Private clubs have the right to restrict their memberships by only admitting people who fit a predetermined demographic profile. This type of exclusionary policy is not the sole province of sports. In fact, many social clubs of the twentieth century had charters that explicitly restricted access. The Rotary Club excluded women, whereas the Business and Professional Women's Club excluded men. Both organizations have since changed their policies and are now open to members of either sex. While this open policy permeates the participation sports market, the isolated cases of apparent discrimination are strongly criticized by advocacy groups and the media. There is no better example of this than the home of the Masters Golf Tournament, the Augusta National Golf Club.

The initial controversy involved the absence of any black members. Indeed, for many years no black players were invited to compete in the famous tournament. These omissions were viewed as a vestige of the racial discrimination that is often associated with the southern region of the United States, where the club is located. Finally, the first black tournament participant, Lee Elder, was invited to play in 1975 by virtue of his status as a winner of a PGA tour event. Then, in 1990, the private club opened its doors to its first African American member. With the controversy of racial discrimination apparently resolved, the critics began to focus on the exclusion of women. Club directors were adamant that they could not be compelled to open their doors to anyone who they wanted to exclude. At the time of these criticisms by the chair of the National Council of Women's Organizations, Martha Burk, there were some 24 private golf clubs in the United States that openly excluded women from being eligible to join their ranks.[1] But none were as widely recognized as the prestigious Augusta National Golf Club. The controversy carried over to the Masters Golf Tournament, with protesters asking the TV network (CBS) to abandon the broadcast while also discouraging consumers from purchasing any of the products advertised during the broadcast. The short-term result was that the 2003 and 2004 Masters Tournaments had no official sponsors and were broadcast without advertisements. This was a voluntary decision on the part of the Masters Tournament organizers; their intent was to insulate their long-standing sponsors from any retribution or criticism by the various critics of the exclusionary policy. By 2005, the tournament welcomed its sponsors back and CBS again made broadcast time available to prospective advertisers. Some of these same criticisms were directed at the Portmarnock Golf Club in Dublin, Ireland. That course hosted the 2004 Irish Open, and it has a similar male-only membership policy.[2]

> **Exclusion based upon gender, race, religion, age, or national origin will inevitably create an outcry by advocacy groups and the media.**

Even in sporting clubs that are open to men and women, some will still restrict access to certain facilities. There may be a restaurant or bar that is open only to the club's male members. Some golf clubs reserve blocks of tee times that overtly exclude female players. Such policies, regardless of the criteria used to implement them, are under increased scrutiny. Exclusion based upon gender, race, religion, age, or national origin will inevitably create an outcry by advocacy groups and the media. As a result, these barriers continue to fall, although they may never be completely eliminated.

Targeting Children

Rather than bemoaning an exclusion of children as a target market, the complaints in this regard tend to emphasize a marketer's decision to direct efforts toward the kid segment. Much such criticism seems to focus on the marketers of athletic shoes. There are few complaints about efforts to get kids to watch more sports or to engage in more sports activities. But attempts to induce these same kids to purchase expensive athletic shoes have made these manufacturers, especially Nike, the object of considerable criticism. Kids who simply cannot afford to buy them want shoes that are endorsed by popular, high-performing athletes. Parents often have to reject their kids' request to buy the newest model of shoes, a decision that can create dissension within the family relationship. Even more problematic is the reality that some kids were stealing the shoes from other kids, in some cases even killing the kids and stripping the shoes from their victims' bodies. While sneakers represent the thieves' most common target, other desirable apparel was also stolen.[3] The 1990 article in *Sports Illustrated* that brought this situation to the public's attention laid much of the blame on the marketing strategies of companies such as Nike, Fila, and Reebok. Though it has been more than 15 years since these complaints were first articulated, little has been done to quell the criticism.

Product Controversies

While the most strongly criticized product in the sports marketing environment is the category of spectator sports, concerns regarding other products abound. Consider the domains that feature the marketing of nonsports products through the use of a sports platform. For instance, when controversial products are sold through sports sponsorship, it is inevitable that the sponsee will bear much of the brunt of the resultant criticism.

Oversaturation of Spectator Sports

Questions have been raised as to whether or not the market has more spectator sports than it can reasonably support. Sports leagues in America have all increased the length of their seasons. This has been accomplished by adding games to the regular season, increasing the length of postseason playoff series, or adding to the number of teams that qualify for post-season playoffs. Even at the collegiate level, recent changes in the rules governing scheduling have allowed for the addition of one or more football games to the regular season. College football in the United States has also witnessed a growth in the number of post-season bowl games. The result has been that teams of marginal quality play in postseason games in stadia that are far from being filled with spectators and fans.

> There is a growing concern that this oversaturation through the media is adversely affecting the demand for minor league sports.

New media options have also made the games more accessible to the viewing and listening public. Local stations broadcast more games involving their local teams; cable TV has made games from distant venues more readily available; sports stations such as ESPN have increased the number of their live broadcasts throughout each sport's season; satellite TV has provided greater access through sports tiers; and new specialized channels feature single sports 24/7. There is a growing concern that this oversaturation through the media is adversely affecting the demand for minor league sports. For example, one note-worthy criticism stated that the tremendous explosion in the broadcast of MLB games is "killing the minor leagues."[4]

Gimmick Sports

While the proliferation of legitimate sports has spawned much criticism, promoters have continued to supplement those competitions with events that represent unusual variations of a sport or that feature athletes in competitions that are best described as novelties. ESPN recently featured a number of professional athletes competing in a 10-pin bowling contest. The winning scores were uninspiring, especially to avid bowlers. Another competition featured football players in a skills competition, and MLB has a home run derby. Promoters may argue that these competitions allow players to be measured on the basis of skills specific to their own sports, but others criticize them as poor measures because the competitions take place in artificial environments that do not simulate actual game conditions.

In other cases, events feature a significant emphasis on sexuality. Beach volleyball is one example. Some of these novel competitions feature celebrities rather than athletes. This category includes TV programming such as the Celebrity Sports Invitational that was recently broadcast on the Fox Sports Network. Then there are events that feature teams comprised of athletes and celebrities; the Legends and Celebrities Softball Game that is played in conjunction with MLB's All-Star Game is an example of what many consider to be a gimmick sport.

Appearance Money

Top players are often paid a significant sum of money just for agreeing to participate in a tournament or event. This money is in addition to any prize money that the players win as a result of their performance. The rationale is that the presence of top players improves the product for the fans. This strategy is most relevant for individual sports such as golf and tennis. For the 2002 New Zealand Tennis Open, Anna Kournikova was paid to participate. She played well, making it to the semifinals and was credited for much of the increase in attendance. That same year, organizers of the New Zealand Open golf tournament paid Tiger Woods $2,000,000 to play.[5] Complaints about the significant increase in the price of tickets in conjunction with Woods's struggle to make the cut called the strategy into question. These facts, along with rainy weather, led to lower than anticipated attendance, thereby creating a financial burden on tournament organizers.

> Organizers of the 2002 New Zealand Open golf tournament paid Tiger Woods $2,000,000 to play.

TV's Role in Spectator Sports

A key component of the spectator sports market is the media-based audience. TV networks pay huge sums of money for the rights to broadcast popular sports events, with those costs offset by the sale of advertising time. Most major sports now incorporate *media timeouts* at designated points during the course of play. While the advertising pays the way for TV viewers to watch for free, the numerous breaks represent idle periods for the players and for those who are part of the live audience.

Another criticism is the role that TV plays in the scheduling of games. Fans of major college football often purchase season tickets that do not specify the exact starting time for some games. Determination of the starting time is often made by TV executives once they decide how important the game will be and assess its potential to attract a large national TV audience. In many cases, games that are scheduled for an afternoon start are rescheduled as evening games because of their ability to attract a large TV audience. Recently, the manager of MLB's St. Louis Cardinals strongly criticized ESPN's decision to reschedule his team's game in San Francisco to a later start to accommodate TV.

Changing the Spectator Sport Core Product

As noted in Chapter 16 in the discussion of product decisions, changes in the rules for spectator sports are often controversial. Despite the criticism that emanates from any changes in the rules, few sports today are played according to the rules that first governed the competition. MLB introduced the designated hitter; the NBA now has a three-point shot; the NFL has new rules that restrict contact with pass receivers; and the NHL now has overtime and a shootout as a way of eliminating tie games. Each rule change was met with opposition, especially among the old-school fans who tend to refer to themselves as purists. To them, any deviation from the long-standing rules with which they are familiar is simply unacceptable and will result in a meaningful level of negative word-of-mouth advertising.

Player Mobility

In the early days of spectator sports, it was not unusual for a star player to retire from the team with which he first played as a professional. There were few options because the interpretation of existing laws favored team management. This changed with a legal

FIGURE 22.1
Beer Sponsorship in NASCAR

challenge in the courts and the advent of free agency. Today, players who have fulfilled the terms of their contracts and meet standards specified in their union's collective bargaining agreement are free to move to a new team. Fans who could at one time anticipate that their favorite players would never play elsewhere now understand that players will move when other teams entice them with lucrative contracts. When such a move occurs, these loyal fans view it as a diminishment of the quality of the sports product that they are being asked to buy.

Unwholesome Nonsports Products Sold through a Sports Platform

It is apparent that sports products are often subjected to considerable criticism. However, concern is also expressed in regard to the unwholesome nature of many of the nonsports products sold using sports as a key marketing platform. Advertising during sports broadcasts or sponsoring a sports property takes advantage of the strategic linkages that allow the marketers to reach their target audiences. Unfortunately, many of the consumers who are exposed to these efforts are not actually part of their target markets. And, in too many cases, the products being marketed are unwholesome, perhaps even dangerous.

Tobacco products and alcoholic beverages have sustained a long relationship with sports. Although recent changes in laws have made it more difficult for tobacco companies to utilize a sports linkage, even today it is not unusual to see signage for Marlboro cigarettes and Foster's beer during the televised broadcast of a Formula One race. Ironically, rules governing promotions of alcoholic beverages have recently been relaxed, thereby creating new opportunities for marketers. For example, Jack Daniel's now has sponsorship involvement with a NASCAR race team. Many critics argue that a partnership featuring fast cars and alcohol simply presents a contradictory picture for those watching the race. Figure 22.1 illustrates the relationship between Coors beer and motor sports.

The second situation, *reaching fans who are not part of the target market*, is not a controversy in its own right. What creates the concern is when these products are of an adult nature, yet kids easily observe the marketing effort. Note that this is a different

FIGURE 22.2
Viagra Signage at an
MLB Stadium

criticism from that involved with the intentional targeting of kids. For example, a recent PGA tournament was identified using its title sponsor's name as the Cialis Western Open. From a traditional sponsorship perspective, Levitra initially signed on as an NFL sponsor beginning with the 2003 season. Similarly, it is not uncommon to see signage promoting Viagra at an MLB stadium (see Figure 22.2). Each of these products is a prescription drug for the treatment of a sexual disorder among men. These promotional efforts can prompt embarrassing questions from inquisitive children. It was this concern that led to the NFL's decision to terminate its relationship with Levitra upon the conclusion of the 2006 Super Bowl. Another common occurrence involves the advertising of adult entertainment clubs and escort services in the sports section of the local newspaper. Clearly, the use of sports in the development of promotional strategies for these types of service providers will have its critics. But in the absence of laws or other regulations that prohibit this type of commercial activity, the marketers that constantly seek the most effective ways of reaching their target markets will not abandon it.

Distribution Controversies

The focus in this section involves the marketing of spectator sports products. For team sports, the controversial issues that most often surface involve franchise relocation and public funding of new sports venues.

Franchise Mobility

As noted earlier, fans are critical of player mobility because they perceive that a star player's departure results in an inferior product. Franchise mobility is even more problematic because the fans lose direct access to the sports product. Teams may move because of the lack of sufficient local fan support; however, they often move because of lucrative deals offered by officials in an alternative location. Such moves may take place even though the fans in the existing location have been loyal supporters. The Cleveland Browns of the NFL are an excellent example. Fans of the team were among the most fervent of any professional sports team. They purchased tickets and logo merchandise; they filled the antiquated stadium and loudly supported their team. BIRGing was a common practice. But the stadium was old and lacked modern amenities. Also absent were the luxury suites that represent a significant revenue stream for most teams today. The inability to convince local authorities to build a new stadium resulted in the team's decision to move to new facilities in a new city, and the Cleveland Browns became the Baltimore Ravens. Fortunately for

TABLE 22.1
Franchise Mobility in North America

League	Year of Move	Old Team	Current Team
MLB	2005	Montreal Expos	Washington Nationals
NBA	2002	Charlotte Hornets	New Orleans Hornets
NHL	1998	Hartford Whalers	Carolina Hurricanes
NFL	1998	Houston Oilers	Tennessee Titans

football fans in Cleveland, the NFL located an expansion franchise there shortly after the original team's departure; however, the new team did little to soothe the pain of having seen their beloved team pack up and leave for economic reasons. Table 22.1 summarizes the most recent franchise move in each of the four major North American sports leagues.

Taxpayer-Funded Venues

Teams may move because of the lack of local fan support; however, any move is virtually certain to depend upon an agreement that provides a new state-of-the-art playing facility for the team. To prevent the loss of a treasured team, some cities have been forced to commit resources for the construction of a new stadium or arena. Critics argue that cities are being held hostage; they must either devise a way to secure funding for a new facility or they lose the team. Such a departure has psychological and economic consequences for a community. The exertion of this type of pressure was in evidence in Miami when MLB imposed a specific deadline on local government for committing $420 million to build a new baseball stadium. Team officials refused to discuss the consequences of the failure to comply, but concurrent discussions with government officials in Las Vegas were interpreted as a veiled threat to move the franchise if an agreement for a new stadium could not be reached.[6]

The most common criticism questions the wisdom of devoting significant resources to build a facility for billionaire owners and their millionaire players. Is this a reasonable way for a community to invest the tax revenues that it has received from its residents, businesses, and visitors? In some cases, new taxes are imposed. Government funding for Comerica Park in Detroit was derived from new taxes imposed on rental cars and hotel visitors. By doing so, the taxes were not a burden on Detroit residents. But it does raise the question as to why visitors to the area should provide funding for a new stadium for the local MLB team. The result is that the team plays in an excellent modern facility; local residents can still take pride in being the home of one of only 30 MLB teams in North America; and local businesses still reap the economic benefits from fan expenditures. Despite these acknowledged benefits, many critics are vocal when expressing their belief that there are better ways to spend tax monies. As discussed later in this chapter, questions are also raised about the actual contributions that sports teams make to local economies.

Pricing Controversies

Generally speaking, any controversy regarding a marketer's pricing strategy reflects the public's sentiment that prices are too high. Earlier in this text, there was a reference to the Fan Cost Index (FCI) for the primary professional sports leagues in North America. The data indicated that the average fan will find it exceedingly difficult to be able to afford many nights at a game with the family. Complaints have also been voiced in regard to the pricing strategies used in the marketing of participation sports, sporting goods, athletic shoes, sports apparel, and sports-related products.

Ticket Prices

According to the FCI, a family of four could enjoy an entertaining NFL game during the 2005 season for an average of $329.82. While this figure takes into account a number of purchases in addition to the tickets, the average price for an NFL game ticket was $58.95. And ticket prices are rising at a rate that substantially exceeds the inflation rate for the economy in general.[7] An article in *Sports Illustrated* entitled "Hey Fans: Sit on It!" captured the essence of the controversy in its first line:

> The high cost of attending games is fattening the owners' wallets while it drives average fans away from arenas, and it may be cooling America's passion for pro sports.[8]

In addition to the higher prices, the article explained how the emphasis on luxury suites in new arenas has resulted in the fans in the less expensive seats being pushed even farther from the action. With the best seats sold in season ticket packages, only high-income consumers and corporate customers can afford them. And the insensitivity to rising prices on the part of these two segments does not bode well for future ticket prices in any of the major professional sports.

> A regular season NFL game in the cheap seats at Ford Field sold for $42; for the Super Bowl, that same seat was priced at $600.

The problem is even more pronounced for special events and league playoffs. The farther a team progress in the playoffs, the more expensive a ticket for the same seat becomes. Special events are generally characterized by exorbitant prices. At the 2005 MLB All-Star Game, a ticket for a seat that cost $35 during the regular season sold for $200. Even more dramatic was the disparity associated with the 2006 Super Bowl. A regular season NFL game in the cheap seats at Ford Field sold for $42; for the Super Bowl, that same seat was priced at $600.

PSLs

PSLs fall into two categories. Though the terms *personal seat license* and *permanent seat license* tend to be used interchangeably, there is one way in which they can be distinguished. That is on the basis of the frequency of the required payment. A personal seat license must be renewed annually, and it provides the right to purchase tickets for the upcoming season. A permanent seat license requires a onetime payment that provides the right to purchase tickets far into the future, perhaps infinitely. While not everyone agrees with this distinction, a PSL basically provides the right to purchase a ticket for a specific seat. The benefit to the marketer is evident; PSLs provide a significant stream of revenue that can be used to fund the construction of a new stadium or arena, offset operational costs such as player salaries, and contribute to the bottom line.[9]

The Dallas Cowboys sold the first PSL in 1968, a 40-year license at prices ranging from a low of $300 to a high of $1,000. The PSL actually outlasted the stadium in which the Cowboys played their games. Professional sports are not the sole domain for PSLs; by 1990, some 90 percent of the major U.S. college football programs had implemented a similar type of priority seating program.[10]

Figure 22.3 illustrates the brochure promoting PSLs for the NFL's St. Louis Rams. It indicates that the cost for the 2005 season varied from $250 to $4,500, with the higher fees being associated with better seats. College football is looking to a form of PSL as a revenue-generating tool as well. Programs that typically play their home games in stadia filled to capacity have seized the opportunity to impose a fee in addition to the cost of the tickets. As noted earlier in this text, these fees are generally positioned as a contribution to the university. Table 22.2 provides an overview of the major college programs and their requirements for purchasing season tickets for the 2005 season.

According to the information posted on the Web site of the NHL's Columbus Blue Jackets, by purchasing a PSL, the fan is "buying ownership of a seat location at Nationwide

FIGURE 22.3
PSLs for the NFL's St. Louis Rams

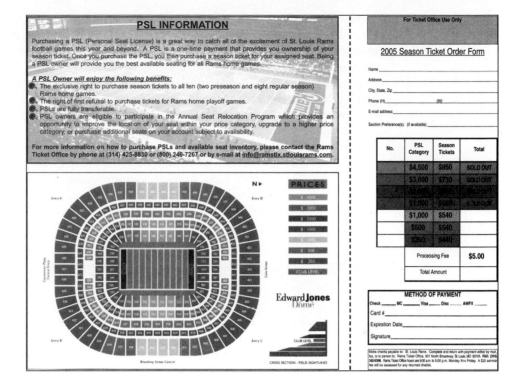

Arena for Blue Jackets games each season."[11] Of course, the fundamental criticism is that the purchase of a season ticket is already expensive and it has historically provided access to the same seat for the entire season. However, without the PSL, there is no guarantee that a fan can purchase the same seat for future seasons. The PSL provides that guarantee in conjunction with an array of additional benefits.

Pay-per-View (PPV)

The controversy surrounding PPV involves decisions regarding two components of the marketing mix: distribution and pricing. However, the primary controversy revolves around the pricing decision, especially when PPV charges are being imposed upon sports programming that has historically been broadcast on free-to-air TV. According to a spokesperson from a leading PPV provider, "I believe it's time for mainstream events to go

TABLE 22.2
PSLs for Major College Football in the United States

Source: D. Ledeman, "Schools Making Fans Give More to Keep Best Seats," *USA Today,* August 25, 2004, pp. 1A, 4A.

University	Annual Contribution	Seat Entitlement
Southern California	$100–25,000	8
Louisiana State	85–400	1
Georgia	200	1
Miami	150–15,000	1
Florida State	125–5,500	1
Michigan	125–500	1
Texas	1,250	1
Ohio State	2,500–3,500	1
Florida	1,200	2
Tennessee	500–1,500	1
Auburn	300–1,500	2 to 10

to pay-per-view for the benefit of the audience, as long as it's accessible and not at an excessive price." His comments followed the awarding of the rights to broadcast the qualifying games of the American basketball team during the 2004 Olympics. Fans could purchase the 10-game package for $59.95 or individual games for $9.95 each.[12]

The part of the quote that should worry fans is the word *mainstream*. It seems to encompass a broad range of popular events that consumers have come to expect on free-to-air TV. Consumers tend to be more amenable to PPV fees when they provide access to sports programming that would not generally have appeared on traditional TV. The fear, however, is that premier events such as the Olympics, the World Cup of Soccer, the Super Bowl, Wimbledon, the Masters Golf Tournament, and the NCAA Final Four may ultimately be distributed solely on a PPV basis. Australia's antisiphoning law is designed to prevent such an occurrence. It mandates that specific events such as the Australian Open and Wimbledon must be broadcast on free-to-air TV. The United States government has hinted at consideration of a similar law if some of the American fans' favorite events seem destined to abandon free-to-air TV in favor of a PPV format.

> The fear is that premier events such as the Olympics, the World Cup of Soccer, the Super Bowl, Wimbledon, the Masters Golf Tournament, and the NCAA Final Four may ultimately be distributed solely on a PPV basis.

Team Scalping of Tickets

Most teams are protected from illegal ticket scalpers who buy, then resell tickets at inflated prices within close proximity of event venues. But even though such scalping is forbidden, several teams have initiated their own practice of selling tickets at prices that exceed their face value. MLB's Chicago Cubs formed a ticket brokerage unit to capitalize on demand that often exceeds the supply of tickets. The team indicated its intention to withhold 200 seats per game and sell them at prices determined by market dynamics. The initial effort resulted in tickets with a face value of $30 being sold for $85 each.[13] It was also reported that a $45 ticket for a game against the New York Yankees sold for $1,500.[14] The controversy was significant enough that a fan filed a lawsuit on the premise that the team was violating the Illinois Ticket Scalping Act. Sports fans were dealt a blow when the courts ruled that such an arrangement did not violate any laws that would prohibit the team from continuing the practice.[15] It is believed that other teams will soon adopt a similar strategy that ultimately has the effect of raising prices for a subset of the premium seats. But marketers need to understand that while the practice is legal, it does not eliminate the controversy surrounding the question of whether or not it constitutes unethical behavior.

High Prices for Participation Sports and Athletic Shoes

Beyond the domain of spectator sports, high prices have attracted the attention of critics of the strategies employed by marketers of some participation sports and athletic shoes. Greens fees for a round of golf at a prestigious course can exceed $350 per round. Athletic shoes endorsed by popular, high-performing athletes have reached levels exceeding $200 per pair. It is also important to acknowledge that sports-related products offered for sale at sports venues sell for prices that substantially exceed those of identical products at nearby shops. Fans complain about prices, but they have few options other than to forgo the purchase. For example, some stadium operators prohibit fans from bringing any beverages into their venues. So fans may pay $8 for a beer, but they will not be happy about it.

Promotion Controversies

More so than with the other elements of the marketing mix, controversies regarding promotional tactics used in both the marketing of sports products and the marketing of nonsports products via the use of a sports platform are abundant. However, the majority of the complaints involve marketing through sports. While most complaints result from some type of sponsorship arrangement, other issues such as virtual advertising and traditional advertising during sports broadcasts raise questions of propriety.

Overcommercialization

Some sports and events have been accused of commercial prostitution. The outcry surfaced in earnest with the 1984 Olympics in Los Angeles. The Centennial Olympic Games in Atlanta in 1996 were also subjected to considerable scrutiny regarding overcommercialization. One critic referred to the Atlanta Olympics as "a third world flea market" that "was condemned by the world's press."[16] NASCAR is so involved with its commercial partners that its race cars have been characterized as 200 mile-per-hour billboards. The reality is that most major events have increased the number of sponsors allowed to promote an official relationship with the sports property. Purists see the overcommercialization as an unacceptable emphasis on the bottom line that may come at the expense of the sport and the competition.

> One critic referred to the Atlanta Olympics as "a third world flea market."

Naming Rights

Staying with the theme of overcommercialization, venue naming rights are often placed in that same category. The vast majority of controversial naming rights deals involve sports venues. Chapter 13 provided a comprehensive overview of the rationale for marketers that pay to have their corporate identity attached to a structure and the operators that benefit from the substantial revenue stream. In general, venues that bear a sponsor's name are not well received by the public. This disdain is even stronger when an existing structure is renamed. Media members often create their own alternative names for venues with a corporate identity, or they simply refuse to identify it by its rightful name. Undoubtedly, this media criticism manifests itself in the form of criticism on the part of the fans.

Naming rights are not confined to buildings, however. Presenting sponsors and title sponsors have their names incorporated within the official designation of an event. The Nokia Sugar Bowl, the Heineken New Zealand Open, and Chicago Bears football presented by Bank One are noteworthy examples of what many deem to be an unacceptable corporate incursion into the world of sports. But vocal criticism can result in the reconsideration of these forms of corporate sponsorship.

On October 26, 2004, it was announced that SBC Communications had reached a two-year agreement with the Ohio State University and the University of Michigan that would provide $530,000 to each school for the right to designate their annual high-profile football game the "SBC Michigan–Ohio State Classic." Within hours of the announcement, intense media criticism had begun. Callers to sports talk radio lamented the two schools' emphasis on the bottom line. Some 80 percent of the e-mails and phone calls to the University of Michigan Athletic Department opposed the deal. Within two days, it was rescinded.[17]

Signage Issues

A common complaint voiced by fans is that there are too many signs inside of sports stadia and arenas. Conversely, some marketers lament the inadequacy of the number of signs that they are allowed to display inside of an event venue. Once more, these concerns generally involve sponsorship issues. Some operators of sports facilities and event organizers severely limit a marketer's access to the inside of sports venues. At the same time, sponsors have clamored for greater access to Olympic venues and some collegiate sports arenas. Coca-Cola, a longtime Olympic sponsor, feels access is justified because some sponsors that provide VIK have their logos readily visible to the live and media-based audiences. The Panasonic brand appears on video screens; the Swatch watch logo is prominently displayed on timing devices; and the IBM logo has been visible on computer equipment located inside of many of the Olympic venues. Coca-Cola believes that its multimillion dollar sponsorship investment entitles it to a more prominent level of exposure. The dilemma lies in the balancing of the public's concern about overcommercialization with the sponsors' expectations regarding the benefits that they should receive in exchange for the sponsorship commitment they make.[18] No matter which direction the IOC takes, criticism is inevitable.

> The dilemma lies in the balancing of the public's concern about overcommercialization with the sponsors' expectations.

Some stadia that once prohibited any signage within the confines of the venue are now more amenable to the idea. MLB's Fenway Park and Wrigley Field were once void of any advertiser's signage. Fenway Park now has considerable signage, and Wrigley Field has begun to allow some behind home plate. Many critics simply cannot accept the idea of signage on Wrigley Field's fabled brick walls. However, according to a team executive, the brick wall "is one of the great icons of Wrigley Field. But for us, it is important that we create a new revenue stream."[19] The disparity between the opinions of management and the fans of the team fuel the controversy.

The issue of clean stadia has also created considerable dissent. As noted earlier in the text, a *clean stadium* is one that is free from any corporate signage or other brand identification. Event organizers have begun to expand the concept beyond the venue by seeking prohibitions on signage on private and public property in close proximity to the venue. This expansion provides even more protection for sponsors from ambush marketers. When the contract was being negotiated for a subset of the 2003 Rugby World Cup games to be played in New Zealand, the requirement was that any signage within each stadium as well as within 500 meters of the stadium would need to be removed or covered.[20] In Detroit, the host city for the 2006 Super Bowl, the city council did not expect all signs to be dismantled; however, new rules were designed to regulate the type and size of temporary signage within one mile of the stadium. Local businesses saw the rules as an infringement on their rights, whereas official sponsors viewed them as a way to reduce the incidence of ambush marketing efforts by nonsponsors that wanted to create the perception that they were officially involved with the NFL and its premier event.[21] Within a week of the announcement that London had been awarded the rights to stage the Olympic Games in 2012, new prohibitions on advertising and signage were discussed by the Department of Culture, Media, and Sport.[22] These situations raise questions as to whether or not the sponsors have too much power within the sports environment.

Athlete Endorsements

> Many youngsters wrongly viewed a pair of Nike's Air Jordan shoes as a key resource that would help make them a better basketball player.

Some people are concerned that kids idolize star athletes and that the athletes' endorsements create demand for products for the wrong reasons. There is also a concern that fees paid to these celebrities inflate prices and that there are superior products sold at lower prices.

Unfortunately, many kids insist that the brand endorsed by their favorite athlete is the only one that they will accept. There is also a concern that the endorsement creates an expectation on the part of the child that is unlikely to be fulfilled. Most everyone can remember at least one advertisement featuring Michael Jordan and the tag line, "be like Mike." Many youngsters wrongly viewed a pair of Nike's Air Jordan shoes as a key resource that would help make them a better basketball player.

Virtual Advertising

This computer-generated signage has yet to be the subject of much criticism simply because most consumers are unaware of technology's role. To them, it is just another sign. The computer-generated images may appear in stadia that prohibit signage. It can utilize animation that will distract the viewers' attention from the game being played. Ambush marketers may also use it. Not only can the technology be used to insert the ambusher's signage, but the official sponsor's signs can also be obscured, modified, or eliminated. Fox TV created an outcry when the broadcaster used virtual imaging technology to eliminate the sponsors' logos from NASCAR vehicles for each sponsor that had not also leveraged its sponsorship by purchasing advertising time during the race broadcast. The criticism was intense, and Fox agreed to refrain from this exclusionary practice in the future.

Broad-Based Controversies

The final category of controversies is comprised of complaints and criticisms that do not fit neatly within any single component of an organization's marketing strategy. Rather, they encompass several dimensions or the overall perception of sports marketers in general. These controversies are not likely to be articulated by sports consumers; instead, they will be voiced by the media, politicians, and consumer advocacy groups.

Estimates of Economic Value Are Overstated

Starting with Chapter 1 and continuing throughout this text has been the acknowledgment that sports make major contributions to the economies in which they operate. Because of this presumed economic impact, cities fight for teams to locate and for major events to be staged within their borders. Countries wage a similar battle for global events such as the World Cup of Soccer. Only recently, we witnessed the emergence of London as the host city for the 2012 Olympics. The people of London felt as though they themselves had won a gold medal. Meanwhile, the competing cities of Madrid, Moscow, New York City, and Paris immediately began to contemplate the next competition for prospective host cities for the 2016 Games. Similarly, we learned how communities place an economic value on the contributions of a new stadium. Government officials often cite these estimates when attempting to portray the commitment of resources or other financial concessions as a positive investment. The critics' argument is that the estimates used to justify these expenditures are overstated. It has been reported that Beijing has committed $36 billion for the 2008 Summer Olympics. The critics doubt that the investment will ever be recouped.[23]

When Baltimore agreed to commit $200 million to entice the move of the NFL's Cleveland Browns to its city, the government cited estimates that the presence of the team would contribute $123 million each year to the local economy.[24] Critics charged that the numbers were inflated, because much of the money would have still been spent locally, even if the team was not there. Although some outsiders are bound to visit, estimates of their numbers and their levels of expenditures were subject to question.

> It has been reported that Beijing has committed $36 billion for the 2008 Summer Olympics; the critics doubt that the investment will ever be recouped.

TABLE 22.3
**Financing of
Recently Completed
Stadia in the United
States**

Source: C. Whalen, "Time for
the Stadium Boom to Go Bust?
Studies Say Arena Subsidies
Are a Bad Investment,"
BusinessWeek, November 20,
2000, p. 150. Reprinted with
permission of *BusinessWeek*

City	Sport	Cost (millions)	Taxpayer Portion
Cincinnati	Baseball	$334	91%
Pittsburgh	Baseball	262	85
San Antonio	Basketball	175	84
Milwaukee	Baseball	394	77
Denver	Football	400	75
Pittsburgh	Football	252	70
Seattle	Football	360	70
Houston	Football	367	69
Dallas	Hockey/basketball	330	38
Detroit	Football	325	35

Proponents of a new stadium, especially in conjunction with the arrival of a new team, point to construction jobs, the presence of highly paid athletes in the community, and the creation of jobs during the sports season. Opponents acknowledge the construction jobs but note that much of the labor needed to fill those jobs is imported from other geographic areas. As for the presence of highly paid athletes, few of them actually live within the borders of the cities where they play. And as for the jobs at the stadium, they are discounted as low-paying, low-skilled, seasonal jobs that contribute very little to the local economy. One report looked at 30 newly constructed stadia. The conclusion was that 27 cities reaped no financial benefit from their new stadium and the other three experienced negative effects. It was acknowledged that the fans, players, and owners benefited; however, the taxpayers who paid the bill for the new stadium reaped no real rewards.[25]

A more recent study looked at the 13 MLB stadia constructed between 1989 and 2001. The conclusion was that the contributions to the team owners were significant and that the increased revenues alone were sufficient to pay for each new stadium. Therefore, team owners should have been motivated to build the facility without seeking external funding.[26] Yet another critic acknowledged that new jobs are created; however, each new job reportedly requires a government investment of $100,000. Further compounding the criticism is that 70 to 80 percent of the $10 billion spent on new sports stadia in the United States between 1990 and 2006 will have come from public funding, and the public will gain little from their investment.[27] Table 22.3 documents the total cost that was borne by taxpayers for recently completed sports venues in the United States. It is important to note that this practice is not limited to American venues; it is a point of contention in many countries across the globe.

Sweatshop Production

One issue that has generated a great deal of public criticism is the series of allegations concerning the use of Asian "sweatshops" for the production of sports equipment, apparel, and athletic shoes. At the forefront of this criticism is Nike, especially in regard to the production of athletic shoes in manufacturing facilities in Vietnam. Low wages, child labor, and abusive labor practices have all been cited. Some of these practices were documented and broadcast on ESPN's "Made in Vietnam: The American Sneaker Controversy."[28]

Students at the University of Michigan, one of many schools that have lucrative contracts with Nike, staged a protest by occupying a university administration building in an effort to persuade the university to implement more stringent policies regarding any marketer with which it is involved. Of specific concern were the establishment of a "living wage" and the elimination of the hostile work environment. Other complaints commonly surface on the Internet; in fact, one genre of Web sites has been designated as "hate Nike" sites.

And while the bulk of such criticism has been directed at Nike, other manufacturers, including adidas and Reebok, have been accused of similar indiscretions. Nike has countered by stating that the outsourcing of labor keeps costs and prices down, that a compensation of $47 per month in Vietnam exceeds minimum wage standards in that country, that its investment has created a positive impact on the Vietnamese economy, and that the company is addressing the issue of the hostile work environment.[29]

Gender Equity

Sports was long deemed to be the province of men. To address this disparity in American universities, critics assessed the applicability of a law that was passed in 1972. Known as Title IX, it was originally conceived to ensure that women had educational opportunities equal to those granted to male students at any university receiving federal funding. Shortly after its implementation, it began to be applied to athletic opportunities at these same universities.

The controversy does not involve any of the efforts to increase opportunities for women. Indeed, Title IX has increased female participation and helped to create a lucrative new market for sports marketers. Instead, the controversy revolves around the fact that many universities have chosen to move toward gender equity, not by increasing opportunities for women, but by reducing the number of sports teams involving male athletes.

> Title IX has increased female participation and helped to create a lucrative new market for sports marketers.

Some schools have cut men's programs in popular sports such as tennis, ice hockey, wrestling, swimming, and soccer. To illustrate the scope of this problem, consider that the number of American universities with a men's wrestling program dropped from 363 to 222 over the past 20 years.[30] Such reductions have resulted in several lawsuits alleging reverse discrimination. In general, the lawsuits have been dismissed as having no merit, and the efforts to achieve gender equity continue. The controversy surrounding Title IX is unlikely to be resolved for years to come.

Handling of Performance Enhancing Drug Violations

While there is a general consensus that performance enhancing drugs (PEDs) are bad for sports, questions have been raised as to whether or not sports officials have imposed sufficient penalties so as to discourage future use. Standards vary significantly from one sports organization to another, with penalties ranging from a suspension of a few days up to two years for the initial violation. One major impediment to stricter drug policies has long been the collective bargaining agreements with unions representing a class of athletes such as NBA players. Conversely, events that feature external oversight such as the World Track and Field Championships have been able to impose standards that result in the immediate suspension of an athlete's eligibility to compete for a longer period of time.

The commissioners of the four major North American sports leagues were recently called before the American Congress to discuss the scope of the problem and the inadequacy of the penalties resulting from a positive test. Testing of MLB players during the 2003 season revealed that 5 to 7 percent of the players tested positive for steroids.[31] As a result, fans have begun to question the legitimacy of the high levels of performance and the new records that were established from the late 1990s through the 2004 season. However, many other people attribute MLB's ability to regain the fans it lost in the aftermath of the work stoppage in 1994 to the excitement generated by the emergence of high-performing athletes within that same time frame. The dilemma faced by league officials is evident; performance enhancing drugs are unacceptable, but the performance of athletes who were alleged to be using steroids played a significant role in baseball's recovery.

Since American sports leagues have not been able to police themselves adequately, Congress has threatened its own intervention. The threat has included significant penalties, the harshest being lifetime banishment. Unions representing players have acknowledged the problem, and some of the existing collective bargaining agreements are being reopened with the objective of imposing stricter standards for testing and more stringent penalties for those who test positive. The good news is that the increased scrutiny has already served to reduce the use of PEDs. In MLB, the number of positive tests during the 2004 season was only 12.[32] But questions remain as to the rigor of the testing. We can anticipate ongoing disagreements among players, unions, leagues, sports federations, fans, and lawmakers regarding this highly charged issue.

Closing Capsule

This chapter has documented that various groups have high expectations regarding the behavior of sports marketers and continuously scrutinize their actions. Furthermore, these groups tend to be vocal critics when some perceived breach of ethical standards has occurred. But marketers can intervene in ways that improve the public's perception of the propriety of their behavior. They can either change their behavior such that it complies with the standards imposed upon them, or they can attempt to influence public opinion as to what constitutes an unacceptable practice.

Each of the primary decision areas in the development of marketing strategy is subject to scrutiny. Likewise, each has been a topic for criticism on the part of fans, consumers, consumer advocacy groups, the media, and politicians. In addition to the criticisms involving target marketing, product, distribution, pricing, and promotional decisions, a number of broad-based concerns regarding sports marketing have become significant points of contention. It is important to understand that the focus is not typically on violations of legal statutes; rather, the emphasis is on perceived breaches of ethical standards. The dilemma faced by sports marketers is that activities that are acceptable to some people are deemed totally inappropriate by others.

As evidenced by the long list of controversial issues discussed in this chapter, numerous concerns confront sports marketers. Among the most controversial are exclusionary membership policies at some private clubs that would be deemed discriminatory, TV's role in spectator sports, taxpayer-funded sports venues, ticket prices, the overcommercialization of sports, and the overstatement of the economic contributions attributable to a new stadium or team.

One compelling criticism that has surfaced in regard to the marketing of athletic shoes has been the outsourcing of manufacturing activities by industry giants such as Nike and adidas. Critics see it as exploitation of cheap labor; for instance, it has been noted that Vietnamese workers in factories producing Nike shoes earn $47 per month while enduring working conditions that would be illegal in more advanced economies. The counterarguments include claims that the companies are complying with all local standards, that lower costs are good for consumers and stockowners, and that their presence represents a contribution to emerging economies. Another major issue has involved what many critics perceive to be the inaction of sports marketers in response to allegations of significant levels of usage of performance enhancing drugs. Is testing rigorous enough? Is it frequent enough? Is the punishment imposed upon the violator sufficient to both discourage future use by the violator and to provide a meaningful disincentive for others, especially kids, to engage in this type of behavior?

As we close this book on sports marketing, we are confronted with the realization that sports marketers face continuous scrutiny. And when perceived breaches of acceptable standards occur, the critics are vocal. Sports marketers, whether marketers of sports products or companies that use sports as a platform for the marketing of nonsports products, must monitor the environment and continually consider the consequences of their behavior. The avoidance of controversies such as those delineated in this chapter will help make the sports marketer's job even more enjoyable.

Review Questions

1. Differentiate between controversies regarding sports and those involving sports marketers. Give an example of each to support your answer.
2. There are several groups that criticize the actions of sports marketers. Identify each group; then for each group, provide an example of an issue that it deems controversial.
3. Provide an argument in support of the all-male membership policy that excludes female members at Augusta National Golf Club.
4. Provide an argument against the exclusionary membership policy of the Augusta National Golf Club.
5. How would you respond to the argument that team relocation in professional sports is an outgrowth of the increased financial emphasis in spectator sports?
6. What can marketers learn from the Fan Cost Index?
7. What is the basis for most of the controversy surrounding pay-per-view TV?
8. Some professional sports teams have started selling their own tickets at prices that exceed the face value printed on the ticket. Why has this practice been so controversial?
9. Explain the concept of a clean stadium. Is this a reasonable demand on the part of a sports property such as the World Cup of Cricket? Why do you feel this way?
10. How are estimates of economic value used by sports marketers?
11. Go to the Internet and find five Web sites that criticize Nike. What are the most common complaints that are articulated in these Web sites?

Endnotes

1. D. Owen, "The Case for All-Male Golf Clubs," *Golf Digest,* March 2003, pp. 113–19.
2. B. Corcoran, "Females Ban Is Diversity Not Bias, Says Golf Captain," *Irish Independent,* November 29, 2003, p. 3.
3. R. Telander and M. Ilic, "Senseless: In America's Cities, Kids Are Killing Kids over Sneakers and Other Sports Apparel Favored by Drug Dealers; Who's to Blame?" *Sports Illustrated,* May 14, 1990, pp. 36–42.
4. R. Neyer, "Greed, Turmoil, and Bad Marketing: Baseball in Great Shape," September 16, 2002, www.espn.go.com/mlb/columns/neyer_rob/1432489.html (accessed October 14, 2005).
5. M. Hosking, "Woods Wasn't Worth It," *The Cut,* February 2002, p. 15.
6. K. Roberts, "Heat Is on for New Miami Stadium," May 18, 2005, www.sportbusiness.com/news/index?news_item_id=1575531 (accessed October 13, 2005).
7. "Team Marketing Report," 2005, www.teammarketing.com/fci.cfm?page=fci_nfl_05.cfm (accessed May 18, 2006).
8. E. Swift, "Hey Fans: Sit on It," *Sports Illustrated,* May 15, 2000, pp. 70–86.
9. L. McCarthy and R. Irwin, "Permanent Seat Licenses (PSLs) as an Emerging Source of Revenue Production," *Sport Marketing Quarterly* 7, no. 3 (1998), pp. 41–46.
10. M. Sperber, *College Sports Inc.* (New York: Henry Holt & Co, 1990).
11. "PSL/Season Tickets," 2005, www.bluejackets.com/arena/seat_season.php (accessed August 16, 2005).
12. C. Britcher, "HF Sports Net PPV Deal," August 6, 2003, www.sportbusiness.com/news/index?news_item_id=152070 (accessed October 14, 2005).

13. D. Rovell, "Sports Fans Feel Pinch in Seat (Prices)," June 21, 2002, www.espn.go.com/sports-business/s/2002/0621/1397693.html (accessed October 14, 2005).

14. G. Couch, "Wicked Ticket: Deceit Is Name of Game," *Chicago Sun-Times,* May 9, 2003. p. 165.

15. D. Rovell, "Judge Decides Business Is Legit," November 24, 2003, www.sports.espn.go.com/mlb/news/story?id=1670041 (accessed October 14, 2005).

16. M. Payne, "As Time Goes By . . . ," *SportBusiness International,* March 2005, p. 37.

17. D. Smith, "Universities Drop Naming Rights Deal," October 28, 2004, www.sportbusiness.com/news/index?news_item_id=155997 (accessed October 13, 2005).

18. B. Horovitz, "Olympic Sponsors Push for More Play," *USA Today,* September 29, 2000, p. B3.

19. Knight Ridder News Service, "Will Cubs Sign Move Hit Brick Wall?" *Decatur Herald & Review,* September 12, 2004, pp. F1, F6.

20. C. Masters, "The Signs Are It's Bad for Business," *New Zealand Herald,* March 13, 2003, p. A18.

21. R. King, "Big Game Restrictions Upset Area Merchants," *Detroit News,* June 15, 2005, pp. 1D, 7D.

22. D. Smith, 2005, "London Olympics to Legislate for Ambush Marketing," July 13, 2005, www.sportbusiness.com/news/index?news_item_id=157994 (accessed October 13, 2005).

23. D. Smith, "Beijing's Olympic Investment," May 24, 2005, www.sportbusiness.com/news/index?newa_item_id=157622 (accessed October 13, 2005).

24. J. Spiers, "Are Sports Teams Worth It?" *Fortune,* January 15, 1996, pp. 29–30.

25. A. Taylor, "Economist Rips Stadiums," *Detroit News,* October 16, 1988, p. 2C.

26. C. Britcher, 2004, "Ballpark Financing Study," March 25, 2004, www.sportbusiness.com/news/index?news_item_id=154136 (accessed October 13, 2005).

27. "The Folly of Taxpayer Funded Stadiums," *Fortune,* December 21, 1998, pp. 41–42.

28. J. Lindqist, "ESPN Laces Them Up in Shoe Investigation," *Richmond Times-Dispatch,* April 2, 1998, www.gateway-va.com (accessed December 2, 1998).

29. T. Clarke, "Made in Vietnam: Nike, Reebok Fire Back," April 6, 1998, www.espn.sportszone.com/gen/features/sneakers/monday.html (accessed April 6, 1998).

30. Associated Press, "Justices Reject Lawsuit against Federal Officials," June 6, 2005, http://sports.espn.go.com/espn/news/story?id=2077321 (accessed October 14, 2005).

31. D. Rovell, "'Roids Put MLB Integrity at Risk," March 4, 2004, http://sports.go.com/espn/sportsbusiness/news/story?id=1750707 (accessed October 14, 2005).

32. K. Roberts, 2005, "U.S. Sports Bosses Face Next Drug Quizzing," May 18, 2005, www.sportbusiness.com/news/index?news_item_id=157550 (accessed October 13, 2005).

URLs of Important Sports Marketing Web Sites

www.allsports.com   General sports

www.americascup.com/en   English language site for America's Cup Yachting Regatta

www.athens2004.gr   Athens 2004 Olympics

www.athletics.org.au   National sports organization for athletics in Australia

www.ausport.gov.au   Australian Sports Commission

www.ballparks.com   Ballparks by Munsey & Suppes; stadium descriptions

www.bonham.com   Sponsorship and naming rights consulting group

www.cbssportline.com   CBS broadcasting; sports information

www.clc.com   The Collegiate Licensing Company

www.collegesports.com   Coverage of U.S. collegiate sports

www.cnnsi.com   CNN/*Sports Illustrated* joint venture; sports information

www.darrellsurvey.com   Information on golf products usage

www.espn.go.com/sportsbusiness/index.html   General sports business

www.e-assm.net   Asian Association for Sport Management

www.easm.org   European Association of Sport Management

www.envisionglobal.com   U.S. consulting firm specializing in venue naming rights and valuation

www.fifa.com   FIFA Soccer

www.thefirsttee.org   The First Tee; youth-oriented golf

www.fitinfotech.com   Publisher of sports-related books and journals

http://formula1zone.com   Formula One and Grand Prix Racing

www.frontrow-marketing.com   Front Row Marketing, a U.S. consulting firm for sponsorship and naming rights valuations

www.garmin.com   Garmin GPS systems

www.gemgroup.com   British PR firm emphasizing leveraging strategies for clients

www.globalsportnet.com   Full-service sport and sponsorship consulting, Germany

www.glsp.com   Great Lakes Sports Publications

http://golf.com   Broad coverage of golf as a participation sport

www.griffith.edu.au/school/gbs/tlhs/smaanz/home.html   Sport Management Association of Australia and New Zealand

www.hillarysport.org.nz   Hillary Commission, New Zealand

www.iaaf.org   International Amateur Athletics Federation

www.jobswithballs.com   Employment opportunities

www.joycejulius.com   Joyce Julius & Associates media equivalency measurement

www.licensing.org   International Licensing Industry Merchandisers' Association (LIMA)

www.mediamonitors.com.au/sis/technology.htm   Sponsorship Information Services (Sportsi)

www.nassm.org   North American sports marketing organization

www.nassm.org/universities.htm   Global list of universities with sports marketing programs

www.ncaasports.com   National Collegiate Athletics Association

www.hoksve.com   HOK +Sport + Venue + Event International architectural firm; sports stadia specialists

www.nzga.co.nz   New Zealand Golf Association

www.octagon.com   Global sports, sponsorship, and leveraging consulting firm

www.performanceresearch.com   Sponsorship market research/consulting firm

www.playgolfamerica.com   Broad coverage of golf participation

http://proquest.umi.com/i-std/lcd/about.htm   ABI-INFORM bibliographic database search service

www.puresportsgames.com   Resources for fantasy-league participants

www.pvimage.com   Princeton Video Image virtual advertising

www.pvieurope.com   Princeton Video Image European site

www.qscores.com   Marketing Evaluations, Inc., Q Score provider

www.randa.org   Royal and Ancient Golf of St. Andrews, Scotland

www.sbrnet.com   Sports research; bibliographic database

www.scomm-research.com   S-Comm, a U.K.-based research and sponsorship evaluation consulting firm

www.sfo.com/~csuppes/Soccer/England/main.htm   Information on English soccer stadiums

www.sfx.co.uk   SFX Sports Group Europe

www.sfx.com   SFX Sports Group USA

www.sgma.com   Sporting Goods Manufacturers Association

www.sirc.ca   Sports Information Research Centre, Canada

www.mediamonitors.com.au/sis/technology.htm   Sponsorship Information Services (Sportsi)

www.snzla.com.au/sports_law.html   New Zealand and Australia sports law

www.sparc.org.nz   Sport and Recreation, New Zealand

www.sponprops.com/en.htm   The Sponsorship Proposal Company, Belgium

www.sponsormap.com   Starfish Research SponsorMap; evaluation of sponsorship effectiveness and ROI

www.sponsorship.ca   Canadian sponsorship data and issues

www.sponsorship.co.uk   BDS Sponsorship; U.K.-based consulting firm

www.sponsorship.com   International Events Group (IEG)

www.sponsorship.org   European Sponsorship Consultants' Association (ESCA)

www.sponsorship-advice.org   Careers in sponsorship

www.sponsorshipintelligence.com   Zenith Media sponsorship service provider

www.sponsortrak.com   Sponsorship/ROI valuation service provider

www.sportaccord.com   Sports services group

www.sportacus.biz   London-based naming rights consulting firm

www.sportbusiness.com   General sports business; U.K.-based

www.sportbusinessjournal.com   Street & Smith's *Sports Business Journal*

www.sportcal.com   Sportcal Global Communications; sports business

www.sportengland.org   Sport England

www.sportmarketingassociation.com   U.S. Sport Marketing Association; academic based

www.sportquest.com   Sport Quest bibliographic search

www.sportscareers.com   Career information

www.sportsmarketingsurveys.com   Sports Marketing Surveys, Ltd.

www.sportsmatch.co.uk   Sports Match; U.K. consulting company

www.sportspoll.com   ESPN Chilton Sports Poll; fan-related research

www.sports-sponsorship.co.uk   U.K. sponsorship

www.sportundmarkt.com   Sport+Markt AG; German sports research company

www.sportvision.com   Sportvision; virtual imaging for TV

www.staff.edu.au/anzla   Australia/New Zealand Association of Leisure Studies

www.starfishresearch.com/au   Australia research, strategy, and sponsorship valuation consulting firm

www.takemefishing.org   Fishing and boating charters, equipment, and trade shows

www.teammarketing.com/fci.cfm   Fan cost indices for major North American sports leagues/teams

www.tsn.ca   The Sports Network, Canada

www.unb.ca/SportManagement   Sport Management Info Centre, Canada

www.usga.org   U.S. Golf Association

www.uspto.gov   U.S. Patent and Trademark Office

www.webgolfer.com   Michigan Golfer magazine

www.wipo.int/madrid/en/general/index.htm   World Intellectual Property Organization

www.womensportsjobs.com   Women sport jobs

www.worldstadiums.com   World Stadiums

University of North Carolina Licensing Information

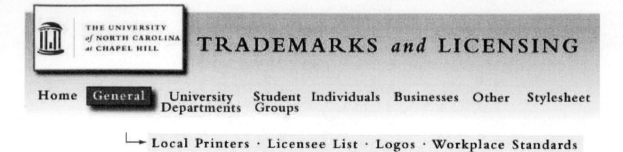

→ **Local Printers · Licensee List · Logos · Workplace Standards**

General Information

The University, like virtually all other institutions and businesses in the United States, has developed policies controlling the use of trademark language and logos because these marks symbolize its purpose, values and traditions. In addition, when businesses make use of these marks to generate revenues, the University shares in the proceeds through its Trademark Licensing Program. At Carolina,100% of the net proceeds from the licensing program is used to help fund need-based and academic scholarships.

The language and logos belonging to the University include, but are not limited to, the words "University of North Carolina", "UNC" and "Tar Heels"; and logos of The Old Well, University Seal, Interlocking NC and Strutting Ram.

If you have questions about using any of these marks please use the topics at left to link to the appropriate category, or contact the Director of Licensing at unc.licensing@unc.edu.

5/3/2004

Source: Reprinted with permission of the University of North Carolina Trademarks & Licensing Committee. www.licensing.unc.edu

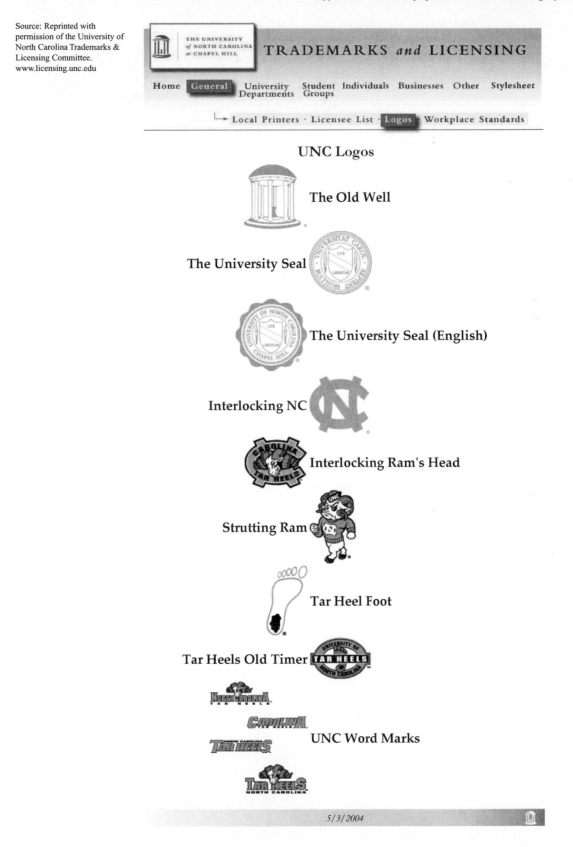

THE UNIVERSITY *of* NORTH CAROLINA *at* CHAPEL HILL

TRADEMARKS *and* LICENSING

Home   General   University Departments   Student Groups   Individuals   Businesses   Other   Stylesheet

→ Local Printers · Licensee List · Logos · Workplace Standards

UNC Logos

The Old Well

The University Seal

The University Seal (English)

Interlocking NC

Interlocking Ram's Head

Strutting Ram

Tar Heel Foot

Tar Heels Old Timer

UNC Word Marks

5/3/2004

THE UNIVERSITY *of* NORTH CAROLINA *at* CHAPEL HILL

TRADEMARKS *and* LICENSING

Home   General   University   Student   Individuals   **Businesses**   Other   Stylesheet
                    Departments Groups

Businesses

In order for a business—which includes individuals—to make a commercial use of the University's name or any of its other marks, that business must have permission to do so. Permission must be acquired either by a formal contract with the University or by obtaining a license through the University's licensing agent, The Collegiate Licensing Company. Contractual permissions are specialized and are negotiated through the University's attorneys, and therefore are not covered on this website.

The University directs The Collegiate Licensing Company (CLC) to contract with a limited number of producers in order to make goods bearing University marks available for retail sale to the public. CLC issues licensing agreements for a limited number of suppliers in each of a broad range of merchandise categories. Both the business and the individual products that business produces must be approved in advance and in writing; when so approved the business becomes a "Licensee" and the individual products become "Licensed Products."

The University, also through CLC, licenses on a very restricted basis the promotional use of University marks.

The normal steps in obtaining a license include the following:

1. A preliminary assessment, first, of the ability of the business to produce and distribute goods in accordance with University expectations; and second, of the market demand and competition levels for the envisioned goods;

2. The signing of a contract between CLC and the business;

3. Approval steps for each individual design.

If you are interested in obtaining a retail license, which allows you to produce goods bearing University marks, or a promotional license, which allows you to use University marks, you should contact Mr. James Parker at Collegiate Licensing Company:

James Parker
The Collegiate Licensing Company
290 Interstate North
Suite 200
Atlanta, GA 30339

Phone: 770-956-0520
Email: jparker@clc.com
Website: www.clc.com

Retailers interested in carrying licensed UNC-CH merchandise should consider using The Collegiate Exchange, an online catalogue and service provided by Collegiate Licensing Company at no charge. Go to www.clc.com and navigate to The Collegiate Exchange.

5/3/2004

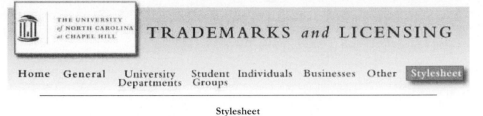

THE UNIVERSITY
of NORTH CAROLINA
at CHAPEL HILL

TRADEMARKS *and* LICENSING

Home   General   University   Student   Individuals   Businesses   Other   Stylesheet
Departments   Groups

Stylesheet

Modification of Logos

As a general rule the University's logos may not be altered. This includes overlaying them with other designs or lettering, displaying only part of a logo, or changing the colors.

Colors

The University's colors are Carolina Blue and White. While there is a range of opinion as to what exactly is the true shade of Carolina Blue, from a licensing standpoint, it is Pantone 278. Three other Pantone colors are used in the logos as well:

Tar Heels Deep Blue: Pantone 282
Tar Heels Silver: Pantone 877
Tar Heels Metallic Silver: Pantone 429

Use with Other Trademarks (Co-branding)

Any use of University marks with other trademarks must be approved by the Director of Trademarks and Licensing, or through a University

Appropriateness

No references to alcohol, drugs or tobacco-related products may be used in conjunction with University marks.

Material that may be demeaning to individuals or institutions (including but not limited to racial, ethnic, gender, or disability-related matters) may not be used in conjunction with University marks.

Profanity may not be used in conjunction with University marks.

Commercially-licensed Usage

The following policies, in addition to those above, apply to the manufacturing of licensed goods. Please note that each item must be approved in advance and in writing through the University's licensing agent; and that factors in addition to those listed herein may be taken into account when deciding whether to grant approval.

Consumables

Must have expiration date on packaging

Current Players

No use of current players' names, images, or likeness is permitted that would violate NCAA rules and regulations.

Workplace Conditions

Merchandise, packaging and advertising of University-logoed goods may not include claims regarding workplace conditions.

Licensing Proceeds

In general, packaging or advertising of University-licensed goods may not make any type of reference to the proceeds from the sale of those goods

Carolina Music and Songs

Any commercial use of UNC music, including but not limited to the following, requires permission through Trademarks and Licensing:
UNC Fight Song
Here Comes Carolina
Hark the Sound

5/3/2004

Index